Leading Cases and Materials on the Social Policy of the EEC

by

Angela Byre

Kluwer Law and Taxation Publishers
Deventer • Boston

Kluwer Law and Taxation Publishers
P.O. Box 23
7400 GA Deventer
The Netherlands

Tel.: 31-5700-47261
Telex: 49295
Fax: 31-5700-22244

Library of Congress Cataloging in Publication Data

Byre, Angela D.
  Leading cases and materials on the social policy of the EEC / by
Angela Byre.
    p.   cm.
  Includes index.
  ISBN 9065443126
  1. Labor laws and legislation—European Economic Community
countries—Cases.   I. Title.
KJE2855.B97   1989
344.4'01—dc19
[344.041]   89-2776
                                                                   CIP

Cover design: Eset

ISBN 90 6544 312 6

LEADING CASES AND MATERIALS
ON THE SOCIAL POLICY OF THE EEC

Table of Contents

Foreword

The social policy of the EEC is having an increasing influence on the development of national labour law frameworks and on labour market practices within the twelve Member States. This influence is likely to expand with the movement to complete the internal market.

There is now an important body of EEC legislation and judgments of the European Court of Justice, in the fields of equal treatment for men and women, employment protection, and health and safety. Practitioners and students in each of the Member States need to be familiar with these provisions, some of which, especially those concerned with discrimination, are being invoked and directly applied in national courts.

The novelty of this subject is indicated by the fact that most of the nearly twenty Directives and 50 key interpretative judgments of the ECJ in this collection of 'leading' cases and legislation are products of the past decade. Not surprisingly, many practitioners and students are, as yet, unfamiliar with these materials. There are many who wish to be acquainted with them, but find it difficult to gain access to the materials through the *Official Bulletin* and law reports. This timely collection meets a pressing need for a systematically arranged, easy-to-use reference book for practitioners and students. The editor, Angela Byre, is a leading expert on European social law, and she has applied her deft touch in bringing together these materials for the first time, as well as providing unintrusive but essential introductions which put the materials into context.

This book will be an indispensable tool for everyone concerned with employment relationships, working conditions, and discrimination throughout the EEC.

Bob Hepple

Professor of Law, University College, London

November 1988

List of Cases

Introduction

'Economic growth and an active programme of social reform are not anti-thetic. The purpose of economic growth should be to widen the range of social options available to the peoples of the European Community by bringing about a continuing rise in living standards and the quality of life. Unless the process of growth can be put more fully at the service of society, growth itself may become politically unacceptable'. These comments from the European Commission, in introducing the EEC's first fully-fledged social action programme in 1974, signalled that a social dimension to Community policies and actions was to be a key part of Community development in the future.

From the very inception of the European Community, the basic EEC Tready provided a starting-point for the development of social provisions by emphasizing the need to promote improved working conditions and an improved standard of living for workers, and to make possible harmonisation across the Community while maintaining such improvements. The Treaty also dealt specifically with the need to secure equal pay for men and women working in the EEC. In the early 1970s, an action programme was formulated bringing together social policy objectives across a wide range of areas and indicating specific actions to be taken at Community and national levels to tackle particular problems which had been identified. The priorities and action areas spelt out in this social action programme were aimed at achieving full and better employment, improved living and working conditions, and participation of workers and social partners in decision-making processes. Community legislation gradually followed to give effect to some of the social action priorities – though some issues, in particular those relating to worker participation, proved too controversial for any consensus to be achieved and for any legislation to be adopted by the Community's Council of Ministers. The social legislation which was adopted took the form of Council Directives on equal treatment for men and women in pay, working conditions and social security; employment protections for workers affected by redundancy, transfer and insolvency situations; and protective provisions linked to aspects of health and safety at the workplace. Broad action programmes to develop Community strategies in the equality and health and safety fields in the medium term were also approved in the 1970s and 1980s.

This growing body of Community measures and social legislation, coupled with the many significant interpretative rulings from the European Court of Justice which have begun to emerge in recent years, are exerting an increasing and discernible influence on labour laws and practices in all parts of the EEC. Preparations for the completion of an internal market without frontiers by 1992, and for a clearly defined social policy in the context of the large single market involving, inter alia, the possible formulation of a Community Charter of fundamental social rights, are likely to ensure that the European dimension continues to influence national policies and practices for many years to come.

This book aims to meet the growing needs of practitioners, lawyers, students and others concerned with the development of social policy and labour law in the EEC. The book brings together the main sources of Community law in this field. It includes framework action programmes indicating the strategic focus for Community measures on particular issues, as well as the relevant Treaty provisions and specific Council Directives which have been adopted in the social field. The emphasis is on mainstream social policy measures rather than those affecting only a particular industry or group of workers, and on legislative provisions which have already been enacted and brought into effect rather than those which are still at the proposal stage and do not directly affect practitioners. The book also includes leading decisions from the European Court interpreting the Community's mainstream social legislation. The Court has already indicated a number of areas where Community labour law is directly effective and may be relied on by individuals before their national courts in the absence of implementing national legislation or to avoid the application of inconsistent national provisions. The Court's basic judgments are given, containing principles of interpretation established by the Court in determining the issues referred to it. The Court has addressed itself to a wide range of questions in its more recent preliminary rulings and has generally adopted the approach suggested by Opinions from its Advocates General. These Opinions are not included here, therefore, to avoid repetition of issues, for reasons of limited space, and to focus attention on decided principles.

This book is intended as a practical, easy-to-use reference tool, and as such it contains brief contextual introductions and summaries of the issues involved and decided principles in particular cases rather than lengthy commentaries. The material is arranged on a subject basis in three main sections, covering equal treatment, employment protection and health and safety. These subjects are followed through on a chronological basis in terms of legislative texts and developing interpretations. The rulings from the European Court arise from its determination of infringement proceedings against governments, brought by the European Commission as guardian of the Treaty, under Article 169 of the EEC Treaty; and from preliminary rulings on issues of interpretation of Community law referred from national courts, in the context of individual cases, under Article 177 of the EEC Treaty. Both channels of access to the European Court have served to advance the interpretative process, though the Article 177 route has produced clarification and examination of issues most directly touching on the application of Community principles to particular workplace situations. The material in the book comprises the relevant official texts and decisions available in English as of 1 January 1989. By bringing together all the main materials relating to EEC social policy and legislation in a single book, it is hoped that practitioners will gain a full appreciation of Community developments in this important area.

General Treaty Extracts
and
Social Action Programme

EEC Treaty Extracts

A. Social provisions

Article 117
Member States agree upon the need to promote improved working conditions and an improved standard of living for workers, so as to make possible their harmonisation while the improvement is being maintained.

They believe that such a development will ensue not only from the functioning of the common market, which will favour the harmonisation of social systems, but also from the procedures provided for in this Treaty and from the approximation of provisions laid down by law, regulation or administrative action.

Article 118
Without prejudice to the other provisions of this Treaty and in conformity with its general objectives, the Commission shall have the task of promoting close cooperation between Member States in the social field, particularly in matters relating to:
- employment;
- labour law and working conditions;
- basic and advanced vocational training;
- social security;
- prevention of occupational accidents and diseases;
- occupational hygiene;
- the right of association, and collective bargaining between employers and workers.

To this end, the Commission shall act in close contact with Member States by making studies, delivering opinions and arranging consultations both on problems arising at national level and on those of concern to international organisations.

Before delivering the opinions provided for in this Article, the Commission shall consult the Economic and Social Committee.

Article 118a[1]
1. Member States shall pay particular attention to encouraging improvements, especially in the working environment, as regards the health and

safety of workers, and shall set as their objective the harmonization of conditions in this area, while maintaining the improvements made.

2. In order to help achieve the objective laid down in the first paragraph, the Council, acting by a qualified majority on a proposal from the Commission, in cooperation with the European Parliament and after consulting the Economic and Social Committee, shall adopt, by means of directives, minimum requirements for gradual implementation, having regard to the conditions and technical rules obtaining in each of the Member States.

Such directives shall avoid imposing administrative, financial and legal constraints in a way which would hold back the creation and development of small and medium-sized undertakings.

3. The provisions adopted pursuant to this Article shall not prevent any Member State from maintaining or introducing more stringent measures for the protection of working conditions compatible with this Treaty.

Article 118b[2]

The Commission shall endeavour to develop the dialogue between management and labour at European level which could, if the two sides consider it desirable, lead to relations based on agreement.

Article 119

Each Member State shall during the first stage ensure and subsequently maintain the application of the principle that men and women should receive equal pay for equal work.

For the purpose of this Article, 'pay' means the ordinary basic or minimum wage or salary and any other consideration, whether in cash or in kind, which the worker receives, directly or indirectly, in respect of his employment from his employer.

Equal pay without discrimination based on sex means:
(a) that pay for the same work at piece rates shall be calculated on the basis of the same unit of measurement;
(b) that pay for work at time rates shall be the same for the same job.

Article 120

Member States shall endeavour to maintain the existing equivalence between paid holiday schemes.

Article 121

The Council may, acting unanimously and after consulting the Economic and Social Committee, assign to be Commission tasks in connection with the implementation of common measures, particularly as regards social security for the migrant workers referred to in Articles 48 to 51.

Article 122

The Commission shall include a separate chapter on social development within the Community in its annual report to the Assembly.

The Assembly may invite the Commission to draw up reports on any particular problems concerning social conditions.

B. General Treaty provisions

Article 100
The Council shall, acting unanimously on a proposal from the Commission, issue directives for the approximation of such provisions laid down by law, regulation or administrative action in Member States as directly affect the establishment or functioning of the common market.

The Assembly and the Economic and Social Committee shall be consulted in the case of directives whose implementation would, in one or more Member States, involve the amendment of legislation.

Article 169
If the Commission considers that a Member State has failed to fulfil an obligation under this Treaty, it shall deliver a reasoned opinion on the matter after giving the State concerned the opportunity to submit its observations.

If the State concerned does not comply with the opinion within the period laid down by the Commission, the latter may bring the matter before the Court of Justice.

Article 177
The Court of Justice shall, have jurisdiction to give preliminary rulings concerning:
(a) the interpretation of this Treaty;
(b) the validity and interpretation of acts of the institutions of the Community;
(c) the interpretation of the statutes of bodies established by an act of the Council, where those statutes so provide.
Where such a question is raised before any court or tribunal of a Member State, that court or tribunal may, if it considers that a decision on the question is necessary to enable it to give judgment, request the Court of Justice to give a ruling thereon.

Where any such question is raised in a case pending before a court or tribunal of a Member State, against whose decisions there is no judicial remedy under national law, that court or tribunal shall bring the matter before the Court of Justice.

Article 235
If action by the Community should prove necessary to attain, in the course of the operation of the common market, one of the objectives of the Community and this Treaty has not provided the necessary powers, the Council shall, acting unanimously on a proposal from the Commission and after consulting the Assembly, take the appropriate measures.

---

1. Article added by Article 21 of the Single European Act.
2. Article added by Article 22 of the Single European Act.

Social Action Programme

Council Resolution

21 January 1974

concerning a social action programme
(74/C13/01)

THE COUNCIL OF THE EUROPEAN COMMUNITIES,

Having regard to the Treaties establishing the European Communities,
Having regard to the draft from the Commission,
Having regard to the Opinion of the European Parliament,
Having regard to the Opinion of the Economic and Social Committee:
    Whereas the Treaties establishing the European Communities assigned to them tasks with relevance to social objectives;
    Whereas, pursuant to Article 2 of the Treaty establishing the European Economic Community, the European Economic Community shall have as a particular task to promote throughout the Community a harmonious development of economic activities, a continuous and balanced expansion, an increase in stability and an acceletated raising of the standard of living;
    Whereas the Heads of state or of Government affirmed at their conference held in Paris in October 1972 that economic expansion is not an end in itself but should result in an improvement of the quality of life as well as of the standard of living;
    Whereas the Heads of State or of Government emphasized as one of the conclusions adopted at the above-mentioned conference that they attach as much importance to vigorous action in the social field as to the achievement of Economic and Monetary Union and invited the Community institutions to draw up a social action programme providing for concrete measures and the corresponding resources particularly in the framework of the European Social Fund on the basis of suggestions put forward by the Heads of State or of Government and the Commission at the said Conference;
    Whereas such a programme involves actions designed to achieve full and better employment, the improvement of living and working conditions and increased involvement of management and labour in the economic and social decisions of the Community, and of workers in the life of undertakings;
    Whereas actions described in the above programme should be imple-

mented in accordance with the provisions laid down in the Treaties, including those of Article 235 of the Treaty establishing the European Economic Community.

Having regard to the wishes expressed by management and labour:

Whereas, irrespective of serious threats to employment which may arise from the situation obtaining at the time of adoption of this Resolution, and without prejudice to the results of any future studies or measures, the Community should decide on the objectives and priorities to be given to its action in the social field over the coming years.

Takes note of the Social Action Programme from the Commission,

Considers that vigorous action must be undertaken in successive stages with a view to realising the social aims of European union, in order to attain the following broad objectives: full and better employment at Community, national and regional levels, which is an essential condition for an effective social policy; improvement of living and working conditions so as to make possible their harmonization while the improvement is being maintained; increased involvement of management and labour in the economic and social decisions of the Community, and of workers in the life of undertakings,

Considers that the Community social policy has an individual role to play and should make an essential contribution to achieving the aforementioned objectives by means of Community measures or the definition by the Community of objectives for national social policies, without however seeking a standard solution to all social problems or attempting to transfer to Community level any responsibilities which are assumed more effectively at other levels,

Considers that social objectives should be a constant concern of all Community policies,

Considers that it is essential to ensure the consistency of social and other Community policies so that measures taken will achieve the objectives of social and other policies simultaneously,

Considers that, to achieve the proposed actions successfully, and particularly in view of the structural changes and imbalances in the Community, the necessary resources should be provided, in particular by strengthening the role of the European Social Fund,

Expresses the political will to adopt the measures necessary to achieve the following objectives during a first stage covering the period from 1974 to 1976, in additior, to measures adopted in the context of other Community policies.

Attainment of full and better employment in the Community

- to establish appropriate consultation between Member States on their employment policies, guided by the need to achieve a policy of full and better employment: in the Community as a whole and in the regions;
- to promote better cooperation by national employment services;
- to implement a common vocational training policy, with a view to attaining progressively the principal objectives thereof, especially approximation

ling standards, in particular by setting up a European Vocational
g Centre;

rtake action for the purpose of achieving equality between men
and women as regards access to employment and vocational training and
advancement and as regards working conditions, including pay, taking into
account the important role of management and labour in this field;
- to ensure that the family reponsibilities of all concerned may be reconciled
with their job aspirations;
- to establish an action programme for migrant workers and members of
their families which shall aim in particular;
  • to improve the conditions of free movement within the Community of
    workers from Member States, including social security, and the social
    infrastructure of the Member States, the latter being an indispensable
    condition for solving the specific problems of migrant workers and
    members of their families, especially problems of reception, housing,
    social services, training and education of children;
  • to humanize the free movement of Community workers and members of
    their families by providing effective assistance during the various phases,
    it being understood that the prime objective is still to enable workers to
    find employment in their own regions;
  • to achieve equality of treatment for Community and non-Community
    workers and members of their families in respect of living and work-
    ing conditions, wages and economic rights, taking into account the
    Community provisions in force;
  • to promote consultation on immigration policies *vis-à-vis* third countries.
- to initiate a programme for the vocational and social integration of handicapped persons, in particular making provisions for the promotion of pilot
experiments, for the purpose of rehabilitating them in vocational life, or
where appropriate, of placing them in sheltered industries, and to undertake a comparative study of the legal provisions and the arrangements
made for rehabilitation at national level;
- to seek solutions to the employment problems contronting certain more
vulnerable categories of persons (the young and the aged);
- to protect workers hired through temporary employment agencies and to
regulate the activities of such firms with a view to eliminating abuses
therein;
- to continue the implementation of the Council's conclusions on employment policy in the Community and particularly those concerning the
progressive integration of the labour markets including those relating to
employment statistics and estimates.

**Improvement of living and working conditions so as to make possible their
harmonization while the improvement is being maintained**

- to establish appropriate consultations between Member States on their
social protection policies with the particular aim of their approximation on
the way of progress;
- to establish an action programme for workers aimed at the humanization of

their living and working conditions, with particular reference to:
- improvement in safety and health conditions at work;
- the gradual elimination of physical and psychological stress which exists in the place of work and on the job, especially through improving the environment and seeking ways of increasing job satisfaction;
- a reform of the organization of work giving workers wider opportunities, especially those of having their own responsibilities and duties and of obtaining higher qualifications.
– to persevere with and expedite the implementation of the European Social Budget;
– gradually to extend social protection, particularly within the framework of social security schemes, to categories of persons not covered or inadequately provided for under existing schemes;
– to promote the coordination of social security schemes for self-employed workers with regard to freedom of establishment and freedom to provide services;
– to invite the Commission to submit a report on the problems arising in connection with coordination of supplementary schemes for employed persons moving within the Community;
– progressively to introduce machinery for adapting social security benefits to increased prosperity in the various Member States;
– to protect workers' interests, in particular with regard to the retention of rights and advantages in the case of mergers, concentrations or rationalization operations;
– to implement, in cooperation with the Member States, specific measures to combat poverty by drawing up pilot schemes.

Increased involvement of management and labour in the economic and social decisions of the Community, and of workers in the life of undertakings

– to refer more extensively to the Standing Committee on Employment for the discussion of all questions with a fundamental influence on employment;
– to help trade union organizations taking part in Community work to establish training and information services for European affairs and to set up a European Trade Union Institute;
– progressively to involve workers or their representatives in the life of undertakings in the Community;
– to facilitate, depending on the situation in the different countries, the conclusion of collective agreements at European level in appropriate fields;
– to develop the involvement of management and labour in the economic and social decisions of the Community,
lays down the following priorities among the actions referred to in this Resolution:

Attainment of full and better employment in the Community

1. The establishment of appropriate consultation between Member States on

their employment policies and the promotion of better cooperation by national employment services.

2. The establishment of an action programme for migrant workers who are nationals of Member States or third countries.
3. The implementation of a common vocational training policy and the setting up of a European Vocational Training Centre.
4. The undertaking of action to achieve equality between men and women as regards access to employment and vocational training and advancement and as regards working conditions including pay.

Improvement of living and working conditions so as to make possible their harmonization while the improvement is being maintained

5. The establishment of appropriate consultation between Member States on their social protection policies.
6. The establishment of an initial action programme, relating in particular to health and safety at work, the health of workers and improved organization of tasks, beginning in those economic sectors where working conditions appear to be the most difficult.
7. The implementation in cooperation with the Member States, of specific measures to combat poverty by drawing up pilot schemes.

Increased involvement of management and labour in the economic and social decisions of the Community, and of workers in the life of undertakings

8. The progressive involvement of workers or their representatives in the life of undertakings in the Community.
9. The promotion of the involvement of management and labour in the economic and social decisions of the Community.

Takes note of the Commission's undertaking to submit to it, during 1974, the necessary proposals concerning the priorities laid down above,
Takes note of the Commission's undertaking to submit to it, before 1 April 1974, proposals relating to:
– an initial action programme with regard to migrant workers;
– the setting up of a European Vocational Training Centre;
– a directive on the harmonization of laws with regard to the retention of rights and advantages in the event of changes in the ownership of undertakings, in particular in the event of mergers.
Notes that the Commission has already submitted to it proposals relating to:
– assistance from the European Social Fund for migrant workers and for handicapped workers;
– an action programme for handicapped workers in an open market economy;
– the setting-up of a European General Industrial Safety Committee and the extension of the competence of the Mines Safety and Health Commission;
– a Directive providing for the approximation of legislation of Member

States concerning the application of the principle of equal pay for men and women;
- the designation as an immediate objective of the overall application of the principle of the standard 40-hour working week by 1975, and the principle of four weeks annual paid holiday by 1976;
- the setting up of a European Foundation for the improvement of the environment and of living and working conditions;
- a Directive on the approximation of the Member Sates legislation on collective dismissals.

Undertakes to act, at the latest five months after the Commission has informed the Council of the results of its deliberations arising from the opinions given by the European Parliament and the Economic and Social Committee, if such consultations have taken place, or, if such consultations have not taken place, at the latest nine months from the date of the transmission of the proposals to the Council by the Commission,

Takes note of the Commission's undertaking to submit to it before 31 December 1976 a series of measures to be taken during a futher phase.

Part I.
Equal Treatment

Contents

Part I. Equal Treatment

Introduction

Action to tackle inequalities in the employment field and to secure equal treatment and equal opportunities as between men and women working in the EEC has long been given a high priority on the Community's social policy agenda. Equality objectives have been incorporated in a growing body of Community legislation, and these provisions (some of which may be directly relied on by individual workers before their national courts) coupled with other Community measures to stimulate positive action to secure equality in practice have exerted a significant influence on policies and practices throughout the Community.

The basic EEC Treaty contains specific provisions designed to ensure application of the principle of equal pay for equal work. These provisions were originally prompted by economic considerations, and, in particular, a concern to ensure that competition in the Member States was not distorted by the employment of women at lower rates of pay than men for the same work. The social significance of such provisions soon became recognised too, and during the 1970s a number of specific Council Directives were enacted amplifying the Treaty provisions on equal pay (most notably by introducing the concept of equal pay for work of equal value) and applying the equal treatment principle to other aspects of employment and working conditions and to social security. The 1980s have seen the formulation of wide-ranging equality action programmes covering many different aspects of employment and working life, and the adoption of further Directives and proposals for others to fill the gaps left by the earlier measures. This growing body of Community legislation in the sex equality field has also led to the development of much important case law by the European Court, particularly in response to requests from national courts for preliminary rulings on the interpretation of the community provisions. As preparations for the completion of the internal market in 1992 proceed apace, the European commission has stressed that equal treatment issues will continue to be a priority on the EEC's social policy agenda, and that 'the fight against discrimination' in its various forms must continue.

The body of Community legislation so far enacted in the equal treatment field is detailed in the following sections. This includes basic Treaty provisions and specific Directives on equal pay, equal treatment in access to

employment and working conditions, and equal treatment in State and occupational social security schemes. Broad framework action programmes
which continue to provide a strategic focus for the direction of Community
law in this area are also included. As already noted, the growing body of EEC
equality legislation has been the subject of some important interpretative
rulings by the European Court. The most important of these rulings are also
included here. The scope of particular Directive and Treaty provisions, the
discretion afforded to Member States in applying Community law objectives
nationally, and the rights of individual workers to rely directly on Treaty
provisions and certain parts of Directives before their national courts to
avoid the application of inconsistent national provisions, are among issues
elaborated on by the European Court. The interaction between provisions in
the EEC Treaty and the various Directives is also explored by the Court. The
case law emerging from interpretation of the EEC's equality legislation also
reflects the practical problems to be addressed in applying Community-wide
principles to particular workplaces and national situations.

This Chapter is essentially concerned with the EEC's general equality
legislation seeking to eliminate discrimination on grounds of sex for workers
in the Community. Cases dealing with equality issues arising from the application of specific staff regulations for EEC officials are not therefore
included, since they do not involve interpretation of mainstream sex equality
legislation – although the principles raised in such cases are often very similar.
Community provisions concerned with other types of equality issues, such as
provisions to eliminate discrimination on grounds of nationality, are also not
included here. They are closely linked to the Community's free movement
rather than social policy provisions, and would require separate and detailed
consideration beyond the scope of this book.

A. EEC Treaty Extracts and Framework Action Programmes

EEC Treaty Extract

Article 119

Each Member State shall during the first stage ensure and subsequently maintain the application of the principle that men and women should receive equal pay for equal work.

For the purpose of this Article, 'pay' means the ordinary basic or minimum wage or salary and any other consideration, whether in cash or in kind, which the worker receives, directly or indirectly, in respect of his employment from his employer.

Equal pay without discrimination based on sex means:
(a) that pay for the same work at piece rates shall be calculated on the basis of the same unit of measurement;
(b) that pay for work at time rates shall be the same for the same job.

Council Resolution

12 July 1982

on the promotion of equal opportunities for women
(82/C 186/03)

THE COUNCIL OF THE EUROPEAN COMMUNITIES,

Having regard to the Treaty establishing the European Economic Community,
Having regard to the draft resolution presented by the Commission,[1]
Having regard to the opinion of the European Parliament,[2]
Having regard to the opinion of the Economic and Social Committee:[3]

Whereas various actions have already been undertaken at Community level to promote equal opportunities for women, in particular the adoption, by the Council, on the basis of Articles 100 and 235 of the Treaty establishing the European Economic Community, of Directive 75/117/EEC,[4] 76/207/EEC[5] and 79/7/EEC[6] concerning equal treatment for men and women;

Whereas all these actions, including those supported by the European Social Fund, have played an important part in improving the situation of women;

Whereas, despite the efforts so far made at both Community and national level, actual inequalities in employment persist and may well become worse in the present economic and social conditions;

Whereas, in a period of economic crisis, the action undertaken at Community and national level should be not only continued but also intensified, in particular in order to promote the achievement of equal opportunities in practice through the implementation of *inter alia* positive measures.

Notes the commission communication concerning a new Community Action Programme on the promotion of equal opportunities for women (1982 to 1985), which covers 'the achievement of equal treatment by strengthening individual rights' and the 'achievement of equal opportunities in practice, particularly by means of positive action programme'; Welcomes the initiative taken by the Commission,

Approves the general objectives of this communication, namely the stepping up of action to ensure observance of the principle of equal treatment for men and women and the promotion of equal opportunities in practice by positive measures; Expresses the will to implement appropriate measures to achieve them,

Notes also the comments which have been made on the Commission communication by the various delegations within the Council and which reveal *inter alia* certain characteristics peculiar to national systems,

Asks the Commission to take account of them in the initiatives which it takes within the framework of its powers,

Recalls the efforts which have been and are still being made in this area in the Member States,

Notes that the Commission communication defines specific objectives and joint courses of action, most of which fall within the follow-up to the implementation of the Directives adopted by the Council in the field of equal treatment for men and women,

Considers that, with due regard to the courses of action proposed, these objectives should guide the Community and the Member States in their efforts to apply on a broader basis and to realize in practice, the principle of equal opportunities without discriminating against women whatever the economic situation obtaining,

Emphasizes the importance, to this end, of strengthning or setting up national bodies for the promotion of women's employment and equal opportunities; Recalls the responsibilities which, in the pursuit of these objectives, also devolve upon workers' and employers' organizations,

Confirms the need to take steps to increase public awareness and disseminate information to support the change in attitudes to sharing occupational, family and social responsibilities; Asks Member States to cooperate fully with the Commission in steps to increase public awareness,

Reaffirms the need to promote the employment of both men and women in all sectors and occupations and a more balanced representation of women at different levels of responsibility at both national and Community level; Considers that the public sector, including the Community institutions and bodies, should set an example in this respect,

Underlines the desirability of avoiding special rules for the protection of women on the labour market and eliminating such rules in cases where originally well-founded concern for their protection is no longer justified,
Considers that account should be taken of the equal-opportunities dimension in preparing and implementing Community policies likely to affect it,
Asks the Commission to present an interim report by 1 January 1984 on progress achieved and on implementation under the new programme, based in particular on information obtained from the Member States, together with, if appropriate, suitable proposals,
Asks the Member States to send a first report to the Commission by 1 January 1985 on progress accomplished at national level; Notes the undertaking by the Commission to present an initial survey of the action undertaken before the end of 1985.

---

1. OJ No. C 22, 29.1.1982, p. 7.
2. OJ No. C 149, 14.6.1982, p. 54.
3. OJ No. C 178, 18.7.1982, p. 22.
4. OJ No. L 45, 19.2.1975, p. 19.
5. OJ No. L 39, 14.2.1976, p. 40.
6. OJ No. L 6, 10.1.1979, p. 24.

Commission Communication to the Council

presented on 14 December 1981

on the new community action programme on the promotion of equal opportunities for women
(1982–1985)*

ANNEX 1

Details of individual actions

ACHIEVEMENT OF EQUAL TREATMENT BY STRENGTHENING INDIVIDUAL RIGHTS

Implementation of existing Community Directives on equal treatment for men and women

Monitoring of the application of the Directives (Action 1)

Aim
To reinforce and to monitor the practical application of the Directives in the ten Member States, their progress and the interpretation given to Community measures at national level, with particular attention to indirect discrimination.

21

Grounds

Whilst the Directives are generally being properly transposed into national legislation, some of their provisions are still not being fully applied. The Commission's reports on the application of the Directives cannot deal exhaustively with the various practical obstacles or go into detail on the progress made in their interpretation or on the comparative results of the various practices and policies. A record of the courts' decisions on this subject needs to be compiled and an analysis made of the administrative mechanisms which are delaying the attainment of equal treatment and those which are promoting it. Particular problems exist regarding the application of the Directives in areas where the provisions are open to interpretation, as is the case with the concept of 'indirect discrimination by reference in particular to marital or family status' (Directives 76/207 and 79/7). A more extensive and systematic body of information in these areas could help to stimulate the activities of bodies promoting women's employment and equal opportunities and provide a basis for comparison across the Community, ensuring a greater consistency in the application of the Directives.

Courses of action

The Member States

• should create new bodies or consolidate existing structures for the promotion of women's employment and/or equal opportunities and should encourage such bodies to set up more systematic networks for information exchanges and consultation.

The Commission

• will develop and foster, through the advisory body on equal opportunities,[1] a network of contacts and exchanges involving representatives of the equal opportunities committees/commissions or equivalent structures existing in the Member States and experts drawn from the various interest groups concerned, in particular from organizations representing management and trade unions;
• will define the concept of indirect discrimination (Article 2(1) of Directive 76/207 and Article 4 of Directive 79/7) on the basis of the analysis and will continue its work on occupational classifications in the context of the practical implementation of the equal pay principle.

Legal redress is respect of equal treatment (Action 2)

Aim

To encourage workers to avail themselves of little-used means of redress (including reversal of the burden of proof).

Grounds

In presenting the reports on the application of Directives 75/117 and 76/207,[2] the Commission noted that workers, and female workers in particular, made little use of the arrangements for redress provided for by the national law.

The inflexibility of the procedures on the one hand, and the difficulty of assembling evidence of discrimination on the other, explain this reticence in part; hish unemployment also discourages female workers from asserting their rights for fear of losing their jobs.

Nevertheless, it appears that in the countries in which special bodies offering advice and assistance have been set up, or more flexible means of redress made available, female workers have become more aware of their rights. This is particularly true of the United Kingdom, where assistance from the equal Opportunities Commission has resulted in a greater number of cases being brought.

The experience of some Member States with respect to reversal of the burden of proof (the onus is placed on the employer or whoever has acted in an allegedly discriminatory fashion) should likewise be brought to the attention of the other Member States. This reversal is provided for in certain specified cases in Belgium, the Federal Republic of Germany, Ireland and the United Kingdom. These arrangements have not yet, however, proved their worth, and their aim and the way they work needs to be further considered.

Courses of action

The Member States
• should intensify their information compaigns and step up their efforts to set up special bodies or encourage existing bodies to advise and assist female workers in availing themselves properly of the means of redress provided for in national legislation on equal treatment.

The Commission
• will conduct a comparative analysis of national procedures with a view to proposing Community action which, by providing a basis for expert advice in this field and in particular by pointing to exmples of good practice, will help Member States to improve their arrangements for legal redress.

Revision of national and Community protective legislation (Action 3)

Aim
To abolish in accordance with Directive 76/207 unjustified protective legislation in the field of access to employment and working conditions and to promote equal standards of protection for men and women.

Grounds
Directive 76/207 stipulates that the Member States should revise protective laws 'when the concern for protection which originally inspired them is no longer well-founded', in particular as a consequence of technological progress and changing customs. In some cases the retention of specific protective measures leads in practice to the exclusion of women from whole sectors of employment or from promotion. Legislation exists in some countries, for

example, which forbids the employment of women in industries where loads of above a certain weight require to be lifted (which is in parctice done mechanically nowadays); in others, the employment of women of Sundays is forbidden.

These changes must not of course obstruct efforts to provide the highest possible level of protection for both men and women and to humanize and improve working conditions in general. These efforts shouls so far as possible be based on the principle of equal treatment.

Courses of action

The Member States
• should continue their efforts to revise protective legislation as provided for in Articles 3(2)(c) and 5(2)(c) of Directive 76/207.

The Commission
• will back up these efforts by determining, on the basis of objective studies at Community level, which protective measures should be abolished on the grounds that the concern for protection which originally inspired them is no longer well-founded. A study is currently being conducted of the current state of legislation in the Member States, which would enable the Commission to define its position in this area and identify whether further study or action would be appropriate;
• will endeavour in future to propose Community measures which provide equal protection for men and women and, if necessary, it will revise existing measures which are no longer in keeping with the position it adopts on the basis of the abovementioned study.[3]

Preparation of additional provisions and extension to new sectors

Equal treatment in matters of social security (Action 4)

Aim
To achieve equal treatment in occupational social security schemes.

To extend the princple of equal treatment provided for in Directive 79/7 to the sector not falling within its present scope (survivors' pensions and family allowances) or in which an exception could be made (retirement age, increases in long-term benefits, maintenance of rights of women who have brought up a child, possibility of contracting out of a statutory scheme).

To establish gradually the individual social security entitlement of married women or women cohabiting.

Grounds
Directive 76/207 provides for the progressive implementation of the principle of equal treatment for men and women in matters of social security.

Directive 79/7 applies only to statutory schemes, and the problems arising in the occupational social security schemes should now be resolved. Directive 79/7 did not seek to cover occupational schemes because they were so numerous and because their administrative machinery required further study. The Commission has now done the preparatory work for the adoption of a Community legal instrument.

The persistence of discrimination in those sectors which either are not covered by the Directive or may be exempted helps to perpetuate inequality of treatment in employment policies as a whole; this is particularly true in respect of retirement ages.

Moreover, the application in several Member States of the head-of-household concept[4] frequently causes direct and indirect discrimination. A number of benefits are either not paid (e.g. widowers' pensions) or are paid out only to one of the spouses (e.g. family allowances) although both partners pay contributions. Despite recent developments in civil law, legislation in the social security sector still reflects the traditional concepts whereby it was the man's responsibility to provide for his family and does not correspond to the present situation in which women and couples work.

Courses of action

The Member States
• should take steps to extend the principle of equal treatment to social security schemes which are exempt from the provisions of Directive 79/7 or which are not covered by it.

The Commission
• will make a proposal for a Community legal instrument relating to the implementation of the principle of equal treatment for men and women in occupational social security schemes;
• will begin the preparatory work for the framing of a legal instrument on the areas which are exempt from or not covered by Directive 79/7;
• will examine the effects of the present system, and in particular those of the application of the head-of-household concept, with a view to formulating Community proposals on the 'individualization' of entitlement in particular to establish the social security entitlement of married women or women cohabiting.[5]

Application of the principle of equal treatment to self-employed women and to women in agriculture, particularly in family enterprises (Action 5)

Aim
To improve the occupational status of self-employed women and of women in agriculture and to affirm equal access to employment, promotion and vocational training and the right to equality as regards certain social security benefits.

Grounds
Directive 76/207 is applicable to the self-employed; yet it appears from a number of studies undertaken by the Commission and the report on the implementation of the Directive that its translation into fact in the self-

employed sector and in family holdings in particular requires special thought and support.

Self-employed women, especially women in agriculture (including wives actively engaged in farming) do not always have a clearly defined occupational status, which makes it difficult, among other things, to identify their contribution to the family income from their earnings; consequently their social security entitlement is also unclear. Even when they play a full part in the family enterprise, their status often remains that of a housewife as defined by matrimonial law. There is, moreover, also a need to improve their opportunities for engaging in vocational training, especially technical and management training, taking account of the Directive of 17 April 1972 on the provision of socio-economic guidance for and the acquisition of occupational skills by persons working in agriculture.[6]

In several countries action is already beginning to be taken, either by improving civil, commercial or tax law or by laying down policies for vocational training or better working conditions and setting up services providing replacements to cover absence for training, participation in the activities of trade organizations, maternity and sickness.

Courses of action

The Member States
• should eliminate in accordance with Directive 76/207 the constraints preventing application of the principle of equal treatment to self-employed women and to women in agriculture.

The Commission
• will continue to scrutinize measures adopted by Member States in various areas recognized as specific to women workers but not covered by Community Directives, with the aim of defining an individual occupational status for self-employed women and women in agriculture including their individual entitlement as regards social security and remuneration. The Commission will seek to improve the conditions for access to training and professional associations and, as regards the agricultural sector, will take account of the equal opportunities dimension in the development of replacement services;
• will propose a Community legal instrument in these areas on the basis of the conclusions of this review.

Taxation and the employment of women (Action 6)

Aim
To implement the principle of equal treatment by revising income tax systems which appear to have an indirect adverse effect on women's employment, their right to work and their promotion in employment.

Grounds
In some Member States the increased proportion of married women in paid employment 'has influenced the development of fiscal legislation, and led to

a questioning of the traditional attitudes built into income tax systems. The question of whether or not the earned incomes of spouses should be aggregated has been reopened after a long period of consensus among fiscal experts that spouses' incomes for tax purposes should be aggregated under progressive tax systems based upon the principle of ability to pay. At the same time, many countries have reviewed the status of married women under fiscal legislation.

Three main issues are involved: the appropriate tax differentials between one and two-earner families (a question of horizontal equity); the status of women under fiscal legislation; work disincentives for married women.[1]

The Commission should focus its attention on these issues, in particular the last-mentioned, in connection with the correct application of equal treatment as regards access to employment and working conditions (Directive 76/207).

'The main features of income tax systems which could have a special impact on the work decisions of married women are whether or not the earned incomes of spouses are aggregated the distribution of allowances between the husband and wife and how these change when the wife enters the labour market, and the progressivity of the tax schedule'.[7]

Courses of action

The Member states
• should eliminate from their taxation systems any provisions constituting indirect discrimination in respect to equal opportunity for women in employment under Article 2(1) of Directive 76/207.

The Commission
• will undertake a comparative analysis of taxation system; if it emerges that the systems in effect in certain Member States have any negative effect, even indirect, on equal opportunities for women, it will take such appropriate measures as are within its competence in this area.

Improvement in living and working conditions

Parental leave, leave for family reasons (Action 7)

Aim
To extend parental leave and leave for family reasons and at the same time to build up the network of public facilities and services.

Grounds
The sharing of family responsibilities is a precondition of the achievement of equal treatment for men and women. Community action should lend support to the change of attitude on this question which is becoming apparent among the younger generation. The extension of family and parental leave is one aspect of a new distribution of time between work and other activities. In this context the reorganization of working time should avoid reinforcing traditional family roles and instead be used to make an important contri-

27

bution in the achievement of equal opportunities. It is however important that the granting of family and parental leave does not serve as a pretext for reducing public facilities and services. There is already a welcome tendency in several Member States to grant leave to men and women to care for children in the period immediately following maternity leave (parental leave), and to care for a sick child or a member of the family, in line with Directive 76/207, which stipulates equal treatment in working conditions.

Courses of action

The Member States
• should examine the possibility of extending parental leave and leave for family reasons (in parallel with efforts to consolidate public facilities and services), taking account of trends towards a new distribution of work and non-work time.

The Commission
• will conduct a survey on experience gained in the Member States, in addition to the work already undertaken, with a view to establishing Community guidelines on the definition of these types of leave, their duration, the conditions on which they are granted, and at the same time will study the evolution of the network of public facilities and services (reduction or extension);
• will disseminate the information thus compiled to the Member States;
• will draft a Community legal instrument to promote parental leave and leave for family reasons while maintaining and extending existing public facilities and services.

Protection of women during pregnancy or motherhood (Action 8)

Aim
To abolish discrimination against pregnant women in recruitment, to improve and harmonize maternity leave and to promote paid leave for antenatal check-ups.
To improve social security cover for pregnant women and mothers, including self-employed women and women in agriculture.

Grounds
In several Member States neither the refusal to recruit pregnant women nor their dismissal on those grounds in sanctioned. Where maternity leave is concerned, there are deficiencies in several countries as regards the duration and payment of various types of leave. Most of the Member States do not assume the cost of the absences from work of pregnant women for medical check-ups, despite the fact that specialists consider these essential for the detection of pregnancies at risk. Self-employed women and women in agriculture often have inadequate social security protection and sometimes none whatsoever during pregnancy or early motherhood.

28

On the other hand, provisions for lengthy maternity leave which is not justified on physiological grounds should be avoided since it overlaps into what should be parental leave and serves to reinforce the inequality of opportunity for women in society and employment. Moreover, when the cost of maternity protection is borne by employers, it has an adverse effect on the recruitment of young women.

Courses of action

The Member States
• should adopt or supplement measures, including social security provisions, for the protection of women during pregnancy and early motherhood, so that mothers are not disadvantaged as regards working life.

The Commission
• will conduct a comparative study and evaluate the financial implications of the measures already adopted by the Member States with a view to identifying the most appropriate protective provisions for motherhood which should take full account of the social function of child-bearing and the financial implications for society as a whole rather than for individual employers;
• will propose Community legislation in this area on the basis of this analysis, if necessary.

ACHIEVEMENT OF EQUAL OPPORTUNITIES IN PRACTICE, PARTICULARLY BY MEANS OF POSITIVE ACTION PROGRAMMES

Development of positive action (Action 9)

Aim
To promote at national level framework legislation to develop positive action.

Grounds
The legal provisions on equal treatment are designed to afford rights to individuals; they are inadequate for the elimination of all forms of discrimination unless parallel action and measures are taken, either by governments or by other bodies responsible for different aspects of social policy, to counteract or compensate for the impact of existing social structures on individual behaviour.

Action may take different forms, some of which will entail the adoption of special budgets, ranging from the provision of information, through action which the public authorities may take in awarding public contracts, policies for diversifying vocational training for women and action to remove existing inequalities which affect women's opportunities.

Article 2(4) of Directive 76/207 provides for the Member States to take such measures. Experience shows that, in the absence of a legal framework of the type existing in the USA[8] to determine the type of action to be taken and the means of implementing it (including the necessary penalties), practical action is generally neglected.

Courses of action

The Member States
• should extend and diversify position action already undertaken in the context of the application of Directive 76/207, in particular Article 2(4).

The Commission
• will lend its support to campaigns undertaken in the Member States to improve knowledge and understanding of this aspect, in particular by organizing seminars;
• will conduct a critical analysis of measures already undertaken in some Member States or in non-Community countries in order to review these measures and prepare a Community instrument on the type of measures to be developed, the resources to be mobilized and the conditions of eligibility.

Preparation for working life, initial and continuing training

Integration into working life (in particular with respect to new technologies) (Action 10)

Aim
To promote the diversification of occupational choices for women and the mastering of new technologies, with particular reference to guidance and initial and continuing training.

Grounds
The traditional stereotyped view of the woman's role, including for example the belief that technical occupations are not 'feminine', tends to be formed from early childhood and continues to be imprinted throughout the training process. This is probably the single biggest factor in hindering the integration of women in the workforce, especially in areas applying the new technologies.

In several Member States, measures are being taken to break down these views. These include efforts to revise school text-books which propagate stereotyped roles and to introduce pilot schemes for training women, in particular unemployed women, for non-traditional occupations, including areas applying the new technologies. These efforts are, however, still on a fairly small scale and have not succeeded in stimulating a thorough reappraisal of the models which often induce girls not to choose training in technical subjects which could lead to interesting and rewarding employment.

Courses of action

The Member States
• should undertake, continue or reinforce positive measures to improve

30

equal opportunity in education, guidance and training, particularly in the following areas (see Articles 2(4) and 4 of Directive 76/207):

training, integration and reintegration of women in employment in general and non-traditional occupations in particular;

further training for women in employment within firms, with a view to improving their prospects for promotion or their access to other than unskilled jobs, especially those involving new technologies;

training of vocational guidance counsellors and instructors to make them aware of the need for diversification in the career choices of both girls and boys; particular attention in training counsellors and instructors should be paid to the special needs of immigrant girls;

development of suitable preparatory training and vocational training programmes for immigrant women, bearing in mind the need to respect their cultural identity;

development of training programmes for couples in rural areas;

training for women with a view to reintegration into working life after a break.

The Commission
• should extend its action especially through the European Social Fund and in liaison with the European Centre for the Development of Vocational Training (Cedefop), which have already played a significant promotional role in these areas, and should place further emphasis on the exchange of experience and the comparative evaluation of innovatory action in this field.

Vocational choices (Action 11)

Aim
To make girls, their families and their schools aware of the job opportunities available to girls.

Grounds
Measures to promote the diversification of women's occupations will be ineffective if no specific provisions are made for informing those concerned and encouraging them to persevere in opening up occupations and training courses hitherto almost entirely the preserve of men.

The Member States should be encouraged at Community level to follow this path, in particular by introducing programmes which are eligible for support from the ESF.

Courses of action

The Member States
• should enable national committees for employment and/or equal opportunities for men and women to conduct a vigorous publicity compaign on opportunities for girls and on their rights in connection with the proper

31

implementation of Directive 76/207, which provides for the abolition of discrimination with regard to access to all types and levels of vocational guidance and training;
• should also do their utmost in accordance with Directive 76/207 to disseminate information on educational and training options available to either girls or boys, or to men or women.

The Commission
• will support measures taken by the Member States by establishing an experimental network of equal opportunities' advisers whose task it will be, complementing the activities of the ESF and of the European Centre for the Development of Vocational Training (Cedefop), to foster integrated national programmes on education and training designed to bring about the desired changes, in particular in collaboration with the social partners;
• will compile information on the action taken and disseminate this information in the Member States through the advisory body on equal opportunities and the two sides of industry.

Employment

Desegregation of employment (Action 12)

Aim
To promote desegregation in employment in all sectors and occupations and at all levels of the occupational hierarchy.

Grounds
Directive 76/207 calls for the opening of all jobs to women. It is a well-known fact, highlighted in particular at the Manchester Conference, that women workers are concentrated in a few sectors of activity and occupations and at lower hierarchical levels. Moreover, this state of affairs persists even when new markets are opened or new jobs created. This is one of the reasons for the high rate of unemployment among women in the Community. In the public sector, the proportion of women in upper-level and managerial posts is still very low. This situation was underlined by the Council, which on 10 June 1981, on the occasion of the adoption of the report on the application of Directive 76/207, called for 'a more balanced representation of women at the various levels of responsibility'.

Nevertheless, it can be shown that change can be brought about where the political will exists and where public or private employers wish to apply Directive 76/207 correctly in practice.

Evidence compiled in studies conducted by the European Centre for the Development of Vocational Training on pilot schemes for integrating women in new jobs or upper-level posts demonstrates the capacity of women to occupy any post that is genuinely open to them. In particular, the studies presented at the Manchester Conference[9] also showed that equal pay and equal conditions of employment are only possible in sectors where desegregation of employment has really been achieved at all levels.

The process of change must be stimulated by starting with key sectors (such as the civil service), sample sectors (such as the banks, where the Commission has already initiated a project) or pilot schemes (such as cooperatives, new activities in craft occupations, restoration of ancient buildings, etc.)

Courses of action

The Member States
• should set an example by taking measures to achieve equal opportunities for men and women in public service;
• should draw up lists of appointments by sex at the highest levels of the hierarchy in the major public sectors (as is already happening in some countries);
• should continue work already begun on the setting up of cooperatives to provide services likely to remedy deficiencies in community services and encourage women to participate in the administration and technical management of these cooperatives.

The Commission
• will conduct a comparative survey with a view to identifying and recommending practical means whereby the Directives can be put into effect in the various public services (e.g. measures to facilitate women's access to upper-level posts, training of women for access to public-sector jobs traditionally reserved for men such as the police force and technical jobs in post and telecommunications offices, entrance examinations restricted to women to redress the balance, in accordance with Directive 76/207);
• will publish, through its existing information network, lists of appointments by sex at the highest levels of the hierarchy in the major public sectors and the Commission itself;
• will support initiatives taken in the Member States to set up cooperatives within the framework of Community priorities for job creation as defined in its October 1981 communication on the priorities for Community action with regard to job creation;[10]
• will establish, with the help of experts, reports on results achieved and factors contributing to change in certain sectors (see, for example, the action-research in progress on employment and equality of opportunity in banks).

Analysis of trends in female employment (Action 13)

Aim
To assess the progress made towards achieving equal treatment in employment and conditions of employment and towards achieving desegregation.

Grounds
In some Member States, the USA and some Scandinavian countries, those responsible for framing employment policies feel that studies should be made of the impact of these policies on the achievement of equal opportunities and the desegregation of employment. Such studies should be based not only on

statistical data but also on a qualitative analysis of the situation. A number of international organizations (including the UN and the OECD) have already made such studies.

Further information is necessary to indicate the particular implications of the economic crisis on the expansion of insecure forms of employment and part-time work which may well accentuate segregation in employment (women are more likely than men to accept these forms of work given that the burden of family responsibilities still rests largely on their shoulders), the provision of public facilities and services, especially nurseries, trends in female migration, often provoked by the inadequacy of social infrastructure, and their effect on regional development.

Courses of action

The Member States
• should cooperate in establishing comparable data by encouraging the collection of data on the basis of common indicators, in order to:

identify the progress in desegregating employment, e.g. in certain representative sectors;
monitor whether the reorganization of working time, especially possible measures to promote part-time work, does not reinforce the segregation of women in employment;
identify the possible obstacles to more women taking up full-time work;
monitor, in some sample regions, the progress of women in the context of regional development.

The Commission
• will convene a group of experts to advise on the setting up of a continuous monitoring system linked with existing international measures and networks (Euridyce, Cedefop, etc.) which would support action by Member States on the basis of common indicators;
• will give priority to the insertion in the computer network (CIRCE), in the existing data banks and in the general production of data, of information concerning the situation of women.

Application of the principle of equal treatment to women immigrants (Action 14)

Aim
To promote the right of immigrant women to equal access to employment and training.

Grounds
Evidence suggests that the application of the principles laid down in Directive 76/207 on equal treatment have had little or no impact on women immigrants and that this will remain the case unless special programmes are adopted.

In view of the double disadvantage of immigrant women (namely as women and as outsiders), special efforts are required to adapt and reaffirm the principles laid down in the Directive to take account of their situation. It is, for example, difficult for immigrant women to gain access in practice to the various forms of adult vocational training because of linguistic differences or the inadequacy of their basic education, which is even more striking than that of local women.

Courses of action

The Member States
• should abolish discrimination which impedes the achievement of the principle of equal treatment for immigrant women in accordance with Directive 76/207 and launch a programme of positive action designed to afford equal opportunities.

The Commission
• will set up an expert panel to ascertain areas in which discrimination against immigrant women exists and identify specific legal difficulties which prevent them from obtaining employment;
• will carry out a comparative analysis of positive measures introduced by the Member States to promote equal opportunities in employment and training for immigrant women with a view to issuing a recommendation on measures to be carried out in this field.

Improvement in the quality of life

Sharing of occupational, family and social responsibilities (Action 15)

Aim
To enable both men and women to find fulfilment in and combine satisfactorily their career, their family and their social life.

Grounds
Up to now the organization of work and many of the other functions of society have been based essentially in the hypothesis that male adults are free of domestic obligations. Although civil law has been increasingly adapted to a more egalitarian analysis of the status of men and women, this has spread neither to social nor to tax law, thereby creating inconsistencies in the legal system and entailing discrimination against women.

Women remain largely absent from trade union, professional governmental and Community advisory and decision-making bodies.

A great deal of thought needs to be given to the means of ensuring overall coherence in the legal field, in the organization of work and society in general (taking account especially of the effects of the new technologies and trends towards adaptation of working time) in order to ensure a more equitable sharing of family responsibilities and, in the same way, a more equal share for women at work and in society.

Basic needs in the area of public services and facilities, especially for the care of young children, are still far from being fully provided for, and this constitutes a major obstacle to the attainment of equality for men and women in employment. The economic crisis has exacerbated difficulties in this respect.

Courses of action

The Member States
• should investigate all possible means to enhance the position of women in decision-making and consultative bodies;
• should attempt to ensure that public services and facilities are organized to take account of working hours, school timetables and the needs of workers and working couples with family responsibilities with a view to promoting equal opportunities for women.

The Commission
• will suggest issues for consideration with regard to the growing inconsistencies between changing social values on the one hand and the organization of work and fiscal and social law on the other hand. This review should be carried out over the medium term, possibly with the cooperation of the European Centre for the Development of Vocational Training in Berlin and the European Foundation for the Improvement of Living and Working Conditions in Dublin;
• will analyse progress achieved as regards the position of women in decision-making bodies, particularly those related to employment, and propose Community guidelines to improve the situation;[12]
• will monitor trends in the area of public services and facilities with a view to identifying guidelines at Community level.

Evolution in public attitudes (Action 16)

Aim
To increase the awareness of the general public and those most directly concerned of positive aspects of the change in attitudes.

Grounds
As with any process of radical change in society, the progress made by women towards achieving equality, which calls into question traditional sex-related roles, has met with stiff resistance. Frequently only the negative aspects of this process are highlighted.

Stereotyped attitudes and discriminatory behaviour continue and tend to be accentuated by the economic crisis. The changing values to which the ten Member States subscribe in principle and the positive changes they entail must therefore be put across to the public, especially through the mass media.

Action in this field should be carried out by special information activities aimed at a number of target audiences (politicians, employers, trade unions, parents, teachers, etc.).

Courses of action

The Member States

• should, in the spirit of Directive 76/207, conduct information campaigns aimed at those parties most directly involved, such as employers, workers, women and parents, in order to accelerate the achievement of equal opportunities for women.

The Commission

• will draw up a programme of information activities aimed at various target audiences, in conjunction with the Member States, in order to improve the impact of national information campaigns;
• will launch measures at Community level to hasten changes in attitudes by involving national information networks (radio, television, women's magazines, the press); and to stimulate cooperation between them (see, for example, the campaigns in women's magazines during the run-up to the elections for the European Parliament).

---

* COM (81)758.
1. *see* Annex III.
2. Bull. EC 1-1979, point 2.1.49; Bull, EC 2-1981, point 2.1.27.
3. Special protection will continue to be afforded to women in connection with pregnancy and maternity.
4. Already abolished in civil law in most Member States.
5. The High-level Conference on the Employment of Women, organised by the OECD in May 1980, issued a statement along these lines.
6. OJ No. L 96, 23.4.1972.
7. Extract from 'The tax/benefit position of selected income groups in OECD member countries, 1974–78', OECD, Paris 1980.
8. Executive Order 11246-1965, as amended by Executive Order 11375-1967.
9. Confirmed by the preparatory documents for the OECD High-level Conference in May 1980.
10. Bull. EC 10-1981, points 2.1.46 to 2.1.49.
11. *See* Convention and Recommendation adopted at the 67th session of the International Labour Conference on equal opportunities and equal treatment for men and women workers with family responsibilities.
12. Bull. EC 6-1981, point 2.1.60.

Second Council Resolution

24 July 1986

on the promotion of equal opportunities for women
(86/C 203/02)

THE COUNCIL OF THE EUROPEAN COMMUNITIES,

Having regard to the Treaties establishing the European Communities,
Having regard to the draft resolution submitted by the Commission,[1]

Having regard to the opinion of the European Parliament,[2]
Having regard to the opinion of the Economic and Social Committee:[3]

Whereas, in order to promote equal opportunities for women, various measures have been taken at Community level, in particular the adoption by the Council of Directive 75/117/EEC of 10 February 1975 on the approximation of the laws of the Member States relating to the application of the principle of equal pay for men and women,[4] Directive 76/207/EEC of 9 February 1976 on the implementation of the principle of equal treatment for men and women as regards access to employment, vocational training and promotion, and working conditions[5] and Directive 79/7/EEC of 19 December 1978 on the progressive implementation of the principle of equal treatment for men and women in matters of social security;[6]

Whereas these Community legal instruments constitute the basis needed for the development of Community action;

Whereas the 1982 to 1985 action programme and the commitments entered into in that connection, in particular the Council resolution of 12 July 1982 concerning the promotion of equal opportunities for women,[7] the Council resolution of 7 June 1984 on action to combat unemployment amongst women[8] and the Council recommendation of 13 December 1984 on the promotion of positive action for women[9] and those adopted in certain related areas,[10] constitute positive contributions to the promotion of equal opportunities;

Whereas, however, inequality persists and seems likely to increase in the present economic climate;

Whereas efforts already under way must be intensified and developed with a view to achieving genuine equality, so that women can approach social, technological and occupational change on an equal footing with men;

Whereas the European Parliament has frequently urged the need for a comprehensive and wide-ranging policy to promote equal opportunities for women;

Whereas it should be noted with approval that the Commission firmly believes that the programme's objective of realizing in practice equal opportunities in economic, social and cultural life can and should be achieved without imposing any unreasonable burden on the economy and undertakings. Considering the conclusions of the European Council of 2 and 3 December 1985 on the matter:

1. *Points to* the Directives, recommendations, resolutions and other instruments adopted concerning the promotion of equal opportunities for women;
2. *Recalls* the proposals for Directives already submitted by the Commission, and agrees to continue its efforts to seek solutions to the problems involved;
3. *Confirms* the need to develop and intensify action at Community and national level through a systematic and coherent wide-ranging policy designed to eliminate de facto inequalities, whatever the economic situation, and to promote genuine equality for opportunity;
4. *Supports* the broad outlines of the Commission communication concerning

a new medium-term programme on equal opportunities for women (1986 to 1990) and supports that programme's objective of realizing in practice equal opportunities in economic, social and cultural life; reiterates in this context, the importance of promoting job creation;

5. *Calls on* the Member States to take appropriate action on the basis of, inter alia, the elements of the Commission communication referred to in point 4 of this resolution and in particular to:

- ensure effective application of existing equal-treatment legislation, particularly through the systematic provision of information, the development of suitable mechanisms to carry through and prepare provisions on equal treatment, and the examination of all aspects of the problems relating to the establishment of proof in this regard;

- develop comprehensive and coordinated action in the fields of education and training in order to create a better balance between men and women in the various types of teaching establishment and to widen career choices to include sectors and trades of the future, in particular those concerned with new technologies, enterprise creation and self-employed occupations, in accordance with the resolution of 3 June 1985;

- adopt adequate measures to increase the number of women in jobs linked to the introduction of new technologies, with a view to promoting desegregation and as a response to the resulting changes;

- develop and intensify specific action promoting the employment of women and, in particular, support local initiatives and adopt measures to ensure that women have equal opportunities to set up businesses, particularly cooperatives, as well as measures to support self-employed women, including those working in agriculture;

- adopt a more systematic policy to promote the presence of both sexes in employment at all levels, particularly through the development of positive action in all fields, the revision of protective legislation which is no longer justified and the search for specific solutions for the most disadvantaged categories;

- review social-protection and social-security provisions, taking into account the changing place of women in employment;

- develop measures to encourage the sharing of family and career responsibilities through measures to increase awareness and steps to adapt and reorganize working time, with due regard for the responsibilities of both sides of industry, development of the social infrastructure, particularly child-minding facilities, and of adequate solutions for groups and persons who particularly need them;

- launch or encourage at all appropriate levels systematic and wide-ranging information and awareness campaigns to highlight the positive aspects of equality, thereby promoting a change in attitudes, especially through the media and by targeting a variety of groups, in order to reach all participants in political, social, occupational and educational life, particularly women themselves;

- encourage both sides of industry to take steps to secure effective equality of opportunity and efficacy of positive measures at the workplace;

39

– actively promote greater participation by women in the public and private sectors, particularly in posts for responsibility, and in decision-making bodies.

6. *Will continue to* promote consistency between specific measures to promote equal opportunities and overall economic and social policy at both Community and national level and instructs the Commission to keep a check on the consistency of its measures at Community level while encouraging positive action to help women within the limits of the means available and avoiding any measure which might discourage women from joining the job market;

7. *Agrees to* develop more systematic cooperation on Member States' policies and actions on equal treatment, and instructs the Commission to organize such cooperation with all bodies concerned, such as national authorities, equal-treatment bodies and committees, both sides of industry;

8. *Requests* the Commission to prepare a progress report and an assessment of the implementation of this programme by 1 January 1991 and accordingly invites the Member States to forward the necessary information to the Commission before 1 January 1990.

---

1. OJ No. C 356, 31.12.1985, p. 28.
2. Opinion delivered on 13 May 1986 (not yet published in the Official Journal).
3. Opinion delivered on 24 April 1986 (not yet published in the Official Journal).
4. OJ No. L 45, 19.2.1976, p. 19.
5. OJ No. L 39, 14.1.1976, p. 40.
6. OJ No. L 6, 10.1.1979, p. 24.
7. OJ No. C 186, 21.7.1982, p. 3.
8. OJ No. C 161, 21.6.1984, p. 4.
9. OJ No. L 331, 19.12.1984, p. 34.
10. Particularly:
    – Council resolution of 2 June 1983 concerning vocational training measures relating to new information technologies (OJ No. C 166, 25.6.1983, p. 1),
    – Council resolution of 11 July 1983 concerning vocational training policies in the European Community in the 1980s (OJ No. C 193, 20.7.1983, p. 2),
    – Resolution of the Council and the Ministers for Education meeting within the Council of 19 September 1983 on measures relating to the introduction of new information technology in education (OJ No. C 256, 24.9.1983, p. 1),
    – Council resolution of 23 January 1984 on the promotion of employment for young people (OJ No. C 29, 4.2.1984, p. 1),
    – Resolution of the Council and the Ministers for Education meeting within the Council of 3 June 1985 containing an action programme on equal opportunities for girls and boys in education (OJ No. C 166, 5.7.1985, p. 1).

Commission Communication to the Council

transmitted on 20 December 1985

on the medium-term community programme on the promotion of equal opportunities for women
(1986–1990)*

Preface

The European Community has played a primary role in the past in the promotion of equal opportunities for men and women. Its legislative activity and the first Action Programme 1982–85 have made a significant contribution to the progress achieved in this area at European level. As a result there has been a shift in attitudes towards a more equal participation by men and women in economic and social life.

However, the evaluation of the first Action Programme 1982–85 made it clear that there is a need for continued and more intensive action by the Community in this area, particularly with a view to adapting it in line with economic and social changes and with technological development.

In this context the Commission has submitted a second Action Programme 1986–90 aimed at pursuing current initiatives and at responding to new economic and social challenges in the equal treatment area. The second Programme deals with an important number of actions concerning women's employment, particularly those which encourage an equal level of participation in employment linked with new technology. The Commission also proposes actions in favour of a more equal sharing of family responsibilities. Particular significance should be accorded to campaigns for information and increasing awareness aimed at the general public and at specific target groups. The Programme identifies the responsibilities of the different parties involved (the Community, national and regional authorities) and underlines the need for intensive cooperation amongst all concerned.

The new Action Programme is part of and will contribute to the achievement of a people's Europe. The Commission hopes that it will show the way to bring about equality of opportunity in concrete terms in economic, social and cultural life.

Explanatory memorandum

General
  1. The Community Action Programme on the Promotion of Equal Opportunities for Women 1982–85[1] has come to an end.
     Pursuant to the Council resolution of 12 July 1982 on this subject,[2] the Commission has taken stock of and assessed the measures taken to implement this Programme at Community and national level.[3]
     The conclusions the Commission has drawn show that, although progress has been made, much remains to be done and that a comprehensive

and diversified policy is needed to achieve concrete results in the equal opportunities field.

A consistent policy is all the more important at a time of economic crisis when the most vulnerable categories are particularly affected by technical and social change and unemployment.

2. On several occasions the European Parliament has emphasized the need for a comprehensive, large-scale policy. Its major resolution of 17 January 1984 on the situation of women in Europe[4] calls on the European institutions and the Member States of the European Community to renew and reinforce action in this field.

3. A similar approach can be observed in work carried out in other areas or by groups particularly concerned by this question.

Thus, the Nairobi Conference, which closed the United Nations Decade for Women, underlined the importance of a comprehensive programme and adopted decisions to this effect.[5]

The International Labour Organization (ILO) has also taken action in this field (Conventions, etc.) and in November 1984 adopted a resolution on this subject. The OECD has likewise been active in this area and in its recent report on the role of women in the economy[6] also calls for a multi-faceted coherent policy.

The Council of Europe is also pursuing action in the legal sphere (European Social Charter) and of a practical nature (positive action, increasing awareness, role of the media, etc.).

4. Lastly, various social and occupational groups have worked to the same end. For example, the European Trade Union Confederation, the European Youth Forum, the family associations which make up the Confederation of Family Organizations in the European Community (Coface) and a variety of women's organizations.

5. Desite the limitations of the 1982–85 Programme and of its actual application, particularly at national level, it is generally acknowledged as having had a very positive and stimulating effect on the development of action to promote equal opportunities for women.

The short implementation period made it possible to launch many actions which must be followed up, to put forward proposals which must be adopted, to finance research, studies and surveys.

6. This is the background against which the Commission is proposing a new medium-term programme (five years) designed to:
• consolidate rights under Community law, particularly by improving the application of existing provisions and adopting the proposals under examination;
• follow-up and develop action launched under the 1982–85 Action Programme, in particular the networks for contacts and exchanges which

represent a new form of social dialogue in this area, and which have made a very positive contribution;

• intensify efforts to involve all those concerned through a broader dialogue and a consciousness-raising campaign aimed at the people involved and at a wider target public;

• develop and intensify support for specific actions, in particular those intended to develop women's employment;

• develop and adopt such action, in particular with regard to the most vulnerable and/or disadvantaged categories;

• examine the situation in the new Member States of the Community.

The details of the proposed actions will be defined, case by case, during the period of application of this programme according to specific guidelines.

The Commission's concern is to highlight ways of realizing equal opportunities in economic, social and cultural life. The Commission firmly believes that this objective may be achieved without imposing any unreasonable burden on industry or on small and medium-sized enterprises in particular.

7. This programme is concerned only with actions within the Community. Needless to say, the Commission is also actively pursuing measures for women, initiated in the context of its development programme pursuant to provisions specifically aimed at the full integration of women into the development process (Article 123, Third Lome Convention).

8. This programme includes actions to be carried out at various levels. The report on the implementation of the 1982–85 Action Programme showed that although sustained efforts had been made, much remained to be done, particularly with regard to the incorporation by the Member States of Community proposals into their national laws and practice. There will have to be a clear definition of the role and responsibilities of the various parties concerned (Community, national, regional and local authorities, social and occupational groups – in particular the two sides of industry – and equal opportunities bodies) together with greater concertation between the latter at Community level on actions and policies pursued in this area.

9. The programme can only be realized if it is supported by the political will of all parties, particularly by the Member States. This will should be demonstrated both by the adoption of the directives proposed in the context of the previous programme, and by a commitment to implement the present programme along the lines laid down in the attached draft resolution.

10. This programme comes under the heading of the development of a 'people's Europe': the Community has played a vital role in promoting equal opportunities for women. Its activities should be developed in a broader context adapted to political, social, cultural and technological changes in the Community.

The need for a multi-faceted policy

11. First of all, the improved application of existing provisions remains one of the Commission's principal responsibilities.

    There are still a number of shortcomings as regards the incorporation into national law of the existing equal opportunities directives; needless to say, the Commission as guardian of the Treaties is taking appropriate action.

    The main problem, however, arises in connection with the application in practice of national legislation implementing Community law.

    The work of the independent expert group set up by the Commission, together with the Conference on 'Equality in law between men and women in the European Community' held at Louvain-la-Neuve in May 1985,[7] has shown that a number of difficulties exist as regards the interpretation of situations that are sometimes difficult to assess objectively, and that there is an inadequate knowledge of both Community and national legislation.

    This has resulted in a low rate of recourse to the courts of potential claimants, which is further aggravated by procedural difficulties and costs and by a fear of dismissal, particularly in view of the present economic situation.

    A comparative analysis of this subject demonstrated the significance of the burden of proof, and the need for a body able to initiate and take charge of proceedings before the courts.

12. Policy to promote equal opportunities cannot be effective unless it tackles problems at the root. For this reason, action in the area of education and training is fundamental, particularly with regard to their adaptation to economic and social change. At Community level, a number of decisions and guidelines concerning principles have been adopted in these areas. In addition, the experience of operations carried out by the European Social Fund and the European Centre for the Development of Vocational Training (Cedefop) provide significant material for consideration regarding the continuation and development of action in this field.

13. Although the aim of the Council Directive of 9 February 1976[8] is to implement the principle of equal treatment, particularly with regard to employment – i.e. to all jobs or posts, whatever the sector of activity, and to all levels of the occupational hierarchy – women remain largely confined to traditional occupations at fairly low levels.

    It is by no means evident that economic and social changes and policies adopted have improved the position of women. The continuing rise in the unemployment rate of women gives particular cause for concern.

    In view of the principle of equal treatment recognized by the Council and demographic considerations related to manpower requirements, it is therefore necessary to intensify, diversify and render coherent the actions taken to promote equal opportunities in this area.

14. The consequences of the introduction and extension of new technologies

deserve special attention. They could constitute an historic opportunity for women to respond to this challenge on an equal footing. In the present circumstances, however, there is a danger that they could give rise to increased segregation on the labour market to the disadvantage of women. This stems partly from inadequate training – often due to the low interest in the area mainly caused by traditional views about the roles of men and women – and partly from the fact that women are generally employed in the positions which are most likely to change in content or be phased out. This means that special efforts must be made on women's behalf, over and above the general measures intended to benefit men and women equally.

15. These traditional stereotypes often underlie social protection and, in particular, social security. In addition, budgetary contraints have led countries to restrict or limit benefits, sometimes in a manner contrary to the principle of equality (for example, by favouring 'heads of family' or 'heads of house-holds', which leads to indirect discrimination against women).

   The Commission is seriously concerned about this situation, which could lead to the incorrect application of the Council Directive of 19 December 1978 on equal treatment in social security matters.[9] Certain areas are excluded from the field of application of this Directive (for example, survivors' pensions) and Member States are allowed to exclude others (e.g. retirement age). Significant problems have now arisen in these areas in particular: it is therefore important to include these areas in Community legislation on equal opportunities.

   Existing provisions and practices relating to the protection of maternity do not always guarantee adequate protection or job security, and they are also in need of a special effort.

16. A *sine qua non* for the promotion of true equality at work is the sharing of family and occupational responsibilities, particularly the development of adequate child-care facilities and a review of social infrastructures in general. In the same area, the development of parental leave and leave for family reasons and the reorganization of working time call for an open and positive approach in connection with the promotion of equality at work, a better quality of life and the campaign against unemployment.

17. Finally, the development of more systematic action to increase aware-ness in order to encourage a change of attitude is vital if the promotion of equal opportunities is not to be imited to the adoption of legislat-ion, the concrete implementation of which is often limited or to policy declarations which have no practical impact.

   The positive aspects of the value of equality at work and in society should be highlighted, and this calls for large-scale action targeted at various sectors of the public; equal opportunities concern society as a whole.

   Coordination between the activities of the Commission and Member

States' activities should be improved: information on Community action is still inadequate.[10]

Actions to be undertaken

Improved application of existing provisions

Action by the Member States

18. (a) The Member States should ensure better information and publicity about legislation on equal treatment, for example:
    • by increasing the training and awareness of the legal profession (seminars, symposia, etc.) and of lawyers, those responsible for social affairs, staff, labour inspectors, etc.;
    • by supporting and encouraging the social partners, particularly in connection with their training programmes.

    (b) The Member States should develop follow-up mechanisms and prepare provisions on equal opportunities, particularly by:
    • a review of the composition and operating procedures of existing committees and bodies in the light of a comparison of their experiences, so as to enable them to provide the motivating force behind the drafting, institution and follow-up of equal opportunities policies, including recourse to the courts;
    • the development of structures at regional and local level;
    • the support for associations and groups promoting equal opportunities and information about them to those sections of the public concerned;
    • a review of the provisions relating to the burden of proof, to ensure that persons subject to discrimination will not be required to undertake a task which is often impossible.

Commission action

19. (a) Using the network of independent experts monitoring the application of the equal opportunities Directives, the Commission will continue and intensify work on the *de jure* and *de facto* application of the existing Directives in terms of legislation, case law, collective agreements and particularly significant *de facto* discriminatory situations.

    The Commission will look into any measures that may be required in the light of information and suggestions provided by the experts, particularly in the context of its duties as guardian of the Treaties. It will disseminate the results of these experts' endeavours in order to stimulate ideas at Community level and in the Member States, especially on complex concepts such as indirect discrimination.

    (b) The Commission will encourage and support measures adopted by the Member States to train, increase the awareness of, inform and advise all sectors of the public concerned, in particular the legal profession, in the context, for example, of national or regional conferences or seminars organized in the wake of the European Conference in Louvain-la-Neuve in May 1985.[11]

(c) The Commission will put forward a Community legal instrument on the principle of the reversal of the burden of proof applying to all equal opportunities measures.

(d) The Commission will relaunch the discussion, notably with the social partners, with a view to giving practical effect to the principle of equal pay, particularly in connection with occupational classifications and the notion of work of equal value in the context of its suggestions for a social dialogue at Community level.

Education and training

Action by the Member States

20. (a) On the basis of the guidelines laid down in the resolution of 3 June 1985[12] containing an action programme on equal opportunities for boys and girls in education, the Member States should develop a general frame of reference for action at national level. It should be systematic, comprehensive and consistent, covering all areas and agents in the education process, and would in particular necessitate:
    • action to increase the awareness of all parties in the education process, particularly by way of information campaigns and the collection and dissemination of practical examples designed to achieve equal opportunities;
    • action to integrate education and vocational guidance in the curriculum for all pupils;
    • action to open up the world of education to the world of work;
    • the promotion of entry-level and in-service training for teachers on the theory and practice of equal opportunities teaching;
    • the reinforcement of coeducation practices in mixed schools;
    • the introduction of measures to ensure a balanced distribution of posts held by men and women at all levels of education (as regards both subject matter and the level of post);
    • the elimination of sex-related stereotypes from all educational material (books, exercises, methods of assessment, guidance material).

    (b) With respect to training, the Member States should:
    • organize campaigns to promote the diversification of occupational choices, including new types of employment, with the support of all the media;
    • assess all experience gained in terms of both placement and innovation;
    • adapt curricula to take account of problems specific to women;
    • provide more adequate guidance;
    • provide the material and social facilities needed to enable women to take training courses (child-minding centres, arrangement of timetables, etc.);
    • promote low-cost and more flexible training arrangements (decentralized, mobile, staggered timetable, etc.);
    • develop adequate expert and advisory facilities on equal opportunities (e.g. equal treatment counsellors, expert networks, etc.) at all

appropriate levels (schools, training bodies, national, regional and local authorities, educational and vocational guidance);

• encourage by every means available (information, increasing awareness, setting up networks, etc.) wider use of the opportunities offered by the European Social Fund to promote equal opportunities.

(c) The Member States should implement the recommendations on education and training by the expert group on the diversification of vocational choices.[1]

These relate to the entire educational process, from pre-school to third-level education, including adult education and training outside the school system *per se*.

Commission action

21. In the context of its measures to bring about equal opportunities in education and training, the Commission will carry out in particular the following actions:

(a) pursuant to the resolution of 3 June 1985[1] the Commission will support – within its budgetary limits – certain measures by the Member states to implement these activities, in particular:

• the introduction of innovative action programmes;

• the collection of parctical examples and the preparation of practical recommendations;

(b) the Commission will organize seminars, meetings, study visits, etc. to bring together the various parties involved in the education process;

(c) the Commission will set up a group of national experts (representatives of the Ministries of Education, equal opportunities committees or bodies, and other experts) to be responsible for implementing the action programme established by the resolution of 3 June 1985;[13]

(d) with the groups of advisors on equality in education and training set up in 1982,[14] the Commission will pursue the promotion of integrated programmes for the diversification of occupational choices;

(e) in the context of the second action programme on the transition of young people from education to working life,[15] the Commission will continue to carry out experiments on equal opportunities for boys and girls, for example promotion of non-sexist education material, training for non-traditional occupations, and the participation of girls of immigrant families in cultural and educational activities; it will organize the dissemination of examples of successful experiments already completed at national and Community level;

(f) Cedefop will pursue the following actions in line with its previous activities relating to:

• network of equal treatment training counsellors;

• network of projects concerning training in new techologies, particularly with a view to career advancement;

• training self-employed women, and will evaluate them with a view to developing guidelines for action.

(g) the Commission will support Member States' activities referred to

48

under point 20 (b) with a view to making wider use of the opportunities offered by the European Social Fund in this field;

(h) the Commission will undertake a study to ascertain whether handicapped girls have access to the same opportunities and the same standard of education and vocational training as handicapped boys;

(i) on the basis of the results and assessment of the above actions, the Commission will propose community guidelines on vocational training for women.

Employment

Actions by the Member States

22. (a) The Member States should improve the quantitative and qualitative data required for the assessment of specific aspects of women's employment (statistics,[16] determination of appropriate indicators to analyse the development of women's employment, qualitative analyses, sample surveys, etc.) and carry out a more systematic analysis of the coherence between overall actions in respect of employment and economic and social policy in general, and of specific actions for women, with particular attention to the development of the so-called 'insecure' forms of employment.

(b) Comprehensive and specific measures[17] should be adopted to promote women's employment and desegregation in employment, particularly through positive action.

(c) Action should be concentrated on certain areas:
    • the public sector as an employer should be seen to set an example;[18]
    • quantitative and qualitative improvement of women's participation in decision-making[19] by means of appropriate measures ('opening-up of political parties, drawing up electoral rolls, encouragement of both sides of industry, active participation by women in government, etc.);
    • the new technologies (through positive action in training, guidance, increasing awareness and recruitment) to avoid increased segregation of women's employment in this sector, and to enable women to respond to technological challenge on an equal footing;
    • promotion of local employment initiatives; these are particularly important for women's employment because they make it possible to respond to certain specific aspects of women's employment and to deal with certain aspects of the promotion of equal opportunities (greater participation in management, the opportunity of finding local employment, more flexible organization of work and advantageous pay conditions) by adopting measures to ensure equal access for women to setting up new undertakings (in particular credit facilities) and positive actions (training, information, setting up) designed to promote women's initiatives in this field.

(d) There should be specific measures to deal with the problems of the most disadvantaged,[20] for example: single-parent families and single

49

women, migrant women, women whose jobs are threatened by the introduction of new technologies, mentally or physically handicapped women, women wishing to return to the labour market after a career break and women who are unemployed or threatened with unemployment at the end of a period of occupational activity, and women working in self-employed occupations, including agriculture.[21]

(e) The necessary measures should be taken to remove the statutory and administrative provisions which are conrary to the principle of equal treatment and which can no longer be justified on the grounds of their original protective purpose.[22] The social partners should similarly be invited to make the appropriate changes to collective agreements of the same nature.

(f) Tax discrimination should be examined with a view to arriving at a neutral system which does not act as a disincentive, particularly with regard to the taxation of the earnings of married women. The Memorandum of 19 December 1984[23] from the Commission to the Council on this matter should serve as a basis for a more detailed examination.

(g) The social protection of home-workers and procedures for their integration into economic and social life should be reexamined with a view to improving participation by these workers in the production process and life in society.

Commission action

23. (a) The work of the expert group on the indicators on women's employment and their analysis will be continued and will stress:
 • the improvement and harmonization of statistics (in conjunction with the Statistical Office);
 • data relating to specific categories;
 • improved coherence between economic and social policies, particularly employment policies on the one hand and measures aimed at advancing women's employment on the other, with better integration of these data in existing information systems – Mutual Information System on Employment Policies in Europe (Misep), European Network for Information Exchange on Local Employment Initiatives (Elise), etc.;
 • the reinforcement of links with the Commission's other activities.

(b) The Commission will organize sample surveys to supplement available data, with particular reference to subjects difficult to assess statistically.

(c) The Commission will organize an exchange of information and experience in respect of:
 • measures to combat unemployment;[24]
 • positive action for women, both through the Advisory Committee on Equal Opportunities and through groups of experts, with a view to carrying out a systematic analysis and assessment of the actions initiated.

(d) The Commission will present to the Council, the Member States, the two sides of industry, and potential promoters of positive actions, a Code of Practice[25] designed to assist and inform them on the often complex implementation of such action.

(e) The Commission will support and encourage positive action in various sectors with a view to the desegregation of employment and better use of human resources, especially in the following areas:
• the public sector (following the studies and the action carried out with the European Institute of Public Administration in Maastricht) and in the context of its own personnel policy;[26]
• the banking sector (follow-up to the pilot scheme initiated in 1980);
• the industrial sector: development of the action launched in six Member States[27] with the help of two industrial management consultants, and its extension to the other Member states;
• the cooperative sector;[28]
• local employment initiatives for women: as well as continuing and developing a policy to support the launch of such initiatives and studies designed to improve the understanding of specific problems of job creation for women, the Commission intends to carry out systematic action in liaison with the overall promotion programme of local employment initiatives,[29] notably by setting up at Community level a network for the exchange of information, experiences and stimuli so as to develop more coherent and systematic activity in this field;
• the media.[30]

(f) Guidelines for Community actions relating to certain categories[31] with special problems will be proposed:
• single-parent families and single women;
• immigrant women;
• women wishing to return to the labour market after a career break;
• physically and mentally handicapped women;
• women in self-employed occupations, including agriculture: the proposal for a directive relating to them will provide an initial legislative response to their problems.

(g) The Commission will ensure that Article 3(2)(b) of the Council Directive of 9 February 1976 is applied, and will submit in this context (following the study carried out in 1982/83) a report on the revision of protective legislation for women, so as to achieve a more even mix in employment; the problems of night work in particular will be examined, because the ban on night work for women only often has a very negative impact on women's employment, for example in the new technologies.[32]

(h) To promote greater neutrality of taxation systems in their impact on women's work, on the basis of the Memorandum which it put before the Council in 1984,[33] the Commission intends to organize discussions with the representatives concerned in the Member

States[34] in order to draw up Community guidelines on this matter.
(i)   When the results of the study on home-working by women and
      young people are available, the Commission will decide whether
      Community guidelines are appropriate in this area.

New technologies

Action by the Member States
The Member States should:

24. (a) produce employment statistics on the new technologies that clearly
        distinguish and number of women workers in the field and the levels
        they have reached in comparison with male workers, and should
        develop a qualitative analysis of the question;
    (b) encourage the preparation of handbooks containing equal opportu-
        nities recommendations regarding schemes to introduce new tech-
        nologies in education, training and employment;
    (c) encourage applications by, and recruitment of, women for jobs using
        new technologies;[35]
    (d) develop pilot schemes for training women in new technologies;
    (e) encourage the institutes, groups and other organizations which dis-
        seminate knowledge and exchange experience and information about
        the impact of new technologies on women's training and employment,
        and increase awareness of such matters among the groups concerned;
    (f) develop measures to increase awareness (prizes, brochures, semi-
        nars, information campaigns, etc.);
    (g) encourage and develop networks of persons involved, and organize
        action research in schools;
    (h) introduce girls and boys to new technologies at the end of primary
        school and in all schools;
    (i) encourage, including the provision of financial incentives, firms
        setting up training courses in new technologies;
    (j) provide for modules within training courses enabling women to take
        greater advantages of the opportunities offered (preliminary train-
        ing, upgrading, etc.);
    (k) analyse the impact of new technology on women's health.

Commission action
25. (a) In the context of implementing the Council resolution concerning
        vocational training-measures relating to new information techno-
        logies[36] and of the resolution of the Council and of the Ministers for
        Education meeting within the Council on measures relating to the
        introduction of new information on technology in education[37] and
        the related work programmes which it has adopted, the Commission[38]
        will give particular attention to the question of equal treatment.
    (b) In connection with education and on the basis of the resolution on
        equal opportunities for girls and boys in education,[39] the Commission
        will support experiments and operations to improve girls' access to

courses in new technologies, and will support action research in this field.

(c) The Commission will endeavour to expand the number of innovative measures affecting women workers in the field of vocational training, and aimed at:
- facilitating the reintegration of women into the labour market in jobs with good prospects; or
- safeguarding their employment when it is threatened by industrial restructuring.

In this context the Commission will focus attention on vocational training operations to promote the upward mobility of women in sectors using new technologies (information technology, office electronics and robotics).

(d) In the framework of the ESF, applications will be encouraged for vocational training or recruitment to additional jobs for women in occupations in which they are under-represented (which often implies the use of new technologies).[40]

(e) On the basis of studies which it has carried out,[41] the Commission will encourage round-table discussions in each Member State with the parties concerned (governments, both sides of industry, training and placement bodies, etc.) to examine how the recommendations made in these studies may be put into practice. The Commission will assess these encounters and any follow-up.

(f) The Commission will carry out studies on the impact on women's employment of collective agreements relating to new technologies'.[42] It should lead to consideration being given to the effects of new technologies on women and the drafting of appropriate provisions in collective agreements.

The Commission will initiate discussion on this question with the two sides of industry on the basis of the findings of these studies.

(g) On the basis of studies under way,[43] the Commission will lay down guidelines for action on tele-commuting and women's employment.

(h) The Commission will organize research and meetings on the impact of new technologies on the distribution of working time and leisure time.

(i) The Commission will analyse the effect of the introduction of new technologies on women's health and safety at work.

(j) On the basis of the results and assessment of the above actions, the Commission will propose Community guidelines in respect of the impact of new technologies on women's employment.

Social protection and social security

Actions by the Member States
The Member States should:

26. (a) draw up measures to reform social security budgets so that they do not have a discriminatory effect as regards women, as laid down in

53

the Council Directive of 19 December 1978 on the progressive implementation of the principle of equal treatment for men and women
in matters of social security[44] and the proposal for a Directive on
equal treatment in occupational social security schemes;[45]
(b) promote the gradual acquisition by women of individual rights so as
to eliminate indirect discrimination;
(c) reinforce provisions for the protection of pregnancy and maternity to
provide adequate protection and eliminate discriminatory effects on
recruitment and career advancement.

Commission action

27. (a) The Commission will ensure that Member States respect in their
measures on budgetary reform the obligations laid down by the
Council Directive of 19 December 1978 to eliminate or avoid any
direct or indirect discrimination on the grounds of sex.
(b) On the basis of the study[46] carried out on areas not covered by this
Directive, the Commission will pursue its preparatory work on a
proposal for a new legal instrument to supplement in particular
the existing provisions in the areas in question with a view to a
progressive individualization of rights.
(c) The Commission will continue its effort to abolish indirect discrimination, particularly in the case of a spouse's derived rights.
(d) In line with the recommendations of the study on 'the protection of
working women during pregnancy and motherhood in the Member
States of the Community', the Commission will define guidelines for
Community action.

Sharing of family and occupational responsibilities

Action by the Member States

28. (a) Starting with the education system and then on a permanent basis,
Member States should carry out action to increase awareness with a
view to changing attitudes and promote the growing trend, especially
among young people, to accept a more equal sharing of family, occupational and social responsibilities, with regard both to couples and
to society in general.
(b) The Member States should rapidly adopt the Commission proposal
for a Directive on parental leave and leave for family reasons[47] and
proceed to implement its provisions.
(c) The Member States should look into various ways of improving child-
minding facilities in the light of a comparative analysis made by the
Commission[48] showing that although the prevailing economic situation seems to have caused some Member States to reduce public
child-care facilities, this was not true of other countries which have
given a degree of priority to improving the situation, including the
promotion of alternative child-care facilities.

(d) Initiatives should be drawn up in respect of the reorganization of working time to promote equal opportunities (for example, by encouraging flexible working hours, the possibility of a system of leave credits spread over a long period, compensation for arduous work in the form of more free time, a review of mobility policies, and a more balanced development of part-time work that will avoid segregation of employment).

(e) The Member States should seek solutions that will help to harmonize the operations of public and private services (including school hours) and occupational activities.

(f) Solutions should be sought for the specific difficulties of groups particularly affected by these problems (single-parent families, persons whose work place is far from home, etc.).

(g) There should be an examination of ways of taking account of the diverse aspirations expressed by women, and increasingly by young parents, with regard to their working, family and social lives, so that the upbringing of children in particular and family activities in general[49] may be better appreciated.

Commission action

29. (a) On the basis of the conclusions of the survey on day-care facilities and services for children under the age of three in the European Community, and the recommendations made by the Conferences held in Bonn in 1984 and Rome in 1985,[50] the Commission will ensure that developments in day-care facilities are followed up by an expert network.

(b) The Commission will propose recommendations for action in the field of day-care facilities along three lines (equal opportunities for children, freedom of choice for parents as regards family, social and occupational responsibilities, demographic impact).

(c) An analysis will be made of infrastructure problems other than those strictly related to day-care facilities (transport, opening hours of public and private services, alternative models) and their impact on women's employment, particularly of young women, in conjunction with their demographic impact.

(d) The Commission will carry out studies on:
 • assistance for elderly and handicapped persons, etc. to find ways of easing the burden of the family (and on women in particular) responsible for their care, and developing employment in this field;
 • the situation of older women and activities that could meet their needs;
 and will propose possible courses of action in this respect.

(e) A study will be made of courses of action to meet the specific needs of certain categories,[51] with a view to establishing Community guidelines.

(f) In its work on the reorganization of working time, the Commission will continue to keep in mind the promotion of equal opportunities.

Increasing awareness – changing attitudes

Action by the Member States

30. (a) More systematic and carefully targeted large-scale information campaigns should be carried out. They should be aimed at decision-makers, individuals and the various groups concerned,[52] those active in politics and in the social occupational and educational fields, while increasing media involvement.

    (b) Equal treatment should figure as a permanent topic in information and awareness campaigns with a broader scope, for example in connection with occupational choices, job creation, the activities of associations, etc.

Commission action

31. (a) The Commission will continue and expand its traditional information activities with regard to women (publications, seminars, booklets, audiovisual presentations, meetings with women's associations and movements, etc.) adjusted in the light of changing needs to ensure that they reach a broader public.

    (b) Contacts and exchanges will be developed with other groups whose activities have an impact on the promotion of equal treatment (family associations, youth forum, consumer groups, organizations combating poverty, parents associations, etc.).

    (c) The Commission will organize specific follow-up to the conference on equality in law of men and women in the Community,[53] attended by representatives of the legal professions, particularly by the promotion of national and regional seminars.

    (d) The field of action with regard to the media will be enlarged following the recommendations of the seminar on women in television held in Brussels in June 1985[54] by:
    • establishing a committee composed of representatives of television channels responsible for stimulating positive action in their organizations;
    • encouraging and supporting meetings at national level;
    • carrying out similar analysis of the situation in the other media with a view to developing action in regard to all the media.

    (e) Action will be developed in connection with the choice of branches of secondary education, and the distribution of tasks between boys and girls, mainly in cooperation with parents' associations.

    (f) More systematic information activities will be conducted with the two sides of industry in conjunction with Member States in order to promote broader consideration of the question of equal opportunities in such activities, for example collective bargaining, particularly when this affects the resturcturing and reorganization of working time and the introduction of new technologies.

Improvement of Community concertation

32. The development of legislation and Community policy has led the Commission to establish mechanisms for the exchange of experience, information and to encourage Community and national action.

    The Advisory Committee on Equal Opportunities for Women and Men was set up in 1981[55] and performs a key role in advising the Commission on the formulation of its equal opportunities policy and in promoting a continuous exchange. Over the course of 1986, the Commission will modify the rules of procedure of the Committee in line with new procedures relating to advisory committees. This exchange will be supplemented and expanded in a number of specific areas by a variety of networks of advisers and experts.

    The social partners have a fundamental role to play in putting into practice a variety of actions established or initiated at Community level. The dialogue with the various movements and associations concerned by the problem should also be developed in a more organized way.

33. The Commission will maintain and develop its contact mechanisms.

    It hopes to promote closer cooperation with government representatives on this subject, by holding regular meetings to exchange information on current and proposed policy, particularly as regards the application of instruments and undertakings at Community level, and to carry out an assessment.

    At the end of the period specified for implementing this programme, a meeting of all those concerned will be held (Advisory Committee, government representatives, the two sides of industry and members of the contact and exchange network) in order to review progress, evaluate action and consider future prospects.

Conclusion

Community action, which sets an example and provides a stimulus in this area – one of the important components of the 'People's Europe' – should be intensified.

For its part, the Commission will continue to carry out its tasks of proposing and encouraging, safe-guarding acquired rights, and concertation.

The Member States have a very special responsibility in implementing and developing actions already initiated and those included in the present progamme. A regular exchange of experience and greater concertation will enable action to become more sustained and developed.

Far from inducing a retreat or blocking progress, the present economic situation should encourage the development of innovatory ideas and initiatives in the context of current social and technological change. Dialogue between all those involved in this field is essential if consistency in action is to be achieved.

Substantial progress in the field of equal treatment in practice is possible only if the Community as a whole comes to feel responsible for dealing with the problem.

The Community has accepted the challenge of a 'People's Europe': the promotion of equal opportunities between men and women is one way of meeting that challenge.

---

* COM (85)801.
1. Supplement 1/82 – Bull. EC.
2. OJ NO. C 186, 21.7.1982.
3. Bull. EC 11-1985, point 2.1.81.
4. OJ No. C 46, 20.2.1984.
5. See document on Forward-looking Strategies adopted by consensus at the Conference cited above.
6. The Integration of Women in the Economy, OECD, 1985.
7. Bull. EC 5/1985, point 2.1.50.
8. OJ No. L. 39, 14.2.1976.
9. OJ No. L. 6, 10.1.1979.
10. See survey on the Situation of European women in paid employment, 1984.
11. Bull. EC 5/1985, point 2.1.50.
12. OJ No. C 166, 5.7.1985.
13. Group created under action B 11 of the 1982–85 Action Programme. Report prepared by Mrs Sullerot, coordinator of the group, October 1984.
14. OJ No. C 166, 5.7.1985.
15. OJ No. C 193, 28.7.1982.
16. A statistical breakdown by sex is not available in a number of areas.
17. In line with existing directives, recommendations and resolutions.
18. See resolution of 12 July 1982: OJ No. C 193, 28.7.1982.
19. See research on this subject carried out by the Commission in 1984 (V/1811/83).
20. In this connection, see the findings of the sample survey carried out by the Commission on Women in Paid Employment, 1984 (V/1240/84).
21. Proposal for a Council Directive on the application of the principle of equal treatment as between men and women engaged in an activity, including agriculture, in a self-employed capacity, and on the protection of self-employed women during pregnancy and motherhood of 15 March 1984: OJ No. C 113, 27.4.1984.
22. Within the meaning of Article 3(2) of the Council Directive of 9 February 1976: OJ No. L 39, 14.2.1976.
23. Bull. EC 12-1984, point 2.1.97.
24. Under the Council resolution of 7 June 1984: OJ No. C 161, 21.6.1984.
25. Examples may be found in certain Member States and certain third countries.
26. See Annex.
27. Belgium, Germany, France, Italy, Netherlands, United Kingdom.
28. In response to the study carried out in 1985 (V/55/86).
29. OJ No. C 161, 21.6.1984.
30. See points 30 and 31 below.
31. In response to studies carried out in these fields and the sample survey on European Women in Paid Employment, 1984.
32. A number of Member States have already denounced ILO Convention 89 on this topic. The others should follow shortly.
33. Bull. EC 12/1984, point 2.1.97.
34. A seminar was held on this topic in the United Kingdom early in 1986.
35. See Council resolution of 7 June 1984 on action to combat unemployment amongst women: OJ No. C 161, 21.6.1984.
36. OJ No. C 166, 25.6.1983.

37. OJ No. C 256, 24.9.1983.
38. Bull. EC 4-1983, point 2.1.57; Bull. EC 1-1985, point 2.1.22.
39. OJ No. C 166, 5.7.1985.
40. *See also* points 20 and 21.
41. With particular reference to 'Office automation and work for women' and 'Vocational training, new technologies and women's employment'.
42. The first study has been started.
43. FAST study by the European Centre for the Development of Vocational Training.
44. OJ No. L 6, 10.1.1979.
45. OJ No. C 134, 21.5.1983.
46. The implementation of equal treatment between men and women in matters of social security for benefits not covered by the Directive of 19 December 1978 (V/1261/1/84 final).
47. OJ No. C 333, 9.12.1983; OJ No. C 316, 27.11.1984.
48. Day-care facilities and services for children under the age of three in the European Community (V/1784/83).
49. There are various Commission surveys and analyses that can provide useful reference points in this respect.
50. Organised jointly by the Commission, the German Government and the Italian Presidency, bringing together representatives of the Ministries concerned (social affairs, health, education and women's rights), equal opportunity bodies and independent experts.
51. *See also* points 22 and 23 above.
52. Namely youth organisations, family associations, consumer groups, etc.
53. Bull. EC 5-1985, point 2.1.50.
54. Bull. EC 6-1985, point 2.1.76.
55. OJ No. L 20, 28.1.1982.

Council Recommendation

13 December 1984

on the promotion of positive action for women
(84/635/EEC)

THE COUNCIL OF THE EUROPEAN COMMUNITIES,

Having regard to the Treaty establishing the European Economic Community, and in particular Article 235 thereof,
Having regard to the draft recommendation submitted by the Commission,[1]
Having regard to the opinion of the European Parliament,[2]
Having regard to the opinion of the Economic and Social Committee:[3]

Whereas various action has been undertaken at Community level to promote equal opportunities for women; whereas, in particular the Council adopted, on the basis of Articles 100 and 235 of the Treaty, Directive 75/117/EEC[4], 76/207/EEC[5] and 79/7/EEC[6] concerning equal treatment for men and women;

Whereas other legal instruments are being prepared;

Whereas Article 2(4) of Council Directive 76/207/EEC provides that it shall be without prejudice to measures to promote equal opportunities for men and women, in particular by removing existing inequalities which affect

59

women's opportunities in the areas referred to in Article 1(1) thereof;

Whereas existing legal provisions on equal treatment, which are designed to afford rights to individuals, are inadequate for the elimination of all existing inequalities unless parallel action is taken by governments, both sides of industry and other bodies concerned, to counteract the prejudicial effects on women in employment which arise from social attitudes, behaviour and structures;

Whereas, by its resolution of 12 July 1982 on the promotion of equal opportunities for women,[7] the Council approved the general objectives of the new Community action programme on the promotion of equal opportunities for women (1982 and 1985), namely the stepping up of action to ensure observance of the principle of equal treatment and the promotion of equal opportunities in practice by positive action (Part B of the programme), and expressed the will to implement appropriate measures to achieve these objectives;

Whereas, in a period of economic crisis, action taken should be not only continued but also intensified at national level and Community level with a view to promoting the achievement of equal opportunities in practice through the implementation of positive actions, more especially in the fields of equal pay and equal treatment as regards access to employment, vocational training and promotion and working conditions;

Whereas the European Parliament has underlined the importance of positive action,

HEREBY RECOMMENDS MEMBER STATES:

1. To adopt a positive action policy designed to eliminate existing inequalities affecting women in working life and to promote a better balance between the sexes in employment, comprising appropriate general and specific measures, within the framework of national policies, while fully respecting the spheres of competence of the two sides of industry, in order:
   (a) to eliminate or counteract the prejudicial effects on women in employment or seeking employment which arise from existing attitudes, behaviour and structures based on the idea of a traditional division of roles in society between men and women;
   (b) to encourage the participation of women in various occupations in those sectors of working life where they are at present under-represented, particularly in the sectors of the future, and at higher levels of responsibility in order to achieve better use of all human resources.
2. To establish a framework containing appropriate provisions designed to promote and facilitate the introduction and extension of such measures.
3. To take, continue or promote positive action measures in the public and private sectors.
4. To take steps to ensure that positive action includes as far as possible actions having a bearing on the following aspects:
   – informing and increasing the awareness of both the general public and

60

the working world of the need to promote equality of opportunity for working women;
- respect for the dignity of women at the workplace;
- qualitative and quantitative studies and analyses of the position of women on the labour market;
- diversification of vocational choice, and more relevant vocational skills, particularly through appropriate vocational training, including the implementation of supporting measures and suitable teaching methods;
- measures necessary to ensure that placement, guidance and counselling services have sufficient skilled personnel to provide a service based on the necessary expertise in the special problems of unemployed women;
- encouraging women candidates and the recruitment and promotion of women in sectors and professions and at levels where they are under-represented, particularly as regards positions of responsibility;
- adapting working conditions; adjusting the organization of work and working time;
- encouraging supporting measures such as those designed to foster greater sharing of occupational and social responsibilities;
- active participation by women in decision-making bodies, including those representing workers, employers and the self-employed.
5. To ensure that the actions and measures described in points 1 to 4 are made known to the public and to the working world, especially to potential beneficiaries, by all appropriate means and as extensively as possible.
6. To enable national equal opportunities committees and organizations to make a significant contribution to the promotion of such measures, which presupposes that these committees and organizations are provided with appropriate means of action.
7. To encourage both sides of industry, wherever possible, to promote positive action within their own organizations and the work place, for example by suggesting guidelines, principles, codes of good conduct or good practice or any other appropriate formula for the implementation of such action.
8. To make efforts also in the public sector to promote equal opportunities which might serve as an example, particularly in those fields where new information technologies are being used or developed.
9. To make appropriate arrangements to gather information on measures taken by public and private bodies, and to follow up and evaluate such measures,

AND TO THIS END REQUESTS THE COMMISSION

1. To promote and organize in liaison with the Member States the systematic exchange and assessment of information and experience on positive action within the Community.
2. To submit a report to the Council, within three years of the adoption of

this recommentation, on progress achieved in its implementation, on the basis of information supplied to it by Member states.

Done at Brussels, 13 December 1984.

For the Council
The President
R. Quinn

---

1. OJ No. C 143, 30.5.1984, p. 3.
2. OJ No. C 315, 26.11.1984, p. 81.
3. Opinion delivered on 12 November 1984 (not yet published in the *Official Journal*).
4. OJ No. L 45, 19.2.1975, p. 19.
5. OJ No. L 39, 14.2.1976, p. 40.
6. OJ No. L 6, 10.1.1979, p. 24.
7. OJ No. C 186, 21.7.1982, p. 3.

B. Specific Equal Treatment Directives

Council Directive

10 February 1975

On the approximation of the laws of the Member States relating to the application of the principle of equal pay for men and women
(75/117/EEC)

THE COUNCIL OF THE EUROPEAN COMMUNITIES,

Having regard to the Treaty establishing the European Economic Community, and in particular Article 100 thereof,
Having regard to the proposal from the Commission,
Having regard to the Opinion of the European Parliament,[1]
Having regard to the Opinion of the Economic and Social Committee:[2]
　　Whereas implementation of the principle that men and women should receive equal pay contained in Article 119 of the Treaty is an integral part of the establishment and functioning of the common market;
　　Whereas it is primarily the responsibility of the Member States to ensure the application of this principle by means of appropriate laws, regulations and administrative provisions;
　　Whereas the Council resolution of 21 January 1974[3] concerning a social action programme, aimed at making it possible to harmonize living and working conditions while the improvement is being maintained and at achieving a balanced social and economic development of the Community, recognized that priority should be given to action taken on behalf of women as regards access to employment and vocational training and advancement, and as regards working conditions, including pay;
　　Whereas it is desirable to reinforce the basic laws by standards aimed at facilitating the practical application of the principle of equality in such a way that all employees in the Community can be protected in these matters;
　　Whereas differences continue to exist in the various Member States despite the efforts made to apply the resolution of the conference of the Member States of 30 December 1961 on equal pay for men and women and whereas, therefore, the national provisions should be approximated as regards application of the principle of equal pay,

63

Has adopted this Directive:

Article 1
The principle of equal pay for men and women outlined in Article 119 of the Treaty, hereinafter called "principle of equal pay", means, for the same work or for work to which equal value is attributed, the elimination of all discrimination on grounds of sex with regard to all aspects and conditions of remuneration.

In particular, where a job classification system is used for determining pay, it must be based on the same criteria for both men and women and so drawn up as to exclude any discrimination on grounds of sex.

Article 2
Member States shall introduce into their national legal systems such measures as are necessary to enable all employees who consider themselves wronged by failure to apply the principle of equal pay to pursue their claims by judicial process after possible recourse to other competent authorities.

Article 3
Member States shall abolish all discrimination between men and women arising from laws, regulations or administrative provisions which is contrary to the principle of equal pay.

Article 4
Member States shall take the necessary measures to ensure that provisions appearing in collective agreements, wage scales, wage agreements or individual contracts of employment which are contrary to the principle of equal pay shall be, or may be declared, null and void or may be amended.

Article 5
Member States shall take the necessary measures to protect employees against dismissal by the employer as a reaction to a complaint within the undertaking or to any legal proceedings aimed at enforcing compliance with the principle of equal pay.

Article 6
Member States shall, in accordance with their national circumstances and legal systems, take the measures necessary to ensure that the principle of equal pay is applied. They shall see that effective means are available to take care that this principle is observed.

Article 7
Member States shall take care that the provisions adopted pursuant to this Directive, together with the relevant provisions already in force, are brought to the attention of employees by all appropriate means, for example at their place of employment.

Article 8
1. Member states shall put into force the laws, regulations and administrative provisions necessary in order to comply with this Directive within one year of its notification and shall immediately inform the Commission thereof.
2. Member States shall communicate to the Commission the texts of the laws, regulations and administrative provisions which they adopt in the field covered by this Directive.

Article 9
Within two years of the expiry of the one-year period referred to in Article 8, Member States shall forward all necessary information to the Commission to enable it to draw up a report on the application of this Directive for submission to the Council.

Article 10
This Directive is addressed to the Member States.

Done at Brussels, 10 February 1975.

For the Council
The President
G. Fitzgerald

---

1. OJ No. C 55, 13.5.1974, p. 43.
2. OJ No. C 88, 26.7.1974, p. 7.
3. OJ No. C 13, 12.2.1974, p. 1.

Council Directive

9 February 1976

on the implementation of the principle of equal treatment for men and women as regards access to employment, vocational training and promotion and working conditions
(76/207/EEC)

THE COUNCIL OF THE EUROPEAN COMMUNITIES,

Having regard to the Treaty establishing the European Economic Community, and in particular Article 235 thereof,
Having regard to the proposal from the Commission,
Having regard to the opinion of the European Parliament,[1]
Having regard to the opinion of the Economic and Social Committee:[2]
    Whereas the Council, in its resolution of 21 January 1974 concerning a social action programme[3] included among the priorities action for the pur-

pose of achieving equality between men and women as regards access to employment and vocational training and promotion and as regards working conditions, including pay;

Whereas, with regard to pay, the Council adopted on 10 February 1975 Directive 75/117/EEC on the approximation of the laws of the Member States relating to the application of the principle of equal pay for men and women;[4]

Whereas Community action to achieve the principle of equal treatment for men and women in respect of access to employment and vocational training and promotion and in respect of other working conditions also appears to be necessary; whereas, equal treatment for male and female workers constitutes one of the objectives of the Community, in so far as the harmonization of living and working conditions while maintaining their improvement are *inter alia* to be furthered; whereas the Treaty does not confer the necessary specific powers for this purpose;

Whereas the definition and progressive implementation of the principle of equal treatment in matters of social security should be ensured by means of subsequent instruments,

HAS ADOPTED THIS DIRECTIVE:

Article 1
1. The purpose of this Directive is to put into effect in the Member States the principle of equal treatment for men and women as regards access to employment, including promotion, and to vocational training and as regards working conditions and, on the conditions referred to in paragraph 2, social security. This principle is hereinafter referred to as 'the principle of equal treatment'.
2. With a view to ensuring the progressive implementation of the principle of equal treatment in matters of social security, the Council, acting on a proposal from the Commission, will adopt provisions defining its substance, its scope and the arrangements for its application.

Article 2
1. For the purposes of the following provisions, the principle of equal treatment shall mean that there shall be no discrimination whatsover on grounds of sex either directly or indirectly by reference in particular to marital or family status.
2. This Directive shall be without prejudice to the right of Member States to exclude from its field of application those occupational activities and, where appropriate, the training leading thereto, for which, by reason of their nature or the context in which they are carried out, the sex of the worker constitutes a determining factor.
3. This Directive shall be without prejudice to provisions concerning the protection of women, particularly as regards pregnancy and maternity.
4. This Directive shall be without prejudice to measures to promote equal opportunity for men and women, in particular by removing existing in-

equalities which affect women's opportunities in the areas referred to in Article 1(1).

Article 3
1. Application of the principle of equal treatment means that there shall be no discrimination whatsover on grounds of sex in the conditions, including selection criteria, for access to all jobs or posts, whatever the sector of branch of activity, and to all levels of the occupational hierarchy.
2. To this end, Member States shall take the measures necessary to ensure that:
   (a) any laws, regulations and administrative provisions contrary to the principle of equal treatment shall be abolished;
   (b) any provisions contrary to the principle of equal treatment which are included in collective agreements, individual contracts of employment, internal rules of undertakings or in rules governing the independent occupations and professions shall be, or may be declared, null and void or may be amended;
   (c) those laws, regulations and administrative provisions contrary to the principle of equal treatment when the concern for protection which originally inspired them is no longer well founded shall be revised; and that where similar provisions are included in collective agreements labour and management shall be requested to undertake the desired revision.

Article 4
Application of the principle of equal treatment with regard to access to all types and to all levels, of vocational guidance, vocational training, advanced vocational training and retraining, means that Member States shall take all necessary measures to ensure that:
(a) any laws, regulations and administrative provisions contrary to the principle of equal treatment shall be abolished;
(b) any provisions contrary to the principle of equal treatment which are included in collective agreements, individual contracts of employment, internal rules of undertakings or in rules governing the independent occupations and professions shall be, or may be declared, null and void or may be amended;
(c) without prejudice to the freedom granted in certain Member States to certain private training establishments, vocational guidance, vocational training, advanced vocational training and retraining shall be accessible on the basis of the same criteria and at the same levels without any discrimination on grounds of sex.

Article 5
1. Application of the principle of equal treatment with regard to working conditions, including the conditions governing dismissal, means that men and women shall be guaranteed the same conditions without discrimination on grounds of sex.

67

2. To this end, Member States shall take the measures necessary to ensure that:
   (a) any laws, regulations and administrative provisions contrary to the principle of equal treatment shall be abolished;
   (b) any provisions contrary to the principle of equal treatment which are included in collective agreements, individual contracts of employment, internal rules of undertakings or in rules governing the independent occupations and professions shall be, or may be declared, null and void or may be amended;
   (c) those laws, regulations and administrative provisions contrary to the principle of equal treatment when the concern for protection which originally inspired them is no longer well founded shall be revised; and that where similar provisions are included in collective agreements labour and management shall be requested to undertake the desired revision.

Article 6
Member States shall introduce into their national legal systems such measures as are necessary to enable all persons who consider themselves wronged by failure to apply to them the principle of equal treatment within the meaning of Articles 3, 4 and 5 to pursue their claims by judicial process after possible recourse to other competent authorities.

Article 7
Member States shall take the necessary measures to protect employees against dismissal by the employer as a reaction to a complaint within the undertaking or to any legal proceedings aimed at enforcing compliance with the principle of equal treatment.

Article 8
Member States shall take care that the provisions adopted pursuant to this Directive, together with the relevant provisions already in force, are brought to the attention of employees by all appropriate means, for example at their place of employment.

Article 9
1. Member States shall put into force the laws, regulations and administrative provisions necessary in order to comply with this Directive within 30 months of its notification and shall immediately inform the Commission thereof.
   However, as regards the first part of Article 3(2)(c) and the first part of Article 5(2)(c), Member States shall carry out a first examination and if necessary a first revision of the laws, regulations and administrative provisions referred to therein within four years of notification on this Directive.
2. Member States shall periodically assess the occupational activities referred to in Article 2(2) in order to decide, in the light of social developments,

whether there is justification for maintaining the exclusions concerned. They shall notify the Commission of the results of this assessment.
3. Member States shall also communicate to the Commission the texts of laws, regulations and administrative provisions which they adopt in the field covered by this Directive.

Article 10
Within two years following expiry of the 30-month period laid down in the first subparagraph of Article 9(1), Member States shall forward all necessary information to the Commission to enable it to draw up a report on the application of this Directive for submission to the Council.

Article 11
This Directive is addressed to the Member States.

Done at Brussels, 9 February 1976.

For the Council
The President
G. Thorn

---

1. OJ No. C 111 of 20 may 1975, p. 14.
2. OJ No. C 286 of 15 December 1975, p. 8.
3. OJ No. C 13 of 12 February 1974, p. 1.
4. OJ No. L 45 of 19 February 1975, p. 19.

Council Directive

19 December 1978

on the progressive implementation of the principle of equal treatment for men and women in matters of social security
(79/7/EEC)

THE COUNCIL OF THE EUROPEAN COMMUNITIES,

Having regard to the Treaty establishing the European Economic Community, and in particular Article 235 thereof,
Having regard to the proposal from the Commission,[1]
Having regard to the opinion of the European Parliament,[2]
Having regard to the opinion of the Economic and Social Committee:[3]
    Whereas Article 1(2) of Council Directive 76/207/EEC of 9 February 1976 on the implementation of the principle of equal treatment for men and women as regards access to employment, vocational training and promotion, and working conditions[4] provides that, withe a view to ensuring the progressive implementation of the principle of equal treatment in matters of social secur-

ity, the Council, acting on a proposal from the Commission, will adopt provisions defining its substance, its scope and the arrangements for its application; whereas the Treaty does not confer the specific powers required for this purpose;

Whereas the principle of equal treatment in matters of social security should be implemented in the first place in the statutory schemes which provide protection against the risks of sickness, invalidity, old age, accidents at work, occupational diseases and unemployment, and in social assistance in so far as it is intended to supplement or replace the abovementioned schemes;

Whereas the implementation of the principle of equal treatment in matters of social security does not prejudice the provisions relating to the protection of women on the ground of maternity; whereas, in this respect, Member States may adopt specific provisions for women to remove existing instances of unequal treatment,

HAS ADOPTED THIS DIRECTIVE:

Article 1
The purpose of this Directive is the progressive implementation, in the field of social security and other elements of social protection provided for in Article 3, of the principle of equal treatment for men and women in matters of social security, hereinafter referred to as 'the principle of equal treatment'.

Article 2
This Directive shall apply to the working population-including self-employed persons, workers and self-employed persons whose activity is interrupted by illness, accident or involuntary unemployment and persons seeking employment-and to retired to invalided workers and self-employed persons.

Article 3
1. This Directive shall apply to:
    (a) statutory schemes which provide protection against the following risks:
        – sickness,
        – invalidity,
        – old age,
        – accidents at work and occupational diseases,
        – unemployment;
    (b) social assistance, in so far as it is intended to supplement or replace the schemes referred to in (a).
2. This Directive shall not apply to the provisions concerning survivors' benefits nor to those concerning family benefits, except in the case of family benefits granted by way of increases of benefits due in respect of the risks referred to in paragraph 1(a).
3. With a view to ensuring implementation of the principle of equal treatment in occupational schemes, the Council, acting on a proposal from the Commission, will adopt provisions defining its substance, its scope and the arrangements for its application.

Article 4
1. The principle of equal treatment means that there shall be no discrimination whatsoever on ground of sex either directly, or indirectly by reference in particular to marital or family status, in particular as concerns:
   - the scope of the schemes and the conditions of access thereto,
   - the obligation to contribute and the calculation of contributions,
   - the calculation of benefits including increases due in respect of a spouse and for dependants and the conditions governing the duration and retention of entitlement to benefits.
2. The principle of equal treatment shall be without prejudice to the provisions relating to the protection of women on the grounds of maternity.

Article 5
Member States shall take the measures necessary to ensure that any laws, regulations and administrative provisions contrary to the principle of equal treatment are abolished.

Article 6
Member States shall introduce into their national legal systems such measures as are necessary to enable all persons who consider themselves wronged by failure to apply the principle of equal treatment to pursue their claims by judicial process, possibly after recourse to other competent authorities.

Article 7
1. This Directive shall be without prejudice to the right of Member State to exclude from its scope:
   (a) the determination of pensionable age for the purposes of granting old-age and retirement pensions and the possible consequences thereof for other benefits;
   (b) advantages in respect of old-age pension schemes granted to persons who have brought up children; the acquisition of benefit entitlement following periods of interruption of employment due to the bringing up of children;
   (c) the granting of old-age or invalidity benefit entitlements by virtue of the derived entitlements of a wife;
   (d) the granting of increases of long-term invalidity, old-age, accidents at work and occupational disease benefits for a dependent wife;
   (e) the consequences of the exercise, before the adoption of this Directive, of a right of option not to acquire rights or incur obligations under a statutory scheme.
2. Member States shall periodically examine matters excluded under paragraph 1 in order to ascertain, in the light of social developments in the matter concerned, whether there is justification for maintaining the exclusions concerned.

Article 8
1. Member States shall bring into force the laws, regulations and adminis-

trative provisions necessary to comply with this Directive within six years of its notification. They shall immediately inform the Commission thereof.

2. Member States shall communicate to the Commission the text of laws, regulations and administrative provisions which they adopt in the field covered by this Directive, including measures adopted pursuant to Article 7(2).

They shall inform the Commission of their reasons for maintaining any existing provisions on the matters referred to in Article 7(1) and of the possibilities for reviewing them at a later date.

Article 9
Within seven years of notification of this Directive, Member States shall forward all information necessary to the Commission to enable it to draw up a report on the application of this Directive for submission to the Council and to propose such further measures as may be required for the implementation of the principle of equal treatment.

Article 10
This Directive is addressed to the Member States.

Done at Brussels, 19 December 1978.

For the Council
The President
H. D. Genscher

---

1. OJ No. C 34 of 11 February 1977, p. 3.
2. OJ No. C 299 of 12 December 1977, p. 13.
3. OJ No. C 180 of 28 July 1977, p. 36.
4. OJ No. L 39 of 14 February 1976, p. 40.

Council Directive

24 July 1986

on the implementation of the principle of equal treatment for men and women in occupational social security schemes
(86/378/EEC)

THE COUNCIL OF THE EUROPEAN COMMUNITIES,

Having regard to the Treaty establishing the European Economic Community, and in particular Articles 100 and 235 thereof,
Having regard to the proposal from the Commission,[1]
Having regard to the Opinion of the European Parliament,[2]
Having regard to the Opinion of the Economic and Social Committee:[3]

Whereas the Treaty provides that each Member State shall ensure the application of the principle that men and women should receive equal pay for equal work; whereas 'pay' should be taken to mean the ordinary basic or minimum wage or salary and any other consideration, whether in cash or in kind, which the worker receives, directly or indirectly, from his employer in respect of his employment;

Whereas, although the principle of equal pay does indeed apply directly in cases where discrimination can be determined solely on the basis of the criteria of equal treatment and equal pay, there are also situations in which implementation of this principle implies the adoption of additional measures which more clearly define its scope;

Whereas Article 1(2) of Council Directive 76/207/EEC of 9 February 1976 on the implementation of the principle of equal treatment for men and women as regards access to employment, vocational training and promotion, and working conditions[4] provides that, with a view to ensuring the progressive implementation of the principle of equal treatment in matters of social security, the Council, acting on a proposal from the Commission, will adopt provisions defining its substance, its scope and the arrangements for it application; whereas the Council adopted to this end Directive 79/7/EEC of 19 December 1978 on the progressive implementation of the principle of equal treatment for men and women in matters of social security;[5]

Whereas Article 3(3) of Directive 79/7/EEC provides that, with a view to ensuring implementation of the principle of equal treatment in occupational schemes, the Council, acting on a proposal from the Commission, will adopt provisions defining its substance, its scope and the arrangements for its application;

Whereas the principle of equal treatment should be implemented in occupational social security schemes which provide protection against the risk specified in Article 3(1) of Directive 79/7/EEC as well as those which provide employees with any other consideration in cash or in kind within the meaning of the Treaty;

Whereas implementation of the principle of equal treatment does not prejudice the provisions relating to the protection of women by reason of maternity,

HAS ADOPTED THIS DIRECTIVE:

Article 1
The object of this Directive is to implement, in occupational social security schemes, the principle of equal treatment for men and women, hereinafter referred to as 'the principle of equal treatment'.

Article 2
1. 'Occupational social security schemes' means schemes not governed by Directive 79/7/EEC whose purpose is to provide workers, whether employees or self-employed, in an undertaking or group of undertakings, area of economic activity or occupational sector or group of such sectors

with benefits intended to supplement the benefits provided by statutory social security schemes or to replace them, whether membership of such schemes is compulsory or optional.

2. This Directive does not apply to:
   (a) individual contracts;
   (b) schemes having only one member;
   (c) in the case of salaried workers, insurance contracts to which the employer is not a party;
   (d) the optional provisions of occupational schemes offered to participants individually to guarantee them:
       – either additional benefits; or
       – a choice of date on which the normal benefits will start, or a choice between several benefits.

Article 3

This Directive shall apply to members of the working population including self-employed persons, persons whose activity is interrupted by illness, maternity, accident or involuntary unemployment and persons seeking employment, and to retired and disabled workers.

Article 4

This Directive shall apply to:
(a) occupational schemes which provide protection against the following risks:
    – sickness;
    – invalidity;
    – old age, including early retirement;
    – industrial accidents and occupational diseases;
    – unemployment.
(b) occupational schemes which provide for other social benefits, in cash or in kind, and in particular survivors' benefits and family allowances, if such benefits are accorded to employed persons and thus constitute a consideration paid by the employer to the worker by reason of the latter's employment.

Article 5

1. Under the conditions laid down in the following provisions, the principle of equal treatment implies that there shall be no discrimination on the basis of sex, either directly or indirectly, by reference in particular to marital or family status, especially as regards:
   – the scope of the schemes and the conditions of access to them;
   – the obligation to contribute and the calculation of contributions;
   – the calculation of benefits, including supplementary benefits due in respect of a spouse or dependants, and the conditions governing the duration and retention of entitlement to benefits.
2. The principle of equal treatment shall not prejudice the provisions relating to the protection of women by reason of maternity.

74

Article 6

1. Provisions contrary to the principle of equal treatment shall include those based on sex, either directly or indirectly, in particular by reference to marital or family status, for:
   (a) determining the persons who may participate in an occupational scheme;
   (b) fixing the compulsory or optional nature of participation in an occupational scheme;
   (c) laying down different rules as regards the age of entry into the scheme or the minimum period of employment or membership of the scheme required to obtain the benefits thereof;
   (d) laying down different rules, except as provided for in subparagraphs (h) and (i), for the reimbursement of contributions where a worker leaves a scheme without having fulfilled the conditions guaranteeing him a deferred right to long-term benefits;
   (e) setting different conditions for the granting of benefits or restricting such benefits to workers of one or other of the sexes;
   (f) fixing different retirement ages;
   (g) suspending the retention or acquisition of rights during periods of maternity leave or leave for family reasons which are granted by law or agreement and are paid by the employer;
   (h) setting different levels of benefit, except insofar as may be necessary to take account of actuarial calculation factors which differ according to sex in the case of benefits designated as contribution-defined;
   (i) setting different levels of worker contribution;
      setting different levels of employer contribution in the case of benefits designated as contribution-defined, except with a view to making the amount of those benefits more nearly equal;
   (j) laying down different standards or standards applicable only to workers of a specified sex, except as provided for in subparagraphs (h) and (i), as regards the guarantee or retention of entitlement to deferred benefits when a worker leaves a scheme.
2. Where the granting of benefits within the scope of this Directive is left to the discretion of the scheme's management bodies, the latter must take account to the principle of equal treatment.

Article 7

Member States shall take all necessary steps to ensure that:
(a) provision contrary to the principle of equal treatment in legally compulsory collective agreements, staff rules of undertaking or any other arrangements relating to occupational schemes are null and void, or may be declared null and void or amended;
(b) schemes containing such provisions may not be approved or extended by administrative measure.

Article 8

1. Member States shall take all necessary steps to ensure that the provisions

of occupational schemes contrary to the principle of equal treatment are revised by 1 January 1993.

2. This Directive shall not preclude rights and obligations relating to a period of membership of an occupational scheme prior to revision of that scheme from remaining subject to the provisions of the scheme in force during that period.

Article 9
Member States may defer compulsory application of the principle of equal treatment with regard to:

(a) determination of pensionable age for the purposes of granting old-age or retirement pensions, and the possible implications for other benefits:
- either until the date on which such equality is achieved in statutory schemes; or,
- at the latest, until such equality is required by a directive.

(b) survivors' pensions until a directive requires the principle of equal treatment in statutory social security schemes in that regard;

(c) the application of the first subparagraph of Article 6(1)(i) to take account of the different actuarial calculation factors, at the latest until the expiry of a thirteen-year period as from the notification of this Directive.

Article 10
Member States shall introduce into their national legal systems such measures as are necessary to enable all persons who consider themselves injured by failure to apply the principle of equal treatment to pursue their claims before the courts, possibly after bringing the matters before other competent authorities.

Article 11
Member States shall take all the necessary steps to protect workers against dismissal where this constitute a response on the part of the employer to a complaint made at undertaking level or to the institution of legal proceedings aimed at enforcing compliance with the principle of equal treatment.

Article 12
1. Member States shall bring into force such laws, regulations and administrative provisions as are necessary in order to comply with this Directive at the latest three years after notification thereof. They shall immediately inform the Commission thereof.

2. Member States shall communicate to the Commission at the latest five years after notification of this Directive all information necessary to enable the Commission to draw up a report on the application of this Directive for submission to the Council.

Article 13
This Directive is addressed to the Member States.

Done at Brussels, 24 July 1986.

For the Council
The President
A. Clark

---

1. OJ No. C 134, 21.5.1983, p. 7.
2. OJ No. 117, 30.4.1984, p. 169.
3. OJ No. 35, 9.2.1984, p. 7.
4. OJ No. L 39, 14.2.1976, p. 40.
5. OJ No. L 6, 10.1.1979, p. 24.

Council Directive

11 December 1986

on the application of the principle of equal treatment between men and women engaged in an activity, including agriculture, in a self-employed capacity, and on the protection of self-employed women during pregnancy and motherhood
(86/613/EEC)

THE COUNCIL OF THE EUROPEAN COMMUNITIES,

Having regard to the Treaty establishing the European Economic Community, and in particular Article 100 and 235 thereof,
Having regard to the proposal from the Commission,[1]
Having regard to the Opinion of the European Parliament,[2]
Having regard to the Opinion of the Economic and Social Committee:[3]
    Whereas, in its resolution of 12 July 1982 on the promotion of equal opportunities for women,[4] the Council approved the general objectives of the Commission communication concerning a new Community action programme on the promotion of equal opportunities for women (1982 to 1985) and expressed the will to implement appropriate measures to achieve them;
    Whereas action 5 of the programme referred to above concerns the application of the principle of equal treatment to self-employed women and to women in agriculture;
    Whereas the implementation of the principle of equal pay for men and women workers, as laid down in Article 119 of the Treaty, forms an integral part of the establishment and functioning of the common market;
    Whereas and 10 February 1975 the Council adopted Directive n° 75/117/EEC on the approximation of the laws of the Member States relating to the application of the principle of equal pay for men and women;[5]
    Whereas, as regards other aspects of equality of treatment between men and women, on 9 February 1976 the Council adopted Directive 76/207/EEC on the implementation of the principle of equal treatment for men and

77

women as regards access to employment, vocational training and promotion, and working conditions[6] and on 19 December 1978 Directive 79/7/EEC on the progressive implementation of the principle of equal treatment for men and women in matters of social security;[7]

Whereas, as regards persons engaged in a self-employed capacity, in an activity in which their spouses are also engaged, the implementation of the principle of equal treatment should be pursued through the adoption of detailed provisions designed to cover the specific situation of these persons;

Whereas differences persist between the Member States in this field, whereas, therefore it is necessary to approximate national provisions with regard to the application of the principle of equal treatment;

Whereas in certain respects the Treaty does not confer the powers necessary for the specific actions required;

Whereas the implementation of the principle of equal treatment is without prejudice to measures concerning the protection of women during pregnancy and motherhood,

HAS ADOPTED THIS DIRECTIVE:

SECTION 1 – Aims and scope

Article 1
The purpose of this Directive is to ensure, in accordance with the following provisions, application in the Member States of the principle of equal treatment as between men and women engaged in an activity in a self-employed capacity, or contribution to the pursuit of such an activity, as regards those aspects not covered by Directives 76/207/EEC and 79/7/EEC.

Article 2
This Directive covers:
(a) self-employed workers, i.e. all persons pursuing a gainful activity for their own account, under the conditions laid down by national law, including farmers and members of the liberal professions;
(b) their spouses, not being employees or partners, where they habitually, under the conditions laid down by national law, participate in the activities of the self-employed worker and perform the same tasks or ancillary tasks.

Article 3
For the purposes of this Directive the principle of equal treatment implies the absence of all discrimination on grounds of sex, either directly or indirectly, by reference in particular to marital or family status.

SECTION 2 – Equal treatment between self-employed male and female workers – position of the spouses without professional status of self-employed workers – protection of self-employed workers or wives of self-employed workers during pregnancy and motherhood

Article 4
As regards self-employed persons, Member States shall take the measures necessary to ensure the elimination of all provisions which are contrary to the principle of equal treatment as defined in Directive 76/207/EEC, especially in respect of the establishment, equipment or extension of a business or the launching or extension of any other form of self-employed activity financial facilities.

Article 5
Without prejudice to the specific conditions for access to certain activities which apply equally to both sexes, Member States shall take the measures necessary to ensure that the conditions for the formation of a company between spouses are not more restrictive than the conditions for the formation of a company between unmarried persons.

Article 6
Where a contributory social security system for self-employed workers exists in a Member State, that Member State shall take the necessary measures to enable the spouses referred to in Article 2(b) who are not protected under the self-employed worker's social security scheme to join a contributory social security scheme voluntarily.

Article 7
Member States shall undertake to examine under what conditions recognition of the work of the spouses referred to in Article 2(b) may be encouraged and, in the light of such examination, consider any appropriate steps for encouraging such recognition.

Article 8
Members States shall undertake to examine whether, and under what conditions, female self-employed workers and the wives of self-employed workers may, during interruptions in their occupational activity owing to pregnancy or motherhood,
– have access to services supplying temporary replacements or existing national social services, or
– be entitled to cash benefits under a social security scheme or under any other public social protection system.

SECTION 3 – General and final provisions

Article 9
Member States shall introduce into their national legal systems such measures as are necessary to enable all persons who consider themselves wronged by failure to apply the principle of equal treatment in self-employed activities to pursue their claims by judicial process, possibly after recourse to other competent authorities.

Article 10

Member States shall ensure that the measures adopted pursuant to this Directive, together with the relevant provisions already in force, are brought to the attention of bodies representing self-employed workers and vocational training centres.

Article 11

The Council shall review this Directive, on a proposal from the Commission, before 1 July 1993.

Article 12

1. Member States shall bring into force the laws, regulations and administrative provisions necessary to comply with this Directive not later than 30 June 1989.

   However, if a Member State which, in order to comply with Article 5 of this Directive, has to amend its legislation on matrimonial rights and obligations, the date on which such Member State must comply with Article 5 shall be 30 June 1991.
2. Member States shall immediately inform the Commission of the measures taken to comply with this Directive.

Article 13

Member States shall forward to the Commission, not later than 30 June 1991, all the information necessary to enable it to draw up a report on the application of this Directive for submission to the Council.

Article 14

This Directive is addressed to the Member States.

Done at Brussels, 11 December 1986.

For the Council
The President
A. Clarke

---

1. OJ No. C 113, 27.4.1984, p. 4.
2. OJ No. C 172, 2.7.1984, p. 90.
3. OJ No. C 343, 24.12.1984, p. 1.
4. OJ No. C 186, 21.7.1982, p. 3.
5. OJ No. L 45, 19.2.1975, p. 19.
6. OJ No. L 39, 14.2.1975, p. 40.
7. OJ No. L 6, 10.1.1979, p. 24.

C. European Court Judgments

1. Equal pay

(a) Infringement proceedings under Article 169, EEC Treaty

Judgment of the Court

9 June 1982 – Case 58/81

Commission of the European Communities
v.
Grand Duchy of Luxembourg

Failure of Member State to fulfil its obligations – equal pay – Member State may not plead provisions, practices or circumstances in its internal legal system to justify failure to comply with obligations arising from Community Directives (Council Directive 75/117/EEC, Article 8(1)).

In Case 58/81

Commission of the European Communities, represented by its Legal Adviser, Jean Amphoux, acting as Agent, with an address for service in Luxembourg at the office of Oreste Montalto, a member of its Legal Department, Jean Monnet Building, Kirchberg,

applicant,

v.

Grand Duchy of Luxembourg, represented by its Agent, Pierre Neyens, Principal Private Secretary to the Minister for the Civil Service, assisted by Paul Béghin, of the Luxembourg Bar,

defendant,

APPLICATION for a declaration that, by not adopting within the period prescribed in Article 8(1) of Council Directive 75/117/EEC of 10 February 1975 on the approximation of the laws of the Member States relating to the application of the principle of equal pay for men and women the measures necessary in order to eliminate discrimination in the conditions for the grant of household allowances to civil servants, the Grand Duchy of Luxembourg has failed to fulfil its obligations under the EEC Treaty,

THE COURT

composed of: J. Mertens de Wilmars, President, G. Bosco, A. Touffait and O. Due (Presidents of Chambers), P. Pescatore, Lord Mackenzie Stuart, A. O'Keeffe, T. Koopmans, U. Everling, A. Chloros and F. Grévisse, Judges,

Advocate General: P. VerLoren van Themaat
Registrar: P. Heim

gives the following JUDGMENT

Decision

1. By application lodged at the Court Registry on 16 March 1981, the Commission of the European Communities brought an action, pursuant to Article 169 of the EEC Treaty, for a declaration that by failing to adopt within the period prescribed in Article 8(1) of Directive 75/117/EEC of 10 February 1975 on the approximation of the laws of the Member States relating to the application of the principle of equal pay for men and women (Official Journal 1975, L 45, p. 19) the measures necessary in order to eliminate discrimination in the conditions for the grant of head of household allowances to civil servants, the Grand Duchy of Luxembourg had failed to fulfil its obligations under the EEC Treaty.

2. Pursuant to Article 8 of the directive, Member States were to put into force the measures necessary in order to comply with its requirements within one year of its notification, a period which expired on 12 February 1976.

3. The Grand Duchy of Luxembourg has not disputed the failure to fulfil its obligations with which it is charged but has confined itself to stating that the delay in adopting the measures necessary to comply with the directive in question resulted on the one hand from the need to enact legislation and, on the other hand, from the fact that implementation of the directive necessitated an assessment of the budgetary consequences. Moreover, it is necessary to make changes to the conditions applicable to part-time working, which involves discussions with the civil service representatives.

4. According to the well-established case-law of the Court, a Member State

may not plead provisions, practices or circumstances existing in its internal legal system in order to justify a failure to comply with obligations resulting from Community directives.

5. It must therefore be declared that by not adopting within the period prescribed in Article 8(1) of Directive 75/117/EEC of 10 February 1975 the measures necessary in order to eliminate discrimination in the conditions for the grant of head of household allowances to civil servants, the Grand Duchy of Luxembourg has failed to fulfil its obligations under the EEC Treaty.

Costs

6. Under Article 69(2) of the Rules of Procedure, the unsuccessful party is to be ordered to pay the costs.

7. Since the Grand Duchy of Luxembourg has failed in its submissions, it must be ordered to pay the costs.

On those grounds,

THE COURT

hereby:

1. **Declares that by not adopting within the period prescribed in Article 8(1) of Directive 75/117/EEC of 10 February 1975, the measures necessary to eliminate discrimination in the conditions for the grant of head of household allowances to civil servants, the Grand Duchy of Luxembourg has failed to fulfil one of its obligations under the EEC Treaty;**

2. **Orders the Grand Duchy of Luxembourg to pay the costs.**

Due	Mertens de Wilmars		Bosco	Touffait	O'Keeffe
Koopmans		Pescatore	Mackenzie Stuart		Grévisse
		Everling	Chloros		

Delivered in open court in Luxembourg on 9 June 1982.

J. A. Pompe   J. Mertens de Wilmars
Deputy Registrar   *President*

Judgment of the Court

6 June 1982 – Case 61/81

Commission of the European Communities
v.
United Kingdom of Great Britain and Northern Ireland

Failure of Member State fully to fulfil its obligations – equal pay – work to which equal value is attributed – responsibility of Member States to guarantee all workers the right to receive equal pay for work of equal value even in the absence of a job classification system – workers should be able to enforce equal value claims (EEC Treaty, Article 119; Council Directive 75/117/EEC, Article 1).

In Case 61/81

Commission of the European Communities, represented by John Forman, a member of the Legal Department, acting as Agent, with an address for service in Luxembourg at the office of Oreste Montalto, a member of the Commission's Legal Department, Jean Monnet Building, Kirchberg,

applicant,

v.

United Kingdom of Great Britain and Northern Ireland, represented by Mrs G. Dagtoglou, of the Treasury Solicitor's Department, acting as Agent, assisted by Peter Scott, QC, with an address for service in Luxembourg at the British Embassy, 28 Boulevard Royal,

defendant,

APPLICATION for a declaration that the United Kingdom has failed to fulfil its obligations under Council Directive 75/117/EEC of 10 February 1975 on the approximation of the laws of the Member States relating to the application of the principle of equal pay for men and women (Official Journal L 45, 1975, p. 19),

THE COURT,

composed of: J. Mertens de Wilmars, President, G. Bosco, A. Touffait and O. Due (Presidents of Chambers), P. Pescatore, Lord Mackenzie Stuart, A. O'Keeffe, T. Koopmans, U. Everling, A. Chloros and F. Grévisse, Judges,

Advocate General: P. VerLoren van Themaat
Registrar: P. Heim

gives the following JUDGMENT

Decision

1. By application lodged at the Court Registry on 18 March 1981 the Commission of the European Communities brought an action under Article 169 of the EEC Treaty for a declaration that the United Kingdom had failed to fulfil its obligations under the Treaty by failing to adopt the laws, regulations or administrative provisions needed to comply with Council Directive 75/117/EEC of 10 February 1975 on the approximation of the laws of the Member States relating to the application of the principle of equal pay for men and women (Official Journal L 45, 1975, p. 19), as regards the elimination of discrimination for work to which equal value is attributed.

2. The first article of the directive, which the Commission considers has not been applied by the United Kingdom, provides that:

   'The principle of equal pay for men and women outlined in Article 119 of the Treaty, hereinafter called "principle of equal pay", means, for the same work or for work to which equal value is attributed, the elimination of all discrimination on grounds of sex with regard to all aspects and conditions of remuneration.
   In particular, where a job classification system is used for determining pay, it must be based on the same criteria for both men and women and so drawn up as to exclude any dicrimination on grounds of sex.'

3. The reference to 'work to which equal value is attributed' is used in the United Kingdom in the Equal Pay Act 1970, as amended by the Sex Discrimination Act 1975. Section 1(5) of the Act provides that:

   'A woman is to be regarded as employed on work rated as equivalent with that of any men if, but only if, her job and their job have been given an equal value, in terms of the demand made on the worker under various headings (for instance effort, skill, decision), on a study undertaken with a view to evaluating in those terms the jobs to be done by all or any of the employees in an undertaking or group of undertakings, or would have been given an equal value but for the evaluation being made on a system setting different values for men and women on the same demand under any heading.'

85

4. Comparison of those provisions reveals that the job classification system is, under the directive, merely one of several methods for determining pay for work to which equal value is attributed, whereas under the provision in the Equal Pay Act quoted above the introduction of such a system is the sole method of achieving such a result.

5. It is also noteworthy that, as the United Kingdom concedes, British legislation does not permit the introduction of a job classification system without the employer's consent. Workers in the United Kingdom are therefore unable to have their work rated as being of equal value with comparable work if their employer refuses to introduce a classification system.

6. The United Kingdom attempts to justify that state of affairs by pointing out that Article 1 of the directive says nothing about the right of an employee to insist on having pay determined by a job classification system. On that basis it concludes that the worker may not insist on a comparative evaluation of different work by the job classification method, the introduction of which is at the employer's discretion.

7. The United Kingdom's interpretation amounts to a denial of the very existence of a right to equal pay for work of equal value where no classification has been made. Such a position is not consonant with the general scheme and provisions of Directive 75/117. The recitals in the preamble to that directive indicate that its essential purpose is to implement the principle that men and women should receive equal pay contained in Article 119 of the Treaty and that it is primarily the responsibility of the Member States to ensure the application of this principle by means of appropriate laws, regulations and administrative provisions in such a way that all employees in the Community can be protected in these matters.

8. To achieve that end the principle is defined in the first paragraph of Article 1 so as to include under the term 'the same work', the case of 'work to which equal value is attributed', and the second paragraph emphasizes merely that where a job classification system is used for determining pay it is necessary to ensure that it is based on the same criteria for both men and women and so drawn up as to exclude any discrimination on grounds of sex.

9. It follows that where there is disagreement as to the application of that concept a worker must be entitled to claim before an appropriate authority that this work has the same value as other work and, if that is found to be the case, to have his rights under the Treaty and the directive acknowledged by a binding decision. Any method which excludes that option prevents the aims of the directive from being achieved.

10. That is borne out by the terms of Article 6 of the directive which provides that Member States are, in accordance with their national circumstances and legal systems, to take the measures necessary to ensure that the principle of equal pay is applied. They are to see that effective means are available to take care that this principle is observed.

11. In this instance, however, the United Kingdom has not adopted the necessary measures and there is at present no means whereby a worker who considers that this post is of equal value to another may pursue his claims if the employer refuses to introduce a job classification system.

12. The United Kingdom has emphasized (particularly in its letter to the Commission dated 19 June 1979) the practical difficulties which would stand in the way of implementing the concept of work to which equal value has been attributed if the use of a system laid down by consensus were abandoned. The United Kingdom believes that the criterion of work of equal value is too abstract to be applied by the courts.

13. The Court cannot endorse that view. The implementation of the directive implies that the assessment of the 'equal value' to be 'attributed' to particular work, may be effected notwithstanding the employer's wishes, if necessary in the context of adversary proceedings. The Member States must endow an authority with the requisite jurisdiction to decide whether work has the same value as other work, after obtaining such information as may be required.

14. Accordingly, by failing to introduce into its national legal system in implementation of the provisions of Council Directive 75/117/EEC of 10 February 1975 such measures as are necessary to enable all employees who consider themselves wronged by failure to apply the principle of equal pay for men and women for work to which equal value is attributed and for which no system of job classification exists to obtain recognition of such equivalence, the United Kingdom has failed to fulfil its obligations under the Treaty.

Costs
15. Under Article 69(2) of the Rules of Procedure the unsuccessful party is to be ordered to pay the costs. Since the defendant has failed in its submissions, it must be ordered to pay the costs.

On those grounds,

THE COURT

hereby:

1. **Declares that, by failing to introduce into its national legal system in implementation of the provisions of Council Directive 75/117/EEC of 10 February 1975 such measures as are necessary to enable all employees who consider themselves wronged by failure to apply the principle of equal pay for men and women for work to which equal value is attributed and for which no system of job classification exists to obtain recognition of such equivalence, the United Kingdom has failed to fulfil its obligations under the Treaty;**

2. **Orders the United Kingdom to pay the costs.**

Due	Mertens de Wilmars		Bosco	Touffait	O'Keeffe
Koopmans	Pescatore	Mackenzie Stuart			Grévisse
	Everling	Chloros			

Delivered in open court in Luxembourg on 6 July 1982.

P. Heim
Registrar

J. Mertens de Wilmars
President

Judgment of the Court

30 January 1985 – Case 143/83

Commission of the European Communities
v.
Kingdom of Denmark

Failure of Member State fully to fulfil its obligations – equal pay – reliance on representatives of management and labour to implement equal pay principle insufficient – Member States must guarantee effective protection for all workers, especially those not protected by other means such as collective agreements – principles of legal certainty and the protection of individuals require unequivocal statement of rights – failure to mention equal pay for work of equal value in national legislation does not satisfy this requirement – Member States not able to rely on unilateral declarations entered in Council minutes when Directive adopted for interpretation of such Community provisions (Council Directive 75/117/EEC, Article 1).

In Case 143/83

Commission of the European Communities, represented by its Legal Adviser, Johannes Føns Buhl, acting as Agent, with an address for service in Luxembourg at the office of Manfred Beschel, a member of its Legal Department, Jean Monnet Building,

applicant,

v.

Kingdom of Denmark, represented by Laurids Mikaelsen, Legal Adviser of the Ministry of Foreign Affairs, with an address for service in Luxembourg at the office of the Danish Chargé d'Affaires, Ib Bodenhagen, at the Danish Embassy, 11 B Boulevard Joseph-II,

defendant,

APPLICATION for a declaration that by failing to adopt within the prescribed period the measures necessary to implement Council Directive No. 75/117/EEC of 10 February 1975 on the approximation of the laws of the Member States relating to the application of the principle of equal pay for men and women (Official Journal L 45, p. 19) the Kingdom of Denmark has failed to fulfil its obligations under the EEC Treaty,

THE COURT

composed of: Lord Mackenzie Stuart, President, O. Due and C. Kakouris (Presidents of Chambers), U. Everling, K. Bahlmann, Y. Galmot and R. Joliet, Judges,

Advocate General: P. VerLoren van Themaat
Registrar: P. Heim

gives the following JUDGMENT

Decision

1. By application lodged at the Court Registry on 18 July 1983 the Commission of the European Communities brought an action pursuant to Article 169 of the EEC Treaty for a declaration that the Kingdom of Denmark has failed to fulfil its obligations under the EEC Treaty by failing to adopt within the prescribed period the measures necessary to implement Council Directive No. 75/117/EEC of 10 February 1975 on the approximation of the laws of the Member States relating to the application of the principle of equal pay for men and women (Official Journal L 45, p. 19).

2. That directive, adopted on the basis of Article 100 of the Treaty, lays down detailed rules regarding certain aspects of the scope of Article 119 and enacts various provisions whose essential purpose is to improve the legal protection of workers who may be wronged by failure to apply the principle of equal pay. In that context it provides in the first paragraph of Article 1 that:

'The principle of equal pay for men and women outlined in
Article 119 of the Treaty ... means, for the same work or for
work to which equal value is attributed, the elimination of all
discrimination on grounds of sex with regard to all aspects and
conditions of remuneration.'

3. Article 2 of the directive requires Member States to introduce into their
national legal systems 'such measures as are necessary to enable all
employees who consider themselves wronged by failure to apply the
principle of equal pay to pursue their claims by judicial process after
possible recourse to other competent authorities'.

4. According to Article 8 the directive was to be implemented within one
year of its notification. That period expired on 12 February 1976 with
regard to the Kingdom of Denmark, and it therefore adopted Law No. 32
of 4 February 1976 on equal pay for men and women (Lovtidende A,
p. 64), which provides in Article 1 that:

'Every person who employs men and women to work at the
same place of work must pay them the same salary for the same
work ("samme arbejde") under this Law if he is not already
required to do so pursuant to a collective agreement.'

5. The Commission considers that the Danish legislation does not fulfil all
the obligations resulting from Directive No. 75/117 inasmuch as on the
one hand it requires employers to pay men and women the same salary
exclusively for the same work but not for work to which equal value is
attributed, and on the other hand it does not provide for any means of
redress enabling workers wronged by the failure to apply the principle of
equal pay for work of equal value to pursue their claims.

6. The Danish Government, for its part, asserts that Danish law is entirely
in conformity with the directive. Danish law does in fact guarantee equal
pay not only for the same work but also for work of equal value.

7. In that regard the Danish Government states that the Law of 4 February
1976, referred to above, is only a subsidiary guarantee of the principle
of equal pay, in cases where observance of that principle is not already
ensured under collective agreements. Collective agreements, which
govern most employment relationships in Denmark, clearly uphold the
idea that the principle of equal pay also applies to work of equal value.
That interpretation is based in particular on the 1971 agreement concluded by the main organizations on the labour market, which provides
expressly that '"equal pay" means that the same salary is to be paid for
work of the same value regardless of sex'. That practice is confirmed by a
decision of the chairman of the Statens Forligsinstitution i Arbejdsstri-
digheder [National Industrial Conciliation Board], acting as arbitrator, of

8 December 1977, in which he applied the principle of equal pay to work 'of the same value to and in production at the place of work'.

8. It is true that Member States may leave the implementation of the principle of equal pay in the first instance to representatives of management and labour. That possibility does not, however, discharge them from the obligation of ensuring, by appropriate legislative and administrative provisions, that all workers in the Community are afforded the full protection provided for in the directive. That State guarantee must cover all cases where effective protection is not ensured by other means, for whatever reason, and in particular cases where the workers in question are not union members, where the sector in question is not covered by a collective agreement or where such an agreement does not fully guarantee the principle of equal pay.

9. In that respect the Danish law in question does not exhibit the clarity and precision necessary for the protection of the workers concerned. Even accepting the assertions of the Danish Government that the principle of equal pay for men and women, in the broad sense required by the directive, is implemented in collective agreements, it has not been shown that the same implementation of that principle is guaranteed for workers whose rights are not defined in such agreements.

10. Since those workers are not unionized and work in small or medium-sized businesses, particular care must be taken to guarantee their rights under the directive. The principles of legal certainty and the protection of individuals thus require an unequivocal wording which would give the persons concerned a clear and precise understanding of their rights and obligations and would enable the courts to ensure that those rights and obligations are observed.

11. In this case it appears that the wording of the Danish law does not fulfil those conditions inasmuch as it sets out the principle of equal pay without speaking of work of equal value, thus restricting the scope of the principle. The fact that in the preamble to the draft law the Government stated that the expression 'same work' was interpreted in Denmark in so broad a sense that the addition of the expression 'work to which equal value is attributed' would not entail any real extension is not sufficient to ensure that the persons concerned are adequately informed.

12. The relevance of those considerations is not affected by the fact that during the preparatory work which led to the adoption of Directive No. 75/117 the Danish Government entered a declaration in the Council minutes to the effect that 'Denmark is of the view that the expression "same work" can continue to be used in the context of Danish labour law'.

13. The Court has consistently held that such unilateral declarations cannot be relied upon for the interpretation of Community measures, since the objective scope of rules laid down by the common institutions cannot be modified by reservations or objections which Member States may have made at the time the rules were being formulated.

14. The conclusion must therefore be that the Kingdom of Denmark has failed to fulfil its obligations under the first paragraph of Article 1 of Directive No. 75/117 by failing, in the text of Law No. 32 of 4 February 1976, to extend the principle of equal pay to work of equal value. Since that finding implies that the law in question does not ensure that employees who consider themselves wronged by failure to apply that principle in a case of work of equal value are able to pursue their claims by judicial process in accordance with Article 3 of the directive, there is no need to make a separate finding on that head.

15. It should be added that during the hearing doubts were expressed with regard to the condition laid down in Article 1 of the Danish law in question, according to which the principle of equal pay for the same work is to be interpreted in relation only to a 'single workplace'. Since, however, the Commission did not formally raise that objection there is no reason to decide that question.

16. For all those reasons it must be declared that by failing to adopt within the prescribed period all the measures necessary to implement Council Directive No. 75/117 of 10 February 1975 on the approximation of the laws of the Member States relating to the application of the principle of equal pay for men and women, the Kingdom of Denmark has failed to fulfil its obligations under the EEC Treaty.

Costs

17. Under Article 69(2) of the Rules of Procedure the unsuccessful party is to be ordered to pay the costs. Since the defendant has failed in its submissions it must be ordered to pay the costs.

On those grounds,

THE COURT

hereby:

1. **Declares that by failing to adopt within the prescribed period the measures necessary to implement Council Directive No. 75/117/EEC of 10 February 1975 on the approximation of the laws of the Member States relating to the application of the principle of equal pay for men and women, the Kingdom of Denmark has failed to fulfil its obligations under the EEC Treaty.**

2. Orders the Kingdom of Denmark to pay the costs.

| Mackenzie Stuart | | Due | | Kakouris | |
| Everling | Bahlmann | | Galmot | | Joliet |

Delivered in open court in Luxembourg on 30 January 1985.

Registrar   *President*
P. Heim   A. J. Mackenzie Stuart

(b) Preliminary rulings under Article 177, EEC Treaty

Judgment of the Court

25 May 1971 – Case 80/70

Cabrielle Defrenne
v.
Belgian State

Equal pay concept – does not include generally applicable social security schemes or benefits directly governed by legislation without any element of agreement in the undertaking or sector concerned – does not therefore include retirement pension schemes which give workers the benefit of a legal system whose levels of financing and contributions from workers, employers and the authorities are determined less by employement relationships than by social policy considerations – employers' contributions to the financing of such schemes do not constitute direct or indirect payments to workers – discrimination arising from application of such schemes not subject to requirements of Article 119, EEC Treaty (EEC Treaty, Article 119).

In Case 80/70

Reference to the Court under Article 177 of the EEC Treaty by the Belgian Conseil d'État for a preliminary ruling in the action pending before that court between

Gabrielle Defrenne, former air hostess with the Belgian Airline Company, Sabena, resident in Brussels,

and

Belgian State, represented by the Minister for Social Security,

on the interpretation of Article 119 of the EEC Treaty with regard to the

93

Royal Decree of 3 November 1969 laying down special rules for the civil aviation air crews on the entitlement to pension and the special conditions of application of Royal Decree No. 50 of 24 October 1967 concerning retirement pensions and survivor's pensions of employed persons,

THE COURT

composed of: R. Lecourt, President, A. M. Donner and A. Trabucchi, Presidents of Chambers, R. Monaco, J. Mertens de Wilmars, P. Pescatore (Rapporteur) and H. Kutscher, Judges,

Advocate-General: A. Dutheillet de Lamothe
Registrar: A. Van Houtte

gives the following JUDGMENT

Decision

1. By order of 4 December 1970, received at the Court Registry on 11 December, the Belgian Conseil d'État referred under Article 177 of the Treaty establishing the European Economic Community three questions relating to the interpretation of Article 119 of the EEC Treaty on the application of the principle of equal pay for men and women for the same work.

The first question

2. The Court is asked in the first place to say 'whether the retirement pension granted under the terms of the social security financed by contribution from workers, employers and by State subsidy, constitutes a consideration which the worker receives indirectly in respect of his employment from his employer'.

3. It appears from the judgment making the reference that this question has been raised in the course of proceedings on the validity of the Belgian Royal Decree of 3 November 1969 concerning retirement pensions to civil aviation air crews – a decree issued within the framework of the general scheme for retirement pensions and survivor's pensions of workers – and more particularly on a provision of this decree excluding air hostesses from the scheme in question.

4. According to the plaintiff in the main action this exclusion is contrary to the principle of equality laid down by Article 119, since the benefit of the pension forms part of the 'pay' as defined in the second paragraph of Article 119 as consideration which the worker receives indirectly from his employer.

5. According to the first paragraph of Article 119 of the EEC Treaty Member States are required to ensure the application of the principle that men and women should receive equal pay for equal work.

6. The provision in the second paragraph of the article extends the concept of pay to any other consideration, whether in cash or in kind, whether immediate or future, provided that the worker receives it, albeit indirectly, in respect of his employment from his employer.

7. Although consideration in the nature of social security benefits is not therefore in principle alien to the concept of pay, there cannot be brought within this concept, as defined in Article 119, social security schemes or benefits, in particular retirement pensions, directly governed by legislation without any element of agreement within the undertaking or the occupational branch concerned, which are obligatorily applicable to general categories of workers.

8. These schemes assure for the workers the benefit of a legal scheme, the financing of which workers, employers and possibly the public authorities contribute in a measure determined less by the employment relationship between the employer and the worker than by considerations of social policy.

9. Accordingly, the part due from the employers in the financing of such schemes does not constitute a direct or indirect payment to the worker.

10. Moreover the worker will normally receive the benefits legally prescribed not by reason of the employer's contribution but solely because the worker fulfils the legal conditions for the grant of benefits.

11. These are likewise characteristics of special schemes which, within the framework of the general system of social security established by legislation, relate in particular to certain categories of workers.

12. It must therefore be found that situations involving discrimination resulting from the application of such a system are not subject to the requirements of Article 119 of the Treaty.

13. It follows from the above that a retirement pension established within the framework of a social security scheme laid down by legislation does not constitute consideration which the worker receives indirectly in respect of his employment from his employer within the meaning of the second paragraph of Article 119.

The second and the third questions
14. The second question asks whether the rules applicable to the worker can

'establish a different age-limit for men and women crew members in civil aviation'.

15. The third question asks in addition whether air hostesses and stewards in civil aviation do 'the same work'.

16. In view of the answer given to the first question the other questions do not call for a reply.

Costs

17/18. The costs incurred by the Commission of the European Communities which has submitted observations to the Court are not recoverable as these proceedings are, in so far as the parties to the main action are concerned, in the nature of a step in the action pending before the Belgian Conseil d'État, the decision as to costs is a matter for that court.

On those grounds,

Upon reading the pleadings;
Upon hearing the report of the Judge-Rapporteur;
Upon hearing the observations of the parties to the main action and of the Commission of the European Communities;
Upon hearing the opinion of the Advocate-General;
Having regard to the Treaty establishing the European Economic Community, especially Articles 119 and 177;
Having regard to the Protocol on the Statute of the Court of Justice of the European Community, especially Article 20;
Having regard to the Rules of Procedure of the Court of Justice of the European Communities;

THE COURT

in answer to the questions referred to it by the Belgian Conseil d'État (section d'administration, IIIrd Chamber) by order of that court of 4 December 1970, hereby rules:

1. **A retirement pension established within the framework of a social security scheme laid down by legislation does not constitute consideration which the worker receives indirectly in respect of his employment from his employer within the meaning of the second paragraph of Article 119 of the EEC Treaty;**

2. **The other question do not call for a reply.**

96

Lecourt	Donner	Trabucchi
Monaco	Mertens de Wilmars	Pescatore	Kutscher

Delivered in open court in Luxembourg on 25 May 1971.

A. Van Houtte   R. Lecourt
Registrar   *President*

Judgment of the Court

8 April 1976 – Case 43/75

Gabrielle Defrenne
v.
Société Anonyme Belge de Navigation Aérienne Sabena

Equal pay principle – Article 119, EEC Treaty, can be directly relied on before national courts – courts have duty to ensure protection of rights which Article 119 vests in individuals, especially where discrimination arises directly from legislative or collectively agreed provisions or where men and women receive unequal pay for equal work carried out in the same establishment or service – time limits for implementing equal pay principle fixed by EEC Treaty – Council Directive 75/117/EEC does not prejudice direct effect of Article 119, nor affect its time limits – given the importance of legal certainty for all involved, the direct effect of Article 119 cannot be relied on to support claims regarding pay periods prior to this judgment except where workers have already made claims – where Article 119 has no direct effect, it may not be interpreted as giving the national legislature exclusive power to implement the equal pay principle, which may be achieved by a combination of Community and national provisions (EEC Treaty, Articles 119 and 236; Council Directive 75/117/EEC).

In Case 43/75

Reference to the Court under Article 117 of the EEC Treaty by the Cour du Travail (Labour Court), Brussels, for a preliminary ruling in the action pending before that court between

Gabrielle Defrenne, former air hostess, residing in Brussels-Jette,

and

Sociéte Anonyme Belge de Navigation Aérienne Sabena, the registered office of which is at Brussels,

97

on the interpretation of Article 119 the EEC Treaty,

THE COURT

composed of: R. Lecourt, President, H. Kutscher and A. O'Keeffe, Presidents of Chambers, A. M. Donner, J. Mertens de Wilmars, P. Pescatore and M. Sørensen, Judges,

Advocate-General: A. Trabucchi
Registrar: A. Van Houtte

gives the following JUDGMENT

Decision

1. By a judgment of 23 April 1975, received at the Court Registry on 2 May 1975, the Cour du travail, Brussels, referred to the Court under Article 177 of the EEC Treaty two questions concerning the effect and implementation of Article 119 of the Treaty regarding the principle that men and women should receive equal pay for equal work.

2. These questions arose within the context of an action between an air hostess and her employer, Sabena S. A., concerning compensation claimed by the applicant in the main action on the ground that, between 15 February 1963 and 1 February 1966, she suffered as a female worker discrimination in terms of pay as compared with male colleagues who were doing the same work as 'cabin steward'.

3. According to the judgment containing the reference, the parties agree that the work of an air hostess is identical to that of a cabin steward and in these circumstances the existence of discrimination in pay to the detriment of the air hostess during the period in question is not disputed.

The first question (direct effect of Article 119)
4. The first question asks whether Article 119 of the Treaty introduces 'directly into the national law of each Member State of the European Community the principle that men and women should receive equal pay for equal work and does it therefore, independently of any national provision, entitle workers to institute proceedings before national courts in order to ensure its observance?'

5. If the answer to this question is in the affirmative, the question further enquires as from what date this effect must be recognized.

6. The reply to the final part of the first question will therefore be given with the reply to the second question.

7. The question of the direct effect of Article 119 must be considered in the light of the nature of the principle of equal pay, the aim of this provision and its place in the scheme of the Treaty.

8. Article 119 pursues a double aim.

9. First, in the light of the different stages of the development of social legislation in the various Member States, the aim of Article 119 is to avoid a situation in which undertakings established in States which have actually implemented the principle of equal pay suffer a competitive disadvantage in intra-Community competition as compared with undertakings established in States which have not yet eliminated discrimination against women workers as regards pay.

10. Secondly, this provision forms part of the social objectives of the Community, which is not merely an economic union, but is at the same time intended, by common action, to ensure social progress and seek the constant improvement of the living and working conditions of their peoples, as is emphasized by the Preamble to the Treaty.

11. This aim is accentuated by the insertion of Article 119 into the body of a chapter devoted to social policy whose preliminary provision, Article 117, marks 'the need to promote improved working conditions and an improved standard of living for workers, so as to make possible their harmonization while the improvement is being maintained'.

12. This double aim, which is at once economic and social, shows that the principle of equal pay forms part of the foundations of the Community.

13. Furthermore, this explains why the Treaty has provided for the complete implementation of this principle by the end of the first stage of the transitional period.

14. Therefore, in interpreting this provision, it is impossible to base any argument on the dilatoriness and resistance which have delayed the actual implementation of this basic principle in certain Member States.

15. In particular, since Article 119 appears in the context of the harmonization of working conditions while the improvement is being maintained, the objection that the terms of this article may be observed in other ways than by raising the lowest salaries may be set aside.

16. Under the terms of the first paragraph of Article 119, the Member States are bound to ensure and maintain 'the application of the principle that men and women should receive equal pay for equal work'.

17. The second and third paragraphs of the same article add a certain number

99

of details concerning the concepts of pay and work referred to in the first paragraph.

18. For the purposes of the implementation of these provisions a distinction must be drawn within the whole area of application of Article 119 between, first, direct and overt discrimination which may be identified solely with the aid of the criteria based on equal work and equal pay referred to by the article in question and, secondly, indirect and disguised discrimination which can only be identified by reference to more explicit implementing provisions of a Community or national character.

19. It is impossible not to recognize that the complete implementation of the aim pursued by Article 119, by means of the elimination of all discrimination, direct or indirect, between men and women workers, not only as regards individual undertakings but also entire branches of industry and even of the economic system as a whole, may in certain cases involve the elaboration of criteria whose implementation necessitates the taking of appropriate measures at Community and national level.

20. This view is all the more essential in the light of the fact that the Community measures on this question, to which reference will be made in answer to the second question, implement Article 119 from the point of view of extending the narrow criterion of 'equal work', in accordance in particular with the provisions of Convention No. 100 on equal pay concluded by the International Labour Organization in 1951, Article 2 of which establishes the principle of equal pay for work 'of equal value'.

21. Among the forms of direct discrimination which may be identified solely by reference to the criteria laid down by Article 119 must be included in particular those which have their origin in legislative provisions or in collective labour agreements and which may be detected on the basis of a purely legal analysis of the situation.

22. This applies even more in cases where men and women receive unequal pay for equal work carried out in the same establishment or service, whether public or private.

23. As is shown by the very findings of the judgment making the reference, in such a situation the court is in a position to establish all the facts which enable it to decide whether a woman worker is receiving lower pay than a male worker performing the same tasks.

24. In such situation, at least, Article 119 is directly applicable and may thus give rise to individual rights which the courts must protect.

25. Furthermore, as regards equal work, as a general rule, the national legislative provisions adopted for the implementation of the principle of

equal pay as a rule merely reproduce the substance of the terms of Article 119 as regards the direct forms of discrimination.

26. Belgian legislation provides a particularly apposite illustration of this point, since Article 14 of Royal Decree No. 40 of 24 October 1967 on the employment of women merely sets out the right of any female worker to institute proceedings before the relevant court for the application of the principle of equal pay set out in Article 119 and simply refers to that article.

27. The terms of Article 119 cannot be relied on to invalidate this conclusion.

28. First of all, it is impossible to put forward an argument against its direct effect based on the use in this article of the word 'principle', since, in the language of the Treaty, this term is specifically used in order to indicate the fundamental nature of certain provisions, as is shown, for example, by the heading of the first part of the Treaty which is devoted to 'Principles' and by Article 113, according to which the commercial policy of the Community is to be based on 'uniform principles'.

29. If this concept were to be attenuated to the point of reducing it to the level of a vague declaration, the very foundations of the Community and the coherence of its external relations would be indirectly affected.

30. It is also impossible to put forward arguments based on the fact that Article 119 only refers expressly to 'Member States'.

31. Indeed, as the Court has already found in other contexts, the fact that certain provisions of the Treaty are formally addressed to the Member States does not prevent rights from being conferred at the same time on any individual who has an interest in the performance of the duties thus laid down.

32. The very wording of Article 119 shows that it imposes on States a duty to bring about a specific result to be mandatorily achieved within a fixed period.

33. The effectiveness of this provision cannot be affected by the fact that the duty imposed by the Treaty has not been discharged by certain Member States and that the joint institutions have not reacted sufficiently energetically against this failure to act.

34. To accept the contrary view would be to risk raising the violation of the right to the status of a principle of interpretation, a position the adoption of which would not be consistent with the task assigned to the Court by Article 164 of the Treaty.

35. Finally, in its reference to 'Member States', Article 119 is alluding to those States in the exercise of all those of their functions which may usefully contribute to the implementation of the principle of equal pay.

36. Thus, contrary to the statements made in the course of the proceedings this provision is far from merely referring the matter to the powers of the national legislative authorities.

37. Therefore, the reference to 'Member States' in Article 119 cannot be interpreted as excluding the intervention of the courts in direct application of the Treaty.

38. Furthermore it is not possible to sustain any objection that the application by national courts of the principle of equal pay would amount to modifying independent agreements concluded privately or in the sphere of industrial relations such as individual contracts and collective labour agreements.

39. In fact, since Article 119 is mandatory in nature, the prohibition on discrimination between men and women applies not only to the action of public authorities, but also extends to all agreements which are intended to regulate paid labour collectively, as well as to contracts between individuals.

40. The reply to the first question must therefore be that the principle of equal pay contained in Article 119 may be relied upon before the national courts and that these courts have a duty to ensure the protection of the rights which this provision vests in individuals, in particular as regards those types of discrimination arising directly from legislative provisions or collective labour agreements, as well as in cases in which men and women receive unequal pay for equal work which is carried out in the same establishment or service, whether private or public.

The second question (implementation of Article 119 and powers of the Community and of the Member States)

41. The second question asks whether Article 119 has become 'applicable in the internal law of the Member States by virtue of measures adopted by the authorities of the European Economic Community', or whether the national legislature must 'be regarded as alone competent in this matter'.

42. In accordance with what has been set out above, it is appropriate to join to this question the problem of the date from which Article 119 must be regarded as having direct effect.

43. In the light of all these problems it is first necessary to establish the chronological order of the measures taken on a Community level to

102

ensure the implementation of the provision whose interpretation is requested.

44. Article 119 itself provides that the application of the principle of equal pay was to be uniformly ensured by the end of the first stage of the transitional period at the latest.

45. The information supplied by the Commission reveals the existence of important differences and discrepancies between the various States in the implementation of this principle.

46. Although, in certain Member States, the principle had already largely been put into practice before the entry into force of the Treaty, either by means of express constitutional and legislative provisions or by social practices established by collective labour agreements, in other States its full implementation has suffered prolonged delays.

47. In the light of this situation, on 30 December 1961, the eve of the expiry of the time-limit fixed by Article 119, the Member States adopted a Resolution concerning the harmonization of rates of pay of men and women which was intended to provide further details concerning certain aspects of the material content of the principle of equal pay, while delaying its implementation according to a plan spread over a period of time.

48. Under the terms of that Resolution all discrimination, both direct and indirect, was to have been completely eliminated by 31 December 1964.

49. The information provided by the Commission shows that several of the original Member States have failed to observe the terms of that Resolution and that, for this reason, within the context of the tasks entrusted to it by Article 155 of the Treaty, the Commission was led to bring together the representatives of the governments and the two sides of industry in order to study the situation and to agree together upon the measures necessary to ensure progress towards the full attainment of the objective laid down in Article 119.

50. This led to be drawing up of successive reports on the situation in the original Member States, the most recent of which, dated 18 July 1973, recapitulates all the facts.

51. In the conclusion to that report the Commission announced its intention to initiate proceedings under Article 169 of the Treaty, for failure to take the requisite action, against those of the Member States who had not by that date discharged the obligations imposed by Article 119, although this warning was not followed by any further action.

52. After similar exchanges with the competent authorities in the new Member States the Commission stated in its report dated 17 July 1974 that, as regards those States, Article 119 had been fully applicable since 1 January 1973 and that from that date the position of those States was the same as that of the original Member States.

53. For its part, in order to hasten the full implementation of Article 119, the Council on 10 February 1975 adopted Directive No. 75/117 on the approximation of the laws of the Member States relating to the application of the principle of equal pay for men and women (OJ L 45, p. 19).

54. This Directive provides further details regarding certain aspects of the material scope of Article 119 and also adopts various provisions whose essential purpose is to improve the legal protection of workers who may be wronged by failure to apply the principle of equal pay laid down by Article 119.

55. Article 8 of this Directive allows the Member States a period of one year to put into force the appropriate laws, regulations and administrative provisions.

56. It follows from the express terms of Article 119 that the application of the principle that men and women should receive equal pay was to be fully secured and irreversible at the end of the first stage of the transitional period, that is, by 1 January 1962.

57. Without prejudice to its possible effects as regards encouraging and accelerating the full implementation of Article 119, the Resolution of the Member States of 30 December 1961 was ineffective to make any valid modification of the time-limit fixed by the Treaty.

58. In fact, apart from any specific provisions, the Treaty can only be modified by means of the amendment procedure carried out in accordance with Article 236.

59. Moreover, it follows from the foregoing that, in the absence of transitional provisions, the principle contained in Article 119 has been fully effective in the new Member States since the entry into force of the Accession Treaty, that is, since 1 January 1973.

60. It was not possible for this legal situation to be modified by Directive No. 75/117, which was adopted on the basis of Article 100 dealing with the approximation of laws and was intended to encourage the proper implementation of Article 119 by means of a series of measures to be taken on the national level, in order, in particular, to eliminate indirect forms of discrimination, but was unable to reduce the effectiveness of that article or modify its temporal effect.

61. Although Article 119 is expressly addressed to the Member States in that it imposes on them a duty to ensure, within a given period, and subsequently to maintain the application of the principle of equal pay, that duty assumed by the States does not exclude competence in this matter on the part of the Community.

62. On the contrary, the existence of competence on the part of the Community, is shown by the fact that Article 119 sets out one of the 'social policy' objectives of the Treaty which form subject of Title III, which itself appears in Part Three of the Treaty dealing with the 'Policy of the Community'.

63. In the absence of any express reference in Article 119 to the possible action to be taken by the Community for the purposes of implementing the social policy, it is appropriate to refer to the general scheme of the Treaty and to the courses of action for which it provided, such as those laid down in Articles 100, 155 and, where appropriate, 235.

64. As has been shown in the reply to the first question, no implementing provision, whether adopted by the institutions of the Community or by the national authorities, could adversely affect the direct effect of Article 119.

65. The reply to the second question should therefore be that the application of Article 119 was to have been fully secured by the original Member States as from 1 January 1962, the beginning of the second stage of the transitional period, and by the new Member States as from 1 January 1973, the date of entry into force of the Accession Treaty.

66. The first of these time-limits was not modified by the Resolution of the Member States of 30 December 1961.

67. As indicated in reply to the first question, Council Directive No. 75/117 does not prejudice the direct effect of Article 119 and the period fixed by that Directive for compliance therewith does not affect the time-limits laid down by Article 119 of the EEC Treaty and the Accession Treaty.

68. Even in the areas in which Article 119 has no direct effect, that provision cannot be interpreted as reserving to the national legislature exclusive power to implement the principle of equal pay since, to the extent to which such implementation is necessary, it may be relieved by a combination of Community and national measures.

The temporal effect of this judgment
69. The Governments of Ireland and the United Kingdom have drawn the Court's attention to the possible economic consequences of attributing direct effect to the provisions of Article 119, on the ground that such

a decision might, in many branches of economic life, result in the intro-duction of claims dating back to the time at which such effect came into existence.

70. In view of the large number of people concerned such claims, which undertakings could not have foreseen, might seriously affect the financial situation of such undertakings and even drive some of them to bankruptcy.

71. Although the practical consequences of any judicial decision must be carefully taken into account, it would be impossible to go so far as to diminish the objectivity of the law and compromise its future application on the ground of the possible repercussions which might result, as regards the past, from such a judicial decision.

72. However, in the light of the conduct of several of the Member States and the views adopted by the Commission and repeatedly brought to the notice of the circles concerned, it is appropriate to take exceptionally into account the fact that, over a prolonged period, the parties concerned have been led to continue with practices which were contrary to Article 119, although not yet prohibited under their national law.

73. The fact that, in spite of the warnings given, the Commission did not initiate proceedings under Article 169 against the Member States con-cerned on grounds of failure to fulfil an obligation was likely to con-solidate the incorrect impression as to the effects of Article 119.

74. In these circumstances, it is appropriate to determine that, as the general level at which pay would have been fixed cannot be known, important considerations of legal certainty affecting all the interests involved, both public and private, make it impossible in principle to reopen the question as regards the past.

75. Therefore, the direct effect of Article 119 cannot be relied on in order to support claims concerning pay periods prior to the date of this judgment, except as regards those workers who have already brought legal pro-ceedings or made an equivalent claim.

Costs

76. The costs incurred by the Commission of the European Communities, which has submitted observations to the Court, are not recoverable.

77. As these proceedings are, in so far as the parties to the main action are concerned, in the nature of a step in the action pending before the Cour du travail, Brussels, the decision as to costs is a matter for that court.

On those grounds,

THE COURT

in answer to the questions referred to it by the Cour du travail, Brussels, by judgment dated 23 April 1975 hereby rules:

1. **The principle that men and women should receive equal pay, which is laid down by Article 119, may be relied on before the national courts. These courts have a duty to ensure the protection of the rights which that provision vests in individuals, in particular in the case of those forms of discrimination which have their origin in legislative provisions or collective labour agreements, as well as where men and women receive unequal pay for equal work which is carried out in the same establishment or service, whether private or public.**

2. **The application of Article 119 was to have been fully secured by the original Member States as from 1 January 1962, the beginning of the second stage of the transitional period, and by the new Member States as from 1 January 1973, the date of entry into force of the Accession Treaty. The first of these time-limits was not modified by the Resolution of the Member States of 30 December 1961.**

3. **Council Directive No. 75/117 does not prejudice the direct effect of Article 119 and the period fixed by that Directive for compliance therewith does not affect the time-limits laid down by Article 119 of the EEC Treaty and the Accession Treaty.**

4. **Even in the areas in which Article 119 has no direct effect, that provision cannot be interpreted as reserving to the national legislature exclusive power to implement the principle of equal pay since, to the extent to which such implementation is necessary, it may be achieved by a combination of Community and national provisions.**

5. **Except as regards those workers who have already brought legal proceedings or made an equivalent claim, the direct effect of Article 119 cannot be relied on in order to support claims concerning pay periods prior to the date of this judgment.**

Lecourt	Kutscher	O'Keeffe
Donner	Mertens de Wilmars	Pescatore	Sørensen

Delivered in open court in Luxembourg on 8 April 1976.

A. Van Houtte   R. Lecourt
Registrar   *President*

Judgment of the Court

15 June 1978 – Case 149/77

Gabrielle Defrenne
v.
Société Anonyme Belge de Navigation Aérienne Sabena

Equal pay principle – scope – Article 119, EEC Treaty, cannot be interpreted as prescribing, in addition to equal pay, equality in respect of other working conditions applicable to men and women – the fact that fixing certain conditions of employment (such as age limits) may have pecuniary consequences is not sufficient to bring such conditions within the scope of Article 119, which is based on the close connection between the nature of the services provided and the amount of remuneration – at the time of the events of this action (ie late 1960s) there was, as regards relationships between employer and employee under national law, no rule of Community law prohibiting discrimination between men and women in working conditions other than the requirements as to pay in Article 119 (EEC Treaty, Articles 117, 118 and 119).

In Case 149/77

REFERENCE to the Court under Article 177 of the EEC Treaty by the Cour de Cassation, Belgium, for a preliminary ruling in the proceedings pending before that court between

Gabrielle Defrenne, a former air hostess, residing in Brussels-Jette,

and

Société Anonyme Belge de Navigation Aérienne Sabena, whose registered office is in Brussels,

on the interpretation of Article 119 of the EEC Treaty,

THE COURT

composed of: H. Kutscher, President, M. Sørensen and G. Bosco (Presidents of Chambers), A. M. Donner, J. Mertens de Wilmars, P. Pescatore, Lord Mackenzie Stuart, A. O'Keeffe and A. Touffait, Judges,

Advocate General: F. Capotorti
Registrar: A. Van Houtte

gives the following JUDGMENT

Decision

1. By judgment of 28 November 1977, received at the Court on 12 December 1977, the Cour de Cassation of Belgium referred to the Court under Article 177 of the EEC Treaty a preliminary question relating to the scope of the principle prohibiting discrimination between men and women workers laid down by Article 119 of the Treaty.

2. That question arose within the context of an action brought before the Belgian labour courts by the appellant in the main action, Miss Gabrielle Defrenne, a former air hostess, against the Société Belge de Navigation Aérienne Sabena following the termination of her employment, in accordance with the terms of her contract, when she reached the age-limit of 40 years.

3. Miss Defrenne had originally brought an action before the Tribunal du Travail, Brussels, on the basis of Article 119 of the EEC Treaty, the object of which was to order Sabena to pay:
   (1) compensation by reason of the fact that, as a woman worker, she had suffered discrimination in the matter of pay as compared with her male colleagues carrying out the same work as cabin stewards;
   (2) a supplementary allowance on termination of service, representing the difference between the allowance actually received by her on her departure and the allowance which would have been received by a cabin steward at the age of 40 with the same seniority who had been declared permanently unfit for employment;
   (3) compensation for the damage suffered by the appellant as regards her pension.

4. By a judgment of 17 December 1970 the Tribunal du Travail dismissed that action in its entirely as unfounded.

5. By a judgment of 23 April 1975 on the appeal lodged by the applicant in the original action the Cour du Travail, Brussels, upheld the judgment at first instance on the second and third heads of claim.

6. For the purpose of giving judgment on the first head of claim that court referred to the Court of Justice two preliminary questions which formed the subject of Case 43/75 on 8 April 1976 ([1976] ECR 455).

7. Following the preliminary ruling, the Cour du Travail by a judgment of 24 November 1976 awarded the applicant the sum of Bfrs 12 716 by way of the arrears of remuneration claimed, increased by interest and costs.

8. Miss Defrenne lodged an appeal in cassation against the judgment of the Cour du Travail as regards the heads of claim which it had dismissed and

the Cour de Cassation in turn referred the matter to the Court of Justice under Article 177 of the Treaty.

9. It must be recalled again that, in the same context, Miss Defrenne had brought an action before the Conseil d'État of Belgium against the Belgian Royal Decree of 3 November 1969 on retirement pensions for civil aviation air crew, which related, in particular, to the validity of a provision of that decree excluding air hostesses from the scheme in question.

10. For its part the Conseil d'État referred to the Court of Justice certain questions relating to the interpretation of Article 119 of the Treaty, which formed the subject of the judgment of 25 May 1971 in Case 80/70 ([1971] ECR 445).

11. In order to resolve the questions at present before it, the Cour de Cassation has referred to the Court a preliminary question, worded in two parts, which requires clear replies inasmuch as it relates, first, to the determination of the field of application of Article 119 of the Treaty and, secondly, to the possible existence of a general principle of Community law, the aim of which is to eliminate discrimination between men and women workers as regards conditions of employment and working conditions other than remuneration in the strict sense.

The first part of the question – scope of Article 119 of the EEC Treaty
12. The first part of the question raised by the Cour de Cassation seeks to discover whether the principle of equal pay laid down by Article 119 may be interpreted as requiring general equality of working conditions for men and women, so that the insertion into the contract of employment of an air hostess of a clause bringing the contract to an end when she reaches the age of 40 years, it being established that no such limit is attached to the contract of male cabin attendants who carry out the same work, constitutes discrimination prohibited by the said provision.

13. According to the appellant in the main action Article 119 must be given a wide interpretation, inasmuch as it is only a specific statement of a general principle against discrimination which has found many expression in the Treaty.

14. In particular she claims that the contested clause contained in the contract of employment of air hostesses, fixing an age-limit of 40, is subject to the rule against discrimination contained in Article 119 by reason of the fact that, first, a woman worker can receive pay equal to that received by men only if the requirement regarding equal conditions of employment is first satisfied and, secondly, that the age-limit imposed on air hostesses by the contract of employment has pecuniary consequences which are

prejudicial as regards the allowance on termination of service and pension.

15. The field of application of Article 119 must be determined within the context of the system of the social provisions of the Treaty, which are set out in the chapter formed by Article 117 et seq.

16. The general features of the conditions of employment and working conditions are considered in Articles 117 and 118 from the point of view of the harmonization of the social systems of the Member States and of the approximation of their laws in that field.

17. There is no doubt that the elimination of discrimination based on the sex of workers forms part of the programme for social and legislative policy which was clarified in certain respects by the Council Resolution of 21 January 1974 (Official Journal C 13, p. 1).

18. The same thought also underlies Council Directive No. 76/207/EEC of 9 February 1976 on the implementation of the principle of equal treatment for men and women as regards access to employment, vocational training and promotion and working conditions (Official Journal L 39, p. 40).

19. In contrast to the provisions of Articles 117 and 118, which are essentially in the nature of a programme, Article 119, which is limited to the question of pay discrimination between men and women workers, constitutes a special rule, whose application is linked to precise factors.

20. In these circumstances it is impossible to extend the scope of that article to elements of the employment relationship other than those expressly referred to.

21. In particular, the fact that the fixing of certain conditions of employment – such as a special age-limit – may have pecuniary consequences is not sufficient to bring such conditions within the field of application of Article 119, which is based on the close connexion which exists between the nature of the services provided and the amount of remuneration.

22. That is *a fortiori* true since the touchstone which forms the basis of Article 119 – that is, the comparable nature of the services provided by workers of either sex – is a factor as regards which all workers are *ex hypothesi* on an equal footing, whereas in many respects an assessment of the other conditions of employment and working conditions involves factors connected with the sex of the workers, taking into account considerations affecting the special position of women in the work process.

23. It is, therefore, impossible to widen the terms of Article 119 to the point, first, of jeopardizing the direct applicability which that provision must be

acknowledged to have in its own sphere and, secondly, of intervening in an area reserved by Articles 117 and 118 to the discretion of the authorities referred to therein.

24. The reply to the first part of the question must therefore be that Article 119 of the Treaty cannot be interpreted as prescribing, in addition to equal pay, equality in respect of the other working conditions applicable to men and women.

The second part of the question – the existence of a general principle prohibiting discrimination based on sex in conditions of employment and working conditions

25. The second part of the question asks whether, apart from the specific provisions of Article 119, Community law contains any general principle prohibiting discrimination based on sex as regards the conditions of employment and working conditions of men and women.

26. The Court has repeatedly stated that respect for fundamental personal human rights is one of the general principles of Community law, the observance of which it has a duty to ensure.

27. There can be no doubt that the elimination of discrimination based on sex forms part of those fundamental rights.

28. Moreover, the same concepts are recognized by the European Social Charter of 18 November 1961 and by Convention No 111 of the International Labour Organization of 25 June 1958 concerning discrimination in respect of employment and occupation.

29. Attention must be drawn in this regard to the fact that in its judgments of 7 June 1972 in Case 20/71 *Sabbatini (née Bertoni)* v. *European Parliament* ([1972] ECR 345) and 20 February 1975 in Case 21/74 *Airola* v. *Commission of the European Communities* ([1975] ECR 221), the Court recognized the need to ensure equality in the matter of working conditions for men and women employed by the Community itself, within the context of the Staff Regulations of Officials.

30. On the other hand, as regards the relationships of employer and employee which are subject to national law, the Community had not, at the time of the events now before the Belgian courts, assumed any responsibility for supervising and guaranteeing the observance of the principle of equality between men and women in working conditions other than remuneration.

31. As has been stated above, at the period under consideration Community law contained only the provisions in the nature of a programme laid down by Articles 117 and 118 of the Treaty, which relate to the general

development of social welfare, in particular as regards conditions of employment and working conditions.

32. It follows that the situation before the Belgian courts is governed by the provisions and principles of internal and international law in force in Belgium.

33. The reply to the second part of the question must therefore be that at the time of the events which form the basis of the main action there was, as regards the relationships between employer and employee under national law, no rule of Community law prohibiting discrimination between men and women in the matter of working conditions other than the requirements as to pay referred to in Article 119 of the Treaty.

Costs
34. The costs incurred by the Government of the United Kingdom, the Government of the Italian Republic and the Commission of the European Communities, which have submitted observations to the Court, are not recoverable.

35. As these proceedings are, in so far as the parties to the main action are concerned, in the nature of a step in the action pending before the Cour de Cassation of Belgium, the decision on costs is a matter for that court.

On those grounds,

THE COURT

in answer to the questions referred to it by the Cour de Cassation of Belgium by judgment of 28 November 1977, hereby rules:

Article 119 of the EEC Treaty cannot be interpreted as prescribing, in addition to equal pay, equality in respect of the other working conditions applicable to men and women.

At the time of the events which form the basis of the main action there was, as regards the relationships between employer and employee under national law, no rule of Community law prohibiting discrimination between men and women in the matter of working conditions other than the requirements as to pay referred to in Article 119 of the Treaty.

Kutscher   Sørensen   Bosco   Donner   Mertens de Wilmars
   Pescatore   Mackenzie Stuart   O'Keeffe   Touffait

Delivered in open court in Luxembourg on 15 June 1978.

A. Van Houtte   H. Kutscher
Registrar   *President*

Judgment of the Court

27 March 1980 – Case 129/79

Macarthys Ltd
v.
Wendy Smith

Equal pay principle – Article 119, EEC Treaty, applies directly, without need for more detailed implementing measures, to all forms of direct and overt discrimination which can be identified solely with aid of criteria of equal work and equal pay referred to in Article 119 – need to establish whether there are differences in treatment between men and women performing equal work – equal work involves nature of services in question and is not confined to contemporaneous performance of equal work – whether differences in pay due to factors unconnected with discrimination on grounds of sex is matter for national courts to decide – where there is actual discrimination within scope of Article 119 as directly applied, comparisons to be based on appraisals of work actually performed by men and women in same establishment or service (EEC Treaty, Article 119; Council Directive 75/117/EEC).

In Case 129/79

REFERENCE to the Court under Article 177 of the EEC Treaty by the Court of Appeal in London for a preliminary ruling in the action pending before that court between

Macarthys Ltd, wholesale dealers in pharmaceutical products, having their registered office in London

and

Mrs Wendy Smith, a former employee of Macarthys Ltd,

on the interpretation of Article 119 of the EEC Treaty and Article 1 of Council Directive No. 75/117/EEC of 10 February 1975 on the approximation of the laws of the Member States relating to the application of the principle of equal pay for men and women,

THE COURT

composed of: H. Kutscher, President, A. O'Keeffe and A. Touffait (Presidents of Chambers), J. Mertens de Wilmars, P. Pescatore, Lord Mackenzie Stuart, G. Bosco, T. Koopmans and O. Due, Judges,

Advocate General: F. Capotorti
Registrar: A. Van Houtte

gives the following JUDGMENT

Decision

1. By order of 25 July 1979, received at the Court on 10 August 1979, the Court of Appeal in London referred to the Court for a preliminary ruling under Article 177 of the EEC Treaty four questions concerning the interpretation of Article 119 of the EEC Treaty and Article 1 of Council Directive No. 75/117 of 10 February 1975 on the approximation of the laws of the Member States relating to the application of the principle of equal pay for men and women (Official Journal No. L 45, p. 19).

2. It appears from the file that the respondent in the main action, Mrs Wendy Smith, was employed as from 1 March 1976 by Macarthys Limited, wholesale dealers in pharmaceutical products, as a warehouse manageress at a weekly salary of £50. She complains of discrimination in pay because her predecessor, a man, whose post she took up after an interval of four months, received a salary of £60 per week.

3. Mrs Wendy Smith brought proceedings before the Industrial Tribunal on the basis of the Equal Pay Act 1970. By its decision of 27 June 1977 that tribunal held that the applicant was employed on like work with her predecessor and ordered Macarthys to pay the applicant a salary equal to his salary.

4. Macarthys appealed to the Employment Appeal Tribunal, which dismissed the appeal by its judgment of 14 December 1977. That judgment, which was based, as was the decision of the Industrial Tribunal, on the Equal Pay Act, made reference also to Article 119 of the EEC Treaty and to the judgment of the Court of Justice of 8 April 1976 in Case 43/75 *Gabrielle Defrenne* v. *Sabena* [1976] ECR 455 which was concerned with the interpretation of that provision.

5. A further appeal was brought before the Court of Appeal by the employer. The employer contended that, according to its natural and ordinary meaning, the Equal Pay Act makes it impermissible for a woman to compare her situation with that of a man formerly in the employment of the same employer. In its submission, such an interpretation would not be inconsistent with the principle of equal pay for men and women laid down in Article 119 of the EEC Treaty.

6. For her part, the respondent in the main action contended that Macarthys' interpretation was contrary to Article 119 and to Article 1 of Directive No. 75/117 in that the principle of equal pay for equal work is not confined to situations in which men and women are contemporaneously doing equal work for their employer but that, on the contrary, that principle also applies where a worker can show that she receives less pay in respect of her employment than she would have received if she were a

115

man doing equal work for the employer or than had been received by a male worker who had been employed prior to her period of employment and who had been doing equal work for her employer.

7. In order to decide the dispute the Court of Appeal formulated four questions worded as follows:

'1. Is the principle of equal pay for equal work, contained in Article 119 of the EEC Treaty and Article 1 of the EEC Council Directive of 10 February 1975 (75/117/EEC), confined to situations in which men and women are contemporaneously doing equal work for their employer?

2. If the answer to Question 1 is in the negative, does the said principle apply where a worker can show that she receives less pay in respect of her employment from her employer:
   (a) than she would have received if she were a man doing equal work for the employer; or
   (b) than had been received by a male worker who had been employed prior to her period of employment and who had been doing equal work for the employer?

'3. If the answer to Question 2(a) or (b) is in the affirmative, is that answer dependent upon the provisions of Article 1 of the said Directive?

4. If the answer to Question 3 is in the affirmative, is Article 1 of the said Directive directly applicable in Member States?'

8. If follows from the wording of these questions, as much as from the reasons given in the order making the reference, that the questions relating to the effect of Directive No. 75/117 and to the interpretation of Article 1 thereof only arise if the application of Article 119 of the Treaty should not permit the issue raised in the proceedings to be resolved. It is therefore appropriate to consider first how Article 119 is to be interpreted having regard to the legal situation in which the dispute has its origin.

The interpretation of Article 119 of the EEC Treaty

9. According to the first paragraph of Article 119 the Member States are obliged to ensure and maintain 'the application of the principle that men and women should receive equal pay for equal work'.

10. As the Court indicated in the *Defrenne* judgment of 8 April 1976, that provision applies directly, and without the need for more detailed implementing measures on the part of the Community or the Member States, to all forms of direct and overt discrimination which may be identified solely with the aid of the criteria of equal work and equal pay referred to by the article in question. Among the forms of discrimination which may be thus judicially identified, the Court mentioned in particular cases

where men and women receive unequal pay for equal work carried out in the same establishment or service.

11. In such a situation the decisive test lies in establishing whether there is a difference in treatment between a man and a woman performing 'equal work' within the meaning of Article 119. The scope of that concept, which is entirely qualitative in character in that it is exclusively concerned with the nature of the services in question, may not be restricted by the introduction of a requirement of contemporaneity.

12. It must be acknowledged, however, that, as the Employment Appeal Tribunal properly recognized, it cannot be ruled out that a difference in pay between two workers occupying the same post but at different periods in time may be explained by the operation of factors which are unconnected with any discrimination on grounds of sex.
    That is a question of fact which it is for the court or tribunal to decide.

13. Thus the answer to the first question should be that the principle that men and women should receive equal pay for equal work, enshrined in Article 119 of the EEC Treaty, is not confined to situations in which men and women are contemporaneously doing equal work for the same employer.

14. The second question put by the Court of Appeal and expressed in terms of alternatives concerns the framework within which the existence of possible discrimination in pay may be established. This question is intended to enable the court to rule upon a submission made by the respondent in the main action and developed by her before the Court of Justice to the effect that a woman may claim not only the salary received by a man who previously did the same work for her employer but also, more generally, the salary to which she would be entitled were she a man, even in the absence of any man who was concurrently performing, or had previously performed, similar work. The respondent in the main action defined this term of comparison by reference to the concept of what she described as 'a hypothetical male worker'.

15. It is clear that the latter proposition, which is the subject of Question 2(a), is to be classed as indirect and disguised discrimination, the identification of which, as the Court explained in the *Defrenne* judgment, cited above, implies comparative studies of entire branches of industry and therefore requires, as a prerequisite, the elaboration by the Community and national legislative bodies of criteria of assessment. From that it follows that, in cases of actual discrimination falling within the scope of the direct application of Article 119, comparisons are confined to parallels which may be drawn on the basis of concrete appraisals of the work actually performed by employees of different sex within the same establishment or service.

117

16. The answer to the second question should therefore be that the principle of equal pay enshrined in Article 119 applies to the case where it is established that, having regard to the nature of her services, a woman has received less pay than a man who was employed prior to the woman's period of employment and who did equal work for the employer.

17. From the foregoing it appears that the dispute brought before the national court may be decided within the framework of an interpretation of Article 119 of the Treaty alone. In those circumstances it is unnecessary to answer the questions submitted in so far as they relate to the effect and to the interpretation of Directive No. 75/117.

Costs

18. The costs incurred by the Government of the United Kingdom and by the Commission of the European Communities, which have submitted observations to the Court, are not recoverable. As these proceedings are, in so far as the parties to the main action are concerned, in the nature of a step in the action pending before the Court of Appeal in London, the decision as to costs is a matter for that court.

On those grounds,

THE COURT

in answer to the questions referred to it by the Court of Appeal, Civil Division, of the Supreme Court of Judicature by order of 25 July 1979, hereby rules:

1. The principle that men and women should receive equal pay for equal work, enshrined in Article 119 of the EEC Treaty, is not confined to situations in which men and women are contemporaneously doing equal work for the same employer.

2. The principle of equal pay enshrined in Article 119 applies to the case where it is established that, having regard to the nature of her services, a woman has received less pay than a man who was employed prior to the woman's period of employment and who did equal work for the employer.

Kutscher	O'Keeffe	Touffait
Mertens de Wilmars	Pescatore	Mackenzie Stuart
Bosco	Koopmans	Due

Delivered in open court in Luxembourg on 27 March 1980.

A. Van Houtte   H. Kutscher
Registrar   *President*

Judgment of the Court

11 March 1981 – Case 69/80

Susan Jane Worringham and Margaret Humphreys
v.
Lloyds Bank Ltd

Equal pay – contributions to retirement benefits scheme paid for employees by employer via additions to gross salary which help to determine the amount of that salary are pay for purposes of Article 119, EEC Treaty – same concept of pay in Article 119 and in Council Directive 75/117/EEC – direct effect of Article 119 – national courts have a duty to ensure protection of rights which Article 119 vests in individuals, as in case where contributions paid by employer for men but not women engaged in same work lead to unequal pay for men and women (EEC Treaty, Article 119; Council Directive 75/117/EEC, Article 1).

In Case 69/80

REFERENCE to the Court under Article 177 of the EEC Treaty by the Court of Appeal (Civil Division), London, for a preliminary ruling in the action pending before that court between

Susan Jane Worringham Margaret Humphreys

and

Lloyds Bank Limited

on the interpretation of Article 119 of the EEC Treaty, Article 1 of Council Directive 75/117/EEC of 10 February 1975 on the approximation of the laws of the Member States relating to the application of the principle of equal pay for men and women (Official Journal 1975, L 45, p. 19) and Article 1(1) and Article 5(1) of Council Directive 76/207/EEC of 9 February 1976 on the implementation of the principle of equal treatment for men and women as regards access to employment, vocational training and promotion, and working conditions (Official Journal 1976, L 39, p. 40),

THE COURT

composed of: J. Mertens de Wilmars, President, P. Pescatore, Lord Mackenzie Stuart and T. Koopmans, Presidents of Chambers, A. O'Keeffe, G. Bosco and A. Touffait, Judges,

Advocate General: J.-P. Warner
Registrar: A. Van Houtte

gives the following JUDGMENT

Decision

1. By order of 19 February 1980, which was received at the Court on 3 March 1980, the Court of Appeal, London, referred to the Court of Justice under Article 177 of the EEC Treaty several questions for a preliminary ruling on the interpretation of Article 119 of the EEC Treaty, Council Directive 75/117/EEC of 10 February 1975 on the approximation of the laws of the Member States relating to the application of the principle of equal pay for men and women (Official Journal L 45, p. 19) and Council Directive 76/207/EEC of 9 February 1976 on the implementation of the principle of equal treatment for men and women as regards access to employment, vocational training and promotion, and working conditions (Official Journal L 38, p. 40).

2. These questions have been raised within the context of proceedings between two female workers and their employer, Lloyds Bank Limited (hereinafter referred to as 'Lloyds'), which they complain was in breach of the clause guaranteeing equal pay for men and women incorporated in their contracts of employment with the bank by virtue of the provisions of Section 1(2)(a) of the Equal Pay Act 1970. The plaintiffs in the main action have claimed in particular that Lloyds has failed to fulfil its obligations under the Equal Pay Act 1970 by not paying female staff under 25 years of age the same gross salary as that of male staff of the same age engaged in the same work.

3. It is clear from the information contained in the order making the reference that Lloyds applies to its staff two retirement benefits schemes, one for men and one for women. Under these retirement benefits schemes, which are the result of collective bargaining between the trade unions and Lloyds and which have been approved by the national authorities under the Finance Act 1970 and certified under the Social Security Pensions Act 1975, the member contracts out of the earnings-related part of the State pension scheme and this part is replaced by a contractual scheme.

4. It follows from the same order that although the two retirement benefits schemes applied by Lloyds do not essentially involve a difference in the treatment of men and women as regards the benefits relating to the retirement pension, they lay down different rules as regards other aspects not related to that pension.

5. The unequal pay alleged in this case before the national court originates, according to the plaintiffs in the main action, in the provisions of these

two retirement benefits schemes relating to the requirement to contribute applicable to staff who have not yet attained the age of 25. In fact, it is clear from the order making the reference that men under 25 years of age are required to contribute 5 per cent of their salary to their scheme whereas women are not required to do so. In order to cover the contribution payable by the men, Lloyds adds an additional 5 per cent to the gross salary paid to those workers which is then deducted and paid directly to the trustees of the retirement benefits scheme in question on behalf of those workers.

6. The order making the reference also shows that workers leaving their employment who consent to the transfer of their accrued rights to the State pension scheme receive a 'contributions equivalent premium' which entitles them to the refund, subject to deductions in respect of a part of the cost of the premium and in respect of income tax, of their past contributions to the scheme of which they were members, with interest; that amount includes, in the case of men under the age of 25, the 5 per cent contribution paid in their name by the employer.

7. Finally, as follows from the information provided by the national court, the amount of the salary in which the above-mentioned 5 per cent contribution is included helps to determine the amount of certain benefits and social advantages such as redundancy payments, unemployment benefits and family allowances, as well as mortgage and credit facilities.

8. The Industrial Tribunal, before which an action was brought at first instance, dismissed by decision of 19 September 1977 the applicants' claim on the ground in particular that the unequal pay for men and women complained of in this instance was the result of a difference in the rules of the bank's retirement benefits schemes for men and women and therefore fell within the exception contained in Section 6(1A)(b) of the Equal Pay Act 1970 which excludes from the operation of the principle of equal pay for men and women terms related to death or retirement or any provision made in connexion with death or retirement.

9. The plaintiffs in the main action appealed to the Employment Appeal Tribunal, contending that the payment of an additional 5 per cent gross salary to male employees of Lloyds aged under 25 raised a problem of discrimination between men and women in respect of pay which fell outside the exception contained in Section 6(1A)(b) of the Equal Pay Act 1970. They also argued that in any case that section could not be interpreted and applied so as to be contrary to Community law, which overrides the provisions of the Equal Pay Act 1970.

10. The Employment Appeal Tribunal allowed the appeal on the grounds that: (a) there was inequality of pay for men and women under the age of 25 in that instance; (b) the terms or provisions in the contract of

employment with reference to pay had to be kept separate from terms or provisions with reference to pensions; and (c) the relevant clause in the contract of employment was not a provision relating to death or retirement as contemplated by Section 6(1A)(b) of the Equal Pay Act 1970.

11. In view of ths legal problem, the Court of Appeal, before which an appeal was brought by Lloyds against the decision of the Employment Appeal Tribunal, decided to refer to the Court of Justice questions on the interpretation of Article 119 of the EEC Treaty, Article 1 of Council Directive 75/117/EEC of 10 February 1975 and Articles 1 and 5 of Council Directive 76/207/EEC of 9 February 1976.

The first question
12. The first question submitted by the national court is worded as follows:

> '1. Are
> (a) contributions paid by an employer to a retirement benefits scheme,
> or
> (b) rights and benefits of a worker under such a scheme "pay" within the meaning of Article 119 of the EEC Treaty?'

13. It is clear from the information supplied by the national court that the first question asks essentially, first, under (a), whether sums of the kind in question paid by the employer in the name of the employee to a retirement benefits scheme by way of an addition to the gross salary come within the concept of 'pay' within the meaning of Article 119 of the Treaty.

14. Under the second paragraph of Article 119 of the EEC Treaty, 'pay' means, for the purpose of that provision, 'the ordinary basic or minimum wage or salary and any other consideration, whether in cash or in kind, which the worker receives, directly or indirectly, in respect of his employment from his employer'.

15. Sums such as those in question which are included in the calculation of the gross salary payable to the employee and which directly determine the calculation of other advantages linked to the salary, such as redundancy payments, unemployment benefits, family allowances and credit facilities, form part of the worker's pay within the meaning of the second paragraph of Article 119 of the Treaty even if they are immediately deducted by the employer and paid to a pension fund on behalf of the employee. This applies *a fortiori* where those sums are refunded in certain circumstances and subject to certain deductions to the employee as being repayable to him if he ceases to belong to the contractual retirement benefits scheme under which they were deducted.

16. Moreover, the argument mentioned by the British Government that the payment of the contributions in question by the employer does not arise out of a legal obligation towards the employee is not in point since that payment is in fact made, it corresponds to an obligation by the worker to contribute and is deducted from this salary.

17. In view of all these facts, it is therefore necessary to reply to Question 1(a) that a contribution to a retirement benefits scheme which is paid by the employer in the name of the employees by means of an addition to the gross salary and which helps to determine the amount of that salary is 'pay' within the meaning of the second paragraph of Article 119 of the EEC Treaty.

18. In view of this reply, there is no need to examine the second part of the first question, Question 1(b), which is subsidiary to Question 1(a).

The second question

19. In its second question, which is almost identical to the first, the national court puts the same problem to the Court with reference to Article 1 of Council Directive 75/117/EEC of 10 February 1975.

20. Since the interpretation of Directive 75/117/EEC was requested by the national court merely subsidiarily to that of Article 119 of the EEC Treaty, examination of the second question is purposeless, having regard to the interpretation given to that article.

21. Moreover, Directive 75/117/EEC, whose objective is, as follows from the first recital of the preamble thereto, to lay down the conditions necessary for the implementation of the principle that men and women should receive equal pay, is based on the concept of 'pay' as defined in the second paragraph of Article 119 of the Treaty. Although Article 1 of the directive explains that the concept of 'same work' contained in the first paragraph of Article 119 of the Treaty includes cases of 'work to which equal value is attributed', it in no way affects the concept of 'pay' contained in the second paragraph of Article 119 but refers by implication to that concept.

The third question

22. The national court asks further in its third question whether, if the answer to Question 1 is in the affirmative, 'Article 119 of the EEC Treaty ... [has] direct effect in the Member States so as to confer enforceable Community rights upon individuals in the circumstances of the present case'.

23. As the Court has states in previous decisions (judgment of 8 April 1976 in Case 43/75, *Defrenne* [1976] ECR 455 and judgment of 27 March 1980 in Case 129/79, *Macarthys Ltd.* [1980] ECR 1275), Article 119 of the Treaty

123

applies directly to all forms of discrimination which may be identified solely with the aid of the criteria of equal work and equal pay referred to by the article in question, without national or Community measures being required to define them with greater precision in order to permit of their application. Among the forms of discrimination which may be thus judicially identified, the Court mentioned in particular cases where men and women receive unequal pay for equal work carried out in the same establishment or service, public or private. In such a situation the court is in a position to establish all the facts enabling it to decide whether a woman receives less pay than a man engaged in the same work or work of equal value.

24. This is the case where the requirement to pay contributions applies only to men and not to women and the contributions payable by men are paid by the employer in their name by means of an addition to the gross salary the effect of which is to give men higher pay within the meaning of the second paragraph of Article 119 than that received by women engaged in the same work or work of equal value.

25. Although, where women are not required to pay contributions, the salary of men after deduction of the contributions is comparable to that of women who do not pay contributions, the inequality between the gross salaries of men and women is nevertheless a source of discrimination contrary to Article 119 of the Treaty since because of that inequality men receive benefits from which women engaged in the same work or work of equal value are excluded, or receive on that account greater benefits or social advantages than those to which women are entitled.

26. This applies in particular where, as in this instance, workers leaving their employment before reaching a given age are, in certain circumstances, refunded in the form of a 'contributions equivalent premium' at least a proportion of the contributions paid in their name by the employer and where the amount of the gross salary paid to the worker determines the amount of certain benefits and social advantages, such as redundancy payments or unemployment benefits, family allowances and mortgage or credit facilities, to which workers of both sexes are entitled.

27. In this case the fact that contributions are paid by the employer solely in the name of men and not in the name of women engaged in the same work or work of equal value leads to unequal pay for men and women which the national court may directly establish with the aid of the pay components in question and the criteria laid down in Article 119 of the Treaty.

28. For those reasons, the reply to the third question should be that Article 119 of the Treaty may be relied upon before the national courts and these courts have a duty to ensure the protection of the rights which this

provision vests in individuals, in particular in a case where, because of the requirement imposed only on men or only on women to contribute to a retirement benefits scheme, the contributions in question are paid by the employer in the name of the employee and deducted from the gross salary whose amount they determine.

The temporal effect of this judgment

29. In its written and oral observations, Lloyds had requested the Court to consider the possibility, if the answer to the third question is in the affirmative, of limiting the temporal effect of the interpretation given by this judgment to Article 119 of the Treaty so that this judgment 'cannot be relied on in order to support claims concerning pay periods prior to the date of the judgment'.

30. It maintains for this purpose, first, that the problem of the compatibility of the national law with Community law was raised only at the stage of the appeal brought before the Employment Appeal Tribunal and, secondly, that acknowledgment by the Court of the direct effect of Article 119 of the Treaty would lead, in a case such as the present, to 'claims for the retrospective adjustment of pay scales covering a period of years'.

31. As the Court acknowledged in its above-mentioned judgment of 8 April 1976, although the consequences of any judicial decision must be carefully taken into account, it would be impossible to go so far as to diminish the objectivity of the law and thus compromise its future application on the ground of the repercussions which might result, as regards the past, from such a judicial decision.

32. In the same judgment the Court admitted that a temporal restriction on the direct effect of Article 119 of the Treaty might be taken into account exceptionally in that case having regard, first, to the fact that the parties concerned, in the light of the conduct of several Member States and the views adopted by the Commission and repeatedly brought to the notice of the circles concerned, had been led to continue, over a long period, with practices which we contrary to Article 119 and having regard, secondly, to the fact that important questions of legal certainty affecting not only the interests of the parties to the main action but also a whole series of interests, both public and private, made it undesirable in principle to reopen the question of pay as regards the past.

33. In this case neither of these conditions has been fulfilled, either in respect of the information available at present to the circles concerned as to the scope of Article 119 of the Treaty, in the light in particular of the decisions of the Court in the meantime on this subject, or in respect of the number of the cases which would be affected in this instance by the direct effect of that provision.

The fourth question
34. As the fourth question was only submitted to the Court of Justice by the national court in case the first two questions were answered in the negative, examination of it has become purposeless.

Costs
The costs incurred by the Government of the United Kingdom and the Commission of the European Communities, which have submitted observations to the Court, are not recoverable. As these proceedings are, in so far as the parties to the main action are concerned, in the nature of a step in the action pending before the national court, the decision on costs is a matter for that court.

On those grounds,

THE COURT

in answer to the questions referred to it by the Court of Appeal, London, by order of 19 February 1980 hereby rules:

1. **A contribution to a retirement benefits scheme which is paid by an employer in the name of employees by means of an addition to the gross salary and which therefore helps to determine the amount of that salary constitutes 'pay' within the meaning of the second paragraph of Article 119 of the EEC Treaty.**

2. **Article 119 of the Treaty may be relied upon before the national courts and these courts have a duty to ensure the protection of the rights which this provision vests in individuals, in particular in a case where, because of the requirement imposed only on men or only on women to contribute to a retirement benefits scheme, the contributions in question are paid by the employer in the name of the employee and deducted from the gross salary whose amount they determine.**

Mertens de Wilmars	Pescatore	Mackenzie Stuart
Koopmans	O'Keeffe	Bosco	Touffait

Delivered in open court in Luxembourg on 11 March 1981.

A. Van Houtte   J. Mertens de Wilmars
Registrar   *President*

Judgment of the Court

31 March 1981 – Case 96/80

J P Jenkins
v.
Kingsgate (Clothing Productions) Ltd

Equal pay principle – hourly rate of pay for part-time worker lower than for full-time work not contrary to Article 119, EEC Treaty, if difference in pay due to objectively justified factors which are not related to discrimination based on sex – difference in pay between full- and part-time workers not discrimination contrary to Article 119 unless in reality an indirect way of reducing the pay of part-timers on the ground that group of workers predominantly composed of women – direct effect of Article 119 – where national court is able, using criteria of equal work and equal pay, without the operation of Community or national measures, to establish that payment of lower hourly rates of pay for part-time than full-time work is discrimination based on sex, Article 119 provisions directly apply – Council Directive 75/117/ EEC, Article 1 does not alter scope of basic equal pay principle in Treaty (EEC Treaty, Article 119; Council Directive 75/117/EEC, Article 1).

In case 96/80

REFERENCE to the Court under Article 177 of the EEC Treaty by the Employment Appeal Tribunal of the United Kingdom for a preliminary ruling in the action pending before that tribunal between

J. P. Jenkins

and

Kingsgate (Clothing Productions) Ltd,

on the interpretation of Article 119 of the EEC Treaty and of Article 1 of Council Directive 75/117/EEC of 10 February 1975 on the approximation of the laws of the Member States relating to the application of the principle of equal pay for men and women,

THE COURT

composed of: J. Mertens de Wilmars, President, P. Pescatore, Lord Mackenzie Stuart and T. Koopmans, Presidents of Chambers, A. O'Keeffe, G. Bosco, A. Touffait, O. Due and U. Everling, Judges,

Advocate General: J.-P. Warner
Registrar: A. Van Houtte

gives the following JUDGMENT

Decision

1. By an order dated 25 February 1980 which was received at the Court on 12 March 1980 the Employment Appeal Tribunal of the United Kingdom referred to the Court for a preliminary ruling under Article 177 of the EEC Treaty several questions as to the interpretation of Article 119 of the EEC Treaty and Article 1 of Council Directive 75/117/EEC of 10 February 1975 on the approximation of the laws of the Member States relating to the application of the principle of equal pay for men and women (Official Journal L 45, p. 19).

2. The questions were raised in the course of a dispute between a female employee working part-time and her employer, a manufacturer of women's clothing, against whom she claimed that she was receiving an hourly rate of pay lower than that paid to one of her male colleagues employed full-time on the same work.

3. Mrs Jenkins took the view that such a difference in pay contravened the equality clause incorporated into her contract of employment by virtue of the Equal Pay Act 1970, Section 1(2)(a) of which provides for equal pay for men and women in every case where 'a woman is employed on like work with a man in the same employment'.

4. The Industrial Tribunal, hearing the case at first instance, held in its decision of 5 February 1979 that in the case of part-time work the fact that the weekly working hours amounted, as in that case, to 75 per cent of the full working hours was sufficient to constitute a 'material difference' between part-time work and full-time work within the meaning of Section 1(3) of the abovementioned Act, according to which:

> 'An enquality clause shall not operate in relation to a variation between the woman's contract and the man's contract if the employer proves that the variation is genuinely due to a material difference (other than the difference of sex) between her case and his.'

5. The plaintiff in the main action appealed against that decision to the Employment Appeal Tribunal, which decided that the dispute raised problems concerning the interpretation of Community law and referred a number of questions to the Court for a preliminary ruling.

6. According to the information in the order making the reference, prior

to 1975 the employer did not pay the same wages to male and female employees but the hourly rates of pay were the same whether the work was part-time or full-time. From November 1975 the pay for full-time work (that is to say, the pay for those working 40 hours per week) became the same for male and female employees but the hourly rate for part-time work was fixed at a rate which was 10 per cent lower than the hourly rate of pay for full-time work.

7. It also appears from the order making the reference that at the time of the proceedings before the Industrial Tribunal the part-time workers employed by the employer in question were all female with the exception of a sole male part-time worker who had just retired and who at the time had been authorized to continue working, exceptionally and for short periods, after the normal age of retirement.

8. On the basis of those facts the Employment Appeal Tribunal referred the following questions to the Court;

> 1. Does the principle of equal pay, contained in Article 119 of the EEC Treaty and Article 1 of the Council Directive of 10 February 1975, require that pay for work at time rates shall be the same, irrespective:
>   (a) of the number of hours worked each week; or
>   (b) of whether it is of commercial benefit to the employer to encourage the doing of the maximum possible hours of work and consequently to pay a higher rate to workers doing 40 hours per week than to workers doing fewer than 40 hours per week?
> 2. If the answer to Question 1(a) or (b) is in the negative, what criteria should be used in determining whether or not the principle of equal pay applies where there is a difference in the time rates of pay related to the total number of hours worked each week?
> 3. Would the answer to Question 1(a) or (b) or 2 be different (and, if so, in what respects) if it were shown that a considerably smaller proportion of female workers than of male workers is able to perform the minimum number of hours each week required to qualify for the full hourly rate of pay?
> 4. Are the relevant provisions of Article 119 of the EEC Treaty or Article 1 of the said directive, as the case may be, directly applicable in Member States in the circumstances of the present case?'

First three questions
9. It appears from the first three questions and the reasons stated in the order making the reference that the national court is principally concerned to know whether a difference in the level of pay for work carried

out part-time and the same work carried out full-time may amount to discrimination of a kind prohibited by Article 119 of the Treaty when the category of part-time workers is exclusively or predominantly comprised of women.

10. The answer to the questions thus understood is that the purpose of Article 119 is to ensure the application of the principle of equal pay for men and women for the same work. The differences in pay prohibited by that provision are therefore exclusively those based on the difference of the sex of the workers. Consequently the fact that part-time work is paid at an hourly rate lower than pay for full-time work does not amount per se to discrimination prohibited by Article 119 provided that the hourly rates are applied to workers belonging to either category without distinction based on sex.

11. If there is no such distinction, therefore, the fact that work paid at time rates is remunerated at an hourly rate which varies according to the number of hours worked per week does not offend against the principle of equal pay laid down in Article 119 of the Treaty in so far as the difference in pay between part-time work and full-time work is attributable to factors which are objectively justified and are in no way related to any discrimination based on sex.

12. Such may be the case, in particular, when by giving hourly rates of pay which are lower for part-time work than those for full-time work the employer is endeavouring, on economic grounds which may be objectively justified, to encourage full-time work irrespective of the sex of the worker.

13. By contrast, if it is established that a considerably smaller percentage of women than of men perform the minimum number of weekly working hours required in order to be able to claim the full-time hourly rate of pay, the inequality in pay will be contrary to Article 119 of the Treaty where, regard being had to the difficulties encountered by women in arranging to work that minimum number of hours per week, the pay policy of the undertaking in question cannot be explained by factors other than discrimination based on sex.

14. Where the hourly rate of pay differs according to whether the work is part-time or full-time it is for the national courts to decide in each individual case whether, regard being had to the facts of the case, its history and the employer's intention, a pay policy such as that which is at issue in the main proceedings although represented as a difference based on weekly working hours is or is not in reality discrimination based on the sex of the worker.

15. The reply to the first three questions must therefore be that a difference

in pay between full-time workers and part-time workers does not amount to discrimination prohibited by Article 119 of the Treaty unless it is in reality merely an indirect way of reducing the level of pay of part-time workers on the ground that that group of workers is composed exclusively or predominantly of women.

Fourth question
16. In the fourth and last question, the national court asks whether the provisions of Article 119 of the Treaty are directly applicable in the circumstances of this case.

17. As the Court has stated in previous decisions (judgment of 8 April 1976 in Case 43/75, *Defrenne* [1976] ECR 455; judgment of 27 March 1980 in Case 129/79, *Wendy Smith* [1980] ECR 1275 and judgment of 11 March 1981 in Case 69/80, *Worringham*), Article 119 of the Treaty applies directly to all forms of discrimination which may be identified solely with the aid of criteria of equal work and equal pay referred to by the article in question, without national or Community measures being required to define them with greater precision in order to permit of their application. Among the forms of discrimination which may be thus judicially identified, the Court mentioned in particular cases where men and women receive unequal pay for equal work carried out in the same establishment or service, public or private.

18. Where the national court is able, using the criteria of equal work and equal pay, without the operation of Community or national measures, to establish that the payment of lower hourly rates of remuneration for part-time work than for full-time work represents discrimination based on difference of sex the provisions of Article 119 of the Treaty apply directly to such a situation.

Article 1 of Council Directive 75/117/EEC of 10 February 1975
19. The national court also raises with regard to Article 1 of Council Directive 75/117/EEC of 10 February 1975 the same question of interpretation as those examined above in relation to Article 119 of the Treaty.

20. As may be seen from the first recital in the preamble the primary objective of the above-mentioned directive is to implement the principle that men and women should receive equal pay which is 'contained in Article 119 of the Treaty'. For that purpose the fourth recital states that 'it is desirable to reinforce the basic laws by standards aimed at facilitating the practical application of the principle of equality'.

21. The provisions of Article 1 of that directive are confined, in the first paragraph, to restating the principle of equal pay set out in Article 119 of the Treaty and specify, in the second paragraph, the conditions for

applying that principle where a job classification system is used for determining pay.

22. It follows, therefore, that Article 1 of Council Directive 75/117/EEC which is principally designed to facilitate the practical application of the principle of equal pay outlined in Article 119 of the Treaty in no way alters the content or scope of that principle as defined in the Treaty.

Costs

The costs incurred by the Government of the Kingdom of Belgium, the Government of the United Kingdom of Great Britain and Northern Ireland and the Commission of the European Communities, which have submitted observations to the Court, are not recoverable. As this case is, in so far as the parties to the main proceedings are concerned, in the nature of a step in the proceedings before the national court, the decision as to costs is a matter for that court.

On those grounds,

THE COURT,

in answer to the questions referred to it by the Employment Appeal Tribunal by an order dated 25 February 1980, hereby rules: -

1. **A difference in pay between full-time workers and part-time workers does not amount to discrimination prohibited by Article 119 of the Treaty unless it is in reality merely an indirect way of reducing the pay of part-time workers on the ground that that group of workers is composed exclusively or predominantly of women.**

2. **Where the national court is able, using the criteria of equal work and equal pay, without the operation of Community or national measures, to establish that the payment of lower hourly rates of remuneration for part-time work than for full-time work represents discrimination based on difference of sex the provisions of Article 119 of the Treaty apply directly to such a situation.**

Mertens de Wilmars   Pescatore   Mackenzie Stuart   Koopmans   O'Keeffe
    Bosco   Touffait   Due   Everling

Delivered in open court in Luxembourg on 31 March 1981.

A. Van Houtte   J. Mertens de Wilmars
Registrar   *President*

Judgment of the Court

9 February 1982 – Case 12/81

Eileen Garland
v.
British Rail Engineering Ltd

Equal pay principle – special travel facilities provided for former male employees after retirement is discrimination within meaning of Article 119, EEC Treaty, against former female employees not receiving same facilities – where such discrimination can be established by national court using criteria of equal work and equal pay, without operation of more detailed Community or national measures, Article 119 directly applies (EEC Treaty, Article 119).

In Case 12/81

REFERENCE to the Court under Article 177 of the EEC Treaty by the House of Lords of the United Kingdom for a preliminary ruling in the action pending between

Eileen Garland

and

British Rail Engineering Limited

on the interpretation of the rules of the EEC Treaty on the principle of equal pay for men and women in connection with a difference in travel benefits enjoyed by male and female employees after retirement,

THE COURT

composed of: G. Bosco, President of the First Chamber, acting as President, A. Touffait and O. Due (Presidents of Chambers), P. Pescatore, Lord Mackenzie Stuart, A. O'Keeffe, T. Koopmans, A. Chloros and F. Grévisse, Judges,

Advocate General: P. Ver Loren van Themaat
Registrar: A. Van Houtte

gives the following JUDGMENT

Decision

1. By order dated 19 January 1981 which was received at the Court on 22

133

January 1981 the House of Lords referred to the Court for a preliminary ruling under Article 177 of the EEC Treaty two questions as to the interpretation of Article 119 of the Treaty, Article 1 of Council Directive 75/117/EEC of 10 February 1975 on the approximation of the laws of the Member States relating to the application of the principle of equal pay for men and women (Official Journal L 45, p. 19) and of Article 1 of Council Directive 76/207/EEC of 9 February 1976 on the implementation of the principle of equal treatment for men and women as regards access to employment, vocational training and promotion, and working conditions (Official Journal L 39, p. 40).

2. Those questions were raised in the context of a dispute between an employee of British Rail Engineering Limited, a subsidiary of the British Railways Board, which is a body created by the Transport Act 1962 charged with the duty of managing the railways in the United Kingdom, and her employer concerning discrimination alleged to be suffered by female employees who on retirement no longer continue to enjoy travel facilities for their spouses and dependent children although male employees continue to do so.

3. It was submitted before the House of Lords that that situation was contrary to Article 119 and the directives implementing it and the House of Lords therefore referred the following two questions to the Court:

> 1. Where an employer provides (although not bound to do so by contract) special travel facilities for former employees to enjoy after retirement which discriminate against former female employees in the manner described above, is this contrary to:
>   (a) Article 119 of the EEC Treaty?
>   (b) Article 1 of Council Directive 75/117/EEC?
>   (c) Article 1 of Council Directive 76/207/EEC?
> 2. If the answer to Questions 1(a), 1(b) or 1(c) is affirmative, is Article 119 or either of the said directives directly applicable in Member States so as to confer enforceable Community rights upon individuals in the above circumstances?'

Question 1
4. To assist in answering the first question it is first of all necessary to investigate the legal nature of the special travel facilities at issue in this case which the employer grants although not contractually bound to do so.

5. It is important to note in this regard that in paragraph 6 of its judgment of 25 May 1971 in Case 80/70 *Defrenne* [1971] ECR 445, at p. 451, the Court stated that the concept of pay contained in the second paragraph of Article 119 comprises any other consideration, whether in cash or in

kind, whether immediate or future, provided that the worker receives it, albeit indirectly, in respect of his employment from his employer.

6. According to the order making the reference for a preliminary ruling, when male employees of the respondent undertaking retire from their employment on reaching retirement age they continue to be granted special travel facilities for themselves, their wives and their dependent children.

7. A feature of those facilities is that they are granted in kind by the employer to the retired male employee or his dependants directly or indirectly in respect of his employment.

8. Moreover, it appears from a letter sent by the British Railways Board to the trade unions on 4 December 1975 that the special travel facilities granted after retirement must be considered to be an extension of the facilities granted during the period of employment.

9. It follows from those considerations that rail travel facilities such as those referred to by the House of Lords fulfil the criteria enabling them to be treated as pay within the meaning of Article 119 of the EEC Treaty.

10. The argument that the facilities are not related to a contractual obligation is immaterial. The legal nature of the facilities is not important for the purposes of the application of Article 119 provided that they are granted in respect of the employment.

11. It follows that where an employer (although not bound to do so by contract) provides special travel facilities for former male employees to enjoy after their retirement this constitutes discrimination within the meaning of Article 119 against former female employees who do not receive the same facilities.

12. In view of the interpretation given to Article 119 of the EEC Treaty, which by itself answers the question posed by the House of Lords, there is no need to consider points (b) and (c) of Question (1) which raise the same question with reference to Article 1 of Directive 75/117/EEC and of Directive 76/207/EEC.

Question 2
13. Since Question (1)(a) has been answered in the affirmative the question arises of the direct applicability of Article 119 in the Member States and of the rights which individuals may invoke on that basis before national courts.

14. In paragraph 17 of its judgment of 31 March 1981 in Case 96/80 *Jenkins* v. *Kingsgate* [1981] ECR 911, at p. 926, the Court stated that Article 119 of

the Treaty applies directly to all forms of discrimination which may be identified solely with the aid of the criteria of equal work and equal pay referred to by the article in question, without national or Community measures being required to define them with greater precision in order to permit of their application.

15. Where a national court is able, using the criteria of equal work and equal pay, without the operation of Community or national meansures, to establish that the grant of special transport facilities solely to retired male employees represents discrimination based on difference of sex, the provisions of Article 119 of the Treaty apply directly to such a situation.

Costs
16. The costs incurred by the Commission of the European Communities and the Government of the United Kingdom of Great Britain and Northern Ireland, which have submitted observations to the Court, are not recoverable. As this case is, in so far as the parties to the main action are concerned, in the nature of a step in the proceedings before the national court, the decision as to costs is a matter for that court.

On those grounds,

THE COURT

hereby rules:

1. **Where an employer (although not bound to do so by contract) provides special travel facilities for former male employees to enjoy after their retirement this constitutes discrimination within the meaning of Article 119 against former female employees who do not receive the same facilities.**

2. **Where a national court is able, using the criteria of equal work and equal pay, without the operation of Community or national measures, to establish that the grant of special travel facilities solely to retired male employees represents discrimination based on difference of sex, the provisions of Article 119 of the Treaty apply directly to such a situation.**

Bosco	Touffait	Due	Pescatore	Mackenzie Stuart
O'Keeffe		Koopmans	Chloros	Grévisse

Delivered in open court in Luxembourg on 9 February 1982.

A. Van Houtte
Registrar

G. Bosco
President of the First Chamber,
Acting as President

Judgment of the Court

18 September 1984 – Case 23/83

W. G. M. Liefting and others
v.
Directie van het Academisch Ziekenhuis bij de Universiteit van Amsterdam

Equal pay principle – social security contributions paid by public authorities and included in calculation of gross salary paid to civil servants constitute pay within meaning of Article 119, EEC Treaty, since they directly determine other salary-linked benefits – scheme where husband and wife civil servants have such contributions paid by State, with contributions calculated on basis of their combined salaries and major part of contributions paid on behalf of busband, contrary to equal pay principle of Article 119 where resulting differences between gross salary of female civil servant whose husband also a civil servant and of male civil servant directly affect calculation of other salary-linked benefits (EEC Treaty, Article 119).

In Case 23/83

REFERENCE to the Court under Article 177 of the EEC Treaty by the Centrale Raad van Beroep [Court of last instance in social security matters], Utrecht, for a preliminary ruling in the case pending before that court between

W. G. M. Liefting and Others

and

Directie van het Academisch Ziekenhuis bij de Universiteit van Amsterdam
[Board of the University Hospital, University of Amsterdam], Amsterdam, and Others

on the interpretation of Article 119 of the EEC Treaty,

THE COURT

composed of: Lord Mackenzie Stuart, President, T. Koopmans, K. Bahlmann and Y. Galmot (Presidents of Chambers), P. Pescatore, A. O'Keeffe, G. Bosco, O. Due and U. Everling, Judges,

Advocate General: Sir Gordon Slynn
Registrar: P. Heim

gives the following JUDGMENT

Decision

1. By order of 20 January 1983, received at the Court Registry on 16 February 1983, the Centrale Raad van Beroep, Utrecht, submitted to the Court for a preliminary ruling under Article 177 of the EEC Treaty two questions on the interpretation of Article 119 of the EEC treaty.

2. That order was made in the context of nine actions brought by the plaintiffs in the main proceedings against the various public authorities which employ them.

3. The plaintiffs in the main proceedings are all women employed as civil servants. They are married and their husbands are also employed in the civil service. Civil servants are covered by two sets of pension rules: the Algemene Ouderdomswet [General Law on Old-Age Insurance Law, hereinafter referred to as the 'Old-Age Law'] and the Algemene Weduwen en Wezenwet [Widows and Orphans General Insurance Law, hereinafter referred to as 'the Widows and Orphans Law'], establishing a general pension scheme for persons residing in the Netherlands, and secondly the Algemene Burgerlijke Pensioenwet [General Civil Pensions Law], laying down pension arrangements for civil servants.

4. In order to avoid any overlapping of pensions, the General Civil Pensions Law provides that a proportion of the general Old-Age Pension is to be regarded as forming part of the pension of civil servants. Consequently, a retired civil servant receives in general only a proportion of the pension payable under the Old-Age Law or the Widows and Orphans Law but, by way of compensation, he is not obliged, while in employment, to pay contributions under those two laws. By virtue of Article N 9 of the General Civil Pensions Law the contribution is paid by the authority by which a civil servant is employed; that article makes the payment of contributions, which in principle is the responsibility of the civil servant, incumbent upon the public authority.

5. Under the Old-Age Law and the Widows and Orphans Law a married couple is treated as one person for the purposes both of benefits and of contributions. Only one contribution is payable on the total of both salaries. The contribution is collected by the collector of direct taxes at the same time as income tax. There is a maximum limit for contributions.

6. Before 1972, if the amounts paid by the public authority exceeded that maximum limit, the surplus (called 'over-compensation') was paid back by the collector of taxes, not to the public authority which paid it but to the civil servants concerned. Obviously, that payment was financially advantageous for them. The recipients of 'over-compensation' were mostly civil servants who worked at the same time for different public authorities, each of which paid separate contributions under the Old-Age

Law and the Widows and Orphans Law, and the wives of civil servants employed by an authority other than the one for which their husbands worked.

7. In 1972 and 1973 legislation was introduced to terminate the so-called 'over-compensation'. It consists of the Wet Gemeenschappelijke Bepalingen Overheidspensioenwetten [Law laying down common provisions with regard to laws governing the pensions of civil servants], the Uitvoeringsbesluit Beperking Meervoudige Overneming AOW/AWW – Premie [Order restricting the payment of contributions due under the Old-Age Insurance Law and the Widows and Orphans General Insurance Law by more than one institution] and various implementing provisions. Those provisions together have created an administrative system under which the various public authorities keep one another informed about the separate payment of contributions for the same civil servant or married couple. Once the maximum amount of contributions has been paid in respect of employment in one place, no further contributions are paid in respect of employment elsewhere.

8. The plaintiffs in the main proceedings, made applications to the Ambtenarengerecht [Public Officials' Tribunal], Amsterdam, the Ambtenarengerecht, Arnhem, the Ambtenarengerecht, 's-Hertogenbosch, and the Ambtenarengerecht, Utrecht, contending that the 'compensation' and 'overcompensation' were pay within the meaning of Article 119 of the EEC Treaty and that, consequently, the abolition of the payment of 'overcompensation' was contrary to that article as it largely affected contributions payable in respect of married female civil servants.

9. Their applications were dimissed at first instance and they appealed to the Centrale Raad van Beroep [Court of last instance in social security matters], Utrecht. Considering that an interpretation of Article 119 was necessary to enable it to give judgment, the Centrale Raad van Beroep stayed the proceedings and submitted the following questions to the Court for a preliminary ruling under Article 177 of the ECC Treaty:

> '1. Must the term "pay" appearing in Article 119 of the EEC Treaty be construed as including the "compensation", or, in certain cases, the amount referred to as 'the overcompensation' which the employing public authority formerly paid to the tax authorities in excess of the maximum contributions due under the Algemene Ouderdomswet and the Algemene Weduwen en Wezenwet but which now no longer need be paid by such an authority?
>
> 2. If the answer to the first question is in the affirmative, must Article 119 of the Treaty be construed as meaning that the system in force in the Netherlands based on the Wet Gemeenschappelijke Bepalingen Overheidspensioenwetten

must be regarded as being contrary to the principle that men and women should receive equal pay for equal work laid down in Article 119 because, under that system, in those cases in which the joint contributions due under the Algemene Ouderdomswet and the Algemene Weduwen en Wezenwet for a married couple employed in the public service exceed the maximum amounts of contributions due, the contributions are primarily paid by the husband's employer while the wife's employer continues to pay contributions only in so far as the maximum amount of contributions due is not exceeded?'

10. Those questions relate to a social security scheme under which:
    1. the contributions are calculated on the basis of the employee's salary but may not exceed a certain limit,
    2. a husband and wife are treated as one person, the contributions being calculated on the basis of their combined salaries, subject once again to the upper limit,
    3. the State is bound to pay on behalf of its employee the contributions owed by him, and
    4. where husband and wife are both civil servants, the authority employing the husband is primarily responsible for paying the contributions and the authority employing the wife is required to pay the contributions only in so far as the upper limit is not reached by the contributions paid on behalf of the husband.

    The answer must enable the national court to appraise the compatibility of such a scheme with the principle of equal pay for male and female employees doing the same work laid down in Article 119 of the Treaty, if a consequence of that scheme is that, in the case of a female civil servant whose husband is also a civil servant, the contribution paid on behalf of the wife is lower than that paid on behalf of a male civil servant doing the same work.

11. Under the system described above a civil servant whose husband is also a civil servant has the same net disposable salary as a male civil servant doing the same work but the latter's gross salary is higher than hers. The reason for that difference is to be found in the way in which the Netherlands old-age insurance scheme and widows' and orphans' pensions scheme operate.

12. It follows from the decisions of the Court, and in particular from the judgment of 11 March 1981 (Case 69/80 *Worringham and Another* v. *Lloyds Bank* [1981] ECR 767), that although the portion which employers are liable to contribute to the financing of statutory social security schemes to which both employees and employers contribute does not constitute pay within the meaning of Article 119 of the Treaty, the same is not true of sums which are included in the calculation of the gross salary

payable to the employee and which directly determine the calculation of other advantages linked to the salary such as redundancy payments, unemployment benefits, family allowances and credit facilities. That is also the case if the amounts in question are immediately deducted by the employer and paid to a pension fund on behalf of the employee.

13. Consequently, the amounts which the public authorities are obliged to pay in respect of contributions owed to the social security scheme by persons working for the State and which are included in the calculation of the gross salary payable to civil servants must be regarded as pay within the meaning of Article 119 since they directly determine the calculation of other advantages linked to the salary.

14. The principle that men and women should receive equal pay for equal work, as laid down in Article 119, has not therefore been complied with in so far as those other advantages linked to the salary and determined by the gross salary are not the same for male civil servants and for female civil servants whose husbands are also civil servants.

15. The reply to the questions raised by the national court must therefore be that a social security scheme under which:
    1. the contributions are calculated on the basis of the employee's salary but may not exceed a certain limit,
    2. a husband and wife are treated as one person, the contributions being calculated on the basis of their combined salaries, subject once again to the upper limit,
    3. the State is bound to pay on behalf of its employee the contributions owed by him, and
    4. where husband and wife are both civil servants, the authority employing the husband is primarily responsible for paying the contributions and the authority employing the wife is required to pay the contributions only in so far as the upper limit is not reached by the contributions paid on behalf of the husband,
    is incompatible with the principle laid down in Article 119 of the EEC Treaty that men and women should receive equal pay for equal work, in so far as the resultant differences between the gross salary of a female civil servant whose husband is also a civil servant and the gross salary of a male civil servant directly affect the calculation of other benefits dependent on salary, such as severance pay, unemployment benefit, family allowances and loan facilities.

Costs
16. The costs incurred by the Government of the Kingdom of the Netherlands and by the Commission of the European Communities, which have submitted observations to the Court, are not recoverable. As these proceedings are, in so far as the parties to the main action are concerned,

in the nature of a step in the action pending before the national court, the decision as to costs is a matter for that court.

On those grounds,

THE COURT

in answer to the questions referred to it by the Centrale Raad van Beroep, Utrecht, by order of 20 January 1983, hereby rules:

A social security scheme under which:
1. **the contributions are calculated on the basis of the employee's salary but may not exceed a certain limit,**
2. **a husband and wife are treated as one person, the contributions being calculated on the basis of their combined salaries, subject once again to the upper limit,**
3. **the State is bound to pay on behalf of its employee the contributions owed by him, and**
4. **where husband and wife are both civil servants, the authority employing the husband is primarily responsible for paying the contributions and the authority employing the wife is required to pay the contributions only in so far as the upper limit is not reached by the contributions paid on behalf of the husband,**
is incompatible with the principle laid down in Article 119 of the EEC Treaty that men and women should receive equal pay for equal work, in so far as the resultant differences between the gross salary of a female civil servant whose husband is also a civil servant and the gross salary of a male civil servant directly affect the calculation of other benefits dependent on salary, such as severance pay, unemployment benefit, family allowances and loan facilities.

Mackenzie Stuart   Koopmans   Bahlmann   Galmot
Prescatore   O'Keeffe   Bosco   Due   Everling

Delivered in open court in Luxembourg on 18 September 1984.

P. Heim   A. J. Mackenzie Stuart
Registrar   *President*

Judgment of the Court

13 May 1986 – Case 170/84

Bilka-Kaufhaus GmbH
v.
Karin Weber von Hartz

Equal pay principle – occupational pension scheme established in accordance with statutory provisions but based on agreement between employer and employee representatives, constituting integral part of contracts of employment, and supplementing social benefits paid under national legislation, is not a social security scheme governed directly by statute and is within scope of Article 119, EEC Treaty – part-timers' exclusion from pension scheme affecting far more women than men is contrary to Article 119, unless employer shows exclusion based on objectively justified factors unrelated to discrimination on grounds of sex – employer may justify pay policy excluding part-timers from pension scheme on grounds that he seeks to employ as few part-timers as possible, where means chosen for achieving that objective correspond to a real need and are appropriate and necessary to that end – Article 119 does not require employer to organise occupational pension scheme to take account of special difficulties of those with family responsibilities in meeting conditions for pension entitlement (EEC Treaty, Articles 117, 118 and 119).

In Case 170/84

REFERENCE to the Court pursuant to Article 177 of the EEC Treaty by the Bundesarbeitsgericht (Federal Labour Court) for a preliminary ruling in the proceedings pending before that court between

Bilka-Kaufhaus GmbH

and

Karin Weber von Hartz

on the interpretation of Article 119 of the EEC Treaty,

THE COURT

composed of: Lord Mackenzie Stuart, President, T. Koopmans, U. Everling, K. Bahlmann and R. Joliet (Presidents of Chambers), G. Bosco, O. Due, Y. Galmot and C. N. Kakouris, Judges,

Advocate General: M. Darmon,
Registrar: D. Louterman, Administrator

gives the following JUDGMENT

Decision

1. By an order of 5 June 1984, which was received at the Court on 2 July 1984, the Bundesarbeitsgericht referred to the Court for a preliminary ruling under Article 177 of the EEC Treaty three questions on the interpretation of Article 119 of that Treaty.

2. Those questions arose in the course of proceedings between Bilka-Kaufhaus GmbH and its former employee Karin Weber von Hartz concerning the payment to Mrs Weber von Hartz of a retirement pension from a supplementary pension scheme established by Bilka for its employees.

3. It appears from the documents before the Court that for several years Bilka, which belongs to a group of department stores in the Federal Republic of Germany employing several thousand persons, has had a supplementary (occupational) pension scheme for its employees. This scheme, which has been modified on several occasions, is regarded as an integral part of the contracts of employment between Bilka and its employees.

4. According to the version in force since 26 October 1973, part-time employees may obtain pensions under the scheme only if they have worked full time for at least 15 years over a total period of 20 years.

5. Mrs Weber was employed by Bilka as a sales assistant from 1961 to 1976. After initially working full time, she chose to work part time from 1 October 1972 until her employment came to an end. Since she had not worked full time for the minimum period of 15 years, Bilka refused to pay her an occupational pension under its scheme.

6. Mrs Weber brought proceedings before the German Labour courts challenging the legality of Bilka's refusal to pay her a pension. She argued *inter alia* that the occupational pension scheme was contrary to the principle of equal pay for men and women laid down in Article 119 of the EEC Treaty. She asserted that the requirement of a minimum period of full-time employment for the payment of an occupational pension placed women workers at a disadvantage, since they were more likely than their male colleagues to take part-time work so as to be able to care for their family and children.

7. Bilka, on the other hand, argued that it was not guilty of any breach of

144

the principle of equal pay since there were objectively justified economic grounds for its decision to exclude part-time employees from the occupational pension scheme. It emphasized in that regard that in comparison with the employment of part-time workers the employment of full-time workers entails lower ancillary costs and permits the use of staff throughout opening hours. Relying on statistics concerning the group to which it belongs, Bilka stated that up to 1980 81.3 per cent of all occupational pensions were paid to women, although only 72 per cent of employees were women. Those figures, it said, showed that the scheme in question does not entail discrimination on the basis of sex.

8. On appeal the proceedings between Mrs Weber and Bilka came before the Bundesarbeitsgericht; that court decided to stay the proceedings and refer the following questions to the Court:

'1. May there be an infringement of Article 119 of the EEC Treaty in the form of "indirect discrimination" where a department store which employs predominantly women excludes part-time employees from benefits under its occupational pension scheme although such exclusion affects disproportionately more women than men?
2. If so:
   (a) Can the undertaking justify that disadvantage on the ground that its objective is to employ as few part-time workers as possible even though in the department store sector there are no reasons of commercial expediency which necessitate such a staff policy?
   (b) Is the undertaking under a duty to structure its pension scheme in such a way that appropriate account is taken of the special difficulties experienced by employees with family commitments in fulfilling the requirements for an occupational pension?'

9. In accordance with Article 20 of the Protocol on the Statute of the Court of Justice of the EEC written observations were submitted by Bilka, Mrs Weber von Hartz, the United Kingdom and the Commission of the European Communities.

The applicability of Article 119
10. The United Kingdom puts forward the preliminary argument that the conditions placed by an employer on the admission of its employees to an occupational pension scheme such as that described by the national court do not fall within the scope of Article 119 of the Treaty.

11. In support of that argument it refers to the judgment of 15 June 1978 (Case 149/77, *Defrenne* v. *Sabena*, [1978] ECR 1365), in which the Court

145

held that Article 119 concerns only pay discrimination between men and women workers and its scope cannot be extended to other elements of the employment relationship, even where such elements may have financial consequences for the persons concerned.

12. The United Kingdom cites further the judgment of 16 February 1982 (Case 19/81, *Burton* v. *British Railways Board* [1982] ECR 555), where the Court held that alleged discrimination resulting from a difference in the ages of eligibility set for men and women for payment under a voluntary redundancy scheme was covered not by Article 119 but by Council Directive 76/207 of 9 February 1976 on the implementation of the principle of equal treatment for men and women as regards access to employment, vocational training and promotion, and working conditions (Official Journal 1976 No. L 39, p. 40).

13. At the hearing the United Kingdom also referred to the proposal for a Council directive on the implementation of the principle of equal treatment for men and women in occupational social security schemes submitted by the Commission on 5 May 1983 (Official Journal 1983 No. C 134, p. 7). According to the United Kingdom, the fact that the Commission considered it necessary to submit such a proposal shows that occupational pension schemes such as that described by the national court are covered not by Article 119 but by Articles 117 and 118, so that the application of the principle of equal treatment for men and women in that area requires the adoption of special provisions by the Community institutions.

14. The Commission, on the other hand, has argued that the occupational pension scheme described by the national court falls within the concept of pay for the purposes of the second paragraph of Article 119. In support of its view it refers to the judgment of 11 March 1981 (Case 69/80, *Worringham and Humphreys* v. *Lloyds Bank*, [1981] ECR 767).

15. In order to resolve the problem of interpretation raised by the United Kingdom it must be recalled that under the first paragraph of Article 119 the Member States must ensure the application of the principle that men and women should receive equal pay for equal work. The second paragraph of Article 119 defines 'pay' as 'the ordinary basic or minimum wage or salary and any other consideration, whether in cash or in kind, which the worker receives, directly or indirectly, in respect of his employment from his employer'.

16. In its judgment of 25 May 1971 (Case 80/70, *Defrenne* v. *Belgium*, [1971] ECR 445), the Court examined the question whether a retirement pension paid under a statutory social security scheme consitutes consideration received by the worker indirectly from the employer in respect of his employment, within the meaning of the second paragraph of Article 119.

17. The Court replied in the negative, taking the view that, although pay within the meaning of Article 119 could in principle include social security benefits, it did not include social security schemes or benefits, in particular retirement pensions, directly governed by legislation which do not involve any element of agreement within the undertaking or trade concerned and are compulsory for generate categories of workers.

18. In that regard the Court pointed out that social security schemes guarantee workers the benefit of a statutory scheme to which workers, employers and in some cases the authorities contribute financially to an extent determined less by the employment relationship between the employer and the worker than by considerations of social policy, so that the employer's contribution cannot be regarded as a direct or indirect payment to the worker for the purposes of the second paragraph of Article 119.

19. The question therefore arises whether the conclusion reached by the Court in that judgment is also applicable to the case before the national court.

20. It should be noted that according to the documents before the Court the occupational pension scheme at issue in the main proceedings, although adopted in accordance with the provisions laid down by German legislation for such schemes, is based on an agreement between Bilka and the staff committee representing its employees and has the effect of supplementing the social benefits paid under national legislation of general application with benefits financed entirely by the employer.

21. The contractual rather than statutory nature of the scheme in question is confirmed by the fact that, as has been pointed out above, the scheme and the rules governing it are regarded as an integral part of the contracts of employment between Bilka and its employees.

22. It must therefore be concluded that the scheme does not constitute a social security scheme governed directly by statute and thus outside the scope of Article 119. Benefits paid to employees under the scheme therefore constitute consideration received by the worker from the employer in respect of his employment, as referred to in the second paragraph of Article 119.

23. The case before the national court therefore falls within the scope of Article 119.

The first question
24. In the first of its questions the national court asks whether a staff policy pursued by a department store company excluding part-time employees from an occupational pension scheme constitutes discrimination contrary

to Article 119 where that exclusion affects a far greater number of women than men.

25. In order to reply to that question reference must be made to the judgment of 31 March 1981 (Case 96/80, *Jenkins* v. *Kingsgate*, [1981] ECR 911).

26. In that judgment the Court considered the question whether the payment of a lower hourly rate for part-time work than for full-time work was compatible with Article 119.

27. Such a practice is comparable to that at issue before the national court in this case: Bilka does not pay different hourly rates to part-time and full-time workers, but it grants only full-time workers an occupational pension. Since, as was stated above, such a pension falls within the concept of pay for the purposes of the second paragraph of Article 119 it follows that, hour for hour, the total remuneration paid by Bilka to full-time workers is higher than that paid to part-time workers.

28. The conclusion reached by the Court in its judgment of 31 March 1981 is therefore equally valid in the context of this case.

29. If, therefore, it should be found that a much lower proportion of women than of men work full time, the exclusion of part-time workers from the occupational pension scheme would be contrary to Article 119 of the Treaty where, taking into account the difficulties encountered by women workers in working full-time, that measure could not be explained by factors which exclude any discrimination on grounds of sex.

30. However, if the undertaking is able to show that its pay practice may be explained by objectively justified factors unrelated to any discrimination on grounds of sex there is no breach of Article 119.

31. The answer to the first question referred by the national court must therefore be that Article 119 of the EEC Treaty is infringed by a department store company which excludes part-time employees from its occupational pension scheme, where that exclusion affects a far greater number of women than men, unless the undertaking shows that the exclusion is based on objectively justified factors unrelated to any discrimination on grounds of sex.

Question 2(a)
32. In its second question the national court seeks in essence to know whether the reasons put forward by Bilka to explain its pay policy may be regarded as 'objectively justified economic grounds', as referred to in the judgment of 31 March 1981, where the interests of undertakings in the department store sector do not require such a policy.

33. In its observations Bilka argues that the exclusion of part-time workers from the occupational pension scheme is intended solely to discourage part-time work, since in general part-time workers refuse to work in the late afternoon and on Saturdays. In order to ensure the presence of an adequate workforce during those periods it was therefore necessary to make full-time work more attractive than part-time work, by making the occupational pension scheme open only to full-time workers. Bilka concludes that on the basis of the judgment of 31 March 1981 it cannot be accused of having infringed Article 119.

34. In reply to the reasons put forward to justify the exclusion of part-time workers Mrs Weber von Hartz points out that Bilka is in no way obliged to employ part-time workers and that if it decides to do so it may not subsequently restrict the pension rights of such workers, which are already reduced by reason of the fact that they work fewer hours.

35. According to the Commission, in order to establish that there has been no breach of Article 119 it is not sufficient to show that in adopting a pay practice which in fact discriminates against women workers the employer sought to achieve objectives other than discrimination against women. The Commission considers that in order to justify such a pay practice from the point of view of Article 119 the employer must, as the Court held in its judgment of 31 March 1981, put forward objective economic grounds relating to the management of the undertaking. It is also necessary to ascertain whether the pay practice in question is necessary and in proportion to the objectives pursued by the employer.

36. It is for the national court, which has sole jurisdiction to make findings of fact, to determine whether and to what extent the grounds put forward by an employer to explain the adoption of a pay practice which applies independently of a worker's sex but in fact affects more women than men may be regarded as objectively justified economic grounds. If the national court finds that the measures chosen by Bilka correspond to a real need on the part of the undertaking, are appropriate with a view to achieving the objectives pursued and are necessary to that end, the fact that the measures affect a far greater number of women that men is not sufficient to show that they constitute an infringement of Article 119.

37. The answer to question 2(a) must therefore be that under Article 119 a department store company may justify the adoption of a pay policy excluding part-time workers, irrespective of their sex, from its occupational pension scheme on the ground that it seeks to employ as few part-time workers as possible, where it is found that the means chosen for achieving that objective correspond to a real need on the part of the undertaking, are appropriate with a view to achieving the objective in question and are necessary to that end.

Question 2(b)

38. Finally, in Question 2(b), the national court asks whether an employer is obliged under Article 119 of the Treaty to organize its occupational pension scheme in such a manner as to take into account the fact that family responsibilities prevent women workers from fulfilling the requirements for such a pension.

39. In her observations Mrs Weber von Hartz argues that the answer to that question should be in the affirmative. She argues that the disadvantages suffered by women because of the exclusion of part-time workers from the occupational pension scheme must at least be mitigated by requiring the employer to regard periods during which women workers have had to meet family responsibilities as periods of full-time work.

40. According to the Commission, on the other hand, the principle laid down in Article 119 does not require employers, in establishing occupational pension schemes, to take into account their employees' family responsibilities. In the Commission's view, that objective must be pursued by means of measures adopted under Article 117. It refers in that regard to its proposal for a Council directive on voluntary part-time work submitted on 4 January 1982 (Official Journal 1982 No. C 62, p. 7) and amended on 5 January 1983 (Official Journal 1983 No. C 18, p. 5), which has not yet been adopted.

41. It must be pointed out that, as was stated in the judgment of 15 June 1978, the scope of Article 119 is restricted to the question of pay discrimination between men and women workers. Problems related to other conditions of work and employment, on the other hand, are covered generally by other provisions of Community law, in particular Articles 117 and 118 of the Treaty, with a view to the harmonization of the social systems of Member States and the approximation of their legislation in that area.

42. The imposition of an obligation such as that envisaged by the national court in its question goes beyond the scope of Article 119 and has no other basis in Community law as it now stands.

43. The answer to Question 2(b) must therefore be that Article 119 does not have the effect of requiring an employer to organize its occupational pension scheme in such a manner as to take into account the particular difficulties faced by persons with family responsibilities in meeting the conditions for entitlement to such a pension.

Costs

44. The costs incurred by the United Kingdom and the Commission of the European Communities, which have submitted observations to the Court, are not recoverable. As these proceedings are, in so far as the

150

parties to the main proceedings are concerned, in the nature of a step in the proceedings pending before the national court, the decision on costs is a matter for that court.

On those grounds,

THE COURT,

in answer to the questions submitted to it by the Bundesarbeitsgericht by order of 5 June 1984, hereby rules:

1. **Article 119 of the EEC Treaty is infringed by a department store company which excludes part-time employees from its occupational pension scheme, where that exclusion affects a far greater number of women than men, unless the undertaking shows that the exclusion is based on objectively justified factors unrelated to any discrimination on grounds of sex.**

2. **Under Article 119 a department store company may justify the adoption of a pay policy excluding part-time workers, irrespective of their sex, from its occupational pension scheme on the ground that it seeks to employ as few part-time workers as possible, where it is found that the means chosen for achieving that objective correspond to a real need on the part of the undertaking, are appropriate with a view to achieving the objective in question and are necessary to that end.**

3. **Article 119 does not have the effect of requiring an employer to organize its occupational pension scheme in such a manner as to take into account the particular difficulties faced by persons with family responsibilities in meeting the conditions for entitlement to such a pension.**

Mackenzie Stuart	Koopmans	Everling
Bahlmann	Joliet	Bosco
Due	Galmot	Kakouris

Delivered in open court in Luxembourg on 13 May 1986.

P. Heim   A. J. Mackenzie Stuart
Registrar   *President*

Judgment of the Court

1 June 1986 – Case 237/85

Gisela Rummler
v.
Dato-Druck GmbH

Equal pay principle – job classification system for determining rates of pay – Council Directive 75/117/EEC does not prohibit use, in such system, of criterion of muscle demand, muscular effort or heaviness of work if, given nature of tasks involved, work to be performed requires use of certain degree of physical strength, provided system as a whole precludes discrimination on grounds of sex by taking into account other criteria – criteria governing pay rate classification must ensure that work which is objectively the same attracts same rate of pay for men and women – use of values reflecting average performance of workers of one sex as basis for determining extent to which work makes demands, requires effort or is heavy, is discrimination on grounds of sex contrary to the Directive – for job classification system not to be discriminatory as a whole, it should take into account criteria for which workers of each sex may show aptitude (Council Directive 75/117/EEC, Article 1).

In Case 237/85

REFERENCE to the Court under Article 177 of the EEC Treaty by the Arbeitsgericht [Labour Court] Oldenburg, Federal Republic of Germany, for a preliminary ruling in the proceedings pending before that court between

Gisela Rummler, residing at Oldenburg,

and

Dato-Druck GmbH, a company incorporated under German law, established in Oldenburg,

on the interpretation of Council Directive 75/117/EEC of 10 February 1975 on the approximation of the laws of the Member States relating to the application of the principle of equal pay for men and women,

THE COURT (FIFTH CHAMBER)

composed of: U. Everling (President of the Chamber), R. Joliet, Y. Galmot, F. Schockweiler and J. C. Moitinho de Almeida, Judges,

Advocate General: C. O. Lenz
Registrar: K. Riechenberg, acting as an Administrator

gives the following JUDGMENT

Decision

1. By an order of 25 June 1985, which was received at the Court on 31 July 1985, the Arbeitsgericht Oldenburg referred to the Court for a preliminary ruling under Article 177 of the EEC Treaty three questions on the interpretation of Council Directive 75/117/EEC of 10 February 1975 on the approximation of the laws of the Member States relating to the application of the principle of equal pay for men and women (Official Journal 1975 No. L 45, p. 19).

2. Those questions were raised in the course of proceedings brought before the Arbeitsgericht by Gisela Rummler against her employer, Dato-Druck GmbH, a printing firm, for the purpose of obtaining classification in a higher category in the pay scale.

3. Conditions of remuneration in the printing industry are governed by the 'Lohnrahmentarifvertrag für die gewerblichen Arbeitnehmer der Druckindustrie im Gebiet der Bundesrepublik Deutschland, einschliesslich Berlin-West' [Framework wage-rate agreement for industrial employees of the printing industry in the territory of the Federal Republic of Germany including West Berlin] of 6 July 1984, which provides for seven wage groups corresponding to the work carried out, determined according to the degree of knowledge, concentration, muscular demand or effort and responsibility. The following aspects are relevant to these proceedings: the activities covered by Wage Group II are described as those which may be executed with slight previous knowledge and after brief instruction or training, require little accuracy, place a slight to moderate demand on the muscles and involve slight or occasionally moderate responsibility; the activities covered by Wage Group III are described as those which may be executed with moderate previous knowledge and instruction or training related to the particular job, require moderate accuracy, require moderate or occasionally great muscular effort and involve slight or occasionally moderate responsibility; the activities falling under Wage Group IV are described as requiring previous knowledge on the basis of instruction or training related to the particular job, occasionally a fair degree of occupational experience requiring moderate accuracy, involving moderate and occasionally great effort of different kinds, particularly as a result of work dependent on machines and involving moderate responsibility. It is specified that the evaluation criteria must not be regarded as cumulative in all cases.

4. The plaintiff in the main proceedings, who is classified in Wage Group III, considers that she ought to be classified in Wage Group IV since she carries out work falling under that wage group; in particular, she is re-

153

quired to pack parcels weighing more than 20 kilogrammes, which for her represents heavy physical work.

5. The defendant in the main proceedings denies that the plaintiff's duties are of the nature described by her; it considers that they do not even fulfil the conditions for classification in Wage Group III, in which the plaintiff is now classified and that having regard to the nature of her duties, which make only slight muscular demands, she should be classified in Wage Group II.

6. The Arbeitsgericht Oldenburg considered that in order to arrive at a decision on the classification of the plaintiff in one of the wage groups in question it needed to know first whether the classification criteria were compatible with Directive 75/117; it therefore stayed the proceedings and referred the following questions to the Court for a preliminary ruling:

'1. Does it follow from the provisions of Council Directive 75/117/EEC on the approximation of the Laws of the Member States relating to the application of the principle of equal pay for men and women that in job classification systems no distinction may be made on the basis of:
   (a) the extent to which a job makes demands on or requires an effort of the muscles;
   (b) whether the work is heavy or not?
2. If Question 1 is answered essentially in the negative:
   As regards the decision as to:
   (a) the extent to which a job makes demands on or requires an effort of the muscles;
   (b) whether the work is heavy or not;
      is reference to be made to the extent to which it makes demands on or requires an effort from women or whether it is heavy for women?
3. If Question 2 is answered in the affirmative:
   Does a job classification system which uses the criterion of demand on or effort of the muscles or the criterion of heaviness of work but does not make clear that it is significant to what extent the work makes demands on or requires an effort of the muscles as regards women or whether the work is heavy for women satisfy the requirements of the directive?'

Question 1
7. By its first question the national court seeks to ascertain whether a job classification system based on the criteria of muscle demand or muscular effort and the heaviness of the work is compatible with the principle of equal pay for men and women.

8. According to Dato-Druck GmbH, pay criteria must in essence be established in accordance with the duties actually performed, and not by refer-

ence to the personal attributes of the worker who carries them out. In its view, the criteria of muscle demand and the heaviness of the work are in no way discriminatory in so far as they correspond to the characteristics of the duties performed and are used in a system which also refers to the criteria of ability, mental effort and responsibility.

9. The United Kingdom considers that the principle of non-discrimination does not preclude the use of a criterion in relation to which one sex has greater natural ability than the other, so long as that criterion is representative of the range of activities involved in the job in question. A system based on the criterion of muscular effort is discriminatory only if it ignores movements of small muscle groups characteristic of manual dexterity.

10. According to the Commission, the criteria of muscle demand and of the heaviness of the work constitute common criteria for the purposes of the second paragraph of Article 1 of Directive 75/117. However, it is also necessary to ascertain whether the system as a whole is discriminatory. The issue whether or not the system is discriminatory must be determined not on the basis of each criterion separately but according to the job classification system as a whole.

11. In replying to Question 1, reference must first be made to the general rule laid down by the first paragraph of Article 1 of Directive 75/117, which provides for the elimination of all discrimination on grounds of sex with regard to all aspects and conditions of remuneration for the same work or for work to which equal value is attributed.

12. That general rule is applied in the second paragraph of Article 1, which provides that a job classification system 'must be based on the same criteria for both men and women and so drawn up as to exclude any discrimination on grounds of sex'.

13. It follows that the principle of equal pay requires essentially that the nature of the work to be carried out be considered objectively. Consequently, the same work or work to which equal value is attributed must be remunerated in the same manner whether it is carried out by a man or by a woman. Where a job classification system is used in determining remuneration, that system must be based on criteria which do not differ according to whether the work is carried out by a man or by a woman and must not be organized, as a whole, in such a manner that it has the practical effect of discriminating generally against workers of one sex.

14. Consequently, criteria corresponding to the duties performed meet the requirements of Article 1 of the directive where those duties by their nature require particular physical effort or are physically heavy. In differentiating rates of pay, it is consistent with the principle of non-discrimination to use a criterion based on the objectively measurable

155

expenditure of effort necessary in carrying out the work or the degree to which, reviewed objectively, the work is physically heavy.

15. Even where a particular criterion, such as that of demand on the muscles, may in fact tend to favour male workers, since it may be assumed that in general they are physically stronger than woman workers, it must, in order to determine whether or not it is discriminatory, be considered in the context of the whole job classification system, having regard to other criteria influencing rates of pay. A system is not necessarily discriminatory simply because one of its criteria makes reference to attributes more characteristic of men. In order for a job classification system as a whole to be non-discriminatory and thus to comply with the principles of the directive, it must, however, be established in such a manner that it includes, if the nature of the tasks in question so permits, jobs to which equal value is attributed and for which regard is had to other criteria in relation to which women workers may have a particular aptitude.

16. It is for the national courts to determine on a case-by-case basis whether a job classification system as a whole allows proper account to be taken of the criteria necessary for adjusting pay rates according to the conditions required for the performance of the various duties throughout the undertaking.

17. The answer to Question 1 must therefore be that Council Directive 75/117 of 10 February 1975 on the approximation of the laws of the Member States relating to the application of the principle of equal pay for men and women does not prohibit the use, in a job classification system for the purpose of determining rates of pay, of the criterion of muscle demand or muscular effort or that of the heaviness of the work if, in view of the nature of the tasks involved, the work to be performed does require the use of a certain degree of physical strength, so long as the system as a whole, by taking into account other criteria, precludes any discrimination on grounds of sex.

Questions 2 and 3
18. It appears from the wording of those questions and from the grounds of the order for reference that the national court wishes in substance to know whether, in the event that the criteria of muscle demand or muscular effort and of the heaviness of the work are compatible with Directive 75/117, the fact that in determining to what extent work requires an effort or is demanding or heavy regard is had to the degree to which the work requires an effort or is demanding or for women workers satisfies the requirements of the directive.

19. The defendant argues that regard must be had only to the objective nature of the work to be carried out and the objectively measurable demands it makes.

20. The United Kingdom adds that to use an absolute level of muscular effort or an absolute degree of heaviness of the work, which in fact amounts to using male points of reference, can constitute no more than indirect discrimination, which is not prohibited by Article 119 of the EEC Treaty insofar as it is based on objectively justifiable grounds. Such grounds exist where an employer must, in order to attract workers to and retain them in a specific job, set the rate of pay for that job in accordance with the particular effort required by it.

21. The Commission considers that in this regard the directive contains no general legal principle, so that national courts are not precluded from basing themselves mainly or exclusively on female values if the principle of non-discrimination so requires in order to avoid discrimination against women.

22. The answer to Questions 2 and 3, seen in those terms, follows from what has already been said in answer to Question 1, that is to say that nothing in the directive prevents the use in determining wage rates of a criterion based on the degree of muscular effort objectively required by a specific job or the objective degree of heaviness of the job.

23. The directive lays down the principle of equal pay for equal work. It follows the work actually carried out must be remunerated in accordance with its nature. Any criterion based on values appropriate only to workers of one sex carries with it a risk of discrimination and may jeopardize the main objective of the directive, equal treatment for the same work. That is true even of a criterion based on values corresponding to the average performance of workers of the sex considered to have less natural ability for the purposes of that criterion, for the result would be another form of pay discrimination: work objectively requiring greater strength would be paid at the same rate as work requiring less strength.

24. The failure to take into consideration values corresponding to the average performance of female workers in establishing a progressive pay scale based on the degree of muscle demand and muscular effort may indeed have the effect of placing women workers, who cannot take jobs which are beyond their physical strength, at a disadvantage. That difference in treatment may, however, be objectively justified by the nature of the job when such a difference is necessary in order to ensure a level of pay appropriate to the effort required by the work and thus corresponds to a real need on the part of the undertaking (see the judgment of 13 May 1986 in Case 170/84 *Bilka-Kaufhaus* v. *Weber von Hartz*, [1986] ECR). As has already been stated, however, a job classification system must, in so far as the nature of the tasks in question permits, include other criteria which serve to ensure that the system as a whole is not discriminatory.

25. The answer to the second and third questions must therefore be that it follows from Directive 75/117 that:

157

(a) the criteria governing pay-rate classification must ensure that work which is objectively the same attracts the same rate of pay whether it is performed by a man or a woman;

(b) the use of values reflecting the average performance of workers of one sex as a basis for determining the extent to which work makes demands or requires effort or whether it is heavy constitutes a form of discrimination on grounds of sex, contrary to the directive;

(c) in order for a job classification system not to be discriminatory as a whole, it must, in so far as the nature of the tasks carried out in the undertaking permits, take into account criteria for which workers of each sex may show particular aptitude.

Costs

26. The costs incurred by the United Kingdom and the Commission of the European Communities, which have submitted observations to the Court, are not recoverable. As these proceedings are, in so far as the parties to the main proceedings are concerned, in the nature of a step in the action pending before the national court, the decision on costs is a matter for that court.

On those grounds,

THE COURT (FIFTH CHAMBER)

in answer to the questions referred to it by the Arbeitsgericht Oldenburg by order of 25 June 1985, hereby rules:

1. **Council Directive 75/117 of 10 February 1975 on the approximation of the laws of the Member States relating to the application of the principle of equal pay for men and women (Official Journal 1975 No. L 45, p. 19) does not prohibit the use, in a job classification system for the purpose of determining rates of pay, of the criterion of muscle demand or muscular effort or that of the heaviness of the work if, in view of the nature of the tasks involved, the work to be performed does require the use of a certain degree of physical strength, so long as the system as a whole, by taking into account other criteria, precludes any discrimination on grounds of sex.**

2. **It follows from Directive 75/117 that:**
   (a) **The criteria governing pay rate classification must ensure that the work which is objectively the same attracts the same rate of pay whether it is performed by a man or a woman;**
   (b) **the use of values reflecting the average performance of workers of one sex as a basis for determining the extent to which work makes demands or requires effort or whether it is heavy constitutes a form of discrimination on grounds of sex, contrary to the directive;**
   (c) **in order for a job classification system not to be discriminatory as a**

whole, it must, in so far as the nature of the tasks carried out in the undertaking permits, take into account criteria for which workers of each sex may show particular aptitude.

Everling   Joliet   Galmot
          Schockweiler   Moitinho de Almeida

Delivered in open court in Luxembourg on 1 July 1986.

P. Heim   U. Everling
Registrar   *President of the Fifth Chamber*

Judgment of the Court

3 December 1987 – Case 192/85

George Noel Newstead
v.
Department of Transport, and Her Majesty's Treasury

Equal pay principle – disparities in men's and women's net pay resulting from deductions from gross salary of contributions to occupational pension scheme which substitutes for statutory scheme come within Article 118 but not Article 119, EEC Treaty – Council Directive 75/117/EEC does not alter scope or content of Article 119 – Council Directive 76/207/EEC not intended to apply to social security and does not prevent employer from paying men and women same gross salary but making deductions only from men's gross salary as contribution to widows' pension fund under occupational scheme which substitutes for statutory scheme (EEC Treaty, Articles 118 and 119; Council Directive 75/117/EEC; Council Directive 76/207/EEC, Article 1(2)).

In Case 192/85

REFERENCE to the Court under Article 177 of the EEC Treaty by the Employment Appeal Tribunal for a preliminary ruling in the proceedings pending before that tribunal between

George Noel Newstead

and

(1) Department of Transport
(2) Her Majesty's Treasury

on the interpretation of Article 119 of the EEC Treaty, Council Directive 75/117 of 10 February 1975 on the approximation of the Laws of the Member

States relating to the application of the principle of equal pay for men and women (Official Journal 1975 No. L 45, p. 19) and Council Directive 76/207 of 9 February 1976 on the implementation of the principle of equal treatment for men and women as regards access to employment, vocational training and promotion, and working conditions (Official Journal 1976 No. L 39, p. 40),

THE COURT

composed of: G. Bosco, President of Chamber, acting as President, O. Due, J. C. Moitinho de Almeida and G. C. Rodriguez Iglesias, (Presidents of Chambers), T. Koopmans, U. Everling, K. Bahlmann, Y. Galmot, C. N. Kakouris, R. Joliet and F. A. Schockweiler, Judges,

Advocate General: M. Darmon
Registrar: H. A. Rühl, Principal Administrator

gives the following JUDGMENT

Decision

1. By an order of 11 June 1985, which was received at the Court Registry on 21 June 1985, the Employment Appeal Tribunal referred to the Court of Justice for a preliminary ruling under Article 177 of the EEC Treaty four questions on the interpretation of Article 119 of that Treaty, Council Directive 75/117 of 10 February 1975 on the approximation of the laws of the Member States relating to the application of the principle of equal pay for men and women (Official Journal 1975 No. L 45, p. 19) and Council Directive 76/207 of 9 February 1976 on the implementation of the principle of equal treatment for men and women as regards access to employment, vocational training and promotion, and working conditions (Official Journal 1976 No. L 39, p. 40).

2. Those questions were raised in the course of proceedings between Mr Newstead, a civil servant employed by the Department of Transport, and the Department of Transport and the Treasury.

3. With regard to social security civil servants employed by the Department of Transport are covered by the Principal Civil Service Pension Scheme 1974, an occupational scheme established by the State for civil servants. Under the applicable United Kingdom legislation it is a substitute for the earnings-related part of the State pension scheme. Persons covered by a scheme of this kind, referred to as a 'contracted-out' scheme, make reduced contributions to the national scheme, corresponding to the basic flat-rate pension payable under the national scheme to all workers regardless of their earnings. On the other hand, they are required to contribute

160

to the occupational scheme, in accordance with the conditions which it lays down.

4. The occupational scheme to which Mr Newstead belongs makes provision for a widows' pension fund. That fund is financed in part by the contributions of civil servants. However, although male civil servants, whatever their marital status, are obliged to contribute to the fund, a deduction of 1.5 per cent being made from their gross salary, female civil servants are never obliged to contribute to the fund but may in certain circumstances be permitted to do so.

5. In the case of civil servant who was at no time married while he was covered by the occupational scheme, it is provided that his contributions to the widow's pension fund should be returned to him, with compound interest at the rate of 4 per cent per annum, when he leaves the Civil Service. Should he die before then, that amount is paid to his estate.

6. Mr Newstead, who is unmarried, argues that the obligation to contribute to the widows' pension fund has the effect of discriminating against him in comparison with a female civil servant in an equivalent post, since she is not obliged to give up 1.5 per cent of her gross salary, albeit temporarily, as a contribution to the fund. He therefore brought proceedings before an industrial tribunal for an order that he should no longer be obliged to make the contribution in question.

7. The industrial tribunal dismissed his application. On appeal, however, the Employment Appeal Tribunal considered that the application raised issues concerning the interpretation of Article 119 of the EEC Treaty and of Directives 75/117 and 76/207, referred to above. It therefore stayed the proceedings and referred the following questions to the Court:

> '(a) Is it a breach of Article 119 (read on its own or together with the Equal Pay Directive 75/117) for the employer to pay men and women the same gross salary but to require an unmarried male pensionable civil servant (such as the appellant) to pay (by way of deduction from his salary) 1½ per cent of his gross salary as a contribution to provision of a widow's pension of the sort in the present case, and which contributions cannot be repaid until his death or he leaves the Civil Service, when a similar requirement is not imposed upon an unmarried female pensionable civil servant for the purposes of a widower's pension?
> (b) If the answer to (a) is in the affirmative does Article 119 (read on its own or together with the Equal Pay Directive) have direct effect in Member States so as to confer enforceable rights on individuals in the circumstances of the present case?

161

(c) Is it a breach of the Equal Treatment Directive 76/207 for the employer to pay men and women the same gross salary but to require an unmarried male pensionable civil servant (such as the appellant) to pay (by way of deduction from his salary) 1½ per cent of his gross salary as a contribution to provision of a widow's pension of the sort in the present case and which contributions cannot be repaid until his death or he leaves the Civil Service, when a similar requirement is not imposed upon a unmarried female pensionable civil servant for the purposes of a widower's pension?

(d) If the answer to (c) is in the affirmative does the Equal Treatment Directive have direct effect in Member States so as to confer enforceable rights on individuals in the circumstances of the present case?'

8. Reference is made to the Report for the Hearing for a more extensive account of the facts of the case, the course of the procedure and the observations submitted to the Court pursuant to Article 20 of the Protocol on the Statute of the Court, which are mentioned or discussed hereinafter only in so far as is necessary for the reasoning of the Court.

The first question
9. In its first question the Employment Appeal Tribunal asks in essence whether it is a breach of Article 119, read together with Directive 75/117, for an employer to pay men and women the same gross salary but to deduct 1.5 per cent of the gross salary of men only as a contribution to a widows' pension fund.

10. In order to reply to that question it must be determined first of all whether the case before the Employment Appeal Tribunal falls within the scope of Article 119.

11. According to the first paragraph of Article 119 the Member States must ensure the application of the principle that men and women should receive equal pay for equal work; pursuant to the second paragraph, 'pay' is to be understood, for the purposes of that article, as 'the ordinary basic or minimum wage or salary and any other consideration, whether in cash or in kind, which the worker receives, directly or indirectly, in respect of his employment from his employer'.

12. It is not disputed that in the case under consideration by the Employment Appeal Tribunal the net pay received by men is less than that received by women doing the same work: only men have 1.5 per cent of their gross salary deducted as a contribution to the widows' pension fund.

13. As the United Kingdom and the Commission rightly pointed out, however, the difference between the net pay of men and women in the case

before the Employment Appeal Tribunal is the result of the fact that only men are required to belong to the widows' pension fund and thus have a deduction made from their salary as a contribution to the fund.

14. It must therefore be concluded that the factor which gives rise to the disparity at issue is neither a benefit paid to workers nor a contribution paid by the employer to a pension scheme on behalf of the employee, which might be regarded as 'consideration . . . which the worker receives, directly or indirectly' as referred to in Article 119.

15. The disparity at issue is in fact the result of the deduction of a contribution to an occupational pension scheme. That scheme contains some provisions which are more favourable than the statutory scheme of general application and is a substitute for the latter. Such a contribution must therefore, like a contribution to a statutory social security scheme, be considered to fall within the scope of Article 118 of the Treaty, not of Article 119.

16. In order to dispute that conclusion Mr Newstead argues that in its judgments of 11 March 1981 (Case 69/80, *Worringham and Humphreys* v. *Lloyds Bank*, [1981] ECR 767) and 18 September 1984 (Case 23/83, *Liefting* v. *Academisch Ziekenhuis bij de Universiteit van Amsterdam*, [1984] ECR 3225) it was from the point of view of Article 119 that the Court examined differences in pay between men and women related to the different conditions applied to them in respect of contributions to the pension schemes, occupational and statutory respectively, at issue in those two cases.

17. It must be borne in mind, however, that in those judgments the Court simply observed that Article 119 was applicable in particular where the gross pay of men was higher than that of women in order to make up for the fact that only men were required to contribute to a social security scheme. The Court emphasized that although the extra pay was subsequently deducted by the employer and paid into a pension fund on behalf of the employee, it determined the calculation of other salary-related benefits (redundancy payments, unemployment benefits, family allowances, credit facilities) and was therefore a component of the worker's 'pay' for the purposes of the second paragraph of Article 119 to which the prohibition of discrimination laid down in the first paragraph of Article 119 was applicable.

18. Those circumstances are not present in the case before the Employment Appeal Tribunal. The deduction in question results in a reduction in net pay because of a contribution paid to a social security scheme and in no way affects gross pay, on the basis of which the other salary related benefits mentioned above are normally calculated. This case cannot

163

therefore be governed by the approach taken by the Court in the judgments referred to.

19. It follows from what has been said that the case before the Employment Appeal Tribunal does not fall within the scope of Article 119 of the Treaty.

20. Council Directive 75/117, which was also mentioned by the Employment Appeal Tribunal in its question, does not affect the conclusion arrived at with regard to Article 119. As the Court stated in its judgment of 31 March 1981 (Case 96/80, *Jenkins* v. *Kingsgate*, [1981] ECR 911), that directive is principally designed to facilitate the practical application of the principle of equal pay laid down in Article 119 and in no way alters its content or scope as defined in that article.

21. The answer to the first question of the Employment Appeal Tribunal must therefore be that Article 119 of the EEC Treaty, read together with Council Directive 75/117 of 10 February 1975, does not prevent an employer from paying men and women the same gross salary but making a deduction of 1.5 per cent of the gross salary of men only, even those who are unmarried, as a contribution to a widows' pension fund provided for under an occupational scheme which is a substitute for a statutory social security scheme.

The second question
22. Since this question was submitted only in the event that the Court should reply to the first question in the affirmative, there is no need to reply to it.

The third question
23. In its third question the Employment Appeal Tribunal asks whether, in circumstances such as those at issue in the main proceedings, there is a breach of Council Directive 76/207 of 9 February 1976 on the implementation of principle of equal treatment for men and women as regards access to employment, vocational training and promotion, and working conditions (Official Journal 1976 No. L 39, p. 40).

24. As the United Kingdom and the Commission correctly observed, Directive 76/207 is not intended to apply in social security matters. That is clear from Article 1(2), according to which 'with a view to ensuring the progressive implementation of the principle of equal treatment in matters of social security, the Council, acting on a proposal from the Commission, will adopt provisions defining its substance, its scope and the arrangements for its application'.

25. None of the directives adopted by the Council pursuant to that provision applies to survivors' pensions, whether provided for under a statutory social security scheme or under an occupational scheme.

26. Article 3(2) of Council Directive 79/7 of 19 December 1978 (Official Journal 1979 No. L 6, p. 24), which is designed to extend the application of principle of equal treatment to statutory schemes providing protection in the case of sickness, invalidity, old-age, accidents at work, occupational diseases and unemployment, and to social assistance in so far as it is intended to supplement or replace such schemes (Article 3(1)), states that the directive "shall not apply to the provisions concerning survivors' benefits". As for occupational social security schemes, Article 3(3) made application to them of the principle of equal treatment subject to the adoption of further provisions by the Council, acting on a proposal from the Commission.

27. While these proceedings were in progress, the Council, acting pursuant to Article 3(3), adopted Directive 86/372 of 24 July 1986 on the implementation of the principle of equal treatment for men and women in occupational social security schemes (Official Journal 1986 No. L 225, p. 40).

   However, Article 9 of that directive – the period for whose implementation by the Member States, laid down in Article 12, has not yet expired – provides that 'Member States may defer compulsory application of the principle of equal treatment with regard to ... (b) survivors' pensions until a directive requires the principle of equal treatment in statutory social security schemes in that regard.'.

28. In the absence of more specific directives extending the application of the principle of equal treatment to benefits for surviving spouses, whether these are provided under a statutory social security scheme or under an occupational scheme, and having regard to the fact that the difference in treatment affecting Mr Newstead as regards the immediate enjoyment of all his net pay is the direct consequence of a difference in treatment in the occupational scheme in question with regard to this type of benefit, it must be concluded that the case before the Employment Appeal Tribunal falls within the exception to the application of the principle of equal treatment provided for in Article 1(2) of Directive 76/207.

29. The answer to the third question of the Employment Appeal Tribunal must therefore be that Council Directive 76/207 of 9 February 1986 does not prevent an employer from paying men and women the same gross salary but making a deduction of 1.5 per cent of the gross salary of men only, even those who are unmarried, as a contribution to a widows' pension fund provided for under an occupational scheme which is a substitute for a statutory social security scheme.

The fourth question
30. Since this question was submitted only in the event that the Court should reply to the third question in the affirmative, it is not necessary to reply to it.

Costs

31. The costs incurred by the United Kingdom and by the Commission, which submitted observations to the Court, are not recoverable. As these proceedings are, in so far as the parties to the main proceedings are concerned, in the nature of a step in the proceedings pending before the Employment Appeal Tribunal, the decision on costs is a matter for that tribunal.

On those grounds,

The Court

in answer to the questions submitted to it by the Employment Appeal Tribunal by an order of 11 June 1985, hereby rules:

1. **Article 119 of the EEC Treaty, read together with Council Directive 75/117 of 10 February 1975, does not prevent an employer from paying men and women the same gross salary but making a deduction of 1.5 per cent of the gross salary of men only, even those who are unmarried, as a contribution to a widows' pension fund provided for under an occupational scheme which is a substitute for a statutory social security scheme.**

2. **Council Directive 76/207 of 9 February 1976 does not prevent an employer from paying men and women the same gross salary but making a deduction of 1.5 per cent of the gross salary of men only, even those who are unmarried, as a contribution to a widows' pension fund provided for under an occupational scheme which is a substitute for a statutory social security scheme.**

Bosco	Due	Moitinho de Almeida
Rodriguez Iglesias	Koopmans	Everling
Bahlmann	Galmot	Kakouris
Joliet	Schockweiler	

Delivered in open court in Luxembourg on 3 December 1987.

P. Heim
Registrar

G. Bosco
Acting as President

Judgment of the Court

4 February 1988 – Case 157/86

Mary Murphy and others
v.
Bord Telecom Eireann

Equal pay principle – Article 119, EEC Treaty, may be directly relied on where worker seeking to obtain equal pay is engaged in work of higher value than that of person with whom comparison is to be made – since equal pay principle prohibits workers of one sex engaged in work of equal value to workers of opposite sex from being paid lower wage on grounds of sex, it must also prohibit such differences in pay where the lower paid category of workers is engaged in work of higher value – contrary interpretation would render equal pay principle ineffective (EEC Treaty, Article 119; Council Directive 75/117/EEC, Article 1).

In Case 157/86

REFERENCE to the Court under Article 177 of the EEC Treaty by the High Court of Ireland for a preliminary ruling in the proceedings pending before that court between

Mary Murphy and Others

and

Bord Telecom Eireann

on the interpretation of Article 119 of the EEC Treaty and Article 1 of Council Directive 75/117/EEC of 10 February 1975 on the approximation of the laws of the Member States relating to the application of the principle of equal pay for men and women (Official Journal 1975 No. L 45, p. 19),

THE COURT

composed of: G. Bosco, President of Chamber, acting as President, O. Due and J. C. Moitinho de Almedia (Presidents of Chambers), U. Everling, K. Bahlmann, Y. Galmot, C. N. Kalouris, T. F. O'Higgins and F. A. Schockweiler, Judges,

Advocate General: C. O. Lenz
Registrar: D. Louterman, Administrator

gives the following JUDGMENT

Decision

1. By an order of 4 March 1986, which was received at the Court on 30 June 1986, the High Court of Ireland referred to the Court for a preliminary ruling, under Article 177 of the EEC Treaty, three questions on the interpretation of Article 119 of the EEC Treaty and Article 1 of Council Directive 75/117/EEC of 10 February 1975 on the approximation of the laws of the Member States relating to the application of the principle of equal pay men and women (Official Journal 1975, No. L 45, p. 19).

2. The questions were raised in the context of proceedings brought by Mary Murphy and 28 other women against their employer, Bord Telecom Eireann. They are employed as factory workers and they are engaged in such tasks as dismantling, cleaning, oiling and reassembling telephones and other equipment. They claim the right to be paid at the same rate as a specified male worker employed in the same factory as a stores labourer and engaged in cleaning, collecting and delivering equipment and components and in lending general assistance as required.

3. It is apparent from the documents before the Court that the Equality Officer to whom the claim was referred in the first instance, under the procedure prescribed by the Anti-Discrimination (Pay) Act 1974, considered the appellants' work to be of higher value taken as a whole than that of the male worker and, consequently, did not constitute "like work" within the meaning of the aforesaid Act. The Equality Officer therefore found herself unable on that ground alone to make a recommendation that the appellants should be paid at the same rate as the male worker; that being so, the Equality Officer decided that it was unnecessary to consider whether the difference in pay amounted to discrimination on grounds of sex.

4. Those conclusions were upheld on appeal by the Labour Court and the appellants then appealed on a point of law to the High Court. That court, whilst upholding the interpretation of the Anti-Discrimination (Pay) Act adopted by the Equality Officer and the Labour Court, examined whether the national legislation was compatible with the Community provisions on equal pay. It therefore stayed the proceedings and referred the following questions to the Court of Justice for a preliminary ruling:

    '1. Does the Community law principle of equal pay for equal work extend to a claim for equal pay on the basis of work of equal value in circumstances where the work of the claimant has been assessed to be of higher value than that of the person with whom the claimant sought comparison?
    2. If the answer to Question 1 is in the affirmative is that answer dependent on the provisions of Article 1 of Council Directive 75/117/EEC of 10 February 1975 on the approximation

of the laws of the Member States relating to the application
of the principle of equal pay for men and women?
3. If so, is Article 1 of the said Directive directly applicable in
Member States?'

5. Reference is made to the Report for the Hearing for a fuller account of
the facts of the main proceedings, the provisions of Community law in
question, the course of the procedure and the observations submitted to
the Court, which are mentioned or discussed hereinafter only in so far as
is necessary for the reasoning of the Corut.

The first question
6. It is apparent from a comparison of the three questions referred to the
Court of Justice and from the explanations given in the grounds of the
order for reference that the first question essentially seeks to ascertain
whether Article 119 of the EEC Treaty must be interpreted as covering
a case where a worker who relies on that provision to obtain equal pay
within the meaning thereof is engaged in work of higher value than that
of the person with whom a comparison is to be made.

7. Under the first paragraph of Article 119 the Member States are to ensure
and maintain 'the application of the principle that men and women should
receive equal pay for equal work'. According to a consistent line of decisions beginning with the Court's judgment of 8 April 1976 (Case 43/75,
Defrenne v. *Sabena*, [1976] ECR 455) Article 119 is directly applicable in
particular in cases where men and women receive unequal pay for equal
work carried out in the same establishment or service, whether public or
private.

8. Bord Telecomm Eireann contends that the principle does not apply in the
situation where a lower wage is paid for work of higher value. In support
of its view it maintains that the term 'equal work' in Article 119 of the
EEC Treaty cannot be understood as embracing unequal work and that
the effect of a contrary interpretation would be that equal pay would have
to be paid for work of different value.

9. It is true that Article 119 expressly requires the application of the
principle of equal pay for men and women solely in the case of equal
work or, according to a consistent line of decisions of the Court, in the
case of work of equal value, and not in the case of work of unequal value.
Nevertheless, if that principle forbids workers of one sex engaged in work
of equal value to that of workers of the opposite sex to be paid a lower
wage than the latter on grounds of sex, it *a fortiori* prohibits such a
difference in pay where the lower-paid category of workers is engaged in
work of higher value.

10. To adopt a contrary interpretation would be tantamount to rendering the

169

principle of equal pay ineffective and nugatory. As the Irish government rightly emphasized, in that case an employer would easily be able to circumvent the principle by assigning additional or more onerous duties to workers of a particular sex, who could then be paid a lower wage.

11. In so far as it is established that the difference in wage levels in question is based on discrimination on grounds of sex, Article 119 of the EEC Treaty is directly applicable in the sense that the workers concerned may rely on it in legal proceedings in order to obtain equal pay within the meaning of the provision and in the sense that national courts or tribunals must take it into account as a constituent part of Community law. It is for the national court, within the limits of its discretion under national law, when interpreting and applying domestic law, to give to it, where possible, an interpretation which accords with the requirements of the applicable Community law and, to the extent that this is not possible, to hold such domestic law inapplicable.

12. For those reasons the reply to the first question must be that Article 119 of the EEC Treaty must be interpreted as covering the case where a worker who relies on that provision to obtain equal pay within the meaning thereof is engaged in work of higher value than that of the person with whom a comparison is to be made.

The second and third questions
13. It follows from the foregoing that the proceedings before the High Court of Ireland are capable of being resolved by means of an interpretation of Article 119 of the EEC Treaty alone. In those circumstances it is unnecessary to reply to the second and third questions concerning the interpretation of Council Directive 75/117/EEC of 10 February 1975.

Costs
14. The costs incurred by the Irish Government and by the Commission of the European Communities, which have sumbitted observations to the Court, are not recoverable. As these proceedings are, in so far as the parties to the main proceedings are concerned, in the nature of a step in the proceedings pending before the national court, the decision on costs is a matter for that court.

On those grounds,

The Court,

in answer to the questions referred to it by the High Court of Ireland, by order of 4 March 1986, hereby rules:

Article 119 of the EEC Treaty must be interpreted as covering the case where a

worker who relies on that provision to obtain equal pay within the meaning thereof is engaged in work of higher value than that of the person with whom a comparison is to be made.

Bosco	Due	Moitinho de Almeida
Everling	Bahlmann	Galmot
Kakouris	O'Higgins	Schockweiler

Delivered in open court in Luxembourg on 4 February 1988.

P. Heim   A. J. Mackenzie Stuart
Registrar   *President*

2. Equal treatment in employment

(a) Infringement proceedings under Article 169, EEC Treaty

Judgment of the Court

26 October 1983 – Case 163/82

Commission of the European Communities
v.
Italian Republic

Equal treatment for men and women – Directive binding as to result to be achieved but Member States have choice of form and method of implementation – in implementing equal treatment principle in Directive 76/207/EEC, Member State not open to criticism for adopting specific provisions regarding most important working conditions and general provisions for all other working conditions, unless result sought by Directive is not in fact achieved – difference in treatment arising from national law provisions under which adoptive fathers unlike adoptive mothers are not entitled to maternity leave for first three months after adoption, though same leave rights thereafter, is not discrimination within meaning of Directive 76/207/EEC – no infringement of Article 6 of Directive where national law implementing Directive limits remedies to infringement of certain of the Directive's provisions, provided general procedural rules of national law still allow individuals to bring any matter covered by Directive before the courts (EEC Treaty, Article 189; Council Directive 76/207/EEC, Articles 5 and 6).

In Case 163/82

Commission of the European Communities, represented by its Legal Adviser, Armando Toledano Laredo, acting as Agent, with an address for service in Luxembourg at the office of Oreste Montalto, a member of the Legal Department of the Commission, Jean Monnet Building, Kirchberg,

applicant,

v.

Italian Republic, represented by Pier Giorgio Ferri, Avvocato dello Stato, with an address for service in Luxembourg at the Italian Embassy,

defendant,

APPLICATION for a declaration that by not adopting within the prescribed period the provisions needed to ensure compliance with Council Directive 76/207/EEC of 9 February 1976 on the implementation of the principle of equal treatment for men and women as regards access to employment, vocational training and promotion, and working conditions (Official Journal, L 39, p. 40), the Italian Republic has failed to fulfil its obligations under the EEC Treaty,

THE COURT

composed of: J. Mertens de Wilmars, President, T. Koopmans, K. Bahlmann and Y. Galmot (Presidents of Chambers), P. Pescatore, Lord Mackenzie Stuart, A. O'Keeffe, G. Bosco, O. Due, U. Everling and C. Kakouris, Judges,

Advocate General: S. Rozès
Registrar: P. Heim

gives the following JUDGMENT

Decision

1. By application received at the Court Registry on 1 June 1982 the Commission of the European Communities brought an action under Article 169 of the EEC Treaty for a declaration that the Italian Republic, by failing to adopt within the prescribed period the provisions necessary to comply with Council Directive 76/207 of 9 February 1976 on the implementation of the principle of equal treatment for men and women as regards access to employment, vocational training and promotion, and working conditions (Official Journal, L 39, p. 40), had failed to fulfil its obligations under the Treaty.

2. Articles 5 and 6 of the directive, which the Commission considers have

172

not been adequately or correctly transposed into Italian law, provide as follows:

'1. Application of the principle of equal treatment with regard to working conditions, including the conditions regarding dismissal, means that men and women shall be guaranteed the same conditions without discrimination on grounds of sex.

2. To this end, Member States shall take the measures necessary to ensure that:

   (a) any laws, regulations and administrative provisions contrary to the principle of equal treatment shall be abolished;

   (b) any provisions contrary to the principle of equal treatment which are included in collective agreements, individual contracts of employment, internal rules of undertakings or in rules governing the independent occupations and profession shall be, or may be declared, null and void or may be amended;

   (c) those laws, regulations and administrative provisions contrary to the principle of equal treatment when the concern for protection which originally inspired them is no longer well founded shall be revised; and that where similar provisions are included in collective agreements labour and management shall be requested to undertake the desired revision.'

Article 6 provides that:

'Member States shall introduce into their national legal systems such measures as are necessary to enable all persons who consider themselves wronged by failure to apply to them the principle of equal treatment within the meaning of Articles 3, 4 and 5 to pursue their claims by judicial process after possible recourse to other competent authorities.'

3. The Italian Republic adopted Law No 903 of 9 December 1977 concerning equal treatment between men and women in relation to employment. Article 1 thereof provides that any discrimination on grounds of sex as regards access to employment, regardless of methods of selection and in any sector or branch of activity whatsoever, at all levels of occupational hierarchy, is prohibited. Such discrimination is likewise prohibited if it is applied on the basis of marital or family status or pregnancy, or indirectly through selection procedures or the press or through any other form of publicity indicating as a requirement of recruitment that a person shall be of a particular sex. The prohibition applies equally to activities undertaken in connection with vocational guidance, vocational training, ad-

173

vanced vocational training and retraining as regards both access to and the content of such activities.

4. Article 2 provides that women are to be entitled to the same remunerationas men for work which is the same or of the same value. Job classification systems for determining remuneration must apply the same criteria for men and for women.

5. Article 3 prohibits any discrimination between men and women as regards the assignment of grading, duties and career development. The leave provided for in Articles 4 and 5 of Law No 1204 of 30 December 1971 is treated for the purposes of career development as days worked when collective agreements do not specify and special conditions in that respect.

6. The first paragraph of Article 4 provides that even if they are eligible for retirement women may elect to continue working up to the retirement age-limit applicable for men. The other paragraphs thereof contain further provisions to which it is not necessary to refer for the purposes of the present judgment.

7. The Commission considers in the first place that the provisions of Law No 903 do not transpose the provisions of Article 5 of the directive into Italian law to an extent and in a manner in conformity with the spirit and letter of the directive. The Law covers certain working conditions such as remuneration, retirement age and the right to take leave from work in the case of adoption, but it does not cover all working conditions in spite of the wider nature of the provisions of Article 5 of the directive.

8. The Government of the Italian Republic replies that consideration of the provisions of the aforesaid Law No 903 shows that discrimination based on sex is prohibited in relation to access to employment, vocational guidance, vocational training, advanced vocational training and retraining (Article 1), remuneration and job classification systems for determining remuneration (Article 2), assignment of grading, duties and career development (Article 3), retirement age (Article 4) and entitlement to leave in certain circumstances (Article 6). The Government of the Italian Republic adds that Article 15 of Law No 300 of 20 May 1970 was amended by Article 13 of Law No 903 of 1977 so as to render void any agreement or measure based on sex aimed at dismissing a worker or adversely affecting him.

9. It must be remembered that according to Article 189 of the Treaty a directive is binding as to the result to be achieved upon each Member State to which it is addressed, but leaves to the national authorities the choice of form and methods. The Italian legislature cannot therefore be criticized for having adopted a number of specific provisions in relation

174

to the most important working conditions and whilst confining itself in relation to other working conditions to a general provision covering, as does Article 15 of the Law of 1970 as amended by Article 13 of the Law of 1977, all other working conditions not specifically mentioned, unless it is shown that the result sought by the directive has not in fact been attained.

10. Since the Commission has not shown that those specific provisions combined with a general supplementing provision have left some areas of the scope of the directive unprovided for, the Commission's first complaint cannot be upheld.

11. The Commission alleges in the second place that the Law of 1977 gives a mother who adopts a child of less than six years of age at the time of adoption the right to compulsory leave and the corresponding financial allowance during the first three months after the child enters the adoptive family and the right to leave for a certain period, without according the adoptive father similar rights. It is said that such different treatment amounts to discrimination in working conditions within the meaning of the directive.

12. Article 6 of Law No 903 of 1977 provides that women who have adopted children or who have obtained custody thereof prior to adoption may claim the maternity leave referred to in Article 4 of Law No 1204 of 1971 and the financial benefits relating thereto for the first three months after the child enters the adoptive family or the family which has been given custody of it, provided the child is not more than six years of age at the time of the adoption or award of custody. The second paragraph of Article 6 adds that such women may also claim the leave provided for in the first paragraph of Article 7 of the Law of 1971 for a period of one year from the actual entry of the child into the family provided that the child is not more than three years of age, and the right to the leave provided for in the second paragraph of Article 7.

13. Article 4 of Law No 1204 of 30 December 1971 provides that women may not be employed:
    (a) During the two months immediately preceding the expected date of confinement;
    (b) If confinement takes place after that date, during the period between the expected date and the actual date of confinement;
    (c) During the three months following confinement.

14. Article 7 of the same Law provides that during the child's first year the woman is entitled, after the above-mentioned maternity leave, to leave from work during a period of six months during which her job is to be kept for her (first paragraph). She is also entitled to leave when a child of less than three years of age is sick, upon submission of a medical certificate (second paragraph).

15. Article 7 of Law No 903 of 1977 gives a working father the right to leave allowed by Article 7 of Law No 1204 of 1971, even if he is a father by adoption or a guardian within the meaning of Article 314/20 of the Civil Code, in lieu of the working mother or where the care and custody of the children are given to the father.

16. However, the adoptive father does not have the right given the adoptive mother of maternity leave for the first three months following the actual entry of the child into the adoptive family. That distinction is justified, as the Government of the Italian Republic rightly contends, by the legitimate concern to assimilate as far as possible the conditions of entry of the child into the adoptive family to those of the arrival of a newborn child in the family during the very delicate initial period. As regards leave from work after the initial period of three months the adoptive father has the same rights as the adoptive mother.

17. In those circumstances the difference in treatment criticized by the Commission cannot be regarded as discrimination within the meaning of the directive.

18. The Commission's last complaint relates to the alleged failure by the Italian Republic to comply with Article 6 of the directive. The Commission states that Article 15 of Law No 903 of 1977 restricts the legal remedies it provides for to cases of breach of the provisions of Articles 1 and 5 of that Law, by not giving a legal remedy to a worker who considers himself adversely affected by failure to comply with the other provisions of the directive.

19. The Government of Italian Republic contends that the procedure referred to in Article 15 of Law No 903 is an emergency one but emphasizes that there is nothing in the directive which requires such a procedure for all cases of discrimination. Article 700 of the Italian Code of Civil Procedure, which is an entirely general rule of procedure, allows the measures required to avoid irremediable damage to be obtained urgently. That provision may be relied upon in all areas where the directive applies and which are not covered by Article 15 of Law No 903.

20. Article 24 of the Italian Constitution, moreover, provides that any person may bring proceedings to protect his rights and lawful interests. That is a constitutional principle of direct application, unchanging and well established in the sense that once the existence of a basic rule protecting an individual interest is established no specific legislative measure is needed to ensure protection thereof since such protection is universally and unconditionally afforded by Article 24 of the Constitution. Workers suffering discrimination may therefore rely on that constitutional provision to ensure observance of the provisions of Law No 903 by means of a court action.

176

21. The Commission has not contested the explanations given by the Government of the Italian Republic. In those circumstances the complaint cannot be upheld.

22. Since none of the complaints made by the Commission has been upheld the application must be dismissed in its entirety.

Costs
23. Under Article 69(2) of the Rules of Procedure the unsuccessful party is to be ordered to pay the costs if a request has been made to that effect.

24. Since the Commission has been unsuccessful it must be ordered to pay the costs.

On those grounds

THE COURT

hereby:

1. Dismisses the application;

2. Orders the Commission to pay the costs.

Mertens de Wilmars		Koopmans	Bahlmann
Galmot	Pescatore	Mackenzie Stuart	O'Keffee
Bosco	Due	Everling	Kakouris

Delivered in open court in Luxembourg on 26 October 1983.

P. Heim
Registrar

J. Mertens de Wilmars
President

Judgment of the Court

8 November 1983 – Case 165/82

Commission of the European Communities
v.
United Kingdom of Great Britain and Northern Ireland

Failure of State fully to fulfil its obligations – equal treatment for men and women – Directive 76/207/EEC covers all collective agreements without distinction as to nature of legal effects they do or do not produce – Members States should ensure that any clauses in such agreements which contradict

177

equal treatment requirements in Directive may be rendered inoperative, eliminated or amended – power of Member States to exclude from scope of Directive certain occupational activities does not extend to general exclusions for employment in private households and small undertakings – midwife exclusion permissible while issue still sensitive (Council Directive 76/207/EEC, Articles 2(2), 4(b) and 9(2)).

In Case 165/82

Commission of the European Communities, represented by John Forman, a member of its Legal Department, acting as Agent, having an address for service in Luxembourg at the office of Oreste Montalto, a member of its Legal Department, Jean Monnet Building, Kirchberg,

applicant,

v.

United Kingdom of Great Britain and Northern Ireland, represented by J. D. Howes, Treasury Solicitor's Department, assisted by I. Glick, with an address for service in Luxembourg at the Embassy of the United Kingdom,

defendant,

APPLICATION for a declaration that the United Kingdom has failed to fulfil its obligations under the EEC Treaty by failing to enact within the prescribed period the provisions needed in order to comply with Council Directive 76/207/EEC of 9 February 1976 on the implementation of the principle of equal treatment for men and women as regards access to employment, vocational training and promotion, and working conditions (Official Journal, L 39, p. 40),

THE COURT

composed of: J. Mertens de Wilmars, President, T. Koopmans, K. Bahlmann and Y. Galmot, (Presidents of Chambers), Lord Mackenzie Stuart, A. O'Keeffe, G. Bosco, O. Due and U. Everling, Judges,

Advocate General: S. Rozès
Registrar: P. Heim

gives the following JUDGMENT

Decision

1. By application lodged at the Court Registry on 3 June 1982 the Commission of the European Communities brought an action before the Court

178

under Article 169 of the EEC Treaty for a declaration that by failing to enact within the prescribed period the provisions needed in order to comply with Council Directive 76/207/EEC of 9 February 1976 on the implementation of the principle of equal treatment of men and women as regards access to employment, vocational training and promotion, and working conditions (Official Journal, L 39, p. 40), the United Kingdom has failed to fulfil its obligations under the Treaty.

2. The Commission charges the United Kingdom with only partially implementing the directive in so far it has failed to amend and supplement the Sex Discrimination Act 1975 [hereinafter referred to as 'the 1975 Act'] which, although abolishing discrimination in certain areas of employment, allows it to continue in other areas in which by virtue of the directive discrimination must be abolished by 12 August 1978 at the latest.

3. The Commission's complaints relate to the following points:
   (a) Neither the 1975 Act nor any other provision of the legislation in force in the United Kingdom provides that provisions contrary to the principle of equal treatment contained in collective agreements, rules of undertakings and rules governing independent occupations and professions are to be, or may be declared, void or may be amended.
   (b) Contrary to the provisions of the directive, section 6(3) of the 1975 Act provides that the prohibition of discrimination does not apply to employment in a private household or where the number of persons employed by an employer does not exceed five (disregarding persons employed in a private household).
   (c) Finally, by virtue of section 20 of the 1975 Act the prohibition of discrimination based on sex does not apply to the employment, promotion and training of midwives.

The first complaint
4. The Government of the United Kingdom considers that this complaint is unfounded. By virtue of section 18 of the Trade Union and Labour Relations Act 1974, any collective agreements made before 1 December 1971 or after the entry into force of that act are to be presumed not to have been intended by the parties to be legally enforceable unless they are in writing and contain a provision in which the parties express their intention that the agreements are to be legally enforceable. In fact, collective agreements are not normally legally binding. The United Kingdom Government is not aware of there being any legally binding collective agreements at present in force in the United Kingdom.

5. Even if collective agreements containing provisions contrary to the principle of equality of treatment do exist, those provisions, in so far as they are not capable of amendment under section 3 of the Equal Pay Act 1970, would be rendered void by section 77 of the 1975 Act.

6. The consequences of any provision in the internal rules of an undertaking

179

or in the rules governing an independent occupation or profession which is contrary to the prohibition of discrimination would similarly be rendered void by the same provision. This would apply to any contract between members of a profession or occupation or between them and an undertaking or any occupational or professional body with legal personality. If any discrimination in employment were to result from the existence of such a discriminatory provision in the internal rules of an undertaking or of an occupational or professional body, that discrimination would be caught by section 6 of the 1975 Act. Moreover, if for example an undertaking whose business was to find employment for workers offered work, by virtue of its internal rules, only to persons of one sex, to the exclusion of persons of the other sex, that would be prohibited by section 15 of the 1975 Act.

7. Finally, if a provision contrary to the principle of equal treatment related to authorization or qualification for a particular profession or occupation, it would be dealt with by section 13(1) of the 1975 Act which, in substance, makes it unlawful for an authority or body which can confer an authorization or qualification 'to discriminate against a woman'.

8. These arguments are not sufficient to nullify the complaints made by the Commission. Whilst it may be admitted that the United Kingdom legislation satisfies the obligations imposed by the directive as regards any collective agreements which have legally binding effects, in so far as they are covered by section 77 of the 1975 Act, it is to be noted on the other hand that the United Kingdom legislation contains no corresponding provision regarding either non-binding collective agreements – which the United Kingdom Government declares to be the only kind in existence – or the internal rules of undertakings or the rules governing independent occupations or professions.

9. The United Kingdom's argument to the effect that the non-binding character of collective agreements removes them from the field of application of that directive cannot be accepted, even if account is taken of the United Kingdom's observation that individual contracts of employment entered into within the framework of a collective agreement are rendered void by section 77 of the 1975 Act.

10. Article 4(b) of Directive 76/207 provides that the application of the principle of equal treatment in the areas to which it relates means that Member States must take the necessary measures to ensure that:

> '(b) any provisions contrary to the principle of equal treatment which are included in collective agreements, individual contracts of employment, internal rules of undertakings or in rules governing the independent occupations and professions shall be, or may be declared, null and void or may be amended.'

11. The directive thus covers all collective agreements without distinction as to the nature of the legal effects which they do or do not produce. The reason for that generality lies in the fact that, even if they are not legally binding as between the parties who sign them or with regard to the employment relationships which they govern, collective agreements nevertheless have important *de facto* consequences for the employment relationships to which they refer, particularly in so far as they determine the rights of the workers and, in the interests of industrial harmony, give undertakings satisfy or need not satisfy. The need to ensure that the directive is completely effective therefore requires that any clauses in such agreements which are incompatible with the obligations imposed by the directive upon the Member States may be rendered inoperative, eliminated or amended by appropriate means.

The second complaint
12. According to the United Kingdom, the exclusions from the prohibition of discrimination provided for in section 6(3) of the 1975 Act in the case of employment in a private household or in undertakings where the number of persons employed does not exceed five are justified by the exception provided for in Article 2(2) of the directive itself, according to which:

> 'This directive shall be without prejudice to the right of Member States to exclude from its field of application those occupational activities and, where appropriate, the training leading thereto, for which, by reason of their nature or the context in which they are carried out, the sex of the worker constitutes a determining factor.'

13. It must be recognized that the provision of the 1975 Act in question is intended, in so far as it refers to employment in a private household, to reconcile the principle of equality of treatment with the principle of respect for private life, which is also fundamental. Reconciliation of that kind is one of the factors which must be taken into consideration in determining the scope of the exception provided for in Article 2(2) of the directive.

14. Whilst it is undeniable that, for certain kinds of employment in private households, that consideration may be decisive, that is not the case for all the kinds of employment in question.

15. As regards small undertakings with not more than five employees, the United Kingdom has not put forward any argument to show that in any undertaking of that size the sex of the worker would be a determing factor by reason of the nature of his activities or the context in which they are carried out.

16. Consequently, by reason of its generality, the exclusion provided for in the contested provision of the 1975 Act goes beyond the objective which

181

may be lawfully pursued within the framework of Article 2(2) of the directive.

The third complaint

17. The Commission's third complaint relates to the fact that the 1975 Act ensures access to the occupation of midwife and to training for that occupation only with certain limits. This is said to entail discrimination based on sex.

18. The United Kingdom acknowledges the facts. By virtue of paragraph (3) of Schedule 4 to the 1975 Act, until a day to be specified by order of the Secretary of State, men are granted access to the occupation in question and may be trained for that purpose only in certain specific places. This situation is due to the fact that in the United Kingdom the occupation in question is not traditionally engaged in by men. In a sphere in which respect for the patient's sensitivities is of particular importance, it considers that at the present time that limitation is in conformity with Article 2(2) of the directive. However, it adds that it intends to proceed by stages and keep the position under review, in accordance with the obligations imposed by Article 9(2) of the directive.

19. That provision requires Member States periodically to assess the occupational activities referred to in Article 2(2) in order to decide, in the light of social developments, whether there is justification for maintaining the permitted exclusions. They are to notify the Commission of the results of that assessment.

20. It is undeniable that in the area in question, as the United Kingdom acknowledges, the Member States are under an obligation to implement the principle of equality of treatment. It must however be recognized that at the present time personal sensitivies may play an important role in relations between midwife and patient. In those circumstances, it may be stated that by failing fully to apply the principle laid down in the directive, the United Kingdom has not exceeded the limits of the power granted to the Member States by Articles 9(2) and 2(2) of the directive. The Commission's complaint in that regard cannot therefore be upheld.

21. It is apparent from all the foregoing considerations that by failing to adopt in accordance with Directive 76/207 of 9 February 1976 the measures needed to ensure that any provisions contrary to the principle of equality of treatment contained in collective agreements or in the internal rules of undertakings or in the rules governing the independent professions or occupations are to be, or may be declared, void or be amended, and by excluding from the application of that principle employment for the purposes of a private household and any case where the number of persons employed does not exceed five, the United Kingdom has failed to fulfil its obligations under the Treaty.

22. In all other respects, the application is dismissed.

Costs

23. Under Article 69(2) of the Rules of Procedure, an unsuccessful party is to be ordered to pay the costs if they have been asked for in the successful party's pleadings. However, by virtue of paragraph (3) of the same article, the Court may order each party to bear its own costs if either of the parties is unsuccessful in one or more of its submissions.

24. It is appropriate to have recourse to that provision in this case, since the Commission has failed in one of its submissions.

For those reasons

THE COURT

1. **Declares that by failing to adopt in accordance with Directive 76/207 of 9 February 1976 the measures needed to ensure that any provisions contrary to the principle of equality of treatment contained in collective agreements or in the rules of undertakings or in the rules governing the independent professions and occupations are to be, or may be declared, void or may be amended, and by excluding from the application of that principle employment for the purposes of a private household and any case where the number of persons employed does not exceed five, the United Kingdom has failed to fulfil its obligations under the Treaty;**

2. **Dismisses the application in all other respects;**

3. **Orders each of the parties to bear its own costs.**

Mertens de Wilmars   Koopmans   Bahlmann   Galmot
Mackenzie Stuart   O'Keeffee   Bosco   Due   Everling

Delivered in open court in Luxembourg on 8 November 1983.

P. Heim   J. Mertens de Wilmars
Registrar   *President*

Judgment of the Court

21 May 1985 – Case 248/83

Commission of the European Communities
v.
Federal Republic of Germany

Failure of State fully to fulfil its obligations – equal treatment for men and women – Directives 76/207/EEC and 75/117/EEC of general application and apply to employment in the public service – general guarantees provided by Constitution and national system of judicial remedies constitute adequate implementation of equal treatment principle for those in public service and the independent professions without need for further legislation – right of Member States to exclude certain occupational activities from scope of Directive 76/207/EEC – duty of Member States to compile complete and verifiable list of any occupational activities they exclude from Directive's scope to enable Commission to carry out its supervisory functions – Directive imposes no obligation on Member States to enact general legislation concerning offers of employment (Council Directive 75/117/EEC; Council Directive 76/207/EEC, Articles 2(2) and 9(2)).

In Case 248/83

Commission of the European Communities, represented by its Legal Adviser, Manfred Beschel, acting as Agent, assisted by Professor Jürgen Schwarze of the University of Hamburg, with an address for service in Luxembourg at the office of Georges Kremlis, a member of the Commission's Legal Department, Jean Monnet Building, Kirchberg,

applicant,

v.

Federal Republic of Germany, represented by Martin Seidel, Ministerialrat im Bundesministerium für Wirtschaft [Ministerial Adviser at the Federal Ministry for Economic Affairs], acting as Agent, assisted by Jochim Sedemund of the Cologne Bar, with an address for service in Luxembourg at the Embassy of the Federal Republic of Germany,

defendant,

APPLICATION for a declaration that the Federal Republic of Germany has failed to fulfil its obligations under the EEC Treaty by not fully transposing into national law Council Directive No. 76/207/EEC of 9 February 1976 on the implementation of the principle of equal treatment for men and women as regards access to employment, vocational training and promotion, and working conditions and Council Directive No. 75/117/EEC of 10 February 1975 on the approximation of the laws of the Member States relating to the application of the principle of equal pay for men and women,

THE COURT

composed of: Lord Mackenzie Stuart, President, G. Bosco, O. Due and C. Kakouris (Presidents of Chambers), P. Pescatore, T. Koopmans, U. Everling, K. Bahlmann and Y. Galmot, Judges,

Advocate General: G. F. Mancini

Registrar: P. Heim

gives the following JUDGMENT

Decision

1. By application lodged at the Court Registry on 9 November 1983, the Commission of the European Communities brought an action before the Court under Article 169 of the EEC Treaty for a declaration that the Federal Republic of Germany has failed to fulfil its obligations under the EEC Treaty by not fully transposing into national law Council Directive No. 76/207/EEC of 9 February 1976 on the implementation of the principle of equal treatment for men and women as regards access to employment, vocational training and promotion, and working conditions (Official Journal 1976, No. L 39, p. 40) and Council Directive No. 75/117/EEC of 10 February 1975 on the approximation of the laws of the Member States relating to the application of the principle of equal pay for men and women (Official Journal 1975 No. L 45, p. 19).

Purpose and legal context of the action
2. It is clear from the documents in the case, and particularly from the letter of 15 January 1982 inviting the submission of observations and the reasoned opinion of 29 October 1982, that the Commission initiated the procedure under Article 169 after the entry into force in the Federal Republic of the Law of 13 August 1980 on equal treatment for men and women in the work place, the Arbeitsrechtliches EG-Anpassungsgesetz [Law aligning labour legislation with Community law] (BGBl 1980, I, p. 1308) The purpose of that law was, in particular, to insert a series of new paragraphs in Book 2, Title 6, of the German Civil Code which deals with contracts of service. Paragraph 611a provides that an employer may not place an employee at a disadvantage by reason of that person's sex on the occasion of the conclusion of a contract of employment or in matters of promotion or dismissal. The same paragraph provides, however, that different treatment is lawful where, for a professional or trade activity,

185

the sex of the employee is an indispensible prerequisite. Paragraph 611b provides that an employer may not advertise posts restricted either to men or to women except where, for the activity in question, the sex of the employee is an indispensible prerequisite. A new provision was added to Paragraph 612, according to which contracts of employment may not provide, in the case of the same work or work of equal value, for the payment to an employee of a remuneration that is lower, on grounds of sex, than that paid to an employee of the opposite sex.

3. It is apparent from the documents before the Court that the Commission charges the Federal Republic essentially with restricting the measures adopted for the implementation of the aforementioned directives to employment relationships governed by private law and, moreover, with failing to give adequate legal effect to a specific provision of the aforementioned law.

4. In those circumstances, the Commission has formulated five complaints against the Federal Republic which may be summarized as follows:
   1. Failure to transpose Directive No. 76/207 into national law as required, with regard to employment relationships in the public service;
   2. Failure to transpose Directive No. 76/207 into national law as required, with regard to the rules governing the independent professions;
   3. Failure to define as required the scope of the exceptions referred to in Article 2(2) of Directive No. 76/207;
   4. Failure to comply fully with Directive No. 76/207 when adopting the provisions concerning offers of employment laid down in Paragraph 611b of the Civil Code;
   5. Failure to transpose Directive No. 75/117 into national law as required, with regard to remuneration in the public service.
   It should be noted that a sixth complaint dealing with the maternity leave introduced by Paragraph 8b of the Mutterschutzgestez [German Law on Protection for Mothers] was withdrawn by the Commission following the judgment of the Court of 12 July 1984 in Case 184/83 (*Hofmann* v. *Barmer Ersatzkasse* [1984] ECR).

5. With a view to determining as accurately as possible the nature of the obligations which the Federal Republic has allegedly failed to fulfil, it is appropriate to recall the purpose and the general structure of the two directives on the basis of which Commission has instituted proceedings, in so far as their provisions are relevant to the dispute.

6. Article 1 of Directive No. 75/117, which defines the scope of the 'principle of equal pay', provides that that principle means, for the same work or for work to which equal value is attributed, the elimination of all discrimination on grounds of sex with regard to all aspects and conditions of remuneration. Article 2 requires the Member States to introduce into their national legal systems 'such measures as are necessary to enable all

employees who consider themselves wronged by failure to apply the principle of equal pay to pursue their claims by judicial process'. That provision is reinforced by Article 6 according to which the Member States are, in accordance with their national circumstances and legal systems, to take the measures necessary to ensure that the principle of equal pay is applied.

7. The structure of Directive No. 76/207 is similar to that of Directive No. 75/117. Article 1, together with Article 2(1) of Directive No. 76/207, defines the scope of the principle of equal treatment for men and women as meaning that 'there shall be no discrimination whatsoever on grounds of sex either directly or indirectly' as regards access to employment and working conditions. Article 2(2) provides that the directive is without prejudice to the right of the Member States to exclude from its field of application those occupational activities for which 'by reason of their nature or the context in which they are carried out, the sex of the worker constitutes a determining factor'. Article 2(3) provides that the directive is without prejudice to the provisions concerning the protection of women, particularly as regards pregnancy and maternity. It should be noted that the scope of the latter provision has in certain respects been defined more precisely by the Court in its aforemention judgment of 12 July 1984.

8. For the purpose of implementing the principle of equal treatment, the directive imposes two kinds of obligations on the Member States. Articles 3, 4 and 5 require the Member States to abolish all forms of discrimination both in their national legislation and in their administrative practices and to establish the necessary legislative machinery to ensure observance of the principle of equal treatment in collective agreements, individual contracts of employment and the rules governing the independent professions.

9. Article 6 requires the Member States to introduce into their national legal systems such measures as are necessary to enable all persons who consider themselves wronged by failure to apply to them the principle of equal treatment to pursue their claims by judicial process.

10. In that regard, it must be borne in mind that in its judgment of 10 April 1984, in Case 14/83 (*Von Colson and Kamann* v. *Land Nordrhein-Westfalen*, [1984] ECR 1891), the Court, in interpreting Directive No. 76/207, emphasized that:

> 'It is impossible to establish real equality of opportunity without an appropriate system of sanctions. That follows not only from the actual purpose of the directive but more specifically from Article 6 thereof which, by granting applicants for a post who have been discriminated against recourse to the courts, acknowledges that those candidates have rights of which they may avail

187

themselves before the courts. Although ... full implementation of the directive does not require any specific form of sanction for unlawful discrimination, it does entail that that sanction be such as to guarantee real and effective judicial protection.'

11. The five complaints formulated by the Commission must be examined in the light of those considerations.

The complaint of failure to apply the principle of equal treatment to the public service

12. The Federal Republic initially denied that Directive No. 76/207 was applicable to the public service (öffentlicher Dienst). Consequently, in its application the Commission dealth with that question first. In its view, Directive No. 76/207 is of general application, as is clear in particular from Article 3(1), which refers to 'all jobs or posts, whatever the sector or branch of activity'. Since employment relationships in the public service are thus within the scope of the directive, the Federal Republic has failed to adopt the legislative provisions needed to ensure that application of the principle of equal treatment in this area. The Commission recognizes that the principle is enshrined in the Basic Law of the Federal Republic of Germany but it considers that the provisions in question need to be given concrete form and to be implemented by ordinary legislation if they are to be effective in practice. In its view, only such legislation could have created the conditions of 'clarity and certainty in legal situations' which are necessary for the proper implementation of directives, as the Court stated in its judgment of 6 May 1980 in Case 102/79 (*Commission v. Belgium*, [1980] ECR 1473, paragraph 11 of the decision). Moreover, the Commission points out that the aforementioned constitutional provisions guarantee equal access and equal treatment for men and women as regards the public service but only subject to the "aptitude" of the applicants, which makes it possible to re-introduce conditions relating to sex. The same observations apply to the legislation concerning the public service. In its view, therefore, provision similar to those of the Law of 13 August 1980 should also have been adopted in relation to the public service.

13. In its defence, the Federal Republic of Germany reaffirms its reservation as regards the applicability of Directive No. 76/207 to the public service. It is clear, however, from the position which the Federal Republic subsequently took in its rejoinder and at the hearing, that the reservation has not in fact been maintained. As far as the substance of the problem is concerned, the Federal Republic contends that both the Basic Law and the legislation concerning the public service expressly guarantee equal access and equal treatment for men and women as regards the public service. Paragraphs (2) and (3) of Article 3 of the Basic Law accordingly provide that:

'(2) Men and women shall have equal rights.
(3) No one may be prejudiced or favoured because of his
sex ...'.

Furthermore, with regard to the public service, Article 33(2) of the Basic
Law provides that:

'(2) Every German shall be equally eligible for any public office
according to his aptitude, qualifications and professional achievements.'.

According to Article 1(3) of the Basic Law:

'(3) The following basic rights shall bind the legislature, the
executive and the judiciary as directly enforceable law.'.

14. Moreover, Paragraph 7 of the Beamtenrechtsrahmengesetz [Framework
Law on the Public Administration] of 1 July 1957 (BGBl I, p. 667, in the
version in force since 3 January 1977, BGBl I, p. 21) provides that:

'Appointments shall be made on the basis of professional aptitude, achievements and qualifications, without any distinction
on grounds of sex ...'.

Paragraph 8 of the Bundesbeàmtengesetz [Federal Law on Public
Servants] of 14 July 1953 (BGBl I, p. 551, in the version in force since
3 January 1977, BGBl I, p. 1) reads as follows:

'Applicants shall be chosen by competition. Selection shall be
on the basis of professional aptitude, qualifications and achievements, without any distinction on grounds of sex ...'.

15. The defendant maintains that all those provisions define rights which are
directly conferred on individuals and which give rise, where they are
infringed, to a right of action before the administrative courts and, if
necessary, before the Constitutional Court. Accordingly, to bring into
force legislative provisions pursuant to Directive No. 76/207 seemed to
be devoid of purpose, particularly as such legislation would merely have
restated the principles already embodied in the Constitution and in the
legislation concerning the public service. From that point of view, employment in the public service differs from employment governed by private
law since, as regards the latter, it was uncertain whether the constitutional
provisions on equal treatment for men and women were of such a nature
as to create direct rights between private individuals (Drittwirkung). In
order to remove that uncertainty, the competent authorities considered it
necessary to adopt the measures contained in the Law of 13 August 1980.

16. In view of the objection initially raised by the Federal Republic of Germany, it must be emphasized that both Directive No. 76/207 and Directive No. 75/117 apply to employment in the public service. Like Article 119 of the EEC Treaty, those directives are of general application, a factor which is inherent in the very nature of the principle which they law down. New cases of discrimination may not be created by exempting certain groups from the provisions intended to guarantee equal treatment for men and women in working life as a whole.

17. With regard to the substance of the problem, it should be noted in the first place that the Commission has not established, or even attempted to establish, that discrimination on grounds of sex exists, either in law or in fact, in the public service of the Federal Republic of Germany. In raising the question whether the constitutional and legislative provisions relied upon by the Federal Republic of Germany constitute an adequate safeguard against possible discrimination and whether Directive No. 76/207 required the adoption of further legislative provisions the Commission considered the problem exclusively in terms of the principles involved.

18. It may be stated in that regard that the categorical affirmation by the Basic Law of the equality of men and women before the law, and the express exclusion of all discrimination on grounds of sex and the guarantee of equal access to employment in the public service for all German nationals, in provisions that are intended be directly applicable, constitute, in conjunction with the existing system of judicial remedies, including the possibility of instituting proceedings before the constitutional Court, an adequate guarantee of the implementation, in the field of the public administration, of the principle of equal treatment laid down in Directive No. 76/207. The same guarantees are reiterated in the legislation concerning the public service, which expressly lays down that appointment to posts in the public service must be based on objective criteria, without any distinction on grounds of sex.

19. It follows that the object of Directive No. 76/207 had already been achieved in the Federal Republic of Germany as regards employment in the public service at the time when the directive entered into force, with the result that no further legislative provisions were required for its implementation.

20. The Commission points out, however, that both Article 33(2) of the Basic Law and the legislation on employment in the public service make access thereto subject to the 'aptitude' of the applicants, which makes it possible to re-introduce discrimination on grounds of sex. The Government of the Federal Republic of Germany contends in that regard that the reference to aptitude constitutes an objective criterion for the selection of applicants and that the principle that there must be no discrimination on grounds of sex also governs the application of that criterion.

21. In that connexion, it must be pointed out in the first place that the criterion of aptitude for office in the public service, as used in the Basic Law and in the legislation of the Federal Republic of Germany, covers a wide variety of criteria of assessment which, having regard to the broad range of duties performed by the public administration, are entirely unconnected with the question of a person's sex. Accordingly, the use of that criterion in the Basic Law and the legislation of the Federal Republic of Germany cannot be contested in principle.

22. The question to be resolved is therefore exclusively concerned with whether the criterion of aptitude, which is in itself an objective criterion, has been applied in practice in such a way as to lead to appointments to the public service based on sex discrimination. The onus was on the Commission to show that such a practice was followed in the German administration. However, it has not established that this was the case.

23. In the light of all the foregoing considerations, the first complaint must be rejected.

The complaint of failure to apply the principle of equal treatment to the independent professions

24. For the same reasons as those on which it relied with regard to employment in the public service, the Commission considers that the Federal Republic of Germany should, in the interests of clarity and certainty in legal situations, have adopted legislative measures to ensure the application of the principle of equal treatment laid down by Directive No. 76/207 in relation to the right to take up the independent professions, particularly as the rules governing those professions are expressly referred to in Articles 3, 4 and 5 of the directive. According to the Commission, the application of the provisions of the Basic Law alone does not create a sufficient degree of legal certainty in the case of the professions at issue. In those circumstances, the Commission fails to understand why the legislation adopted to implement the directive was limited to employment relationships and was not extended to the activities carried on by self-employed persons. As an example of discrimination in this area, the Commission refers to the occupation of midwife, which, it maintains, is still not entirely open to men.

25. The Federal Republic of Germany denies that charge on the ground that the relevant provisions of the Basic Law constitute an adequate safeguard against sex discrimination also in the case of the independent professions. In addition to the general provisions already mentioned, which are concerned with the equality of men and women before the law and with the abolition of sex discrimination, the Government of the Federal Republic draws attention to Article 12(1) of the Basic Law, which provides as follows:

'(1) All Germans shall have the right freely to choose their trade, occupation or profession, their place of work and their place of training.'.

26. According to the Government of the Federal Republic of Germany, the relevant constitutional provisions are directly applicable in this area in view of the fact that, in so far as the right to take up an independent profession is subject to an admission procedure, admission is in the nature of an administrative measure adopted by a body governed by public law. Consequently, the principle laid down in Article 1(3) of the Basic Law applies without exception to the rules governing the various independent professions, in accordance with the requirements of the directive. Examination of the rules governing each of the various professions concerned reveals the absence in the Federal Republic of any provisions which are contrary to the requirements of the directive. Admission to all the independent professions is therefore open to persons of either sex, provided that they possess the required professional qualifications.

27. With regard to the occupation of midwife, in particular, the Government of the Federal Republic of Germany states that access to the appropriate training was extended to men with effect from 1 January 1983 as a result of the adoption of the Ausbildungs- und Prüfungsordnung für Hebammen [Rules Governing the Training and Examination of Midwives] of 3 September 1981 (BGBl I, p. 923). Consequently, the Hebammengesetz [Law on the Pursuit of the Occupation of Midwife] of 21 December 1938 (RGBL I, p. 1893) is under review. Such action on the part of the authorities of the Federal Republic corresponds fully with action of the kind which the Court held to be compatible with the directive in its judgment of 8 November 1983 in Case 165/82 (*Commission* v. *United Kingdom*, [1983] ECR 3431).

28. It should be noted that during the proceedings, the Commission indicated that it did not attach much importance to the question of midwives, which it cited only by way of illustration and which was not in reality the subject of the application.

29. Having regard to that clarification, it must be stated, as with the first complaint, that the Commission has produced no evidence from which it may be inferred that the rules governing the independent professions in the Federal Republic of Germany actually give rise to discrimination. This charge was included in the application as a matter of principle, as was the preceding charge, since the Commission considered that the existing legal situation did not provide sufficient clarity and certainty for legal purposes to satisfy the requirements of the directive.

30. For the reasons already given in connexion with the first complaint, this head of the application also appears to be unfounded. In view of the

guarantees provided by the Basic Law and by the existing system of judicial remedies as regards the freedom for all German nationals to take up an independent profession, subject only to the possession of qualifications that are objectively determined without any reference to sex, it must be held that, as far as the rules governing the independent professions are concerned, the object of Directive No. 76/207 had already been achieved in the Federal Republic of Germany at the time when that directive came into force, with the result that no further legislative measures were required for its implementation.

31. Therefore this complaint must also be rejected.

The complaint of failure to define the scope of the exceptions provided for in Article 2(2) of Directive No. 76/207

32. In its third complaint, the Commission charges the Federal Republic of Germany with failing to implement the provisions of Article 2(2) and Article 9(2) of Directive No. 76/207 regarding occupational activities which may be excluded from the scope of the principle of equal treatment by reason of their nature or the context in which they are carried on. It is not clear from the application whether the Commission requires those exceptions to be legally determined or whether a list or a catalogue of such exceptions is to be established by other means. In any event, the Commission considers that Paragraph 611a of the Civil Code, which makes it possible to derogate from the principle of equal treatment where a person's sex constitutes a condition for carrying on a given occupational activity, is inadequate since that provision does not contain a catalogue setting out precisely the exceptions permitted. Moreover, the Federal Republic is charged with failing to create an adequate basis for enabling the Commission to exercise the right of supervision which is conferred upon it by Article 9(2) of Directive No. 76/207. The Commission points out that a study of comparative law shows that most of the other Member States have embodied in legislation the exceptions which they consider justified under Article 2(2) of the directive.

33. The Federal Republic of Germany denies that charge on the ground that Article 2(2) of Directive No. 76/207 does not contain any indication which suggests that the Member States are obliged to determine exhaustively by way of legislation the exceptions permitted by that provision. It considers that the relevant provision embodied in Paragraph 611a of the Civil Code fully satisfies the requirements of the directive. The existence of a list established by law is not essential for the exercise by the Commission of its right of supervision. Moreover, the requirement laid down by the Commission is impracticable since the occupational activities excluded from the scope of the principle of equal treatment by Article 2(2) of the directive are largely the result of specific prohibitions of access to certain posts, which are laid down for the purpose of providing protection related to the nature of the activity carried on, in accordance with the provisions

of Article 2(3). Finally, the Federal Republic casts doubt on the Commission's statements regarding the implementation of the directive by other Member States, particularly as it is uncertain whether the provisions enacted by those States were adopted in pursuance of a legal obligation or in the exercise of their discretion.

34. In order to clarify that aspect of the dispute, the Court requested the Commission to provide it with a summary of the results of its investigation as to the implementation of Article 2(2) of Directive No. 76/207 by the various Member States and to indicate whether, on the basis of that information, it had been able to draw up a list of the occupational activities exempted by the aforementioned provision which was valid for the whole Community. The Commission did not reply to that question. It is clear from the information which it supplied concerning the practice followed by the Member States that, although the laws and practices of the various States are similar with regard to certain clearly-defined occupations (such as singing, acting, dancing and artistic or fashion modelling), the Member States maintain a wide variety of other exceptions based on social, moral or, in certain cases, religious considerations, that a substantial number of those exceptions are based on considerations relating to the physical and moral protection of women and, finally, that certain important exemptions are bound up with the question of military service and the organization of the police and similar bodies. The basis for the exemptions is also variable, inasmuch as some owe their existence to voluntary and unwritten customs, others to provisions laid down by law or regulation, and others still to international conventions. Finally, it has become apparent that the provisions of certain Member States are limited to general clauses similar to Article 2(2) of Directive No. 76/207. The Commission has pointed out that it intends to take action against several Member States for failure to fulfil their obligations.

35. In order to determine the scope of the Commission's complaint and the grounds on which it is based, it is necessary to refer first of all to the relevant provisions of Directive No. 76/207. Article 2(2) provides that:

> 'This directive shall be without prejudice to the right of Member States to exclude from its field of application those occupational activities and, where appropriate, the training leading thereto, for which, by reason of their nature or the context in which they are carried out, the sex of the worker constitutes a determining factor.'.

Article 2(3) provides that:

> 'This directive shall be without prejudice to provisions concerning the protection of women, particularly as regards pregnancy and maternity.'.

194

Article 9(2) provides as follows.

'Member States shall periodically assess the occupation activities referred to in Article 2(2) in order to decide, in the light of social developments, whether there is justification for maintaining the exclusions concerned. They shall notify the Commission of the results of this assessment.'.

36. It must be pointed out in the first place that the purpose of Article 2(2) is not to oblige but to permit the Member States to exclude certain occupational activities from the field of application of the directive. That provision does not have as its object or as its effect to require the Member States to exercise that power of derogation in a particular manner, especially since, as is clear from the study of comparative law submitted by the Commission, the exceptions in question serve widely differing purposes and several of them are closely linked to the rules governing certain occupations or activities.

37. However, it is necessary to ascertain what obligations Article 9(2) of the directive imposes on the Member States. That provision provides for supervision in two stages, namely a periodic assessment by the Member States themselves of the justification for maintaining exceptions to the principle of equal treatment, and supervision by the Commission based on the notification of the results of that assessment. That twofold supervision serves to eliminate progressively existing exceptions which no longer appear justified, having regard to the criteria laid down in Article 2(2) and (3).

38. It follows from those provisions that it is primarily for the Member States to compile a complete and verifiable list, in whatever form, of the occupations and activities excluded from the application of the principle of equal treatment and to notify the results to the Commission. For its part, the Commission has the right and the duty, by virtue of the powers conferred on it by Article 155 of the EEC Treaty, to adopt the measures necessary to verify the application of that provision of the directive.

39. It became apparent during the proceedings that at no time since the entry into force of the directive has the Federal Republic of Germany adopted the necessary measures to create even a minimum of transparency with regard to the application of Article 2(2) and (3) and Article 9 of Directive No. 76/207. The Federal Republic has thus prevented the Commission from exercising effective supervision and has made it more difficult for any persons wronged by discriminatory measures to defend their rights.

40. It must therefore be held that, by failing to take the measures necessary to implement Article 9(2) of Directive No. 76/207, in relation to the occupational activities excluded from the scope of the principle of equal

treatment by virtue of Article 2(2) of that directive, the Federal Republic of Germany has failed to fulfil its obligations under the EEC Treaty.

The complaint of failure to give legal effect to the provisions concerning offers of employment

41. This complaint is concerned with Paragraph 611a of the Civil Code, according to which an employer may not advertise offers of employment which are not 'impartial' as regards the sex of the employees. The Commission considers that, since offers of employment precede access to employment, they come within the scope of Directive No. 76/207. It charges the Federal Republic of Germany with failing to make Paragraph 611a a binding provision. It considers that the choice of the contested provision, which has no legal effect, does not satisfy the requirement laid down in Article 6 of the directive to the effect that persons who consider themselves wronged by failure to apply the principle of equal treatment to them must be able to pursue their claims by judicial process.

42. The Federal Republic of Germany refutes that charge on the ground that, since offers of employment merely precede access to employment, they do not come within the scope of the directive. It points out that none of the provisions of the directive refers to offers of employment. In its view, it is only at the stage of access to employment that the directive comes into operation, that obligations are imposed on the Member States and that persons seeking employment can assert their right to equal treatment. The Federal Republic cannot therefore be criticized for enacting Paragraph 611a of the Civil Code as a non-binding rule.

43. In response to that argument, it must be observed first of all that offers of employment cannot be excluded *a priori* from the scope of Directive No. 76/207, inasmuch as they are closely connected with access to employment and can have a restrictive effect thereon. It must also be recognized, however, that the directive imposes no obligation on the Member States to enact general legislation concerning offers of employment, particularly as this question is in turn closely linked to that of the exceptions permitted by Article 2(2) of the directive, given that the application of Article 9(2) in full will have the effect of creating the necessary transparency also as regards offers of employment.

44. Consequently, Paragraph 611a of the German Civil Code cannot be regarded as implementing an obligation imposed by Directive No. 76/207 but must be treated as an independent legislative measure adopted for the purpose of giving effect to the principle of equal treatment.

45. This complaint must therefore be rejected.

The complaint of failure to transpose Directive No. 75/117 into national law with regard to remuneration in the public service

46. Finally, the Commission charges the Federal Republic of Germany with failing to transpose into national law the provisions of Directive No. 75/117 concerning equal pay for male and female public servants. The Commission therefore considers that the legislation of the Federal Republic in this area also lacks the legal clarity which is essential for effective implementation of the directive.

47. The Government of the Federal Republic of Germany has linked its arguments on this point to those which it put forward in connexion with the first complaint. It contends, in particular, that the remuneration of public servants and judges is determined according to post and grade, without reference to the sex of the officials concerned.

48. That argument must be upheld. The Commission has not been able to produce the slightest evidence of sex discrimination with regard to the remuneration of public servants in the Federal Republic of Germany; such remuneration is, as the defendant has correctly explained, based exclusively on post and grade, regardless of the sex of the officials concerned.

49. Thus it would appear that in that respect the object of Directive No. 75/117 had already been achieved in the Federal Republic of Germany at the time when that directive entered into force, with the result that no specific measure was required for its implementation.

50. Therefore this complaint must also be rejected.

51. It follows from the foregoing considerations that the Commission's application must be dismissed as regards the first, second, fourth and fifth complaints, but with regard to the third complaint, it must be held that the Federal Republic has failed to fulfil its obligations under the Treaty.

Costs
52. Under Article 69(2) of the Rules of Procedure the unsuccessful party is to be ordered to pay the costs. Since the Commission has largely failed in its submissions it must be ordered to pay the costs.

On those grounds,

THE COURT

hereby:

1. Declares that, by failing to adopt the measures necessary to apply Article 9(2) of Council Directive No. 76/207/EEC of 9 February 1976 on the implementation of the principle of equal treatment for men and women as regards access to employment, vocational training and promotion, and working

conditions, in relation to the occupational activities excluded from the scope of that principle by virtue of Article 2(2) of the same directive, the Federal Republic of Germany has failed to fulfil its obligations under the EEC Treaty;

2. For the rest, dismisses the application;

3. Orders the Commission to pay the costs.

Mackenzie Stuart   Bosco   Due   Kakouris

Pescatore   Koopmans   Everling   Bahlmann

Galmot

Delivered in open court in Luxembourg on 21 May 1985.

P. Heim   A. J. Mackenzie Stuart
Registrar   *President*

(b) Preliminary rulings under Article 177, EEC Treaty

Judgment of the Court

16 February 1982 – Case 19/81

Arthur Burton
v.
British Railways Board

Equal treatment for men and women – equal treatment principle in Article 5, Council Directive 76/207/EEC, on access to working conditions applies to conditions of access to voluntary redundancy benefits paid by employer to worker wishing to leave his employment – where access to voluntary redundancy available only in five years before minimum pensionable age set by national social security legislation, fact that minimum age is different for men and women does not in itself constitute discrimination within meaning of Article 5, Directive 76/207/EEC – determination of minimum pensionable age for social security purposes which is not the same for men and women is not discrimination prohibited by Community law (Council Directive 76/207/EEC, Article 5; Council Directive 79/7/EEC, Article 7).

In Case 19/81

REFERENCE to the Court under Article 177 of the EEC Treaty by the Employment Appeal Tribunal for a preliminary ruling in the action pending before that court between

Arthur Burton

and

British Railways Board

on the interpretation of Article 119 of the Treaty and Article 1 of Council Directive 75/117/EEC of 10 February 1975 on the approximation of the laws of the Member States relating to the application of the principle of equal pay for men and women (Official Journal L 45, p. 19) and Articles 1(1), 2(1) and 5(1) of Council Directive 76/207/EEC of 9 February 1976 on the implementation of the principle of equal treatment for men and women as regards access to employment, vocational training and promotion, and working conditions (Official Journal L 39, p. 40), with regard to payment of a voluntary redundancy benefit,

THE COURT

composed of: G. Bosco, President of the First Chamber, acting as President, A. Touffait and O. Due (Presidents of Chambers), P. Pescatore, Lord Mackenzie Stuart, A. O'Keeffe, T. Koopmans, A. Chloros and F. Grévisse, Judges,

Advocate General: P. VerLoren van Themaat
Registrar: A. van Houtte

gives the following JUDGMENT

Decision

1. By an order of 16 January 1981 which was received at the Court on 4 February 1981 the Employment Appeal Tribunal referred to the Court for a preliminary ruling under Article 177 of the EEC Treaty three questions concerning the interpretation, with regard to payment of voluntary redundancy benefit, of Article 119 of the Treaty, Article 1 of Council Directive 75/117/EEC of 10 February 1975 on the approximation of the laws of the Member States relating to the application of the principle of equal pay for men and women (Official Journal L 45, p. 19) and Articles 1(1), 2(1) and 5(1) of Council Directive 76/207/EEC of 9 February 1976 on the implementation of the principle of equal treatment for men and women as regards access to employment, vocational training and promotion, and working conditions (Official Journal L 39, p. 40).

2. According to the case-file Mr Burton, the plaintiff in the main action, is an employee of the British Railways Board (hereinafter referred to as 'the Board'), a body established by the Transport Act 1962 and responsible for operating the railway system in Great Britain.

199

3. As a result of an internal reorganization the Board made an offer of voluntary redundancy to some of its employees. A memorandum was drawn up embodying the terms of a collective agreement between management and the recognized trade unions on the terms on which certain aspects of the reorganization were to be carried out. Paragraph 6 of the memorandum provides as follows:

> 'Staff aged 60/55 (Male/Female) may leave the service under the Redundancy and Resettlement arrangements when the Function in which [they are] employed has been dealt with under Organization Planning.'.

4. In August 1979 Mr Burton applied for voluntary redundancy but his application was rejected on the ground that he was under the minimum age of 60 specified for male employees by the above-mentioned memorandum. Mr Burton therefore claimed that he was treated less favourably than female employees inasmuch as the benefit would have been granted to a woman of his age (58).

5. After the rejection of his application Mr Burton complained to an Industrial Tribunal under the provisions of the Equal Pay Act 1970, as last amended by the Sex Discrimination Act 1975. The Industrial Tribunal rejected Mr Burton's claim and he appealed to the Employment Appeal Tribunal. In the course of the appeal it was conceded on his behalf that by virtue of section 6 (4) of the Sex Discrimination Act 1975 it is not contrary to the Act for an employer to treat a male employee less favourably than he treats a female employee as regards access to voluntary redundancy benefit. However, Mr Burton contended that section 6(4) must be construed as subject to the enforceable Community rights conferred by Article 119 of the Treaty, Article 1 of Directive 75/117 on equal pay and Articles 1, 2, and 5 of Directive 76/207 on equal treatment.

6. In order to resolve the issue the Employment Appeal Tribunal referred to the Court three questions worded as follows:

> '(1) Is a voluntary redundancy benefit, which is paid by an employer to a worker wishing to leave his employment, within the scope of the principle of equal pay contained in Article 119 of the EEC Treaty and Article 1 of Council Directive 75/117/EEC of 10 February 1975?
> (2) If the answer to Question (1) is in the affirmative, does the principle of equal pay have direct effect in Member States so as to confer enforceable Community rights upon individuals in the circumstances of the present case?
> (3) If the answer to Question (1) is in the negative:
>   (i) is such a voluntary redundancy benefit within the scope of the principle of equal treatment for men and women

as regards 'working conditions' contained in Article 1(1), Article 2(1) and Article 5(1) of Council Directive 76/207/EEC of 9 February 1976?

(ii) if so, does the said principle have direct effect in Member States so as to confer enforceable Community rights upon individuals in the circumstances of the present case?'

7. The principal issue raised by those questions is whether the requirement that a male worker should have reached the age of 60 in order to be eligible for payment of a voluntary redundancy benefit whereas women workers become eligible at the age of 55 amounts to discrimination prohibited by Article 119 of the Treaty or by Article 1 of Directive 75/117 or, at least, by Directive 76/207 and, if so, whether the relevant provision of Community law may be relied upon in the national courts.

8. Consequently the question of interpretation which has been referred to the Court concerns not the benefit itself, but whether the conditions of access to the voluntary redundancy scheme are discriminatory. That is a matter covered by the provisions of Directive 76/207 to which reference was made by the national court, and no by those of Article 119 of the Treaty or Directive 75/117.

9. According to Article 5(1) of Directive 76/207 application of the principle of equal treatment with regard to working conditions, including the conditions governing dismissal, means that men and women are to be guaranteed the same conditions without discrimination on grounds of sex. In the context of the directive the word "dismissal" must be widely construed so as to include termination of the employment relationship between a worker and his employer, even as part of a voluntary redundancy scheme.

10. In deciding whether the difference in treatment of which the plaintiff in the main action complains is discriminatory within the meaning of that directive account must be taken of the relationship between measures such as that at issue and national provisions on normal retirement age.

11. Under United Kingdom legislation the minimum qualifying age for a State retirement pension is 60 for women and 65 for men.

12. From the information supplied by the United Kingdom Government in the course of the proceedings it appears that a worker who is permitted by the Board to take voluntary early retirement must do so within the five years preceding the normal minimum age of retirement, and that he may receive the following benefits: (1) the lump sum calculated in accordance with the provisions of the Redundancy Payments Act 1965, (2) a lump sum calculated on the basis of the total length of his employment with

the Board, and (3) 25 per cent of the sum of the first two amounts. In addition he is entitled up to the minimum retiring age to an early retirement pension equal to the pension to which he would have been entitled had he attained the minimum statutory retirement age and to an advance, repayable at the minimum retiring age, equal to the sum to which he becomes entitled at that age.

13. Council Directive 79/7/EEC of 19 December 1978 on the progressive implementation of the principle of equal treatment for men and women in matters of social security (Official Journal 1979, L 6, p. 24), which was adopted with particular reference to Article 235 of the Treaty, provides in Article 7 that the directive shall be without prejudice to the right of Member States to exclude from its scope the determination of pensionable age for the purposes of granting old-age and retirement pensions and the possible consequences thereof for other benefits.

14. It follows that the determination of a minimum pensionable age for social security purposes which is not the same for men as for women does not amount to discrimination prohibited by Community law.

15. The option given to workers by the provisions at issue in the present instance is tied to the retirement scheme governed by United Kingdom social security provisions. It enables a worker who leaves his employment at any time during the five years before he reaches normal pensionable age to receive certain allowances for a limited period. The allowances are calculated in the same manner regardless of the sex of the worker. The only difference between the benefits for men and those for women stems from the fact that the minimum pensionable age under the national legislation is not the same for men as for women.

16. In the circumstances the different age conditions for men and women with regard to access to voluntary redundancy cannot be regarded as discrimination within the meaning of Directive 76/207.

17. In the light of that answer to the first part of the third question it is not necessary to give a reply to the second part.

18. The answers to be given to the questions which have been raised by the Employment Appeal Tribunal are therefore as follows:

'1. The principle of equal treatment contained in Article 5 of Council Directive 76/207 of 9 February 1976 applies to the conditions of access to voluntary redundancy benefit paid by an employer to a worker wishing to leave his employment.
2. The fact that access to voluntary redundancy is available only during the five years preceding the minimum pensionable age fixed by national social security legislation and that

that age is not the same for men as for women cannot in itself be regarded as discrimination on grounds of sex within the meaning of Article 5 of Directive 76/207.'.

Costs

19. The costs incurred by the Government of the United Kingdom, the Government of the Kingdom of Denmark and the Commission of the European Communities, which have submitted observations to the Court, are not recoverable. As the proceedings are, in so far as the parties to the main action are concerned, in the nature of a step in the proceedings before the national court, the decision as to costs is a matter for that court.

On those grounds,

THE COURT

in answer to the questions referred to it by the Employment Appeal Tribunal by order of 16 January 1981, hereby rules:

1. **The principle of equal treatment contained in Article 5 of Council Directive 76/207 of 9 February 1976 (Official Journal L 39, p. 40) applies to the conditions of access to voluntary redundancy benefit paid by an employer to a worker wishing to leave his employment.**

2. **The fact that access to voluntary redundancy is available only during the five years preceding the minimum pensionable age fixed by national social security legislation and that that age is not the same for men as for women cannot in itself be regarded as discrimination on grounds of sex within the meaning of Article 5 of Directive 76/207.**

Bosco   Touffait   Due   Pescatore   Mackenzie Stuart
      O'Keeffe   Koopmans   Chloros   Grévisse

Delivered in open court in Luxembourg on 16 February 1982.

P. Heim   G. Bosco
Registrar   *President of the First Chamber,*
                                                              acting as President

Judgment of the Court

10 April 1984 – Case 14/83

Sabine von Colson and Elisabeth Kamann
v.
Land Nordrhein-Westfalen

Equal treatment for men and women – Member States free to choose ways and means of achieving result envisaged by a Directive, but must adopt measures which ensure Directive is fully effective – Directive 76/207/EEC does not require discrimination on grounds of sex regarding access to employment to be made the subject of a sanction requiring employer who has discriminated to conclude contract of employment with candidate discriminated against – Directive 76/207/EEC does not include any unconditional and sufficiently precise obligation which, in absence of national implementing measures adopted within set time limits, may be relied on by individuals to obtain specific compensation where that is not provided for under national law – a Member State is free to choose appropriate sanctions for breach of discrimination prohibition – if it chooses to penalise such breach by award of compensation, that compensation must be adequate in relation to damage sustained and amount to more than purely nominal compensation in order to be effective and have a deterrent effect – a national court should interpret and apply legislation adopted to implement Directive in accordance with requirements of Community law, so far as it is given discretion to do so under national law (EEC Treaty, Articles 5 and 189; Council Directive 76/207/EEC).

In Case 14/83

REFERENCE to the Court under Article 177 of the EEC Treaty by the Arbeitsgericht [Labour Court] Hamm for a preliminary ruling in the action pending before that court between

Sabine von Colson and Elisabeth Kamann

and

Land Nordrhein-Westfalen [North-Rhine Westphalia],

on the interpretation of Council Directive No 76/207/EEC of 9 February 1976 on the implementation of the principle of equal treatment for men and women as regard access to employment, vocational training and promotion, and working conditions (Official Journal 1976, L 39, p. 40).

THE COURT

composed of: J. Mertens de Wilmars, President, T. Koopmans, K. Bahlmann and Y. Galmot, Presidents of Chambers, P. Pescatore, Lord Mackenzie Stuart, A. O'Keeffe, G. Bosco, O. Due, U. Everling and C. Kakouris, Judges,

Advocate General: S. Rozès
Registrar: H. A. Rühl, Principal Administrator

gives the following JUDGMENT

Decision

1. By order of 6 December 1982, which was received at the Court on 24 January 1983, the Arbeitsgericht [Labour Court] Hamm referred to the Court for a preliminary ruling pursuant to Article 177 of the EEC Treaty several questions on the interpretation of Council Directive No. 76/207/EEC of 9 February 1976 on the implementation of the principle of equal treatment for men and women as regards access to employment, vocational training and promotion, and working conditions (Official Journal 1976, L 39, p. 40).

2. Those questions were raised in the course of proceedings between two qualified social workers, Sabine von Colson and Elisabeth Kamann, and the Land Nordrhein-Westfalen. It appears from the grounds of the order for reference that Werl prison, which caters exclusively for male prisoners and which is administered by the Land Nordrhein-Westfalen, refused to engage the plaintiffs in the main proceedings for reasons relating to their sex. The officials responsible for recruitment justified their refusal to engage the plaintiffs by citing the problems and risks connected with the appointment of female candidates and for those reasons appointed instead male candidates who were however less well-qualified.

3. The Arbeitsgericht Hamm held that there had been discrimination and took the view that under German law the only sanction for discrimination in recruitment is compensation for 'Vertrauensschaden', namely the loss incurred by candidates who are victims of discrimination as a result of their belief that their would be no discrimination in the establishment of the employment relationship. Such compensation is provided for under Paragraph 611a(2) of the Bürgerliches Gesetzbuch.

4. Under that provision, in the event of discrimination regarding access to employment, the employer is liable for 'damages in respect of the loss incurred by the worker as a result of his reliance on the expectation that the establishment of the employment relationship would not be precluded by such a breach [of the principle of equal treatment]'. That provision purports to implement Council Directive No. 76/207.

5. Consequently the Arbeitsgericht found that, under German law, it could order the reimbursement only of the travel expenses incurred by the

plaintiff von Colson in pursuing her application for the post (DM 7.20) and that it could not allow the plaintiffs' other claims.

6. However, in order to determine the rules of Community law applicable in the event of discrimination regarding access to employment, the Arbeitsgericht referred the following questions to the Court of Justice:

'1. Does Council Directive No. 76/207/EEC of 9 February 1976 on the implementation of the principle of equal treatment for men and women as regards access to employment, vocational training and promotion, and working conditions imply that discrimination on grounds of sex in relation to access to employment (failure to conclude a contract of employment on account of the candidate's sex; preference given to another candidate on account of his sex) must be sanctioned by requiring the employer in question to conclude a contract of employment with the candidate who was discriminated against?

2. If Question 1 is answered in the affirmative, in principle:
    (a) Is the employer required to conclude a contract of employment only if, in addition to the finding that he made a subjective decision on the basis of criteria relating to sex, it can be established that the candidate discriminated against is objectively – according to acceptable selection criteria – better qualified for the post than the candidate with whom a contract of employment was concluded?
    (b) Or, is the employer also required to engage the candidate discriminated against if, although it can be established that the employer made a subjective decision on the basis of criteria relating to sex, the candidate discriminated against and the successful candidate are objectively equally well qualified?
    (c) Finally, does the candidate discriminated against have the right to be engaged even if objectively he is less well qualified than the successful candidate, but it is established that from the outset the employer, on account of the sex of the candidate discriminated against, disregarded that candidate in making his decision on the basis of acceptable criteria?

3. If the essential issue is the objective assessment of the candidate's qualifications within the meaning of Questions 2(a), (b) and (c):
    Is that issue to be decided wholly by the court and what criteria and procedural rules relating to evidence and burden of proof are applicable in that regard?

4. If Question 1 is answered in the affirmative, in principle:

where there are more than two candidates for a post and from the outset more than one person is on the ground of sex disregarded for the purposes of the decision made on the basis of acceptable criteria, is each of those persons entitled to be offered a contract of employment?

Is the court in such a case obliged to make its own choice between the candidates discriminated against?

If the question contained in the first paragraph is answered in the negative, what other sanction of substantive law is available?

5. If Question 1 is answered in the negative, in principle:
Under the provisions of Directive No. 76/207/EEC what sanction applies where there is an established case of discrimination in relation to access to employment?

In that regard must a distinction be drawn between the situations described in Question 2(a), (b) and (c)?

6. Does Directive No. 76/207/EEC as interpreted by the Court of Justice in its answers to the questions set out above constitute directly applicable law in the Federal Republic of Germany?'

7. Those questions are intended primarily to establish whether Directive No. 76/207 requires Member States to lay down legal consequences or specific sanctions in the event of discrimination regarding access to employment (Questions 1 to 5) and whether individuals may, where appropriate, rely on the provisions of the directive before the national courts where the directive has not been transposed into the national legal order within the periods prescribed (Question 6).

(a) Question 1

8. In its first question the Arbeitsgericht asks essentially whether Directive No. 76/207 requires discrimination on grounds of sex in the matter of access to employment to be penalized by an obligation, imposed on an employer who is guilty of discrimination to conclude a contract of employment with the candidate who was the victim of discrimination.

9. According to the Arbeitsgericht, it is clear from the recitals in the preamble to and from the actual provisions of the directive that the directive requires Member States to adopt legal provisions which provide effective sanctions. In its view only compensation in kind, entailing, the appointment of the persons who were the victims of discrimination, is effective.

10. According to the plaintiffs in the main action, by restricting the right to compensation solely to 'Vertrauensschaden', Paragraph 611a(2) of the Bürgerliches Gesetzbuch excluded the possibilities of compensation afforded by the general rules of law. Directive No. 76/207 requires

207

Member States to introduce appropriate measures with a view to avoiding discrimination in the future. It should, therefore, be accepted that Paragraph 611a(2) must be left out of account. The result of that would be that the employer would be required to conclude a contract of employment with the candidate discriminated against.

11. The Government of the Federal Republic of Germany is aware of the need for an effective transposition of the directive but stresses the fact that, under the third paragraph of Article 189 of the EEC Treaty, each Member States has a margin of discretion as regards the legal consequences which must result from a breach of the principle of equal treatment. The German Government submits, moreover, that it is possible for the German courts to work out, on the basis of private national law and in conformity with the substance of the directive, adequate solutions which satisfy both the principle of equal treatment and the interests of all the parties. Finally an appreciable legal consequence is in its view sufficient to ensure compliance with the principle of equal treatment and that consequence should follow only if the victim of discrimination was better qualified for the post than the other candidates; it should not apply where the candidates' qualifications were equal.

12. The Danish Government considers that the directive deliberately left to Member States the choice of sanctions, in accordance with their national circumstances and legal systems. Member States should penalize breaches of the principle of equal treatment in the same way as they penalize similar breaches of national rules in related areas not governed by Community law.

13. The United Kingdom is also of the opinion that it is for Member States to choose the measures which they consider appropriate to ensure the fulfilment of their obligations under the directive. The directive gives no indication as to the measures which Member States should adopt and the questions referred to the Court themselves clearly illustrate the difficulties encountered in laying down appropriate measures.

14. The Commission considers that although the directive is intended to leave to Member States the choice and the determination of the sanctions, the transposition of the directive must nevertheless produce effective results. The principle of the effective transposition of the directive requires that the sanctions must be of such a nature as to constitute appropriate compensation for the candidate discriminated against and for the employer a means of pressure which it would be unwise to disregard and which would prompt him to respect the principle of equal treatment. A national measure which provides for compensation only for losses actually incurred through reliance on a expectation ('Vertrauensschaden') is not sufficient to ensure compliance with that principle.

15. According to the third paragraph of Article 189: 'A directive shall be binding, as to the result to be achieved, upon each Member State to which it is addressed, but shall leave to the national authorities the choice of form and methods'. Although that provision leaves Member States to choose the ways and means of ensuring that the directive is implemented, that freedom does not affect the obligation imposed on all the Member States to which the directive is addressed, to adopt, in their national legal systems, all the measures necessary to ensure that the directive is fully effective, in accordance with the objective which it pursues.

16. It is therefore necessary to examine Directive No. 76/207 in order to determine whether it requires Member States to provide for specific legal consequences or sanctions in respect of a breach of the principle of equal treatment regarding access to employment.

17. The object of that directive is to implement in the Member States the principle of equal treatment for men and women, in particular by giving male and female real equality of opportunity as regards access to employment. With that end in view, Article 2 defines the principle of equal treatment and its limits, while Article 3(1) sets out the scope of the principle specifically as regards access to employment. Article 3(2)(a) provides that Member States are to take the measures necessary to ensure that any laws, regulations and administrative provisions contrary to the principle of equal treatment are abolished.

18. Article 6 requires Member States to introduce into their national legal systems such measures as are necessary to enable all persons who consider themselves wronged by discrimination 'to pursue their claims by judicial process'. It follows from the provision that Member States are required to adopt measures which are sufficiently effective to achieve the objective of the directive and to ensure that those measures may in fact be relied on before the national courts by the persons concerned. Such measures may include, for example, provisions requiring the employer to offer a post to the candidate discriminated against or giving the candidate adequate financial compensation, backed up where necessary by a system of fines. However the directive does not prescribe a specific sanction; it leaves Member States free to choose between the different solutions suitable for achieving its objective.

19. The reply to the first question should therefore be that Directive No. 76/207 does not require discrimination on grounds of sex regarding access to employment to be made the subject of a sanction by way of an obligation imposed upon the employer who is the author of the discrimination to conclude a contract of employment with the candidate discriminated against.

(b) Questions 2, 3 and 4

20. It is not necessary to answer the second, third and fourth questions since they are put only on the supposition that an employer is required to offer a post to the candidate discriminated against.

(c) Questions 5 and 6

21. In its fifth question the Arbeitsgericht essentially asks whether it is possible to infer from the directive any sanction in the event of discrimination other than the right to the conclusion of a contract of employment. Question 6 asks whether the directive, as properly interpreted, may be relied on before national courts by persons who have suffered injury.

22. It is impossible to establish real equality of opportunity without an appropriate system of sanctions. That follows not only from the actual purpose of the directive but more specifically from Article 6 thereof which, by granting applicants for a post who have been discriminated against recourse to the courts, acknowledges that those candidates have rights of which they may avail themselves before the courts.

23. Although, as has been stated in the reply to Question 1, full implementation of the directive does not require any specific form of sanction for unlawful discrimination, it does entail that that sanction be such as to guarantee real and effective judicial protection. Moreover it must also have a real deterrent effect on the employer. It follows that where a Member State chooses to penalize the breach of the prohibition of discrimination by the award of compensation, that compensation must in any event be adequate in relation to the damage sustained.

24. It consequence it appears that national provisions limiting the right to compensation of persons who have been discriminated against as regards access to employment to a purely nominal amount, such as, for example, the reimbursement of expenses incurred by them in submitting their application, would not satisfy the requirements of an effective transposition of the directive.

25. The nature of the sanctions provided for in the Federal Republic of Germany in respect of discrimination regarding access to employment and in particular the question whether the rule in Paragraph 611a(2) of the Bürgerliches Gesetzbuch excludes the possibility of compensation on the basis of the general rules of law were the subject of lengthy discussion before the Court. The German Government maintained in the oral procedure that that provision did not necessarily exclude the application of the general rules of law regarding compensation. It is for the national court alone to rule on that question concerning the interpretation of its national law.

26. However, the Member States' obligation arising from a directive to achieve the result envisaged by the directive and their duty under Article 5 of the Treaty to take all appropriate measures, whether general or particular, to ensure the fulfilment of that obligation, is binding on all the authorities of Member States including, for matters within their jurisdiction, the courts. It follows that, in applying the national law and in particular the provisions of a national law specifically introduced in order to implement Directive No. 76/207, national courts are required to interpret their national law in the light of the wording and the purpose of the directive in order to achieve the result referred to in the third paragraph of Article 189.

27. On the other hand, as the above considerations show, the directive does not include any unconditional and sufficiently precise obligation as regards sanctions for discrimination which, in the absence of implementing measures adopted in good time may be relied on by individuals in order to obtain specific compensation under the directive, where that is not provided for or permitted under national law.

28. It should, however, be pointed out to the national court that although Directive No. 76/207/EEC, for the purpose of imposing a sanction for the breach of the prohibition of discrimination, leaves the Member States free to choose between the different solutions suitable for achieving its objective, it nevertheless requires that if a Member States chooses to penalize breaches of that prohibition by the award of compensation, then in order to ensure that it is effective and that it has a deterrent effect, that compensation must in any event be adequate in relation to the damage sustained and must therefore amount to more than purely nominal compensation such as, for example, the reimbursement only of the expenses incurred in connection with the application. It is for the national court to interpret and apply the legislation adopted for the implementation of the directive in conformity with the requirements of Community law, in so far as it is given discretion to do so under national law.

Costs
29. The costs incurred by the Governments of Denmark and the Federal Republic of Germany, by the United Kingdom and by the Commission of the European Communities, which have submitted observations to the Court, are not recoverable. As the proceedings are, in so far as the parties to the main action are concerned, in the nature of a step in the proceedings pending before the national court, the decision on costs is a matter for that court.

On those grounds,

THE COURT

in answer to the questions referred to it by the Arbeitsgericht Hamm by order of 6 December 1982, hereby rules:

1. **Directive No. 76/207/EEC does not require discrimination on grounds of sex regarding access to employment to be made the subject of a sanction by way of an obligation imposed on the employer who is the author of the discrimination to conclude a contract of employment with the candidate discriminated against.**

2. **As regards sanctions for any discrimination which may occur, the directive does not include any unconditional and sufficiently precise obligation which, in the absence of implementing measures adopted within the prescribed time-limits, may be relied on by an individual in order to obtain specific compensation under the directive, where that is not provided for or permitted under national law.**

3. **Although Directive No. 76/207/EEC, for the purpose of imposing a sanction for the breach of the prohibition of discrimination, leaves the Member States free to choose between the different solutions suitable for achieving its objective, it nevertheless requires that if a Member State chooses to penalize breaches of that prohibition by the award of compensation, then in order to ensure that it is effective and that it has a deterrent effect, that compensation must in any event be adequate in relation to the damage sustained and must therefore amount to more than purely nominal compensation such as, for example, the reimbursement only of the expenses incurred in connection with the application. It is for the national court to interpret and apply the legislation adopted for the implementation of the directive in conformity with the requirements of Community law, in so far as it is given discretion to do so under national law.**

Mertens de Wilmars	Koopmans	Bahlmann
Galmot Pescatore	Mackenzie Stuart	O'Keeffe
Bosco Due	Everling	Kakouris

Delivered in open court in Luxembourg on 10 April 1984.

P. Heim
Registrar

J. Mertens de Wilmars
President

Judgment of the Court

10 April 1984 – Case 79/83

Dorit Harz
v.
Deutsche Tradax GmbH

Equal treatment for men and women – Member States free to choose ways and means of achieving result envisaged by a Directive, but must adopt measures which ensure Directive is fully effective – Directive 76/207/EEC does not require discrimination on grounds of sex regarding access to employment to be made the subject of a sanction requiring employer who has discriminated to conclude contract of employment with candidate discriminated against – Directive 76/207/EEC does not include any unconditional and sufficiently precise obligation which, in absence of national implementing measures adopted within set time limits, may be relied on by individuals to obtain specific compensation where that is not provided for under national law – a Member State is free to choose appropriate sanctions for breach of discrimination prohibition – if it chooses to penalise such breach by award of compensation, that compensation must be adequate in relation to damage sustained and amount to more than purely nominal compensation in order to be effective and have a deterrent effect – a national court should interpret and apply legislation adopted to implement Directive in accordance with requirements of Community law, so far as it is given discretion to do so under national law (EEC Treaty, Articles 5 and 189; Council Directive 76/207/EEC).

In Case 79/83

REFERENCE to the Court under Article 177 of the EEC Treaty by the Arbeitsgericht [Labour Court] Hamburg for a preliminary ruling in the action pending before that court between

Dorit Harz

and

Deutsche Tradax GmbH,

on the interpretation of Council Directive No. 76/207/EEC of 9 February 1976 on the implementation of the principle of equal treatment for men and women as regards access to employment, vocational training and promotion, and working conditions (Official Journal 1976, L 39, p. 40),

THE COURT

composed of: J. Mertens de Wilmars, President, T. Koopmans, K. Bahlmann and Y. Galmot, Presidents of Chambers, P. Pescatore, Lord Mackenzie Stuart, A. O'Keeffe, G. Bosco, O. Due, U. Everling and C. Kakouris, Judges,

Advocate General: S. Rozès
Registrar: H. A. Rühl, Principal Administrator

gives the following JUDGMENT

Decision

1. By order of 5 July 1982, which was received at the Court on 3 May 1983, the Arbeitsgericht [Labour Court] Hamburg referred to the Court for a preliminary ruling pursuant to Article 177 of the ECC Treaty several questions on the interpretation of Council Directive No. 76/207/EEC of 9 February 1976 on the implementation of the principle of equal treatment for men and women as regards access to employment, vocational training and promotion, and working conditions (Official Journal 1976, L 39, p. 40).

2. Those questions were raised in the course of proceedings between Dorit Harz, a graduate in business studies, and Deutsche Tradax GmbH. It appears from the grounds of the order for reference that the Arbeitsgericht considers that the defendant undertaking practised sex discrimination in the recruitment procedure commenced by it in which Mrs Harz was a candidate.

3. In the Arbeitsgericht's view, under German law, the only sanction for discrimination in a recruitment procedure is compensation for 'Vertrauensschaden', namely the loss incurred by candidates who are victims of discrimination as a result of their belief that there would be no discrimination in the establishment of the employment relationship. Such compensation is provided for in Paragraph 611a(2) of the Bürgerliches Gesetzbuch.

4. Under that provision, in the event of discrimination regarding access to employment, the employer is liable for 'damages in respect of the loss incurred by the worker as a result of his reliance on the expectation that the establishment of the employment relationship would not be precluded by such a breach [of the principle of equal treatment]'. That provision purports to implement Council Directive No. 76/207.

5. Consequently the Arbeitsgericht found that, under German law, it could order the payment only of minimal compensation, of DM 2.31 in the case

in point, in respect of expenses incurred by Mrs Harz in relation to her application. It considered that such compensation was not sufficient to ensure compliance with the Community directive, since it would not serve to ensure that employers conduct themselves in conformity with the law.

6. In order to determine the rules of Community law applicable in the event of discrimination regarding access to employment, the Arbeitsgericht referred the following questions to the Court of Justice:

       '1. In an established case of discrimination, does the principle of equal treatment for men and women as regards access to employment contained in Articles 1(2), 2(1) and 2(3) of Council Directive No. 76/207/EEC of 9 February 1976 on the implementation of the principle of equal treatment for men and women as regards access to employment, vocational training and promotion, and working conditions (Official Journal 1976, L 39, p. 40) confer on a female applicant a right to a contract of employment against an employer who has refused to engage her on account of her sex?

      2. In the case of an affirmative reply to Question 1 does that answer apply only:

        (a) where the female applicant discriminated against is the best qualified of all the applicants, whether male or female, or

        (b) also where, although there was discrimination in the selection procedure, in the result a better qualified male applicant was appointed?

      3. If Questions 1, 2(a) and 2(b) are answered in the negative, does it follow, as a legal consequence, from the principle of equal treatment for men and women as laid down by the provisions of Directive No. 76/207/EEC that a financially appreciable sanction is necessary, for example a right in favour of the female worker discriminated against to damages to be assessed, according to the position in the particular case, in a sum not exceeding the earnings which she could properly have expected to receive for the period of six months, the period in which under the law of the Federal Republic of Germany workers may not plead socially un-justified dismissal, and/or that the State must impose penalties or administrative fines?

      4. If Question 3 is answered in the affirmative, does that answer apply only:

        (a) where the female applicant discriminated against is the best qualified of all the candidates, whether male or female, or

        (b) also where, even though there was discrimination in the

> selection procedure, in the result a better qualified male candidate was appointed?
> 5. If Questions 1, 2, 3 or 4 are answered in the affirmative, are Articles 1, 2 and 3 of Directive No. 76/207/EEC directly applicable in the Member States?'

7. Those questions are intended primarily to establish whether Directive No. 76/207 requires Member States to lay down legal consequences or specific sanctions in the event of discrimination regarding access to employment (Questions 1 to 4) and whether individuals may, where appropriate, rely on the provisions of the directive before the national courts where the directive has not been transposed into the national legal order within the periods prescribed. (Question 5).

(a) Question 1
8. In its first question the Arbeitsgericht asks essentially whether Directive No. 76/207 requires discrimination on grounds of sex in the matter of access to employment to be penalized by an obligation, imposed on an employer who is guilty of discrimination, a conclude a contract of employment with the candidate who was the victim of discrimination.

9. According to the Arbeitsgericht the sanctions which may be envisaged in order to enforce the principle of equal treatment for men and women regarding access to employment are an automatic right to be given a post or a right to damages, which in German law are classified as compensation for a 'positive interest' [Ersatz des positiven Interesses]. The Arbeitsgericht considers that Directive No. 76/207 has not yet been transposed into German law inasmuch as the sanction provided for in Paragraph 611a(2) of the Bürgerliches Gesetzbuch is not, in its view, sufficent in that respect.

10. According to the plaintiff in the main action, by restricting the right to compensation solely to 'Vertrauensschaden', Paragraph 611a(2) of the Bürgerliches Gesetzbuch excluded the possibilities of compensation afforded by the general rules of law. Directive No. 76/207 requires Member States to introduce appropriate measures with a view to avoiding discrimination in the future. It should, therefore, at least be accepted that Paragraph 611a(2) must be left out of account. The result of that would be that the employer would be required to conclude a contract of employment with the candidate discriminated against or, if that proves impossible or out of the question in the particular case, at least to pay him appreciable damages.

11. The Government of the Federal Republic of Germany is aware of the need for an effective transposition of the directive but stresses the fact that, under the third paragraph of Article 189 of the EEC Treaty, each Member State has a margin of discretion as regards the legal consequences

216

which must result from a breach of the principle of equal treatment. The German Government submits, moreover, that it is possible for the German courts to work out, on the basis of private national law and in conformity with the substance of the directive, adequate solutions which satisfy both the principle of equal treatment and the interests of all the parties. Finally an appreciable legal consequence is in its view sufficient to ensure compliance with the principle of equal treatment and that consequence should follow only if the victim of discrimination was better qualified for the post than the other candidates; it should not apply where the candidates' qualifications were equal.

12. The Netherlands Government takes the view that the directive does not require a specific sanction, for example by giving victims of discrimination the automatic right to be offered a post. On the other hand, an order requiring the employer to pay a purely nominal sum does not satisfy the requirement that the person discriminated against must be able to rely on his rights under the directive.

13. The United Kingdom is also of the opinion that it is for Member States to choose the measures which they consider appropriate to ensure the fulfilment of their obligations under the directive. The directive gives no indication as to the measures which Member States should adopt and the questions referred to the Court themselves clearly illustrate the difficulties encountered in laying down appropriate measures.

14. The Commission considers that although the directive is intended to leave to Member States the choice and the determination of the sanctions, nevertheless the transposition of the directive must produce effective results. The principle of the effective transposition of the directive requires that the sanctions must be of such a nature as to constitute, for the candidate discriminated against, appropriate compensation and, for the employer, a means of pressure which it would be unwise to disregard and which would prompt him to respect the principle of equal treatment. A national measure which provides for compensation only for losses actually incurred through reliance on an expectation ('Vertrauensschaden') is not sufficient to ensure compliance with that principle.

15. According to the third paragraph of Article 189: 'A directive shall be binding, as to the result to be achieved, upon each Member State to which it is addressed, but shall leave to the national authorities the choice of form and methods'. Although that provision leaves Member States free to choose the ways and means of ensuring that the directive is implemented, that freedom does not affect the obligation, imposed on all the Member States to which the directive is addressed, to adopt, within the framework of their national legal systems, all the measures necessary to ensure that the directive is fully effective, in accordance with the objective which it pursues.

217

16. It is therefore necessary to examine Directive No. 76/207 in order to determine whether it requires Member States to provide for specific legal consequences or sanctions in respect of a breach of the principle of equal treatment regarding access to employment.

17. The object of that directive is to implement in the Member States the principle of equal treatment for men and women, in particular by giving male and female workers real equality of opportunity as regards access to employment. With that end in view. Article 2 defines the principle of equal treatment and its limits, while Article 3(1) sets out the scope of the principle specifically as regards access to employment. Article 3(2)(a) provides that Member States are to take the measures necessary to ensure that any laws, regulations and administrative provisions contrary to the principle of equal treatment are abolished.

18. Article 6 requires Member States to introduce into their national legal systems such measures as are necessary to enable all persons who consider themselves wronged by discrimination 'to pursue their claims by judicial process'. It follows from that provision that Member States are required to adopt measures which are sufficiently effective to achieve the objective of the directive and to ensure that those measures may in fact be relied on before the national courts by the persons concerned. Such measures may include, for example, provisions requiring the employer to offer a post to the candidate discriminated against or giving the candidate adequate financial compensation, reinforced where necessary by a system of fines. However the directive does not prescribe a specific sanction; it leaves Member States free to choose between the different solutions suitable for achieving its objective.

19. The reply to the first question should therefore be that Directive No. 76/207 does not require discrimination on grounds of sex regarding access to employment to be made the subject of a sanction by way of an obligation imposed upon the employer who is the author of the discrimination to conclude a contract of employment with the candidate discriminated against.

(b) Question 2
20. It is not necessary to answer the second question, since it is put only on the supposition that an employer is required to offer a post to the candidate discriminated against.

(c) Questions 3, 4 and 5
21. In its third and fourth questions the Arbeitsgericht essentially asks whether it is possible to infer from the directive that a financially appreciable sanction is necessary. The fifth question asks whether the directive, as properly interpreted, may be relied on before national courts by persons who have suffered injury.

22. In that respect it must be remarked that it is impossible to establish real equality of opportunity without an appropriate system of sanctions. That follows not only from the actual purpose of the directive but more specifically from Article 6 thereof which, by granting applicants for a post who have been discriminated against recourse to the courts, acknowledges that those candidates have rights of which they may avail themselves before the courts.

23. Although, as has been stated in the reply to the first question, full implementation of the directive does not require a specific form of sanction for breach of the prohibition of discrimination, it does entail that that sanction be such as to guarantee real and effective judicial protection. Moreover it must also have a real deterrent effect on the employer. It follows that where a Member State chooses to penalize the breach of the prohibition of discrimination by the award of compensation, that compensation must in any event be adequate in relation to the damage sustained.

24. In consequence national provisions limiting the rights to compensation of persons who have been discriminated against as regards access to employment to a purely nominal amount, such as for example the reimbursement of expenses incurred in connexion with their application, would not satisfy the requirements of an effective transposition of the directive.

25. The nature of the sanction provided for in the Federal Republic of Germany in respect of discrimination regarding access to employment and in particular the question whether the rule in Paragraph 611a(2) of the Bürgerliches Gesetzbuch excludes the possibility of compensation on the basis of the general rules of law were the subject of lengthy discussion before the Court. The German Government maintained in the oral procedure that that provision did not necessarily exclude the application of general rules of law regarding compensation. It is for the national court alone to rule on that question concerning the interpretation of its national law.

26. However, the Member States' obligation arising from a directive to achieve the result envisaged by the directive and their duty under Article 5 of the Treaty to take all appropriate measures, whether general or particular, to ensure the fulfilment of that obligation, is binding on all the authorities of Member States including, for matters within their jurisdiction, the courts. It follows that, in applying national law and in particular the provisions of a national law specifically introduced in order to implement Directive No. 76/207, the national court is required to interpret its national law in the light of the wording and the purpose of the directive in order to achieve the result referred to in the third paragraph of Article 189.

27. On the other hand, as the above considerations show, the directive does not include any unconditional and sufficiently precise obligation as regards sanctions for discrimination which, in the absence of implementing measures adopted in good time, may be relied on by individuals in order to obtain specific compensation under the directive, where that is not provided for or permitted under national law.

28. It should, however, be pointed out to the national court that although Directive No. 76/207/EEC, for the purpose of imposing a sanction for the breach of the prohibition of discrimination, leaves the Member States free to choose between the different solutions suitable for achieving its objective, it nevertheless requires that if a Member State chooses to penalize breaches of that prohibition by the award of compensation, then in order to ensure that it is effective and that it has a deterrent effect, that compensation must in any event be adequate in relation to the damage sustained and must therefore amount to more than purely nominal compensation such as, for example, the reimbursement only of the expenses incurred in connection with the application. It is for the national court to interpret and apply the legislation adopted for the implementation of the directive in conformity with the requirements of Community law, in so far as it is give discretion to do so under national law.

Costs
29. The costs incurred by the Governments of the Federal Republic of Germany and the Netherlands, by the United Kingdom and by the Commission of the European Communities, which have submitted observations to the Court, are not recoverable. As the proceedings are, in so far as the parties to the main action are concerned, in the nature of a step in the proceedings pending before the national court, the decision on costs is a matter for that court.

On those grounds,

THE COURT

in answer to the questions referred to it by the Arbeitsgericht Hamburg by order of 5 July 1982, hereby rules:

1. **Directive No. 76/207/EEC does not require discrimination on grounds of sex regarding access to employment to be made the subject of a sanction by way of an obligation imposed on the employer who is the author of the discrimination to conclude a contract of employment with the candidate discriminated against.**

2. **As regards sanctions for any discrimination which may occur, the directive does not include any unconditional and sufficiently precise obligation which,**

in the absence of implementing measures adopted within the prescribed time-limits, may be relied on by an individual in order to obtain specific compensation under the directive, where that is not provided for or permitted under national law.

3. Although Directive No. 76/207/EEC, for the purpose of imposing a sanction for the breach of the prohibition of discrimination, leaves the Member States free to choose between the different solution suitable for achieving its objective, it nevertheless requires that if a Member State chooses to penalize breaches of that prohibition by the award of compensation, then in order to ensure that it is effective and that it has a deterrent effect, that compensation must in any event be adequate in relation to the damage sustained and must therefore amount to more than purely nominal compensation such as, for example, the reimbursement only of the expenses incurred in connection with the application. It is for the national court to interpret and apply the legislation adopted for the implementation of the directive in conformity with the requirements of Community law, in so far as it is given discretion to do so under national law.

Mertens de Wilmars	Koopmans	Bahlmann
Galmot Pescatore	Mackenzie Stuart	O'Keeffe
Bosco Due	Everling	Kakouris

Delivered in open court in Luxembourg on 10 April 1984.

P. Heim   J. Mertens de Wilmars
Registrar   *President*

Judgment of the Court

12 July 1984 – Case 184/83

Ulrich Hofmann
v.
Barmer Ersatzkasse

Equal treatment for men and women – Directive 76/207/EEC not designed to settle questions regarding organisation of the family or to alter division of responsibility between parents – Member States' rights under the Directive to retain or introduce provisions to protect women with regard to pregnancy and maternity recognise the legitmacy of protecting women's biological condition during pregnancy and the special mother-child relationship after pregnancy – maternity leave granted to women after statutory protective period is within scope of Directive's maternity-linked provisions as it seeks to protect women with regard to effects of pregnancy and motherhood – Member States have reasonable margin of discretion as to nature of protective measures they introduce and detailed arrangements for their implementation – Articles 1, 2 and 5(1) of Directive 76/207/EEC to be interpreted as meaning that a Member State may, after a protective period has expired, grant mothers a period of maternity leave which the State encourages them to take by payment of an allowance, and State is not obliged as an alternative to allow such leave to be granted to fathers even where parents so decide (Council Directive 76/207/EEC, Article 1, 2(3) & (4), and 5(1)).

In Case 184/83

REFERENCE to the Court under Article 177 of the EEC Treaty by the Landessozialgericht [Higher Social Court] Hamburg for a preliminary ruling in the proceedings pending before that court between

Ulrich Hofmann, residing in Hamburg,

and

Barmer Ersatzkasse, Wuppertal,

on the interpretation of Articles 1, 2 and 5(1) of Council Directive 76/207 of 9 February 1976 on the implementation of the principle of equal treatment for men and women as regards access to employment, vocational training and promotion, and working conditions,

THE COURT

composed of: Lord Mackenzie Stuart, President, T. Koopmans, K. Bahlmann and Y. Galmot (Presidents of Chambers), P. Pescatore, A. O'Keeffe, G. Bosco, O. Due, U. Everling, C. Kakouris and R. Joliet, Judges,

Advocate General: M. Darmon
Registrar: P. Heim

gives the following JUDGMENT

Decision

1. By an order of 9 August 1983, received at the Court Registry on 29 August 1983, the Landessozialgericht [Higher Social Court] Hamburg referred to the Court for a preliminary ruling under Article 177 of the EEC Treaty two questions concerning the interpretation of Council Directive 76/207/EEC of 9 February 1976 on the implementation of the principle of equal treatment for men and women as regards access to employment, vocational training and promotion, and working condi-

tions (Official Journal 1976, L 39, p. 40), in order to determine whether Paragraph 8a of the Mutterschutzgesetz [Law for the Protection of Working Mothers] of 18 April 1968, as amended by the Laws of 25 June 1979 and 22 December 1981 (Bundesgesetzblatt I, 1968, p. 315, 1979, p. 797, and 1981, p. 1523), is compatible with Community law.

2. The order making the reference to the Court discloses that Mr Hofmann, the plaintiff in the main proceedings, is the father of an illegitimate child, of which he has acknowledged paternity. He obtained unpaid leave from his employer for the period between the expiry of the statutory protective period of eight weeks which was available to the mother and the day on which the child reached the age of six months; during that time he took care of the child while the mother continued her employment.

3. At the same time the plaintiff submitted to the Barmer Ersatzkasse, the defendant in the main proceedings, a claim for payment, during the period of maternity leave provided for by Paragraph 8a of the Mutters-chutzgesetz, of an allowance pursuant to the combined provisions of Paragraph 13 thereof and Paragraph 200(4) of the Reichsversicherung-sordnung [German Insurance Regulation].

4. The defendant refused the plaintiff's request, and his appeal against that refusal was also unsuccessful. An action brought before the Sozialgericht [Social Court] Hamburg was dismissed by a judgment of 19 October 1982, on the ground that the wording of Paragraph 8(a) of the Mutters-chutzgesetz and the intention of the legislature indicated that only mothers could claim maternity leave. According to the Sozialgericht, it was the deliberate intent of the legislature not to creat 'parental leave'.

5. The plaintiff appealed against that decision to the Landessozialgericht Hamburg, arguing that the maternity leave introduced by the Mutter-schutzgesetz was not in fact designed to protect the mother's health but was concerned exclusively with the mother's care of the child. In the course of the proceedings before the Landessozialgericht, he requested primarily that the proceedings should be stayed and that certain questions on the interpretation of Directive 76/207 should be referred to the Court of Justice.

6. In view of the doubts which had arisen as to the compatibility of the national legislation on maternity leave with the aforesaid directive, the Landessozialgericht granted Mr Hofmann's request, particularly since it had learned that the Commission had brought proceedings on the same issue against the Federal Republic of Germany claiming that the latter had failed to fulfil its Treaty obligations (Case 248/83). It therefore referred two questions to the Court, worded as follows:

'1. Are Articles 1, 2 and 5(1) of Council Directive 76/207/EEC

223

on the implementation of the principle of equal treatment for men and women as regards access to employment, vocational training and promotion, and working conditions (Official Journal of the European Communities, L 39, pp. 40 to 42) infringed if, on the expiry of the eight-week protective period for working mothers following childbirth, a period of leave which the State encourages by payment of the net remuneration of the person concerned, subject to a maximum of DM 25 per calendar day, and which lasts until the day on which the child reaches the age of six months can be claimed solely by working mothers and not, by way of alternative, if the parents so decide, by working fathers?

2. If the answer to Question 1 is in the affirmative, are Articles 1, 2 and 5(1) of Council Directive 76/207/EEC directly applicable in the Member states?'

7. In its order, the Landessozialgericht points out that the plaintiff, at the same time, lodged a Verfassungsbeschwerde [an objection on a point of constitutional law] with the Bundesverfassungsgericht [Federal Constitutional Court], pleading that some of the provisions of the Law instituting the maternity leave were unconstitutional, on the ground that they infringed the rule of the equality of men and women before the law, enshrined in Article 3(2) and (3) of the Grundgesetz [Basic Law].

First question (scope and limits of the principle of equal treatment)

8. It is appropriate first of all to set out the legislative provisions on maternity leave which form the subject-matter of the proceedings pending before the Landessozialgericht.

9. Under Paragraph 6(1) of the Mutterschutzgesetz, women may not be employed during the eight weeks which follow childbirth. According to Paragraph 8a of that Law, mothers are entitled to maternity leave from the end of the protective period provided for by Paragraph 6(1) until the day on which the child attains the age of six months. The leave must be claimed by the mother at least four weeks prior to the expiry of the protective period and is subject to the condition that the mother must have held employment for a period of, generally speaking, nine months before the birth. If the child dies during the period of leave, the leave is, as a general rule, terminated three weeks after the death. Under Paragraph 9a, the employer is forbidden to terminate the employment contract during the maternity leave and for a period of two months thereafter. Under Paragraph 13 of the Law, the mother receives an allowance from the State which is equal to her earnings, but subject to an upper limit of DM 25 per day, according to the provisions in force at the material time.

10. The plaintiff claims, essentially, that the main object of the disputed legislative provisions, in contrast with the protective period provided

for by Paragraph 6, is not to give social protection to the mother on biological and medical grounds but rather to protect the child. The plaintiff draws that conclusion, on the one hand, from the *travaux préparatoires* relating to the Law introducing maternity leave and, on the other hand, from certain objective characteristics of the Law. He draws particular attention to three characteristics:

  (i) The fact that the leave is withdrawn in the event of the child's death, which demonstrates that the leave was created in the interests of the child and not of the mother;
 (ii) The optional nature of the leave, which means that it cannot be said to have been introduced to meet imperative biological or medical needs;
(iii) Lastly, the requirement that the woman should have been employed for a minimum period prior to childbirth; this indicates that it was not considered necessary to grant the leave in the interests of the mother, otherwise it ought to have been extended to all women in employment irrespective of the date on which their employment commenced.

11. According to the plaintiff, the protection of the mother against the multiplicity of burdens imposed by motherhood and her employment could be achieved by non-discriminatory measures, such as enabling the father to enjoy the leave or creating a period of parental leave, so as to release the mother from the responsibility of caring for the child and thereby allow her to resume employment as soon as the statutory protective period had expired. The plaintiff further claims that the choice between the options thereby created should, in conformity with the principle on non-discrimination between the sexes, be left completely at the discretion of the parents of the child.

12. The plaintiff's viewpoint is supported by the Commission, which takes the view that the proviso in Article 2(3) of Directive 76/207, which permits Member States to maintain provisions concerning the protection of women, particularly as regards pregnancy and maternity, calls for a restrictive interpretation inasmuch as it derogates from the principle of equal treatment. Since that principle constitutes a 'fundamental right', its application cannot be limited except by provisions which are objectively necessary for the protection of the mother. If national legislation, such as that in this instance, serves the interests of the child as well, its purpose should preferably be achieved by non-discriminatory means. In the present instance, however, the protection provided for by Article 2(3) of the directive may equally well be attained by a reduction of the mother's domestic duties, achieved by granting the leave to the father.

13. The Commission draws attention to the fact that, in a number of Member States, social legislation is moving towards the grant of 'parental leave' or of 'child-care leave', which is to be preferred to leave which is available to the mother alone. It stated that it was considering whether

to bring actions for failure to fulfil a Treaty obligation against a number of Member States which, in various forms, retained measures which were comparable to the maternity leave provided for by the German legislation.

14. The Government of the Federal Republic of Germany, supporting the viewpoint of the Barmer Ersatzkasse, argues that legal protection afforded to the mother by the disputed legislation aims to reduce the conflict between a woman's role as a mother and her role as a wage-earner, in order to preserve her health and that of the child. It admits that there are differing views on the length of time for which a woman should enjoy special treatment following pregnancy and childbirth, but it argues that the period in question, although varying from woman to woman, extends considerably beyond the end of the statutory eight-week period of protection laid down by the Law. Hence the creation of maternity leave is justified for reasons which are connected with a woman's biological characteristics, since its aim is to avoid placing the mother, on expiry of the statutory protective period, under an obligation to decide whether or not to resume her employment. Indeed, experience and statistics demonstrate that a considerable number of working women were compelled, under earlier legislation, to give up their employment as a result of motherhood.

15. In reply to the arguments put forward in particularly by the plaintiff in the main proceedings, the Government of the Federal Republic of Germany maintains that maternity leave under German legislation constitutes an uninterrupted continuation of the protection given to a mother beyond the end of the protective period provided for by Paragraph 6(1) of the Mutterschutzgesetz. The withdrawal of the leave in the event of the child's death is justified by the fact that its death puts an end to the multiplicity of burdens borne by the woman as a result of motherhood and her employment. The fact that the leave is optional and may be claimed by the mother is consistent with its objective, namely to enable the woman to choose freely, in the light of her physical condition and of other family and social factors, in the light of her physical condition and of other family and social factors, the solution which is better suited to her personal circumstances; by virtue of that provision the purpose of the leave, namely to protect the mother, may be better achieved than by the adoption of other solutions, such as the grant of leave to the father or the assumption by other members of the family of responsibility for looking after the child. Finally, the provision which makes the grant of leave subject to the prerequisite that the mother shall have been in employment for a minimum period prior to giving birth is explained by the concern to avoid abuses whereby expectant mothers take up employment during pregnancy for the purpose of enjoying leave and the pecuniary benefits attaching to it.

226

16. The Government of the United Kingdom, after setting out the arrangements for protecting mothers under the social legislation of the United Kingdom, supports the viewpoint of the German Government. It reacts critically to the contentions put forward by the Commission, which in its view places too restrictive an interpretation on Article 2(3) of the directive, thereby discouraging Member States from availing themselves of the possibilities offered by that provision.

17. For the purpose of answering the question raised by the Landessozialgericht, it is appropriate in the first instance to set out the provisions of Directive 76/207 to which reference had been made.

18. The directive is designed to implement the principle of equal treatment for men and women as regards *inter alia* 'working conditions', with a view to attaining the social policy aims of the EEC Treaty to which the third recital in the preamble to the directive refers.

19. To that end, Article 1 defines 'the principle of equal treatment' as meaning that the directive seeks to put into effect in the Member States the principle of equal treatment for men and women as regards access to employment, promotion, vocational training and working conditions. According to Article 2(1), the principle of equal treatment means 'that there shall be no discrimination whatsoever on grounds of sex either directly or indirectly by reference in particular to marital or family status.' Under Article 5(1), application of the principle of equal treatment with regard to working conditions 'means that men and women shall be guaranteed the same conditions without discrimination on grounds of sex'; paragraph (2) of the article requires Member States to abolish any laws, regulations and administrative provisions contrary to the principle of equal treatment and to amend those which conflict with the principle 'when the concern for protection which originally inspired them is no longer well founded'.

20. Paragraphs (2), (3) and (4) of Article 2 indicate, in various respects, the limits of the principle of equal treatment laid down by the directive.

21. Under paragraph (2), which is of no relevance to the present case, the directive is expressed to be without prejudice to the right of Member States to exclude from its field of application those occupational activities for which, 'by reason of their nature or the context in which they are carried out, the sex of the worker constitutes a determining factor'.

22. Paragraph (3) makes the following provision:

'This directive shall be without prejudice to provisions concerning the protection of women, particularly as regards pregnancy and maternity.'.

227

23. Reference should also be made in the present context to paragraph (4), according to which the directive is to be without prejudice to measures to promote equal opportunity for men and women, 'by removing existing inequalities which affect women's opportunities in the areas referred to in Article 1(1)', that is to say, as regards access to employment, promotion and other working conditions.

24. It is apparent from the above analysis that the directive is not designed to settle questions concerned with the organization of the family, or to alter the division of responsibility between parents.

25. It should further be added, with particular reference to paragraph (3), that, by reserving to Member States the right to retain, or introduce provisions which are intended to protect women in connection with 'pregnancy and maternity', the directive recognizes the legitimacy, in terms of the principle of equal treatment, of protecting a woman's needs in two respects. First, it is legitimate to ensure the protection of a woman's biological condition during pregnancy and thereafter until such time as her physiological and mental functions have returned to normal after childbirth; secondly, it is legitimate to protect the special relationship between a woman and her child over the period which follows pregnancy and childbirth, by preventing that relationship from being disturbed by the multiple burdens which would result from the simultaneous pursuit of employment.

26. In principle, therefore, a measure such as maternity leave granted to a woman on expiry of the statutory protective period falls within the scope of Article 2(3) of Directive 76/207, inasmuch as it seeks to protect a woman in connection with the effects of pregnancy and motherhood. That being so, such leave may legitimately be reserved to the mother to the exclusion of any other person, in view of the fact that it is only the mother who may find herself subject to undesirable pressures to return to work prematurely.

27. Furthermore, it should be pointed out that the directive leaves Member States with a discretion as to the social measures which they adopt in order to guarantee, within the framework laid down by the directive, the protection of women in connection with pregnancy and maternity and to offset the disadvantages which women, by comparison with men, suffer with regard to the retention of employment. Such measures are, as the Government of the United Kingdom has rightly observed, closely linked to the general system of social protection in the various Member States. It must therefore be concluded that the Member States enjoy a reasonable margin of discretion as regards both the nature of the protective measures and the detailed arrangements for their implementation.

28. It follows from the foregoing that the reply to be given to the question submitted by the Landessozialgericht Hamburg is that Articles 1, 2 and

5(1) of Council Directive 76/207 must be interpreted as meaning that a Member State may, after the statutory protective period has expired, grant to mothers a period of maternity leave which the State encourages them to take by the payment of an allowance. The directive does not impose on Member States a requirement that they shall, as an alternative, allow such leave to be granted to fathers, even where the parents so decide.

29. Since the reply to the first question submitted by the Landessozialgericht is in the negative, the second question, concerning the effect of Directive 76/207 in the event of its provisions being disregarded by a Member State, is otiose.

Costs
30. The costs incurred by the Government of the Federal Republic and by the Commission of the European Communities, which have submitted observations to the Court, are not recoverable. As these proceedings are, in so far as the parties to the main proceedings are concerned, in the nature of a step in the proceedings pending before the national court, the decision on costs is a matter for that court.

On those grounds,

THE COURT,

in answer to the questions referred to it by the Landessozialgericht Hamburg, by order dated 9 August 1983, hereby rules:

Articles 1, 2 and 5(1) of Council Directive 76/207 of 9 February 1976 on the implementation of the principle of equal treatment for men and women as regards access to employment, vocational training and promotion, and working conditions must be interpreted as meaning that a Member State may, after the protective period has expired, grant to mothers a period of maternity leave which the State encourages them to take by the payment of an allowance. The directive does not impose on Member States a requirement that they shall, as an alternative, allow such leave to be granted to fathers, even where the parents so decide.

Mackerzie Stuart		Koopmans		Bahlmann
Galmot	Pescatore		O'Keeffe	Bosco
Due	Everling		Kakouris	Joliet

Delivered in open court in Luxembourg on 12 July 1984.

For the Registrar   A. J. Mackenzie Stuart
H. A. Rühl   *President*
Principal Administrator

Judgment of the Court

26 February 1986 – Case 151/84

Joan Roberts
v.
Tate & Lyle Industries Ltd

Equal treatment for men and women – Article 5(1) of Directive 76/207/EEC applies equal treatment principle to working conditions including dismissal – dismissal must be given wide meaning and can include age limit for compulsory redundancy of workers as part of mass redundancy, even if redundancy involves grant of early retirement pension – Article 1(2) of Directive 76/207/EEC, which excludes from scope social security matters, must be strictly interpreted – exception to prohibition of discrimination on grounds of sex in Article 7(1)(a) of Directive 79/7/EEC applies only to determination of pensionable age for purposes of granting old age and retirement pensions and its consequences for other social security benefits – Article 5(1) of Directive 76/207/EEC to be interpreted as meaning that a contractual provision which sets single age for dismissal of men and women under a mass redundancy involving grant of an early retirement pension, whereas normal pensionable age is different for men and women, is not discrimination on grounds of sex contrary to Community law (Council Directive 76/207/EEC, Articles 1(2) and 5(1); Council Directive 79/7/EEC, Article 7(1)).

In Case 151/84

REFERENCE to the Court under Article 177 of the EEC Treaty by the Court of Appeal of England and Wales for a preliminary ruling in the proceedings pending before that court between

Joan Roberts

and

Tate & Lyle Industries Limited

on the interpretation of Council Directive No. 76/207/EEC of 9 February 1976 on the implementation of the principle of equal treatment for men and women as regards access to employment, vocational training and promotion, and working conditions (Official Journal 1976 No. L 39, p. 40),

THE COURT

composed of: Lord Mackenzie Stuart, President, U. Everling and K. Bahlmann (Presidents of Chambers), G. Bosco, T. Koopmans, O. Due and T. F. O'Higgins, Judges,

Advocate General: Sir Gordon Slynn
Registrar: D. Loutermann, Administrator

gives the following JUDGMENT

Decision

1. By an order of 12 March 1984, which was received at the Court on 19 June 1984, the Court of Appeal of England and Wales referred to the Court for a preliminary ruling under Article 177 of the EEC Treaty two questions on the interpretation of Council Directive No. 76/207/EEC of 9 February 1976 on the implementation of the principle of equal treatment for men and women as regards access to employment, vocational training and promotion, and working conditions (Official Journal 1976 No. 39, p. 40).

2. The questions were raised in the course of proceedings between Joan Roberts (hereinafter referred to as 'the appellant') and Tate & Lyle Industries Limited, previously Tate & Lyle Food and Distribution Limited, (hereinafter referred to as 'the respondents') concerning the question whether the appellant's dismissal was in accordance with section 6(4) of the Sex Discrimination Act 1975 and with Community law.

3. The appellant was employed by the respondents at their Liverpool depot for 28 years and, at the age of 53, was made redundant on 22 April 1981, following the closure of the depot, together with other employees, under a mass redundancy.

4. The appellant was a member of an occupational pension scheme, which had been created in 1978 by the respondents for their employees and which was contracted out of the State retirement pension scheme. That scheme is funded partly by the respondents themselves and partly by voluntary contributions by employees. It provides for compulsory retirement with a pension at the age of 65 for men and 60 for women. Nevertheless, men and women over the age of 50 may, with the respondents' consent, retire before attaining the aforementioned normal retirement age, in which case they are entitled to a reduced pension immediately. An employee who has been a member of the scheme for ten years may choose to retire at any time up to five years before the normal retirement age and receive the pension earned up to that date.

5. On the closure of the Liverpool depot the respondents agreed severance terms with the trade union of which the appellant was a member. Under those terms all employees made redundant were to be offered either a cash payment or an early pension out of the pension scheme up to five years before the date of their entitlement under the scheme. The pension was therefore payable immediately to women over the age of 55 and men over the age of 60. Nevertheless, as a result of representations made

231

by male employees against the allegedly discriminatory nature of those arrangements with regard to men aged between 55 and 60, the respondents amended them by agreeing to grant an immediate pension to both men and women over the age of 55, with the amount of their cash payment reduced.

6. The appellant, who was aged 53 at the date of redundancy, brought proceedings against the respondents before an Industrial Tribunal, claiming that her dismissal constituted unlawful discrimination contrary to the Sex Discrimination Act and to Community law, since under the new arrangements, a male employee was entitled to receive an immediate pension 10 years before the normal retirement age for men whereas a female employee was not so entitled until five years before the normal retirement age for women.

7. After her case was dismissed by the Industrial Tribunal she appealed to the Employment Appeal Tribunal, which held that, even if it was assumed that the appellant had been treated in a discriminatory manner, the respondents had not acted unlawfully since, in the first place, section 6(4) of the Sex Discrimination Act provided that the provisions of the Act concerning the prohibition of discrimination on the basis of sex did not apply to 'provision in relation to death or retirement', and, in the second place, Directive No. 76/207 was not directly applicable before the courts of the United Kingdom.

8. The appellant appealed to the Court of Appeal, which decided to refer the following questions to the Court of Justice for a preliminary ruling:

'(1) Whether or not the respondents discriminated against the appellant contrary to the Equal Treatment Directive by arranging for male employees who were made redundant to receive a pension from the occupational pension fund ten years prior to their normal retirement age of 65 but arranging for female employees (such as the appellant) who were made redundant to receive a pension only five years prior to their normal retirement age of 60, thereby arranging for both men and women to receive an immediate pension at the age of 55.

(2) If the answer to (1) above is in the affirmative, whether or not the Equal Treatment Directive can be relied upon by the appellant in the circumstances of the present case in national courts and tribunals notwithstanding the inconsistency (if any) between the directive and section 6(4) of the Sex discrimination Act 1975.'

Relevant legal provisions
9. Article 1(1) of Directive No. 76/207 provides as follows:

232

'The purpose of this directive is to put into effect in the Member States the principle of equal treatment for men and women as regards access to employment, including promotion, and to vocational training and as regards working conditions and, on the conditions referred to in paragraph (2), social security. This principle is hereinafter referred to as "the principle of equal treatment".'.

10. Article 2(1) of the directive provides that:

'... the principle of equal treatment shall mean that there shall be no discrimination whatsoever on grounds of sex either directly or indirectly by reference in particular to marital or family status.'.

11. Article 5(1) of the directive provides that:

'Application of the principle of equal treatment with regard to working conditions, including the conditions governing dismissal, means that men and women shall be guaranteed the same conditions without discrimination on grounds of sex.'.

12. Article 1(2) of the directive provides that:

'With a view to ensuring the progressive implementation of the principle of equal treatment in matters of social security, the Council, acting on a proposal from the Commission, will adopt provisions defining its substance, its scope and the arrangements for its application.'.

13. Pursuant to the last-mentioned provision, the Council adopted Directive No. 79/7/EEC of 19 December 1978 on the progressive implementation of the principle of equal treatment for men and women in matters of social security (Official Journal 1979 No. L 6, p. 24), which Member States were to transpose into national law, according to Article 8(1) thereof, within six years of its notification. The directive applies, according to Article 3(1) thereof, to:

'(a) statutory schemes which provide protection against the following risks:
sickness, ·
invalidity,
old age,
accidents at work and occupational diseases,
unemployment;
(b) social assistance, in so far as it is intended to supplement or replace the schemes referred to in (a).'.

233

14. According to Article 7(1) thereof, the directive is to be:

> 'without prejudice to the right of Member States to exclude from its scope:
> (a) the determination of pensionable age for the purposes of granting old-age and retirement pensions and the possible consequences thereof for other benefits.'.

15. With regard to occupational social security schemes, Article 3(3) of the directive provides that with a view to ensuring implementation of the principle of equal treatment in such schemes 'the Council, acting on a proposal from the Commission, will adopt provisions defining its substance, its scope and the arrangements for its application.' On 5 May 1983 the Commission submitted to the Council a proposal for a directive on the implementation of the principle of equal treatment for men and women in occupational social security schemes (Official Journal 1983 No. C 134, p. 7). The proposed directive would, according to Article 2(1) thereof, apply to 'benefits intended to supplement the benefits provided by statutory social security schemes or to replace them'. The Council has not yet responded to that proposal.

16. The minimum qualifying age for a State retirement pension under United Kingdom legislation is 60 for women and 65 for men.

17. Observations were submitted to the Court by the United Kingdom, the Kingdom of Denmark and the Commission, in addition to the appellant and the respondents.

The first question
18. By the first question the Court of Appeal seeks to ascertain whether Article 5(1) of Directive No. 76/207 must be interpreted as meaning that a contractual provision which lays down a single age for the dismissal of both men and women under a mass redundancy involving the grant of an early retirement pension, whereas the normal retirement age is different for men and women, namely 65 for the former and 60 for the latter, constitutes discrimination on grounds of sex contrary to that directive.

19. The appellant considers that the first question must be answered in the affirmative.

20. According to her the question falls to be considered, by virtue of the Court's judgment of 16 February 1982 (Case 19/81, *Burton* v. *British Railways Board*, [1982] ECR 555), under Directive No. 76/207. The terms 'working conditions' and 'conditions governing dismissal' contained in that directive also encompass the grant of an early retirement pension under a mass redundancy.

21. The appellant claims that she suffered discrimination as a result of the respondents' failure to take into account the fact that its normal retirement scheme it linked to the State retirement scheme, which provides for a different normal retirement age for men and women. Although the first variation of the respondents' scheme adopted that age difference in respect of access to early retirement, in accordance with the principles stated by the Court in the *Burton* case, those principles were not taken account of in the second variation.

22. The appellant claims that she is entitled, according to the judgment in the *Burton* case, to compare her treatment with that of a male employee who is an equal number of years away from the normal retirement age. A scheme which applies an age differential with regard to the retirement of men and of women, and which departs from that differential in the case of a mass redundancy in a manner less favourable to women than to men, gives rise to discrimination on grounds of sex, contrary to the provisions of the directive.

23. In contrast, the respondents argue first of all that it is unnecessary to reply to the first question in view of the fact that they propose that the reply to the second question should be in the negative.

24. They contend that they did not, in any event, discriminate against the appellant, because men and women of the same age (55) are treated in an identical manner.

25. According to the respondents, a woman cannot demand to be treated differently in all cases for the sole reason that there is a difference in treatment with regard to the normal retirement age applied by the employer under its occupational social security scheme. On the contrary, such a difference of treatment should not be reflected in other matters prior to the normal date of retirement.

26. The fact that the Court held in its judgment in the *Burton* case that a difference in the age which men and women must have attained for access to voluntary retirement cannot be regarded as discrimination does not mean, according to the respondents, that identical age conditions are necessarily discriminatory. In any event, the treatment applied in this case is justified objectively by the need to ensure that all employees who are dismissed and are over the age of 55 receive a pension.

27. The United Kingdom is also of the opinion that there is no discrimination, either direct or indirect, in this case. It considers that the normal way to ensure equality of treatment is to base the right to benefits linked to employment on the same age requirement for men and women and that the *Burton* judgment is not relevant to this case.

235

28. The Commission also maintains that there is no discrimination in this case and that the reply to the question is to be found in Article 5 of Directive No. 76/207 and in an analysis of the Court's judgment in the *Burton* case. In that judgment the Court recognized the existence of a link between access to voluntary redundancy and national social security schemes.

29. According to the Commission, Article 7(1) of Directive No. 79/7 does not aim to entrench the difference between the pensionable ages for men and women but merely creates an exception in a case where national law provides for such a difference. In the absence of a provision to that effect national provisions imposing such a difference might be incompatible with the directive. The position might be the same with regard to Article 9(1)(a) of the proposed directive concerning occupational social security schemes.

30. The Court observes in the first place that the question of interpretation which has been referred to it does not concern the conditions for the grant of the normal old-age or retirement pension but the termination of employment in connexion with a mass redundancy caused by the closure of part of an undertaking's plant. The question therefore concerns the conditions governing dismissal and falls to be considered under Directive No. 76/207.

31. Article 5(1) of Directive No. 76/207 provides that application of the principle of equal treatment with regard to working conditions, including the conditions governing dismissal, means that men and women are to be guaranteed the same conditions without discrimination on grounds of sex.

32. In its judgment in the *Burton* case the Court has already stated that the term 'dismissal' contained in that provision must be given a wide meaning. Consequently, an age limit for the compulsory redundancy of workers as part of a mass redundancy falls within the term 'dismissal' construed in that manner, even if the redundancy involves the grant of an early retirement pension.

33. Even though the retirement scheme at issue does not *prima facie* discriminate between men and women with regard to the conditions for dismissal, it is still necessary to consider whether the fixing of the same age for the grant of an early pension nevertheless constitutes discrimination on grounds of sex in view of the fact that under the United Kingdom statutory social security scheme the pensionable age for men and women is different. Under United Kingdom legislation the minimum qualifying age for a State retirement pension is 60 for women and 65 for men.

34. As the Court emphasized in its judgment in the *Burton* case, Article 7

of Directive No. 79/7 expressly provides that the directive does not prejudice the right of Member States to exclude from its scope the determination of pensionable age for the purposes of granting old-age and retirement pensions and the possible consequences thereof for other benefits falling within the statutory social security schemes. The Court thus acknowledged that benefits linked to a national scheme which lays down a different minimum pensionable age for men and women may lie outside the ambit of the aforementioned obligation.

35. However, in view of the fundamental importance of the principle of equality of treatment, which the Court has reaffirmed on numerous occasions, Article 1(2) of Directive No. 76/207, which excludes social security matters from the scope of that directive, must be interpreted strictly. Consequently, the exception to the prohibition of discrimination on grounds of sex provided for in Article 7(1)(a) of Directive No. 79/7 applies only to the determination of pensionable age for the purposes of granting old-age and retirement pensions and to the consequences thereof for other social security benefits.

36. In that respect it must be emphasized that, whereas the exception contained in Article 7 of Directive No. 79/7 concerns the consequences which pensionable age has for social security benefits, this case is concerned with dismissal within the meaning of Article 5 of Directive No. 76/207. In those circumstances the grant of a pension to persons of the same age who are made redundant amounts merely to a collective measure adopted irrespective of the sex of those persons in order to guarantee them all the same rights.

37. Consequently, the answer to the first question referred to the Court of Justice by the Court of Appeal must be that Article 5(1) of Directive No. 76/207 must be interpreted as meaning that a contractual provision which lays down a single age for the dismissal of men and women under a mass redundancy involving the grant of an early retirement pension, whereas the normal retirement age is different for men and women, does not constitute discrimination on grounds of sex, contrary to Community law.

The second question
38. Since the second question is contingent upon the reply to the first question being in the affirmative, it is not necessary to give a reply to it.

Costs
39. The costs incurred by Denmark, the United Kingdom and the Commission of the European Communities, which have submitted observations to the Court, are not recoverable. As these proceedings are, in so far as the parties to the main proceedings are concerned, in the nature of a step in the action before the national court, the decision as to costs is a matter for that court.

237

On those grounds,

THE COURT,

in answer to the questions referred to it by the Court of Appeal by an order of 12 March 1984, hereby rules:

Article 5(1) of Directive No. 76/207 must be interpreted as meaning that a contractual provision which lays down a single age for the dismissal of men and women under a mass redundancy involving the grant of an early retirement pension, whereas the normal retirement age is different for men and women, does not constitute discrimination on grounds of sex, contrary to Community law.

Mackenzie Stuart   Everling   Bahlmann

Bosco   Koopmans   Due   O'Higgins

Delivered in open court in Luxembourg on 26 February 1986.

P. Heim   A. J. Mackenzie Stuart
Registrar   *President*

Judgment of the Court

26 February 1986 – Case 152/84

M. H. Marshall
v.
Southampton and South West Hampshire Area Health Authority
(Teaching)

Equal treatment for men and women – Article 5(1) of Directive 76/207/EEC applies equal treatment principle to working conditions including dismissal – dismissal must be given wide meaning, and can include age limit for compulsory dismissal of workers in accordance with an employer's general policy on retirement, even if dismissal involves grant of a retirement pension – Article 1(2) of Directive 76/207/EEC, which excludes from scope social security matters, must be strictly interpreted – exception to prohibition of discrimination on grounds of sex in Article 7(1)(a) of Directive 79/7/EEC applies only to determination of pensionable age for purposes of granting old age and retirement pensions and its consequences for other social security benefits – Article 5(1) of Directive 76/207/EEC to be interpreted as meaning that a general policy concerning dismissal, involving dismissal of a woman solely because she has attained the qualifying age for a State pension, such

238

age being different under national legislation for men and women, constitutes discrimination on grounds of sex contrary to the Directive – where a Directive's provisions are unconditional and sufficiently precise, they may be directly relied on by individuals against State which fails to implement Directive in time or correctly in national law – Directive provisions may not be directly relied on against individuals – Article 5(1) of Directive 76/207/EEC may be directly relied on against a State authority acting in capacity as employer to avoid application of national provisions contrary to that Article (EEC Treaty, Article 189; Council Directive 76/207/EEC, Articles 1(2) and 5(1); Council Directive 79/7/EEC, Article 7(1)).

In Case 152/84

REFERENCE to the Court under Article 177 of the EEC Treaty by the Court of Appeal of England and Wales for a preliminary ruling in the proceedings pending before that court between

M. H. Marshall

and

Southampton and South West Hampshire Area Health Authority (Teaching)

on the interpretation of Council Directive No. 76/207/EEC of 9 February 1976 on the implementation of the principle of equal treatment for men and women as regards access to employment, vocational training and promotion, and working conditions (Official Joural 1976 No. L 39, p. 40),

THE COURT

composed of: Lord Mackenzie Stuart, President, U. Everling and K. Bahlmann (Presidents of Chambers), G. Bosco, T. Koopmans, O. Due and T. F. O'Higgins, Judges,

Advocate General: Sir Gordon Slynn
Registrar: D. Loutermann, Administrator

gives the following JUDGMENT

Decision

1. By an order of 12 March 1984, which was received at the Court on 19 June 1984, the Court of Appeal of England and Wales referred to the Court for a preliminary ruling under Article 177 of the EEC Treaty two questions on the interpretation of Council Directive No. 76/207/EEC of 9 February 1976 on the implementation of the principle of equal treat-

ment for men and women as regards access to employment, vocational training and promotion, and working conditions (Official Journal 1976 No. L 39, p. 40).

2. The questions were raised in the course of proceedings between Miss M. H. Marshall (hereinafter referred to as 'the appellant') and Southampton and South West Hampshire Area Health Authority (Teaching) hereinafter referred to as 'the respondent') concerning the question whether the appellant's dismissal was in accordance with section 6(4) of the Sex Discrimination Act 1975 and with Community law.

3. The appellant, who was born on 4 February 1918, was employed by the respondent from June 1966 to 31 March 1980. From 23 May 1974 she worked under a contract of employment as Senior Dietician.

4. On 31 March 1980, that is to say approximately four weeks after she had attained the age of 62, the appellant was dismissed, notwithstanding that she had expressed her willingness to continue in the employment until she reached the age of 65, that is to say until 4 February 1983.

5. According to the order for reference, the sole reason for the dismissal was the fact that the appellant was a woman who had passed 'the retirement age' applied by the respondent to women.

6. In that respect it appears from the documents before the Court that the respondent has followed a general policy since 1975 that 'the normal retirement age will be the age at which social security pensions become payable'. The Court of Appeal states that, although that policy was not expressly mentioned in the appellant's contract of employment, it none the less constituted an implied term thereof.

7. Sections 27(1) and 28(1) of the Social Security Act 1975, the United Kingdom legislation governing pensions, provide that State pensions are to be granted to men from the age of 65 and to women from the age of 60. However, the legislation does not impose any obligation to retire at the age at which the State pension becomes payable. Where an employee continues in employment after that age, payment of the State pension or of the pension under an occupational pension scheme is deferred.

8. However, the respondent was prepared, in its absolute discretion, to waive its general retirement policy in respect of a particular individual in particular circumstances and it did in fact waive that policy in respect of the appellant by employing her for a further two years after she had attained the age of 60.

9. In view of the fact that she suffered financial loss consisting of the difference between her earnings as an employee of the respondent and

her pension and since she had lost the satisfaction she derived from her work, the appellant instituted proceedings against the respondent before an Industrial Tribunal. She contended that her dismissal at the date and for the reason indicated by the respondent constituted discriminatory treatment by the respondent on the ground of sex and, accordingly, unlawful discrimination contrary to the Sex Discrimination Act and Community law.

10. The Industrial Tribunal dismissed the appellant's claim in so far as it was based on infringement of the Sex Discrimination Act, since section 6(4) of that Act permits discrimination on the ground of sex where it arises out of 'provision in relation to retirement'; the Industrial Tribunal took the view that the respondent's general policy constituted such provision. However, the claim that the principle of equality of treatment laid down by Directive No. 76/207 had been infringed was upheld by the Industrial Tribunal.

11. On appeal to the Employment Appeal Tribunal that decision was confirmed as regards the first point but was set aside as regards the second point on the ground that, although the dismissal violated the principle of equality of treatment laid down in the aforementioned directive, and individual could not rely upon such violation in proceedings before a United Kingdom court or tribunal.

12. The appellant appealed against that decision to the Court of Appeal. Observing that the respondent was constituted under section 8(1)A(b) of the National Health Service Act 1977 and was therefore an 'emanation of the State', the Court of Appeal referred the following questions to the Court of Justice for a preliminary ruling:

> '1. Whether the respondent's dismissal of the appellant after she had passed her sixtieth birthday pursuant to the policy [followed by the respondent] and on the grounds only that she was a woman who had passed the normal retiring age applicable to women was an act of discrimination prohibited by the Equal Treatment Directive.
> 2. If the answer to (1) above is in the affirmative, whether or not the Equal Treatment Directive can be relied upon by the appellant in the circumstances of the present case in national courts or tribunals notwithstanding the inconsistency (if any) between the directive and section 6(4) of the Sex Discrimination Act.'.

Relevant legal provisions
13. Article 1(1) of Directive No. 76/207 provides as follows:

241

'The purpose of this directive is to put into effect in the Member States the principle of equal treatment for men and women as regards access to employment, including promotion, and to vocational training and as regards working conditions and, on the conditions referred to in paragraph (2), social security. This principle is hereinafter referred to as "the principle of equal treatment".'.

14. Article 2(1) of the directive provides that:

'. . . the principle of equal treatment shall mean that there shall be no discrimination whatsoever on grounds of sex either directly or indirectly by reference in particular to marital or family status.'.

15. Article 5(1) of the directive provides that:

'Application of the principle of equal treatment with regard to working conditions, including the conditions governing dismissal, means that men and women shall be guaranteed the same conditions without discrimination on grounds of sex.'.

Article 5(2) thereof provides that:

'To this end, Member States shall take the measures necessary to ensure that:
(a) any laws, regulations and administrative provisions contrary to the principle of equal treatment shall be abolished;
(b) any provisions contrary to the principle of equal treatment which are included in collective agreements, individual contracts of employment, internal rules of undertakings or in rules governing the independent occupations and professions shall be, or may be declared, null and void or may be amended;
(c) those laws, regulations and administrative provisions contrary to the principle of equal treatment when the concern for protection which originally inspired them is no longer well founded shall be revised; and that where similar provisions are included in collective agreements labour and management shall be requested to undertake the desired revision.'.

16. Article 1(2) of the directive provides that:

'With a view to ensuring the progressive implementation of the principle of equal treatment in matters of social security, the Council, acting on a proposal from the Commission, will adopt

242

provisions defining its substance, its scope and the arrangements for its application.'.

17. Pursuant to the last-mentioned provision, the Council adopted Directive No. 79/7/EEC of 19 December 1978 on the progressive implementation of the principle of equal treatment for men and women in matters of social security (Official Journal 1979 No. L 6, p. 24), which the Member States were to transpose into national law, according to Article 8(1) thereof, within six years of its notification. The directive applies, according to Article 3(1) thereof, to:

'(a) statutory schemes which provide protection against the following risks:
sickness,
invalidity,
old age,
accidents at work and occupational diseases,
unemployment;
(b) social assistance, in so far as it is intended to supplement or replace the schemes referred to in (a)'.

18. According to Article 7(1) thereof, the directive is to be:

'without prejudice to the right of Member States to exclude from its scope:
(a) the determination of pensionable age for the purposes of granting old-age and retirement pensions and the possible consequences thereof for other benefits'.

19. With regard to occupational social security schemes, Article 3(3) of the directive provides that with a view to ensuring implementation of the principle of equal treatment in such schemes 'the Council, acting on a proposal from the Commission, will adopt provisions defining its substance, its scope and the arrangements for its application.' On 5 May 1983 the Commission submitted to the Council a proposal for a directive on the implementation of the principle of equal treatment for men and women in occupational social security schemes (Official Journal 1983 No. C 134, p. 7). The proposed directive would, according to Article 2(1) thereof, apply to 'benefits intended to supplement the benefits provided by statutory social security schemes or to replace them'. The Council has not yet responded to that proposal.

20. Observations were submitted to the Court by the United Kingdom and the Commission, in addition to the appellant and the respondent.

21. By the first question the Court of Appeal seeks to ascertain whether or not Article 5(1) of Directive No. 76/207 must be interpreted as meaning

that a general policy concerning dismissal, following by a State authority, involving the dismissal of a woman solely because she has attained or passed the qualifying age for a State pension, which age is different under national legislation for men and for women, constitutes discrimination on grounds of sex, contrary to that directive.

22. The appellant and the Commission consider that the first question must be answered in the affirmative.

23. According to the appellant, the said age limit falls within the term 'working conditions' within the meaning of Articles 1(1) and 5(1) of Directive No. 76/207. A wide interpretation of that term is, in her opinion, justified in view of the objective of the EEC Treaty to provide for "the constant improving of the living and working conditions of [the Member States'] peoples" and in view of the wording of the prohibition of discrimination laid down in the above-mentioned articles of Directive No. 76/206 and in Article 7(1) of Regulation No. 1612/68 of the Council of 15 October 1968 on freedom of movement of workers within the Community (Official Journal, English Special Edition 1968 (II), p. 475).

24. The appellant argues furthermore, that the elimination of discrimination on grounds of sex forms part of the *corpus* of fundamental human rights and therefore of the general principles of Community law. In accordance with the case-law of the European Court of Human Rights, those fundamental principles must be given a wide interpretation and, conversely, any exception thereto, such as the reservation provided for in Article 1(2) of Directive No. 76/207 with regard to social security, must be interpreted strictly.

25. In addition, the appellant considers that the exception provided for in Article 7(1) of Directive No. 79/7 with regard to the determination of pensionable age for the purposes of granting old-age and retirement pensions, is not relevant since, unlike Case 19/81 (*Burton* v. *British Railways Board*, [1982] ECR 555), this case does not relate to the determination of pensionable age. Moreover, in this case there is no link between the contractual retirement age and the qualifying age for a social security pension.

26. The Commission emphasizes that neither the respondent's employment policy nor the State social security schemes makes retirement compulsory upon a person's reaching pensionable age. On the contrary, the provisions of national legislation take into account the case of continued employment beyond the normal pensionable age. In those circumstances, it would be difficult to justify the dismissal of a woman for reasons based on her sex and age.

27. The Commission also refers to the fact that the Court has recognized that

equality of treatment for men and women constitutes a fundamental principle of Community law.

28. The respondent maintains, in contrast, that account must be taken, in accordance with the *Burton* case, of the link which it claims exists between the retirement ages imposed by it in the context of its dismissal policy, on the one hand, and the ages at which retirement and old-age pensions become payable under the State social security scheme in the United Kingdom, on the other. The laying down of different ages for the compulsory termination of a contract of employment merely reflects the minimum ages fixed by that scheme, since a male employee is permitted to continue in employment until the age of 65 precisely because he is not protected by the provision of a State pension before that age, whereas a female employee benefits from such protection from the age of 60.

29. The respondent considers that the provision of a State pension constitutes an aspect of social security and therefore falls within the scope not of Directive No. 76/207 but of Directive No. 79/7, which reserves to the Member States the right to impose different ages for the purpose of determining entitlement to State pensions. Since the situation is therefore the same as that in the *Burton* case, the fixing by the contract of employment of different retirement ages linked to the different minimum pensionable ages for men and women under national legislation does not constitute unlawful discrimination contrary to Community law.

30. The United Kingdom, which also takes that view, maintains, however, that treatment is capable of being discriminatory even in respect of a period after retirement in so far as the treatment in question arises out of employment or employment continues after the normal contractual retirement age.

31. The United Kingdom maintains, however, that in the circumstances of this case there is no discrimination in working conditions since the difference of treatment derives from the normal retirement age, which in turn is linked to the different minimum ages at which a State pension is payable.

32. The Court observes in the first place that the question of interpretation which has been referred to it does not concern access to a statutory or occupational retirement scheme, that is to say the conditions for payment of an old-age or retirement pension, but the fixing of an age limit with regard to the termination of employment pursuant to general policy concerning dismissal. The question therefore relates to the conditions governing dismissal and falls to be considered under Directive No. 76/207.

33. Article 5(1) of Directive No. 76/207 provides that application of the

principle of equal treatment with regard to working conditions, including the conditions governing dismissal, means that men and women are to be guaranteed the same conditions without discrimination on grounds of sex.

34. In its judgment in the *Burton* case the Court has already stated that the term 'dismissal' contained in that provision must be given a wide meaning. Consequently, an age limit for the compulsory dismissal of workers pursuant to an employer's general policy concerning retirement falls within the term 'dismissal' construed in that manner, even if the dismissal involves the grant of a retirement pension.

35. As the Court emphasized in its judgment in the *Burton* case, Article 7 of Directive No. 79/7 expressly provides that the directive does not prejudice the right of Member States to exclude from its scope the determination of pensionable age for the purposes of granting old-age and retirement pensions and the possible consequences thereof for other benefits falling within the statutory social security schemes. The Court thus acknowledged that benefits tied to a national scheme which lays down a different minimum pensionable age for men and women may lie outside the ambit of the aforementioned obligation.

36. However, in view of the fundamental importance of the principle of equality of treatment, which the Court has reaffirmed on numerous occasions, Article 1(2) of Directive No. 76/207, which excludes social security matters from the scope of that directive, must be interpreted strictly. Consequently, the exception to the prohibition of discrimination on grounds of sex provided for in Article 7(1)(a) of Directive No. 79/7 applies only to the determination of pensionable age for the purposes of granting old-age and retirement pensions and the possible consequences thereof for other benefits.

37. In that respect it must be emphasized that, whereas the exception contained in Article 7 of Directive No. 79/7 concerns the consequences which pensionable age has for social security benefits, this case is concerned with dismissal within the meaning of Article 5 of Directive No. 76/207.

38. Consequently, the answer to the first question referred to the Court by the Court of Appeal must be that Article 5(1) of Directive No. 76/207 must be interpreted as meaning that a general policy concerning dismissal involving the dismissal of a woman solely because she has attained the qualifying age for a State pension, which age is different under national legislation for men and for women, constitutes discrimination on grounds of sex, contrary to that directive.

The second question
39. Since the first question has been answered in the affirmative, it is neces-

sary to consider whether Article 5(1) of Directive No. 76/207 may be relied upon by an individual before national courts and tribunals.

40. The appellant and the Commission consider that that question must be answered in the affirmative. They contend in particular, with regard to Articles 2(1) and 5(1) of Directive No. 76/207, that those provisions are sufficiently clear to enable national courts to apply them without legislative intervention by the Member States, at least so far as overt discrimination is concerned.

41. In support of that view, the appellant points out that directives are capable of conferring rights on individuals which may be relied upon directly before the courts of the Member States; national courts are obliged by virtue of the binding nature of a directive, in conjunction with Article 5 of the EEC Treaty, to give effect to the provisions of directives where possible, in particular when construing or applying relevant provisions of national law (judgment of 10 April 1984 in Case 14/83, *von Colson and Kamann* v. *Land Nordrhein-Westfalen*, [1984] ECR 1891). Where there is any inconsistency between national law and Community law which cannot be removed by means of such a construction, the appellant submits that a national court is obliged to declare that the provision of national law which is inconsistent with the directive is inapplicable.

42. The Commission is of the opinion that the provisions of Article 5(1) of Directive No. 76/207 are sufficiently clear and unconditional to be relied upon before a national court. They may therefore be set up against section 6(4) of the Sex Discrimination Act, which, according to the decisions of the Court of Appeal, has been extended to the question of compulsory retirement and has therefore become ineffective to prevent dismissals based upon the difference in retirement ages for men and for women.

43. The respondent and the United Kingdom propose, conversely, that the second question should be answered in the negative. They admit that a directive may, in certain specific circumstances, have direct effect as against a Member State in so far as the latter may not rely on its failure to perform its obligations under the directive. However, they maintain that a directive can never impose obligations directly on individuals and that it can only have direct effect against a Member State *qua* public authority and not against a Member State *qua* employer. As an employer a State is no different from a private employer. It would not therefore be proper to put persons employed by the State in a better position than those who are employed by a private employer.

44. With regard to the legal position of the respondent's employees the United Kingdom states that they are in the same position as the em-

ployees of a private employer. Although according to United Kingdom constitutional law the health authorities, created by the National Health Service Act 1977, as amended by the Health Services Act 1980 and other legislation, are Crown bodies and their employees are Crown servants, nevertheless the administration of the National Health Service by the health authorities is regarded as being separate from the Government's central administration and its employees are not regarded as civil servants.

45. Finally, both the respondent and the United Kingdom take the view that the provisions of Directive No. 76/207 are neither unconditional nor sufficiently clear and precise to give rise to direct effect. The directive provides for a number of possible exceptions, the details of which are to be laid down by the Member States. Furthermore, the wording of Article 5 is quite imprecise and requires the adoption of measures for its implementation.

46. It is necessary to recall that, according to a long line of decisions of the Court (in particular its judgment of 19 January 1982 in Case 8/81, *Becker* v. *Finanzamt Münster-Innenstadt*, [1982] ECR 53), wherever the provisions of a directive appear, as far as their subject-matter is concerned, to be unconditional and sufficiently precise, those provisions may be relied upon by an individual against the State where that State fails to implement the directive in national law by the end of the period prescribed or where it fails to implement the directive correctly.

47. That view is based on the consideration that it would be incompatible with the binding nature which Article 189 confers on the directive to hold as a matter of principle that the obligation imposed thereby cannot be relied on by those concerned. From that the Court deduced that a Member State which has not adopted the implementing measures required by the directive within the prescribed period may not plead, as against individuals, its own failure to perform the obligations which the directive entails.

48. With regard to the argument that a directive may not be relied upon against an individual, it must be emphasized that according to Article 189 of the EEC Treaty the binding nature of a directive, which constitutes the basis for the possibility of relying on the directive before a national court, exists only in relation to 'each Member State to which it is addressed'. It follows that a directive may not of itself impose obligations on an individual and that a provision of a directive may not be relied upon as such against such a person. It must therefore be examined whether, in this case, the respondent must be regarded as having acted as an individual.

49. In that respect it must be pointed out that where a person involved in legal proceedings is able to rely on a directive as against the State he may

do so regardless of the capacity in which the latter is acting, whether employer or public authority. In either case it is necessary to prevent the State from taking advantage of its own failure to comply with Community law.

50. It is for the national court to apply those considerations to the circumstances of each case; the Court of Appeal has, however, stated in the order for reference that the respondent, Southampton and South West Hampshire Area Health Authority (Teaching), is a public authority.

51. The argument submitted by the United Kingdom that the possibility of relying on provision of the directive against the respondent *qua* organ of the State would give rise to an arbitrary and unfair distinction between the rights of State employees and those of private employees does not justify any other conclusion. Such a distinction may easily be avoided if the Member State concerned has correctly implemented the directive in national law.

52. Finally, with regard to the question whether the provision contained in Article 5(1) of Directive No. 76/207, which implements the principle of equality of treatment set out in Article 2(1) of the directive, may be considered, as far as its contents are concerned, to be unconditional and sufficiently precise to be relied upon by an individual as against the State, it must be stated that the provision, taken by itself, prohibits any discrimination on grounds of sex with regard to working conditions, including the conditions governing dismissal, in a general manner and in unequivocal terms. The provision is therefore sufficiently precise to be relied on by an individual and to be applied by the national courts.

53. It is necessary to consider next whether the prohibition of discrimination laid down by the directive may be regarded as unconditional, in the light of the exceptions contained therein and of the fact that according to Article 5(2) thereof the Member States are to take the measures necessary to ensure the application of the principle of equality of treatment in the context of national law.

54. With regard, in the first place, to the reservation contained in Article 1(2) of Directive No. 76/207 concerning the application of the principle of equality of treatment in matters of social security, it must be observed that, although the reservation limits the scope of the directive *ratione materiae*, it does not lay down any condition on the application of that principle in its field of operation and in particular in relation to Article 5 of the directive. Similarly, the exceptions to Directive No. 76/207 provided for in Article 2 thereof are not relevant to this case.

55. It follows that Article 5 of Directive No. 76/207 does not confer on the Member States the right to limit the application of the principle of

equality of treatment in its field of operation or to subject it to conditions and that that provision is sufficiently precise and unconditional to be capable of being relied upon by an individual before a national court in order to avoid the application of any national provision which does not conform to Article 5(1).

56. Consequently, the answer to the second question must be that Article 5(1) of Coucil Directive No. 76/207 of 9 February 1976, which prohibits any discrimination on grounds of sex with regard to working conditions, including the conditions governing dismissal, may be relied upon as against a State authority acting in its capacity as employer, in order to avoid the application of any national provision which does not conform to Article 5(1).

Costs
57. The costs incurred by the United Kingdom and the Commission of the European Communities, which have submitted observations to the Court, are not recoverable. As these proceedings are, in so far as the parties to the main proceedings are concerned, in the nature of a step in the action before the national court, the decision as to costs is a matter for that court.

On those grounds,

THE COURT,

in answer to the questions referred to it by the Court of Appeal by an order of 12 March 1984, hereby rules:

1. **Article 5(1) of Directive No. 76/207 must be interpreted as meaning that a general policy concerning dismissal involving the dismissal of a woman solely because she has attained or passed the qualifying age for a State pension, which age is different under national legislation for men and for women, constitutes discrimination on grounds of sex, contrary to that directive.**

2. **Article 5(1) of Council Directive No. 76/207 of 9 February 1976, which prohibits any discrimination on grounds of sex with regard to working conditions, including the conditions governing dismissal, may be relied upon as against a State authority acting in its capacity as employer, in order to avoid the application of any national provision which does not conform to Article 5(1).**

Mackenzie Stuart   Everling   Bahlmann

Bosco   Koopmans   Due   O'Higgins

Delivered in open court in Luxembourg on 26 February 1986.

P. Heim
Registrar

A. J. Mackenzie Stuart
President

Judgment of the Court

26 February 1986 – Case 262/84

Vera Mia Beets-Proper
v.
F. van Lanschot Bankiers N. V.

Equal treatment for men and women – Article 5(1) of Directive 76/207/EEC applies equal treatment principle to working conditions including dismissal – dismissal must be given wide meaning, and can include age limit for compulsory dismissal of workers in accordance with an employer's general policy on retirement, even if dismissal involves grant of a retirement pension – Article 1(2) of Directive 76/207/EEC, which excludes from scope social security matters, must be strictly interpreted – exception to prohibition of discrimination on grounds of sex in Article 7(1)(a) of Directive 79/7/EEC applies only to determination of pensionable age for purposes of granting old age and retirement pensions and its consequences for other social security benefits – Article 5(1) of Directive 76/207/EEC to be interpreted as meaning that Member States not free to exempt from scope of equal treatment principle an express or implied condition in a contract of employment based on a collective agreement, if that condition has the effect of terminating the contract on grounds of the age attained by an employee, where the relevant age is determined by the age, different for men and women, at which employee becomes entitled to retirement pension (Council Directive 76/207/ EEC, Articles 1(2) and 5(1); Council Directive 79/7/EEC, Article 7(1)).

In Case 262/84

REFERENCE to the Court under Article 177 of the EEC Treaty by the Hoge Raad der Nederlanden [Supreme Court of the Netherlands] for a preliminary ruling in the proceedings pending before that court between

Vera Mia Beets-Proper, residing in Amsterdam,

and

F. van Lanschot Bankiers N. V., whose registered office is in 's-Hertogenbosch,

on the interpretation of Council Directive No. 76/207 of 9 February 1976 on the implementation of the principle of equal treatment for men and women as regards access to employment, vocational training and promotion, and working conditions (Official Journal 1976 No. L 39, p. 40),

THE COURT

composed of: Lord Mackenzie Stuart, President, U. Everling and K. Bahlmann (Presidents of Chambers), G. Bosco, T. Koopmans, O. Due and T. F. O'Higgins, Judges,

Advocate General: Sir Gordon Slynn
Registrar: D. Louterman, Administrator

gives the following JUDGMENT

Decision

1. By an order of 2 November 1984, which was received at the Court on 9 November 1984, the Hoge Raad der Nederlanden referred to the Court for a preliminary ruling under Article 177 of the EEC Treaty a question concerning the interpretation of Council Directive No. 76/207 of 9 February 1976 on the implementation of the principle of equal treatment for men and women as regards access to employment, vocational training and promotion, and working conditions (Official Journal 1976 No. L 39, p. 40).

2. The question was raised in the course of proceedings between V. M. Beets-Proper (hereinafter referred to as 'the appellant') and F. van Lanschot Bankiers N.V. (hereinafter referred to as 'the respondent') concerning the compatibility of the appellant's dismissal with Article 1637ij of the Netherlands Civil Code and with Community law.

3. The appellant worked as a secretary with Vermeer & Co., bankers, of Amsterdam, from 1969 until that company's amalgamation in 1972 with the respondent, and from then until the end of August 1982 with the latter. The employment relationship between the parties was governed by the collective labour agreement for the banking sector for the years 1980 and 1981 and the pension scheme of the 'F. van Lanschot Pension Fund'.

4. Article 3 of that scheme provides that the persons affiliated to it are entitled to an old-age pension 'from the date of retirement'. That date is defined in Article 1 as 'the first day of the month following the month in which a person affiliated to the scheme attains the age of 65 in the case of a man and 60 in the case of a woman'.

5. Since the appellant reached the age of 60 in August 1982, the respondent took the view that the employment relationship automatically ended on 1

252

September 1982 by virtue of an implied condition to that effect in the contract of employment, without the need for any notice of dismissal. By a letter dated 2 August 1982 the respondent informed the appellant that she was entitled to an old-age pension together with a supplementary pension payable until she attained the age of 65. She has not been admitted to work since 1 September 1982.

6. In May 1981 the appellant had expressed her wish to continue her employment, possibly on a part-time basis, after the date on which she was due to retire. In November 1981 the respondent had informed her that her wish could not be satisfied.

7. By a writ of 16 September 1982 the appellant applied to the president of the Arrondissementsrechtbank [District Court], Amsterdam, for an interlocutory injunction requiring the respondent to allow her to resume her work as an executive secretary in the respondent's offices and to pay her salary from 1 September 1982 until such time as the contract of employment should be terminated in a legally valid manner.

8. The appellant also submitted a complaint to the *Commissie Gelijke Behandeling van Mannen en Vrouwen bij de Arbeid* [Commission on Equal Treatment of Men and Women in Employment at Work], established by the *Wet gelijk loon voor vrouwen en mannen* [Law on equal pay for men and women] (*Staatsblad* 1975, p. 129). In its opinion of 14 February 1983 on that complaint, the Commission concluded 'that a direct distinction is made, to the disadvantage of the applicant, between men and women with regard to the termination of the contract of employment by the application of different age limits'.

9. After the dismissal of the appellant's application by the Arrondissementsrechtbank she appealed to the Gerechtshof [Regional Court of Appeal], Amsterdam, which, by judgment of 19 May 1983, confirmed the judgment of the lower court on the ground 'that the exception referred to in the second sentence of paragraph (1) of Article 1637ij [of the Civil Code] is applicable in this case'.

10. Article 1637ij of the Netherlands Civil Code provides as follows:

'(1) As regards the conclusion of a contract of employment, staff training, the terms of employment, promotion and the termination of the contract of employment, an employer may not make any distinction between men and women, either directly or indirectly, for example by reference to marital status or family circumstances. The terms of employment do not include benefits or entitlements under pension schemes. The first sentence of this paragraph shall not apply in those cases in which an employee's sex is a decisive factor.

(2) Any clause which is contrary to the first sentence of paragraph (1) shall be void.

(3) The first sentence of paragraph (1) shall not apply as far as concerns clauses relating to the protection of women, in particular in connexion with pregnancy and maternity.

(4) The first sentence of paragraph (1) shall not apply as far as concerns clauses which are intended to place employees of a particular sex in a privileged position in order to eliminate factual inequalities.

(5) The termination of a person's employment by an employer on account of the fact that the employee has invoked the provisions of paragraph (1), whether before a court or otherwise, shall be void. An employee shall be entitled to invoke the nullity of the termination of his employment during a period of two months after he was given notice or after his employment was terminated if his employer terminated it otherwise than by giving notice. He shall do so by serving notice on the employer. The termination of employment referred to in the first sentence of this paragraph shall not make the employer liable in damages.

(6) When concluding or terminating a contract of employment, an employer may not make any distinction between married and unmarried persons.'.

11. The Gerechtshof, Amsterdam, based its judgment on the existence of a 'close connexion between the termination of the contract of employment and the commencement of the pension', and in particular on the fact that the respondent's female employees, who retire at the age of 60, acquire pension rights, on a non-contributory basis, at a rate of 2 per cent of the basic salary for each year of service, whereas male employees, whose retirement age is fixed at 65, acquire such rights at the rate of 1.75 per cent.".

12. The appellant brought an appeal on a point of law against that judgment before the Hoge Raad der Nederlanden, which referred the following question to the Court of Justice for a preliminary ruling:

'Does Council Directive No. 76/207/EEC of 9 February 1976 allow the Member States the freedom not to include among the conditions of employment in respect of which equal treatment for men and women must be laid down pursuant to that directive an express or implied condition concerning the termination of the contract of employment on the ground of the age attained by the employee, where that condition relates to the age at which the employee becomes entitled to a pension?'.

Relevant legal provisions
13. Article 1(1) of Directive No. 76/207 provides as follows:

> 'The purpose of this directive is to put into effect in the Member States the principle of equal treatment for men and women as regards access to employment, including promotion, and to vocational training and as regards working conditions and, on the conditions referred to in paragraph (2), social security. This principle is hereinafter referred to as "the principle of equal treatment".'.

14. Article 2(1) of the directive provides that:

> 'The principle of equal treatment shall mean that there shall be no discrimination whatsoever on grounds of sex either directly or indirectly by reference in particular to marital or family status.'.

15. Article 5(1) of the directive provides that:

> 'Application of the principle of equal treatment with regard to working conditions, including the conditions governing dismissal, means that men and women shall be guaranteed the same conditions without discrimination on grounds of sex.'.

16. Article 1(2) of the directive provides that:

> 'With a view to ensuring the progressive implementation of the principle of equal treatment in matters of social security, the Council, acting on a proposal from the Commission, will adopt provisions defining its substance, its scope and the arrangements for its application.'.

17. Pursuant to the last-mentioned provision, the Council adopted Directive No. 79/7/EEC of 19 December 1978 on the progressive implementation of the principle of equal treatment for men and women in matters of social security (Official Journal 1979 No. L 6, p. 24), which Member States were to transpose into national law, according to Article 8(1) thereof, within six years of its notification. The directive applies, according to Article 3(1) thereof, to:

> '(a) statutory schemes which provide protection against the following risks:
> sickness,
> invalidity,
> old age,
> accidents at work and occupational diseases,
> unemployment;

255

(b) social assistance, in so far as it is intended to supplement or replace the schemes referred to in (a).'.

18. According to Article 7(1) thereof, the directive is to be:

'without prejudice to the right of Member States to exclude from its scope:
(a) the determination of pensionable age for the purposes of granting old-age and retirement pensions and the possible consequences thereof for other benefits.'.

19. With regard to occupational social security schemes, Article 3(3) of the directive provides that with a view to ensuring implementation of the principle of equal treatment in such schemes 'the Council, acting on a proposal from the Commission, will adopt provisions defining its substance, its scope and the arrangements for its application'. On 5 May 1983 the Commission submitted to the Council a proposal for a directive on the implementation of the principle of equal treatment for men and women in occupational social security schemes (Official Journal 1983 No. C 134, p. 7). The proposed directive would, according to Article 2(1) thereof, apply to 'benefits intended to supplement the benefits provided by statutory social security schemes or to replace them'. The Council has not yet responded to that proposal.

20. It is evident from the documents before the Court that Article 7 of the *Algemene Ouderdomswet* [General Law an Old-age] (for the version in force at the material time, *see Staatsblad* 1956, p. 281; for the version now in force, *see Staatsblad* 1985, p. 181) lays down a single pensionable age for persons of either sex, namely 65.

21. Observations were submitted to the Court in this case by the Government of the Kingdom of the Netherlands, the Government of the Kingdom of Denmark, the United Kingdom and the Commission, in addition to the appellant and the respondent.

The question referred to the Court
22. The appallent, the Danish Government and the Commission considered that the reply to the question must be in the negative.

23. In essence the appellant contends that the case before the Court concerns a difference of treatment not with regard to the conditions for the grant of an old-age and retirement pension, in respect of which an age differential may be maintained provisionally under Article 1(2) of Directive No. 76/207 and Article 7(1) of Directive No. 79/7, but with regard to the conditions governing dismissal within the meaning of Article 5(1) of Directive No. 76/207.

24. In the appellant's view, since the Community legislature intended the principle of equality of treatment for men and women to be applied as extensively as possible in employment matters as a fundamental principle of Community law, the expression 'conditions of employment' must be construed widely so as to encompass the conditions on which a contract of employment is terminated, whereas the exception to that principle must be interpreted narrowly and extends to pension benefits only.

25. According to the appellant, an express or implied condition concerning the termination of a contract of employment does not cease to be a "condition of employment" because it relates to the age at which the employee becomes entitled to an old-age pension, since a link between those two fields is unknown to Community law. Furthermore, such a link may not be deduced from the Court's judgment of 16 February 1982 (Case 19/81, *Burton* v. *British Railways Board*, [1982] ECR 555), which concerned the different question of the conditions of access to a voluntary redundancy scheme.

26. The Commission likewise contends that the termination of a contract of employment, whether by way of dismissal or automatically, is included in the concept 'conditions of employment' and does not fall within the exceptions to the principle of equality of treatment referred to in Article 2 of Directive No. 76/207 or within the scope of Directive No. 79/7. In that connexion it states that in the national legal systems termination of a contract of employment also falls within the sphere of labour law rather than of social security law. The fact that the termination of such a contract coincides with the retirement age cannot have the effect of excluding it from the scope of Directive No. 76/207.

27. The Danish Government, which in essence shares that view, adds that when implementing Directive No. 76/207 in national law the Danish legislature interpreted the prohibition of discrimination contained in Article 5(1) of the directive as meaning that the age at which a person's contract of employment terminates for the purposes of retirement can no longer vary according to the employee's sex.

28. In contrast, the respondent contends that in order to resolve the question whether or not the difference in treatment in question is discriminatory, within the meaning of Directive No. 76/207, it is necessary to take into account, in accordance with the judgment in the *Burton* case, the link which the respondent considers to exist between the contractual provisions applicable in this case and the rule on pensionable age under the occupational retirement scheme.

29. In that connexion the respondent points out that its pension scheme provides that members of the scheme become entitled to a pension at the age of 65 in the case of male employees and at the age of 60 in the case of

female employees and that the fixing of different ages for compulsory termination of the contract of employment is directly linked to that difference in pensionable age since, under Netherlands law, termination of the contract of employment is the immediate and automatic consequence of the operation of the pension scheme and the reaching of pensionable age. A contract of employment for an unlimited period has a maximum term determined by reference to pensionable age, so that it terminates automatically on the date at which the pension becomes payable; it is therefore unnecessary to include an express term to that effect in the contract. Consequently, as long as pension schemes provide for pensionable ages which are different for men and women, their contracts of employment will terminate at different ages.

30. In the respondent's opinion, it follows from the judgment in the *Burton* case that, in view of that link between pensionable age and retirement age, the difference of treatment accorded to men and women in this case does not fall within the prohibition of discrimination contained in Directive No. 76/207 but is compatible with Community law in so far as the Member States retain the power, by virtue of the exception in favour of social security matters contained in Article 1(2) of Directive No. 76/207, to fix different retirement ages for men and women.

31. It is possible to conclude, in the respondent's view, that Directive No. 76/207 leaves the Member States free not to include, among the conditions of employment in respect of which equal treatment for men and women must be laid down pursuant to that directive, an express or implied condition concerning termination of the contract of employment on the ground of the age attained by the employee where that condition is linked to the age at which the employee becomes entitled to a pension.

32. The Government of the Netherlands and the United Kingdom are also of the opinion that the difference in treatment in question is not contrary to Community law in view of the link between termination of the contract of employment and the retirement age fixed in the pension scheme and in view of the fact that there is no directive providing that such an age differential in occupational social security schemes is discriminatory.

33. The Netherlands Government also contends that in view of the close relationship between the date of termination of the contract of employment, on the one hand, and the date of retirement and the terms of the pension scheme, on the other, any other interpretation could have the effect of forcing employers and pension funds in many cases to fix the terms of their pension schemes and the retirement date according to their own perceptions.

34. The Court observes in the first place that the question of interpretation referred to it does not concern access to a statutory or occupational

retirement scheme, that is to say the conditions for the payment of an old-age or retirement pension, but the fixing of an age limit with regard to the termination of employment. That question concerns the conditions governing dismissal and therefore falls to be considered under Directive No. 76/207.

35. Article 5(1) of Directive No. 76/207 provides that application of the principle of equal treatment with regard to working conditions, including the conditions governing dismissal, means that men and women are to be guaranteed the same conditions without discrimination on grounds of sex.

36. In its judgment in the *Burton* case the Court has already stated that the word 'dismissal' contained in that provision must be given a wide meaning. Consequently, an age limit for the compulsory dismissal of workers pursuant to an employer's general policy concerning retirement falls within the term 'dismissal' construed in that manner, even if the dismissal involves the grant of a retirement pension.

37. As the Court emphasized in that judgment, Article 7 of Directive No. 79/7 expressly provides that the directive does not prejudice the right of Member States to exclude from its scope the determination of retirement age for the purpose of granting old-age and retirement pensions and the possible consequences thereof for other benefits falling within the statutory social security schemes. The Court thus acknowledged that benefits linked to a national scheme which lays down a different pensionable age for men and women may lie outside the ambit of the aforementioned obligation.

38. However, in view of the fundamental importance of the principle of equality of treatment, which the Court has reaffirmed on numerous occasions, Article 1(2) of Directive No. 76/207, which excludes social security matters from the scope of that directive, must be interpreted strictly. Consequently, the exception to the prohibition of discrimination on grounds of sex contained in Article 7(1)(a) of Directive No. 79/7 applies only to the determination of pensionable age for the purposes of granting old-age and retirement pensions and to the consequences thereof for other social security benefits.

39. In that respect it must be emphasized that, whereas the exception contained in Article 7 of Directive No. 79/7 concerns the consequences which pensionable age has for social security benefits, this case is concerned with dismissal within the meaning of Article 5 of Directive No. 76/207.

40. Consequently, the answer to the question referred to the Court of Justice by the Hoge Raad der Nederlanden must be that Article 5(1) of Directive No. 76/207 must be interpreted as meaning that it does not allow the

259

Member States the freedom to exempt from the application of the principle of equality of treatment an express or implied condition in a contract of employment concluded on the basis of a collective agreement, if that condition has the effect of terminating the contract of employment on the ground of the age attained by the employee and the relevant age is determined by the age – which is different for men and women – at which the employee becomes entitled to a retirement pension.

Costs

41. The costs incurred by Denmark, the Netherlands, the United Kingdom and the Commission of the European Communities, which have submitted observations to the Court, are not recoverable. As these proceedings are, in so far as the parties to the main proceedings are concerned, in the nature of a step in the action before the national court, the decision as to costs is a matter for that court.

On those grounds,

THE COURT,

in answer to the question referred to it by the Hoge Raad der Nederlanden by an order of 2 November 1984, hereby rules:

Article 5(1) of Directive No. 76/207 must be interpreted as meaning that it does not allow the Member States the freedom to exempt from the application of the principle of equality of treatment an express or implied condition in a contract of employment concluded on the basis of a collective wage agreement, if that condition has the effect of terminating the contract of employment on the ground of the age attained by the employee and the relevant age is determined by the age – which is different for men and women – at which the employee becomes entitled to a retirement pension.

Mackenzie Stuart		Everling		Bahlmann
Bosco	Koopmans		Due	O'Higgins

Delivered in open court in Luxembourg on 26 February 1986.

P. Heim
Registrar

A. J. Mackenzie Stuart
President

Judgment of the Court

15 May 1986 – Case 222/84

Marguerite Johnston
v.
Chief Constable of the Royal Ulster Constabulary

Equal treatment for men and women – principles on which European Human Rights Convention based to be taken into consideration in Community law – principle of effective judicial control in Article 6 of Directive 76/207/EEC, also in European Convention, does not allow certificate issued by national authority, stating that conditions for derogating from equal treatment principle to protect public safety are satisfied, to be treated as conclusive evidence so as to exclude exercise of any review power by courts – Article 6 provision, entitling those wronged by discrimination to an effective judicial remedy, may be relied on by individuals against a Member State which has not ensured its implementation nationally – acts of sex discrimination done for reasons related to public safety must be examined in light of derogations from equal treatment principle in Directive – Article 2(2) and 2(3) derogations relating to access to employment and working conditions should be strictly interpreted – Article 2(2) of Directive to be interpreted as meaning that in deciding whether, because of context in which police officer's activities carried out, sex of the officer is determining factor for that occupational activity, Member State may take account of requirements of public safety to restrict general policing duties, in an internal situation involving frequent assassinations, to men with fire-arms – differences in men's and women's treatment allowed by Article 2(3) of Directive so as to protect women do not include risks and dangers, such as those to which any armed police officer is exposed, which do not specifically affect women – individuals may claim application, against State authority charged with maintenance of public order and safety acting in capacity as employer, of equal treatment principle in Article 2(1) of Directive to matters concerning access to posts and training, so as to set aside any national derogation which exceeds limits of Directive's permissible exceptions (EEC Treaty, Article 224; Council Directive 76/207/EEC, Articles 2(1), (2), (3), 3(1), 4(1) and 6).

In Case 222/84

REFERENCE to the Court under Article 177 of the EEC Treaty by the Industrial Tribunal of Northern Ireland, for a preliminary ruling in the action pending before that court between

Marguerite Johnston

and

The Chief Constable of the Royal Ulster Constabulary

on the interpretation of Council Directive No. 76/207/EEC of 9 February 1976 on the implementation of the principle of equal treatment for men and women (Official Journal 1976 No. L 39, p. 40) and of Article 224 of the EEC Treaty,

THE COURT

composed of: Lord Mackenzie Stuart, President, T. Koopmans, U. Everling, K. Bahlmann and R. Joliet, Presidents of Chamber, O. Due, Y. Galmot, C. N. Kakouris and T. F. O'Higgins, Judges,

Advocate General: M. Darmon
Registrar: P. Heim

gives the following JUDGMENT

Decision

1. By a decision dated 8 August 1984, which was received at the Court on 4 September 1984, the Industrial Tribunal of Northern Ireland, Belfast, referred to the Court for a preliminary ruling under Article 177 of the EEC Treaty several questions on the interpretation of Council Directive No. 76/207/EEC of 9 February 1976 on the implementation of the principle of equal treatment for men and women (Official Journal 1976 No. L 39, p. 40) and of Article 224 of the EEC Treaty.

2. Those questions were raised in a dispute between Mrs Marguerite I. Johnston and the Chief Constable of the Royal Ulster Constabulary (the 'RUC'). The Chief Constable is the competent authority for appointing reserve constables to the RUC Reserve in Northern Ireland and to full-time posts in the RUC full-time Reserve under three-year renewable contracts. The dispute concerns the Chief Constable's refusal to renew Mrs Johnston's contract as a member of the RUC full-time Reserve and to allow her to be given training in the handling and use of fire-arms.

3. According to the decision making the reference for a preliminary ruling, the provisions of the Royal Ulster Constabulary Reserve (Appointment and Conditions of Service) Regulations (Northern Ireland) 1973, which govern the appointment and conditions of service of members of the reserve police force, do not make any distinction between men and women which is of important in this case. It is also clear from Articles 10 and 19 of the Sex Discrimination (Northern Ireland) Order 1976 (S.I. 1976 No. 1042 (N.I. 15)), which lays down rules to eliminate sex discrimination and implements the principle of equal treatment as regards access to employment, vocational training and promotion and working conditions, that the ban on discrimination applies to employ-

ment with the police and that men and women are not to be treated differently in this respect, except as regards requirements relating to height, uniform or equipment, or allowances in lieu of uniform or equipment. Article 53(1) of the Sex Discrimination Order provides that none of its provisions prohibiting discrimination

> 'shall render unlawful an act done for the purpose of safeguarding national security or of protecting public safety or public order',

whilst Article 53(2) provides that

> 'a certificate signed by or on behalf of the Secretary of State and certifying that an act specified in the certificate was done for a purpose mentioned in paragraph (1) shall be conclusive evidence that it was done for that purpose'.

4. In the United Kingdom police officers do not as a general rule carry fire-arms in the performance of their duties except for special operations and no distinction is made in this regard between men and women. Because of the high number of police officers assassinated in Northern Ireland over a number of years, the Chief Constable of the RUC considered that he could not maintain that practice. He decided that, in the RUC and the RUC Reserve, men should carry fire-arms in the regular course of their duties but that women would not be equipped with them and would not receive training in the handling and use of fire-arms.

5. In those circumstances, the Chief Constable decided in 1980 that the number of women in the RUC was sufficient for the particular tasks generally assigned to women officers. He took the view that general police duties, frequently involving operations requiring the carrying of fire-arms, should no longer be assigned to women and decided not to offer or renew any more contracts for women in the RUC full-time Reserve except where they had to perform duties assigned only to women officers. Since that decision, no woman in the RUC full-time Reserve has been offered a contract or had her contract renewed, save in one case.

6. According to the decision making the reference for a preliminary ruling, Mrs Johnston had been a member of the RUC full-time Reserve from 1974 to 1980. She had efficiently performed the general duties of a uniformed police officer, such as acting as station-duty officer, taking part in mobile patrols, driving the patrol vehicle and assisting in searching persons brought to the police station. She was not armed when carrying out those duties and was ordinarily accompanied in duties outside the police station by an armed male officer of the RUC full-time Reserve. In 1980 the Chief Constable refused to renew her contract because of his new policy, mentioned above, with regard to female members of the RUC full-time Reserve.

7. Mrs Johnston lodged an application with the Industrial Tribunal challenging the decision, taken pursuant to that new policy, to refuse to renew her contract and to give her training in the handling of fire-arms. She contended that she had suffered unlawful discrimination prohibited by the Sex Discrimination Order.

8. In the proceedings before the Industrial Tribunal the Chief Constable produced a certificate issued by the Secretary of State in which that Minister of the United Kingdom Government certified in accordance with Article 53 of the Sex Discrimination Order, cited above, that 'the act consisting of the refusal of the Royal Ulster Constabulary to offer further full-time employment to Mrs Marguerite I. Johnston in the Royal Ulster Constabulary Reserve was done for the purpose of (a) safeguarding national security; and (b) protecting public safety and public order'.

9. Mrs Johnston referred to Directive No. 76/207. The purpose of that directive, according to Article 1 thereof, is to put into effect the principle of equal treatment for men and women as regards access to employment, including promotion, and to vocational training and as regards working conditions. According to Article 2(1), the principle of equal treatment means that there shall be no discrimination whatsoever on grounds of sex, subject, however, to the exceptions allowed by Article 2(2) and (3). For the purposes of the application of that principle in different spheres, Articles 3 to 5 require the Member States in particular to abolish any laws, regulations or administrative provisions contrary to the principle of equal treatment and to revise laws, regulations and administrative provisions where the concern for protection which originally inspired them is no longer well founded. Article 6 provides that all persons who consider themselves wronged by discrimination must be able to pursue their claims by judicial process.

10. In order to be able to rule on that dispute, the Industrial Tribunal referred the following questions to the Court for a preliminary ruling:
    1. On the proper construction of Council Directive No. 76/207 and in the circumstances of this case, can a Member State exclude from the directive's field of application acts of sex discrimination as regards access to employment done for the purpose of safeguarding national security or of protecting public safety or public order?
    2. On the proper construction of the directive and in the circumstances of this case, is full-time employment as an armed member of a police reserve force, or training in the handling and use of fire-arms for such empolyment, capable of constituting one of those occupational activities and, where appropriate, the training leading thereto for which, by reason of their nature or the context in which they are carried out, the sex of the worker constitutes a determining factor, within the meaning of Article 2(2)?
    3. What are the principles and criteria by which Member States should

determine whether 'the sex of a worker constitutes a determining factor' within the meaning of Article 2(2) in relation to (a) the 'occupational activities' of an armed member of such a force and (b) 'the training leading thereto', whether by reason of their nature or by reason of the context in which they are carried out?

4. Is a policy applied by a chief constable of police, charged with a statutory responsibility for the direction and control of a police force, that women members of that force should not carry fire-arms capable, in the circumstances of this case, of constituting a 'provision concerning the protection of women', within the meaning of Article 2(3), or an 'administrative provision' inspired by 'concern for protection' within the meaning of Article 3(2)(c) of the directive?

5. If the answer to question 4 is affirmative, what are the principles and criteria by which Member States should determine whether the 'concern for protection' is 'well founded', within the meaning of Article 3(2)(c)?

6. Is the applicant entitled to rely upon the principle of equal treatment contained in the relevant provisions of the directive before the national courts and tribunals of Member States in the circumstances of the present case?

7. If the answer to question 6 is affirmative:
    (a) Does Article 224 of the EEC Treaty, on its proper construction, permit Member States when confronted with serious internal disturbances affecting the maintenance of law and order to derogate from any obligations which would otherwise be imposed on them or on employers within their jurisdiction by the directive?
    (b) If so, is it open to an individual to rely upon the fact that a Member State did not consult with other Member States for the purpose of preventing the first Member State from relying on Article 224 of the EEC Treaty?

11. To enable answers to be given which will be of assistance in resolving the dispute in the main proceedings, it is necessary to explain the situation in which the Industrial Tribunal is required to adjudicate. As is clear from the decision by which the case was referred to the Court, the Chief Constable acknowledged before the Industrial Tribunal that, of all the provisions in the Sex Discrimination Order, only Article 53 could justify his position. Mrs Johnston, for her part, conceded that the certificate issued by the Secretary of State would deprive her of any remedy if national law was applied on its own; she relied on the provisions of the directive in order to have the effects of Article 53 of the Sex Discrimination Order set aside.

12. It therefore appears that the questions raised by the Industrial Tribunal are intended to ascertain first of all whether it is compatible with Community law and Directive No. 76/207 for a national court or tribunal

to be prevented by a rule such as that laid down in Article 53(2) of the Sex Discrimination Order from fully exercising its powers of judicial review (part of question 6). The next object of the questions submitted by the Industrial Tribunal is to enable it to decide whether and under what conditions the provisions of the directive, in a situation such as that which exists in the present case, allow men and women employed with the police to be treated differently on grounds of the protection of public safety mentioned in Article 53(1) of the Sex Discrimination Order (questions 1 to 5). The questions submitted are also intended to enable the Industrial Tribunal to ascertain whether or not the provisions of the directive may, in an appropriate case, be relied upon as against a conflicting rule of national law (remainder of question 6). Finally, depending on the answers to be given to those questions, the question might arise whether a Member State may avail itself of Article 224 of the EEC Treaty in order to derogate from obligations which the directive imposes on it in a case such as this (question 7).

The right to an effective judicial remedy

13. It is therefore necessary to examine in the first place the part of the sixth question which raises the point whether Community law, and more particularly Directive No. 76/207, requires the Member States to ensure that their national courts and tribunals exercise effective control over compliance with the provisions of the directive and with the national legislation intended to put it into effect.

14. In *Mrs Johnston*'s view, a provision such as Article 53(2) of the Sex Discrimination Order is contrary to Article 6 of the directive inasmuch as it prevents the competent national court or tribunal from exercising any judicial control.

15. The *United Kingdom* observes that Article 6 of the directive does not require the Member States to submit to judicial review every question which may arise in the application of the directive, even where national security and public safety are involved. Rules of evidence such as the rule laid down in Article 53(2) of the Sex Discrimination Order are quite common in national procedural law. Their justification is that matters of national security and public safety can be satisfactorily assessed only by the competent political authority, namely the minister who issues the certificate in question.

16 The *Commisssion* takes the view that to treat the certificate of a minister as having an effect such as that provided for in Article 53(2) of the Sex Discrimination Order is tantamount to refusing all judicial control or review and is therefore contrary to a fundamental principle of Community law and to Article 6 of the directive.

266

17. As far as this issue is concerned, it must be borne in mind first of all that Article 6 of the directive requires Member States to introduce into their internal legal systems such measures as are needed to enable all persons who consider themselves wronged by discrimination 'to pursue their claims by judicial process'. It follows from that provision that the Member States must take measures which are sufficiently effective to achieve the aim of the directive and that they must ensure that the rights thus conferred may be effectively relied upon before the national courts by the persons concerned.

18. The requirement of judicial control stipulated by that article reflects a general principle of law which underlies the constitutional traditions common to the Member States. That principle is also laid down in Articles 6 and 13 of the European Convention for the Protection of Human Rights and Fundamental Freedoms of 4 November 1950. As the European Parliament, Council and Commission recognized in their Joint Declaraton of 5 April 1977 (Official Journal No. C 103, p. 1) and as the Court has recognized in its decisions, the principles on which that Convention is based must be taken into consideration in Community law.

19. By virtue of Article 6 of Directive No. 76/207, interpreted in the light of the general principle stated above, all persons have the right to obtain an effective remedy in a competent court against measures which they consider to be contrary to the principle of equal treatment for men and women laid down in the directive. It is for the Member States to ensure effective judicial control as regards compliance with the applicable provisions of Community law and of national legislation intended to give effect to the rights for which the directive provides.

20. A provision which, like Article 53(2) of the Sex Discrimination Order, requires a certificate such as the one in question in the present case to be treated as conclusive evidence that the conditions for derogating from the principle of equal treatment are fulfilled allows the competent authority to deprive an individual of the possibility of asserting by judicial process the rights conferred by the directive. Such a provision is therefore contrary to the principle of effective judicial control laid down in Article 6 of the directive.

21. The answer to this part of the sixth question put by the Industrial Tribunal must therefore be that the principle of effective judicial control laid down in Article 6 of Council Directive No. 76/207 of 9 February 1976 does not allow a certificate issued by a national authority stating that the conditions for derogating from the principle of equal treatment for men and women for the purpose of protecting public safety are satisfied to be treated as conclusive evidence so as to exclude the exercise of any power of review by the courts.

The applicability of Directive No. 76/207 to measures taken to protect public safety

22. It is necessary to examine next the Industrial Tribunal's first question by which it seeks to ascertain whether, having regard to the fact that Directive No. 76/207 contains no express provision concerning measures taken for the purpose of safeguarding national security or of protecting public order, and more particularly public safety, the directive is applicable to such measures.

23. In *Mrs Johnston's* view, no general derogation from the fundamental principle of equal treatment unrelated to particular occupational activities, their nature and the context in which they are carried out, exists for such purposes. By being based on the sole ground that a discriminatory act is done for purposes such as the protection of public safety, such a derogation would enable the Member States unilaterally to avoid the obligations which the directive imposes on them.

24. The *United Kingdom* takes the view that the safeguard clauses contained in Articles 36, 48, 56, 66, 223 and 224 of the EEC Treaty show that neither the Treaty nor, therefore, the law derived from it apply to the fields mentioned in the Industrial Tribunal's question and do not restrict the Member States' power to take measures which they can consider expedient or necessary for those purposes. The measures referred to in the first question do not therefore fall within the scope of the directive.

25. The *Commission* suggests that the directive should be interpreted with reference to Article 224 of the EEC Treaty so that considerations of public safety could, in the special conditions envisaged by that article and subject to judicial review, justify derogations from the principle of equal treatment even where the strict conditions laid down in Article 2(2) and (3) of the directive are not fulfilled.

26. It must be observed in this regard that the only articles in which the Treaty provides for derogations applicable in situations which may involve public safety are Articles 36, 48, 56, 223 and 224 which deal with exceptional and clearly defined cases. Because of their limited character those articles do not lend themselves to a wide interpretation and it is not possible to infer from them that there is inherent in the Treaty a general proviso covering all measures taken for reasons of public safety. If every provision of Community law were held to be subject to a general proviso, regardless of the specific requirements laid down by the provisions of the Treaty, this might impair the binding nature of Community law and its uniform application.

27. It follows that the application of the principle of equal treatment for men and women is not subject to any general reservation as regards measures taken on grounds of the protection of public safety, apart from the

possible application of Article 224 of the Treaty which concerns a wholly exceptional situation and is the subject-matter of the seventh question. The facts which induced the competent authority to invoke the need to protect public safety must therefore if necessary be taken into consideration, in the first place, in the context of the application of the specific provisions of the directive.

28. The answer to the first question must therefore be that acts of sex discrimination done for reasons related to the protection of public safety must be examined in the light of the exceptions to the principle of equal treatment for men and women laid down in Directive No. 76/207.

The derogations allowed on account of the context in which the occupational activity is carried out

29. The Industrial Tribunal's second and third questions are concerned with the interpretation of the derogation, provided for in Article 2(2) of the directive, from the principle of equal treatment and are designed to enable the Tribunal to decide whether a difference in treatment, such as that in question, is covered by that derogation. It asks to be informed of the criteria and principles to be applied for determining whether an activity such as that in question in the present case is one of the activities for which 'by reason of their nature or the context in which they are carried out, the sex of the worker constitutes a determining factor'.

30. *Mrs Johnston* takes the view that a reply to this question is not possible in terms so general. She states that she has always worked satisfactorily in performing her duties with the police and maintains that women are quite capable of being trained in the handling of fire-arms. It is for the Industrial Tribunal to determine whether a derogation is possible under Article 2(2) of the directive, having regard to the specific duties which she is required to carry out. That provision does not make it possible for her to be completely excluded from any employment in the RUC full-time Reserve.

31. The *United Kingdom* submits that the Member States have a discretion in deciding whether, owing to requirements of national security and public safety or public order, the context in which an occupational activity in the police is carried out prevents that activity from being carried out by an armed policewoman. In determining that question the Member States may take into consideration criteria such as the difference in physical strength between the sexes, the probable reaction of the public to the appearance of armed policewomen and the risk of their being assassinated. Since the decision taken by the Chief Constable was taken on the application of such criteria, it is covered by Article 2(2) of the directive.

32. The *Commission* takes the view that, owing to the context in which it is carried out but not to its nature, the occupational activity of an armed

police officer could be considered an activity for which the sex of the officer is a determining factor. A derogation must, however, be justified in relation to specific duties and not in relation to an employment considered in its entirety. In particular, the principle of proportionality must be observed. The national court must look at the discrimination in question from that point of view.

33. In this regard it must be stated first of all that, in so far as the competent police authorities in Northern Ireland have decided, because of the requirements of public safety, to depart from the principle, generally applied in other parts of the United Kingdom, of not arming the police in the ordinary course of their duties, that decision does not in itself involve any discrimination between men and women and is therefore outside the scope of the principle of equal treatment. It is only in so far as the Chief Constable decided that women would not be armed or trained in the use of fire-arms, that general policing duties would in future be carried out only be armed male officers and that contracts of women in the RUC full-time Reserve who, like Mrs Johnston, had previously been entrusted with general policing duties, would not be renewed, that an appraisal of those measures in the light of the provisions of the directive is relevant.

34. Since, as is clear from the Industrial Tribunal's decision, it is expressly provided that the Sex Discrimination Order is to apply to employment in the police and since in this regard no distinction is made between men and women in the specific provisions that are applicable, the nature of the occupational activity in the police force is not a relevant ground of justification for the discrimination in question. What must be examined, however, is the question whether, owing to the specific context in which the activity described in the Industrial Tribunal's decision is carried out, the sex of the person carrying out that activity constitutes a determining factor.

35. As is clear from the Industrial Tribunal's decision, the policy towards women in the RUC full-time Reserve was adopted by the Chief Constable because he considered that if women were armed they might become a more frequent target for assassination and their fire-arms could fall into the hands of their assailants, that the public would not welcome the carrying of fire-arms by women, which would conflict too much with the ideal of an unarmed police force, and that armed policewomen would be less effective in police work in the social field with families and children in which the services of policewomen are particularly appreciated. The reasons which the Chief Constable thus gave for his policy were related to the special conditions in which the police must work in the situation existing in Northern Ireland, having regard to the requirements of the protection of public safety in a context of serious internal disturbances.

36. As regards the question whether such reasons may be covered by Article

2(2) of the directive, it should first be observed that that provision, being a derogation from an individual right laid down in the directive, must be interpreted strictly. However, it must be recognized that the context in which the occupational activity of members of an armed police force are carried out is determined by the environment in which that activity is carried out. In this regard, the possibility cannot be excluded that in a situation characterized by serious internal disturbances the carrying of fire-arms by policewomen might create additional risks of their being assassinated and might therefore be contrary to the requirements of public safety.

37. In such circumstances, the context of certain policing activities may be such that the sex of police officers constitutes a determining factor for carrying them out. If that is so, a Member State may therefore restrict such tasks, and the training leading thereto, to men. In such a case, as is clear from Article 9(2) of the directive, the Member States have a duty to assess periodically the activities concerned in order to decide whether, in the light of social developments, the derogation from the general scheme of the directive may still be maintained.

38. It must also be borne in mind that, in determining the scope of any derogation from an individual right such as the equal treatment of men and women provided for by the directive, the principle of proportionality, one of the general principles of law underlying the Community legal order, must be observed. That principle requires that derogations remain within the limits of what is appropriate and necessary for achieving the aim in view and requires the principle of equal treatment to be reconciled as far as possible with the requirements of public safety which constitute the decisive factor as regards the context of the activity in question.

39. By reason of the division of jurisdiction provided for in Article 177 of the EEC Treaty, it is for the national court to say whether the reasons on which the Chief constable based his decision are in fact well founded and justify the specific measure taken in Mrs Johnston's case. It is also for the national court to ensure that the principle of proportionality is observed and to determine whether the refusal to renew Mrs Johnston's contract could not be avoided by allocating to women duties which, without jeopardizing the aims pursued, can be performed without fire-arms.

40. The answer to the Industrial Tribunal's second and third questions should therefore be that Article 2(2) of Directive No. 76/207 must be interpreted as meaning that in deciding whether, by reason of the context in which the activities of a police officer are carried out, the sex of the officer constitutes a determining factor for that occupational activity, a Member State may take into consideration requirements of public safety in order to restrict general policing duties, in an internal situation characterized by frequent assassinations, to men equipped with fire-arms.

The derogations allowed on the ground of a concern to protect women

41. In its fourth and fifth question the Industrial Tribunal then asks the Court for an interpretation of the expressions 'protection of women' in Article 2(3) of the directive and 'concern for protection' in Article 3(2)(c), which inspired certain provisions of national law, so that it can decide whether the difference in treatment in question may fall within the scope of the derogations from the principle of equal treatment laid down for those purposes.

42. In *Mrs Johnston's* view, those provisions must be interpreted strictly. Their sole purpose is to assure women special treatment in order to protect their health and safety in the case of pregnancy or maternity. That is not the case where women are completely excluded from service in an armed police force.

43. The *United Kingdom* states that the aim of the policy with regard to women in the RUC full-time Reserve is to protect women by preventing them from becoming targets for assassination. The expression 'protection of women' may cover such an aim in a period of serious disturbances. The *Commission* also takes the view that an exceptional situation such as exists in Northern Ireland and the resultant dangers for armed women police officers may be taken into consideration from the viewpoint of the protection of women.

44. It must be observed in this regard that, like Article 2(2) of the directive, Article 2(3), which also determines the scope of Article 3(2)(c), must be interpreted strictly. It is clear from the express reference to pregnancy and maternity that the directive is intended to protect a woman's biological condition and the special relationship which exists between a woman and her child. That provision of the directive does not therefore allow women to be excluded from a certain type of employment on the ground that public opinion demands that women be given greater protection than men against risks which affect men and women in the same way and which are distinct from women's specific needs of protection, such as those expressly mentioned.

45. It does not appear that the risks and dangers to which women are exposed when performing their duties in the police force in a situation such as exists in Northern Ireland are different from those to which any man is also exposed when performing the same duties. A total exclusion of women from such an occupational activity which, owing to a general risk not specific to women, is imposed for reasons of public safety is not one of the differences in treatment that Article 2(3) of the directive allows out of a concern to protect women.

46. The answer to the Industrial Tribunal's fourth and fifth questions must therefore be that the differences in treatment between men and women

that Article 2(3) of Directive No. 76/207 allows out of a concern to protect women do not include risks and dangers, such as those to which any armed police officer is exposed when performing his duties in a given situation, that do not specifically affect women as such.

The effects of Directive No. 76/207

47. By its sixth question the Industrial Tribunal also seeks to ascertain whether an individual may rely upon the provisions of the directive in proceedings brought before a national court. In view of the foregoing, this question arises more particularly with regard to Articles 2 and 6 of the directive.

48. *Mrs Johnston* considers that Article 2(1) of the directive is unconditional and sufficiently clear and precise to have direct effect. It may be relied upon as against the Chief Constable acting as a public authority. In any event, the directive has horizontal direct effect even in regard to private persons.

49. In the view of the *United Kingdom*, Article 2(1) of the directive is a conditional provision inasmuch as it is subject to derogations which the Member State may determine in a discretionary manner. The Chief Constable is constitutionally independent of the State and in the present case is involved only as an employer; the directive has no direct effect in such relationships.

50. The *Commission* takes the view that the case may be dealt with within the scope of national law and that a ruling on the direct effect of Articles 2 and 3 of the directive is not necessary.

51. On this point it must be observed first of all that in all cases in which a directive has been properly implemented its effects reach individuals through the implementing measures adopted by the Member States concerned. The question whether Article 2(1) may be relied upon before a national court therefore has no purpose since it is established that the provision has been put into effect in national law.

52. The derogation from the principle of equal treatment which, as stated above, is allowed by Article 2(2) constitutes only an option for the Member States. It is for the competent national court to see whether that option has been exercised in provisions of national law and to construe the content of those provisions. The question whether an individual may rely upon a provision of the directive in order to have a derogation laid down by national legislation set aside arises only if that derogation went beyond the limits of the exceptions permitted by Article 2(2) of the directive.

53. In this context it should be observed first of all that, as the Court has

already stated in its judgments of 10 April 1984 (Case 14/83, *von Colson and Kamann* v. *Land Nordrhein-Westfalen* [1984] ECR 1891 and Case 79/83, *Harz* v. *Deutsche Tradax GmbH* [1984] ECR 1921), the Member States' obligation under a directive to achieve the result envisaged by that directive and their duty under Article 5 of the Treaty to take all appropriate measures, whether general or particular, to ensure the fulfilment of that obligation, is binding on all the authorities of Member States including, for matters within their jurisdiction, the courts. It follows that, in applying national law, and in particular the provisions of national legislation specifically introduced in order to implement Directive No. 76/207, national courts are required to interpret their national law in the light of the wording and the purpose of the directive in order to achieve the result referred to in the third paragraph of Article 189 of the EEC Treaty. It is therefore for the Industrial Tribunal to interpret the provisions of the Sex Discrimination Order, and in particular Article 53(1) thereof, in the light of the provisions of the directive, as interpreted above, in order to give it its full effect.

54. In the event that, having regard to the foregoing, the question should still arise whether an individual may rely on the directive as against a derogation laid down by national legislation, reference should be made to the established case-law of the Court (see in particular its judgment of 19 January 1982 in Case 8/81, *Becker* v. *Finanzamt Münster-Innenstadt*, [1982] ECR 53). More particularly, the Court recently held in its judgment delivered on 26 February 1986 in Case 152/84 (*Marshall* v. *Southampton and South West Hampshire Area Health Authority*, [1986] ECR) that certain provisions of Directive No. 76/207 are, as far as their subject-matter is concerned, unconditional and sufficiently precise and that they may be relied upon by individuals as against a Member State where it fails to implement it correctly.

55. That statement was made, in the aforesaid judgment of 26 February 1986, with regard to the application of the principle of equal treatment laid down in Article 2(1) of the directive to the conditions governing dismissal referred to in Article 5(1). The same applies as regards the application of the principle contained in Article 2(1) to the conditions governing access to jobs and access to vocational training and advanced vocational training referred to in Articles 3(1) and 4(1) which are in question in this case.

56. The Court also held in the aforesaid judgment that individuals may rely on the directive as against an organ of the State whether it acts *qua* employer or *qua* public authority. As regards an authority like the Chief Constable, it must be observed that, according to the Industrial Tribunal's decision, the Chief Constable is an official responsible for the direction of the police service. Whatever its relations may be with other organs of the State, such a public authority, charged by the State with the maintenance of public order and safety, does not act as a private

274

individual. It may not take advantage of the failure of the State, of which it is an emanation, to comply with Community law.

57. The answer to the sixth question should therefore be that individuals may claim the application, as against a State authority charged with the maintenance of public order and safety acting in its capacity of an employer, of the principle of equal treatment for men and women laid down in Article 2(1) of Directive No. 76/207 to the matters referred to in Articles 3(1) and 4(1) concerning the conditions for access to posts and to vocational training and advanced vocational training in order to have a derogation from that principle under national legislation set aside in so far as it exceeds the limits of the exceptions permitted by Article 2(2).

58. As regards Article 6 of the directive which, as explained above, is also applicable in this case, the Court has already held in its judgments of 10 April 1984, cited above, that that article does not contain, as far as sanctions for any discrimination are concerned, any unconditional and sufficiently precise obligation which may be relied upon by an individual. On the other hand, in so far as it follows from that article, construed in the light of a general principle which it expresses, that all persons who consider themselves wronged by sex discrimination must have an effective judicial remedy, that provision is sufficiently precise and unconditional to be capable of being relied upon as against a Member State which has not ensured that it is fully implemented in its internal legal order.

59. The answer to this part of the sixth question must therefore be that the provision contained in Article 6 to the effect that all persons who consider themselves wronged by discrimination between men and women must have an effective judicial remedy may be relied upon by individuals as against a Member State which has not ensured that it is fully implemented in its internal legal order.

Article 224 of the EEC Treaty
60. As far as concerns the seventh question, on the interpretation of Article 224, it follows from the foregoing that Article 2(2) of Directive No. 76/207 allows a Member State to take into consideration the requirements of the protection of public safety in a case such as the one before the Court. As regards the requirement that the question whether the rules laid down by the directive have been complied with must be amenable to judicial review, none of the facts before the Court and none of the observations submitted to it suggest that the serious internal disturbances in Northern Ireland make judicial review impossible or that measures needed to protect public safety would be deprived of their effectiveness because of such review by the national courts. In those circumstances, the question whether Article 224 of the EEC Treaty may be relied upon by a Member State in order to avoid compliance with the obligations imposed

on it by Community law and in particular by the directive does not arise in this case.

61. The seventh question therefore has no purpose in view of the answers to the other questions.

Costs

62. The costs incurred by the United Kingdom, the Government of Denmark and the Commission of the European Communities, which have submitted observations to the Court, are not recoverable. Since these proceedings are, in so far as the parties to the main proceedings are concerned, in the nature of a step in the proceedings pending before the national tribunal, the decision on costs is a matter for that tribunal.

On those grounds,

THE COURT,

in answer to the questions submitted to it by the Industrial Tribunal of Northern Ireland by decision of 8 August 1984, hereby rules:

1. **The principle of effective judicial control laid down in Article 6 of Council Directive No. 76/207 of 9 February 1976 does not allow a certificate issued by a national authority stating that the conditions for derogating from the principle of equal treatment for men and women for the purposes of protecting public safety are satisfied to be treated as conclusive evidence so as to exclude the exercise of any power of review by the courts. The provision contained in Article 6 to the effect that all persons who consider themselves wronged by discrimination between men and women must have an effective judicial remedy may be relied upon by individuals as against a Member State which has not ensured that it is fully implemented in its internal legal order.**

2. **Acts of sex discrimination done for reasons related to the protection of public safety must be examined in the light o the derogations from the principle of equal treatment for men and women which are laid down in Directive No. 76/207.**

3. **Article 2(2) of Directive No. 76/207 must be interpreted as meaning that in deciding whether, by reason of the context in which the activities of a police officer are carried out, the sex of the officer constitutes a determining factor for that occupational activity, a Member State may take into consideration requirements of public safety in order to restrict general policing duties, in an internal situation characterized by frequent assassinations, to men equipped with fire-arms.**

4. The differences in treatment between men and women that Article 2(3) of Directive No. 76/207 allows out of a concern to protect women do not include risks and dangers, such as those to which any armed police officer is exposed in the performance of his duties in a given situation, that do not specifically affect women as such.

5. Individuals may claim the application, as against a State authority charged with the maintenance of public order and safety acting in its capacity as employer, of the principle of equal treatment for men and women laid down in Article 2(1) of Directive No. 76/207 to the matters referred to in Articles 3(1) and 4(1) concerning the conditions for access to posts and to vocational training and advanced vocational training in order to have a derogation from that principle contained in national legislation set aside in so far as it exceeds the limits of the exceptions permitted by Article 2(2).

Mackenzie Stuart	Koopmans	Everling
Bahlmann	Joliet	Due
Galmot	Kakouris	O'Higgins

Delivered in open court in Luxembourg on 15 May 1986.

P. Heim   A. J. Mackenzie Stuart
Registrar   *President*

3. Equal treatment in social security

(a) Preliminary rulings under Article 177, EEC Treaty

Judgment of the Court

24 June 1986 – Case 150/85

Jacqueline Drake
v.
Chief Adjudication Officer

Equal treatment in social security – scope of Directive 79/7/EEC – 'working population' included in scope of Directive by Article 2 to be interpreted as including a person who has interrupted work to provide necessary care for disabled relative – Article 3(1) of Directive to be interpreted as including within scope of Directive any benefit which broadly forms part of one of statutory schemes mentioned or a social assistance provision intended to supplement or replace such scheme – benefit provided by Member State and paid to person caring for disabled person thus forms part of a statutory scheme providing protection against invalidity covered by Article 3(1)(a) – discrimination on grounds of sex contrary to Article 4(1) of Directive arises where legislation provides that a benefit which forms part of a statutory scheme mentioned in Article 3(1) is not payable to married woman living with or maintained by husband, though it is paid in similar situation to married man (Council Directive 79/7/EEC, Articles 2, 3(1)(a) and 4(1)).

In Case 150/85

REFERENCE to the Court under Article 177 of the EEC Treaty by the Chief Social Security Commissioner for a preliminary ruling in the proceedings pending before him between

Jacqueline Drake

and

Chief Adjudication Officer

on the interpretation of Council Directive 79/7/EEC of 10 January 1979 on the progressive implementation of the principle of equal treatment for men and women in matters of social security (Official Journal 1979 No. L 6, p. 24),

THE COURT (FOURTH CHAMBER)

composed of: K. Bahlmann, President of Chamber, T. Koopmans, G. Bosco, T.F. O'Higgins and F. A. Schockweiler, Judges,

Advocate General: G. F Mancini
Registrar: P. Heim

gives the following JUDGMENT

Decision

1. By an order of 15 May 1985, which was received at the Court on 20 May 1985, the Chief Social Security Commissioner referred to the Court for a preliminary ruling under Article 177 of the EEC Treaty two questions regarding the interpretation of Council Directive 79/7/EEC of 10 January 1979 on the progressive implementation of the principle of equal treatment for men and women in matters of social security, with a view to determining the compatibility with that directive of a provision of national law laying down conditions for the granting of an invalid care allowance.

2. Those questions were raised in the course of proceedings before the Commissioner between Mrs Drake and the Adjudication Officer concerning the latter's refusal to grant Mrs Drake the said invalid care allowance.

3. Mrs Drake is married and lives with her husband. Over a number of years, until the middle of 1984, she held a variety of full-time and part-time jobs. In June 1984 her mother, a severely disabled person who receives an attendance allowance under section 35(1) of the Social Security Act 1975, came to live with her. Mrs Drake thereupon gave up her work in order to look after her mother.

4. The British legislation on invalidity benefits is laid down in the Social Security Act 1975. Section 37(1) of that Act provides for the payment of an invalid care allowance where (a) the applicant is regularly and substantially engaged in caring for a severely disabled person; (b) the applicant is not gainfully employed; (c) the severely disabled person is such relative of his or such other person as may be prescribed by the law. For the purposes of the application of that provision, section 37(2) defines 'severely disabled person' as a person entitled to an attendance allowance under section 35 of that Act or to any other benefit of the same nature. Under section 37(3) the invalid care allowance is not paid: to any person who is under the age of 16 or is engaged in full-time education; to a married woman who lives with her husband or to whose maintenance her husband contributes a weekly sum not less than the weekly rate of the allowance; to a woman where she and a man to whom she is not married are living together as husband and wife.

5. On 5 February 1985 Mrs Drake applied for the allowance in respect of the care provided by her to her mother. The Adjudication Officer responsible for the award of the benefit stated that under section 37(3)(a)(i) the benefit was not payable to a married woman residing with her husband. In order to accelerate the proceedings, however, he referred the claim to the Social Security Appeal Tribunal.

6. By a decision of 1 March 1985 the Tribunal held that that rule constituted discrimination on grounds of sex contrary to Directive 79/7. The Adjudication Officer appealed against that decision to the Chief Social Security Commissioner. In his order referring the matter to the Court of Justice, the Chief Social Security Commissioner states that the sole point at issue between the parties concerns section 37(3)(a)(i) of the Social Security Act 1975 and that the other conditions laid down in that Act for the grant of the invalid care allowance are fulfilled.

7. The Chief Social Security Commissioner also states in his order that section 37(3) of the Act has not been repealed or amended since the entry into force of Directive 79/7, the relevant provisions of which are set out below.

279

8. Article 1 states that the purpose of the directive is the:

> '... progressive implementation, in the field of social security and other elements of social protection provided for in Article 3, of the principle of equal treatment for men and women in matters of social security, hereinafter referred to as the "principle of equal treatment".'.

According to Article 2, the directive applies to:

> '... the working population – including self-employed persons, workers and self-employed persons whose activity is interrupted by illness, accident or involuntary unemployment and persons seeking employment – and to retired or invalided workers and self-employed persons'.

Under Article 3(1), the directive applies to:

> '(a) statutory schemes which provide protection against the following risks:
> – sickness,
> – invalidity,
> – old age,
> – accidents at work and occupational diseases,
> – unemployment;
> (b) social assistance, in so far as it is intended to supplement or replace the schemes referred to in (a).'.

Article 4(1) provides that:

> 'The principle of equal treatment means that there shall be no discrimination whatsoever on ground of sex either directly, or indirectly by reference in particular to marital or family status, in particular as concerns:
> – the scope of the schemes and the conditions of access thereto,
> – the obligation to contribute and the calculation of contributions,
> – the calculation of benefits including increases due in respect of a spouse and for dependants and the conditions governing the duration and retention of entitlement to benefits.'.

9. The Chief Social Security Commissioner considered that a decision on the interpretation of the directive was necessary for his decision in the case; he therefore stayed the proceedings and referred the following questions to the Court for a preliminary ruling:

> '1. If a Member State provides a benefit payable (provided

certain residence and other conditions are met) to a person who is not gainfully employed and is regularly and substantially engaged in caring for a person in respect of whom a benefit is payable as a severely disabled person by reason of that person requiring attention or supervision as prescribed (and provided that that person meets certain residence and other conditions), does the benefit payable to the first-mentioned person constitute the whole or part of a statutory scheme which provides protection against invalidity to which Article 3(1)(a) of Directive 79/7/EEC applies?

2. If the answer to the first question is yes, does a condition that a married woman is not entitled to that benefit if she is residing with her husband or he is contributing to her maintenance above a certain level constitute discrimination contrary to Article 4(1) of that Directive in circumstances where married men do not have to meet a corresponding condition?'.

10. Observations were submitted by Mrs Drake, the Adjudication Officer and the Commission.

Question 1
11. By his first question the Chief Social Security Commissioner seeks to know whether the right to the payment of a benefit to a person who cares for a disabled person constitutes part of a statutory scheme providing protection against the risk of invalidity to which Directive 79/7 applies under Article 3(1)(a) of that directive.

12. Mrs Drake and the Commission consider that the answer to Question 1 should be in the affirmative.

13. Mrs Drake submits in the first place that the expression 'working population' used in Article 2 of the directive must be interpreted as including individuals who have worked, who wish to return to work, who are of working age, but who are temporarily unable to work because of some particular risk covered by the social security system, which is precisely her situation. She considers that she is therefore a person to whom the directive applies.

14. Secondly, Mrs Drake argues that Article 3(1)(a) of the directive must be interpreted as applying to any benefit which forms part of a national statutory scheme providing protection against the risks referred to in that provision. She argues that in the United Kingdom the statutory scheme of protection against the risk of invalidity is provided by two benefits, the attendance allowance payable to the disabled person and the invalid care allowance payable to the person who cares for him. It would thus be

impossible to describe the relevant statutory scheme without describing both benefits.

15. The Commission argues first of all that a person belongs to the working population for the purposes of Article 2 of the directive if he is in fact working, is unemployed and seeking work, is a former or retired worker, or is prevented from working by reason of illness or invalidity, whether his own or that of a person for whom he is caring. The Commission considers that Mrs Drake gave up work by reason of invalidity, albeit that of her mother, and that she should therefore be regarded as a member of the working population for the purposes of the directive.

16. The Commission argues that the fact that the benefit in question is paid to a third party and not directly to the disabled person does not put it outside the scope of the risk of invalidity, the scheme for which is covered by the directive. It points out that the effectiveness of the directive might be seriously compromised if it were to be held that the way in which the benefit is paid could determine whether or not the benefit was covered by the directive.

17. The Adjudication Officer, on the other hand, considers that the invalid care allowance cannot in itself be regarded as providing protection against the risk of invalidity within the meaning of Article 3(1)(a) of Directive 79/7. In his view, that provision is directed at schemes providing persons with protection against risks to them, not, as in the case of the invalid care allowance, against risks to third parties. He argues that Article 2, which defines the persons to whom the directive applies, is concerned only with persons who are directly affected by one of those risks and thus excludes from the scope of the directive benefits made available to other persons.

18. The Adjudication Officer goes on to point out that it is clear from Article 2 and from the preamble to the directive that the benefits to which the directive refers are all work-related. Since the allowance in question is intended for persons who do not work and therefore do not belong to the working population it cannot be regarded as one of those benefits.

19. Finally, the Adjudication Officer states that far from being an all-embracing code for the implementation of the principle of equal treatment in matters of social security, Directive 79/7 is only a first step towards equal treatment for men and women in that area. He argues that the scope of the directive is restricted to the working population as defined in Article 2. Allowances such as those at issue in the main proceedings therefore fall outside its scope.

20. It must be pointed out first of all that according to the first and second recitals in the preamble to Directive 79/7, the aim of that directive is the

progressive implementation of the principle of equal treatment for men and women in matters of social security.

21. According to Article 3(1), Directive 79/7 applies to statutory schemes which provide protection against, *inter alia*, the risk of invalidity (sub-paragraph (a)) and social assistance in so far as it is intended to supplement or replace the invalidity scheme (subparagraph (b)). In order to fall within the scope of the directive, therefore, a benefit must constitute the whole or part of a statutory scheme providing protection against one of the specified risks or a form of social assistance having the same objective.

22. Under Article 2, the term 'working population', which determines the scope of the directive, is defined broadly to include 'self-employed persons, workers and self-employed persons whose activity is interrupted by illness, accident or involuntary employment and persons seeking employment ... [and] retired or invalided workers and self-employed persons'. That provision is based on the idea that a person whose work has been interrupted by one of the risks referred to in Article 3 belongs to the working population. That is the case of Mrs Drake, who has given up work solely because of one of the risks listed in Article 3, namely the invalidity of her mother. She must therefore be regarded as a member of the working population for the purposes of the directive.

23. Furthermore, it is possible for the Member States to provide protection against the consequences of the risk of invalidity in various ways. For example, a Member State may, as the United Kingdom has done, provide for two separate allowances, one payablee to the disabled person himself and the other payable to a person who provides care, while another Member State may arrive at the same result by paying an allowance to the disabled person at a rate equivalent to the sum of those two benefits. In order, therefore, to ensure that the progressive implementation of the principle of equal treatment referred to in Article 1 of Directive 79/7 and defined in Article 4 is carried out in a harmonious manner throughout the Community, Article 3(1) must be interpreted as including any benefit which in a broad sense forms part of one of the statutory schemes referred to or a social assistance provision intended to supplement or replace such a scheme.

24. Moreover, the payment of the benefit to a person who provides care still depends on the existence of a situation of invalidity inasmuch as such a situation is a condition *sine qua non* for its payment, as the Adjudication Officer admitted during the oral procedure. It must also be emphasized that there is a clear economic link between the benefit and the disabled person, since the disabled person derives an advantage from the fact that an allowance is paid to the person caring for him.

25. It follows that the fact that a benefit which forms part of a statutory

283

invalidity scheme is paid to a third party and not directly to the disabled person does not place it outside the scope of Directive 79/7. Otherwise, as the Commission emphasized in its observations, it would be possible, by making formal changes to existing benefits covered by the directive, to remove them from its scope.

26. The answer to the first question referred by the Chief Social Security Commissioner must therefore be that a benefit provided by a Member State and paid to a person caring for a disabled person forms part of a statutory scheme providing protection against invlaidity which is covered by Directive 79/7 pursuant to Article 3(1)(a) of that directive.

Question 2
27. Since Question 1 has been answered in the affirmative, it is necessary to examine Question 2, which concerns the issue whether discrimination on grounds of sex contrary to Article 4(1) of Directive 79/7 arises where legislation provides that a benefit which forms part of one of the statutory schemes referred to in Article 3(1) of the directive is not payable to a married woman who lives with or is maintained by her husband, although it is paid in corresponding circumstances to a married man.

28. Mrs Drake, the Commission and the Adjudication Officer all suggest that that question should be answered in the affirmative.

29. Mrs Drake and the Commission argue that the exclusion of married women from such a benefit, where married men residing with their wives are not excluded, constitutes a clear example of direct discrimination on grounds of sex.

30. The Adjudication Officer himself has recognized that the provision governing the benefit in question places certain categories of women (married women living with their husbands and women who live with a man as husband and wife) at a disadvantage by precluding them from obtaining that benefit.

31. It should be noted that Article 4(1) of Directive 79/7 provides that the implementation of the principle of equal treatment, with regard in particular to the scope of schemes and the conditions of access to them, means that there should be no discrimination whatsoever on grounds of sex.

32. That provision embodies the aim of the directive, set out in Article 1, that is to say the implementation, in the field of social security and between men and women, of the principle of equal treatment, a principle which the Court has frequently described to as fundamental.

33. It follows from the foregoing that a national provision such as that at issue

284

before the Chief Social Security Commissioner is contrary to the aim, as stated above, of the directive, which under Article 189 of the Treaty is binding on the Member States as to the result to be achieved.

34. The answer to Question 2 must therefore be that discrimination on grounds of sex contrary to Article 4(1) of Directive 79/7 arises where legislation provides that a benefit which forms part of one of the statutory schemes referred to in Article 3(1) of that directive is not payable to a married woman who lives with or is maintained by her husband, although it is paid in corresponding circumstances to a married man.

Costs
35. The costs incurred by the Commission of the European Communities, which submitted observations to the Court, are not recoverable. As these proceedings are, in so far as the parties to the main proceedings are concerned, in the nature of a step in the action before the Chief Social Security Commissioner, the decision as to costs is a matter for him.

On those grounds,

THE COURT (FOURTH CHAMBER),

in answer to the questions referred to it by the Chief Social Security Commissioner by an order of 15 May 1985, hereby rules:

1. **A benefit provided by a Member State and paid to a person caring for a disabled person forms part of a statutory scheme providing protection against invalidity which is covered by Directive 79/7/EEC pursuant to Article 3(1)(a) of that directive.**

2. **Discrimination on grounds of sex contrary to Article 4(1) of Directive 79/7/EEC arises where legislation provides that a benefit which forms part of one of the statutory schemes referred to in Article 3(1) of that directive is not payable to a married woman who lives with or is maintained by her husband, although it is paid in corresponding circumstances to a married man.**

Bahlmann   Koopmans   Bosco

            O'Higgins   Schockweiler

Delivered in open court in Luxembourg on 24 June 1986.

P. Heim   K. Bahlmann
Registrar   *President of the Fourth Chamber*

Judgment of the Court

4 December 1986 – Case 71/85

State of the Netherlands
v.
Federatie Nederlandse Vakbeweging

Equal treatment in social security – provisions of a Directive which appear unconditional and sufficiently precise as regards subject matter may be directly relied on by individuals – where no national implementing measures adopted within required time, Article 4(1) of Directive 77/7/EEC is unconditional and sufficiently precise to allow individuals to rely on it before national courts to preclude application of inconsistent national provisions – until national government adopts necessary measures to implement Directive, women entitled to be treated in same way and via application of same rules as men in same situation in line with Directive, whose rules remain only valid point of reference – a Member State may not invoke its discretion regarding choice of methods for implementing equal treatment principle in social security matters to deny all effect to Article 4(1) of Directive, which may be invoked in legal proceedings even though Directive has not been implemented in its entirety (Council Directive 79/7/EEC, Articles 4(1), 5 and 7).

In Case 71/85

REFERENCE to the Court under Article 177 of the EEC Treaty by the Gerechtshof [Regional Court of Appeal], The Hague, for a preliminary ruling in the case pending before that court between

State of the Netherlands

and

Federatie Nederlandse Vakbeweging

on the interpretation of Article 4(1) of Council Directive 79/7/EEC of 19 December 1978 on the progressive implementation of the principle of equal treatment for men and women in matters of social security (Official Journal 1979 No. L 6, p. 24),

THE COURT,

composed of: Lord Mackenzie Stuart, President, Y. Galmot, C. N. Kakouris, T. F. O'Higgins and F. A. Schockweiler (Presidents of Chambers), G. Bosco, T. Koopmans, O. Due, U. Everling, K. Bahlmann, R. Joliet, J. C. Moitinho de Almeida and G. C. Rodriguez Iglesias, Judges,

Advocate General: G. F. Mancini
For the Registrar: D. Louterman, Administrator

gives the following JUDGMENT

Decision

1. By order of 13 March 1985, which was received at the Court on 18 March 1985, the Gerechtshof [Regional Court of Appeal], The Hague, referred to the Court for a preliminary ruling under Article 177 of the EEC Treaty three questions on the interpretation of Article 4 of Council Directive 79/7/EEC of 19 December 1978 on the progressive implementation of the principle of equal treatment for men and women in matters of social security (Official Journal 1979 No. L 6, p. 24) in order to determine whether that provision may be regarded as having had direct effects in the Netherlands since 23 December 1984, the date on which the Member States should have adopted the measures needed to comply therewith.

2. Those questions were raised in connexion with an action brought by Federatie Nederlandse Vakbeweging [Netherlands Trades Union Federation] against the State of the Netherlands. The purpose of that action is to obtain a finding that the State of the Netherlands acted unlawfully by maintaining in force or refusing to cease to apply after 23 December 1984 Article 13(1), point 1, of the Wet Werkloosheidsvoorziening [Law on Unemployment Benefit], which excludes from 'the right to benefit workers who, having the status of married women, may not be described as wage-earners ("kostwinster") under rules adopted by the competent minister after consulting the central commission, or who do not live permanently separated from their husbands'. The Federatie Nederlandse Vakbeweging maintains that married women disqualified from receiving unemployment benefit under that provision acquired a right to those benefits under the combined provisions of the Wet Werkloosheidsvoorziening and Article 4 of Directive 79/7/EEC.

3. It is not contested that Article 13(1), point 1, of the Wet Werkloosheidsvoorziening is contrary to the principle of equal treatment as defined in Article 4 of the directive.

4. It appears from the documents before the Court that the Netherlands Government initially intended, as part of a wide-ranging reform of the social security system, simultaneously to transpose the directive into national law and to merge the Wet Werkloosheids voorziening and the Werkloosheidswet [Law on Unemployment]. That reform was to include the repeal of the wage-earner requirement.

5. When it appeared that that merger could not be effected by 23 December 1984, a provisional bill amending Article 13(1), point 1, of the Wet

287

Werkloosheidsvoorziening and designed to extend the wage-earner requirement to unemployed males was tabled by the Government but rejected by the Second Chamber of the States General on 13 December 1984. By letter dated 18 December 1984, the State Secretary for Social Affairs and Employment informed the President of the Second Chamber of the States General that a new bill would be submitted whose provisions would take effect retroactively from 23 December 1984, in order to implement the directive within the period prescribed. The States General was asked to approve the bill by 1 March 1985 (Bill No. 18849 submitted on 6 February 1985).

6. Furthermore, the State Secretary notified the competent authorities, by circular dated 21 December 1984, that the contested provisions of the Wet Werkloosheidsvoorziening had to continue to be applied pending the retroactive amending law.

7. The respondent in the main proceedings, the Federatie Nederlandse Vakbeweging, whose statutory objects include safeguarding workers and their families, summoned the State in interlocutory proceedings before the President of the Arrondissementsrechtbank [District Court], The Hague, seeking an order requiring the State to suspend, or at least not to give effect until new published legislation entered into force to, Article 13(1), point 1, of the Wet Werkloosheidsvoorziening as far as concerns the wage-earner rule. By order of 17 January 1985 the President ordered the State to amend the relevant Article 13 before 1 March 1985. The State and the Federatie Nederlandse Vakbeweging appealed against that decision.

8. The Gerechtshof, on appeal, considered that the effect of Directive 79/7/EEC was unclear and so it suspended the proceedings and referred to the Court for a preliminary ruling the following three questions:

'1. Has Article 4 of Directive 79/7/EEC had direct effect since 23 December 1984 and does this mean that from that date Article 13(1), point 1, of the Wet Werkloosheidsvoorziening is inapplicable and that the women excluded by that provision acquired entitlement to benefit as from that same date?

2. In that respect, does it matter whether, apart from having the possibility of simply repealing the provision referred to in Question 1, the State had alternative possibilities for complying with the directive? For example, in repealing the aforesaid provision and in order to finance the extra costs involved, it could have made more rigorous the conditions for the acquisition of entitlement to benefit and limited it to unemployed persons under 35 years of age.

3. Does it matter, in that respect, that a transitional provision

is necessary owing to the repeal of that provision and that a choice must be made between alternative measures?'.

9. It appears from the documents before the Court that Article 13(1), point 1, of the Wet Werkloosheidsvoorziening has been repealed, with retroactive effect from 23 December 1984, by the Law of 24 April 1985, Staatsblad 230, which entered into force on 1 May 1985. That Law provides that the abolition of the wage-earner requirement is not to apply to workers whose unemployment commenced before 23 December 1984. In order to secure the funding of the benefits scheme under the Wet Werkloosheidsvoorziening, the Law also reduces the duration of such benefits in the case of unemployed persons – male and female alike – of under 35 years of age.

10. It follows that since the entry into force of the Law of 24 April 1985 male and female unemployed persons are subject to the same system, also as regards the period between 23 December 1984 and the date of entry into force of the new Law; however, differences based on the status of wage-earner continue to affect the entitlement to benefit of unemployed persons whose unemployment commenced before 23 December 1984.

11. Reference is made to the Report for the Hearing for the detailed arguments of the parties.

The first question
12. In its first question the Gerechtshof essentially seeks to establish whether Article 4(1) of the directive causes individuals to acquire rights as from the expiry of the period granted to the Member States in which to comply with the directive and, if so, whether married women excluded by national legislation acquired entitlement to benefit as from that date on the same conditions as men.

13. As the Court has consistently held, in particular in its judgment of 19 January 1982 in Case 8/81, *Becker* v. *Finanzamt Münster-Innenstadt*, [1982] ECR 53, wherever the provisions of a directive appear, as far as their subject-matter is concerned, to be unconditional and sufficiently precise, individuals may rely on those provisions in the absence of implementing measures adopted within the prescribed period as against any national provision which is incompatible with the directive or in so far as the provisions define rights which individuals are able to assert against the State.

14. That principle is based on the fact that it would be incompatible with the binding effect which Article 189 of the EEC Treaty ascribes to directives to exclude in principle the possibility of the obligation imposed by them being relied on by persons concerned. The Court therefore considered that a Member State which has not taken measures to implement the

directive within the prescribed period may not, as against individuals, plead its own failure to perform the obligations which the directive entails.

15. The Gerechtshof wishes to know whether Article 4(1) of the directive may be held to have the characteristics described above and whether, as a result, that article caused individuals in the Netherlands to acquire rights between 23 December 1984, the date on which the directive should have been transposed into national law, and the date on which the new national legislation on that matter was adopted.

16. Article 1 of Directive 79/7/EEC sets out its aims in the following terms:

'The purpose of this directive is the progressive implementation, in the field of social security and other elements of social protection provided for in Article 3, of the principle of equal treatment for men and women in matters of social security, hereinafter referred to as "the principle of equal treatment".'

17. As the Court recently held its judgment of 24 June 1986 in Case 150/85 (*Drake* v. *Chief Adjudication Officer*, [1986] ECR 2002), the objective set out in Article 1 of Directive 79/7/EEC is given practical expression by Article 4(1), which provides that in matters of social security there shall be no discrimination whatsoever on ground of sex, either directly, or indirectly by reference in particular to marital or family status, in particular as concerns the scope of social security schemes and the conditions of access thereto.

18. It must be pointed out that, standing by itself, and in the light of the objective and contents of Directive 77/7/EEC, Article 4(1) precludes, generally and unequivocally, all discrimination on ground of sex. The provision is therefore sufficiently precise to be relied upon in legal proceedings by an individual and applied by the courts. However, it remains to be considered whether the prohibition of discrimination which it contains may be regarded as unconditional having regard to the exceptions provided for in Article 7 and to the fact that according to the wording of Article 5 Member States are to take certain measures in order to ensure that the principle of equal treatment is applied in national legislation.

19. As regards, in the first place, Article 7, it must be observed that that provision merely reserves to Member States the right to exclude from the scope of the directive certain clearly defined areas but lays down no condition with regard to the application of the principle of equal treatment as regards Article 4 of the directive. It follows that Article 7 is not relevant in this case.

20. As for Article 5, which obliges Member States to take 'the measures necessary to ensure that any laws, regulations and administrative provisions contrary to the principle of equal treatment are abolished', it cannot be inferred from the wording of that article that it lays down conditions to which the prohibition of discrimination is subject. Whilst Article 5 leaves the Member States a discretion with regard to methods, it prescribes the result which those methods must achieve, that is to say, the abolition of any provisions contrary to the principle of equal treatment.

21. Consequently, Article 4(1) of the directive does not confer on Member States the power to make conditional or to limit the application of the principle of equal treatment within its field of application and it is sufficiently precise and unconditional to allow individuals, in the absence of implementing measures adopted within the prescribed period, to rely upon it before the national courts as from 23 December 1984 in order to preclude the application of any national provision inconsistent with that article.

22. It follows that until such time as the national government adopts the necessary implementing measures women are entitled to be treated in the same nmanner, and to have the same rules applied to them, as men who are in the same situation, since, where the directive has not been implemented, those rules remain the only valid point of reference.

23. The answer to the first question should therefore be that, where no measures have been adopted to implement Council Directive 79/7/EEC, Article 4(1) thereof, which prohibits all discrimination on grounds of sex in matters of social security, could be relied on as from 23 December 1984 in order to preclude the application of any national provision inconsistent with that article. In the absence of measures implementing that article women are entitled to be treated in the same manner, and to have the same rules applied to them, as men who are in the same situation, since, where the said directive has not been implemented, those rules remain the only valid point of reference.

The second and third questions
24. As regards the second and third questions which have been referred to the Court by the Gerechtshof and which seek to ascertain whether, in order to adapt its legislation in accordance with the principles of the directive, a Member State may have recourse to methods other than the straightforward repeal of the rule which is incompatible with the directive and, in particular, whether a transitional provision is necessary, it is sufficient to observe, as the Court has already held in its judgment of 19 January 1982 in *Becker*, cited above, that the fact that a directive leaves chocie of the form and methods for achieving the desired result to the Member States may not be relied upon in order to deny all effect to those

provisions of the directive which may be invoked in legal proceedings even though the said directive has not been implemented in its entirety.

25. The answer to the second and third questions must therefore be that a Member State may not invoke its discretion with regard to the choice of methods for implementing the principle of equal treatment in the field of social security laid down in Directive 79/7/EEC in order to deny all effect to Article 4(1) thereof, which may be invoked in legal proceedings even though the said directive has not been implemented in its entirety.

Costs

26. The costs incurred by the United Kingdom and by the Commission of the European Communities, which have submitted observations to the Court, are not recoverable. As these proceedings are, in so far as the parties to the main proceedings are concerned, in the nature of a step in the proceedings pending before the national court, the decision on costs is a matter for that court.

On those grounds,

THE COURT,

in answer to the questions submitted to it by the Gerechshof, The Hague, by order of 13 March 1985,

hereby rules:

1. **Where no measures have been adopted to implement Council Directive 79/7/EEC, Article 4(1) thereof, which prohibits all discrimination on grounds of sex in matters of social security, could be relied on as from 23 December 1984 in order to preclude the application of any national provision inconsistent with that article. In the absence of measures implementing that article women are entitled to be treated in the same manner, and to have the same rules applied to them, as men who are in the same situation, since, where the directive has not been implemented, those rules remain the only valid point of reference.**

2. **A Member State may not invoke its discretion with regard to the choice of methods for implementing the principle of equal treatment in the field of social security laid down in Directive 79/7/EEC in order to deny all effect to Article 4(1) thereof, which may be invoked in legal proceedings even though the said directive has not been implemented in its entirety.**

Mackenzic Stuart	Galmot	Kakouris
O'Higgins	Schockweiler	Bosco

292

Koopmans   Due   Everling

Bahlmann   Joliet   Moitinho de Almeida

                   Rodriguez Iglesias

Delivered in open court in Luxembourg on 4 December 1986.

P. Heim   A. J. Mackenzie Stuart
Registrar   *President*

Judgment of the Court

24 March 1987 – Case 286/85

McDermott and Cotter
v.
The Minister for Social Welfare and the Attorney General

Equal treatment in social security – provisions of a Directive which appear unconditional and sufficiently precise as regards subject matter may be directly relied on by individuals – where no national implementing measures adopted within required time, Article 4(1) of Directive 79/7/EEC is unconditional and sufficiently precise to allow individuals to rely on it before national courts to preclude application of inconsistent national provisions – until national government adopts necessary measures to implement Directive, women entitled to have same rules applied to them as are applied to men in same situation in line with Directive, whose rules remain only valid point of reference (Council Directive 79/7/EEC, Article 4(1).)

In Case 286/85

REFERENCE to the Court under Article 177 of the EEC Treaty by the High Court, Dublin, for a preliminary ruling in the proceedings pending before that court between

McDermott and Cotter

and

The Minister for Social Welfare and the Attorney General,

on the interpretation of Council Directive 79/7/EEC of 19 December 1978 on the progressive implementation of the principle of equal treatment for men and women in matters of social security (Official Journal 1979 No. L 6, p. 24),

293

THE COURT

composed of: Lord Mackenzie Stuart, President, Y. Galmot, C. N. Kakouris, T. F. O'Higgins and F. A. Schockweiler (Presidents of Chambers), G. Bosco, T. Koopmans, O. Due, U. Everling, K. Bahlmann, R. Joliet, J. C. Moitinho de Almeida and G. C. Rodriguez Iglesias, Judges,

Advocate General: G. F. Mancini
Registrar: D. Louterman, Administrator

gives the following JUDGMENT

Decision

1. By an order of 13 May 1985, which was received at the Court Registry on 23 September 1985, the High Court, Dublin, referred to the Court for a preliminary ruling under Article 177 of the EEC Treaty two questions on the interpretation of Article 4 of Council Directive 79/7 of 19 December 1978 on the progressive implementation of the principle of equal treatment for men and women in matters of social security (Official Journal 1979 No. L 6, p. 24), in order to determine whether that provision could be regarded as having direct effect in the Republic of Ireland as from 23 December 1984, the date on which the Member States should have taken the measures necessary to implement it.

2. Those questions were raised in the course of two actions brought before the High Court by Mrs McDermott and Mrs Cotter against the Minister for Social Welfare and the Attorney General. In those actions the High Court was asked to quash decisions made by or on behalf of the Minister for Social Welfare terminating the payment of unemployment benefit to the prosecutrices after a period of 312 days and hence, in the case of Mrs Cotter, to restore the pay-related benefit automatically withdrawn. The prosecutrices in the main proceedings argued that if they had been men or single women they would have been entitled to unemployment benefit for a further period of 78 days. They also pointed out that, as married women, they received lower unemployment benefits than men in respect of all contribution periods.

3. On 4 February 1985 the prosecutrices made application to the High Court for an order to quash those decisions terminating the payment of benefits, on the ground that the decisions infringed their rights under Article 4(1) of Council Directive 79/7 (hereinafter referred to as 'the directive').

4. It is not disputed that under the provisions of Chapters 4 and 6 of Part 2 of the Social Welfare (Consolidation) Act 1981 the unemployment benefit received by married women is less than that paid to married men and single persons and is paid for a shorter period.

5. However, it appears from the documents before the Court that before the national court the respondents argued that Article 4 of the directive did not impose clear and precise obligations on Ireland and that Ireland thus had considerable discretion in determining the manner of implementation. In their view Article 4 could not therefore be relied on in the Irish courts.

6. Since the High Court entertained doubts as to the effect of the directive, it stayed the proceedings and submitted the following questions to the Court for a preliminary ruling:

   '1. Do the provisions of Directive 79/7/EEC, and in particular Article 4 thereof, have direct effect in the Republic of Ireland as and from the 23rd day of December 1984 so as to confer enforceable Community rights upon married women such as the prosecutrices in the circumstances of the present cases?
   2. If the answer to question 1 is in the affirmative, does this mean that national provisions such as those contained in Chapters 4 and 6 of Part 2 of the Social Welfare (Consolidation) Act 1981, as amended, are inactable and that the prosecutrices as married women living in a Member State which had failed to repeal or adapt such provisions are entitled to equal treatment in relation to the relevant social welfare benefits as and from the 23rd day of December 1984 and have rights of action in that regard which are enforceable by them against such Member States?'.

7. It appears from the documents before the Court that section 34(6) of the Social Welfare (Consolidation) Act 1981 was repealed by section 6(c) of the Social Welfare (No. 2) Act 1985, which provides that married women are to be entitled to unemployment benefits and pay-related benefits for the same period as other claimants. Section 6 of the 1985 Act came into force on 15 May 1986, and gave limited retroactive effect to the repeal inasmuch as only married women who had received unemployment benefits within the period of 78 days ending on the date on which the section came into force were entitled to take advantage of it. Consequently, the two prosecutrices in the main proceedings, who ceased to receive unemployment benefits in January 1985, were unable to benefit.

8. It also appears that section 2 of the 1985 Act amended in particular Chapters 4 and 6 of the 1981 Act by providing that the rate of unemployment benefit was to be the same for men and for women. That section also came into force on 15 May 1986 in so far as it concerns unemployment benefits.

9. Reference is made to the Report for the Hearing for the observations

295

submitted to the Court, which are mentioned or discussed hereinafter only in so far as is necessary for the reasoning of the Court.

Question 1

10. In its first question the High Court seeks in essence to ascertain whether Article 4(1) of the directive confers rights on individuals in a Member State upon the expiry of the period within which the Member States were to implement it.

11. As the Court has consistently held, in particular in its judgment of 19 January 1982 (Case 8/81, *Becker* v. *Finanzamt Münster-Innenstadt*, [1982] ECR 53), wherever the provisions of a directive appear, as far as their subject-matter is concerned, to be unconditional and sufficiently precise, individuals may rely on those provisions in the absence of implementing measures adopted within the prescribed period as against any national provision which is incompatible with the directive or in so far as the provisions define rights which individuals are able to assert against the State.

12. That conclusion is based on the fact that directives are binding on the Member States and on the principle that a Member State which has not taken measures to implement the directive within the prescribed period may not, as against individuals, plead its own failure to fulfil such obligations.

13. As the Court pointed out in its judgment of 24 June 1986 (Case 150/85, *Drake* v. *Chief Adjudication Officer*, [1986] ECR 2002), the objective set out in Article 1 of Directive 79/7 is given practical expression by Article 4(1), which provides that in matters of social security there shall be no discrimination whatsoever on ground of sex, either directly, or indirectly by reference in particular to marital or family status, in particular as concerns the scope of social security schemes and the conditions of access thereto.

14. Furthermore, in its judgment of 4 December 1986 (Case 71/85, *Netherlands* v. *FNV*, [1986] ECR) the Court held that standing by itself, and in the light of the objective and contents of the directive, Article 4(1) is sufficiently precise to be relied upon in legal proceedings and applied by a court. Moreover, that article in no way permits Member States to restrict or place conditions on the application of the principle of equal treatment in its particular area of application.

15. With regard to the argument to the effect that the multiplicity of alternatives available for the purpose of achieving equal treatment makes it impossible for the directive to confer rights on individuals, it will suffice

to point out that, as the Court has already held in its aforesaid judgment of 19 January 1982 in *Becker*, the fact that directives leave to the national authorities the choice of the form and methods for achieving the required result cannot constitute a ground for denying all effect to those provisions which may be relied upon before a court.

16. It follows from the foregoing that Article 4(1) is sufficiently precise and unconditional to allow individuals, in the absence of implementing measures, to rely upon it before the national courts as from 23 December 1984, in order to preclude the application of any national provision inconsistent with that article.

17. The answer to the first question must therefore be that where Council Directive 79/7/EEC of 19 December 1978 has not been implemented Article 4(1) of the directive, which prohibits all discrimination on grounds of sex in matters of social security, could be relied upon as from 23 December 1984 in order to preclude the application of any national provision inconsistent with it.

Question 2
18. With regard to the second question raised by the High Court, which seeks in essence to determine whether, where no measures have been taken to implement Article 4(1) of the directive, married women barred by national legislation are entitled as from 23 December 1984 to benefits under the same conditions as men, it will suffice to point out that, as the Court held in its judgment of 4 December 1986 referred to above, until such time as the national government adopts the necessary implementing measures women are entitled to have the same rules applied to them as are applied to men who are in the same situation, since in such circumstances those rules remain the only valid point of reference.

19. The answer to the second question must therefore be that in the absence of measures implementing Article 4(1) of the directive women are entitled to have the same rules applied to them as are applied to men who are in the same situation, since, where the directive has not been implemented, those rules remain the only valid point of reference.

Costs
20. The costs incurred by the Netherlands Government and the Commission of the European Communities, which have submitted observations to the Court, are not recoverable. As these proceedings are, in so far as the parties to the main proceedings are concerned, in the nature of a step in the proceedings pending before the national court, the decision on costs is a matter for that court.

On those grounds,

THE COURT

in answer to the questions submitted to it by the High Court, Dublin, by order of 13 May 1985, hereby rules:

1. **Where Council Directive 79/7/EEC of 19 December 1978 has not been implemented, Article 4(1) of the directive, which prohibits all discrimination on grounds of sex in matters of social security, could be relied on as from 23 December 1984 in order to preclude the application of any national provision inconsistent with it.**

2. **In the absence of measures implementing Article 4(1) of the directive women are entitled to have the same rules applied to them as are applied to men who are in the same situation, since, where the directive has not been implemented, those rules remain the only valid point of reference.**

Mackenzie Stuart	Galmot	Kakouris
O'Higgins	Schockweiler	Bosco
Koopmans	Due	Everling
Bahlmann	Joliet	Moitinho de Almeida
	Rodriguez Iglesias	

Delivered in open court in Luxembourg on 24 March 1987.

P. Heim   A. J. Mackenzie Stuart
Registrar   *President*

Judgment of the Court

11 June 1987 – Case 30/85

J. W. Teuling
v.
Bedrijfsvereniging voor de Chemische Industrie

Equal treatment in social security – a system of social security benefits in which supplements are not directly based on sex of beneficiaries but take account of their marital status or family situation, and where a considerably smaller proportion of women than men are entitled to the supplements, is contrary to Article 4(1) of Directive 79/7/EEC if the system cannot be justified by reasons which exclude discrimination on grounds of sex – where supplements correspond to the greater burdens borne by beneficiaries with dependent spouses or children as compared with single persons, serve to ensure an adequate minimum subsistence income for those beneficiaries and are necessary for that purpose, the fact that they are paid to considerably more men than women does not mean that the grant of such supplements is contrary to the Directive – a benefits system concerning incapacity for work, under which benefit amounts determined in part by marital status and income earned from or in connection with work of spouse, is consistent with Article 4 of Directive if system seeks to ensure adequate minimum subsistence income for beneficiaries with dependent spouses or children by a supplement to benefit which compensates for greater burdens they bear compared with single persons – Community law does not prevent Member State, in controlling its social expenditure, from taking account of fact that need of beneficiaries with dependent children or spouses with very small incomes is greater than that of single persons – legislation restricting to persons with a dependent spouse or child, or a spouse with a very small income, a guarantee, previously applicable to all workers suffering from incapacity for work whose income was equal to the statutory minimum wage, that their benefits would be at least equal to the statutory minimum wage, is compatible with Article 4(1) of the Directive (Council Directive 79/7/EEC, Article 4(1)).

In Case 30/85

REFERENCE to the Court under Article 177 of the EEC Treaty by the Raad van Beroep ((Social Security Court)), Amsterdam, for a preliminary ruling in the proceedings pending before that court between

J. W. Teuling, Amsterdam,

and

Bedrijfsvereniging voor de Chemische Industrie (Professional and Trade Association for the Chemical Industry)

on the interpretation of Council Directive 79/7/EEC of 19 December 1978 on the progressive implementation of the principle of equal treatment for men and women in matters of social security (Official Journal 1979 No. L 6, p. 24),

THE COURT (SIXTH CHAMBER)

composed of: C. N. Kakouris, President of the Chamber, T. F. O'Higgins, T. Koopmans, K. Bahlmann and G. C. Rodriguez Iglesias, Judges,

Advocate General: G. F. Mancini
Registrar: H. A. Rühl, Principal Administrator

gives the following JUDGMENT

Decision

1. By an order of 4 February 1985, which was received at the Court on 6 February 1985, the Raad van Beroep, Amsterdam, referred to the Court for a preliminary ruling under Article 177 of the EEC Treaty four questions on the interpretation of Council Directive 79/7 of 19 December 1978 on the progressive implementation of the principle of equal treatment for men and women in matters of social security (Official Journal 1979 No. L 6, p. 24) and Council Directive 76/207 of 9 February 1976 on the implementation of the principle of equal treatment for men and women as regards access to employment, vocational training and promotion, and working conditions (Official Journal 1976 No. L 39, p. 40).

2. Those questions were raised in the course of proceedings between Mrs Teuling and the Bedrijfsvereniging voor de Chemische Industrie concerning the decision of the latter to calculate her invalidity pension with effect from 1 January 1984 on the basis not of the legal minimum wage but of the last wage paid to her, in accordance with the amendments made to the insurance scheme by the law of 29 December 1982.

3. According to the Wet op de Arbeidsongeschiktheidsverzekering (Law on Insurance against Incapacity for Work, hereinafter referred to as 'the Insurance Law'), in the version in force prior to the adoption of the Law of 29 December 1982, all employed persons suffering from an incapacity for work, regardless of their sex or civil status, were entitled to a net minimum benefit equal to the net amount of the statutory minimum wage as laid down by the law of 27 November 1968 (Staatsblad 657) on the minimum wage and minimum holiday entitlement for employed persons. The Law of 29 December 1982 (Staatsblad 737) abolished that right with effect from 1 January 1984 and provided for the gradual transfer of the beneficiaries thereof from the minimum benefit provided for under the Insurance Law to the (lower) minimum benefit provided for under the Algemene Arbeidsongeschiktheidswet (General law on Incapacity for Work, hereinafter referred to as 'the General Law'), namely 70 per cent of the statutory minimum wage. By means of supplements that minimum could be increased to 100 per cent only for beneficiaries fulfilling the conditions laid down in Article 10(4) of the General Law, that is to say, in practice, those having family responsibilities.

4. The Law of 30 December 1983 (Staatsblad 698) introduced a new article (Article 97) into the General Law under which a right to benefits under that law was granted to women entitled to benefits under the Insurance Law in respect of an incapacity for work which had already arisen on 1 October 1976 (the date on which the General Law came into force); such women had previously been excluded from those benefits simply by virtue of being married. With effect from 1 January 1984, they became

entitled to those benefits where the amount of the benefits awarded under the Insurance Law was less than the amount to which they would have been entitled under the General Law if they had not been excluded from benefits thereunder.

5. Mrs Teuling, who has been unable to work since 1972, received, from 1975 onwards, benefits under the Insurance Law equal to the net statutory minimum wage, irrespective of the fact that she was married and of her husband's income. However, from 1 January 1984 that benefit was reduced in accordance with the Law of 29 December 1982 to 70 per cent of the statutory minimum wage. Moreover, she was not entitled to benefit supplements under Article 10(4) of the General Law because of the income arising from or in connexion with her husband's work. Her husband died on 28 April 1984 and the period in dispute is therefore that between January and April 1984.

6. The applicant in the main proceedings claims that under the Law of 29 December 1982 the invalidity benefit which she receives was reduced from 100 per cent to 70 per cent of the statutory minimum wage. Since, at the material time, she was married, and her husband's income was above the maximum laid down in Article 10(4), she was not entitled to the benefit supplements of 15 per cent or 30 per cent. She claims in essence that that system of supplements, which takes account of income arising from or in connexion with the work of a spouse and of the presence of dependent children, constitutes indirect discrimination against women and is therefore incompatible with Article 4(1) of Directive 79/7.

7. However, the competent Netherlands institution considers that only persons with a dependent spouse or children are entitled to the guaranteed minimum income equal to the full amount of the net statutory minimum wage.

8. Since it considered the scope of the directive to be unclear, the Raad van Beroep, Amsterdam, before which the matter had been brought, stayed the proceedings and referred the following four questions to the Court of Justice for a preliminary ruling:

   '1. Is a system of entitlement to benefits in respect of incapacity for work under which the amount of the benefit is determined in part by marital status and by the income earned from or in connexion with work of the spouse, or by the existence of a dependent child, consistent with Article 4(1) of Council Directive No. 79/7/EEC of 19 December 1978?
   2. (a) Is the Law of 29 December 1982 (Staatsblad 737) abolishing the guarantee for all persons covered by the Wet op de Arbeidsongeschiktheidsverzekering

that the (net) benefits are to be at least equal to the (net) statutory minimum wage, with the result that the guarantee now applies only to persons who satisfy the conditions of Article 10(4) of the Algemene Arbeids-ongeschiktheidswet consistent with Article 4(1) of the directive referred to in Question 1?

2. (b) Having regard to the period referred to in Article 8 of the directive and to the provisions of Article 5 thereof and Article 5 of the Treaty establishing the European Economic Community, is it relevant to the answer to be given to Question 2(a) that the said law was adopted on 29 December 1982 and entered into force partially on 1 January 1983, whilst provision is made for its material consequences to take effect in stages both before and after the expiry of the period referred to in Article 8 of the directive?

3. Are the provisions of Council Directive No. 76/207/EEC of 9 February 1976 also relevant as regards the answers to the foregoing questions?

4. If Question 1 or Question 2(a), or both, are answered in the negative, does that mean that the relevant provision of Community law – which is thus deemed to have been infringed – may be relied upon directly by the persons concerned as against the national authorities?'.

9. Reference is made to the Report for the Hearing for the Netherlands legislation at issue and the detailed arguments of the parties, which are mentioned or discussed hereinafter only in so far as is necessary for the reasoning of the Court.

Question 1
10. In the first question, the Raad van Beroep seeks to know whether a system of entitlement to benefits in respect of incapacity for work under which the amount of the benefit is determined in part by marital status and by the income earned from or in connexion with work of the spouse or by the existence of a dependent child constitutes discrimination within the meaning of Article 4(1) of the directive.

11. As the Court decided in its judgment of 24 June 1986 (Case 150/85, *Drake* v. *Chief Adjudication Officer*, (1986) ECR 1995, the aim set out in Article 1 of Directive 79/7 is given effect in Article 4(1). That Article provides, in regard to social security, that there shall be no discrimination whatsoever on ground of sex either directly, or indirectly by reference in particular to marital or family status, in particular as concerns the calculation of benefits including increases due in respect of a spouse or for dependents and the conditions governing the duration and retention of entitlement to benefits.

12. It is thus clear from the very words of Article 4(1) that increases are prohibited if they are directly or indirectly based on the sex of the beneficiary.

13. In that regard, it should be pointed out that a system of benefits in which, as in this case, supplements are provided for which are not directly based on the sex of the beneficiaries but take account of their marital status or family situation and in respect of which it emerges that a considerably smaller proportion of women than of men are entitled to such supplements is contrary to Article 4(1) of the directive if that system of benefits cannot be justified by reasons which exclude discrimination on grounds of sex.

14. It appears from the documents before the Court that according to statistics provided to the Commission by the Netherlands Government a significantly greater number of married men than married women receive a supplement linked to family responsibilities. According to the plaintiff and the Commission, that results from the fact that in the Netherlands there are at present considerably more married men than married women who carry on occupational activities, and therefore considerably fewer women who have a dependent spouse.

15. In such circumstances a supplement linked to family responsibilities is contrary to Article 4(1) of the directive if the grant thereof cannot be justified by reasons which exclude discrimination on grounds of sex.

16. In that regard, the purpose of the supplements at issue must be considered. According to the Netherlands Government, the General Law does not link benefits to the salary previously earned by the beneficiaries but seeks to provide a minimum subsistence income to persons with no income from work. It must be observed that such a guarantee granted by Member States to persons who would otherwise be destitute is an integral part of the social policy of the Member States.

17. Consequently, if supplements to a minimum social security benefit are intended, where beneficiaries have no income from work, to prevent the benefit from falling below the minimum subsistence level for persons who, by virtue of the fact that they have a dependent spouse or children, bear heavier burdens than single persons, such supplements may be justified under the directive.

18. If a national court, which has sole jurisdiction to assess the facts and interpret the national legislation, finds that supplements such as those in this case correspond to the greater burdens which beneficiaries having a dependent spouse or children must bear in comparison with persons living alone, serve to ensure an adequate minimum subsistence income for those beneficiaries and are necessary for that purpose, the fact that

303

the supplements are paid to a significantly higher number of married men than married women is not sufficient to support the conclusion that the grant of such supplements is contrary to the directive.

19. The reply to the first question raised by the Raad van Beroep must therefore be that Article 4(1) of Council Directive 79/7 of 19 December 1978 is to be interpreted as meaning that a system of benefits in respect of incapacity for work under which the amount of the benefit is determined in part by marital status and by the income earned from or in connexion with work of a spouse is consistent with that provision if the system seeks to ensure an adequate minimum subsistence income for beneficiaries who have a dependent spouse or children, by means of a supplement to the social security benefit which compensates for the greater burdens they bear in comparison with single persons.

Question 2(a)
20. In part (a) of the second question, the national court seeks to determine whether legislation such as the Netherlands Law of 29 December 1982, cited above, under which the guarantee previously applicable to all workers suffering from an incapacity for work whose income was approximately equal to the statutory minimum wage that their (net) benefits would be at least equal to the (net) statutory minimum wage is restricted to persons having a dependent spouse or child, or whose spouse has a very small income, is compatible with Article 4(1) of the directive.

21. It appears from the order for reference that after the entry into force of the Law of 29 December 1982 the position of married persons entitled to benefits under the Insurance Law at the minimum rate who could not produce evidence that they had a dependent spouse became less favourable, since their benefits were reduced to 70 per cent of the statutory minimum wage with effect from 1 January 1984. It is also clear that within the group of persons entitled to benefits under the Insurance Law, a much greater number of (married) men than (married) women came within the scope of Article 10(4) of the General Law.

22. As the Netherlands Government emphasized, the Law of 29 December 1982 embodies a policy which seeks to ensure, having regard to available resources, a minimum subsistence income for all workers suffering from an incapacity for work. In that regard, it must be recognized that Community law does not prevent a Member State, in controlling its social expenditure, from taking account of the fact that the need of beneficiaries who have a dependent child or spouse or whose spouse has a very small income is greater than that of single persons.

23. The reply to part (a) of the second question must therefore be that Article 4(1) of Directive 79/7 is to be interpreted as meaning that legislation under which the guarantee previously applicable to all workers suffering from an incapacity for work whose income was approximately

equal to the statutory minimum wage that their (net) benefits would be at least equal to the (net) statutory minimum wage is restricted to persons having a dependent spouse or child or whose spouse has a very small income is compatible with that provision.

Questions 2(b), 3 and 4
24. Having regard to the replies given to questions 1 and 2(a), it is no longer necessary to consider questions 2(b), 3 or 4.

Costs
25. The costs incurred by the Netherlands Government and by the Commission of the European Communities, which have submitted observations to the Court, are not recoverable. As these proceedings are, in so far as the parties to the main proceedings are concerned, in the nature of a step in the action pending before the national court, the decision as to costs is a matter for that court.

On those grounds,

THE COURT (SIXTH CHAMBER)

in answer to the questions referred to it by the Raad van Beroep, Amsterdam, by order of 4 February 1985, hereby rules:

1. **Article 4(1) of Council Directive 79/7/EEC of 19 December 1978 is to be interpreted as meaning that a system of benefits in respect of incapacity for work under which the amount of the benefit is determined in part by marital status and by the income earned from or in connexion with work of a spouse is consistent with that provision if the system seeks to ensure an adequate minimum subsistence income for beneficiaries who have a dependent spouse or children, by means of a supplement to the social security benefit which compensates for the greater burdens they bear in comparison with single persons.**

2. **Article 4(1) of Directive 79/7/EEC is to be interpreted as meaning that legislation under which the guarantee previously applicable to all workers suffering from an incapacity for work whose income was approximately equal to the statutory minimum wage that their (net) benefits would be at least equal to the (net) statutory minimum wage is restricted to persons having a dependent spouse or child or whose spouse has a very small income is compatible with that provision.**

Kakouris, O'Higgins, Koopmans, Bahlmann, Rodriguez Iglesias

Delivered in open court in Luxembourg on 11 June 1987.

P. Heim   C. N. Kakouris
Registrar   *President of the Sixth Chamber*

Judgment of the Court

24 June 1987 – Case 384/85

Mrs Borrie Clarke
v.
The Chief Adjudication Officer

Equal treatment in social security – Article 4(1) of Directive 79/7/EEC is sufficiently precise and unconditional to be relied on in legal proceedings and applied by national courts – Article 5 of Directive requires Member States to abolish any provisions contrary to equal treatment principle, but allows discretion as to their methods for achieving this result – Directive does not provide for any derogation from equal treatment principle so as to authorise extension of discriminatory effects of earlier provisions of national law – Article 4(1) of Directive 79/7/EEC may be relied on as from 22 December 1984 (expiry date for implementation nationally) to prevent extension beyond that date of effects of earlier inconsistent national provisions – in absence of appropriate national measures implementing Directive, women are entitled to be treated in same way and via application of same rules as men in same situation in line with Directive, whose rules remain only valid point of reference (Council Directive 79/7/EEC, Articles 4(1) and 5).

In Case 384/85

REFERENCE to the Court under Article 177 of the EEC Treaty by the Social Security Commissioner, London, for a preliminary ruling in the proceedings pending before the Commissioner between

Mrs Borrie Clarke,

and

The Chief Adjudication Officer,

on the interpretation of Council Directive 79/7/EEC of 19 December 1978 on the progressive implementation of the principle of equal treatment for men and women in matters of social security (Official Journal 1979 No. L 6, p. 24),

THE COURT (SECOND CHAMBER)

composed of: T. F. O'Higgins, President of Chamber, O. Due and K. Bahlmann, Judges,

Advocate General: J. L. Da Cruz Vilaça
Registrar: H. A. Rühl, Principal Administrator

gives the following JUDGMENT

Decision

1. By order of 25 November 1985, which was received at the Court Registry on 29 November 1985, the Social Security Commissioner, London, referred to the Court for a preliminary ruling under Article 177 of the EEC Treaty a question concerning the interpretation of Article 4 of Council Directive 79/7/EEC of 19 December 1978 on the progressive implementation of the principle of equal treatment for men and women in matters of social security, in which the Commissioner seeks to ascertain whether Article 4 may be regarded as having direct effect in the United Kingdom since 22 December 1984, the date by which the Member States should have adopted all the measures necessary for its implementation.

2. That question was raised in appeal proceedings between Mrs Borrie Clarke and the Chief Adjudication Officer concerning the question whether Article 4(1) of the aforesaid directive precludes the effects of a discriminatory rule abolished before 22 December 1984, the date of the expiry of the period within which the Member States were to comply with the directive, from continuing beyond that date, pursuant to national transitional provisions adopted in connexion with the introduction of a new invalidity benefit.

3. It appears from the documents before the Court that in April 1983 Mrs Borrie Clarke was refused a non-contributory invalidity pension on the basis of a condition concerning ability to perform normal household duties, which was not imposed on persons of the opposite sex. Non-contributory invalidity pensions were abolished as from 29 November 1984 and a new benefit was introduced, known as the severe disablement allowance, which is available to claimants of either sex on the same conditions. The appointed date for the entry into force of the severe disablement allowance was in principle 29 November 1985. However, Regulation 20(1) of the Social Security (Severe Disablement Allowance) Regulations 1984 (hereinafter referred to as 'the transitional provisions') allowed persons who were entitled to the non-contributory invalidity pension formerly available to qualify automatically, as from 29 November 1984, for the new severe disablement allowance without having to show that they satisfied all the new conditions. It follows, therefore, that automatic entitlement to the payment of that new allowance pursuant to the transitional provisions was subject to the same criteria as those which determined entitlement to the old non-contributory invalidity pension.

4. According to Mrs Borrie Clarke, the effect of the aforesaid transitional provisions is to perpetuate in respect of automatic entitlement to the new severe disablement allowance the discriminatory basis of entitlement to

the old non-contributory invalidity pension. She maintains that since 22 December 1984 she has been entitled, by virtue of Article 4(1) of the directive, to the severe disablement allowance without having to show that she satisfies the additional condition concerning her ability to perform normal household duties, which applies exclusively to married women living with their husbands. The United Kingdom, on the other hand, states that the aim of the transitional provisions is to enable persons who qualified for the old non-contributory invalidity pension to qualify for the new allowance without having to satisfy the new conditions and thus to safeguard the legitimate expectation of those persons that they would not be deprived of benefits owing to the change in the rules.

5. As is clear from the documents before the Court, it is not disputed that the provisions at issue, including the transitional provisions concerning the severe disablement allowance, are contrary to the principle of equal treatment laid down in Article 4(1) of the directive.

6. Taking the view that the effect of Article 4(1) of the directive was unclear in that regard, the Social Security Commissioner, hearing the appeal, stayed the proceedings and referred to the Court the following question:

'Does Article 4(1) of Council Directive 79/7/EEC have a direct effect such that a woman can from 22 December 1984 qualify for an invalidity benefit by reason of her having before that date satisfied conditions sufficient to enable a man to qualify for that benefit notwithstanding that she did not also before that date satisfy a further condition applicable under domestic law only to a class of women of whom she was one?'.

7. Reference is made to the Report for the Hearing for a more detailed account of the national legislation at issue and the observations submitted to the Court, which are mentioned or discussed hereinafter only in so far as is necessary for the reasoning of the Court.

8. The Social Security Commissioner's question seeks essentially to ascertain whether Article 4(1) of the directive may be relied upon by individuals in a Member State in order to prevent the extension beyond 22 December 1984, the date of the expiry of the period prescribed for the implementation of the directive, of the effects of an earlier national provision inconsistent with Article 4(1) and, if so, whether the women concerned acquired entitlement to benefits as from that date on the same conditions as men.

9. It should be noted, as the Court held in its judgments of 4 December 1986 in Case 71/85 (*FNV*, [1986] ECR) and of 24 March 1987 in Case 286/85 (*Mc Dermott and Cotter*, [1987] ECR), that standing by itself, and in the light of the objective and contents of the directive, Article 4(1) is

sufficiently precise to be relied upon in legal proceedings and applied by a court. Moreover, whilst Article 5 of the directive leaves to the Member States a discretion with regard to methods, it prescribes the result which those methods must achieve, namely the abolition of any provisions contrary to the principle of equal treatment.

10. Furthermore, it must be emphasized that the directive does not provide for any derogation from the principle of equal treatment laid down in Article 4(1) in order to authorize the extension of the discriminatory effects of earlier provisions of national law. It follows that a Member State may not maintain beyond 22 December 1984 any inequalities of treatment which have their origin in the fact that the conditions for entitlement to benefit are those which applied before that date. That is so notwithstanding the fact that those inequalities are the result of transitional provisions adopted at the time of the introduction of a new benefit.

11. Consequently, Article 4(1) of the directive in no way confers on Member States the power to make conditional or to limit the application of the principle of equal treatment within its field of application and it is sufficiently precise and unconditional to allow individuals, in the absence of appropriate implementing measures, to rely upon it before the national courts as from 22 December 1984 in order to preclude the application of any provision of national law inconsistent with that article.

12. As is also apparent from the judgments of 4 December 1986 in *FNV* and of 24 March 1987 in *McDermott and Cotter*, it follows from Article 4(1) of the directive that, as from 22 December 1984, women are entitled to be treated in the same manner, and to have the same rules applied to them, as men who are in the same situation, since, where the directive has not been implemented correctly, those rules remain the only valid point of reference. In this case, that means that if, as from 22 December 1984, a man in the same position as a woman was automatically entitled to the new severe disablement allowance under the aforesaid transitional provisions without having to re-establish his rights, a woman was also entitled to that allowance without having to satisfy an additional condition applicable before that date exclusively to married women.

13. The answer to the question submitted must therefore be that Article 4(1) of Council Directive 79/7/EEC of 19 December 1978 on the progressive implementation of the principle of equal treatment for men and women in matters of social security could be relied upon as from 22 December 1984 in order to prevent the extension beyond that date of the effects of an earlier national provision inconsistent with Article 4(1). In the absence of appropriate measures for the implementation of that article, women are entitled to be treated in the same manner, and to have the same rules applied to them, as men who are in the same situation, since, where the

309

directive has not been implemented, those rules remain the only valid point of reference.

Costs

14. The costs incurred by the United Kingdom and by the Commission of the European Communities, which have submitted observations to the Court, are not recoverable. As these proceedings are, in so far as the parties to the main proceedings are concerned, in the nature of a step in the proceedings pending before the national court, the decision on costs is a matter for that court.

On those grounds,

THE COURT (SECOND CHAMBER),

in answer to the question referred to it by the Social Security Commissioner, London, by order of 25 November 1985, hereby rules:

Article 4(1) of Council Directive 79/7/EEC of 19 December 1978 on the progressive implementation of the principle of equal treatment for men and women in matters of social security could be relied upon as from 22 December 1984 in order to prevent the extension beyond that date of the effects of an earlier national provision inconsistent with Article 4(1). In the absence of appropriate measures for the implementation of that article, women are entitled to be treated in the same manner, and to have the same rules applied to them, as men who are in the same situation, since, where the directive has not been implemented, those rules remain the only valid point of reference.

O'Higgins   Due   Bahlmann

Delivered in open court in Luxembourg on 24 June 1987.

P. Heim   T. F. O'Higgins
Registrar   *President of the Second Chamber*

Part II.
Employment Protection

Contents

Part II. Employment Protection

Introduction

The improvement of working conditions for employees throughout the EEC, and the establishment of common basic standards of protection for workers, have long been at the heart of the EEC's social policies. From the very inception of the Community, the basic Treaty of Rome numbered among its explicit objectives the improvement of living and working conditions.

During the 1970s, these objectives were elaborated on in a broad social action programme and in subsequent measures proposed by the European Commission. Many issues were discussed during this period, including working time provisions and various employment protection and harmonisation measures. However, the deteriorating economic and employment climate concentrated attentions on job security issues, and the legislative provisions which were actually adopted by the Community's Council of Ministers reflected this preoccupation. The three Directives enacted sought to safeguard employees' rights and offer certain protections to those threatened by collective redundancies, company takeovers or employers' insolvencies. The emphasis of the 1980s has been on labour market flexibility and deregulation, and there has thus been no further employment protection legislation enacted at Community level – apart from specific provisions relating to health and safety at work, which has increasingly been affected by new technological developments. However, with the approach of 1992 and the need to consider the social implications of the completion of the internal market, attention has again focussed on basic standards of protection for employees in the Community. As the European Commission has stated, in making the improvement of living and working conditions a continuing priority objective for the 1990s, 'there is a greater need than ever for effective measures to protect workers in a labour market which is becoming more flexible'.

The body of general employment protection legislation already enacted at Community level is detailed in the following sections. Essentially, this comprises general Treaty provisions and specific Council Directives on collective redundancy procedures, employees' rights where transfers of undertakings occur, and protections for employees on the insolvency of their employer. Some case law interpreting these provisions has also begun to emerge in the last few years. Although not as developed or wide-ranging as the case law on the Community's equality legislation (see previous Chapter), the rulings by the European Court in this area have clarified several issues concerning the scope of the collective redundancies and transfers Directives. These clarifications have been given by the Court in the course of determining proceedings brought against Governments by the European Commission (under Article 169 of the EEC Treaty), and in preliminary rulings on questions of interpretation referred from national courts (under Article 177 of the Treaty). The relevant Court rulings are included in this chapter.

This Chapter is essentially concerned with the EEC's general, mainstream employment legislation. EEC provisions not directly concerned with social policy but touching on social issues for particular groups of workers (for example, transport regulations governing drivers' hours, or redundancy provisions for iron and steel workers) are not included here as they are outside the mainstream of the Community's social legislation. Much specific Community legislation has been enacted concerning the health and safety aspects of working conditions. These special protective measures affecting workplace health and safety have been developed in the context of distinct programmes for action in the health and safety field. They are dealt with separately, therefore, in the next chapter.

A. General: EEC Treaty Extracts

Social Provisions

Article 117
Member States agree upon the need to promote improved working conditions and an improved standard of living for workers, so as to make possible their harmonization while the improvement is being maintained.

They believe that such a development will ensue not only from the functioning of the common market, which will favour the harmonization of social systems, but also from the procedures provided for in this Treaty and from the approximation of provisions laid down by law, regulation or administrative action.

Article 118
Without prejudice to the other provisions of this Treaty and in conformity with its general objectives, the Commission shall have the task of promoting close cooperation between Member States in the social field, particularly in matters relating to:
- employment;
- labour law and working conditions;
- basic and advanced vocational training;
- social security:
- prevention of occupational accidents and diseases;
- occupational hygiene;
- the right of association, and collective bargaining between employers and workers.

B. Specific Employment Protection Directives

Council Directive

of 17 February 1975

on the approximation of the laws of the Member States relating to collective redundancies
(75/129/EEC)

The Council of the European Communities,

Having regard to the Treaty establishing the European Economic Community, and in particular Article 100 thereof,
Having regard to the proposal from the Commission,
Having regard to the Opinion of the European Parliament;[1]
Having regard to the Opinion of the Economic and Social Committee:[2]

Whereas it is important that greater protection should be afforded to workers in the event of collective redundancies while taking into account the need for balanced economic and social development within the Community;

Whereas, despite increasing convergence, differences still remain between the provisions in force in the Member States of the Community concerning the practical arrangements and procedures for such redandancies and the measures designed to alleviate the consequences of redundancy for workers;

Whereas these differences can have a direct effect on the functioning of the common market;

Whereas the Council resolution of 21 January 1974[3] concerning a social action programme makes provision for a Directive on the approximation of Member States' legislation on collective redundancies;

Whereas this approximation must therefore be promoted while the improvement is being maintained within the meaning of Article 117 of the Treaty,

Has adopted this Directive:

SECTION 1 – **Definitions and scope**

Article 1
1. For the purposes of this Directive:
    (a) 'collective redundancies' means dismissals effected by an employer

for one or more reasons not related to the individual workers concerned where, according to the choice of the Member States, the number of redundancies is:
- either, over a period of 30 days:
    (1) at least 10 in establishments normally employing more than 20 and less than 100 workers;
    (2) at least 10 per cent of the number of workers in establishments normally employing at least 100 but less than 300 workers;
    (3) at least 30 in establishments normally employing 300 workers or more;
- or, over a period of 90 days, at least 20, whatever the number of workers normally employed in the establishments in question;
(b) 'workers' representatives' means the workers' representatives provided for by the laws or practices of the Member States.
2. This Directive shall not apply to:
(a) collective redundancies affected under contracts of employment concluded for limited periods of time or for specific tasks except where such redundancies take place prior to the date of expiry or the completion of such contracts;
(b) workers employed by public administrative bodies or by establishments governed by public law (or, in Member States where this concept is unknown, by equivalent bodies);
(c) the crews of sea-going vessels;
(d) workers affected by the termination of an establishment's activities where that is the result of a judicial decision.

SECTION 2 – Consultation procedure

Article 2
1. Where an employer is contemplating collective redundancies, he shall begin consultations with the workers' representatives with a view to reaching an agreement.
2. These consultations shall, at least, cover ways and means of avoiding collective redundancies or reducing the number of workers affected, and mitigating the consequences.
3. To enable the workers' representatives to make constructive proposals the employer shall supply them with all relevant information and shall in any event give in writing the reasons for the redundancies, the number of workers to be made redundant, the number of workers normally employed and the period over which the redundancies are to be effected.

   The employer shall forward to the competent public authority a copy of all the written communications referred to in the preceding subparagraph.

SECTION 3 – Procedure for collective redundancies

Article 3
1. Employers shall notify the competent public authority in writing of any projected collective redundancies.

This notification shall contain all relevant information concerning the projected collective redundancies and the consultations with workers' representatives provided for in Article 2, and particularly the reasons for the redundancies, the number of workers to be made redundant, the number of workers normally employed and the period over which the redundancies are to be effected.

2. Employers shall forward to the workers' representatives a copy of the notification provided for in paragraph 1.

The workers' representatives may send any comments they may have to the competent public authority.

Article 4

1. Projected collective redundancies notified to the competent public authority shall take effect not earlier than 30 days after the notification referred to in Article 3(1) without prejudice to any provisions governing individual rights with regard to notice of dismissal.

Member States may grant the competent public authority the power to reduce the period provided for in the preceding subparagraph.

2. The period provided for in paragraph 1 shall be used by the competent public authority to seek solutions in the problems raised by the projected collective redundancies.

3. Where the initial period provided for in paragraph 1 is shorter than 60 days, Member States may grant the competent public authority the power to extend the initial period to 60 days following notification where the problems raised by the projected collective redundancies are not likely to be solved within the initial period.

Member States may grant the competent public authority wider powers of extension.

The employer must be informed of the extension and the grounds for it before expiry of the initial period provided for in paragraph 1.

SECTION 4 – Final provisions

Article 5

This Directive shall not affect the right of Member States to apply or to introduce laws, regulations or administrative provisions which are more favourable to workers.

Article 6

1. Member States shall bring into force the laws, regulations and administrative provisions needed in order to comply with this Directive within two years following its notification and shall forthwith inform the Commission thereof.

2. Member States shall communicate to the Commission the texts of the laws, regulations and administrative provisions which they adopt in the field covered by this Directive.

Article 7
Within two years following expiry of the two year period laid down in Article 6, Member States shall forward all relevant information to the Commission to enable it to draw up a report for submission to the Council on the application of this Directive.

Article 8
This Directive is addressed to the Member States.

Done at Brussels, 17 February 1975.

For the Council
The President
R. Ryan

---

1. OJ No. C 19, 12.4.1973, p. 10.
2. OJ No. C 100, 22.11.1973, p. 11.
3. OJ No. C 13, 12.2.1974, p. 1.

Council Directive

of 14 February 1977

on the approximation of the laws of the Member States relating to the safeguarding of employees' rights in the event of transfers of undertakings, businesses or parts of businesses
(77/187/EEC)

THE COUNCIL OF THE EUROPEAN COMMUNITIES,

Having regard to the Treaty establishing the European Economic Community, and in particular Article 100 thereof,
Having regard to the proposal from the Commission,
Having regard to the opinion of the European Parliament,[1]
Having regard to the opinion of the Economic and Social Committee:[2]
    Whereas economic trends are bringing in their wake, at both national and Community level, changes in the structure of undertakings, through transfers of undertakings, businesses or parts of businesses to other employers as a result of legal transfers or mergers;
    Whereas it is necessary to provide for the protection of employees in the event of a change of employer, in particular, to ensure that their rights are safeguarded;
    Whereas differences still remain in the Member States as regards the extent of the protection of employees in this respect and these differences should be reduced;

Whereas these differences can have a direct effect on the functioning of the common market;

Whereas it is therefore necessary to promote the approximation of laws in this field while maintaining the improvement described in Article 117 of the Treaty,

HAS ADOPTED THIS DIRECTIVE:

SECTION 1 – Scope and definitions

Article 1

1. This Directive shall apply to the transfer of an undertaking, business or part of a business to another employer as a result of a legal transfer or merger.
2. This Directive shall apply where and in so far as the undertaking, business or part of the business to be transferred is situated within the territorial scope of the Treaty.
3. This Directive shall not apply to sea-going vessels.

Article 2

For the purposes of this Directive:

(a) 'transferor' means any natural or legal person who, by reason of a transfer within the meaning of Article 1(1), ceases to be the employer in respect of the undertaking, business or part of the business;
(b) 'transferee' means any natural or legal person who, by reason of a transfer within the meaning of Article 1(1), becomes the employer in respect of the undertaking, business or part of the business;
(c) 'representatives of the employees' means the representatives of the employees provided for by the laws or practice of the Member States, with the exception of members of administrative, governing or supervisory bodies of companies who represent employees on such bodies in certain Member States.

SECTION 2 – Safeguarding of employees' rights

Article 3

1. The transferor's rights and obligations arising from a contract of employment or from an employment relationship existing on the date of a transfer within the meaning of Article 1(1) shall, by reason of such transfer, be transferred to the transferee.

   Member States may provide that, after the date of transfer within the meaning of Article 1(1) and in addition to the transferee, the transferor shall continue to be liable in respect of obligations which arose from a contract of employment or an employment relationship.
2. Following the transfer within the meaning of Article 1(1), the transferee shall continue to observe the terms and conditions agreed in any collective

agreement on the same terms applicable to the transferor under that agreement, until the date of termination or expiry of the collective agreement or the entry into force or application of another collective agreement.

Member States may limit the period for observing such terms and conditions, with the provison that it shall not be less than one year.

3. Paragraphs 1 and 2 shall not cover employees' rights to old-age, invalidity or survivors' benefits under supplementary company or inter-company pension schemes outside the statutory social security schemes in Member States.

Member States shall adopt the measures necessary to protect the interests of employees and of persons no longer employed in the transferor's business at the time of the transfer within the meaning of Article 1(1) in respect of rights conferring on them immediate or prospective entitlement to old-age benefits, including survivors' benefits, under suplementary schemes referred to in the first subparagraph.

Article 4

1. The transfer of an undertaking, business or part of a business shall not in itself constitute grounds for dismissal by the transferor or the transferee. This provision shall not stand in the way of dismissals that may take place for economic, technical or organizational reasons entailing changes in the workforce.

Member States may provide that the first subparagraph shall not apply to certain specific categories of employees who are not covered by the laws or practice of the Member States in respect of protection against dismissal.

2. If the contract of employment or the employment relationship is terminated because the transfer within the meaning of Article 1(1) involves a substantial change in working conditions to the detriment of the employee, the employer shall be regarded as having been responsible for termination of the contract of employment or of the employment relationship.

Article 5

1. If the business preserves its autonomy, the status and function, as laid down by the laws, regulations or administrative provisions of the Member States, of the representatives or of the representation of the employees affected by the transfer within the meaning of Article 1(1) shall be preserved.

The first subparagraph shall not apply if, under the laws, regulations, administrative provisions or practice of the Member States, the conditions necessary for the re-appointment of the representatives of the employees or for the reconstitution of the representation of the employees are fulfilled.

2. If the term of office of the representatives of the employees affected by a transfer within the meaning of Article 1(1) expires as a result of the transfer, the representatives shall continue to enjoy the protection provided by the laws, regulations, administrative provisions or practice of the Member States.

SECTION 3 – **Information and consultation**

Article 6

1. The transferor and the transferee shall be required to inform the representatives of their respective employees affected by a transfer within the meaning of Article 1(1) of the following:
   – the reasons for the transfer,
   – the legal, economic and social implications of the transfer for the employees,
   – measures envisaged in relation to the employees.
   The transferor must give such information to the representatives of his employees in good time before the transfer is carried out.
   The transferee must give such information to the representatives of his employees in good time, and in any event before his employees are directly affected by the transfer as regards their conditions of work and employment.

2. If the transferor or the transferee envisages measures in relation to his employees, he shall consult his representatives of the employees in good time on such measures with a view to seeking agreement.

3. Member States whose laws, regulations or administrative provisions provide that representatives of the employees may have recourse to an arbitration board to obtain a decision on the measures to be taken in relation to employees may limit the obligations laid down in paragraphs 1 and 2 to cases where the transfer carried out gives rise to a change in the business likely to entail serious disadvantages for a considerable number of the employees.
   The information and consultations shall cover at least the measures envisaged in relation to the employees.
   The information must be provided and consultations take place in good time before the change in the business as referred to in the first subparagraph is effected.

4. Member States may limit the obligations laid down in paragraphs 1, 2 and 3 to undertakings or businesses which, in respect of the number of employees, fulfil the conditions for the election or designation of a collegiate body representing the employees.

5. Member States may provide that where there are no representatives of the employees in an undertaking or business, the employees concerned must be informed in advance when a transfer within the meaning of Article 1(1) is about to take place.

SECTION 4 – **Final provisions**

Article 7

This Directive shall not affect the right of Member States to apply or introduce laws, regulations or administrative provisions which are more favourable to employees.

Article 8
1. Member States shall bring into force the laws, regulations and administrative provisions needed to comply with this Directive within two years of its notification and shall forthwith inform the Commission thereof.
2. Member States shall communicate to the Commission the texts of the laws, regulations and administrative provisions which they adopt in the field covered by this Directive.

Article 9
Within two years following expiry of the two-year period laid down in Article 8, Member States shall forward all relevant information to the Commission in order to enable it to draw up a report on the application of this Directive for submission to the Council.

Article 10
This Directive is addressed to the Member States.

Done at Brussels, 14 February 1977.

For the Council
The President
J. Silkin

---

1. OJ No. C 95, 28.4.1975, p. 17.
2. OJ No. C 255, 7.11.1975, p. 25.

Council Directive

of 20 October 1980

On the Approximation of the Laws of the Member States Relating to the Protection of Employees in the Event of the Insolvency of their Employer (80/987/EEC)

THE COUNCIL OF THE EUROPEAN COMMUNITIES,

Having regard to the Treaty establishing the European Economic Community, and in particular Article 100 thereof,
Having regard to the proposal from the Commission,[1]
Having regard to the Opinion of the European Parliament,[2]
Having regard to the Opinion of the Economic and Social Committee:[3]
    Whereas it is necessary to provide for the protection of employees in the event of the insolvency of their employer, in particular in order to guarantee payment of their outstanding claims, while taking account of the need for balanced economic and social development in the Community;

325

Whereas differences still remain between the Member States as regards the extent of the protection of employees in this respect; whereas efforts should be directed towards reducing these differences, which can have a direct effect on the functioning of the common market;

Whereas the approximation of laws in this field should, therefore, be promoted while the improvement within the meaning of Article 117 of the Treaty is maintained;

Whereas as a result of the geographical situation and the present job structure in that area, the labour market in Greenland is fundamentally different from that of the other areas of the Community;

Whereas to the extent that the Hellenic Republic is to become a member of the European Community on 1 January 1981, in accordance with the Act concerning the Conditions of Accession of the Hellenic Republic and the Adjustments to the Treaties, it is appropriate to stipulate in the Annex to the Directive under the heading 'Greece,' those categories of employees whose claims may be excluded in accordance with Article 1(2) of the Directive,

HAS ADOPTED THIS DIRECTIVE:

SECTION 1 – **Scope and definitions**

Article 1

1. This Directive shall apply to employees' claims arising from contracts of employment or employment relationships and existing against employers who are in a state of insolvency within the meaning of Article 2(1).
2. Member States may, by way of exception, exclude claims by certain categories of employee from the scope of this Directive, by virtue of the special nature of the employee's contract of employment or employment relationship or of the existence of other forms of guarantee offering the employee protection equivalent to that resulting from this Directive.

   The categories of employee referred to in the first sub-paragraph are listed in the Annex.
3. This Directive shall not apply to Greenland. This exception shall be re-examined in the event of any development in the job structures in that region.

Article 2

1. For the purposes of this Directive, an employer shall be deemed to be in a state of insolvency:
   (a) where a request has been made for the opening of proceedings involving the employer's assets, as provided for under the laws, regulations and administrative provisions of the Member State concerned, to satisfy collectively the claims of creditors and which make it possible to take into consideration the claims referred to in Article 1(1), and
   (b) where the authority which is competent pursuant to the said laws, regulations and administrative provisions has:

- either decided to open the proceedings,
- or established that the employer's undertaking or business has been definitively closed down and that the available assets are insufficient to warrant the opening of the proceedings.

2. This Directive is without prejudice to national law as regards the definition of the terms 'employee,' 'employer,' 'pay,' 'right conferring immediate entitlement' and 'right conferring prospective entitlement'.

SECTION 2 – **Provisions concerning guarantee institutions**

Article 3
1. Member States shall take the measures necessary to ensure that guarantee institutions guarantee, subject to Article 4, payment of employees' outstanding claims resulting from contracts of employment or employment relationships and relating to pay for the period prior to a given date.
2. At the choice of the Member States, the date referred to in paragraph 1 shall be:
   - either that of the onset of the employer's insolvency;
   - or that of the notice of dismissal issued to the employee concerned on account of the employer's insolvency;
   - or that of the onset of the employer's insolvency or that on which the contract of employment or the employment relationship with the employee concerned was discontinued on account of the employer's insolvency.

Article 4
1. Member States shall have the option to limit the liability of guarantee institutions, referred to in Article 3.
2. When Member States exercise the option referred to in paragraph 1, they shall:
   - in the case referred to in Article 3(2), first indent, ensure the payment of outstanding claims relating to pay for the last three months of the contract of employment or employment relationship occurring within a period of six months preceding the date of the onset of the employer's insolvency;
   - in the case referred to in Article 3(2), second indent, ensure the payment of the outstanding claims relating to pay for the last three months of the contract of employment or employment relationship preceding the date of the notice of dismissal issued to the employee on account of the employer's insolvency;
   - in the case referred to in Article 3(2), third indent, ensure the payment of outstanding claims relating to pay for the last 18 months of the contract of employment or employment relationship preceding the date of the onset of the employer's insolvency or the date on which the contract of employment or the employment relationship with the employee was discontinued on account of the employer's insolvency. In this case, Member States may limit the liability to make payment to pay

corresponding to a period of eight weeks or to several shorter periods totalling eight weeks.

3. However, in order to avoid the payment of sums going beyond the social objective of this Directive, Member States may set a ceiling to the liability for employees' outstanding claims.

When Member States exercise this option, they shall inform the Commission of the methods used to set the ceiling.

Article 5

Member States shall lay down detailed rules for the organisation, financing and operation of the guarantee institutions, complying with the following principles in particular:

(a) the assets of the institutions shall be independent of the employers' operating captial and be inaccessible to proceedings for insolvency;

(b) employers shall contribute to financing, unless it is fully covered by the public authorities;

(c) the institutions' liabilities shall not depend on whether or not obligations to contribute to financing have been fulfilled.

SECTION 3 – Provisions concerning social security

Article 6

Member States may stipulate that Articles 3, 4 and 5 shall not apply to contributions due under national statutory social security schemes or under supplementary company or inter-company pension schemes outside the national statutory social security schemes.

Article 7

Members States shall take the measures necessary to ensure that nonpayment of compulsory contributions due from the employer, before the onset of his insolvency, to their insurance institutions under national statutory social security schemes does not adversely affect employees' benefit entitlement in respect of these insurance institutions inasmuch as the employees' contributions were deducted at source from the remuneration paid.

Article 8

Members States shall ensure that the necessary measures are taken to protect the interests of employees and of persons having already left the employer's undertaking or business at the date of the onset of the employer's insolvency in respect of rights conferring on them immediate or prospective entitlement to old age benefits, including survivors' benefits, under supplementary company or inter-company pension schemes outside the national statutory social security schemes.

SECTION 4 – General and final provisions

Article 9

This Directive shall not affect the option of Member States to apply or intro-

328

duce laws, regulations or administrative provisions which are more favourable to employees.

Article 10
This Directive shall not affect the option of Member States:
(a) to take the measures necessary to avoid abuses;
(b) to refuse or reduce the liability referred to in Article 3 or the guarantee obligation referred to in Article 7 if it appears that fulfilment of the obligation is unjustifiable because of the existence of special links between the employee and the employer and of common interests resulting in collusion between them.

Article 11
1. Member States shall bring into force the laws, regulations and administrative provisions necessary to comply with this Directive within 36 months of its notification. They shall forthwith inform the Commission thereof.
2. Member States shall communicate to the Commission the texts of the laws, regulations and administrative provisions which they adopt in the field governed by this Directive.

Article 12
Within 18 months of the expiry of the period of 36 months laid down in Article 11(1), Member States shall forward all relevant information to the Commission in order to enable it to draw up a report on the application of this Directive for submission to the Council.

Article 13
This Directive is addressed to the Member States.
Done at Luxembourg, October 20, 1980.

ANNEX

Categories of employees whose claims may be excluded from the scope of this Directive, in accordance with Article 1(2)

I. Employees having a contract of employment, or an employment relationship, of a special nature

a. Greece
The master and the members of a crew of a fishing vessel, if and to the extent that they are remunerated by a share in the profits or gross earnings of the vessel.
b. Ireland
1. Out-workers (i.e. persons doing piece-work in their own homes), unless they have a written contract of employment.
2. Close relatives of the employer, without a written contract of employment,

whose work has to do with a private dwelling or farm in, or on, which the employer and the close relatives reside.
3. Persons who normally work for less than 18 hours a week for one or more employers and who do not derive their basic means of subsistence from the pay for this work.
4. Persons engaged in share fishing on a seasonal, casual or part-time basis.
5. The spouse of the employer.

c. Netherlands
Domestic servants employed by a natural person and working less than three days a week for the natural person in question.

d. United Kingdom
1. The master and the members of the crew of a fishing vessel who are remunerated by a share in the profits or gross earnings of the vessel.
2. The spouse of the employer.

II. Employees covered by other forms of guarantee

a. Greece
The crews of sea-going vessels.

b. Ireland
1. Permanent and pensionable employees of local or other public authorities or statutory transport undertakings.
2. Pensionable teachers employed in the following: national schools, secondary schools, comprehensive schools, teachers' training colleges.
3. Permanent and pensionable employees of one of the voluntary hospitals funded by the Exchequer.

c. Italy
1. Employees covered by benefits laid down by law guaranteeing that their wages will continue to be paid in the event that the undertaking is hit by an economic crisis.
2. The crews of sea-going vessels.

d. United Kingdom
1. Registered dock workers other than those wholly or mainly engaged in work which is not dock work.
2. The crews of sea-going vessels.

---

1. OJ No. C 135.
2. OJ No. C 39.
3. OJ No. C 105.

C. European Court Judgments

1. Collective redundancies

(a) Infringement proceedings under Article 169, EEC Treaty

Judgment of the Court

8 June 1982 – Case 91/81

Commission of the European Communities
v.
Italian Republic

Failure of State to fulfil its obligations – collective redundancies – aim of Directive to establish common body of rules for all Member States – power of Member States to apply more favourable provisions – insufficient national provisions to meet totality of Directive's requirements (EEC Treaty Article 117; Council Directive 75/129/EEC).

In Case 91/81

Commission of the European Communities, represented by Armando Toledano Laedo, its Legal Adviser, acting as Agent, with an address for service in Luxembourg at the office of Oreste Montalto, a member of its Legal Department, Jean Monnet Building, Kirchberg.

applicant,

v.

Italian Republic, in the person of its Agent, Arnaldo Squillante, head of the Department for Contentious Diplomatic Affairs, Treaties and Legislative Matters, represented by Pier Giorgio Ferri, Avvocato dello Stato, with an address for service in Luxembourg at the Italian Embassy,

defendant,

APPLICATION for a declaration that the Italian Republic, by not adopting within the prescribed period the provisions needed to comply with Council Directive 75/129/EEC of 17 February 1975 on the approximation of the laws of the Member States relating to collective redundancies (Official Journal L 48, p. 29), has failed to fulfil its obligations under the EEC Treaty,

THE COURT

composed of: J. Mertens de Wilmars, President, G. Bosco and A. Touffait (Presidents of Chambers), Lord Mackenzie Stuart, A. O'Keeffe, T. Koopmans and U. Everling, Judges,

Advocate General: P. VerLoren van Themaat
Registrar: P. Heim

gives the following JUDGMENT

Decision

1. By application lodged at the Court Registry on 15 April 1981 the Commission of the European Communities brought an action before the Court under Article 169 of the EEC Treaty for a declaration that the Italian Republic has failed to fulfil its obligations under the Treaty by not adopting within the prescribed period the measures needed to comply with Council Directive 75/129/EEC of 17 February 1975 on the approximation of the laws of the Member States relating to collective redundancies (Official Journal L 48, p. 29).

2. Directive 75/129/EEC was adopted by the Council on the basis of Article 100 of the Treaty concerning the approximation of such provisions laid down by law, regulation or administrative action in Member States as directly affect the establishment or functioning of the common market. The recitals in the preamble to the directive state that it is important that greater protection should be afforded to workers in the event of collective redundancies whilst taking into account the need for balanced economic and social development within the Community; that, despite increasing convergence, differences still remain between the provisions in force in the Member States of the Community concerning the practical arrangements and procedures for such redundancies and the measures designed to alleviate the consequences of redundancy for workers; that these differences may have a direct effect on the functioning of the common market; that the Council Resolution of 21 January 1974 makes provision for a directive on the approximation of Member States' legislation on collective redundancies, and that it is therefore necessary to promote that approximation within the meaning of Article 117 of the Treaty which is intended to promote improved working conditions and an improved

standard of living for workers, so as to make possible their harmonization while the improvement is being maintained.

3. With this in view the directive determines the scope of the concept of 'collective redundancies' whilst leaving the Member States to choose between the two criteria which it lays down.

4. Article 2 of the directive provides that where an employer is contemplating collective redundancies, he must begin consultations with the workers' representatives with a view to reaching an agreement. He is required to supply them with all relevant information and in any event to give in writing the reasons for the redundancies, the number of workers to be made redundant, the number of workers normally employed and the period over which the redundancies are to be effected. He is required to forward to the competent public authority a copy of that written communication.

5. Articles 3 and 4 of the directive contain provisions concerning the measures to be taken by the competent public authority. The employer is required to notify that authority in writing of any projected collective redundancies. The notification must contain all relevant information on the matters specified in Article 2 and, in addition, on the consultations with the workers' representatives. A copy of that notification must be forwarded to the workers' representatives. As a general rule collective redundancies may not take effect earlier than 30 days after notification. The competent public authority must use this period to seek solutions to the problems raised by the collective redundancies and the above-mentioned period may be extended for that purpose.

6. Article 6 of the directive requires the Member States to bring into force, within a period of two years following notification of the directive, the laws, regulations and administrative provisions needed in order to comply therewith.

7. Article 5 states that the directive is not to affect the right of Member States to apply or introduce laws, regulations or administrative provisions which are more favourable to workers.

8. The Italian Government has observed that, having regard to the whole of the Italian system of protection in the case of dismissals which is provided both by the wide scope given by Italian legislation to the concept of individual redundancy, which is heavily weighted in favour of workers, to the specific provisions laid down by regulation relating to collective redundancies and by the provisions of collective agreements, that system creates conditions and establishes procedures making it possible to attain the objectives of the directive and indeed, in various respects, exceeding its requirements.

9. Nevertheless the Italian Government does not dispute that in certain sectors especially in agriculture and commerce, Italian legislation is not as comprehensive as the provisions of the directive. It is furthermore common ground that Italian collective agreements do not require the notification in writing on the part of the employer which is provided for by the directive and that the Italian system does not provide, as is required by the directive, that the competent public authority must be notified of any collective redundancy and that the competent public authority is not compelled to intervene in order to seek solutions to the problems raised by the projected collective redundancies.

10. It is clear from the foregoing that the provisions in this field which are in force in Italy do not suffice to meet the totality of the requirements of the directive.

11. In this connection it should be emphasized that the directive, which the Council considers corresponds to the need, stated in Article 117 of the Treaty, to promote improved working conditions and an improved standard of living for workers, is intended to approximate the provisions laid down in this field by the Member States by law, regulation or administrative action. The provisions of the directive are thus intended to serve to establish a common body of rules applicable in all the Member States, whilst leaving to the Member States power to apply or introduce provisions which are more favourable to workers.

12. It is clear from these considerations that by not adopting within the prescribed period the measures needed in order fully to comply with the directive the Italian Republic has failed to fulfil its obligations under the Treaty.

Costs
13. Under Article 69(2) of the Rules of Procedure the unsuccessful party must be ordered to bear the costs.

14. Since the defendant has been unsuccessful it must be ordered to pay the costs.

On those grounds,

THE COURT

hereby:

1. **Declares that, by not adopting within the prescribed period the measures needed in order to comply with Council Directive 75/129/EEC of 17 February 1975 on the approximation of the laws of the Member States relating to**

collective redundancies (Official Journal L 48, p. 29), the Italian Republic
has failed to fulfil its obligations under the Treaty;

2. Orders the defendant to pay the costs.

Mertens de Wilmars   Bosco   Touffait
Mackenzie Stuart   O'Keeffe   Koopmans   Everling

Delivered in open court in Luxembourg on 8 June 1982.

P. Heim   J. Mertens de Wilmars
Registrar   *President*

Judgment of the Court

6 November 1985 – Case 131/84

Commission of the European Communities
v.
Italian Republic

Failure of State to implement Court judgment – collective redundancies – no
mandatory period for implementing Court judgments – measures should
be adopted as soon as possible – Member States may not plead internal
circumstances to justify failure to comply (EEC Treaty Article 171; Council
Directive 75/129/EEC).

In Case 131/84

Commission of the European Communities, represented by its Legal Adviser,
Armando Toledano Laredo, acting as Agent, with an address for service in
Luxembourg at the office of Manfred Beschel, a member of the Commission's
Legal Department, Jean Monnet Building, Kirchberg,

applicant,

v.

Italian Republic, represented by Arnaldo Squillante, acting as Agent, assisted
by Ivo Braguglia, Avvocato dello Stato, with an address for service in
Luxembourg at the Italian Embassy,

defendant,

APPLICATION for a declaration that by not having complied with the judgment
delivered by the Court of justice on 8 June 1982 in Case 91/81 the Italian

335

Republic has failed to fulfil its obligations under Article 171 of the EEC Treaty,

THE COURT

composed of: Lord Mackenzie Stuart, President, K. Bahlmann and R. Joliet (Presidents of Chambers), G. Bosco, T. Koopmans, O. Due and T. F. O'Higgins, Judges,

Advocate General: P. Ver Loren van Themaat
Registrar: D. Louterman, Administrator,

after hearing the Opinion of the Advocate General delivered at the sitting on 10 July 1985,

gives the following JUDGMENT

Decision

1. By an application lodged at the Court Registry on 17 May 1984, the Commission of the European Communities brought an action before the Court under Article 169 of the EEC Treaty for a declaration that by not having complied with the judgment delivered by the Court on 8 June 1982 (Case 91/81, *Commission* v. *Italian Republic*, [1982] ECR 2133) the Italian Republic has failed to fulfil its obligations under Article 171 of the EEC Treaty.

2. In that judgment, the Court held as follows:

   '. . . by not adopting within the prescribed period the measures needed in order to comply with Council Directive No. 75/129/EEC of 17 February 1975 on the approximation of the laws of the Member States relating to collective redundancies (Official Journal 1975 No. L 48, p. 29), the Italian Republic has failed to fulfil its obligations under the Treaty.'.

3. The Commission considers that, in breach of Article 171 of the Treaty, the Italian Republic has not taken the measures required for implementation of the Court's judgment. Therefore, after an exchange of letters with the Italian Government, on 28 February 1984 it delivered a reasoned opinion under the first paragraph of Article 169 of the Treaty. Since that opinion was not acted upon, the Commission brought the present action.

4. The Commission claims that, by not taking the measures necessary for implementation of the above-mentioned judgment, the Italian Republic has failed to fulfil its obligations. It considers that although Article 171

does not lay down a mandatory period within which a Member State must take the measures required for compliance with judgments of the Court, it should be taken to mean that those measures must be adopted as soon as possible. In its judgment of 28 March 1980 (Joined Cases 24 and 97/80, *Commission* v. *French Republic*, [1980] ECR 1319, the Court stated that by reason solely of the judgment declaring the Member State to be in default, the State concerned is required to take the necessary measures to remedy its default and may not create any impediment whatsoever.

5. The Italian Republic contends that Directive No. 75/129 has not yet been fully implemented for objective reasons. In Italy's present social and economic situation, legislative activity must be directed primarily towards maintaining the level of employment and it would be inappropriate to adopt rules concerning collective redundancies at a time when there is an emergency which must be dealt with in order to safeguard employment.

6. It has been consistently held by the Court that a Member State may not plead provisions, practices or circumstances existing in its internal legal system in order to justify failure to comply with obligations and time-limits laid down in directives. According to Directive No. 75/129, the measures should have been adopted by 19 February 1977. In its judgment of 8 June 1982 the Court held that by failing fully to implement the directive within the prescribed period, the Italian Republic had failed to fulfil its obligations under the Treaty.

7. Article 171 of the EEC Treaty does not lay down a time-limit within which a judgment must be complied with. However, it is well established that the implementation of a judgment must be commenced immediately and must be completed as soon as possible. In the present case, there has been unreasonable delay.

8. In view of all the foregoing considerations, it must be stated that by not having complied with the judgment delivered by the Court on 8 June 1982 (Case 91/81, *Commission* v. *Italian Republic*, [1982] ECR 2133), the Italian Republic has failed to fulfil its obligations under Article 171 of the EEC Treaty.

Costs
9. Under Article 69(2) of the Rules of Procedure the unsuccessful party is to be ordered to pay the costs. Since the Italian Republic has failed in its submissions, it must be ordered to pay the costs.

On those grounds,

THE COURT

hereby

1. **Declares that by not having complied with the judgment delivered by the Court of Justice on 8 June 1982 in Case 91/81, the Italian Republic has failed to fulfil its obligations under Article 171 of the EEC Treaty;**

2. **Orders the Italian Republic to pay the costs.**

Mackenzie Stuart   Bahlmann   Joliet   Bosco

Koopmans   Due   O'Higgins

Delivered in open court in Luxembourg on 6 November 1985.

P. Heim   A. J. Mackenzie Stuart
Registrar   *President*

Judgment of the Court

28 March 1985 – Case 215/83

Commission of the European Communities
v.
Kingdom of Belgium

Failure of State to fulfil its obligations – collective redundancies – closures and workers' protections – insufficient legal certainty regarding such protections – over-broad exclusions for certain categories fo workers – need for Member States to fulfil obligations under Community Directives in every respect (EEC Treaty Article 117; Council Directive 75/129/EEC, Articles 1(a) & (d), 3 & 4).

In Case 215/83

Commission of the European Communities, represented by its Legal Adviser, J. Griesmar, acting as Agent, with an address for service in Luxembourg at the office of Manfred Beschel, a member of the Commission's Legal Department, Jean Monnet Building, Kirchberg,

applicant,

v.

Kingdom of Belgium, in the person of the Minister for Foreign Relations, represented by Robert Hoebaer, Director at the Ministry for Foreign Relations, Foreign Trade and Co-operation with Developing Countries, acting as

Agent, with an address for service in Luxembourg at the Belgian Embassy, 4 Rue des Girondins,

defendant,

APPLICATION for a declaration that by failing to adopt within the precribed period all the measures necessary to comply fully with Council Directive 75/129/EEC of 17 February 1975 on the approximation of the laws of the Member States relating to collective redundancies (Official Journal 1975 No. L 48, p. 29), the Kingdom of Belgium has failed to fulfil its obligations under the EEC Treaty,

THE COURT

composed of: G. Bosco, President of the First Chamber, for the President, C. Kakouris (President of Chamber), T. Koopmans, U. Everling, Y. Galmot, R. Joliet and T. F. O'Higgins, Judges,

Advocate General: Sir Gordon Slynn
Registrar: D. Louterman, Administrator,

gives the following JUDGMENT

Decision

1. By application lodged at the Court Registry on 27 September 1983 the Commission of the European Communities has brought an action under Article 169 of the EEC Treaty for a declaration that by failing to adopt within the prescribed period all the measures necessary to comply fully with Council Directive 75/129/EEC of 17 February 1975 on the approximation of the laws of the Member States relating to collective redundancies, the Kingdom of Belgium has failed to fulfil its obligations under the EEC Treaty.

2. That directive, which was adopted pursuant to Article 100 of the EEC Treaty, has as its purpose, according to the preamble, to ensure 'that greater protection should be afforded to workers in the event of collective redundancies while taking into account the need for balanced economic and social development within the Community' and to promote 'approximation ... while the improvement is being maintained within the meaning of Article 117 of the Treaty'.

3. The scope of the directive is defined in Article 1 as follows:

   '1. For the purposes of this directive:
   (a) "collective redundancies" means dismissals effected by

339

an employer for one or more reasons not related to the individual workers concerned where, according to the choice of the Member States, the number of redundancies is:

either, over a period of 30 days:

1. at least 10 days in establishments normally employing more than 20 and less than 100 workers;
2. at least 10 per cent of the number of workers in establishments normally employing at least 100 but less than 300 workers;
3. at least 30 in establishments normally employing 300 workers or more;

or, over a period of 90 days, at least 20, whatever the number of workers normally employed in the establishments in questions;

2. This directive shall not apply to:
   (a) collective redundancies effected under contracts of employment concluded for limited periods of time or for specific tasks except where such redundancies take place prior to the date of expiry or the completion of such contracts;
   (b) workers employed by public administrative bodies or by establishments governed by public law (or, in Member States where this concept is unknown, by equivalent bodies);
   (c) the crews of sea-going vessels;
   (d) workers affected by the termination of an establishment's activities where that is the result of a judicial decision.'.

4. The directive provides in substance that: 'Where an employer is contemplating collective redundancies, he shall begin consultations with the workers' representatives with a view to reaching an agreement (Article 2(1)) ... Employers shall notify the competent public authority in writing of any projected collective redundancies' (Article 3(1)). It further states that projected redundancies so notified are to 'take effect not earlier than 30 days after the notification ...' (Article 4(1)).

5. Under Article 6(1) the Member States are required to bring into force the laws, regulations and administrative provisions needed in order to comply with the directive within two years following its notification. Since the directive was notified to the Kingdom of Belgium on 19 February 1975, that period expired on 19 February 1977.

6. The Kingdom of Belgium incorporated Directive 75/129 into national law first by Collective Labour Agreement No. 24, concluded on 20 October 1975 within the Conseil National du Travail [National Labour Council]

340

concerning the procedure for informing and consulting workers' representatives in the matter of collective redundancies and given the force of law by the Royal Decree of 21 January 1976 (Moniteur Belge of 17 February 1976, p. 1716) and, secondly, by the Royal Decree of 24 May 1976 on collective redundancies (Moniteur Belge of 17 September 1976, p. 11663) concerning the notification of projected collective redundancies to the Office National de l'Emploi [National Employment Office].

7. Those measures were amended by Collective Labour Agreement No. 24a of 6 December 1983, which was given the force of law by the Royal Decree of 7 February 1984 (Moniteur Belge of 22 February 1984, p. 2395), and by the Royal Decree of 26 March 1984 (Moniteur Belge of 18 April 1984, p. 5036), respectively.

8. The scope of Collective Labour Agreement No. 24, as amended by Collective Labour Agreement No. 24a, is defined as follows:

> 'Article 2. A collective redundancy for the purpose of this collective labour agreement means any dismissal for one or more reasons not related to the individual workers concerned which affects over a period of 60 days:
> 1. at least 10 workers in undertakings employing more than 20 and less than 100 workers during the calendar year preceding the dismissal;
> 2. at least 10 per cent of the number of workers in undertakings employing on average at least 100 but less than 300 workers during the calendar year preceding the dismissal;
> 3. at least 30 workers in undertakings employing on average 300 workers or more during the calendar year preceding the dismissal.
>
> Article 3. This agreement shall apply to undertakings which employed on average more than 20 workers during the calendar year preceding the collective redundancy.
>
> Article 5. The obligations arising from this collective labour agreement shall not apply to the following categories of workers:
> 1. workers employed by undertakings under contracts of employment concluded for limited periods of time or for specific tasks except where such collective redundancies take place prior to the date of expiry or the completion of such contracts;
> 2. workers employed by undertakings as port workers, ship repairers, sea fishermen or sailors in the merchant navy;
> 3. manual workers employed by undertakings in the building industry.'.

9. The scope of the Royal Decree of 24 May 1976, as amended by the Royal Decree of 26 march 1984, is defined by similar provisions:

> 'Article 1. For the purposes of this decree:
> 3. 'Collective redundancy' means any dismissal for one or more reasons not related to the individual workers concerned which affects over a period of 60 days:
>   – at least 10 workers in undertakings employing more than 20 and less than 100 workers;
>   – at least 10 per cent of the number of workers in undertakings employing on average at least 100 but less than 300 workers;
>   – at least 30 workers in undertakings employing on average 300 workers or more.
>
> Article 2. This decree shall apply to undertakings employing more than 20 workers.
>
> Article 3. The following categories of workers shall be excluded from the scope of this decree:
> 1. workers employed by undertakings under contracts of employment concluded for limited periods of time or for a clearly-defined piece of work except where such collective redundancies take place prior to the date of expiry of the contract or the completion of the work;
> 2. workers employed by undertakings as port workers, ship repairers, sea fishermen or sailors in the merchant navy;
> 3. manual workers employed by undertakings in the building industry.'.

10. Taking the view that the Belgian provisions did not satisfy all the requirements of Directive 75/129 and following an exchange of letters with the Belgian Government, on 5 July 1982 the Commission delivered a reasoned opinion under the first paragraph of Article 169 of the EEC Treaty. By letter of 13 October 1982 the Belgian Government informed the Commission that 'the Minister of Labour and Employment has decided that legislative action is necessary in that respect and a draft law on collective redundancies is at present being drafted'.

11. Since no further information was forthcoming, the Commission has brought this action against Belgium for failure to fulfil its obligations under the Treaty, seeking essentially a declaration that the aforesaid Belgian rules, which were adopted in order to give effect to Directive 75/129, are narrower in scope than that directive.

12. Since the contested rules were amended during these proceedings in the manner set out above, the Commission has restricted the scope of

its action to two complaints, first that Belgian law does not meet the requirements of the directive as regards the protection of workers in the event of collective redundancies arising from the closure of undertakings where such closure did not come about as the result of a judicial decision, and secondly that certain categories of workers, namely ship repairers, port workers, and manual workers in the building industry are excluded from the benefit of the directive.

Collective redundancies arising from the closure of an undertaking
13. The Commission contends in the first place that Belgian law traditionally draws a distinction between the concepts of closure of an undertaking and collective redundancy. The effect of that distinction is that redundancies arising from the closure of undertakings, whether or not such closure comes about as a result of a judicial decision, are governed not by the legislation adopted in order to give effect to Directive 75/129 but by the special provisions of the Law of 28 June 1966 concerning compensation for workers dismissed as a result of the closure of undertakings (Moniteur Belge of 2 July 1966, p. 6879) and of the Royal Decree of 20 September 1967 implementing that law (Moniteur Belge of 5 October 1967, p. 10463).

14. The Commission points out that although those provisions, where appropriate in conjunction with those of Collective Labour Agreement No. 9 of 9 March 1972, require the employer, in the event of the closure of an undertaking, to provide certain information to the workers' representatives and to the public authorities, the scope of that obligation does not satisfy all the requirements of the directive, particularly those embodied in Articles 3 and 4 concerning what information is to be provided and within what periods.

15. The Belgian Government points out that the distinction drawn in Belgium between the closure of undertakings and collective redundancies has historical origins. In Belgium the position of workers dismissed as a result of the closure of an undertaking has been regulated by legislation since 1960, whilst collective redundancies were regulated for the first time by Collective Labour Agreement No. 10 of 8 May 1973 which sought to mitigate the consequences of collective redundancies by the grant of a special allowance the cost of which was to be borne by the employer.

16. The Belgian Government maintains that the vast majority of closures of undertakings which are likely to lead to collective redundancies come about as a result of a judicial decision, within the meaning of the exception in Article 1(2)(d) of the directive, and are consequently excluded from the scope of the directive. It also states that Belgian law does not rule out the interpretation that the rules adopted to give effect to the directive also apply in the event of collective redundancies arising from

the closure of undertakings. It acknowledges, however, that this point has not yet been decided by the courts.

17. It must be noted that even if the defendant's contention is accepted that in Belgium only a relatively small number of closures of undertakings do not come about as a result of a judicial decision within the meaning of Article 1(2)(d) of Directive 75/129, that does not relieve the Kingdom of Belgium of its duty to provide workers with the protection envisaged by the directive in the event of collective redundancies arising from such closures.

18. That duty is not fully discharged by the Law of 28 June 1966 concerning compensation for workers dismissed as a result of the closure of undertakings and by the Royal Decree of 20 September 1967 implementing that law. Contrary to the requirements of Articles 3 and 4 of the directive, the above-mentioned provisions do not require the employer to provide information relating to the reasons for the collective redundancies, the number of workers to be dismissed and the period over which the redundancies are to be effected, nor do they stipulate that the collective redundancies envisaged are not to take effect before the expiry of a period of 30 days from the date of notification of the projected redundancy to the competent public authority.

19. As the Belgian Government has itself conceded, Belgian law may be interpreted as meaning that in the event of collective redundancies arising from the closure of an undertaking, only the specific legislation adopted in 1966 and 1967 is applicable, to the exclusion of the subsequent, though general, rules adopted in order to give effect to the directive. It follows that Belgian law does not offer a sufficient degree of legal certainty as regards the protection of workers envisaged by the directive.

20. This complaint must therefore be upheld.

System applicable to certain categories of workers
21. Secondly, the Commission contends that the exclusion of ship repairers, port workers and manual workers in the building industry from the benefit of Directive 75/129, as decided by the Kingdom of Belgium, is contrary to Article 1 which defines the directive's scope. Under Article 1(2) only collective redundancies affecting certain categories of workers, which are listed exhaustively and which do not include the categories excluded by the Belgian legislation, are not covered by the directive.

22. The Commission acknowledges that the workers falling within the categories at issue can be excluded from the benefit of the directive, pursuant to Article 1(2)(a) thereof, in so far as they are engaged on a day-to-day basis or their contract of employment is concluded for a limited period or for a clearly-defined piece of work, on condition that, however, the

benefit of the directive is extended to them where the collective redundancies take place prior to the date of expiry or the completion of their contract of employment. The Belgian rules therefore wrongly exclude workers in those categories who are engaged for an indefinite period or are affected by collective redundancies arising during the performance of their task. The Commission adds that workers in the 'hard core' of undertakings in the building industry are by definition engaged for an indefinite period and are therefore capable of coming within the scope of the directive.

23. Ship repairers and port workers are, according to the Belgian Government, normally engaged for a specific task or for a clearly-defined piece of work, as provided for by Article 1(2)(a) of Directive 75/129. However, there is nothing to prevent such workers from entering into contracts of employment for an indefinite period. In its view, their exclusion from the benefit of the directive is justified on two grounds. First of all, they are covered by specific conditions of employment based on their own system for securing their livelihood. Secondly, in view of the small number of such workers engaged under contracts of employment for an indefinite period, the concept of collective redundancy does not apply to them in practice. The exclusion of workers in the building industry is justified, in the Belgian Government's view, by their natural mobility and also by the fact that they are covered by a special social security scheme which is characterized by the grant of various allowances designed to offset the disadvantages resulting from periods of temporary unemployment.

24. It must be noted that, even assuming that the majority of workers belonging to the categories at issue are engaged for a limited period, as the Belgian Government maintains, there is none the less a core of workers who enter into contracts of employment for an indefinite period and to whom the rules of the directive must therefore be applied. Furthermore, the exemption provided for by Article 1(2)(a) of Directive 75/129 in the case of workers engaged for limited periods of time or for specific tasks cannot be relied upon 'except where such redundancies take place prior to the date of expiry or the completion of such contracts'. The Belgian Government does not deny that Belgian law does not contain any rule corresponding to the directive in that respect.

25. The Court has consistently held that the Member States must fulfil their obligations under Community directives in every respect and may not plead provisions, practices or circumstances existing in their internal legal system in order to justify a failure to comply with those obligations. The Kingdom of Belgium cannot, therefore, plead in its defence that the circumstances at issue are of little practical significance. Nor is its failure to comply fully with Directive 75/129 justified by the fact that Belgian law provides the workers in question with other forms of social security.

345

26. Consequently this complaint must also be upheld.

27. It must therefore be held that by failing to adopt within the prescribed period all the measures necessary to comply fully with Council Directive 75/129/EEC of 17 February 1975 on the approximation of the laws of the Member States relating to collective redundancies (Official Journal 1975 No. L 48, p. 29), the Kingdom of Belgium has failed to fulfil its obligations under the EEC Treaty.

Costs
28. Under Article 69(2) of the Rules of Procedure, the unsuccessful party is to be ordered to pay the costs. Since the defendant has been unsuccessful in its submissions, it must be ordered to pay the costs.

On those grounds,

THE COURT

hereby:

1. **Declares that by failing to adopt within the prescribed period all the measures necessary to comply fully with Council Directive 75/129/EEC of 17 February 1975 on the approximation of the laws of the Member States relating to collective redundancies (Official Journal 1975 No. L 48, p. 29), the Kingdom of Belgium has failed to fulfil its obligations under the EEC Treaty.**

2. **Orders the Kingdom of Belgium to pay the costs.**

Bosco   Kakouris   Koopmans

          Everling   Galmot

Joliet   O'Higgins

Delivered in open court in Luxembourg on 28 March 1985.

P. Heim   *For the President*
Registrar   G. Bosco
                         President of the First Chamber

346

(b) Preliminary rulings under Article 177, EEC Treaty

Judgment of the Court

12 February 1985 – Case 284/83

Dansk Metalarbejderforbund and Specialarbejderforbundet i Danmark
v.
H. Nielsen & Son, Maskinfabrik A/S, in liquidation

Collective redundancies – termination of contracts of employment by workers where employer suspends payment of debts – such terminations not to be treated as dismissal by the employer under the Directive – Directive applies only where employer has in fact contemplated or drawn up plan for collective redundancies – no obligation on employer to contemplate collective redundancies in the event of financial difficulties (Council Directive 75/129/EEC Articles 1(1)(a), 2(1) and 3(1)).

In Case 284/83

REFERENCE to the Court under Article 177 of the EEC Treaty by the Højesteret [Supreme Court of Denmark] for a preliminary ruling in the proceedings pending before that court between

(1) Dansk Metalarbejderforbund, acting as agent for Ali Altin and Jan Benny Hansen,

and

H. Nielsen & Søn, Maskinfabrik A/S, in liquidation

Intervener:
LØNMODTAGERNES GARANTIFOND

and between

(2) Specialarbejderforbundet i Danmark, acting as agent for Finn Walther Sørensen, Harry Larsen and Erik Sørensen,

and

H. Nielsen & Søn, Maskinfabrik A/S, in liquidation,

Intervener:
LØNMODTAGERNES GARANTIFOND

347

on the interpretation of Council Directive No. 75/129/EEC of 17 February 1975 on the approximation of the laws of the Member States relating to collective redundancies (Official Journal 1975 L 48, p. 29),

THE COURT (FIFTH CHAMBER)

composed of: O. Due, President of Chamber, C. Kakouris, U. Everling, Y. Galmot and R. Joliet, Judges,

Advocate General: C. O. Lenz
Registrar: H. A. Rühl, Principal Administrator

*

gives the following JUDGMENT

---

* after considering the observations submitted on behalf of the plaintiff Specialarbejderforbundet i Danmark by Mr J. Bjørst, the intervener Lønmodtagernes Garantifond by Mr U. Andersen, the Commission of the European Communities by Mr H. P. Hartvig, acting as Agent, after hearing the Opinion of the Advocate General delivered at the sitting on 27 November 1984.

Decision

1. By a letter of 15 December 1983, which was received at the Court Registry on 20 December 1983, the Højesteret referred to the Court for a preliminary ruling under Article 177 of the EEC Treaty two questions on the interpretation of Council Directive No. 75/129 of 17 February 1975 on the approximation of the laws of the Member States relating to collective redundancies.

2. Those questions were raised in proceedings brought by two trade unions, namely Dansk Metalarbejderforbund and Specialarbejderforbundet Danmark, both acting on behalf of some of their members, against H. Nielsen & Son, Maskinfabrik A/S, in liquidation, (hereinafter referred to as 'the Company'). The Company is supported by the Lonmodtagernes Garantifond [Wage-earners' Guarantee Fund].

3. It appears that in February 1980 the Company informed the staff representatives of its financial difficulties. On 14 March 1980 it informed the bankruptcy court that it was suspending payment of its debts. The two trade unions thereupon asked the company to provide a bank guarantee for the future payment of wages. No such guarantee was forthcoming and on 19 March 1980 the workers stopped work on the advice of their trade unions. On 21 March 1980 the Company informed the competent Danish Employment Office that it was considering dismissing all its workers. On

25 March 1980 it was declared insolvent on its own application. On 26 March 1980 the workers were given due notice of dismissal.

4. The two trade unions claim from the Company special allowances in reliance on Article 102a(2) of the Danish Law on the Procurement of Employment and Unemployment Insurance. That provision states that if an employer does not give the competent authorities 30 days notice of proposed collective redundancies he must pay the workers an allowance equal to their salary for that period. In the event of the employer's insolvency the Wage-earners' Guarantee Fund is responsible for payment of the allowance.

5. The aforesaid provision of Danish Law is part of the legislation implementing Directive No. 75/129, which provides that the Member States must impose certain obligations on employers contemplating collective redundancies. Article 2(1) of the directive states: 'Where an employer is contemplating collective redundancies, he shall begin consultation with the workers' representatives with a view to reaching an agreement.' Article 3(1) provides: 'Employers shall notify the competent public authority in writing of any projected collective redundancies.' Under Article 4, the redundancies referred to in Article 3 are to take effect not earlier than 30 days after notification unless the competent authority reduces that period.

6. When the actions came before the Danish Højesteret as the court of last instance, it queried whether the cessation of work by the workers in the circumstances of the case constituted a repudiation of their contract amounting to dismissal attributable to the employer and thereby falling under the directive. It also queried whether the employer ought to have contemplated collective redundancies within the meaning of the directive, on announcing that it was suspending payment of its debts, since that announcement was followed by the Company's winding-up and the collective redundancy of the workers. The Højesteret therefore referred the following questions to the Court of Justice:

'(1) May a termination of employment which is effected by the employees because the employer has notified the bankruptcy court that he is suspending payment of his debts be treated as dismissal by the employer, with the consequences that the employment falls within the scope of Council Directive No. 75/129/EEC of 17 February 1975 on the approximation of the laws of the Member States relating to collective redundancies, provided that the conditions therefore are otherwise satisfied? The reply should be based on the assumption that the employees' termination of their employment was justified under Danish law.

(2) Does Council Directive No. 75/129/EEC apply not only

349

where the employer in fact contemplated large-scale redundancies, but also where he ought to have contemplated
large-scale redundancies and to have given advance notice
thereof but failed to do so?'.

First question

7. The purpose of the first question is to ascertain whether, under the
directive, termination of a contract of employment by the employees in
such circumstances may be treated as dismissal by the employer and as
such falling under the directive.

8. The answer to that question must first of all be sought in the wording of
the directive. As Specialarbejderforbundet i Danmark, the Guarantee
Fund and the Commission point out, Article 1(1)(a) of the directive
states '"collective redundancies" means dismissal effected by an employer'. No other provision of the directive supports an extension of its
scope to termination of employment by the employees.

9. Nevertheless, according to Specialarbejderforbundet i Danmark, the
objective of the directive, which is to strengthen the protection of workers
in the event of collective dismissal, implies that the termination by the
workers of their employment on the ground that payment of their wages
is no longer guaranteed should be treated as dismissal effect by the
employer.

10. That argument cannot be accepted. The directive does not affect the
employer's freedom to effect or refrain from effecting collective dismissals. Its sole object is to provide for consultation with the trade unions
and for notification of the competent public authority prior to such dismissals. Article 2(2) provides that consultation with the trade unions
must, at least, cover 'ways and means of avoiding collective redundancies
or reducing the number of workers affected, and mitigating the consequences.' Article 4 provides that projected collective redundancies
notified to the competent authority are to take effect only after a particular period has elapsed. The competent public authority is to use
that period to seek solutions to the problems raised by the projected
collective redundancies. As the Guarantee Fund and the Commission
rightly observe, to treat termination of their employment by the workers
in the manner advocated by Specialarbejderforbundet i Danmark would
give the workers the possibility of bringing about dismissals against the
will of the employer and without his being in a position to discharge his
obligations under Articles 2 and 3 of the directive. It would lead to a
result precisely contrary to that sought by the directive, namely to avoid
or reduce collective redundancies.

11. For those reasons the reply to the first question must be that the termination by workers of their contract of employment following an an-

nouncement by the employer that he is suspending payment of his debts cannot be treated as dismissal by the employer for the purposes of Council Directive No. 75/129 of 17 February 1975 on the approximation of the laws of the Member States relating to collective redundancies.

Second question

12. By the second question the national court asks whether the directive applies where, because of the financial state of the undertaking, the employer ought to have contemplated collective redundancies but did not do so.

13. There is nothing in the wording of Articles 2(1) and 3(1) of the directive to justify an affirmative reply to the second question. The employer must consult the unions only when he 'contemplates' redundancies and must inform the public authority only of 'projected' redundancies.

14. Specialarbejderforbundet i Danmark contends, however, that the effectiveness of the directive would be impaired if the employer were not obliged, by implication, to foresee collective redundancies as soon as he encounters serious financial difficulties.

15. As the Guarantee Fund and the Commission rightly state, there is no implied obligation under the directive to foresee collective redundancies. It does not stipulate the circumstances in which the employer must contemplate collective redundancies and in no way affects his freedom to decide whether and when he must formulate plans for collective dismissals.

16. Moreover, as the Commission rightly observes, the effect of the interpretation proposed by Specialarbejderforbundet i Danmark would be that any employer who ceased to trade as a result of insolvency and who failed to notify the public authority of any projected collective redundancy would incur the penalties laid down by national law, since he would not have foreseen collective redundancies in sufficient time. Such an interpretation would run counter to the wording of Article 1(2), which excludes from the scope of the directive collective redundancies caused 'by the termination of an establishment's activities where that is the result of a judicial decision.'

17. For those reasons the reply to the second question must be that Council Directive No. 75/129 of 17 February 1975 on the approximation of the laws of the Member States relating to collective redundancies applies only where the employer has in fact contemplated collective redundancies or has drawn up a plan for collective redundancies.

Costs

18. The costs incurred by the Commission of the European Communities,

which submitted observations to the Court, are not recoverable. As these proceedings are, in so far as the parties to the main proceedings are concerned, in the nature of a step in the action pending before the national court, the decision on costs is a matter for that court.

On those grounds,

THE COURT (FIFTH CHAMBER),

in reply to the questions referred to it by the Højesteret by letter of 15 December 1983, hereby rules:

(1) **The termination by workers of their contract of employment following an announcement by the employer that he is suspending payment of his debts cannot be treated as dismissal by the employer for the purposes of Council Directive No. 75/129 of 17 February 1975 on the approximation of the laws of the Member States relating to collective redundancies.**

(2) **Council Directive No. 75/129 of 17 February 1975 on the approximation of the laws of the Member States relating to collective redundancies applies only where the employer has in fact contemplated collective redundancies or has drawn up a plan for collective redundancies.**

	Due		Kakouris	
Everling		Galmot		Joliet

Delivered in open court in Luxembourg on 12 February 1985.

P. Heim   O. Due
Registrar   *President of the Fifth Chamber*

2. Transfer of undertakings

(a) Infringement proceedings under Article 169, EEC Treaty

Judgment of the Court

15 April 1986 – Case 237/84

Commission of the European Communities
v.
Kingdom of Belgium

Failure of State fully to fulfil its obligations – transfer of undertakings – dismissal protection for employees – categories excluded from protection – permissible exclusions only those who have no protection against dismissal under national law – Directive applied to any situation where employees affected by a transfer enjoy some, albeit limited, protection against dismissal under national law – Member States may not unilaterally determine scope of Directive (Council Directive 77/187/EEC Article 4(1)).

In Case 237/84

Commission of the European Communities, represented by Joseph Griesmar, Legal Adviser, acting as Agent, with an address for service in Luxembourg at the office of G. Kremlis, a member of the Commission's Legal Department, Jean Monnet Building,

applicant,

v.

Kingdom of Belgium, represented by the Minister for Foreign Relations and by Robert Hoebaer, Director at the Ministry for Foreign Affairs, Foreign Trade and Development Co-operation, acting as Agent, with an address for service in Luxembourg at the Belgian Embassy, 4 Rue des Girondins,

defendant,

APPLICATION for a declaration that, by failing to adopt within the prescribed period all the measures necessary to comply in full with the provisions of council Directive No. 77/187/EEC of 14 February 1977 on the approximation of the laws of the Member States relating to the safeguarding of employees' rights in the event of transfers of undertakings, businesses or parts of businesses (Official Journal 1977 No. L 61, p. 26), the Kingdom of Belgium has failed to fulfil its obligations under the EEC Treaty,

353

THE COURT

composed of: Lord Mackenzie Stuart, President, T. Koopmans, U. Everling and R. Joliet, Presidents of Chambers, G. Bosco, Y. Galmot and C. N. Kakouris, Judges,

Advocate General: Sir Gordon Slynn
Registrar: P. Heim,

after hearing the Opinion of the Advocate General delivered at the sitting on 18 February 1986,

gives the following JUDGMENT

Decision

1. By application lodged at the court Registry on 18 September 1984 the Commission of the European Communities brought an action under Article 169 of the EEC Treaty for a declaration that, by failing to adopt within the prescribed period all the measures necessary to comply in full with the provisions of Council Directive No. 77/187/EEC of 14 February 1977 on the approximation of the laws of the Member States relating to the safeguarding of emloyees' rights in the event of transfers of undertakings, businesses or parts of businesses (Official Journal 1977 No. L 61, p. 26), the Kingdom of Belgium had failed to fulfil its obligations under the EEC Treaty.

2. According to its preamble, Directive No. 77/187/EEC, which was adopted on the basis in particular of Article 100 of the Treaty, seeks to 'provide for the protection of employees in the event of a change of employer, in particular, to ensure that their rights are safeguarded'. It is based on the principle that as far as possible the employment relationship should be maintained unchanged with the transferee.

3. More specifically, Article 3(1) of the directive provides for the transfer of the transferor's rights and obligations arising from a contract of employment or from an employment relationship. The directive protects the employees concerned against dismissal by providing in the first subparagraph of Article 4(1) that 'the transfer of an undertaking, business or part of a business shall not in itself constitute grounds for dismissal by the transferor or the transferee'; this is without prejudice to 'dismissals that may take place for economic, technical or organizational reasons entailing changes in the workforce.' However, according to the second subparagraph of Article 4(1), 'Member States may provide that the first subparagraph shall not apply to certain specific categories of employees who are not covered by the laws or practice of the Member States in respect of protection against dismissal'.

4. As regards the latter provisions, it appears from the documents before the Court that, according to a statement recorded in the Council minutes, Member States undertook to inform the Commission within six months of the notification of the directive of the categories of employee excluded from the scope of Article 4(1) pursuant to the second subparagraph of that provision. In accordance with that undertaking, the Belgian Government informed the Commission, by letter of 4 August 1977, that in Belgium employees undergoing a trial period and employees dismissed at the approach of pensionable age would be so excluded.

5. Article 8 provided that Member States were to comply with Directive No. 77/187/EEC within two years of its notification. Since the directive was notified to the Kingdom of Belgium on 16 February 1977, that period expired on 16 February 1979.

6. The Commission considered that, despite the expiry of that period, the Kingdom of Belgium had not adopted legislation meeting all the requirements arising from the directive. First, the Belgian legislation in force did not protect rights to old-age benefits under supplementary social security schemes (second subparagraph of Article 3(3) of the directive). Secondly, it excluded certain categories of employees from the protection against dismissal in the event of transfers of undertakings (Article 4(1)) of the directive. As a result, following an exchange of letters with the Belgian Government and after delivering a reasoned opinion pursuant to the first paragraph of Article 169 of the Treaty, the Commission brought this action for a declaration that the Kingdom of Belgium has failed to fulfil its obligations.

7. By notice of 6 January 1986, which was received at the Court on 8 January 1986, the Commission stated that it would abandon that part of its action relating to the first complaint, namely the alleged infringement of the second subparagraph of Article 3(3) of the directive. It explained that on 1 January 1986 three royal decrees, of such a nature as to make Belgian law compatible with the directive, had entered into force and that, in consequence, the complaint in question was redundant.

8. Accordingly, the Court has to adjudicate on the second complaint only, namely the alleged failure fully to transpose the whole of Article 4(1) of Directive No. 77/187/EEC into Belgian law.

9. On 19 April 1978, the Kingdom of Belgium adopted, for the purposes of the implementation of, *inter alia*, Article 4(1) of the directive, the Royal Decree making obligatory Collective Bargaining Agreement No. 32 of 28 February 1978 on the safeguarding of employees' rights in the event of a change of employer as a result of an agreed transfer of an undertaking concluded within the National Labour Council (Moniteur Belge of 25 August 1978). Article 6 of that Agreement provides that 'a change of

employer shall not in itself constitute grounds for dismissal'. However, Article 7 of the Agreement provides as follows:

'the following persons shall not be covered by the provisions of Article 6:

(1) employees undergoing a trial period;
(2) employees dismissed at the approach of pensionable age;
(3) persons bound by a student's employment contract pursuant to the Law of 9 June 1970 on the employment of students.'.

10. The Commission submits that the provision quoted above has the effect of excluding from the protection afforded by Article 4(1) of the directive categories of employee whose exclusion is not covered by the derogation set out in the second subparagraph of Article 4(1). That derogation should be interpreted strictly so as to cover only employees who have no protection under national law against dismissal. In its view, that is not the case with the categories of employee specified in Article 7 of Collective Bargaining Agreement No. 32 since each of those three categories of employee are protected by some period of notice, even though the periods of notice due to them are shorter than those due to other categories of worker.

11. The Belgian Government objects of that interpretation. It argues that protection against dismissal, within the meaning of the second subparagraph of Article 4(1) of the directive, means a measure to dissuade employers from dismissing employees so that employees do not suffer an interruption of their working life. In its view, no such dissuasive effect exists in the case of the categories of employees excluded by the Belgian legislation, in particular employees dismissed at the approach of pensionable age and employees undergoing a trial period. The former are at the end of their working lives and the element of dissuasion no longer operates. As for employees undergoing a trial period, they are subject to a very short period of notice for the reason that the employer must remain entirely at liberty to dismiss employees when they are not suited to the job.

12. That objection of the Belgian Government cannot be upheld. It is clear both from the wording of Article 4(1) and from the scheme of the directive that the provision in question is designed to ensure that employees' rights are maintained by extending the protection against dismissal by the employer afforded by national law to cover the case in which a change in employer occurs upon the transfer of an undertaking.

13. Consequently, that provision applies to any situation in which employees affected by a transfer enjoy some, albeit limited, protection against dismissal under national law, with the result that, under the directive, that protection may not be taken away from them or curtailed solely because of the transfer.

14. In this case, the Belgian Law of 3 July 1978 on contracts of employment (Moniteur Belge of 22 August 1978) makes the dismissal of the three categories of employee mentioned in Article 7 of Collective Bargaining Agreement No. 32 subject to specific minimum periods of notice. It is common ground that, under that Law, employees undergoing a trial period may be lawfully dismissed only if given at least seven days' notice in the absence of serious cause; however, the termination of the employment contract may not take effect before the last day of the first month of the trial period in the case of employees' and commercial travellers' employment contracts (Articles 48(4), 6; and 81 in conjunction with Article 87 of the Law of 3 July 1978). Moreover, employees dismissed at the approach of pensionable age are entitled to a period of notice of between 28 days and 6 months, depending on the case (Articles 59 and 83 in conjunction with Article 87 of the Law of 3 July 1978). Lastly, the dismissal of persons bound by a student's employment contract is subject to a period of notice of 3 or 7 days, depending on the length of employment (Article 130 of the Law of 3 July 1978); however, the provisions more favourable to employees, relating to the contracts of employment of manual workers serving a trial period, apply where the student's employment contract includes a trial period clause (Article 48(4) in conjunction with Article 127 of the Law of 3 July 1978).

15. Consequently, Article 4(1) of Directive No. 77/187/EEC requires the above-mentioned periods of notice to be complied with also in the case where the transferor or the transferee dismisses the employees concerned in connexion with the transfer of an undertaking.

16. The Belgian Government further argues in this connexion that the Kingdom of Belgium was entitled to exclude from the protection afforded by Article 4(1) of Directive No. 77/187/EEC at least employees undergoing a trial period and employees dismissed at the approach of pensionable age. It notified those two categories of employee to the Commission on 4 August 1977 in accordance with the statement to that effect inserted in the Council minutes. Since the Commission did not signify its disagreement within a reasonable time, it thus allowed it to be believed that the notified categories of employee could in fact be covered by the exception provided for in the second subparagraph of Article 4(1).

17. That argument is irrelevant. The court has consistently held that the true meaning of rules of Community law can be derived only from those rules themselves, having regard to their context. That meaning cannot therefore be affected by such a statement.

18. Consequently, the Kingdom of Belgium cannot effectively rely on such an uncontested notification in order to alter the scope of its obligations under Article 4(1) of Directive No. 77/187/EEC.

19. For those reasons, it must be concluded that, by failing to adopt within

the prescribed period all the measures necessary to comply in full with Article 4(1) of Council Directive No. 77/187/EEC of 14 February 1977 on the approximation of the laws of the Member States relating to the safeguarding of employees' rights in the event of transfers of under-takings, businesses or parts of businesses (Official Journal 1977 No. L 61, p. 26), the Kingdom of Belgium has failed to fulfil its obligations under the EEC Treaty.

Costs
20. Under Article 69(2) of the Rules of Procedure, the unsuccessful party is to be ordered to pay the costs; under Article 69(4), a party who discontinues or withdraws from proceedings is to be ordered to pay the costs, unless the discontinuance or withdrawal is justified by the conduct of the opposite party. In this case, the defendant was unsuccessful as regards the second complaint whilst the withdrawal of the first complaint was justified by its conduct. It should therefore be ordered to pay the whole of the costs.

On those grounds,

THE COURT

hereby:

1. Declares that, by failing to adopt within the prescribed period all the measures necessary to comply in full with Article 4(1) of Council Directive No. 77/187/EEC of 14 February 1977 on the approximation of the laws of the Member States relating to the safeguarding of employees' rights in the event of transfers of undertakings, businesses or parts of businesses (Official Journal 1977 No. L 61, p. 26), the Kingdom of Belgium has failed to fulfil its obligations under the EEC Treaty.

2. Orders the Kingdom of Belgium to pay the costs.

Mackenzie Stuart   Koopmans   Everling

Joliet   Bosco

Galmot   Kakouris

Delivered in open court in Luxembourg on 15 April 1986.

P. Heim   A. J. Mackenzie Stuart
Registrar   *President*

Judgment of the Court

10 July 1986 – Case 235/84

Commission of the European Communities
v.
Italian Republic

Failure of State fully to fulfil its obligations – transfer of undertakings – protection of employees' supplementary pension rights – information and consultation with employees' representatives in event of transfer of undertaking – Member States must ensure that all workers who might be affected by a transfer and are not covered by protections under collective agreements are covered by information and consultation mechanisms (Council Directive 77/187/EEC, Articles 3(3) and 6(1) & (2)).

In Case 235/84

Commission of the European Communities, represented by its Legal Adviser, Armando Toledano Laredo, and by Enrico Traversa, a member of its Legal Department, acting as Agents, with an address for service in Luxembourg at the office of Kremlis, also a member of its Legal Department, Jean Monnet Building,

applicant,

v.

Italian Republic, represented by Luigi Ferrari Bravo, Head of the Department for Contentious Diplomatic Affairs, acting as Agent, assisted by Oscar Fiumara, Avvocato dello Stato, with an address for service in Luxembourg at the Italian Embassy,

defendant,

APPLICATION for a declaration that, by failing to adopt within the prescribed period all the measures necessary for the implementation of Council Directive 77/187 of 14 February 1977 on the approximation of the laws of the Member States relating to the safeguarding of employees' rights in the event of transfers of undertakings, businesses or parts of businesses (Official Journal 1977, No. L 61, p. 26), the Italian Republic has failed to fulfil its obligations under the EEC Treaty,

THE COURT

composed of: Lord Mackenzie Stuart, President, T. Koopmans, U. Everling and R. Joliet (Presidents of Chambers), G. Bosco, Y. Galmot and C. N. Kakouris, Judges,

Advocate General: Sir Gordon Slynn
Registrar: D. Louterman, Administrator,

after hearing the Opinion of the Advocate General delivered at the sitting on 17 April 1986,

gives the following JUDGMENT

Decision

1. By an application lodged at the Court Registry on 19 September 1984, the Commission of the European Communities brought an action under Article 169 of the EEC Treaty for a declaration that, by failing to adopt within the period prescribed all the measures necessary for the implementation of Council Directive 77/187 of 14 February 1977 on the approximation of the laws of the Member States relating to the safeguarding of employees' rights in the event of transfers of undertakings, businesses or parts of businesses, the Italian Republic has failed to fulfil its obligations under the EEC Treaty.

2. Directive 77/187, which was adopted on the basis of, in particular, Article 100 of the EEC Treaty, is intended, according to its preamble, 'to provide for the protection of employees in the event of a change of employer, in particular to ensure that their rights are safeguarded'. Its purpose is to ensure, as far as possible, that the employment relationship continues unchanged with the transferee.

3. More particularly, Article 3(1) provides that the transferor's rights and obligations arising from a contract of employment or from an employment relationship shall be transferred to the transferee; Article 3(2) provides that following the transfer the transferee shall continue to observe the terms and conditions agreed in any collective agreement. However, according to the first subparagraph of Article 3(3), 'paragraphs 1 and 2 shall not cover employees' rights to old-ago, invalidity or survivors' benefits under supplementary or inter-company pension schemes outside the statutory social security schemes in Member States'. With regard to such rights the second subparagraph of Article 3(3) provides:

    'Member States shall adopt the measures necessary to protect the interests of employees and of persons no longer employed in the transferor's business at the time of the transfer within the meaning of Article 1(1) in respect of rights conferring on them immediate or prospective entitlement to old-age benefits, including survivors' benefits, under supplementary schemes referred to in the first subparagraph.'.

4. In addition Article 6 of the directive requires the transferor and the transferee to inform and consult the workers affected by the transfer. The prescribed information relates to the reasons for the transfer, its implications for the employees and the measures envisaged in relation to them; the information must be given to representatives of the employees in good time and in any event before the employees are directly affected by the transfer as regards their conditions of work and employment (paragraph (1)). If the transferor or the transferee envisages measures in relation to his employees, he must consult the employees' representatives in good time on such measures with a view to seeking agreement (paragraph (2)).

5. Under Article 8, Member States were required to comply with the directive within two years of its notification. Since the directive was notified to the Italian Republic on 16 February 1977, that period expired on 16 February 1979.

6. The Commission considers that the Italian legislation does not satisfy the requirements of the directive in two respects. Firsts the legislation in force does not ensure protection of the rights of employees and former employees to old-age benefits under supplementary schemes of social security pursuant to the second subparagraph of Article 3(3) of the directives; secondly, the duty imposed on transferors and transferees to inform and consult employees' representatives does not satisfy the requirements of Article 6(1) and (2) of the directive. In consequence, the Commission, after an exchange of letters with the Italian Government and after delivering a reasoned opinion pursuant to the first paragraph of Article 169 of the Treaty, brought the present action for a declaration that the Italian Republic has failed to fulfil its obligations in respect of the two above-mentioned matters.

Implementation of the second subparagraph of Article 3(3) of Directive 77/187

7. First of all, with regard to the alleged failure fully to transpose into national law the second subparagraph of Article 3(3) of Directive 77/187, the Italian Republic does not deny that it has not adopted specific rules for the implementation thereof. The parties take issue, however, on the question whether existing Italian law already satisfied the obligations arising from that provision.

8. In that respect the Italian Government refers to two provisions of the Italian Civil Code, namely Articles 2112 and 2117, and claims that those provisions, as interpreted by the Corte Suprema di Cassazione, guarantee employees protection at least equal to that required by the directive. The provisions read as follows:

361

'Article 2112. Transfer of the undertaking

> Where an undertaking is transferred, contracts of employment will continue to be valid as against the transferee unless the transferor has given the required notice and employees retain the rights flowing from the seniority acquired before the transfer.
>
> The transferee is liable for any debt which the transferor may have vis-à-vis employees at the time of the transfer arising from work carried out, including debts arising from notice given by the transferor, to the extent that the transferee had knowledge of them at the time of the transfer or that the debts appear in the books of the undertaking transferred or on the employee's personal file.

Article 2117. Special insurance and aid funds

> The special insurance and aid funds established by the employer, even if the employees have not contributed thereto, may not be used for purposes other than those for which they were intended and may not be attached by the creditors of the employer or the employee.'.

9. The Italian Government states that Article 2112 lays down the general rule that the new proprietor of the undertaking is to replace the former proprietor in the contract of employment. Under established case-law that provision also applies to rights arising under supplementary pension schemes since such schemes confer rights upon employees within the framework of their employment relationship. In support of that assertion the Italian Government refers to several judgments of the Corte Suprema di Cassazione, copies of which it has forwarded to the Court. It claims that those judgments show that the benefits payable under supplementary pension schemes represent debts arising out of employment and that the contract of employment guarantees that such schemes will continue with the transferee, irrespective of whether the funds in question are internal or external to the undertaking.

10. The Italian Government explains that Article 2117 provides an additional guarantee that employees or former employees shall receive amounts due to them.

11. The Commission challenges those contentions mainly on the ground that there is no sufficiently clear and established case-law which extends the scope of the provisions cited by the Italian Government to rights to old-age and survivors' benefits under supplementary schemes.

12. The Commission considers that Article 2112 excludes supplementary pension schemes set up outside the undertaking in the form of funds

which are legally separate, since in such case the rights to benefits may not be asserted against the employer or undertaking but against a third party who is not privy to the employment relationship.

13. According to the Commission, it is true that the effect of Article 2117 is to put special pension funds outside the reach of the undertaking's creditors; that provision does not, however, safeguard the rights of employees should the new employer decide not to retain the supplementary pension scheme.

14. The parties are thus at issue on the scope of the aforesaid national provisions and in particular on the question whether under those provisions rights of employees and former employees under supplementary pension schemes are to be regarded in all cases as rights arising from the employment relationship and, as such, are transferred in their entirety from the transferor to the transferee in accordance with the requirements of the second subparagraph of Article 3(3) of the directive. The answer to that question depends on how those provisions have been applied in practice, in particular by the national courts. The Italian Government has cited several cases. The Commission, on the other hand, has submitted no evidence to justify its doubts and in particular has not cited any case-law to support its views or referred to any specific instance in which employees' rights have not been fully safeguarded to the extent prescribed by the directive.

15. In those circumstances it must be concluded that the Commission has not established, to the required standard of proof, that Italian law does not provide the full degree of protection prescribed by the second subparagraph of Article 3(3) of Directive 77/187.

16. In consequence, the first complaint must be rejected.

Implementation of Article 6(1) and (2) of Directive 77/187
17. With regard to the alleged failure fully to transpose into national law Article 6(1) and (2) of Directive 77/187, it is clear from the documents before the Court that Italian law prescribes certain procedures for informing and consulting employees' representatives in the event of the transfer of an undertaking. Those procedures are laid down on the one hand by collective agreements and on the other by Law No. 215 of 26 May 1978 on rules to facilitate the mobility of workers and rules concerning unemployment funds.

18. The Commission claims that the said measures do not ensure general and unconditional fulfilment of the obligations arising under the directive. The scope of the collective agreements is limited to specific economic sectors and to employers' associations or undertakings and trade unions which are parties to the agreements. Law No. 215 of 25 May 1978 lays

down special rules to cover particular circumstances and is therefore of limited scope.

19. The Italian Government does not deny the facts alleged by the Commission. It simply emphasized in the proceedings before the Court that the most important and most widespread collective agreements have for years recognized the right of workers to information and laid down appropriate procedures for the benefit of the workers concerned; moreover, there are similar obligations under Law No. 25 of 26 May 1978 for undertakings which are declared to be in a state of crisis.

20. With regard to those observations it must be remembered that, as the Court held in its judgment of 30 January 1985 in Case 143/83 (*Commission* v. *Denmark* [1985] ECR 432), it is true that the Member States may leave the implementation of the social policy objectives pursued by a directive in this area in the first instance to management and labour. That possibility does not, however, discharge them from the obligation of ensuring that all workers in the Community are afforded the full protection provided for in the directive. The State guarantee must cover all cases where effective protection is not ensured by other means.

21. The Italian Government itself has admitted that only certain collective agreements lay down procedures for informing and consulting representatives of employees affected by the transfer of an undertaking. However widespread and important such agreements may be, they cover only specific economic sectors and, owing to their contractual nature, create obligations only between members of the trade union in question and employers or undertakings bound by the agreements.

22. It is moreover common ground that Law No. 215 of 26 May 1978 does not fully satisfy the requirements of the directive, since that law applies only where an undertaking is declared by order of the Employment Minister to be 'in a state of crisis' and where a solution to the crisis is possible by means of a transfer.

23. In those circumstances the Italian Republic was required to adopt appropriate laws, regulations or administrative measures to ensure that all workers who might be affected by the transfer of an undertaking and who were not covered by collective agreements received the protection provided for in Article 6(1)(2) of the directive.

24. For those reasons it must be concluded, with regard to the second claim made by the Commission, that, by failing to adopt within the prescribed period all the measures needed to comply fully with Article 6(1) and (2) of Council Directive 77/187 of 14 February 1977 on the approximation of the laws of the Member States relating to the safeguarding of employees' rights in the event of transfers of undertakings, businesses or parts of

businesses (Official Journal 1977 No. L 61, p. 26), the Italian Republic has failed to fulfil its obligations under the Treaty.

Costs

25. Under Article 69(2) of the Rules of Procedure, the unsuccessful party is to be ordered to pay the costs. However, Article 69(3) provides that, where each party succeeds on some and fails on other heads, the Court may order that the parties bear their own costs in whole or in part. Since in the present case each party has failed in some of its submission, the parties must bear their own costs.

On those grounds,

THE COURT

hereby:

1. **Declares that, by failing to adopt within the prescribed period all the measures needed to comply fully with Article 6(1) and (2) of Council Directive 77/187 of 14 February 1977 on the approximation of the laws of the Member States relating to the safeguarding of employees' rights in the event of transfers of undertakings, businesses or parts of businesses (Official Journal 1977 No. L 61, p. 26), the Italian Republic has failed to fulfil its obligations under the Treaty;**

2. **For the rest, dismisses the application;**

3. **Orders the parties to bear their own costs.**

Mackenzie Stuart   Koopmans

              Everling   Joliet

Bosco   Galmot   Kakouris

Delivered in open court in Luxembourg on 10 July 1986.

P. Heim   A. J. Mackenzie Stuart
Registrar   *President*

(b) Preliminary rulings under Article 177, EEC Treaty

Judgment of the Court

7 February 1985 – Case 135/83

H. B. M. Abels
v.
The Administrative Board of the Bedrijfsvereniging voor de Metaalindustrie en de Electrotechnische Industrie*

Transfer of undertakings – safeguarding employees' rights – scope of Directive – transfer of undertaking in liquidation excluded – transfer of undertaking in course of a procedure where court grants leave to suspend payment of debts included – Directive applies to obligations of transferor arising before the date of the transfer (Council Directive 77/187/EEC, Articles 1(1) and 3(1)).

In Case 135/83

REFERENCE to the Court under Article 177 of the Treaty by the Raad van Beroep [Social Security Court], Zwolle, for a preliminary ruling in the proceedings pending before that court between

H. B. M. Abels

and

The Administrative Board of the Bedrijfsvereniging voor de Metaalindustrie en de Electrotechnische Industrie [Professional and Trade Association for the Metal and Electrotechnical Industries],

on the interpretation of Council Directive No. 77/187/EEC of 14 February 1977 on the approximation of the laws of the Member States relating to the safeguarding of employees' rights in the event of transfers of undertakings, businesses or parts of businesses (Official Journal 1977 L 61, p. 26),

THE COURT

composed of: Lord Mackenzie Stuart, President, G. Bosco, O. Due and C. Kakouris (Presidents of Chambers), T. Koopmans, U. Everling, K. Bahlmann, Y. Galmot and R. Joliet, Judges,

Advocate General: Sir Gordon Slynn
Registrar: H. A. Rühl, Principal Administrator

**

gives the following JUDGMENT

---

* – Language of the Case: Dutch.
** after considering the observations submitted on behalf of the plaintiff Abels by Mr J. van der
   Hel, the defendant Bedrijfsvereniging voor de Metaalindustrie en de Electrotechnische
   Industrie by Mr J. H. Meijs, in the written proceedings, and by Mr W. M. Levelt-Overmars,
   in the oral proceedings, the Netherlands Government by Mr. I. Verkade in the written
   proceedings, and by Mr A. Bos, acting as Agent, in the oral proceedings, the latter being
   assisted by Mr L. A. D. Keus, the Danish Government by Mr L. Mikaelsen, acting as Agent,
   the French Government by Mr G. Boivineau, acting as Agent, the Commission of the
   European Communities by Mr M. Beschel, acting as Agent, assisted by Mr F. Herbert, after
   hearing the Opinion of the Advocate General delivered at the sitting on 8 November 1984.

Decision

1. By order dated 28 June 1983, which was received at the Court on 11
   July 1983, the Raad van Beroep, Zwolle, referred to the Court for a
   preliminary ruling under Article 177 of the EEC Treaty two questions as
   to the interpretation of Articles 1(1) and 3(1) of Council Directive No.
   77/187/EEC of 14 February 1977 on the approximation of the laws of the
   Member States relating to the safeguarding of employees' rights in the
   event of transfers of undertakings, businesses or parts of businesses
   (Official Journal 1977 L 61, p. 26).

2. Those questions were raised in proceedings instituted by H. B. M.
   Abels against the Administrative Board of the Bedrijfsvereniging voor de
   Metaalindustrie en de Electrotechnische Industrie.

3. The plaintiff in the main proceedings was employed by the private
   limited company Machinefabriek Thole BV (hereinafter referred to as
   'Thole'), Enschede, when, by successive decisions of the Arrondissementsrechtbank [District Court] Almelo, Thole was granted a 'surséance
   van betaling' [judicial leave to suspend payment of debts], first provisionally, on 2 September 1981, and then definitively on 17 March 1982,
   before being put into liquidation on 9 June 1982. It was during the
   liquidation proceedings that, pursuant to an agreement concluded by the
   liquidator, Thole's business was transferred with effect from 10 June 1982
   to the private limited company Transport Toepassing en Produktie BV
   (hereinafter referred to as 'TTP'), Enschede, which continued to operate
   the undertaking and took over most of its work-force, including Mr Abels.

4. Since Mr Abels had not received his wages for the period from 1 to 9
   June 1982 from either Thole or TTP, or any payment for his accrued
   holiday entitlement during the year in question or a proportional part of
   his end-of-year allowance, he sought payment of those sums from the
   Bedrijfsvereniging, which, in his view, was subsidiarily liable to pay
   them to him under Netherlands legislation.

367

5. His request was rejected on the ground that under Articles 1639(aa) and 1639(bb) of the Netherlands Civil Code, which were inserted therein by the Law of 15 May 1981 to implement Directive No. 77/187, TTP was required to fulfil Thole's obligations towards its workers under the contract of employment and it was therefore inappropriate for the Bedrijfsvereniging to intervene.

6. Directive No. 77/187, which was adopted by the Council on the basis of, in particular, Article 100 of the Treaty, is intended, in the terms of its preamble, 'to provide for the protection of employees in the event of a change of employer, in particular, to ensure that their rights are safeguarded'. For that purpose, Article 3(1) thereof provides that: 'The transferor's rights and obligations arising from a contract of employment or from an employment relationship existing on the date of a transfer . . . shall, by reason of such transfer, be transferred to the transferee'. Article 4(1) provides for the protection of the workers concerned against dismissal by the transferor or the transferee, but does not stand in the way of 'dismissals that may take place for economic, technical or organizational reasons entailing changes in the work-force'. In addition, Article 6 of the directive requires the transferor and the transferee to inform and consult the representatives of the workers affected by the transfer. Finally, Article 7 provides that the directive is not to 'affect the right of Member States to apply or introduce laws, regulations or administrative provisions which are more favourable to employees'.

7. Mr Abels appealed against the Bedrijfsvereniging's negative decision to the Raad van Beroep, Zwolle, which, considering that the judgment to be given depended on the interpretation of certain provisions of Directive No. 77/187, stayed the proceedings and referred the following questions to the Court for a preliminary ruling:

'(1) Does the scope of Article 1 (1) of Directive No. 77/187/ EEC extend to a situation in which the transferor of an undertaking is adjudged insolvent or is granted a "sur-séance van betaling"?

(2) If the answer to Question 1 is in the affirmative, must Article 3 (1) of Directive No. 77/187/EEC be interpreted as meaning that the transferor's obligations which are assigned to the transferee by reason of the transfer of the undertaking also include the debts which arose from the contract of employment or the employment relationship before the date of the transfer within the meaning of Article 1 (1)?'.

The first question
Determination of the scope of the directive

8. It should be observed in the first place, with regard to the first question, that under Article 1(1) of Directive No. 77/187, which determines the

scope of the directive *ratione materiae*, the directive is to 'apply to the transfer of an undertaking, business or part of a business to another employer as a result of a legal transfer or merger'. It follows that the directive applies only to transfers resulting from a legal transfer or merger, the latter not being relevant to this case. The question is intended to determine whether that definition includes cases where the transferor of the undertaking has been adjudged insolvent or has been granted a 'surséance van betaling' and the undertaking in question forms part of the assets of the insolvent transferor or is covered by the 'surséance van betaling'.

9. According to the plaintiff in the main proceedings, the Netherlands Government and the Commission, the term 'overdracht krachtens overeenkomst' in the Dutch-language version of the directive indicates that its scope is confined to transfers effected on the basis of agreements entered into voluntarily, to the exclusion of any transfer resulting from legal proceedings whose purpose is the collective and compulsory liquidation of the debtor's assets or the overcoming of the debtor's financial difficulties in order to prevent such liquidation. Those procedures, it is maintained, are excluded, even in cases of sales by private agreement since the essential factor of contractual autonomy is lacking by virtue of the fact that the transfer involves the intervention of the Court and that the form and the subject matter of the sale are determined by weighing up the various interests involved in such procedures.

10. The Bedrijfsvereniging and the Danish Government, on the other hand, claim that the provision at issue, interpreted textually, contains no factor on which to base the assumption that the directive does not cover transfers made as the result of a sale by a liquidator or by a debtor to whom a 'surséance van betaling' has been granted.

11. A comparison of the vrious language versions of the provision in question shows that there are terminological divergencies between them as regards the transfer of undertakings. Whilst the German ('vertragliche Übertragung'), French ('cession conventionnelle'), Greek ('συμβατική εκχώρηση'), Italian ('cessione contrattuale') and Dutch ('overdracht krachtens overeenkomst') versions clearly refer only to transfers resulting from a contract, from which it may be concluded that other types of transfers such as those resulting from an administrative measure or judicial decision are excluded, the English ('legal transfer') and Danish ('overdragelse') versions appear to indicate that the scope is wider.

12. Moreover, it should be noted that the concept of contractual transfer is different in the insolvency laws of the various Member States, as has become apparent in these proceedings. Whilst certain Member States consider that in certain circumstances a sale effected in the context of liquidation proceedings is a normal contractual sale, even if judicial intervention is a preliminary requirement for conclusion of such a contract,

under other legal systems the sale is in certain circumstances regarded as taking place by virtue of a measure adopted by a public authority.

13. In view of those divergencies, the scope of the provision at issue cannot be appraised solely on the basis of a textual interpretation. Its meaning must therefore be clarified in the light of the scheme of the directive, its place in the system of Community law in relation to the rules on insolvency, and its purpose.

The relationship between the directive and insolvency law

14. As is apparent from the above-mentioned recitals in the preamble to Directive No. 77/187, the directive is intended to protect workers in order to safeguard their rights when an undertaking is transferred.

15. Insolvency law is characterized by special procedures intended to weigh up the various interests involved, in particular those of the various classes of creditors; consequently, in all the Member States there are specific rules which may derogate, at least partially, from other provisions, of a general nature, including provisions of social law.

16. The specificity of insolvency law, encountered in all the legal systems of the Member States, is confirmed in Community law. Article 1(2)(d) of Council Directive No. 75/129/EEC of 17 February 1975 on the approximation of the laws of the Member States relating to collective redundancies (Official Journal 1975 L 48, p. 29), which, like Directive No. 77/187, was adopted to attain the objectives of Article 117 of the Treaty, expressly excludes from its scope workers affected by termination of an establishment's activities 'where that is the result of a judicial decision'. Moreover, the specificity of insolvency law was also reflected in the adoption of Council Directive No. 80/987 of 20 October 1980 on the approximation of the laws of the Member States relating to the protection of employees in the event of the insolvency of their employer (Official Journal 1980 L 283, p. 23). That directive creates a system to ensure the payment of outstanding claims relating to pay which applies equally to undertakings which have been adjudged insolvent.

17. In addition, the rules on liquidation proceedings and analogous proceedings are very different in the various Member States. For that reason, and in view of the fact that insolvency law is the subject of specific rules both in the legal systems of the Member States and in the Community legal order, it may be concluded that if the directive had been intended to apply also to transfers of undertakings in the context of such proceedings, an express provision would have been included for that purpose.

The purpose of the directive

18. That interpretation of Directive No. 77/187 also follows necessarily from a consideration of its purpose. The preamble to the directive indicates that the directive's aim of affording protection to workers in the event of transfers of undertakings is to be seen against the background of 'economic trends' and the need referred to in Article 117 of the Treaty 'to promote improved working conditions and an improved standard of living for workers, so as to make possible their harmonization while the improvement is being maintained'. As the Commission has correctly explained, the purpose of the directive is therefore to ensure that restructuring of undertakings within the common market does not adversely affect the workers in the undertakings concerned.

19. The parties are divided as to whether, if the directive were held to be applicable to liquidation or similar proceedings, the resulting social and economic effects would be favourable or prejudicial to the interests of employees.

20. The Bedrijfsvereniging and the Danish Government consider that the directive is applicable to such a situation on the ground that employees whose employer has been adjudged insolvent are precisely those who are most in need of protection; moreover, where such protection is provided, both the workers and the liquidator are normally more inclined to ensure that the undertaking continues to operate until a transfer takes place.

21. On the other hand, the Netherlands Government and the Commission refer to certain economic consequences which would detract from the protection of workers if the directive were to be applied to transfers of undertakings in the event of insolvency or a 'surséance van betaling'. In their opinion, such an extension of the scope of the directive might dissuade a potential transferee from acquiring an undertaking on conditions acceptable to the creditors thereof, who, in such a case, would prefer to sell the assets of the undertaking separately. That would entail the loss of all the jobs in the undertaking, detracting from the usefulness of the directive.

22. That difference of opinion shows that, at the present stage of economic development, considerable uncertainty exists regarding the impact on the labour market of transfers of undertakings in the event of an employer's insolvency and the appropriate measures to be taken in order to ensure the best protection of the workers' interests.

23. It is apparent from the foregoing considerations that a serious risk of general deterioration in working and living conditions of workers, contrary to the social objectives of the Treaty, cannot be ruled out. It cannot therefore be concluded that Directive No. 77/187 imposes on the Member States the obligation to extend the rules laid down therein to transfers of undertakings, businesses or parts of businesses taking place

in the context of insolvency proceedings instituted with a view to the liquidation of the assets of the transferor under the supervision of the competent judicial authority.

24. It must nevertheless be made clear that, even though, in view of the considerations set out above, transfers of that kind do not fall within the scope of the above-mentioned directive, the Member States are at liberty independently to apply the principles of the directive, wholly or in part, on the basis of their national law alone.

The application of the directive to cases of 'surséance van betaling'

25. Although in this case the transfer of the undertaking was effected in liquidation proceedings, the question submitted by the national court relates also to the case of a transfer taking place in proceedings such as a 'surséance van betaling' (judicial leave to suspend payment of debts).

26. The parties disagree as to whether such a transfer must conform to the same rules, as far as the application of Directive No. 77/187 is concerned, as a transfer effected as a result of a sale by a liquidator. In that respect, the Netherlands Government and the Commission take the view that the reasons for not extending the scope of the directive to transfers of undertakings occurring in liquidation proceedings also militate against its application to a case where a court has given the transferor leave to suspend payment of debts.

27. On the other hand, the Bedrijfsvereniging and the Danish Government appear to consider that Directive No. 77/187 should apply where the transferor has obtained leave to suspend payment of debts, even if the directive is not applicable to a transfer effected in liquidation proceedings. Otherwise, leave to suspend payment of debts might be applied for specifically with a view to a transfer, to the detriment of the rights of the workers.

28. It is to be noted that proceedings such as those relating to a 'surséance van betaling' have certain features in common with liquidation proceedings, in particular inasmuch as the proceedings are, in both cases, of a judicial nature. They are, however, different from liquidation proceedings in so far as the supervision exercised by the Court over the commencement and the course of such proceedings is more limited. Moreover, the object of such proceedings is primarily to safeguard the assets of the insolvent undertaking and, where possible, to continue the business of the undertaking by means of a collective suspension of the payment of debts with a view to reaching a settlement which will ensure that the undertaking is able to continue operating in the future. If no such settlement is reached, proceedings of this kind may, as in the present case, lead to the debtor's being put into liquidation.

29. It follows that the reasons for not applying the directive to transfers of undertakings taking place in liquidation proceedings are not applicable to proceedings of this kind taking place at an earlier stage.

30. For all those reasons, the reply to the first question must be that Article 1(1) of Council Directive No. 77/187 of 14 February 1977 does not apply to the transfer of an undertaking, business or part of a business where the transferor has been adjudged insolvent and the undertaking or business in question forms part of the assets of the insolvent transferor, although the Member States are at liberty to apply the principles of the directive to such a transfer on their own initiative. The directive does, however, apply where an undertaking, business or part of a business is transferred to another employer in the course of a procedure such as a 'surséance van betaling'.

The second question
31. The second question is intended essentially to determine whether Article 3(1) of Directive No. 77/187 must be interpreted as extending to the obligations of a transferor resulting from an employment contract or employment relationship and arising prior to the date of the transfer.

32. The first subparagraph of Article 3(1) provides that: 'The transferor's rights and obligations arising from a contract of employment or from an employment relationship existing on the date of a transfer within the meaning of Article 1(1) shall, by reason of such transfer, be transferred to the transferee'. The second subparagraph states, however, that 'Member States may provide that, after the date of transfer within the meaning of Article 1(1) and in addition to the transferee, the transferor shall continue to be liable in respect of obligations which arose from a contract of employment or an employment relationship'.

33. The Bedrijfsvereniging and the Commission maintain that the provision in question covers all obligations attaching to the transferor by reason of a contract of employment or an employment relationship, including claims of workers already enforceable against the previous employment. That follows from the purpose of the directive, which is intended to protect workers and, more particularly, to safeguard their rights upon a change of employer.

34. On the other hand, the Netherlands Government considers that the provision must be interpreted as not entailing the transfer of debts arising before the transfer of the undertaking, since by virtue of a recognized principle of contract law a debtor cannot transfer his debts to a third party without the concurrence of his creditors. The national legislature is, however, free to declare the new employer to be liable for those debts, together with the old employer, in order to eliminate the risk to which workers might be exposed if the transferor disappeared after the transfer.

373

35. The Danish Government, for its part, distinguishes between the transfer of an undertaking following a normal sale, including cases where the payment of debts has been suspended, and the transfer of an undertaking by a liquidator. Whereas in the first case the transferee becomes subject to all the obligations of the transferor arising from an employment relationship, in the second case the transferee is not obliged to take over the existing liabilities attaching to the insolvent transferor by virtue of the legislation relating to insolvency.

36. It should be borne in mind that the first subparagraph of Article 3(1) of Directive No. 77/187 refers in general terms and unreservedly to the 'transferor's rights and obligations arising from a contract of employment or from an employment relationship existing on the date of a transfer'. The second subparagraph thereof, which authorizes the Member States to provide that the transferor is to continue to be liable 'after the date of the transfer', in addition to the transferee, indicates that it is the transferee who is primarily liable for bearing the burdens resulting from employees' rights existing at the time of the transfer.

37. That interpretation is confirmed by the fact that Article 3(3) expressly excludes from the scope of paragraph (1), the provision at issue, 'employees' rights to oldage, invalidity or survivors' benefits under supplementary company or intercompany pension schemes outside the statutory social security schemes in Member States'. The existence of such a specific clause, limiting the scope of the basic rule, leads to the conclusion that Article 3(1) relates to all the rights of employees which are not covered by that exception, whether those rights arose after or before the transfer of the undertaking.

38. The reply to the second question must therefore be that Article 3(1) of Directive No. 77/187 must be interpreted as covering obligations of the transferor resulting from a contract of employment or an employment relationship and arising before the date of the transfer, subject only to the exceptions provided for in Article 3(3).

Costs

39. The costs incurred by the Netherlands and Danish Governments and by the Commission of the European Communities, which have submitted observations to the Court, are not recoverable. Since these proceedings are, in so far as the parties to the main proceedings are concerned, in the nature of a step in the action before the national court, the decision on costs is a matter for that court.

On those grounds,

The Court,

in reply to the questions submitted to it by the Raad van Beroep, Zwolle, by order of 28 June 1983, hereby rules:

(1) **Article 1(1) of Council Directive No. 77/187/EEC of 14 February 1977 does not apply to the transfer of an undertaking, business or part of a business where the transferor has been adjudged insolvent and the undertaking or business in question forms part of the assets of the insolvent transferor, although the Member States are at liberty to apply the principles of the directive to such a transfer on their own initiative. The directive does, however, apply where an undertaking, business or part of a business is transferred to another employer in the course of a procedure such as a 'surséance van betaling' (judicial leave to suspend payment of debts).**

(2) **Article 3(1) of Directive No. 77/187 must be interpreted as covering obligations of the transferor resulting from a contract of employment or an employment relationship and arising before the date of the transfer, subject only to the exceptions provided for in Article 3(3).**

Mackenzie Stuart		Bosco	Due	Kakouris	
Koopmans	Everling	Bahlmann		Galmot	Joliet

Delivered in open court in Luxembourg on 7 February 1985.

P. Heim   A. J. Mackenzie Stuart
Registrar   *President*

Judgment of the Court

7 February 1985 – Case 179/83

Industriebond FNV and Federatie Nederlandse Vakbeweging (FNV)
v.
The Netherlands State*

Transfer of undertakings – safeguarding employees' rights – scope of Directive – transfer of an undertaking in liquidation excluded – transfer of undertaking in course of a procedure where a court grants leave to suspend payment of debts included (Council Directive 77/187/EEC, Article 1(1)).

In Case 179/83

Reference to the Court under Article 177 of the EEC Treaty by the President of the Arrondissementsrechtbank [District Court], The Hague, for a preliminary ruling in the proceedings pending before that court between

(1) Industriebond FNV, an incorporated association,
(2) Federatie Nederlandse Vakbeweging (FNV), an incorporated association,

and

The Netherlands State,

on the interpretation of Council Directive No. 77/187/EEC of 14 February 1977 on the approximation of the laws of the Member States relating to the safeguarding of employees' rights in the event of transfers of undertakings, business or parts of businesses (Official Journal 1977 L 61, p. 26),

THE COURT

composed of: Lord Mackenzie Stuart, President, G. Bosco, O. Due and C. Kakouris (Presidents of Chambers), T. Koopmans, U. Everling, K. Bahlmann, Y. Galmot and R. Joliet, Judges,

Advocate General: Sir Gordon Slynn
Registrar: H. A. Rühl, Principal Administrator

**

gives the following JUDGMENT

---

* – Lanugage of the Case: Dutch.
** after considering the observations submitted by the plaintif FNV by Mr S. de Laat, the Netherlands Government by Mr I. Verkade in the written proceedings, and by Mr A. Bos, acting as Agent, in the oral proceedings, the latter being assisted by Mr L. A. D. Keus, the Danish Government by Mr L. Mikaelsen, acting as Agent, the French Government by Mr G. Boivineau, acting as Agent, the Commission of the European Communities by Mr M. Beschel, acting as Agent, assisted by Mr F. Herbert, after hearing the Opinion of the Advocate General delivered at the sitting on 8 November 1984.

Decision

1. By order dated 16 August 1983, which was received at the Court on 19 August 1983, the President of the Arrondissementsrechtbank, The Hague, referred to the Court for a preliminary ruling under Article 177 of the EEC Treaty a question as to the interpretation of Article 1(1) of Council Directive No. 77/187/EEC of 14 February 1977 on the approximation of the laws of the Member States relating to the safeguarding of employees' rights in the event of transfers of undertakings, businesses or parts of businesses (Official Journal 1977 L 61, p. 26).

2. That question was raised in connection with an application for the adoption of interim measures made by Industriebond FNV and Federatie Nederlandse Vakbeweging against the Netherlands State, the purpose of which was to obtain an order 'annulling, rendering ineffective or declaring inapplicable the part of the circular from the Minister for Social Affairs and Employment of 17 May 1983 requesting Chief Inspectors and Directors for Employment to instruct the Directors of the Regional Employment Offices to disregard Article 1639(aa) *et seq.* of the Netherlands Civil Code when considering applications for permission to dismiss employees in the event of insolvency or "surséance van betaling" (judicial leave to suspend the payment of debts)'.

3. Articles 1639(aa) and 1639(bb) of the Netherlands Civil Code provide that upon the transfer of an undertaking, as defined in those provisions, 'the employer's rights and obligations resulting from a contract of employment between the employer and any of his employees on the date of the transfer shall pass by operation by law to the transferee of the undertaking. However, in addition to the transferee, the employer shall continue to be liable for a further year following the transfer in respect of any obligation which arose from the contract of employment before the date of the transfer.' Those provisions were introduced by the Law of 15 May 1981 in order to implement Council Directive No. 77/187 of 14 February 1977.

4. Directive No. 77/187, which was adopted by the Council on the basis of, in particular, Article 100 of the Treaty, is intended, in the terms of its preamble, 'to provide for the protection of employees in the event of a change of employer, in particular, to ensure that their rights are safeguarded'. For that purpose, Article 3(1) thereof provides that: 'The transferor's rights and obligations arising from a contract of employment or from an employment relationship existing on the date of a transfer ... shall, by reason of such transfer, be transferred to the transferee'. Article 4(1) provides for the protection of the workers concerned against dismissal by the transferor or the transferee, but does not stand in the way of 'dismissals that may take place for economic, technical or organizational reasons entailing changes in the work-force'. In addition, Article 6 of the directive requires the transferor and transferee to inform and consult the representatives of the workers affected by the transfer. Finally, Article 7 provides that the directive is not to 'affect the right of Member States to apply or introduce laws, regulations or administrative provisions which are more favourable to employees'.

5. Considering that the decision to be given depended on the interpretation of Directive No. 77/187, the President of the Arrondissementsrechtbank, The Hague, stayed the proceedings and submitted the following question to the Court for a preliminary ruling:

'Does the scope of Article 1 (1) of Directive No. 77/187/EEC extend to a situation in which the transferor of an undertaking is adjudged insolvent or is granted a "surséance van betaling"?'.

6. That question is identical to a question submitted in Case 135/83 (*Abels*), in which judgment has today been delivered.

7. In that judgment, the Court ruled that:

'Article 1 (1) of Council Directive No. 77/187/EEC of 14 February 1977 does not apply to the transfer of an undertaking, business or part of a business where the transferor has been adjudged insolvent and the undertaking or business in question forms part of the assets of the insolvent transferor, although the Member States are at liberty to apply the principles of the directive to such a transfer on their own initiative. The directive does, however, apply where an undertaking, business or part of a business is transferred to another employer in the course of a procedure such as a "surséance van betaling" (judicial leave to suspend payment of debts).'.

8. For the grounds of the ruling, reference should be made to the judgment in that case, the text of which is annexed to this judgment.

Costs

9. The costs incurred by the Netherlands and Danish Governments and by the Commission of the European Communities, which have submitted observations to the Court, are not recoverable. Since these proceedings are, in so far as the parties to the main proceedings are concerned, in the nature of a step in the action before the national court, the decision on costs is a matter for that court.

On those grounds,

THE COURT,

in answer to the question submitted to it by the President of the Arrondissementsrechtbank, The Hague, by order of 16 August 1983, hereby rules:

Article 1(1) of Council Directive No. 77/187/EEC of 14 February 1977 does not apply to the transfer of an undertaking, business or part of a business where the transferor has been adjudged insolvent and the undertaking or business in question forms part of the assets of the insolvent transferor, although the Member States are at liberty to apply the principles of the directive to such a transfer on their own initiative. The directive does, however, apply where an undertaking, business or part of a business is transferred to another employer in the course of a procedure such as a 'surséance van betaling' (judicial leave to suspend payment of debts).

Mackenzie Stuart   Bosco   Due   Kakouris
Koopmans   Everling   Bahlmann   Galmot   Joliet

Delivered in open court in Luxembourg on 7 February 1985.

P. Heim   A. J. Mackenzie Stuart
Registrar   *President*

Judgment of the Court

7 February 1985 – Case 186/83

Arie Botzen and Others
v.
Rotterdamsche Droogdok Maatschappij BV*

Transfer of undertakings – safeguarding employees' rights – scope of Directive – transfer of an undertaking in liquidation excluded – transfer of undertaking in course of a procedure where court grants leave to suspend payment of debts included – workers not employed in transferred part of undertaking excluded (Council Directive 77/187/EEC, Articles 1(1) and 3(1)).

in Case 186/83

REFERENCE to the Court under Article 177 of the EEC Treaty by the Kantonrechter [Cantonal Court], Rotterdam, for a preliminary ruling in the proceedings pending before that court between

Arie Botzen and Others

and

Rotterdamsche Droogdok Maatschappij BV

on the interpretation of Council Directive No. 77/187/EEC of 14 February 1977 on the approximation of the laws of the Member States relating to the safeguarding of employees' rights in the event of transfers of undertakings, businesses or parts of businesses (Official Journal 1977 L 61, p. 26),

THE COURT

composed of: Lord Mackenzie Stuart, President, G. Bosco, O. Due and C. Kakouris (Presidents of Chambers), T. Koopmans, U. Everling, K. Bahlmann, Y. Galmot and R. Joliet, Judges,

Advocate General: Sir Gordon Slynn
Registrar: H. A. Rühl, Principal Administrator

**

gives the following JUDGMENT

---

* – Language of the Case: Dutch.
** after considering the observations submitted on behalf of the plaintiffs A. Botzen and Others
by Mr S. de Laat, the defendant Rotterdamsche Droogdok Maatschappij by Mr A. F. de
Savornin Lohan and Mr A. J. Braakman, in the written proceedings, and by Mr E. W. J. H.
de Liagre Böhl and Mr A. J. Braakman, in the oral proceedings, the Netherlands
Government by Mr I. Verkade, in the written proceedings, and by Mr A. Bos, acting as
Agent, in the oral proceedings, the latter being assisted by Mr L. A. D. Keus, the Danish
Government by Mr L. Mikaelsen, acting as Agent, the French Government by Mr G.
Boivineau, acting as Agent, the Commission of the European Communities by Mr M.
Beschel, acting as Agent, assisted by Mr F. Herbert, after hearing the Opinions of the
Advocate General delivered at the sitting on 16 January 1985.

Decision

1. By judgment of 25 August 1983, which was received at the Court on
   1 September 1983, the Kantonrechter, Rotterdam, referred to the Court
   for a preliminary ruling under Article 177 of the EEC Treaty three
   questions as to the interpretation of certain provisions of Council Directive No. 77/187 of 14 February 1977 on the approximation of the laws of
   the Member States relating to the safeguarding of employees' rights in
   the event of transfers of undertakings, business or parts of businesses
   (Official Journal 1977 L 61, p. 26).

2. Those questions were raised in proceedings instituted by Arie Botzen and
   Others against Rotterdamsche Droogdok Maatschappij BV.

3. The plaintiffs in the main proceedings were employees of Rotterdamsche
   Droogdok Maatschappij Heijplaat BV (hereinafter referred to as 'the old
   RDM'), which was declared insolvent by judgment of 6 April 1983. In
   order to avoid total liquidation of that undertaking and with a view of
   safeguarding as large a proportion as possible of the jobs, a new company, Rotterdamsche Droogdok Maatschappij BV (hereinafter referred
   to as 'the new RDM') was constituted on 30 March 1983.

4. On 7 April 1983, an agreement was concluded between the old RDM
   and the new RDM. Under that agreement, the new RDM took over
   certain departments of the old RDM and all the staff assigned thereto,
   and in addition took over a number of employees of the departments
   not transferred to it, namely the general and administrative departments. However, the other workers, including the plaintiffs in the main
   proceedings, were dismissed by the liquidators of the old RDM.

380

5. Considering their dismissal to be invalid on the ground that they had *ipso jure* entered the service of the new RDM on the date of the transfer, the plaintiffs in the main proceedings brought an action against the new RDM before the Kantonrechter, Rotterdam, seeking payment of the salary due from 7 April 1983 until such time as their employment relationship might be terminated. They also requested, as an interim measure, that the new RDM should be ordered to pay them, as from 7 April 1983, or, in the alternative, as from the date of the decision to be given, a monthly amount equivalent to their salary and to allow them to carry out their usual work. In support of their action, they claimed that the transaction at issue was to be regarded as a transfer of a business or part of a business within the meaning of Articles 1639aa and 1639bb of the Netherlands Civil Code, introduced by the Law of 15 May 1981 for the purpose of implementing Council Directive No. 77/187 of 14 February 1977.

6. Directive No. 77/187, which was adopted by the Council on the basis of, in particular, Article 100 of the Treaty, is intended, in the terms of its preamble, 'to provide for the protection of employees in the event of a change of employers, in particular, to ensure that their rights are safeguarded'. For that purpose, Article 3(1) thereof provides that: 'The transferor's rights and obligations arising from a contract of employment or from an employment relationship existing on the date of a transfer ... shall, by reason of such transfer, be transferred to the transferee.' Article 4(1) provides for the protection of the workers concerned against dismissal by the transferor or the transferee, but does not stand in the way of 'dismissals that may take place for economic, technical or organizational reasons entailing changes in the work-force'. In addition, Article 6 of the directive requires the transferor and the transferee to inform and consult the representatives of the workers affected by the transfer. Finally, Article 7 provides that the directive is not to 'affect the right of Member States to apply or introduce laws, regulations or administrative provisions which are more favourable to employees'.

7. Considering that the decision to be given depended on the interpretation of Directive No. 77/187, the Kantonrechter, Rotterdam, stayed the proceedings and submitted the following questions to the Court of a preliminary ruling:

'(1) Does the scope of Article 1 (1) of Directive No. 77/187/EEC extend to a situation in which the transferor of an undertaking is adjudged insolvent or is granted a "surséance van betaling" [judicial leave to suspend payment of debts]?
(2) Does the scope of the directive extend to the rights conferred upon and the obligations imposed upon the transferor by contracts of employment which exist at the date of transfer and which are made with employees whose duties are

not performed exclusively with the aid of assets which belong to the transferred part of the undertaking?

(3) Does the scope of the directive extend to the rights conferred upon and the obligations imposed upon the transferor by contracts of employment which exist at the time of transfer and which are made with employees who are employed in an administrative department of the undertaking (for example, general management services, personnel matters, etc.), where that administrative department carried out duties for the benefit of the transferred part of the undertaking but has not itself been transferred?'.

The first question

8. The first question is identical to a question submitted in Case 135/83 (*Abels*), in which judgment has today been delivered.

9. In that judgment, the Court ruled, with respect to that question, that:

'Article 1 (1) of Council Directive No. 77/187/EEC of 14 February 1977 does not apply to the transfer of an undertaking, business or part of a business where the transfer has been adjudged insolvent and the undertaking or business in question forms part of the assets of the insolvent transferor, although the Member States are at liberty to apply the principles of the directive to such a transfer on their own initiative. The directive does, however, apply where an undertaking, business or part of a business is transferred to another employer in the course of a procedure such as a "surséance van betaling" (judicial leave to suspend payment of debts).'.

10. For the grounds of that ruling, reference should be made to the judgment in that case, the text of which is annexed to this judgment.

The second and third questions

11. The second and third questions are essentially intended to ascertain whether Article 3(1) of Directive No. 77/187 must be interpreted as extending to a transferor's rights and obligations arising from a contract of employment or employment relationship existing on the date of the transfer and entered into with employees who, although not belonging to the part of the undertaking which was transferred, carry on certain activities using the assets assigned to the transferred part, or who, being assigned to an administrative department of the undertaking which was not itself transferred, carried out certain duties for the benefit of the transferred part of the undertaking.

12. Article 3(1) provides that: 'The transferor's rights and obligations arising from a contract of employment or from an employment relationship existing on the date of a tranfer within the meaning of Article 1(1) shall, by reason of such transfer, be transferred to the transferee'.

13. In that connection, Rotterdamsche Droogdok Maatschappij claims that only employees working full-time or substantially full-time in the transferred part of the undertaking are covered by the transfer of employment relationships, to the exclusion of those engaged in partial tasks in various businesses or parts of businesses and those who, although working for several businesses or parts of businesses, form part of the remaining staff.

14. On the other hand, the Commission considers that the only decisive criterion regarding the transfer of employees' rights and obligations is whether or not a transfer takes place of the department to which they were assigned and which formed the organizational framework within which their employment relationship took effect.

15. The Commission's view must be upheld. An employment relationship is essentially characterized by the link existing between the employee and the part of the undertaking or business to which he is assigned to carry out his duties. In order to decide whether the rights and obligations under an employment relationship are transferred under Directive No. 77/187 by reason of a transfer within the meaning of Article 1(1) thereof, it is therefore sufficient to establish to which part of the undertaking or business the employee was assigned.

16. The answer to the second and third questions must therefore be that Article 3(1) of Directive No. 77/187 must be interpreted as not covering the transferor's rights and obligations arising from a contract of employment or an employment relationship existing on the date of the transfer and entered into with employees who, although not employed in the transferred part of the undertaking, performed certain duties which involved the use of assets assigned to the part transferred or who, whilst being employed in an administrative department of the undertaking which has not itself been transferred, carried out certain duties for the benefit of the part transferred.

Costs

17. The costs incurred by the Netherlands and Danish Governments and by the Commission of the European Communities, which have submitted observations to the Court, are not recoverable. Since these proceedings are, in so far as the parties to the main proceedings are concerned, in the nature of a step in the action before the national court, the decision on costs is a matter for that court.

On those grounds,

THE COURT,

in reply to the questions submitted to it by the Kantonrechter, Rotterdam, by judgment of 25 August 1983, hereby rules:

383

(1) Article 1(1) of Council Directive No. 77/187/EEC of 14 February 1977 does not apply to the transfer of an undertaking, business or part of a business where the transferor has been adjudged insolvent and the undertaking or business in question forms part of the assets of the insolvent transferor, although the Member States are at liberty to apply the principles of the directive to such a transfer on their own initiative. The directive does, however, apply where an undertaking, business or part of a business is transferred to another employer in the course of a procedure such as a 'surséance van betaling' (judicial leave to suspend payment of debts).

(2) Article 3(1) of Directive No. 77/187/EEC must be interpreted as not covering the transferor's rights and obligations arising from a contract of employment or an employment relationship existing on the date of the transfer and entered into with employees who, although not employed in the transferred part of the undertaking, performed certain duties which involved the use of assets assigned to the part transferred or who, whilst being employed in an administrative department of the undertaking which has not itself been transferred, carried out certain duties for the benefit of the part transferred.

| Mackenzie Stuart | | Bosco | Due | Kakouris | |
| Koopmans | Everling | Bahlmann | | Galmot | Joliet |

Delivered in open court in Luxembourg on 7 February 1985.

P. Heim   A. J. Mackenzie Stuart
Registrar   *President*

Judgment of the Court

7 February 1985 Case 19/83

Knud Wendelboe and Others
v.
L. J. Music ApS, in liquidation

Transfer of undertakings – safeguarding employees' rights – transferee's obligations concerning holiday pay and compensation – Member States not required to enact provisions for transferee to be liable for holiday pay and compensation obligations for employees who were not employed on the date of transfer – existence of contracts of employment on date of transfer to be established according to national law (Council Directive 77/187/EEC, Articles 3(1) and 4(1)).

In Case 19/83

REFERENCE to the Court under Article 177 of the EEC Treaty by the Vestre Landsret [Western Division of the Danish High Court] for a preliminary ruling in the proceedings pending before that court between

(1) **Knud Wendelboe,**
(2) **Foreningen af Arbejdsledere i Danmark [Association of Supervisory Staff, Denmark]**, acting on behalf of Ib Jensen,
(3) **Handels- og Kontorfunktionærernes Forbund i Danmark [Union of Commercial and Clerical Employees, Denmark]**, acting on behalf of Jørn Holst Jeppesen,

and

L. J. Music ApS, in liquidation,

on the interpretation of Council Directive No 77/187/EEC of 14 February 1977 on the approximation of the laws of the Member States relating to the safeguarding of employees' rights in the event of transfers of undertakings, business or parts of business (Official Journal 1977 L 61, p. 26),

THE COURT

composed of: Lord Mackenzie Stuart, President, G. Bosco, O. Due and C. Kakouris (Presidents of Chambers), T. Koopmans, U. Everling, K. Bahlmann, Y. Galmot and R. Joliet, Judges,

Advocate General: Sir Gordon Slynn
Registrar: H. A. Rühl, Principal Administrator

*

gives the following JUDGMENT

---

* after considering the observations submitted on behalf of the plaintiff Wendelboe by Mr J. Glusted Madsen, the plaintiffs Foreningen af Arbejdsledere i Danmark and Handels- og Kontorfunktionaererenes Forbund i Danmark by Mr L. Svenning Andersen, the Danish Government by Mr L. Mikaelsen, acting as Agent, the Netherlands Government by Mr I. Verkade, acting as Agent, the French Government by Mr J.-P. Costes, in the written proceedings, and by Mr G. Boivineau, in the oral proceedings, both acting as Agents, the United Kingdom by Mr R. N. Ricks, acting as Agent, the Commission of the European Communities by Mr H. P. Hartvig, acting as Agent, after hearing the Opinion of the Advocate General delivered at the sitting on 8 November 1984.

Decision

1. By order of 3 February 1983, which was received at the Court on 7 February 1983, the Vestre Landsret [Western Division of the Danish

385

High Court] referred to the Court for a preliminary ruling under Article 177 of the EEC Treaty a questions as to the interpretation of certain provisions of Council Directive No 77/187 of 14 February 1977 on the approximation of the laws of the Member States relating to the safeguarding of employees' rights in the event of transfers of undertakings, businesses or parts of businesses (Official Journal 1977 L 61, p. 26).

2. That question was raised in proceedings instituted by Knud Wendelboe, by the Forening af Arbejdsledere i Danmark [Association of Supervisory Staff, Denmark], acting on behalf of Ib Jensen, and by the Handels- og Kontorfunktionærernes Forbund i Danmark [Union of Commercial and Clerical Employees, Denmark], acting on behalf of Jorn Holst Jeppesen, against L. J. Music ApS, a company in liquidation.

3. Messrs Wendelboe, Jensen and Jeppesen were employed by L. J. Music ApS, whose business consisted in making cassette recordings. On 28 February 1980, faced with impending insolvency, L. J. Music ApS ceased production and dismissed the majority of its work-force, including the plaintiffs in the main proceedings, who were informed that they would not be required to work out their notice.

4. By order of 4 March 1980, the Skifteret [Bankruptcy Court], Hjørring, declared L. J. Music ApS involvent. On the same day, in the course of the hearing at which the company was declared insolvent, the Skifteret, having notice of an offer to buy the undertaking made by the company SPKR No. 534 ApS, authorized that company to use the insolvent undertaking's premises and equipment as from 5 March 1980. The final agreement on the transfer was concluded on 27 March 1980, but in that agreement it was stated that the company's business was deemed to have been carried on on behalf, and at the risk, of the transferee as from 4 March 1980.

5. On 6 March, Messrs Wendelboe, Jensen and Jeppesen were engaged by the new company; they were paid a higher salary by the company but lose their seniority.

6. The plaintiffs in the main proceedings then brought an action against L. J. Music ApS before the Skifteret, Hjørring, for a declaration that they were entitled, as preferential creditors, to compensation for unlawful dismissal and holiday pay.

7. In judgments of 29 September 1980, the Skifteret, although upholding the claim relating to holiday pay, dismissed the claim for compensation for unlawful dismissal on the ground that the transferor of the undertaking was discharged, after the transfer, from his obligations towards his employees, since those obligations had been transferred to the transferee pursuant to Article 2(1) of Danish Law No. 111 of 21 March 1979 on the Rights of Employees on the Transfer of Undertakings. That Law had

been adopted in order to implement Council Directive No. 77/187 of 14 February 1977.

8. That directive, which was adopted on the basis, in particular, of Article 100 of the Treaty, is intended, according to its preamble, to provide for 'the protection of employees in the event of a change of employer, in particular, to ensure that their rights are safeguarded'. For that purpose, Article 3(1) thereof provides that 'the transferor's rights and obligations arising from the contract of employment or from an employment relationship existing on the date of a transfer . . . shall, by reason of such transfer, be transferred to the transferee'. Article 4(1) provides for protection of the employees concerned against dismissal by the transferor or the transferee, but does not stand in the way of 'dismissals that may take place for economic, technical or organizational reasons entailing changes in the work-force'. Moreover, Article 6 of the directive requires the transferor and the transferee to inform and consult the representatives of the employee affected by the transfer. Finally, Article 7 states that the directive is not to 'affect the right of Member States to apply or introduce . . . provisions which are more favourable to employees'.

9. The plaintiffs in the main proceedings appealed against the judgments of the Skifteret to the Vestre Landsret, which, considering that the decision to be given depended on the interpretation of Directive No. 77/187, stayed the proceedings and submitted the folllowing question to the Court for a preliminary ruling:

> 'Does the Council directive of 14 February 1977 on the approximation of the laws of the Member States relating to the safeguarding of employees' rights in the event of transfers of undertakings, businesses or parts of businesses require the Member States to enact provisions under which the transferee of an undertaking becomes liable in respect of obligations concerning holiday pay and compensation to employees who were not employed in the undertaking on the date of transfer?'.

The applicability of Directive No. 77/187 in cases of insolvency

10. Since the transfer of the undertaking in question took place in liquidation proceedings, it must be noted in the first place that, as the Court held in its judgment delivered today in Case 135/83 (*Abels*):

> 'Article 1(1) of Council Directive No. 77/187/EEC of 14 February 1977 does not apply to the transfer of an undertaking, business or part of a business where the transferor has been adjudged insolvent and the undertaking or business in question forms part of the assets of the insolvent transferor, although the Member States are at liberty to apply the principles of the

directive to such a transfer on their own initiative. The directive does, however, apply where an undertaking, business or part of a business is transferred to another employer in the course of a procedure such as a "surséance van betaling" (judicial leave to suspend payment of debts).'.

11. In this case, it is apparent from the grounds of the order for reference that the Vestre Landsret seeks an interpretation of Directive No 77/187 so that it will be in a position to interpret and apply its national law in conformity with the principles laid down in that directive. It is therefore appropriate, in pursuance of the cooperation between national courts and this Court provided for in Article 177, to reply to the question submitted in such a manner as to enable the national court to apply the principles of that directive where national legislation has made them applicable to cases of insolvency.

The question submitted for a preliminary ruling
12. It should be noted in the first place that Article 3(1) of Directive No. 77/187 provides that: 'The transferor's rights and obligations arising from a contract of employment or from an employment relationship existing on the date of a transfer ... shall, by reason of such transfer, be transferred to the transferee'.

13. It follows from a textual interpretation of that provision in the various language versions that it refers only to the rights and obligations of workers whose contract of employment or employment relationship is in force on the date of the transfer and not to those who have ceased to be employed by the undertaking in question at the time of the transfer. This is apparent from the fact that in the Dutch, French, German, Greek and Italian versions the phrase 'existing on the date of the transfer' relates unequivocally to the expression 'contract of employment or ... employment relationship' and that, in the English and Danish language versions, the same interpretation is in any event possible.

14. That interpretation is confirmed by comparison of Article 3(1) with Article 3(3); the latter provision, which relates to certain old-age, invalidity and survivors' benefits, makes an express distinction between 'employees' and 'persons no longer employed in the transferor's business at the time of the transfer'. The fact that no such distinction is drawn in Article 3(1) indicates that former employees are excluded therefrom.

15. That interpretation of the scope of Article 3(1) is also in conformity with the scheme and the purposes of the directive, which is intended to ensure, as far as possible, that the employment relationship continues unchanged with the transferee, in particular by obliging the transferee to continue to observe the terms and conditions of any collective agreement (Article

3(2)) and by protecting workers against dismissals motivated solely by the fact of the transfer (Article 4 (1)). Those provisions relate only to employees in the service of the undertaking on the date of the transfer, to the exclusion of those who have already left the undertaking on that date.

16. The existence or otherwise of a contract of employment or an employment relationship on the date of the transfer within the meaning of Article 3(1) of the directive must be established on the basis of the rules of national law, subject however to observance of the mandatory provisions of the directive and, more particularly, Article 4(1) thereof, concerning the protection of employees against dismissal by the transferor or the transferee by reason of the transfer. It is for the national court to decide, on the basis of those factors, whether or not, on the date of the transfer, the employees in question were linked to the undertaking by virtue of a contract of employment or employment relationship.

17. For all those reasons, it is necessary to state in reply to the question submitted that Council Directive No. 77/187 of 14 February 1977 does not require the Member States to enact provisions under which the transferee of an undertaking becomes liable in respect of obligations concerning holiday pay and compensation to employees who were not employed in the undertaking on the date of the transfer.

Costs
18. The costs incurred by the Danish, United Kingdom, French and Netherlands Governments and by the Commission of the European Communities, which have submitted observations to the Court, are not recoverable. As these proceedings are, in so far as the parties to the main proceedings are concerned, in the nature of a step in the action before the national court, the decision on costs is a matter for that court.

On those grounds,

THE COURT,

in reply to the questions submitted to it by the Vestre Landsret, by order of 3 February 1983, hereby rules:

Council Directive No. 77/187/EEC of 14 February 1977 does not require the Member States to enact provisions under which the transferee of an undertaking becomes liable in respect of obligations concerning holiday pay and compensation to employees who were not employed in the undertaking on the date of the transfer.

Mackenzie Stuart		Bosco	Due	Kakouris	
Koopmans	Everling	Bahlmann		Galmot	Joliet

389

Delivered in open court in Luxembourg on 7 February 1985.

P. Heim
Registrar

A. J. Mackenzie Stuart
President

Judgment of the Court

11 July 1985 – Case 105/84

Foreningen af Arbejdsledere i Danmark
v.
A/S Danmols Inventar, in liquidation

Transfer of undertakings – safeguarding employees' rights – scope of Directive – transfer of an undertaking in liquidation excluded – transfer of undertaking after suspension of payment of debts included – employees who by their own decision do not work as employees of the transferee not covered – meaning of employee to be determined by reference to national law (Council Directive 77/187/EEC, Articles 1(1) and 3(1)).

In Case 105/84

REFERENCE to the Court under Article 177 of the EEC Treaty by the Vestre Landsret [Western Division of the Danish High Court] for a preliminary ruling in the proceedings pending before that court between

Foreningen af Arbejdsledere i Danmark [Association of Supervisory Staff, Denmark], acting on behalf of Hans Erik Mikkelsen,

and

Danmols Inventar A/S, in liquidation,

on the intepretation of Council Directive No. 77/187/EEC of 14 February 1977, on the approximation of the laws of the Member States relating to the safeguarding of employees' rights in the event of transfers of undertakings, businesses or parts of businesses (Official Journal 1977 No. L 61, p. 26),

THE COURT (FIFTH CHAMBER)

composed of: Lord Mackenzie Stuart, President, O. Due (President of Chamber), U. Everling, Y. Galmot and R. Joliet, Judges,

Advocate General: Sir Gordon Slynn
Registrar: H. A. Rühl, Principal Administrator,

after considering the observations submitted on behalf of

Foreningen af Arbejdsledere i Danmark, by L. Svenning Andersen,

Danmols Inventar A/S, in liquidation, by Mr Søgaard-Christensen,

the Commission of the European Communities, by H. P. Hartvig and J. F. Buhl,

after hearing the Opinion of the Advocate General delivered at the sitting on 30 April 1985,

gives the following JUDGMENT

Decision

1. By a request dated 10 April 1984, which was received at the Court on 16 April 1984, the Vestre Landsret [Western Division of the Danish High Court] referred to the Court for a preliminary ruling under Article 177 of the EEC Treaty two questions concerning the interpretation of Council Directive No. 77/187/EEC of 14 February 1977 on the approximation of the laws of the Member States relating to the safeguarding of employees' rights in the event of transfers of undertakings, businesses or parts of businesses (Official Journal 1977 No. L 61, p. 26).

2. Those questions were raised in proceedings instituted by the Foreningen af Arbejdsledere i Danmark, acting on behalf of Hans Erik Mikkelsen, against Danmols Inventar A/S, a company in liquidation.

3. Mr Mikkelsen was employed by Danmols Inventar A/S as works foreman. On 3 September 1981 that company announced that it was suspending payment of its debts and dismissed Mr Mikkelsen with effect from 31 December 1981.

4. With effect from 19 October 1981, the undertaking was transferred to Danmols Inventar – og Møbelfabrik A/S, a company in formation, of which Mr Mikkelsen became a co-owner, acquiring a 33 per cent shareholding and 50 per cent of the voting rights at the General Meeting; in addition he was appointed Chairman of the Board of Directors. He continued to carry out his duties at works foreman in the new company, doing the same work and receiving the same salary as prior to the transfer.

5. On 2 December 1981 Danmols Inventar A/S was adjudged insolvent, whereupon Mikkelsen filed a claim against the company for compensation corresponding to two months' pay, from 1 November to 31 December 1981, for the premature termination of his employment contract, and for holiday pay for the period from 1 January to 31 October 1981.

391

6. By a judgment of 6 September 1982 the bankruptcy court ruled that Mikkelsen had no claim against the company because, 'in the light of the background to the Law on the transfer of undertakings and, in particular, the EEC directive on which it is based and the explanatory memorandum to the bill, Article 2 of the Law must be interpreted to the effect that the transferor of the undertaking is released from all his obligations towards the employees of the undertaking since all those obligations are transferred to the transferee.' The Danish Law in question, namely Law No. 111 of 21 March 1979 on the rights of employees on the transfer of undertakings, was adopted in order to implement Council Directive No. 77/187 of 14 February 1977.

7. That directive, which was adopted on the basis of, in particular, Article 100 of the Treaty, is intended, according to its preamble, 'to provide for the protection of employees in the event of a change of employer, in particular, to ensure that their rights are safeguarded'. To that end, Article 3(1) provides for the transfer of the transferor's rights and obligations arising from a contract of employment or from an employment relationship. Article 4(1) provides for the protection of the workers concerned against dismissal by the transferor or the transferee where the dismissal is due solely to the transfer. In addition, Article 6 of the directive requires the transferor and the transferee to inform and consult the representatives of the workers affected by the transfer. Finally, Article 7 provides that the directive is not to 'affect the right of Member States to apply or introduce laws, regulations or administrative provisions which are more favourable to employees'.

8. On appeal the case came before the Vestre Landsret, which took the view that its decision depended upon the interpretation to be given to Directive No. 77/187. It therefore stayed the proceedings and referred the case to the Court for a preliminary ruling on the following questions:

'Must the expression "employee" in Council Directive No. 77/187/EEC of 14 February 1977 on the approximation of the laws of the Member States relating to the safeguarding of employees' rights in the event of transfers of undertakings, businesses or parts of businesses be interpreted to mean that it is sufficient for the person concerned to have been an employee of the transferor or must he also occupy a position as employee with the transferee?

If the Court takes the view that the person concerned must also be an employee of the transferee, does the expression "employee" contained in the directive cover a person who has a 50 per cent interest in the company in question?'.

The applicability of Directive No. 77/187 where an undertaking suspends payment of its debts

9. Since the transfer of the undertaking in question took place after the transferor had announced that it was suspending payment of its debts but before it was adjudged insolvent, it is appropriate to refer in the first place to the judgment of 7 February 1985 (Case 135/83, *Abels*, [1985] ECR 479), in which the Court held that:

> 'Article 1(1) of Council Directive No. 77/187/EEC of 14 February 1977 does not apply to the transfer of an undertaking, business or part of a business where the transferor has been adjudged insolvent and the undertaking or business in question forms part of the assets of the involvent transferor, although the Member States are at liberty to apply the principles of the directive to such a transfer on their own initiative. The directive does, however, apply where an undertaking, business or part of a business is transferred to another employer in the course of a procedure such as a "surséance van betaling" (judicial leave to suspend the payment of debts.)'.

10. It follows that the mere fact that the transfer of an undertaking, business or part of a business has occurred after the transferor has suspended payment of its debts is not enough to exclude the said transactions from the scope of Directive No. 77/187. It therefore applies to a transfer as defined in Article 1(1) which is effected in the course of a procedure or at a stage prior to the commencement of liquidation proceedings.

The first question
11. By the first question the Vestre Landsret asks essentially whether Article 3(1) of Council Directive No. 77/187 of 14 February 1977 must be interpreted as applying also to the transfer of the rights and obligations of persons who were employed by the transferor at the date of the transfer but who do not continue to work as employees of the transferee.

12. The parties to the main proceedings and the Commission suggest that question should be answered in the negative. That follows both from a linguistic interpretation of the provision and from an interpretation based on the objectives of the directive. The actual wording of the provision in question shows that it applies only where there is a change of employer, in other words where the person concerned continues as an employee of the transferee. That conclusion is in their view supported by reference to the aim of the directive, which is to ensure the continuity of the employment relationship of the employee vis-à-vis the person acquiring the undertaking.

13. It must be noted that, according to the first subparagraph of Article 3(1) of the directive, 'the transferor's rights and obligations arising from a contract of employment or from an employment relationship existing on the date of a transfer within the meaning of Article 1(1) shall, by reason

393

by such transfer, be transferred to the transferee'. The second subparagraph states however that 'Member States may provide that, after the date of transfer within the meaning of Article 1(1) and in addition to the transferee, the transferor shall continue to be liable in respect of obligations which arose from a contract of employment or an employment relationship'. Moreover, according to Article 3(2) 'the transferee shall continue to observe the terms and conditions agreed in any collective agreement on the same terms applicable to the transferor under that agreement, until the date of termination or expiry of the collective agreement or the entry into force or application of another collective agreement'.

14. In this connexion it is also necessary to refer to Article 4(1) of Directive No. 77/187, which provides that 'the transfer of an undertaking, business or part of a business shall not in itself constitute grounds for dismissal by the transferor or the transferee'. However, that provision is not to 'stand in the way of dismissals that may take place for economic, technical or organizational reasons entailing changes in the work-force'.

15. Taken together those provisions show that the directive is intended to safeguard the rights of workers in the event of a change of employer by making it possible for them to continue to work for the transferee under the same conditions as those agreed with the transferor. As the Court stated in its judgment of 7 Feburary 1985 (Case 19/83, *Wendelboe* [1985] ECR 457), it is intended to ensure, as far as possible, that the employment relationship continues unchanged with the transferee, in particular by obliging the transferee to continue to observe the terms and conditions of any collective agreement Article 3(2)) and by protecting workers against dismissals motivated solely by the fact of transfer (Article 4(1)).

16. The protection which the directive is intended to guarantee is however redundant where the person concerned decides of his own accord not to continue the employment relationship with the new employer after the transfer. That is the case where the employee in question terminates the employment contract or employment relationship of his own free will with effect from the date of the transfer, or where that contract or relationship is terminated with effect from the date of the transfer by virtue of an agreement voluntarily concluded between the worker and the transferor or the transferee of the undertaking. In that situation Article 3(1) of the directive does not apply.

17. For those reasons it must be held in reply to the first question that Article 3(1) of Council Directive No. 77/187 of 14 February 1977 must be construed as not covering the transfer of the rights and obligations of persons who were employed by the transferor at the date of the transfer, but who, by their own decision, do not continue to work as employees of the transferee.

18. The second question concerns the meaning of the term 'employee' in Directive No. 77/187.

19. By that question the Vestre Landsret seeks to establish whether or not a person who holds a large stake in a company and who is also the Chairman of its Board of Directors may be regarded as 'an employee' of that company within the meaning of the directive.

20. In that regard the plaintiff in the main proceedings claims that the term 'employee' means a person who works for an employer and is subject to the instructions and orders of that employer. That does not apply to a person who carries out work for a company in which he holds a large percentage of the shares.

21. The defendant in the main proceedings, on the other hand, maintains that the term 'employee' within the meaning of Directive No. 77/187 does extend to a person who holds shares in, or is a member of the Board of Directors of, the company by which he is employed, provided that he does not occupy a dominant position on that Board.

22. The Commission observes in the first place that it is necessary to establish a Community definition of the term 'employee' within the meaning of Directive No. 77/187. It takes the view that the term covers any person who in return for remuneration carries out work on behalf of, and as the subordinate party in a relationship with, another person. That definition does not mean that a person cannot be regarded as an employee within the meaning of the directive because he possesses a certain, or even a substantial, shareholding in the undertaking. On the other hand, the directive does not apply where the person's position in the undertaking is such that he is no longer the subordinate party in an employment relationship.

23. It is common ground that Directive No. 77/187 does not contain an express definition of the term 'employee'. In order to establish its meaning it is necessary to apply generally recognized principles of interpretation by referring in the first place to the ordinary meaning to be attributed to that term in its context and by obtaining such guidance as may be derived from Community texts and from concepts common to the legal systems of the Member States.

24. It may be recalled that the Court, *inter alia* in its judgment of 23 March 1982 (Case 53/81, *Levin*, [1982] ECR 1035), held that the term 'worker',[1] as used in the Treaty, may not be defined by reference to the national

---

1. **Translator's note:** It will be noted that the English-language version of Directive No. 77/87 uses a different word ('employee') from that used in the Treaty ('worker'). In other language versions the same word is used in both texts.

laws of the Member States but has a Community meaning. If that were not the case, the Community rules on freedom of movement for workers would be frustrated, since the meaning of the term could be decided upon and modified unilaterally, without any control by the Community institutions, by the Member States, which would thus be able to exclude at will certain categories of persons from the benefit of the Treaty.

25. It is necessary to consider whether similar considerations apply to the definition of the term 'employee' in the context of Directive No. 77/187. According to its preamble, the directive is intended to ensure that employees' rights are safeguarded in the event of a change of employer by providing for, *inter alia*, the transfer from the transferor to the transferee of the employees' rights arising from a contract of employment or from an employment relationship (Article 3) and by protecting employees against dismissals motivated solely by the fact of the transfer of the undertaking (Article 4).

26. It is clear from those provisions that Directive No. 77/187 is intended to achieve only partial harmonization essentially by extending the protection guaranteed to workers independently by the laws of the individual Member States to cover the case where an undertaking is transferred. Its aim is therefore to ensure, as far as possible, that the contract of employment or the employment relationship continues unchanged with the transferee so that the employees affected by the transfer of the undertaking are not placed in a less favourable position solely as a result of the transfer. It is not however intended to establish a uniform level of protection throughout the Community on the basis of common criteria.

27. It follows that Directive No. 77/187 may be relied upon only by persons who are, in one way or another, protected as employees under the law of the Member State concerned. If they are so protected, the directive ensures that their rights arising from a contract of employment or an employment relationship are not diminished as a result of the transfer.

28. In reply to the second question it must therefore be held that the term 'employee' within the meaning of Directive No. 77/187 must be interpreted as covering any person who, in the Member State concerned, is protected as an employee under national employment law. It is for the national court to establish whether that is the case in this instance.

Costs
29. The costs incurred by the Commission of the European Communities, which has submitted observations to the Court, are not recoverable. As these proceedings are, in so far as the parties to the main proceedings are concerned, in the nature of a step in the proceedings before the national court, the decision on costs is a matter for that court.

On those grounds,

THE COURT (FIFTH CHAMBER),

in answer to the questions referred to it by the Vestre Landsret by a request of 10 April 1984, hereby rules:

1. Article 3(1) of Council Directive No. 77/187 of 14 February 1977 must be construed as not covering the transfer of the rights and obligations of persons who were employed by the transferor at the date of the transfer, but who, by their own decision, do not continue to work as employees of the transferee.

2. The expression 'employee' within the meaning of Directive No. 77/187 must be interpreted as covering any person who, in the Member State concerned, is protected as an employee under national employment law. It is for the national court to establish whether that is the case in this instance.

Mackenzie Stuart   Due   Everling

Galmot   Joliet

Delivered in open court in Luxembourg on 11 July 1985.

P. Heim   A. J. Mackenzie Stuart
Registrar   *President*

Judgment of the Court

18 March 1986 – Case 24/85

Jozef Maria Antonius Spijkers
v.
Gebroeders Benedik Abattoir C. V. & Alfred Benedik en Zonen B. V.

Transfer of undertakings – safeguarding employees' rights – scope of Directive – criterion for establishing whether there is a transfer for the purposes of the Directive is whether the business retains its identity – a transfer does not occur merely because the assets are disposed of – necessary to consider whether, having regard to all the facts of the transaction, the business was disposed of as a going concern – a going concern would be indicated, for example, where the operation was continued or resumed by the new employer with the same or similar activities (Council Directive 77/187/EEC, Article 1(1)).

In Case 24/85

REFERENCE to the Court under Article 177 of the EEC Treaty by the Hoge

Raad der Nederlanden [Supreme Court of the Netherlands] for a preliminary ruling in the proceedings pending before the court between

Jozef Maria Antonius Spijkers

and

1. Gebroeders Benedik Abattoir C. V.
2. Alfred Benedik en Zonen B. V.,

on the interpretation of Council Directive No. 77/187/EEC of 14 February 1977 on the approximation of the laws of the Member States relating to the safeguarding of employees' rights in the event of transfers of undertakings, businesses or parts of businesses (Official Journal 1977 No. L 61, p. 26),

The Court (Fifth Chamber)

composed of: U. Everling, President of Chamber, R. Joliet, O. Due, Y. Galmot and C. N. Kakouris, Judges,

Advocate General: Sir Gordon Slynn
Registrar: H. A. Rühl, Principal Administrator,

after considering the observations submitted on behalf of

Jozef Maria Antonius Spijkers, by J. Groen and J. A. Van Veen, Advocaten at The Hague,

the Netherlands Government, by I. Verkade, Secretary-General at the Ministry of Foreign Affairs,

The United Kingdom, by S. J. Hay, of the Treasury Solicitor's Department, and by C. Symons, Barrister,

The Commission of the European Communities, by T. van Rijn and F. Grondman, members of its Legal Department,

after hearing the Opinion of the Advocate General delivered at the sitting on 22 January 1986,

gives the following Judgment

Decision

1. By a judgment of 18 January 1985, which was received at the Court on 25 January 1985, the Hoge Raad der Nederlanden referred to the Court

398

for a preliminary ruling under Article 177 of EEC Treaty three questions concerning the interpretation of Article 1(1) of Council Directive No. 77/187 of 14 February 1977 on the approximation of the laws of the Member States relating to the safeguarding of employees' rights in the event of transfers of undertakings, businesses or parts of businesses.

2. Those questions were raised in the course of proceedings brought by Jozef Maria Antonius Spijkers against Gebroeders Benedik Abattoir C. V. (hereinafter referred to as 'Benedik Abattoir') and Alfred Benedik en Zonen B.V. (hereinafter reffered to as 'Alfred Benedik').

3. The Hoge Raad found that Mr Spijkers was employed as an assistant manager by Gebroeders Colaris Abattoir B.V. (hereinafter referred to as 'Colaris') at Ubach over Worms (The Netherlands), a company whose business consisted in the operation of a slaughter-house. The Hoge Raad also found that on 27 December 1982, by which date the business activities of Colaris 'had entirely ceased and there was no longer any goodwill in the business', the entire slaughter-house, with various rooms and offices, the land and certain specified goods, were purchased by Benedik Abattoir. 'Since that date, although in fact only since 7 February 1983', Benedik Abattoir has operated a slaughter-house for the joint account of Alfred Benedik and itself. All the employees of Colaris were taken over by Benedik Abattoir, apart from Mr Spijkers and one other employee. The Hoge Raad also states that the business activity which Benedik Abattoir carries on in the buildings is of the same kind as the activity previously carried on by Colaris and that the transfer of the business assets enabled Benedik Abattoir to continue the activities of Colaris, although Benedik Abattoir did not take over Colaris's customers.

4. By a judgment of the Rechtbank [District Court], Maastricht, of 3 March 1983, Colaris was declared insolvent. By a writ of 9 March 1983 Mr Spijkers summoned Benedik Abattoir and Alfred Benedik to appear in proceedings for interim relief before the President of the Rechtbank, Maastricht, and sought an order that they should pay him his salary from 27 December 1982, or at least from such date as the President thought fit, and should provide him with work within two days of the order. In support of his claims he contended that there had been a transfer of an undertaking within the meaning of the Netherlands legislation enacted in order to implement Directive No. 77/187 and that this entailed, by operation of law, a transfer to Benedik Abattoir of the rights and obligations arising from his contract of employment with Colaris.

5. The application for interim relief was dismissed by the President of the Rechtbank, Maastricht, whose decision was confirmed on appeal by the Gerechtshof [Regional Court of Appeal], 's-Hertogenbosch. Mr Spijkers then appealed in cassation to the Hoge Raad der Nederlanden, which

stayed the proceedings and referred the following questions to the Court of Justice:

'1. Is there a transfer within the meaning of Article 1(1) of Council Directive No. 77/187 where buildings and stock are taken over and the transferee is thereby enabled to continue the business activities of the transferor and does in fact subsequently carry on business activities of the same kind in the buildings in question?

2. Does the fact that at the time when the buildings and stock were sold the business activities of the vendor had entirely ceased and that in particular there was no longer any good-will in the business prevent there being a 'transfer' as defined in Question 1?

3. Does the fact that the circle of customers is not taken over prevent there being such a transfer?'.

6. In order to understand the purpose of those questions, it is necessary to consider them in the light of Directive No. 77/187. That directive, which was adopted on the basis, *inter alia*, of Article 100 of the Treaty, is intended, according to the terms of its preamble, 'to provide for the protection of employees in the event of a change of employer, in particular, to ensure that their rights are safeguarded'. For that purpose Article 3(1) of the directive provides for the transfer of the transferor's rights and obligations arising from a contract of employment or from an employment relationship, and Article 4(1) provides for the protection of the workers concerned against dismissal by the transferor or the transferee solely by reason of the transfer. Article 1(1), which the Court has been requested to interpret in this case, defines the scope of the directive; it provides that the directive 'shall apply to the transfer of an undertaking, business or part of a business to another employer as a result of a legal transfer or merger'.

7. It therefore appears that by its questions the Hoge Raad seeks a ruling on the scope of and the criteria for applying the expression 'transfer of an undertaking, business or part of a business to another employer' in Article 1(1) of the directive in relation to a case such as that described in the Hoge Raad's judgment. The questions must therefore be considered together.

8. Mr Spijkers maintains that there is a transfer of an undertaking within the meaning of Article 1(1) where the undertaking's assets and business are transferred as a unit from one employer to another; it is immaterial whether at the time of the transfer the business activities of the transferor have ceased and the goodwill has already disappeared.

9. The Netherlands and United Kingdom Governments and the Commis-

sion, on the other hand, consider that the question whether there is a transfer of an undertaking for the purposes of Article 1(1) must be considered in the light of all the circumstances characterizing the transaction, such as whether or not the tangible assets (buildings, movable property and stocks) and the intangible assets (know-how and goodwill) were transferred, the nature of the activities engaged in and whether or not those activities had ceased at the time of the transfer. However, none of those factors is in itself decisive.

10. The United Kingdom Government and the Commission suggest that the essential criterion is whether the transferee is put in possession of a going concern and is able to continue its activities or at least activities of the same kind. The Netherlands government emphasizes that, having regard to the social objective of the directive, it is clear that the term 'transfer' implies that the transferee actually carries on the activities of the transferor as part of the same business.

11. That view must be accepted. It is clear from the scheme of Directive No. 77/187 and from the terms of Article 1(1) thereof that the directive is intended to ensure the continuity of employment relationships existing within a business, irrespective of any change of ownership. It follows that the decisive criterion for establishing whether there is a transfer for the purposes of the directive is whether the business in question retains its identity.

12. Consequently, a transfer of an undertaking, business or part of a business does not occur merely because its assets are disposed of. Instead it is necessary to consider, in a case such as the present, whether the business was disposed of as a going concern, as would be indicated, *inter alia*, by the fact that its operation was actually continued or resumed by the new employer, with the same or similar activities.

13. In order to determine whether those conditions are met, it is necessary to consider all the facts characterizing the transaction in question, including the type of undertaking or business, whether or not the business's tangible assets, such as buildings and movable property, are transferred, the value of its intangible assets at the time of the transfer, whether or not the majority of its employees are taken over by the new employer, whether or not its customers are transferred and the degree of similarity between the activities carried on before and after the transfer and the period, if any, for which those activities were suspended. It should be noted, however, that all those circumstances are merely single factors in the overall assessment which must be made and cannot therefore be considered in isolation.

14. It is for the national court to make the necessary factual appraisal, in the light of the criteria for interpretation set out above, in order to establish whether or not there is a transfer in the sense indicated above.

401

15. Consequently, in reply to the questions submitted it must be held that Article 1(1) of Directive No. 77/187 of 14 February 1977 must be interpreted as meaning that the expression 'transfer of an undertaking, business or part of a business to another employer' envisages the case in which the business in question retains its identity. In order to establish whether or not such a transfer has taken place in a case such as that before the national court, it is necessary to consider whether, having regard to all the facts characterizing the transaction, the business was disposed of as a going concern, as would be indicated *inter alia* by the fact that its operation was actually continued or resumed by the new employer, with the same or similar activities.

Costs

16. The costs incurred by the Netherlands and United Kingdom Governments and by the Commission of the European Communities, which have submitted observations to the Court, are not recoverable. Since these proceedings are, in so far as the parties to the main proceedings are concerned, in the nature of a step in the proceedings pending before the national court, the decision as to costs is a matter for that court.

On those grounds,

THE COURT (FIFTH CHAMBER),

in answer to the questions referred to it by the Hoge Raad der Nederlanden by a judgment dated 18 January 1985,

hereby rules:

Article 1(1) of Directive No. 77/187 of 14 February 1977 must be interpreted to the effect that the expression 'transfer of an undertaking, business or part of a business to another employer' envisages the case in which the business in question retains its identity. In order to establish whether or not such a transfer has taken place in a case such as that before the national court, it is necessary to consider whether, having regard to all the facts characterizing the transaction, the business was disposed of as a going concern, as would be indicated *inter alia* by the fact that its operation was actually continued or resumed by the new employer, with the same or similar activities.

Everling		Joliet		Due
	Galmot		Kakouris	

Delivered in open court in Luxembourg on 18 March 1986.

P. Heim
Registrar

U. Everling
President of the Fifth Chamber

Part III.
Health and Safety at Work

Contents

Part III. Health and Safety at Work

Introduction

Improving working conditions and standards of health and safety at work have long been among the EEC's key social policy objectives. The development of new processes and technologies in recent years has also served to focus increasing attention on the importance of ensuring safe working conditions and adequate general protections for workers in all parts of the European Community.

The original social provisions in the EEC Treaty emphasised 'the need to promote improved working conditions and an improved standard of living for workers ...' and made specific mention of 'occupational hygiene' and the 'prevention of occupational accidents and diseases' as key areas for the attentions of Member States and the European Commission (Articles 117 and 118). Building on these basic provisions, wide-ranging framework programmes for action have been approved by the Community's Council of Ministers, and legislative and other measures have been enacted especially during the 1970s and 1980s to give detailed effect to aspects of these programmes. There has also been a noticeable flurry of legislative activity from the European Commission since amendments to the EEC Treaty, introduced by the Single European Act, came into force in July 1987, enabling measures in the health and safety field to be approved by qualified majority voting by the Council of Ministers rather than requiring unanimity among Ministers from all countries as previously. The Commission submitted seven new draft Directives to the Council in respect of health and safety at work in 1988 alone.

The EEC legislation which has been enacted in the health and safety field ranges from general framework programmes to specific Directives dealing in detail with particular industrial activities and the risks associated with them. The detailed provisions are often very precise – for example, specifying maximum daily exposure levels for workers exposed to particular risks. There is thus little scope for interpretation by the courts. This Chapter contains the main legislative texts which the EEC has enacted in the health and safety field – provisions of importance as affecting the rights and obligations of employers and workers throughout the Community. In contrast to preceding Chapters, however, there is no case law as none has yet emerged in this field.

The basic sources of EEC law governing workplace health and safety are detailed in the following sections. Broad safety action programmes and specific implementing Directives are included. The Directives cover such subjects as the provision of safety signs at the workplace, protections for workers against harmful exposure to various chemical, physical and biological agents at work (including protections against the risks associated with lead, asbestos and noise), and provisions to prevent or limit the consequences of major accidents in certain industrial activities. It may be noted that the latest of the worker protection Directives to be adopted (a proscriptions Directive, banning certain specified agents and/or work activities) was adopted on 9 June 1988 by a qualified majority vote of the Council of Ministers – the first Directive in the social and labour field to be adopted on this basis since the EEC Treaty was amended to allow for majority voting in this field by the 1987 Single European Act.

The main Directives which have been enacted affecting workers and their workplaces are included here. Other Directives with less of a social emphasis – concerned, for instance, with the design and use of certain equiment (e.g. a Directive on electrical equipment for use in potentially explosive atmospheres), or the classification, packaging and labelling of dangerous substances – are not included. Provisions outside the scope of the EEC Treaty and directed more generally at health protection of the general public as well as workers (e.g. Euratom Directives on protection against the dangers of ionizing radiation) are also omitted.

A. General: EEC Treaty Extracts and Framework Action Programmes

Social Provisions

Article 117

Member States agree upon the need to promote improved working conditions and an improved standard of living for workers, so as to make possible their harmonization while the improvement is being maintained.

They believe that such a development will ensue not only from the functioning of the common market, which will favour the harmonization of social systems, but also from the procedures provided for in this Treaty and from the approximation of provisions laid down by law, regulation or administrative action.

Article 118

Without prejudice to the other provisions of the Treaty and in conformity with its general objectives, the Commission shall have the task of promoting close cooperation between Member States in the social field, particularly in matters relating to:
- employment;
- labour law and working conditions;
- basic and advanced vocational training;
- social security;
- prevention of occupational accidents and diseases;
- occupational hygiene;
- the right of association, and collective bargaining between employers and workers.

To this end, the Commission shall act in close contact with Member States by making studies, delivering opinions and arranging consultations both on problems arising at national level and on those of concern to international organisations.

Before delivering the opinions provided for in this Article, the Commission shall consult the Economic and Social Committee.

Article 118a*

1. Member States shall pay particular attention to encouraging improvements, especially in the working environment, as regards the health and safety of workers, and shall set as their objective the harmonization of conditions in this area, while maintaining the improvements made.

2. In order to help achieve the objective laid down in the first paragraph, the Council, acting by a qualified majority on a proposal from the Commission, in cooperation with the European Parliament and after consulting the Economic and Social Committee, shall adopt, by means of directives, minimum requirements for gradual implementation, having regard to the conditions and technical rules obtaining in each of the Member States.

Such directives shall avoid imposing administrative, financial and legal constraints in a way which would hold back the creation and development of small and medium-sized undertakings.

3. The provisions adopted pursuant to this Article shall not prevent any Member State from maintaining or introducing more stringent measures for the protection of working conditions compatible with this Treaty.

---

* Article added by Article 21 of the Single European Act 1987.

Council Resolution

29 June 1978

on an action programme of the European Communities on safety and health at work

THE COUNCIL OF THE EUROPEAN COMMUNITIES,

Having regard to the Treaties establishing the European Communities,
Having regard to the draft resolution submitted by the Commission,
Having regard to the opinion of the European Parliament,[1]
Having regard to the opinion of the Economic and Social Committee:[2]

Whereas the Council resolution of 21 January 1974 concerning a social action programme[3] provides for the establishment of an action programme on safety and health at work;

Whereas, under Article 2 of the Treaty establishing the European Economic Community, the Community shall have among its tasks, by establishing a common market and progressively approximating the economic policies of Member States, that of promoting throughout the Community a harmonious development of economic activities, a continuous and balanced expansion and an accelerated raising of the standard of living;

Whereas at the Conference held in Paris in October 1972 the Heads of State or of Government affirmed that the first aim of economic expansion, which is not an end in itself, should be to enable disparities in living conditions to be reduced and that it should result in an improvement in the quality of life as well as in standards of living;

Whereas moreover, in Article 117 of the said Treaty, the Member States agree upon the need to promote improved working conditions and an improved standard of living for workers, so as to make possible their harmonization while the improvement is being maintained;

Whereas prevention of occupational accidents and diseases and also occupational hygiene fall within the fields and objectives referred to in Article 118 of the said Treaty; whereas in this context collaboration should be strengthened between the Member States and the Commission and between the Member States themselves;

Whereas suitable health protection for the public and effective prevention of accidents at work and occupational diseases would meet these general objectives;

Whereas in spite of sustained efforts the continuing high level of accidents at work and of occupational diseases remains a serious problem;

Whereas efforts made in the field of accident prevention and health protection at the work place have beneficial effects which are reflected in the economic sphere and in industrial relations;

Whereas a considerable effort is needed at Community level to search for and implement suitable means for maintaining or creating a working environment tailored to the needs of man and his legitimate aspirations;

Whereas both the effectiveness of the measures and their cost should be taken into account in the choice of action at Community level to be undertaken and of the measures to be taken to implement it;

Whereas the improvement of working conditions and the working environment must be envisaged in overall terms and must concern all sectors of the economy;

Whereas the actions should be implemented in accordance with the provisions of the Treaties, including those of Article 235 of the Treaty establishing the European Economic Community;

Whereas it is essential also to encourage the increasing participation of management and labour in the decisions and initiatives in the field of safety, hygiene and health protection at work at all levels, particularly at the level of the undertaking;

Whereas the Advisory Committee on Safety, Hygiene and Health Protection at Work, set up by Council Decision 74/325/EEC of 27 June 1974,[4] must be closely associated with this work;

Whereas the European Foundation for the Improvement of Living and Working Conditions and the European Centre for the Development of Vocational Training may have a role to play in the implementation of certain aspects of the programme;

Whereas, in implementing the actions, account must be taken of work undertaken in other fields, notably in the context of the Council resolution of 17 December 1973 on industrial policy[5] and of the Declaration of the Council of the European Communities and of the representatives of the Governments of the Member States meeting in the Council of 22 November 1973 on the programme of action of the European Communities on the environment,[6] in order to ensure the closest possible coordination of actions and proposals;

Whereas, in order to carry out the actions, it is important to ensure that

411

concepts, terminology and also methods of identification, measurement and assessment relating to safety and health risks are harmonized; whereas such a task is of major importance in the context of these actions.

Notes the action programme from the Commission annexed hereto and approves its general objective, which is to increase protection of workers against occupational risks of all kinds by improving the means and conditions of work, knowledge and human attitudes,

Expresses the political will to take, in keeping with the urgency of the matter and bearing in mind what is feasible at national and Community level, the measures required so that between now and the end of 1982 the following actions in particular can be undertaken:

Accident and disease aetiology connected with work – Research
1. Establish, in collaboration with the Statistical Office of the European Communities, a common statistical methodology in order to assess with sufficient accuracy the frequency, gravity and causes of accidents at work, and also the mortality, sickness and absenteeism rates in the case of diseases connected with work.
2. Promote the exchange of knowledge, establish the conditions for close cooperation between research institutes and identify the subjects for research to be worked on jointly.

Protection against dangerous substances
3. Standardize the terminology and concepts relating to exposure limits for toxic substances.
   Harmonize the exposure limits for a certain number of substances, taking into account the exposure limits already in existence.
4. Develop a preventive and protective action for substances recognized as being carcinogenic, by fixing exposure limits, sampling requirements and measuring methods, and satisfactory conditions of hygiene at the work place, and by specifying prohibitions where necessary.
5. Establish, for certain specific toxic substances such as asbestos, arsenic, cadmium, lead and chlorinated solvents, exposure limits, limit values for human biological indicators, sampling requirements and measuring methods, and satisfactory conditions of hygiene at the work place.
6. Establish a common methodology for the assessment of the health risks connected with the physical, chemical and biological agents present at the work place, in particular by research into criteria of harmfulness and by determining the reference values from which to obtain exposure limits.
7. Establish information notices on the risks relating to and handbooks on the handling of a certain number of dangerous substances such as pesticides, herbicides, carcinogenic substances, asbestos, arsenic, lead, mercury, cadmium and chlorinated solvents.

Prevention of the dangers and harmful effects of machines
8. Establish the limit levels for noise and vibrations at the work place and

412

determine practical ways and means of protecting workers and reducing sound levels at places of work.

Establish the permissible sound levels of building-site equipment and other machines.

9. Undertake a joint study of the application of the principles of accident prevention and of ergonomics in the design, construction and utilization of the plant and machinery, and promote this application in certain pilot sectors, including agriculture.

10. Analyse the provisions and measures governing the monitoring of the effectiveness of safety and protection arrangements and organize an exchange of experience in this field.

Monitoring and inspection – improvement of human attitudes

11. Develop a common methodology for monitoring both pollutant concentrations and the measurement of environmental conditions at places of work; carry out intercomparison programmes and establish reference methods for the determination of the most important pollutants.

Promote new monitoring and measuring methods for the assessment of individual exposure, in particular through the application of sensitive biological indicators. Special attention will be given to the monitoring of exposure in the case of women, especially of expectant mothers, and adolescents.

Undertake a joint study of the principles and methods of application of industrial medicine with a view to promoting better protection of workers' health.

12. Establish the principles and criteria applicable to the special monitoring relating to assistance or rescue teams in the event of accident or disaster, maintenance and repair teams and the isolated worker.

13. Exchange experience concerning the principles and methods of organization of inspection by public authorities in the fields of safety, hygiene at work and occupational medicine.

14. Draw up outline schemes at a Community level for introducing and providing information on safety and hygiene matters at the work place to particular categories of workers such as migrant workers, newly recruited workers and workers who have changed jobs.

Notes that the Commission will take the necessary initiatives for the implementation of this resolution,

Invites the Commission to submit an annual report to it on the progress made in implementing this resolution.

---

1. Opinion delivered on 12 June 1978 (not yet published in the *Official Journal*).
2. Opinion delivered on 21 June 1978 (not yet published in the *Official Journal*).
3. OJ No. C 13, 12.2.1974, p. 1
4. OJ No. L 185, 9.7.1974, p. 15.
5. OJ No. C 117, 31.12.1973, p. 1
6. OJ No. C 112, 20.12.1973.

ANNEX

Action programme of the European Communities on health and safety at work

INTRODUCTION

A high percentage of the population of the nine Member States is exposed to varying degrees of many and widely divergent occupational risks which could threaten their health and personal safety. Occupational pathology is habitually concerned with accidents and diseases resulting from work, the prevention or diagnosis of which have been the subject of action within the Community for several years, and the harmful effects of which are partly or totally compensated through various schemes.

Despite the efforts made in the Member States of the Community, the number of accidents and diseases resulting from work remains high. Quite apart from their financial importance, the human and social consequences of occupational accidents and diseases are incalculable, since it is not easy to assess the psychological damage done or to take into account the long-term factors connected with accidents and disease. Thus there is good reason to believe that the total social and financial cost of occupational accidents and diseases is far greater than the quantitative estimates at our disposal suggest.

Modern technology uses increasingly advanced processes which present new dangers. They produce or use chemical substances which are inadequately tested for their harmful effects on man. All chemical, physical, mechanical and biological agents and the psychosocial factors connected with work must be readily recognizable and brought under control or eliminated by suitable means so as to avoid any damage to health or a significant reduction in safety.

The prevention, limitation and, where possible, elimination of occupational risks constitute major elements of a policy to protect the health and safety of the workers.

Of course, the Member States have a long tradition in the organization of industrial safety and health but they must also agree to shoulder a joint programme of positive and effective actions to improve the conditions under which man performs his job and do everything possible to ensure his well-being and guarantee the quality of his working environment. In order to implement such a programme, it is necessary not only to harmonize ideas and basic principles, but also to plan and guide technical progress and the organization of work in such a way as to take account of the requirement of health and safety.

In view of the persisting gravity of the problem, the Commission must initiate, promote and develop a common preventive policy with regard to all occupational risks, especially by obtaining fresh knowledge, by encouraging cooperation and coordination and by developing appropriate actions at different levels of responsibility or competence. In addition to promoting exchanges and the improvement of reciprocal information, such a programme should

414

aim to persuade responsible authorities in the Member States and the social partners to join forces against risks of all kinds which the work environment brings to bear on the health and safety of workers and on society at large.

The present programme takes account of the guidelines proposed by the Commission and of several studies made and consultations held over the past two years. It also takes into consideration the experience gained by the Commission in the coal and steel industries and the nuclear field where, under the terms of the ECSC and Euratom Treaties, research programmes and work on harmonization and standardization in accident and disease prevention and protection with regard to specific risks in these three sectors have been carried out for many years.

This programme does not effect other programmes such as those for the elimination of technical barriers to trade and for the protection of the environment. In proposing specific actions within the framework of this programme, the work undertaken by other research programmes, notably in the environmental field will be taken into account, so that maximum coordination is ensured.

Some action could be taken in collaboration or conjunction with other organizations, such as the European Foundation for the Improvement of Living and Working Conditions and the European Centre for the Development of Vocational Training.

I. General objectives of the action programme on safety and health

The main aim of the programme is to increase the level of protection against occupational risks of all types by increasing the efficiency of measures for preventing, monitoring and controlling these risks.

One of the primary conditions for the implementation of such a programme is the full participation of both sides of industry in preventive and protective measures.

Each of the actions proposed in the programme must be seen as an element contributing to the better organization of preventive and protective measures for workers and to closer collaboration between the social partners towards that end. Furthermore, in order to take account of the experience obtained by international organizations and to avoid duplication of effort in the surveys or actions undertaken, liaison between Member States must be improved with a view to organizing joint action in international agencies responsible for occupational health and safety.

Such a programme should make it possible to achieve the following general objectives:

(a) Improvement of the working situation with a view to increased safety and with due regard to health requirements in the organization of the work. Such an improvement should cover not only the existing situation but also new technical developments. Technical progress which contributes to the creation of a new working situation or to the improvement of an existing

415

situation is not always conceived and directed in line with the dictates of safety and health; where machinery, premises and plant are concerned, safety aspects should be considered at the design stage and integrated into the subsequent stages of their production and commissioning. Due attention must also be paid to health considerations at every stage in the production and use of chemical substances.

There is a close link between occupational accident and disease prevention on the one hand, and the organization of work and safety and health training and information at the place of work on the other. There is an urgent need to review and redefine a more effect accident and disease prevention strategy in order to up-date traditional methods.

Where is it not possible to eliminate it, exposure to occupational risks must be kept to permissible levels applicable to all workers within the Community and based on common concepts and references.

So as to monitor more effectively the application of preventive measures, surveillance of health and working conditions must be intensified, notably in line with the exigencies of occupational medicine, hygiene and safety appropriate to present-day conditions.

(b) Improvement of knowledge in order to identify and assess risks and prefect prevention and control methods.

In view of the complexity and diversity of the factors it embraces, aetiology is a priority subject for research and analysis. Valid and comparable statistics must be prepared and existing research coordinated. The promotion of new research is an essential corollary to any Community action in occupational medicine, hygiene and safety.

(c) Improvement of human attitudes in order to promote and develop safety and health consciousness.

Alongside the technical aspects of accident prevention and health protection, a real system of safety instruction and health education must be created. This has yet to be introduced and will be taught in different ways at the various educational levels and at the various levels of responsibility and action within undertakings.

II. Description of the initiatives to be taken at Community level

Attainment of the general objectives requires many initiatives involving various scientific disciplines. Such initiatives presuppose the effective participation of individuals in managing their own health and safety and should encourage the social partners and the various professional associations and bodies to take a more active part in the formulation and implementation of a policy for the prevention of dangers at the workplace.

The following six concrete initiatives are planned within various time limits for the attainments of these general objectives:

1. incorporation of safety aspects into the various stages of design, production and operation;

416

2. determination of exposure limits for workers with regard to pollution and harmful substances present or likely to be present at the workplace;
3. more extensive monitoring of workers' safety and health;
4. accident and disease aetiology and assessment of the risks connected with work;
5. coordination and promotion of research on occupational safety and health;
6. development of safety and health consciousness by education and training.

Initiative 1 – Incorporation of safety aspects into the various stages of design, production and operation

Aim

In order to promote this incorporation the Commission will consider actions aimed essentially at harmonizing, from the safety point of view, the principles and designs of workplaces, machinery, equipment and plant and at the formulation or coordination of rules for their use and guidance on the use of dangerous substances.

The principle of integrated safety is today generally regarded as essential for all preventive measures and it is receiving increasing attention at national and international level. In all decisions with regard to undertakings (planning and construction of the undertaking, purchase and operation of plant, organization of production, working methods, etc.) more attention must be paid to safety. Similarly operational safety should be studied in advance for the design and manufacture of machinery and tools so as to guarantee protection of the worker's health as far as possible. As concerns the production and distribution of dangerous substances, the same principles have to be taken into account.

The principles of ergonomics are not yet sufficiently well applied in the search for better safety. In particular design ergonomics which is already widespread in the Community has not been sufficiently adopted, as compared with the work carried out in the Scandinavian countries and in the United States.

The results of research carried out over several years in the coal and steel industries indicate the measures which should be planned at Community level in other sectors of industry.

In this field the Commission is planning to propose a certain number of measures which will encourage the application of the principles and which could progressively form a basis of legal, regulatory and administrative provisions or of up-to-date technical guides drawn up at Community level in order to improve the current situation in many industrial or agricultural spheres. These measures concern in particular:

(a) Setting up of undertakings and planning of layout and equipment

The Commission has selected the following points from amongst the numerous factors which must be taken into consideration: ventilation and lighting, temperature, protection against falling from heights and against falling heavy objects, protection against fire, noise and vibrations, gases, vapours and

417

dusts, design of general and emergency thoroughfares and location of doors and windows.

(b) Organization of work within undertakings or between several undertakings

The following points are to receive special attention: equipment and layout of workplaces, outdoor workplaces, warning signs, dangerous jobs, no-access and limited access areas, transport within the undertaking, inspections, maintenance work, plant testing, coordination of work within the undertaking, coordination of the work of various departments belonging to the same undertaking or to different undertakings, etc.

(c) Manufacture and use of machinery, equipment and tools

This is the chief area for the application of technical accident and disease prevention which is of paramount social and economic importance. In this sector harmonization measures require lengthy preparation. With regard to the manufacture of machinery and equipment the concept of their safety was already considered in the general programme of 28 May 1969 on the elimination of technical barriers to trade.[1] However, there exist inherent dangers in the use of machinery and equipment and a procedure should be introduced for the exchange of experience and information so that such dangers are recognized and identified. Furthermore, since 1969 the Council had already pointed out that it would be possible, if necessary, to lay down rules on use supplementing Community Directives on harmonization with regard to the manufacture of machinery and equipment. Guidelines and rules must be drawn up with a view to determining appropriate legislation at Community level.

(d) Handling of dangerous substances and preparations

In this field Community harmonization action must be taken with regard to the handling of dangerous substances and preparations, with a view to improving the practical organization of safety, that is, handling at the workplace, storage, marking of containers and pipes. Technical and health protection measures, working restrictions and prohibitions, the number of hours worked and medical protection measures should also be harmonized at Community level. The distribution of dangerous substances (classification, identification and packaging) is taken into account in the programmes for the 'elimination of the technical barriers to trade' and 'environment'.

Contents

Some of the objectives set out above can be achieved only in the medium and long-term. The problems will be selected for study on the basis of the wishes expressed or guidance given by relevant bodies who should above all bear in mind practical considerations and on the basis of urgent needs which may arise from unforeseen dangerous situations such as accidents or disaster, or which may be recognized as a result of the acquisition of fresh knowledge on the effects of chemical substances and the need to control their use with a view to protecting health.

418

The Commission plans to being work in this field by studying the following matters:

(a) Setting up of undertakings and planning of layout and equipment
1. Organization and layout of agricultural holdings. There is reason to consider that modern agricultural holdings should meet requirements similar to those imposed upon industrial enterprises. So far these requirements have generally not been taken into account in national regulations and it would be appropriate to take the necessary steps at Community level.
2. Noise and vibration control. This requires special medium and long-term attention. The main task consists in setting an optimum machine-noise level on the basis of health data and an assessment of results obtained to date by research and the examination of practical experiments (for example the use of machinery with a low-noise level, which has already been perfected). Noise emission levels, designed to take account especially of the practical problems involved in occupational protection, will be established after national experts have been consulted and will be published in the form of Directives.

(b) Organization of work within undertakings
1. Transport within undertakings. Internal transport, particularly the safe organization of general thoroughfares, needs to be examined and suitable practical instructions should be drawn up. This sector has a particularly high accident rate.
2. Safety signs at workplaces. Council Directive 77/576/EEC of 25 July 1977 on safety signs at workplaces provides that these signs must be able to keep up with technical progress and meet recommendations for harmonization at international level.
   In this connection provision is made for a committee to meet at regular intervals. This action was initiated in 1977 and will be continued in 1978 and 1979 by means of proposals for Directives.
3. Coordination of the work of principal and secondary undertakings. The internal and external collaboration of principal and secondary undertakings (subcontracts) requires special technical examination from the point of view of safety. In practice – especially for the coordination of collaboration between several independent undertakings – there are many problems still to be solved. A Community examination of these questions leading to such coordination by means of suitable legal instruments is required.

(c) Manufacture and use of machinery, equipment and tools
In addition to the work completed within the context of the elimination of technical barriers to trade which is concerned with the design and manufacture of machines, equiment and tools it seems essential to examine in the short and medium-term the need for joint rules on the use of the following: agricultural machinery, lifting gear, machinery used in construction, metal scaffolding and

419

woodworking machines. Depending on the circumstances and on the results of the collaboration to be organized such rules would take the form of guidelines or Directives.

(d) Handling of dangerous substances and preparations

An urgent study must be made of the handling of dangerous or toxic substances and agreement reached on common standards which will then be proposed to the Member States. An essentially practical approach is required and attention will initially be directed towards the problems of health protection connected with the use of pesticides and herbicides in agriculture. Similar problems arise with other products, e.g. arsenic, lead, mercury, cadmium, chrome, nickel, vegetable dusts, biological pollution, etc.

As information is obtained on the toxicological effect of these substances, as outlined in paragraph 5 of Initiative 2, practical guidelines will be drawn up for all products which involve handling problems or health risks.

Initiative 2 – Determination of exposure limits for workers with regard to pollutants and harmful substances present or likely to be present at the workplace

Aim

With a view to the organization of disease prevention and to the monitoring of many occupational risks it is essential to have data on exposure limits for workers with regard to pollutants and harmful substances. It is therefore important for the Commission to achieve, at Community level, harmonization of the concepts, methodologies and references on the basis of which the Member States determine their permissible exposure limits.

There are already standards for protection against radiation at Community level which have been in force since 1959 (Directive) and which were recently revised by a Directive issued in June 1976. They are an example of a joint health policy concerned with an industrial risk facing workers and the general public and based on uniform standards for the whole Community. This example should be extended to other pollutants present at the workplace.

Moreover the studies carried out by the Commission over the past four years in particular in relation to the environment programme and the experience acquired with regard to certain environmental pollutants now make it possible to present concrete proposals for action with regard to certain specific pollutants affecting workplaces in particular.

In addition to these short-term actions, however, the Commission plans to make an objective analysis at Community level of the harmful or undesirable effects of exposure to pollutants in given circumstances – taking account of the results already obtained at international level, in particular by the WHO and the ILO. From this analysis it is proposed to deduce criteria of noxiousness on which to base acceptable exposure limits for workers. Such a project would cover a large number of substances and would be extended as industrial toxicity studies currently in progress are completed.

The protection of human health against chemical substances requries a complex toxicological evaluation which at present is incomplete. The Commission must take priority action with regard to carcinogens, since it is generally accepted that a high proportion of human cancer is caused by external factors including chemicals present at the workplace.

Contents
The Commission is planning the following initiatives:

1. Non-ionizing radiation and other physical agents
With regard to non-ionizing radiation, proposals for Directives will be submitted to the Council on microwaves, laser radiation, ultra-violet radiation and ultrasound, on the basis of the procedure followed for standards in protection against radiation.

2. Harmonization of exposure limits
The Commission plans, at the earliest possible opportunity, to make a comparative study of existing regulations and recommendations in Member States with regard to permissible exposure levels of workers to toxic substances or physically harmful substances.

The values adopted in different countries vary, the terminology used is not the same and the concepts used to determine the limits are not based on the same principles. Harmonization is therefore essential and a general Directive coordinating and harmonizing exposure levels, possibly updated later on in accordance with the latest scientific data and international information available to the Commission, could be prepared between now and 1979.

This short-term initiative would have the advantage of achieving harmonization at Community level and avoiding the delay of waiting for the completion of on-going research projects in the field of occupational toxicology, whether within the Commission or in the Member States.

3. Directives on specific pollutants
The general harmonization discussed in paragraph 2 must be supplemented by the preparation of specific Directives such as those proposed by the Commission for vinyl chloride monomer and those shortly to be put forward on asbestos, lead, mercury, solvents, carbon monoxide, noise and vibrations. The studies in progress within the Commission and the state of knowledge have now reached the stage where they can be used to determine the permissible exposure levels for the abovementioned pollutants from the point of view of health protection.

4. Carcinogens
Specific Commission action with regard to carcinogens present at workplaces will consist in:
– collecting data on the distribution of carcinogens and their concentration at the workplace,
– collecting and analysing medical data,
– perfecting readily applicable detection,

421

– fixing the lowest possible levels or, if necessary, prohibit a certain number of carcinogens present at the workplace.

5. Toxicological evaluation

Toxicological evaluation is central to the assessment of the health risks due to the presence of many chemical and biological agents in the working environment. This can be carried out only if sufficient knowledge is available on the effects of the agents under consideration on man. The methodology adopted by the Commission for assessing the dangers from environmental pollutants in general is based on research into criteria for noxiousness from which permissible human exposure levels may be deduced. The data already collected by the Commission on the effects on health of urban atmospheric pollutants and certain water pollutants provide a basis for the action planned in industry, but it needs to be considerably extended and developed. Priority will be given to the following substances: arsenic, cadmium, chromium, iron oxides, nickel, vegetable dusts, ozone, nitrogen oxides and biological pollutants.

The Commission, while taking account of studies already carried out and projects being planned at international level, is to give priority to the extension and development of information relating to the objective evaluation of risks associated with toxic substances present at the workplace. This action will lead to Directives on exposure levels for workers and also to the compilation of handbooks on the safe handling of such substances at the workplace. The Commission intends to carry out this action by means of a series of studies and scientific and technical consultations. It will be assisted in this action by a Scientific Committee on Toxicology planned for the end of 1977.

Initiative 3 – More extensive monitoring of workers' safety and health

Aims
Whereas exposure limits for workers and safety and health protection measures are essential factors in the organization of accident and disease prevention, various permanent and well-adapted methods are also required with which to monitor the measures adopted and the exposure levels prescribed for the workplace.

These monitoring methods must be harmonized and coordinated at Community level.

The monitoring of workers' health and safety depends upon several types of monitoring which complement each other:
(a) monitoring of the effectiveness of individual or group safety and protection measures with regard to machinery, equipment and plant;
(b) monitoring of hygiene and working conditions from which the types of exposure to different physical, chemical and biological agents present in the working environment are derived;
(c) monitoring of the state of health and behaviour of the workers as part of occupational medicine;
(d) special monitoring as a result of work entailing special risks;

(e) industrial toxico-vigilance;

(f) inspections.

The Commission feels that it is essential to harmonize at Community level principles and methods applicable to monitoring. Moreover, efforts should be made to interest workers in monitoring within the undertaking, either by direct means or by means of existing bodies or institutions.

Any proposed solutions must allow workers' and employers' representatives to play a fuller part in the practical organization of such monitoring at various levels of action and responsibility.

Contents

1. Monitoring of the effectiveness of safety and protection measures

Planning and execution of this form of monitoring varies at present from country to country and according to the regulations and activities concerned. Once the provisions currently governing such monitoring have been analysed, suitable proposals will be submitted to the Council for adoption in order to harmonize and strengthen the organization of this type of monitoring in which the workers' and employers' representatives should play a greater role.

2. Monitoring of hygiene and working conditions

Monitoring of pollutant concentrations at workplaces and the intensity of environmental factors is essential for the organization of disease prevention and monitoring

Measuring programmes do exist in Member States but they are based on different methods and sometimes different principles. These measures must be harmonized at Community level with regard to sampling, techniques and measuring intervals.

When the Commission has analysed these different methods, it will draw up intercomparison programmes and prepare reference methods for the determination of the major pollutants present at workplaces.

Special attention will be paid to promoting the development of new monitoring and measuring methods for individual exposure.

The Commission will make a similar effort to apply the human biological indicators already in existence and will carry out research for new indicators which will make it possible to detect any changes in the state of health at any early stage. The European list of occupational diseases will be used as a reference document for drawing up the priorities from this action scheduled to take place as from 1978. Account will have to be taken not only of individual sensitivity, which may be very high for some pollutants, and of workplaces so that groups with a high occupational exposure risk may be identified, but also of some special groups of workers such as adolescents and women.

3. Monitoring of workers' health

In accordance with the terms of Article 118 of the Treaty establishing the EEC, occupational medicine must be considered as an area in which the

Commission has the task of promoting close cooperation between Member States in the social field, particularly in matters relating to working conditions and to the prevention of occupational accidents and diseases. The term 'occupational medicine', as stated in the 1962 recommendation on occupational medicine in the undertaking, refers to a service established in or near a place of employment for the purposes of:

(a) protecting the workers against any health hazard which may arise out of their work or conditions in which it is carried on;
(b) contributing towards the workers' physical and mental adjustment, in particular by the adaptation of the work to the workers and their assignment to jobs for which they are suited; and
(c) contributing to the establishment and maintenance of the highest possible degree of physical and mental well-being of the workers.

In addition, Recommendation 112 of the ILO stated that the role of occupational health services should be essentially preventive and defined their functions so as to include the prevention of accidents and occupational diseases, the rehabilitation of workers, job analysis in the light of physiological and psychological considerations, surveillance of hygiene, advice on the placement of workers, medical supervision, emergency treatment and research in occupational health.

Consideration must be given to closer harmonization of the methods used by occupational health services in undertakings in order that the work of the industrial medical officer may be more fully integrated into the system for monitoring workers' safety and health, as recommended in this programme.

This revision will be carried out with effect from 1978 by consultation with the relevant bodies and should culminate in a directive on the organization of occupational medicine in the Member States of the Community, to be proposed in 1979.

4. Special monitoring

In many undertakings there are some jobs which present higher than average risks; certain types of casual work may also involve exposure to risk which is higher than that present in normal working conditions or than the exposure levels laid down. Such jobs are done, for example, by members of rescue teams or of maintenance and repair teams and by workers in virology laboratories and in institutes producing sera or viruses, etc.

Exchanges of information and experience for cases involving these aspects should be organized at Community level and should lead to a definition of the principles and criteria for this particular type of monitoring.

5. Industrial toxico-vigilance

The Commission plans to set up an industrial toxico-vigilance system along the lines proposed by the ILO and which is aimed at establishing a central information system for all observations made in industrial activity concerning the harmful effects of toxic substances. This system should be based on

424

a network of highly specialized centres which could analyse information received from occupational health services and transmit it when required to interested persons or institutions.

The Commission will make an appropriate proposal to the Council, after holding the necessary consultations.

6. Inspections

Inspections carried out for the purposes of occupational safety, medicine and hygiene should be organized so that they assume full responsibility and control by placing the emphasis on preventive measures. With this end in view the necessary provisions must be made in close collaboration with the competent authorities in Member States for the strengthening and development of the work of inspection at national level. The Commission intends to review the role of the inspectorate responsible for implementing in each Member State the regulations of occupational health, hygiene and safety. This review will cover diplomas, certificates and other qualifications, and the powers and scope of their responsibilities in this field.

Initiative 4 – Accident and disease aetiology and assessment of risks connected with work

Aims

The risk of accident or disease may be estimated objectively only if reliable methods are available which make it possible to determine the scope, seriousness and development in time and, in a general way, to acquire greater knowledge of the various factors involved in the cause of accidents at work and of diseases due to work.

Statistics are essential tools for the analysis and interpretation of facts and for assessment of the results obtained from an accident and disease prevention policy.

The improvement of statistics and their comparability, the harmonization of methodologies and the more precise interpretation of the data they provide are important steps in the development of an improved organization of work with regard to accident and disease prevention. Since so many different approaches are used a distinction must be drawn between action in respect of accidents at work and action in respect of disease due to work.

Such actions must provide a clearer picture of the different causative factors of accidents at work and of diseases due to work and must use them as a basis for practical preventive and protective measures against hazards connected with work. It will then be possible to provide preventive-type protection for men at work, on an objective and realistic basis.

In addition, special attention will be paid to calculating the economic and social cost of accidents at work and diseases due to work so as to establish the order of priority for preventive measures.

Account will be taken of the harmonization work already carried out by other international organizations and of work completed or in progress, particularly by the ILO.

Contents

These initiatives deal separately with accidents at work and diseases resulting from work.

As regards accidents at work the two sectors for which Community statistics are already available are the iron and steel industry and mining. Drawing on the experience gained in the sectors the Commission plans to draw up Community statistics concerning other sectors, to launch sectoral in-depth studies and to harmonize accident definitions and methods of reporting accidents in order to establish more precisely the aetiology of accidents. Preparatory surveys are in progress and the first results will be available in 1979.

With regard to diseases due to work, statistics collected at national level usually concern only occupational diseases and are drawn up on different bases so that it is not possible to compare them. There are no Community statistics in this field and it would be appropriate to devise a joint methodology as soon as possible so that existing national statistics may be processed. The Commission therefore plans to gather and analyse national statistical information and to draw up proposals for methodologies with a view to a common approach, so that calculations may be made of mortality, sickness and absenteeism rates and their evolution over a period of time.

Close collaboration must be instituted with the national statistical offices and the national social security offices with regard to these new problems.

This is a medium-term initiative and the first results will become available only after two or three years.

Initiatives 5 – Coordination and promotion of research on occupational safety and health

Aims

The action planned in the programme must find its scientific support in a research programme which is coordinated and/or carried out jointly and which deals on the one hand with the measurement and effects on health of pollutants and harmful substances and, on the other hand, with the development within undertakings of safer, 'cleaner' technologies which do not threaten the general environment.

Collaboration must be organized and strengthened between the institutes and laboratories of Member States in order to avoid duplication of work, to derive greater benefit from the financial resources available and where necessary to bring together highly specialized laboratories to work on problems which cannot be solved in a single Member State.

Moreover, research must be carried out in fields where little or no work has been done, such as agriculture and the tertiary industries.

Contents

Two permanent inventories of research in progress or planned (occupational safety and medicine) at national level are already being prepared at Community level. From 1978 the inventories will make it possible to set up a reciprocal

426

information system on responsible bodies in order to promote the exchange of knowledge and create conditions for close collaboration between research institutes. These permanent inventories will also mention fields in which there are gaps. Three pilot studies are in progress on inflammable substances, occupational risks in the building industry and certain carcinogens. During 1978 these studies will also indicate which subjects should be covered by joint research.

On the basis of these inventories the data bank being compiled within the Commission should be progressively supplemented and should include details of new research; account is taken of the fact that this data bank will subsequently be linked to the information system on medical research which is being set up at Commission level.

Research work aimed at closing the gaps in knowledge on toxic agents and their effects on health or at improving methods for measuring these agents is of major importance for the success of several parts of the programme – in particular the section on the determination of criteria for harmfulness. It will also help to determine as accurately as possible the potential and actual effect on health of pollutants and nuisances present or likely to be present at the workplace.

The results of the implementation of the various inititatives making up the programme will be analysed by the Commission with effect from 1979 and could form a basis for the preparation of a detailed and precise Community research and development programme which could be the subject of a future Commission proposal for adoption by the Council.

Initiative 6 – Development of safety and health consciousness by means of education and training

Aims
This initiative is aimed at developing safety and health consciousness by means of education and training. It is of paramount importance for the success of the promotion of safety and hygiene at workplaces. It is based on instruction and training and involves various levels of education and the undertaking itself. It also concerns in a general way occupational and social sectors involved in problems of accident prevention and health protection at work.

This is a medium and long-term initiative in view of the different sectors involved and of the absence to date of any real methodology and common principles. Various studies and consultations will be required before results and concrete proposals are obtained at Community level.

This action concerns educational bodies, undertakings and society in general.

As for education the basic principles of safety and of health education must be taught in schools. Knowledge of and the correct attitudes towards occupational safety and hygiene must be taught at various levels of education as an integral part of the curriculum and at the same time attention must be paid to the requirements of prevention in relation to real life situations. The question

427

is one of establishing at Community level a safety training scheme which takes account of the differences between national characteristics and traditions but which is based on common principles and a common approach.

Within undertakings steps for the elimination of risks must be systematically organized and coordinated at all levels of responsibility and management. Principles of safety must be consolidated, developed and made public. Action designed to sharpen the awareness of industrialists and heads of undertakings must be taken together with the campaign aimed at workers.

For the training of society in general the action taken in education must be supplemented by action aimed at certain population groups. The use of audio-visual aids is one of the most modern and most effective means of inform-ing the public of the importance and significance of accident and disease prevention.

Contents

1. Education

The Commission plans to carry out, together with the bodies responsible for national education, preparatory studies for the purpose of defining harmonized planning at Community level.

In general education – starting at the earliest age and continuing through-out school life – instruction must be on two levels:
- theoretical and practical instruction to give children and young people an awareness of the risk of accidents,
- instruction to develop a sense of moral and public responsibility with regard to safety and health protection.

In technical education relevant training in safety and health protection should accompany all levels of technical instruction and vocational training. Special attention should be paid to the training of persons particularly concerned with safety and health protection who have a specific task or responsibility in this field.

The Commission plans to propose Community training models for persons in certain occupations and concerned with specific tasks, such as industrial medical officer, occupational safety officer, engineer, architect, member of a company safety committee or union official.

2. Undertaking

Within an undertaking training in safety must be under the control of the undertaking itself since general and technical training cannot take the place of appropriate action at the workplace. This type of training must supplement the instruction received in schools and it must also be given to those who have not previously received any such instruction.

Such training, to be carried out within industry, will be more specialized and more detailed. In many cases it will be organized by specialist bodies whose work must be coordinated at Community level. It should be remembered that education covers a broad span of learning situations – for example instruction given by experienced workers and learning on-the-job.

Beginning in 1978, the Commission intends:
– to draw up Community models for safety training and refresher courses for certain categories of staff: administrative grades, executive grades, instructors for courses on safety and health education and safety delegates,
– to draw up Community models for presenting various aspects of safety to newly recruited workers, migrant workers and workers who have changed jobs,
– to draw up manuals and codes of practice with regard to sectoral activities or dangerous jobs,
– to organize safety campaigns of limited duration with a specific aim, in which workers will feel fully and actively involved,
– to extend the group training courses already in existence to other groups of persons concerned with accident prevention and safety measures.

This action will be furthered by making available to both management and labour knowledge or concepts acquired either by exchange of experience within specialist groups in the elevant sectors or by research projects jointly agreed and financed. Such knowledge could be included in instructions, regulations or codes of practice, to be distributed with commentaries in the appropriate quarters and to be kept constantly up to date.

The Commission will support this type of cooperation and promotion of safety by providing information gathered from specific aspects of the action programme, such as information on accidents and on technical progress in the design, manufacture and use of machinery and plant, and by making available the industrial toxicovigilance results.

3. Population groups

In addition to the action taken in education, general information for certain population-groups (such as parent's associations, professional bodies, women's associations) must be organized with regard to the importance of accident and disease prevention. Some steps have already been taken in this field at national level. Audiovisual aids are already used to provide this information. The Commission plans to coordinate these initiatives and develop them jointly, to produce films and set up a permanent file on audiovisual aids available on an exchange basis.

---

1. OJ No. C 76, 17.6.1969.

Council Resolution

of 27 February 1984

on a second programme of action of the European Communities on safety and health at work

THE COUNCIL OF THE EUROPEAN COMMUNITIES,

Having regard to the Treaties establishing the European Communities,
Having regard to the draft resolution submitted by the Commission,[1]
Having regard to the opinion of the European Parliament,[2]
Having regard to the opinion of the Economic and Social Committee:[3]

Whereas the Council resolution of 21 January 1974 concerning a social action programme[4] provides for the establishment of an action programme on safety and health at work;

Whereas, under Article 2 of the Treaty establishing the European Economic Community, the Community shall have in particular as its task, by establishing a common market and progressively approximating the economic policies of Member States, that of promoting throughout the Community a harmonious developing of economic activities, a continuous and balanced expansion and an accelerated raising of the standard of living;

Whereas, at the Conference held in Paris in October 1972, the Heads of State or of Government affirmed that the first aim of economic expansion, which is not an end in itself, should be to enable disparities in living conditions to be reduced and that it should result in an improvement in the quality of life as well as in standards of living;

Whereas, moreover, under Article 117 of the said Treaty the Member States agreed upon the need to promote improved working conditions and an improved standard of living for workers, so as to make possible their harmonization while the improvement was being maintained;

Whereas prevention of accidents at work and occupational diseases and also occupational hygiene fall within the fields and objectives referred to in Article 118 of the said Treaty; whereas in this context collaboration should be strengthened between the Member States and the Commission and between the Member States themselves;

Whereas suitable health protection for the public and effective prevention of accidents at work and occupational diseases would be in conformity with these general objectives;

Whereas, in spite of sustained efforts, the continuing high level of accidents at work and of occupational diseases remains a serious problem;

Whereas efforts made in the field of accident prevention and health protection at the work place have beneficial effects which are reflected in the economic sphere and in industrial relations;

Whereas a considerable effort is needed at Community level to search for and implement suitable means for maintaining or creating a working environment tailored to the needs of man and his legitimate aspirations;

Whereas both the effectiveness of the measures and the cost of implementing them should be taken into account in the choice of action to be undertaken at Community level and of the measures to be taken to implement it;

Whereas the improvement of working conditions and the working environment must be envisaged in overall terms and must concern all sectors of the economy;

Whereas it is also essential to encourage the increasing participation of management and labour, at all levels and particularly at the level of the undertaking, in decisions and initiatives in the field of safety, hygiene and health protection at work;

Whereas the Advisory Committee on Safety, Hygiene and Health Protection at Work, set up by Decision 74/325/EEC,[5] must be closely associated with this work;

Whereas the European Foundation for the Improvement of Living and Working Conditions and the European Centre for the Development of Vocational Training may have a role to play in the implementation of certain aspects of the programme;

Whereas, in implementing the actions, account must be taken of work undertaken in other fields, especially in the context of the Council resolution of 17 December 1973 on industrial policy[6] and of the Declaration of 22 November 1973[7] and resolutions of 17 May 1977[8] and of 7 February 1983[9] of the Council of the European Communities and of the representatives of the Governments of the Member States, meeting within the Council, concerning a European Community action programme on the environment, in order to ensure the closest possible coordination of actions and proposals;

Whereas, in order to carry out the actions successfully, it is important to ensure that concepts, terminology and methods of identification, measurement and assessment relating to safety and health risks are harmonized; whereas such a task is of major importance in the context of these actions.

Notes that this second action programme takes into account the first action programme annexed to the Council resolution of 29 June 1978 on an action programme of the European Communities on safety and health at work,[10]

Expresses the political will to take, in keeping with the urgency of the matter and bearing in mind what is feasible at national and Community level, the measures required so that between now and the end of 1988 the following priority actions in particular can be undertaken:

I. Protection against dangerous substances

1. Continue with the establishment of Community provisions based on Council Directive 80/1107/EEC of 27 November 1980 on the protection of workers from the risks related to exposure to chemical, physical and biological agents at work.[11]
2. Establish common methodologies for the assessment of the health risks of physical, chemical and biological agents present at the work place.
3. Develop a standard approach for the establishment of exposure limits for toxic substances by applying the methodologies referred to in point 2.

Make recommendations for the harmonization of exposure limits for a certain number of substances, taking into account existing exposure limits.

4. Establish for toxic substances standard methods for measuring and evaluating work place air concentrations and biological indicators of the workers involved, together with quality control programmes for their use.

5. Develop preventive and protective measures for substances recognized as being carcinogenic and other dangerous substances and processes which may have serious harmful effects on health.

6. Establish Community rules for limiting exposure to noise and continue work on developing a basis for Community measures on vibrations and non-ionizing radiation.

II. Ergonomic measures, protection against accidents and dangerous situations

7. Work out safety proposals, particularly for certain high-risk activities, including proposals on specific measures for the prevention of accidents involving falls, manual lifting, handling and dangerous machinery.

8. Examine the major-accident hazards of certain industrial activities covered by Directive 82/501/EEC.[12]

9. Work out ergonomic measures and accident prevention principles with the aim of determining the limits of the constraints imposed on various groups of the working population by the design of equipment, the tasks required and the working environment so that they are not prejudicial to their health and safety.

10. Work out proposals on lighting at the work place.

11. Organize exchanges of experience with a view to establishing more clearly the principles and methods of organization and training of the departments responsible for inspection in the fields of safety, health and hygiene at work.

III. Organization

12. Make recommendations on the organizational and advisory role of the departments responsible for dealing with health and safety problems in small and medium-sized undertakings, by defining, in particular, the role of specialists in occupational medicine, hygiene and safety.

13. Draw up the principles and criteria for monitoring workers whose health and safety are likely to be seriously at risk, such as certain maintenance and repair workers, certain migrant workers and certain workers in sub-contracting undertakings.

14. Draw up the principles for participation by workers and their representatives in the improvement of health and safety measures at the work place.

IV. Training and information

15. Ensure that employers and workers who are liable to be exposed to chemicals and other substances at their work place have adequate information on those substances.

    Prepare information notices and manuals on the handling of certain dangerous substances, particularly those covered by Community Directives. If need be, and taking account of existing Community regulations on the matter, draw up proposals on the establishment of systems and codes for the identification of dangerous substances at the work place.

16. (a) Draw up programmes aimed at better training as regards occupational hazards and measures for the safety of those at work (safety training) and
    (b) Training schemes intended for specific groups:
        – young workers,
        – groups who have special need of up-to-date information, i.e. workers doing a job to which they are not accustomed or who have difficulty in acquiring information through the usual channels, or to whom it is difficult to communicate information,
        – workers in key positions, i.e. people who lay down working conditions, communicate information, etc.

V. Statistics

17. Establish comparable data on mortality and occupational diseases and collect data from existing sources on the frequency, gravity and causes of accidents at work and occupational diseases, including, as far as possible, data on vulnerable groups of workers and absenteeism due to illness.
18. Compile an inventory of existing cancer registers at local, regional and national level in order to assess the comparability of the data contained in them and to ensure better coordination at Community level.

VI. Research

19. Identify and coordinate topics for applied research in the field of safety and health at work which can be the subject of future Community action.

VII. Cooperation

20. Within the framework of existing procedures, continue to cooperate with international organizations such as the World Health Organization and the International Labour Office and with national organizations and institutes outside the Community.
21. Continue to cooperate on other action by the Community and by Member States, where it proves worthwhile,

433

Requests the Commission to prepare annually, after consulting the Member States, a forward outline of the work it intends to carry out on the implementation of this resolution.

---

1. OJ No. C 308, 25.11.1982, p. 11.
2. OJ No. C 57, 29.2.1984.
3. OJ No. C 176, 4.8.1983, p. 16.
4. OJ No. C 13, 12.2.1974, p. 1.
5. OJ No. L 185, 9.7.1974, p. 15.
6. OJ No. C 117, 31.12.1973, p. 1.
7. OJ No. C. 112, 20.12.1973, p. 1.
8. OJ No. C. 139, 13.6.1977, p. 1.
9. OJ No. C 46, 17.2.1983, p. 1.
10. OJ No. C 165, 11.7.1978, p. 1.
11. OJ No. L 327, 3.12.1980, p. 8.
12. OJ No. L 230, 5.8.1982, p. 1.

Commission Communication

on its third programme concerning safety, hygiene and health at work
(88/C 28/02)

SUMMARY

In order to remain coherent and achieve its full impact, the creation of the internal market, 'the heart of the strategy to relaunch the construction of Europe', must incorporate a significant element of social policy, within which the physical and mental protection of workers stands high on the list of priorities. Taking full advantage of the opportunities afforded by the provisions of the Article 118A of the Single Act concerning the improvement of health and safety at work, and confirming its commitment to making full and rapid use of all the resources put at its disposal by this legal provision, the Commission has adopted the following action programme.

I. INTRODUCTION

A. The situation in the Member States

1. Despite the absence of sufficiently reliable statistics for Europe as a whole, the data available at national level are adequate demonstration of the high cost in human and social terms of industrial accidents. The estimated level of compensation paid out in 1984 for occupational accidents and diseases was around 16 000 million ECU in the EEC as a whole, amounting to 7 per cent of total sickness insurance payments.

434

2. An analysis of efforts made within the Member States to reduce occupational accidents and diseases shows that many means of increasing awareness of health and safety have been employed, not only at manager and worker level within firms, but also among the public at large. Cooperation between management, health and safety services and workers and their representatives within firms has been constantly improved and more efficiently organized. The inclusion of safety considerations, right from the planning stage, is recognized as a necessity.

3. National legislation is increasingly reflecting the work carried out at Community level; at the same time, there is a growing tendency to life restrictions intended to protect women at work, in the interests of equal employment opportunities for men and women.

4. General measures can be divided into those which, while not necessarily legislative, are aimed at improving installations in respect of work safety, removing the hazards presented by the use of tools and machinery, and protecting workers engaged in particularly dangerous tasks; secondly, protective measures for handling dangerous substances and finally, those enabling the appropriate advisory committees to ensure proper implementation of the legal and administrative provisions.

B. Community action

Under the EEC Treaty, the Commission has implemented two action programmes on safety and health at work since 1978.
These programmes were the subject of two Council resolutions:
The first of these, of 29 June 1978,[1] expressed the political will to enable a series of actions to be taken up to 1982 focussing on the aetiology substances, prevention of the dangers and harmful effects of machines, monitoring and inspection, and the improvement of human attitudes.
The second resolution, adopted on 27 February 1984,[2] was a continuation of the first action programme.
In this context, the Commission drafted 10 directives – seven of which have been adopted by the Council – on the protection of workers exposed to physical and chemical agents at work and the prevention of major accident hazards related to chemicals.

C. Legal bases and content of the new work programme

In order to confirm its will to reinforce the social dimension of the completion of the internal market, the Commission intends to develop its initiatives in the field of safety, hygiene and health at work, on the basis of Articles 117 and 118 of the EEC Treaty concerning social policy, and the specific provisions of the Single Act given in Article 118A(1) on the harmonization of improvements in the conditions of protection of the health and safety of workers, and

435

Article 118B which stresses the need to promote the dialogue between the two sides of industry.

The Commission has therefore decided, without awaiting the expiry of the second action programme, to draw up a new work programme concentrating chiefly on the following five subjects:
- safety and ergonomics,
- health and hygiene,
- information and training,
- initatives specifically directed at small and medium-sized enterprises,
- social dialogue.

II. THE PROGRAMME

A. Safety and ergonomics at work

1. Completion of the internal market – removal of technical barriers

In the White Paper on completing the internal market, the Commission took into account the 'underlying reasons for the existence of barriers to trade' and recognized in particular 'the overall equivalence of Member States legislative objectives in the protection of health and safety'.

In Commission has established and will continue close cooperation in defining essential safety requirements at the design and construction stages of new equipment.

Legislative harmonization will enable principal safety requirements to be established progressively, the necessary technical specifications being entrusted to organizations competent to deal with standardization. In view of the importance of the technical specifications for meeting the essential requirements for products used at work and the need to fully guarantee the dialogue between the two sides of industry on this question, the Commission will ensure adequate involvement of the trade unions in European standardization work and related activities.

2. Promotion of safety at work and application of ergonomic principles

(a) The Commission will prepare directives covering the organization of safey at work as well as the selection and use of appropriate plant, equipment, machinery and substances. In addition, the Commission will prepare a proposal for a Council decision regarding a system for the rapid exchange of information on specific safety hazards at work and the resulting restrictions placed on the use of dangerous substances, tools, equipment, etc.
(b) The Commission will prepare directives on personal protective equipment provided at the work place by the employer, with particular regard to appropriate use, user acceptability, availability, maintenance and testing.
(c) The Commission will revise the 1977 Directive on safety signs at work to bring it up to date and extend its scope.

436

(d) The Commission will put forward recommendations on the selection and use of equipment resulting from the development of new technologies and process control systems, with particular regard to the intrinsic safety of the equipment and ergonomic factors in its use.

(e) The Commission will prepare recommendations on good working practices aimed at avoiding back pain and back injury caused by bad work place design resulting in physical strain, faulty handling of materials, incorrect lifting and falls.

3. Safety in high-risk sectors

From the high-risk sectors the Commission has focussed its attention on the three with the highest accident rate and highest level of serious injury.

(a) Work at sea:
Working and living conditions on board are particularly difficult: movement of the work area, limited space, long duration and high intensity of work, noise multiplicity of individual workers' tasks, geographic or meteorological isolation of the vessel, limiting the possibilities of assistance and thus exacerbating the consequences of accidents, all contribute to a higher fatal accident rate in the seafaring occupations than in other 'high-risk' jobs.

In view of this situation, which affects around 500 000 workers, urgent measures are envisaged in order to make safety a more integral part of the design of vessels and the definition of tasks and to ensure the availability of adequate medical assistance and emergency services at sea.

(b) Agriculture:
Agriculture employs around 10 million people in the Community. More than half of all work accidents occur in farmyards and farm buildings, in particular during the handling of animals, horizontal or vertical movements and the handling of tools, loads and pesticides. However, owing to their self-employed status, farmers are not covered or concerned by the regulations governing health and safety at work, even when such regulations apply to agriculture.

The Commission is drawing up a directive on plant-protection products and recommendations concerning the design of farm buildings and electrical installations in agriculture.

(c) The construction industry:
The construction industry (building and civil engineering) is an essential element of economic activity in the European Community and employs almost 10 million workers. The building sector is characterized by a high proportion of small firms, attracted by the low level of capital outlay needed. It is also an activity with a higher-than-average risk of accidents and occupational diseases. In addition, as the current system of bidding for contracts gives no specific indication of safety and health costs, it may encourage tenderers to propose working methods which are apparently cheaper but less safe, or to adopt such

437

methods once the contract has been won. For these reasons, the traditional tripartite approach must be broadened to include designers and clients.

The Commission will prepare a directive on safety in the construction industry, which will stress the need to incorporate safety requirements right from the initial design stage, to make health and safety aspects clearer in the tenders, to closely define responsability on construction sites and to establish safety-related qualification requirements for certain tasks.

B. Occupational health and hygiene

1. In order to guarantee that exposure of workers to physical factors, bio-logical organisms and chemical substances is as low as reasonably achiev-able, and to enable the level of exposure to be monitored and measured, the Commission has forwarded to the Council a proposal for a directive establishing the basis for a Community list of exposure limit values for 100 agents.[3]

   The lists already drawn up by the Member States contain over 1 000 substances and the European Inventory of Existing Chemical Substances (EINECS) contains 100 000 entries.

   The Commission intends to extend this list accordingly, and will carry out studies to collect and evaluate toxicological and health data for in-dividual agents and their absorption pathways. The Commission will also examine ways and means of improving the collection of such data. In the case of special protective measures which may be required for those chemical agents which can be absorbed through the skin, the Commission will propose modifications to the existing directives.

2. In the case of agents likely to cause cancer, the Commission intends to submit to the Council a directive laying down general and specific mea-sures relating to occupational carcinogens. Subsequent directives will be proposed for the other carcinogenic agents in line with ongoing work on the classification and labelling of chemical substances. The Commission will also submit proposals for directives on certain groups of compounds such as pesticides. A proposal for a directive will also have to be made on biological agents which cause ill health, such as pathogenic micro-organisms, and genetic engineering techniques which may present a risk to health.

3. Once the proposal for a Council directive on exposure limit values for 100 agents (see B(2)) has been adopted by the Council, detailed examination of the measures required – for example, technical analyses – must be carried out to ensure accurate determination of exposure levels. To this end, the Commission will request technical assistance from competent organizations such as CEN. Account will also be taken of the current work of the Inter-national Organizations Standards in this area. The Commission will also study ways of improving the measurement methods available.

438

4. For very dangerous agents or work activities, the Commission has already submitted a proposal for a directive to the Council, in which the conditions to be applied for the proscription of specific agents are set out. Studies will be carried out to determine the other agents and/or processes to be added to this directive.

5. The Commission is working on the technical aspects of the directive on noise, which will be implemented from 1990. A proposal will be submitted extending its field of application by including workers not currently covered and by re-evaluating the threshold values.

6. The proposed directive on the harmonizations of classification and labelling of dangerous preparations[4] emphasizes the need for information on the composition of such preparations and the hazards they present. The Commission will investigate what supplementary measures are required for the health protection of workers under Article 118A.

7. In 1962 and 1966 the Commission made recommendations to the Member States concerning a European Schedule of Industrial Diseases.[5] This list must be revised to take account of subsequent improvements in the diagnosis of occupational diseases. The competent advisory committee is considering what improvements should be made to the Schedule and the Commission will make new recommendations to the Member States on the basis of its findings.

8. Legal provisions relating to occupational health services and their role in the protection of workers' health vary considerably between Member States. The appropriate advisory committee is currently preparing an opinion on the organization of these services and the respective roles of the various health and safety specialists, taking into account the previous work of the Economic and Social Committee. On the basis of this, the Commission intends to draft a recommendation on the subject.

C. Information

1. In its joint opinion on information and consultation, the Val Duchesse Working Party stated: 'When technological changes which imply major consequences for the work-force are introduced in the firm, workers and/or their respresentatives should be informed and consulted in accordance with the laws, agreements and practices in force in the Community countries'. The Commission considers this objective to be particularly important where such practices have a potential impact on health and safety.

2. In order to overcome the disparity of available information on chemical substances, the Commission intends to provide information on all the substances for which directives are proposed in the field of health and

439

safety. This information, together with that provided by the labelling system for dangerous substances and preparations, will be examined in order to determine its best use.

3. The protection of workers requires that research results and technical innovations aimed at improving working conditions are applied with the cooperation of all parties involved.

    To this end, the Commission will step up its work in the following fields:
    - the evaluation of recent research, to select the most promising for application in pilot projects,
    - the establishment of evaluating programmes with the cooperation in each case of two or more Member States,
    - the development of methods of disseminating the results, particularly for high-risk activities such as deep-sea diving or offshore exploration.

4. Finally, the Commission intends to increase information, training and exchange of experience between senior labour inspectors responsible for national implementation of regulations derived from Community directives.

    To this end, the regular meetings of the labour inspectors currently taking place of Community level will be formalized, seminars will be organized on specific topics, and the programme of exchange of inspectors between Member States will be expanded.

D. Training

1. The Commission recently submitted to the Council two communications on adult training in firms and vocational training for women. On the basis of the conclusions adopted by the Council, new action programmes will be drawn up in these areas, in which health and safety training at the workplace could be included.

    In addition, with the assistance of the European Centre of the Development of Vocational Training (CEDEFOP), the Commission will give special priority to the development of courses for the training of safety instructors.

2. Considerable differences exist between the Member States in the safety training and official recognition of those responsible for safety and health protection (company managers, safety officers, ergonomics and health specialist, first aiders, workers representatives, etc.). The Commission proposes to continue to encourage training initiatives for these various groups based upon generally accepted principles and practice.

3. When developing and during the course of special youth training schemes aimed particularly at the unemployed the Commission will study the provisions necessary to ensure the safety of participants, including those combined work/training schemes.

4. At university, or in higher level technical education, the Commission will

440

investigate ways of providing a full course of training in the appropriate safety precautions required for the future specialization of those who will be responsible for the safety of others, e.g. engineers, industrial chemists, and physicists.

5. In the high-risk sectors, the Commission has already developed a series of training modules for certain dangerous agricultural activities, and these have been tested in pilot projects. For sea fishing, financial and technical assistance has been provided for the development of the 'Medical Advice Centres Network' (Macnet), to extend the availability of medical assistance. The Commission intends to further develop these activities, which have a direct impact on these high-risk sectors.

6. To develop the training resources necessary to meet these various needs, the Commission intends to establish a network of collaboration centres involved in teaching the various disciplines and training workers and their representatives.

E. Small and medium-sized enterprises

1. The Community is devoting special attention to small and medium-sized enterprises, which are considered an essential element in economic recovery and job creation. The 'Action Programme for SMEs' stresses the need to keep regulations down to a necessary minimum. For its part, Article 118A of the Single European Act recognizes the special needs of SMEs in respect of safety and health problems.
   In order to fulfil both these essential requirements, and in order to keep the directives from imposing administrative, financial and legal constraints which may hold back the creation and development of SMEs, the Commission intends:
   – to undertake a study of how existing regulations on health and safety are interpreted and applied in a sample of SMEs,
   – to undertake a review of the special rules and exceptions which exist in national legislation regarding health, hygiene and safety at work, and to assess the need for harmonization of legislation in this field in accordance with Article 118A of the Single European Act.

2. When faced with activities which have a high health and safety risk, SMEs do not always possess the technical know-how in accident prevention, training and monitoring are difficult to carry out and accidents can have serious economic consequences.
   Any impetus towards new patterns of working can pose additional problems for such enterprises. Moreover, longer working hours in SMEs may lead to increased fatigue and a slackening of vigilance, increasing the risk of accidents. In addition, the measurement of exposure limits to dangerous agents, normally calculated on an eight-hour working day, may have to be adjusted.

The Commission therefore intends to study the effect of new patterns of working on safety, hygiene and health in SMEs.

3. The Commission is aware of the limited impact of information campaigns on the special rules and expections in health and safety legislation in SMEs. Furthermore, it would appear that efforts made within the Member States to provide advice and training on safety are not having the expected results.

To counter this, the Commission intends:
- to consider how health and safety regulations can be made clearer for proprietors of SMEs,
- to include advice on safety, hygiene and health at work in information manuals to be prepared for creators of SMEs,
- to prepare training modules on safety specifically for creators of SMEs, develop pilot projects integrating these modules into general training and provide for specific safety counselling,
- to develop a system for providing readily accessible information to SMEs on safety equipment and personal protective equipment.

F. Social dialogue

Development of Community action on health and safety and the balance which must be achieved between economic and social policy, as the large internal market is developed, both necessitate close collaboration between employer and worker representatives during the stages leading up to Commission decisions.

The Commission therefore intends to develop the dialogue between the two sides of industry in this field pursuant to Article 118B of the Single Act.

The Advisory Committee on Safety, Hygiene and Health Protection at Work, which has existed since 1974,[6] provides a highly appropriate forum for consultation between the two sides of industry. This Committee must play fully its part in assisting the Commission in defining the action it will take in this field. As in the past, the Commission will continue to consult the Committee on the proposals which it intends to present to the Council.

---

1. OJ No. C 165, 11.7.1978.
2. OJ No. C 67, 8.3.1984.
3. OJ No. C 164, 2.7.1986.
4. OJ No. C 196, 16.8.1967.
5. OJ No. 80, 31.8.1962 and OJ No. 147, 9.8.1966.
6. OJ No. L 185, 9.7.1974.

B. Specific Occupational Health and Safety Directives

Council Directive

of 25 July 1977

on the approximation of the laws, regulations and administrative provisions of the Member States relating to the provision of safety signs at places of work
(77/576/EEC)

THE COUNCIL OF THE EUROPEAN COMMUNITIES,

Having regard to the Treaty establishing the European Economic Community, and in particular Article 100 thereof,
Having regard to the proposal from the Commission,
Having regard to the opinion of the European Parliament,[1]
Having regard to the opinion of the Economic and Social Committee:[2]

Whereas, in its resolution of 21 January 1974 concerning a social action programme,[3] the Council affirmed the need to improve safety and protection of health in places of work, as part of the improvement of living and working conditions;

Whereas the freedom of movement of persons and services has considerably increased the risk of accidents at work and occupational diseases, in particular because of the differences in the organization of work within the Member States, the different languages and the resulting misunderstandings and errors; whereas these difficulties, which constitute an obstacle to the functioning of the common market, can be reduced by the introduction of a Community system of safety signs;

Whereas the use of uniform safety signs has positive effects both for workers at places of work, inside or outside undertakings, and for other persons having access to such places;

Whereas a Community system of safety signs can be effective only if it is ensured by means of unified provisions, if the presentation of the signs is as simple and striking as possible, if it makes the minimum use of explanatory texts and, furthermore, if those concerned receive full and repeated information thereon;

Whereas technical progress and the future development of international methods of signposting require that safety signs be brought up to date; whereas, in order to facilitate the carrying out of the necessary measures with

443

regard to Community signs, close collaboration should be instituted between the Member States and the Commission; whereas a Special Committee should be set up for the purpose,

HAS ADOPTED THIS DIRECTIVE:

Article 1
1. This Directive shall apply to safety signs at places of work.
2. This Directive shall not apply to:
    (a) signs used in rail, road, inland waterway, marine or air transport;
    (b) signs laid down for the placing of dangerous substances and preparations on the market;
    (c) coal mines.

Article 2
1. For the purposes of this Directive:
    (a) *system of safety signs*
        means a system of signs referring to a specific object or situation and providing safety information by means of a safety colour or sign;
    (b) *safety colour*
        means a colour to which a specific safety meaning is assigned;
    (c) *contrasting colour*
        means a colour contrasting with the safety colour and providing additional information;
    (d) *safety sign*
        means a sign combining geometrical shape, colour and symbol to provide specific safety information;
    (e) *prohibition sign*
        means a safety sign prohibiting behaviour likely to cause danger;
    (f) *warning sign*
        means a safety sign giving warning of a hazard;
    (g) *mandatory sign*
        means a safety sign prescribing a specific obligation;
    (h) *emergency sign*
        means a safety sign indicating, in the event of danger, an emergency exit, the way to an emergency installation or the location of a rescue appliance;
    (i) *information sign*
        means a safety sign providing safety information other than that referred to in points (e) to (h);
    (j) *additional sign*
        means a safety sign used only in conjunction with one of the safety signs referred to in points (e) to (h) and providing additional information;
    (k) *symbol*
        means a pictural representation, describing a specific situation, used on one of the safety signs referred to in points (e) to (h).

2. The meaning and use of safety and contrast colours and the shape, design and meaning of safety signs shall be as defined in Annex I.

Article 3

Member States shall take all necessary measures to ensure that:
– safety signs at all places of work conform to the principles laid down in Annex I,
– only those safety signs defined in Annex II are used to indicate the dangerous situations and to provide the information specified in that Annex;
– road traffic signs in force are used to regulate internal works traffic.

Article 4

Any amendments required to adapt Annex I, points 2 to 6, and Annex II to technical progress and to future developments in international methods regarding signs shall be adopted in accordance with the procedure laid down in Article 6.

Article 5

1. A Committee of Representatives of the Member States, with a Commission representative as chairman, is hereby set up.
2. The Committee shall establish its rules of procedures.

Article 6

1. Where the procedure laid down in this Article is invoked, the matter shall be referred to the Committee by its chairman, either on his own initiative or at the request of a representative of a Member State.
2. The Commission representative shall submit to the Committee a draft of the measures to be taken. The Committee shall give its opinion on the draft within the time laid down by the chairman, having regard to the urgency of the matter. Decisions shall be taken by a majority of 41 votes, the votes of the Member States being weighted as laid down in Article 148(2) of the Treaty. The chairman shall not vote.
3. (a) Proposed measures which are in accordance with the opinion of the Committee shall be taken by the Commission.
   (b) Where the proposed measures are not in accordance with the opinion of the Committee, or if no opinion is delivered, the Commission shall forthwith submit to the Council a proposal on the measures to be taken. The Council shall act by a qualified majority.
   (c) if the Council has not acted within three months of receiving the proposal, the proposed measures shall be adopted by the Commission.

Article 7

1. Member States shall adopt and publish by 1 January 1979 the measures necessary to comply with this Directive and shall inform the Commission immediately thereof. They shall apply these measures from 1 January 1981 at the latest.
2. Member States shall communicate to the Commission the text of any national provisions which they adopt in the field covered by this Directive.

445

Article 8
This Directive is addressed to the Member States.

Done at Brussels, 25 July 1977.

For the Council
The President
H. Simonet

---

1. OJ No. C 178, 2.8.1976, p. 57.
2. OJ No. C 278, 24.11.1976, p. 3.
3. OJ No. C 13, 12.2.1974, p. 1.

ANNEX 1

Basic principles of the system of safety signs

1. GENERAL

1.1. The objective of the system of safety signs is to draw attention rapidly and unambiguously to objects and situations capable of causing specific hazards.
1.2. Under no circumstances is the system of safety signs a substitute for the requisite protective measures.
1.3. The system of safety signs may be used only to give information related to safety.
1.4. The effectiveness of the system of safety signs is dependent in particular on the provision of full and constantly repeated information to all persons likely to benefit therefrom.

2. SAFETY COLOURS AND CONTRASTING COLOURS

2.1 Meaning of safety colours

TABLE 1

Safety colour	Meaning or purpose	Examples of use
Red	Stop Prohibition	Stop signs Emergency shutdown devices Prohibition signs
	This colour is also used to identify fire-fighting equipment.	
Yellow	Caution! Possible danger	Identification of dangers (fire, explosion, radiation, chemical hazards, etc.) Identification of steps, dangerous passages, obstacles

Safety colour	Meaning or purpose	Examples of use
Green	No danger First aid	Identification of emergency routes and emergency exits Safety showers First aid stations and rescue points
Blue[1]	Mandatory signs Information	Obligation to wear individual safety equipment Location of telephone

1. Counts as a safety colour only when used in conjunction with a symbol or words on a mandatory sign or information sign bearing instructions relating to technical prevention.

2.2 Contrasting colours and symbol colours

TABLE 2

Safety colour	Contrasting colour	Symbol colour
Red	White	Black
Yellow	Black	Black
Green	White	White
Blue	White	White

3. GEOMETRICAL FORM AND MEANING OF SAFETY SIGNS

TABLE 3

Geometrical form	Meaning
⬭	Mandatory and prohibition signs
△	Warning signs
▢ ▢	Emergency, information and additional signs

447

4. COMBINATIONS OF SHAPES AND COLOURS AND THEIR MEANINGS FOR SIGNS

TABLE 4

Shape / Colour	◯	△	▭
Red	Prohibition		Fire-fighting equipment
Yellow		Caution, possible danger	
Green			No danger Rescue equipment
Blue	Mandatory		Information or instruction

5. DESIGN OF SAFETY SIGNS

5.1 Prohibition signs

Background: white; symbol or wording: black.
   The safety colour red must appear around the edge and in a transverse bar and must cover at least 35 per cent of the surface of the sign.

5.2 Warning, mandatory, emergency and information signs

Background: safety colour; symbol or wording: contrasting colour.
   A yellow triangle must have a black edge. The safety colour must cover at least 50 per cent of the surface of the sign.

5.3 Additional signs

Background: white; wording: black;
or
background: safety colour; wording: contrasting colour.

448

5.4 Symbols

The design must be as simple as possible and details not essential to comprehension must be left out.

6. Yellow/black danger identification

Identification of permanent risk locations such as:
– locations where there is a risk of collision,
  falling, stumbling or of falling loads,
– steps, holes in floors, etc.
(Proportion of safety colour at least 50 per cent)

BILAG II – ANLAGE II – ANNEX II –
ANNEXE II – ALLEGATO II – BIJLAGE II

Særlig sikkerhedsskiltning – besondere Sicherheitskennzeichnung – Special system of safety signs – Signalisation particulière de sécurité – Segnaletica particolare di sicurezza – Bijzondere veiligheidssignalering

1. Forbudstavler – Verbotszeichen – Prohibition signs – Signaux d'interdiction – Segnali di divieto – Verbodssignalen

a)

b)

c)

Rygning forbudt	Rygning og åben ild forbudt	Ingen adgang for fodgængere
Rauchen verboten	Feuer, offenes Licht und Rauchen	Für Fußgänger verboten
No smoking	verboten	Pedestrians forbidden
Défense de fumer	Smoking and naked flames forbidden	Interdit aux piétons
Vietato fumare	Flamme nue interdite et défense de fumer	Vietato ai pedoni
Verboden te roken	Vietato fumare o usare fiamme libere	Verboden voor voetgangers
	Vuur, open vlam en roken verboden	

d)

e)

Sluk ikke med vand	Ikke drikkevand
Verbot, mit Wasser zu löschen	Kein Trinkwasser
Do not extinguish with water	Not drinkable
Défense d'éteindre avec de l'eau	Eau non potable
Divieto di spegnere con acqua	Acqua non potabile
Verboden met water te blussen	Geen drinkwater

450

2. Advarselstavler – Warnzeichen – Warning signs – Signaux d'avertissement – Segnali di avvertimento – Waarschuwingssignalen

a)

Brandfarlige stoffer
Warnung vor feuerfährlichen
Stoffen
Flammable matter
Matières inflammables
Materiale infiammabile
Ontvlambare stoffen

b)

Eksplosionsfarlige stoffer
Warnung vor explosionsgefährlichen
Stoffen
Explosive matter
Matières explosives
Materiale esplosivo
Explosieve stoffen

c)

Giftige stoffer
Warnung vor giftigen Stoffen
Toxic matter
Matières toxiques
Sostanze velenose
Giftige stoffen

d)

Ætsende stoffer
Warnung vor ätzenden Stoffen
Corrosive matter
Matières corrosives
Sostanze corrosive
Bijtende stoffen

e)

Ioniserende stråling
Radioaktivitet/Røntgenstråling
Warnung vor radioaktiven Stoffen oder
ionisierenden Strahlen
Radioactive matter
Matières radioactives
Radiazioni pericolose
Radioactieve stoffen

f)

Kran i arbejde
Warnung vor schwebender Last
Beware, overhead load
Charges suspendues
Attenzione ai carichi sospesi
Hangende lasten

g)

Pas på kørende transport
Warnung vor Flurförderzeugen
Beware, industrial trucks
Chariots de manutention
Carrelli di movimentazione
Transportvoertuigen

h)

Farlig elektrisk spænding
Warnung vor gefährlicher elektrischer
Spannung
Danger: electricity
Danger électrique
Tensione elettrica pericolosa
Gevaar voor elektrische spanning

i)

Giv agt
Warnung vor einer Gefahrenstelle
General danger
Danger générale
Pericolo generico
Gevaar

451

3. Påbudstavler – Gebotszeichen – Mandatory signs – Signaux d'obligation –
Segnali di prescrizione – Gebodssignalen

a)

b)

c)

Øjenværn påbudt
Augenschutz tragen
Eye protection must be worn
Protection obligatoire de la vue
Protezione degli occhi
Oogbescherming verplicht

Hovedværn påbudt
Schutzhelm tragen
Safety helmet must be worn
Protection obligatoire de la tête
Casco di protezione
Veiligheidshelm verplicht

Høreværn påbudt
Gehörschutz tragen
Ear protection must be worn
Protection obligatoire de l'ouïe
Protezione dell'udito
Gehoorbescherming verplicht

d)

e)

f)

Åndedrætsværn påbudt
Atemschutz tragen
Respiratory equipment must be used
Protection obligatoire des voies
respiratoires
Protezione vie respiratorie
Adembescherming verplicht

Fodværn påbudt
Schutzschuhe tragen
Safety boots must be worn
Protection obligatoire des pieds
Calzature di sicurezza
Veiligheidsschoenen verplicht

Beskyttelseshandsker påbudt
Schutzhandschuhe tragen
Safety gloves must be worn
Protection obligatoire des mains
Guanti di protezione
Veiligheidshandschoenen verplicht

452

4. Redningstavler – Rettungszeichen – Emergency signs – Signaux de sauvetage
– Segnali di salvataggio – Reddingssignalen

a)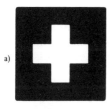

b)

Føstehjælp
Hinweis auf 'Erste Hilfe'
First aid post
Poste premiers secours
Pronto soccorso
Eerste hulp-post

c)

eller/oder/or/ou/o/of

d)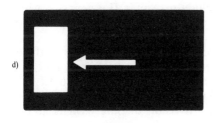

e)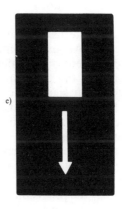

Retningsangivelse til nødudgang
Fluchtweg (Richtungsangabe für Fluchtweg)
Emergency exit to the left
Issue de secours vers la gauche
Uscita d'emergenza a sinistra
Nooduitgang naar links

Nødudgang
(anbringes over udgangen)
Fluchtweg
(über dem Fluchtausgang anzubringen)
Emergency exit
(to be placed above the exit)
Sortie de secours
(à placer au-dessus de la sortie)
Uscita d'emergenza
(da collocare sopra l'uscita)
Nooduitgang
(te plaatsen boven de uitgang)

Commission Directive

of 21 June 1979

amending the Annexes to Council Directive 77/576/EEC on the approximation of the laws, regulations and administrative provisions of the Member States relating to the provision of safety signs at places of work
(79/640/EEC)

THE COMMISSION OF THE EUROPEAN COMMUNITIES,

Having regard to the Treaty establishing the European Economic Community,
Having regard to Council Directive 77/576/EEC of 25 July 1977 on the approximation of the laws, regulations and administrative provisions of the Member States relating to the provisions of safety signs at places of work,[1] and in particular Articles 4, 5 and 6 thereof:

Whereas the provisions in the Annexes to the abovementioned Directive relating to a uniform system of safety signs at places of work need to be regularly adapted to take account of technical progress and the future development of international methods of signposting;

Whereas Annex I contains no regulations concerning the relationship between dimensions of safety signs and distance of observation and no precise definition of the colorimetric and photometric properties of the materials used for such signs; whereas, when approving the Directive, the Council asked that these omissions be promptly rectified; whereas the addition which has accordingly been made to Annex I is in line with the current international standards in this field;

Whereas it seems necessary to include in Annex II a new sign warning of the presence of laser beams; whereas here also the sign on which there is unanimous international agreement can serve as a model;

Whereas the provisions of this Directive are in accordance with the opinion of the Committee for the Adjustment to Technical Progress and to Future Development in International Methods of Directive 77/576/EEC on the Approximation of the Laws, Regulations and Administrative Provisions of the Member States Relating to the Provision of Safety Signs at Places of Work,

HAS ADOPTED THIS DIRECTIVE:

Article 1
The Annexes to Council Directives 77/576/EEC are amended as provided in the following Articles.

Article 2
In Annex I:

1. the following paragraph shall be inserted after paragraph 5.4 of section 5, 'Design of safety signs':

454

'5.5. Dimensions of safety signs

The dimensions of safety signs may be determined in accordance with the formula:

$$A \geq \frac{1^2}{2000}$$

where A is the area of the sign in m^2 and 1 the greastest distance in m from which the sign must be understood.

Note: This formula is applicable for distances up to about 50 m.'

2. after section 5, 'Design of safety signs', the following new section 6 shall be inserted:

'6. COLORIMETRIC AND PHOTOMETRIC PROPERTIES OF MATERIALS

As regards the colour and photometric properties of working substances the ISO standards and the standards of the International Lighting Commission (CIE – Commission international de l'éclairage) are recommended.'

3. The existing section 6 'Yellow/back danger identification' shall become section 7.

Article 3
In Annex II, No. 2, 'Warning signs' the following sign is added:

j)

Laserstråler
Warnung vor Laserstrahl
Laser beam
Rayonnements laser
Raggio laser
Laserstraal

Article 4
Member States shall bring into force the laws, regulations or administrative provisions necessary to comply with the provisions of this Directive by 1 January 1981 at the latest. They shall forthwith inform the Commission thereof.

Article 5

This Directive is addressed to the Member States.

Done at Brussels, 21 June 1979.

For the Commission
Henk Vredeling
Vice-President

---

1. OJ No. L 229, 7.9.1977, p. 12.

Council Directive

29 June 1978

on the approximation of the laws, regulations and administrative provisions of the Member States on the protection of the health of workers exposed to vinyl chloride monomer
(78/610/EEC)

THE COUNCIL OF THE EUROPEAN COMMUNITIES,

Having regard to the Treaty establishing the European Economic Community, and in particular Article 100 thereof,
Having regard to the proposal from the Commission,
Having regard to the opinion of the European Parliament,[1]
Having regard to the opinion of the Economic and Social Committee:[2]
Whereas, in the past it was recognized that vinyl chloride monomer was capable of giving rise only to the generally reversible disease known as 'occupational acro-osteolysis'; whereas more recent evidence from epidemiological studies and animal experimentation indicates that prolonged and/or repeated exposure to high concentrations of vinyl chloride monomer in the atmosphere may give rise to 'vinyl chloride monomer' syndrome encompassing, in addition to occupational acro-osteolysis, the skin disease scleroderma and liver disorders;
Whereas vinyl chloride monomer should also be regarded as a carcinogen which may cause angiosarcoma, a rare malignant tumour which can also occur without any known cause;
Whereas, although working conditions are considerably better than those under which the above syndrome formerly occurred, a comparison of protective measures taken by each Member State reveals certain differences; whereas, therefore, in the interests of balanced economic and social development, these national laws, which directly affect the functioning of the common market, should be harmonized and improved;
Whereas the first step should be to take technical preventive and protective measures based on the latest scientific knowledge so that the values of

456

concentrations of vinyl chloride monomer in the atmosphere in the works can be reduced to an extremely low figure;

Whereas medical surveillance of workers in the vinyl chloride monomer and vinyl chloride polymer industry should take account of the latest medical knowledge, in order that the health of workers in this important sector of the chemical industry may be protected;

Whereas the urgent need to harmonize laws in this field is recognized by both sides of industry which took part in the discussion on this specific problem; whereas efforts must therefore be made towards the approximation, while the improvement is being maintained, of the laws, regulations and administrative provisions of the Member States as envisaged in Article 117 of the Treaty;

Whereas the provisions of this Directive constitute minimal requirements which may be re-examined in the light of the experience gained and of progress in medical techniques and knowledge in this field, the final objective being to achieve optimum protection of workers,

Has adopted this Directive:

Article 1

1. The object of this Directive is the protection of workers:
   - employed in works in which vinyl chloride monomer is produced, reclaimed, stored, discharged into containers, transported or used in any way whatsoever, or in which vinyl chloride monomer is converted into vinyl chloride polymers; and
   - exposed to the effects of vinyl chloride monomer in a working area.
2. This protection shall comprise:
   - technical preventive measures;
   - the establishment of limit values for the atmospheric concentration of vinyl chloride monomer in the working area;
   - the definition of measuring methods and the fixing of provisions for monitoring the atmospheric concentration of vinyl chloride monomer in the working area;
   - if necessary, personal protection measures;
   - adequate information for workers on the risks to which they are exposed and the precautions to be taken;
   - the keeping of a register of workers with particulars of the type and duration of their work and the exposure to which they have been subjected;
   - medical surveillance provisions.

Article 2

For the purpose of this Directive:

(a) 'working area' means a section of a works with defined boundaries which may comprise one or more workplaces. It is characterized by the fact that the individual worker spends irregular periods of time there at various workplaces in the course of his duty or duties, that the length of time

457

spent at these individual workplaces cannot be more closely defined and that further subdivision of the working area into smaller units is not possible;

(b) 'technical long-term limit value' means the value which shall not be exceeded by the mean concentration, integrated with respect to time, of vinyl chloride monomer in the atmosphere of a working area, the reference period being the year, with account being taken only of the concentrations measured during the periods in which the plant is in operation and of the duration of such periods.

For guidance and for practical reasons, Annex I contains a table of the corresponding limit values obtained from statistics with a view to being able to detect, over shorter periods, the risk of the technical long-term limit value's being exceeded.

The concentration values recorded during the alarm periods referred to in Article 6 shall not be taken into account in the calculation of the mean concentration;

(c) 'competent doctor' means the doctor responsible for the medical surveillance of the workers referred to in Article 1(1).

Article 3

1. The fundamental aim of the technical measures adopted to meet the requirements of this Directive shall be to reduce to the lowest possible levels the concentrations of vinyl chloride monomer to which workers are exposed. All working areas in works referred to in Article 1(1) shall therefore be monitored for the atmospheric concentration of vinyl chloride monomer.

2. For the works referred to in Article 1(1), the technical long-term limit value shall be three parts per million.

An adjustment period not exceeding one year in which to comply with the technical long-term limit value of three parts per million shall be provided for in the case of existing plant at such works.

Article 4

1. The concentration of vinyl chloride monomer in the working area may be monitored by continuous or discontinuous methods. The permanent sequential method shall be regarded as being a continuous method.

However, the use of a continuous or permanent sequential method shall be obligatory in enclosed vinyl chloride monomer polymerization plant.

2. In the case of continuous or permanent sequential measurements over a period of one year, the technical long-term limit value shall be considered as having been complied with if the arithmetic mean concentration is found not to exceed this value.

In the case of discontinuous measurements, the number of values measured shall be such that it is possible to predict with a confidence coefficient of at least 95 per cent – accepting the relevant assumptions made in Annex I – that the actual mean annual concentration will not exceed the technical long-term limit value.

458

3. Any measurment system which records accurately for the purposes of analysis at least one third of the technical long-term limit value concentration shall be regarded as suitable.

4. If non-selective systems of measurment are used for measuring vinyl chloride monomer, the measurement recorded shall be taken as the total vinyl chloride monomer concentration value.

5. Measuring instruments shall be calibrated at regular intervals. Calibration shall be carried out by suitable methods based on the latest state of the art.

Article 5
1. Measurments of the atmospheric concentration of vinyl chloride monomer in a working area for the purpose of verifying compliance with the technical long-term limit value shall be carried out using measuring points chosen so that the results obtained are as representative as possible of the individual vinyl chloride monomer exposure level of workers in that area.

2. Depending on the size of the working area, there may be one or more measuring points. If there is more than one measuring point, the mean value for the various measuring points shall be considered in principle as the representative value for the whole working area.

    If the results obtained are not representative of the vinyl chloride monomer concentration in the working area, the measuring point for checking compliance with the technical long-term limit value shall be that point in the working area where the worker is exposed to the highest mean concentration.

3. Measurements carried out as described in this Article may be combined with measurements based on individual sampling, i.e. using devices worn by exposed persons for the purpose of verifying the suitability of the measuring points chosen and of obtaining any other information relevant to technical prevention and medical surveillance.

Article 6
1. In order that abnormal increases in vinyl chloride monomer concentration levels may be detected, a monitoring system capable of detecting such increases shall be provided in places where they may occur.

    In cases involving such an increase in the concentration level, technical measures shall be taken without delay to determine and to remedy the causes thereof.

2. The value corresponding to the alarm threshold shall not exceed, at a measuring point, 15 parts per million for mean values measured over a period of one hour, 20 parts per million for mean values measured over 20 minutes or 30 parts per million for mean values measured over two minutes. If the alarm threshold is exceeded, personal protection measures shall be taken without delay.

Article 7

Appropriate personal protection measures shall be provided for certain operations (e.g. cleaning of autoclaves, servicing and repairs) during which it cannot be guaranteed that concentrations will be kept below the limit values through operational or ventilation measures.

Article 8

Employers shall inform the workers referred to in Article 1(1), both upon recruitment or prior to their taking up their activities and at regular intervals thereafter, of the health hazards associated with vinyl chloride monomer and of the precautions to be taken when this substance is being handled.

Article 9

1. Employers shall keep a register of the workers referred to in Article 1(1), with particulars of the type and duration of work and the exposure to which they have been subjected. This register shall be given to the competent doctor.

2. A worker shall, at his request, be given the opportunity to note the particulars in the register concerning him.

3. Employers shall make available to workers' representatives at the undertaking, at their request, the results of the measurments taken at the places of work.

Article 10

1. Employers shall be required to ensure that the workers referred to in Article 1(1) are examined by the competent doctor, both upon recruitment or prior to their taking up their activities and subsequently.

2. Without prejudice to national provisions, the competent doctor shall determine in each individual case the frequency and type of the examination provided for in paragraph 1. The necessary guidelines are given in Annex II.

3. Member States shall take the necessary steps to ensure that the registers referred to in Article 9 and the medical records are kept for at least 30 years from the date on which the activity of the workers referred to in Article 1(1) was taken up.

    For workers already engaged in such activity on the date of entry into force of the provisions adopted pursuant to this Directive, the 30-year period shall commence on that date.

    Member States shall determine how the registers and the medical records are to be used for study and research purposes.

Article 11

1. Member States shall bring into force the laws, regulations and admini-

460

strative provisions necessary to comply with this Directive within 18 months of its notification and shall forthwith inform the Commission thereof.

2. Member States shall communicate to the Commission the texts of the provisions of national law which they adopt in the field covered by this Directive.

Article 12
This Directive is addressed to the Member States.

Done at Luxembourg, 29 June 1978.

For the Council
The President
S. Auken

---

1. OJ No. C 163, 11.7.1977, p. 11.
2. OJ No. C 287, 30.11.1977, p.11.

ANNEX I

Statistical basis for the technial long-term limit value

(Article 2(b))
1. Owing to differences in definition, the recommended values for the permissible atmospheric concentration substances injurious to health at the workplace currently vary from country to country.

This Directive is concerned with a new, statistically-defined reference value – the technical long-term limit value – which should be regarded as a means annual value.

2. The limit values for shorter reference periods are based on data obtained by extensive measurement of vinyl chloride monomer concentrations in the vinyl chloride polymer industry. These measurements accord with the data resulting from observations both on other substances injurious to health and for other sectors of industry.

The data can be summarized as follows:
(a) the distributions of concentrations of substances injurious to health can be represented log normally;
(b) the logarithmic variance $\sigma^2 (\tau, T)$ is a function of the reference period τ from which the mean of the individual values is calculated and of the assessment period T over which all individual values extend.

This relationship can, with a degree of approximation, be expressed by the following equation:
$$\sigma^2 (\tau, T) = 2 \cdot 5 \cdot 10^{-2} \log (T/\tau).$$

461

3. Assuming these data, a mean ratio of the limit values for shorter reference periods to the technical long-term limit value can be established:

Reference period	Limit value in parts per million (rounded off)	Ratio of short-term value to technical long-term limit value
One year	3	1
One month	5	1.7
One week	6	1.95
Eight hours	7	2.3
One hour	8	2.55

4. The above limit values for reference periods shorter than one year must have a maximum 5 per cent probability of being exceeded when the annual arithmetic mean of atmospheric vinyl chloride monomer concentrations is three parts per million.

ANNEX II

Guidelines for the medical surveillance of workers

(Article 10(2))
1. Current knowledge indicates that over-exposure to vinyl chloride monomer can give rise to the following disorders and diseases:
    – sclerodermatous skin disorders,
    – circulatory disorders in the hands and feet (similar to Raynaud's syndrome),
    – acro-osteolysis (affecting certain bone structures, particularly the phalanges in the hand),
    – liver and spleen fibroses (similar to perilobular fibrosis, known as Banti's syndrome),
    – lung function disorders,
    – thrombocytopenia,
    – hepatic angiosarcoma.

2. Medical surveillance of the workers should take account of all symptoms and syndromes, with particular emphasis on the area of greatest risk. As far as is known at present, no symptoms occurring separately or in combination have been identified as precursors or transitional stages of hepatic sarcoma. As no specific methods of preventive analysis are known for this disease, medical action shall include at least the following measures as minimum requirements:
    (a) records of the worker's medical and occupational history,
    (b) clinical examination of the extremities, the skin and the abdomen,
    (c) X-ray of the hand bones (every two years).

Further tests, particularly laboratory tests, are desirable. These should be decided by the competent doctor in the light of the most recent developments in industrial medicine.

The following laboratory tests are suggested at present for prognostic epidemiological surveys:
- urinalysis (glucose, proteins, salts, bile pigments, urobilinogen),
- erythrocyte sedimentation rate,
- blood platelet count,
- determination of total bilirubin level,
- determination of transaminase levels (SGOT, SGPT),
- determination of gamma glutamyl transferase (GT) level,
- thymol turbidity test,
- alkaline phospatase level,
- determination of cryoglobulin.

3. As in the case of all biological examinations, the results of the tests shall be interpreted in the light of the laboratory techniques used and their normal values. Generally speaking, the significance of a functional disorder is assessed after joint consideration of the results obtained from various examinations and by developments in the anomalies observed. As a general rule, abnormal results shall be investigated and, if necessary, additional specialist examinations carried out.

4. The competent doctor shall decide in each case whether a worker is suitable for a working area.

The competent doctor shall also decide what contra-indications apply. The most important of these are:
- typical vascular and neurovascular lesions,
- lung function disorders,
- clinical or biological hepatic insufficiency,
- diabetes,
- chronic renal insufficiency,
- thrombocytopenia and hemorrhagic disorders,
- certain chronic skin diseases such as scleroderma,
- abuse of alcohol and/or addiction to drugs.

This list, which is intended merely for guidance, has been drawn up using pathological data obtained from previous retrospective studies.

Council Directive

27 November 1980

on the protection of workers from the risks related to exposure to chemical, physical and biological agents at work
(80/1107/EEC)

THE COUNCIL OF THE EUROPEAN COMMUNITIES,

Having regard to the Treaty establishing the European Economic Community, and in particular Article 100 thereof,

Having regard to the proposal from the Commission,[1] drafted following consultation with the Advisory Committee on Safety, Hygiene and Health Protection at work,

Having regard to the opinion of the European Parliament,[2]

Having regard to the opinion of the Economic and Social Committee:[3]

Whereas the Council resolution of 29 June 1978 on an action programme of the European Communities on safety and health at work,[4] provides for the harmonization of provisions and measures regarding the protection of workers with respect to chemical, physical and biological agents; whereas efforts must therefore be made towards approximation, while the improvement is being maintained, of the laws, regulations and administrative provisions of the Member States in accordance with Article 117 of the Treaty;

Whereas certain differences are revealed by an examination of the measures taken by Member States to protect workers from the risks related to exposure to chemical, physical and biological agents at work; whereas, therefore, in the interests of balanced development, these measures, which directly affect the functioning of the common market, should be approximated and improved; whereas this approximation and improvement should be based on common principles;

Whereas the said protection should as far as possible be ensured by measures to prevent exposure or keep it at as low a level as is reasonably practicable;

Whereas to this end it is appropriate that the Member States should, when they adopt provisions in this field, comply with a set of requirements, including in particular the laying down of limit values; whereas an initial list of agents may be adopted in this Directive for the application of further more specific requirements; whereas the Member States will determine whether and to what extent each of these requirements is applicable to the agent concerned;

Whereas provision should be made, within the time limits set by this Directive, for the implementation, in respect of a limited number of agents, of provisions to ensure, for the workers concerned, appropriate surveillance of their state of health during exposure and the provision of appropriate information;

464

Whereas the Council will lay down the limit values and other specific requirements for certain agents in individual Directives;

Whereas certain technical aspects concerning the specific requirements established in the individual directives can be reviewed in the light of experience and progress made in the technical and scientific fields;

Whereas representatives of employers and workers have a role to play in the protection of workers;

Whereas, since the Hellenic Republic is to become a member of the European Economic Community on the 1 January 1981 in accordance with the 1979 Act of Accession, it should be granted a longer period in which to implement this Directive so as to enable it to set up the necessary legislative, social and technical structures, in particular those concerning consultation of both sides of industry, the setting up of a system for monitoring the health of workers as well as the supervision of such implementation,

HAS ADOPTED THIS DIRECTIVE:

Article 1
1. The aim of this Directive is the protection of workers against risks to their health and safety, including the prevention of such risks, arising or likely to arise at work from exposure to chemical, physical and biological agents considered harmful.

2. This Directive shall not apply to:
   - workers exposed to radiation covered by the Treaty establishing the European Atomic Energy Community;
   - sea transport;
   - air transport.

Article 2
For the purposes of this Directive:
(a) 'agent' means any chemical, physical or biological agent present at work and likely to be harmful to health;
(b) 'worker' means any employed person exposed or likely to be exposed to such agents at work;
(c) 'limit value' means the exposure limit or biological indicator limit in the appropriate medium, depending on the agent.

Article 3
1. In order that the exposure of workers to agents be avoided or kept at as low a level as is reasonably practicable, Member States shall, when they adopt provisions for the protection of workers, concerning an agent, take:
   - the measures set out in Article 4;
   - the additional measures set out in Article 5, where the agent appears in the initial list in Annex I.

465

2. For the purposes of paragraph 1, the Member States shall determine the extent, if any, to which each of the measures provided for in Articles 4 and 5 is to apply, taking into account the nature of the agent, the extent and duration of the exposure, the gravity of the risk and the available knowledge concerning it, together with the degree of urgency of the measures to be adopted.

3. Member States shall adopt the measures necessary to ensure:
   - in the case of the agents listed in Annex II, Part A, appropriate surveillance of the state of health of workers during the period of exposure;
   - in the case of the agents listed in Annex II, Part B, access for workers and/or their representatives at the place of work to appropriate information on the dangers which these agents present.

4. The adoption of the measures referred to in paragraph 3 by the Member States shall not oblige them to apply paragraphs 1 and 2.

Article 4
The measures referred to in the first indent of Article 3(1) shall be:
1. limitation of the use of the agent at the place of work;
2. limitation of the number of workers exposed or likely to be exposed;
3. prevention by engineering control;
4. establishment of limit values and of sampling procedures, measuring procedures and procedures for evaluating results;
5. protection measures involving the application of suitable working procedures and methods;
6. collective protection measures;
7. individual protection measures, where exposure cannot reasonably be avoided by other means;
8. hygiene measures;
9. information for workers on the potential risks connected with their exposure, on the technical preventive measures to be observed by workers, and on the precautions taken by the employer and to be taken by workers;
10. use of warning and safety signs;
11. surveillance of the health of workers;
12. keeping updated records of exposure levels, lists of workers exposed and medical records;
13. emergency measures for abnormal exposures;
14. if necessary, general or limited ban on the agent, in cases where use of the other means available does not make it possible to ensure adequate protection.

Article 5
The additional measures referred to in the second indent of Article 3(1) shall be:
1. providing medical surveillance of workers prior to exposure and thereafter

466

at regular intervals. In special cases, it shall be ensured that a suitable form of health surveillance is available to workers who have been exposed to the agent, after exposure has ceased;

2. access by workers and/or their representatives at the place of work to the results of exposure measurements and to the anonymous collective results of the biological tests indicating exposure when such tests are provided for;

3. access by each worker concerned to the results of his own biological tests indicating exposure;

4. informing workers and/or their representatives at the place of work where the limit values referred to in Article 4 are exceeded, of the causes thereof and of the measures taken or to be taken in order to rectify the situation;

5. access by workers and/or their representatives at the place of work to appropriate information to improve their knowledge of the dangers to which they are exposed.

Article 6
Member States shall see to it that:
– workers' and employers' organizations are consulted before the provisions for the implementation of the measures referred to in Article 3 are adopted and that workers' representatives in the undertakings or establishments, where they exist, can check that such provisions are applied or can be involved in their application;
– any worker temporarily suspended on medical grounds in accordance with national laws or practices from exposure to the action of an agent is, where possible, provided with another job;
– the measures adopted in implementation of this Directive are consistent with the need to protect public health and the environment.

Article 7
This Directive and the individual Directives referred to in Article 8 shall not prejudice the right of Member States to apply or introduce laws, regulations or administrative provisions ensuring greater protection for workers.

Article 8
1. In the individual Directives which it adopts on the agents listed in Annex I, the Council shall, acting on a proposal from the Commission, lay down the limit value or values and the other specific requirements applicable.

2. The titles of the individual Directives shall include serial numbers.

3. Adaption to technical progress in accordance with the procedure in Article 10 shall be restricted to the technical aspects listed in Annex III under the conditions laid down in the individual Directives.

Article 9

1. With a view to the adaptation to technical progress referred to in Article 8(3) a committee is hereby established consisting of representatives of the Member States and presided over by a representative of the Commission.

2. The Committee shall draw up its own rules of procedure.

Article 10

1. Where the procedure laid down in this Article is invoked, matters shall be referred to the Committee by the chairman, either on his own initiative or at the request of the representative of a Member State.

2. The representative of the Commission shall submit to the Committee a draft of the measures to be taken. The Committee shall deliver its opinion on this draft within a time limit which the chairman may set according to the urgency of the matter. Decisions shall be taken by a majority of 41 votes, the votes of Member States being weighted as provided for in Article 148(2) of the Treaty. The chairman shall not vote.

3. (a) The Commission shall take the proposed measures where they are in accordance with the opinion of the Committee.
   (b) Where the proposed measures are not in accordance with the opinion of the Committee, or if no opinion is delivered the Commission shall without delay propose to the Council the measures to be taken. The Council shall act by a qualified majority.
   (c) If the Council has not acted within three months of receiving the proposal, the proposed measures shall be adopted by the Commission.

Article 11

1. Member States shall bring into force the laws, regulations and administrative provisions necessary to comply with this Directive within a period of three years of its notification and shall forthwith inform the Commission thereof.

   However, in the case of Article 3(3), first indent, this period shall be four years.

   In derogation from the above provisions, the time limits laid down in the first and second subparagraphs shall be four and five years respectively in the case of the Hellenic Republic.

2. Member States shall communicate to the Commission the provisions of the national law which they adopt in the field governed by this Directive.

Article 12

This Directive is addressed to the Member States.

468

Done at Brussels, 27 November 1980.

For the Council
The President
J. Santer

1. OJ No. C 89, 5.4.1979, p. 6.
2. OJ No. C 59, 10.3.1980, p. 73.
3. OJ No. C 297, 28.11.1979, p. 5.
4. OJ No. C 165, 11.7.1978, p. 1.

ANNEX I

List of agents referred to in Article 3(1), second indent, and Article 8(1)

Acrylonitrile
Asbestos
Arsenic and Compounds
Benzene
Cadmium and compounds
Mercury and compounds
Nickel and compounds
Lead and compounds
Chlorinated hydrocarbons: – chloroform
– paradichlorobenzene
– carbon tetrachloride

ANNEX II

A. List of agents referred to in Article 3(3), first indent

1. Asbestos
2. Lead and compounds

B. List of agents referred to in Article 3(3), second indent

1. Asbestos
2. Arsenic and compounds
3. Cadmium and compounds
4. Mercury and compounds
5. Lead and compounds

ANNEX III

Technical aspects referred to in Article 8(3)

1. Sampling procedures and measuring methods (including quality control) with respect to the limit values in so far as such procedures and methods have no effect on the quantitative significance of those limit values.

2. Practical recommendations on medical surveillance before and during exposure and after such exposure has ceased and keeping of records on the results of such medical surveillance.

3. Practical procedures regarding the establishment and keeping of records concerning ambient measurement results and lists of exposed workers.

4. Practical recommendations for alarm systems to be installed at workplaces where abnormal exposures are likely to occur.

5. Practical recommendations for emergency measures to be taken in the event of abnormal emissions.

6. Collective and individual protection measures for certain operations (e.g. servicing and repairs) during which it cannot be guaranteed that concertrations or intensities of the agents will be kept below the limit values.

7. Procedures regarding general hygiene requirements, and means of ensuring personal hygiene.

8. Signs to identify areas where significant exposure is likely to occur and to indicate the precautions which have to be taken.

Council Directive

28 July 1982

on the protection of workers from the risks related to exposure to metallic lead and its ionic compounds at work (first individual Directive within the meaning of Article 8 of Directive 80/1107/EEC)
(82/605/EEC)

THE COUNCIL OF THE EUROPEAN COMMUNITIES,

Having regard to the Treaty establishing the European Economic Community, and in particular Article 100 thereof,
Having regard to the proposal from the Commission,[1]

Having regard to the opinion of the European Parliament,[2]
Having regard to the opinion of the Economic and Social Committee:[3]

Whereas the Council resolution of 29 June 1978 on an action programme of the European Communities on safety and health at work,[4] provides for the establishment of specific harmonized procedures regarding the protection of workers with respect to lead;

Whereas Council Directive 80/1107/EEC of 27 November 1980 on the protection of workers from the risks related to exposure to chemical, physical and biological agents at work,[5] lays down certain provisions which have to be taken into account for this protection; whereas that Directive provides for the laying down in individual Directives of limit values and specific requirements for those agents listed in Annex I, which included lead;

Whereas metallic lead and its ionic compounds are toxic agents found in a large number of circumstances at work; whereas many workers are therefore exposed to a potential health risk;

Whereas, therefore, preventive measures for the protection of the health of workers exposed to lead and the committment envisaged for Member States with regard to the surveillance of their health are important;

Whereas workers exposed to lead in the extractive industries must enjoy a level of health protection similar to that laid down in this Directive; whereas, given the specific nature of such activities, the implementation of such protection will need to be covered by special provisions embodied in a subsequent Directive;

Whereas this Directive includes minimum requirements which will be reviewed on the basis of experience acquired and of developments in technology and medical knowledge in this area, the objective being to attain greater protection of workers,

HAS ADOPTED THIS DIRECTIVE:

Article 1
1. This Directive, which is the first individual Directive within the meaning of Article 8 of Directive 80/1107/EEC has as its aim the protection of workers against risks to their health, including the prevention of such risks, arising or likely to arise at work from exposure to metallic lead and its ionic compounds; it shall not apply to alkylated lead compounds. It shall lay down limit values and other specific requirements.

2. This Directive shall not apply to:
   - sea transport;
   - air transport;
   - mining and quarrying of lead-containing ores and the preparation of lead-ore concentrate at the site of the mine or quarry.

3. This Directive shall not prejudice the right of Member States to apply or introduce laws, regulations or administrative provisions ensuring greater protection for workers or for a particular category of workers.

471

Article 2

1. Any work likely to involve a risk of absorbing lead shall be assessed in such a way as to determine the nature and degree of the exposure to lead of the workers.

   Annex I contains an indicative, non-exhaustive list of activities where there is reason to consider that there may be a risk of absorbing lead.

2. If the assessment provided for in paragraph 1 reveals the presence of at least one of the following conditions:
   - exposure to a concentration of lead in air greater that 40 $\mu g/m^3$, calculated as a time-weighted average over 40 hours per week;
   - a blood-lead level greater than 40 μg Pb/100 ml blood in individual workers,

   the provisions regarding information set out in Article 11(1) shall apply and appropriate measures shall be taken to minimize the risk of absorbing lead which arises through smoking, eating and drinking at the place of work.

3. If the assessment provided for in paragraph 1 reveals that the blood-lead level of workers due to lead absorption is between 40 μg and 50 μg Pb/100 ml blood, Member States shall endeavour to carry out biological monitoring of the workers concerned in accordance with the procedures laid down by the Member States.

4. If the assessment provided for in paragraph 1 reveals the presence of at least one of the following conditions:
   - exposure to a concentration of lead in air greater than 75 $\mu g/m^3$, calculated as a time-weighted average over 40 hours per week,
   - a blood-lead level greater than 50 μg Pb/100 ml blood in individual workers,

   the protection provided for in this Directive, in particular the lead-in-air monitoring and the medical surveillance set out in Articles 3 and 4, is to be given to the workers concerned.

5. The assessment provided for in paragraph 1 shall be the subject of consultation with the workers and/or their representatives within the undertaking or establishment and shall be revised where there is reason to believe that it is incorrect or there is a material change in the work.

Article 3

1. All lead-in-air measurements shall be representative of worker exposure to particles containing lead.

   Particles containing lead within the meaning of this Directive shall be those particles captured by equipment having the sampling characteristics specified in Annex II, point 1, and analyzed in accordance with the methods indicated in Annex II, point 2.

2. Monitoring of the concentration of lead in air shall take place at least every three months.

This frequency may, however, be reduced in the cases listed in paragraph 3.

3. Frequency of monitoring may be reduced to once a year, provided that there is no material change in the work and conditions of exposure, where:
   (i) the results of the measurements for individual workers or for groups of workers have shown that on the previous two consecutive occasions on which monitoring was carried out:
   – the lead-in-air concentration did not exceed 100 $\mu g/m^3$; or
   – the conditions or exposure did not fluctuate appreciably; or
   (ii) the blood-lead level of any worker does not exceed 60 μg Pb/100 ml blood.

4. The monitoring for a worker or group of workers, as stipulated in paragraph 2, shall entail taking one or more air samples.

Without prejudice to the second indent of Article 7(b), sampling shall be carried out in such a way as to permit assessment of the probable maximum risk to which the individual worker or workers are exposed, account being taken of the work done, the working conditions and the length of exposure during the course of the work. The workers concerned and/or their representatives within the undertaking or establishment shall be consulted to this end.

For the initial monitoring, after it has been established that the values laid down in Article 2(4) have been exceeded, the duration of the sampling period shall not be less than four hours.

Subsequently this duration shall not be less than four hours if the results obtained on the occasion of the preceding monitoring have shown higher lead-in-air concentration values than those obtained before that monitoring.

Where groups of workers are performing identical or similar tasks in the same location and are thus being exposed to the same health risk, sampling may be carried out on a group basis. In such a case, sampling shall be carried out for at least one worker out of 10.

5. The specifications referred to in paragraph 1 and Annex II, with the exception of the specification concerning the air intake velocity given at point 1(a) of the Annex, and the technical aspects of this Article shall be adapted in the light of technical progress in accordance with the procedure set out in Article 10 of Directive 80/1107/EEC, within the limits laid down in Annex III to that Directive.

Article 4
1. Workers shall be subject to medical (clinical and biological) surveillance. This surveillance must start prior to or at the beginning of the exposure.

The frequency of clinical assessment shall be at least once a year during the period of employment. Biological monitoring shall be carried out, in accordance with paragraph 2, at least every six months.

This surveillance shall take account not only of the magnitude of the exposure but also of the individual worker's susceptibility to lead.

2. The biological monitoring shall, apart from the exception mentioned in paragraph 3, include measuring the blood-lead level (PbB).

   This monitoring may also include measuring one or more of the following biological indicators:
   – delta aminolæ vulinic acid in urine (ALAU);
   – zinc protoporphyrin (ZPP);
   – delta aminolæ vulinic acid dehydratase in blood (ALAD).

   The methods of measuring the biological indicators referred to above are listed in Annex III and may be adapted in accordance with the procedure specified in Article 10 of Directive 80/1107/EEC.

3. The PbB measurement referred to in paragraph 2 may be replaced by that of ALAU when dealing with workers who have been subjected for a period of less than one month to risks of high exposure.

4. The frequency of biological monitoring may be reduced to once a year where at the same time:
   – the results of the measurements for individuals or for groups of workers have shown, on the previous two consecutive occasions on which monitoring was carried out, a lead-in-air concentration higher than the value laid down in the first indent of Article 2(4) and lower than 100 $\mu g/m^3$;
   – the PbB level of any individual worker does not exceed the value laid down in the second indent of Article 2(4).

5. Practical recommendations to which Member States may refer for clinical assessment are set out in Annex IV and may be adapted in accordance with the procedure set out in Article 10 of Directive 80/1107/EEC.

Article 5
1. Where the biological monitoring carried out in accordance with Article 4(2) reveals an individual PbB level higher than 60 μg Pb/100 ml blood but lower than the limit value set out in Article 6(1)(b), a clinical examination shall be carried out as soon as possible. However, this clinical examination may be deferred until a repeat determination of the PbB level, undertaken within one month, shows that the value of 60 μg Pb/100 ml blood continues to be exceeded.

   Thereafter, biological monitoring and clinical assessment shall be carried out at shorter intervals than those laid down in Article 4(1) at least until the PbB level is below 60 μg Pb/100 ml blood.

2. Following the clinical examination referred to in paragraph 1, the doctor or authority responsible for the medical surveillance of the workers should advise on any protective or preventive measures to be taken on an individual basis; these may include, where appropriate, the withdrawal of the worker concerned from exposure to lead or a reduction in the period of his exposure.

Article 6
1. The following limit values shall be applied:
   (a) lead-in-air concentration:
       150 µg/m^3, calculated as a time-weighted average over 40 hours per week;
   (b) value of the biological parameters:
       PbB level in individual workers: 70 µg/Pb/100 ml blood.[6] However, a PbB level of between 70 and 80 µg Pb/100 ml blood shall be allowed if the ALAU level remains lower than 20 mg/g creatinine or the ZPP level remains lower than 20 µg/g haemoglobin or the ALAD level remains greater than six European units.

2. Where biological monitoring is based solely on ALAU measurement in accordance with Article 4(3), the following limit value shall be applied for ALAU: 20 mg/g creatinine.

3. The Council, acting on a proposal from the Commission, and taking into account in particular progress made in scientific knowledge and technology as well as experience gained in the application of this Directive, shall reexamine the limit values for the biological parameters within five years of adoption of this Directive, with a view to setting a maximum blood-lead limit value of 70 µg Pb/100 ml blood.

Article 7
For the purpose of establishing whether or not the lead-in-air limit value fixed in Article 6(1)(a) has been exceeded, it is appropriate to proceed as follows:
(a) If the total sampling period is of 40 hours in one week then the lead-in-air concentrations obtained can be compared directly with the limit value laid down in Article 6(1)(a);
(b) If the total sampling period is less than 40 hours in one week then:
    – the limit value laid down in Article 6(1)(a) shall not be considered as having been exceeded if the concentration obtained by sampling in accordance with Article 3(4) is below the numerical level of the limit value;
    – if the concentration referred to in the first indent exceeds the numerical level of the limit value then at least three additional lead-in-air samples shall be taken which are representative of average exposure to lead; the total period over which each of these three samples is taken shall be at least four hours.

475

If, from four samples taken over a period of one week, it is found that three levels of concentration are below the numerical level of the limit value, then it shall be deemed that this limit value has not been exceeded.

Article 8

1. Where the lead-in-air limit value laid down in Article 6(1)(a) is exceeded the reasons for the limit being exceeded shall be identified and appropriate measures to remedy the situation shall be taken as soon as possible.

   The doctor or authority responsible for the medical surveillance of the workers shall judge whether an immediate determination of the biological parameters of the workers concerned should be carried out.

   In order to check the effectiveness of the measures mentioned in the first subparagraph, a further determination of the lead-in-air concentrations on the basis of the procedures laid down in Articles 3 and 7 shall be carried out.

2. Where the measures referred to in the first subparagraph of paragraph 1 cannot, owing to their nature or magnitude, be taken within one month and a further determination of lead-in-air concentrations shows that the lead-in-air limit values continue to be exceeded, work may not be continued in the affected area until adequate measures have been taken for the protection of the workers concerned, in the light of the opinion of the doctor or authority responsible for medical surveillance.

   Where the exposure cannot reasonably be reduced by other means and where the wearing of individual respiratory protective equipment proves necessary, this may not be permanent and shall be kept to the strict minimum necessary for each worker.

3. In the case of incidents likely to lead to significant increases in exposure to lead, workers shall be immediately evacuated from the affected area. Only workers whose presence is required to carry out the necessary repairs may enter the affected area on condition that they use suitable protective apparatus.

4. In the case of certain operations in respect of which it is foreseen that the limit value set out in paragraph 1 will be exceeded and in respect of which technical preventive measures for limiting concentrations in the air are not reasonably practicable, the employer shall define the measures intended to ensure protection of the workers during operations of this kind. The workers and/or their representatives in the undertaking or establishment shall be consulted on these measures before such operations are effected.

Article 9

1. Where the biological limit value laid down in Article 6(1)(b) has been exceeded:
   - the necessary steps shall be taken immediately to ascertain the reasons for this excess and to remedy the situation. Such measures may, de-

pending on the magnitude of the excess, and where it is considered desirable by the doctor or authority responsible for the medical surveillance of the workers include the immediate with drawal of the worker concerned from all exposure to lead;
- a further determination of the PbB level shall be made within three months. Following this determination, the worker concerned must not continue at his work or at any other work involving an equal or greater risk of exposure to lead if the biological limit value continues to be exceeded. The worker concerned may be assigned, following an opinion from the doctor or authority responsible for medical surveillance, to other work involving a lesser risk of exposure. In this case, he shall be subject to more frequent medical assessments.

However, Member States may take different measures for workers who, having been exposed to lead over a number of years, have a very high body burden of lead when this Directive becomes applicable.

2. The worker concerned or the employer may ask for a review of the assessments referred to in paragraph 1.

Article 10
1. For all work carried out under the conditions set out in Article 2(4), appropriate measures shall be taken to ensure that:
   (a) (i) the risk of absorbing lead through smoking, eating or drinking is avoided;
   (ii) areas are set aside where workers can eat and drink without risking contamination by lead;
   (iii) in very hot workplaces where workers should be encouraged to drink, workers are provided with drinking water or other drinks not contaminated by the lead present in the workplace.
   (b) (i) workers are provided with appropriate working or protective clothing, taking into account the physico-chemical properties of the lead compounds to which they are exposed;
   (ii) this working or protective clothing remains within the undertaking. It may, however, be laundered in establishments outside the undertaking which are equipped for this sort of work, if the undertaking itself does not carry out cleaning; where this is the case, the clothing shall be transported in closed containers;
   (iii) working or protective clothing and street clothes are stored separately;
   (iv) workers are provided with adequate and appropriate washing facilities, including showers in the case of dusty operations.

2. The cost of the measures taken pursuant to paragraph 1 shall not be borne by the workers.

Article 11
1. For all work carried out under the conditions set out in Article 2(2),

477

appropriate measures shall be taken so that workers and their representatives in the undertaking or establishment are provided with adequate information on:
- the potential risks to health from lead exposure, including the potential risks for the foetus and infants being breast-fed;
- the existence of statutory limit values and the need for biological and atmospheric monitoring;
- hygiene requirements, including the need to refrain from smoking, eating or drinking at the workplace,
- the precautions to be taken as regards the wearing and use of protective equipment and clothing;
- the special precautions to be taken to minimize exposure to lead.

2. In addition to the measures referred to in paragraph 1, for all work carried out under the conditions set out in Article 2(4), appropriate measures shall be taken so that;
   (a) workers and/or their representative within the undertaking or establishment have access to:
      - the results of lead-in-air measurements;
      - the statistical (non-personalized) results of biological monitoring, and explanations of the significance of these results are available to them;
   (b) if the results exceed the lead-in-air limit value laid down in Article 6(1)(a) the workers concerned and their representatives in the undertaking or establishment are informed as quickly as possible of the excess and the reason for it and the workers and/or their representatives in the undertaking or establishment are consulted on the measures to be taken or, in an emergency, are informed of the measures which have been taken;
   (c) each time PbB tests, ALAU tests or any other biological measurements for assessing lead exposure are carried out, the workers concerned are informed, on the authority of the doctor responsible, of the results of those measurements and the interpretation placed on the results.

Article 12
The doctor or authority responsible for medical surveillance of the workers shall have access to all information necessary for determining the extent of workers' exposure to lead, including the results of the lead-in-air monitoring.

Article 13
Steps shall be taken to ensure that individual data relating to the exposure of workers and their clinical and biological examinations are recorded and stored in an appropriate form, in accordance with national laws and practices.

Article 14
1. Member States shall bring into force the laws, regulations and admini-

strative provisions necessary to comply with this Directive by 1 January 1986 at the latest and shall forthwith inform the Commission thereof.

2. Member States shall communicate to the Commission the texts of the provisions of national law which they adopt in the field covered by this Directive.

Article 15
This Directive is addressed to the Member States.

Done at Brussels, 28 July 1982.

For the Council
The President
O. Møller

---

1. OJ No. C 324, 28.12.1979, p. 3.
2. OJ No. C 101, 4.5.1981, p. 14.
3. OJ No. C 300, 18.11.1980, p. 22.
4. OJ No. C 165, 11.7.1978, p. 1.
5. OJ No. L. 327, 3.12.1980, p. 8.
6. Correspondends in SI units to 3.4 mu mol lead per litre blood.

ANNEX I

List of activities referred to in the second subparagraph of Article 2(1)

1. Handing of lead concentrate.
2. Lead and zinc smelting and refining (primary and secondary).
3. Lead arsenate spray manufacture and handling.
4. Manufacture of lead oxides.
5. Production of other lead compounds (including that part of the production of alkyl lead compounds, where it includes exposure to metallic lead and its ionic compounds).
6. Manufacture of paints, enamels, mastics and colours containing lead.
7. Battery manufacture and recycling.[1]
8. Craftwork in tin and lead.
9. Manufacture of lead solder.
10. Lead ammunition manufacture.
11. Manufacture of lead-based or lead-alloy objects.
12. Use of paints, enamels, mastics and colours containing lead.
13. Ceramic and craft pottery industries.[1]
14. Crystal glass industries.
15. Plastic industries using lead additives.
16. Frequent use of lead solder in an enclosed space.
17. Printing work involving the use of lead.
18. Demolition work, especially the processes of scraping off, burning off

and flame-cutting executed on materials coated with paint containing lead, as well as the breaking up of plant (e.g. lead furnaces).[1]
19. Use of lead ammunition in an enclosed space.
20. Automobile construction and repair work.[1]
21. Manufacture of leaded steel.
22. Lead tempering of steel.
23. Lead coating.
24. Recovery of lead and metallic residues containing lead.

---

1. Inasmuch as lead is used or is present.

ANNEX II

Technical specifications referred to in the second subparagraph of Article 3(1)

1. The equipment is that which complies with the technical specifications listed below:
   (a) Air intake velocity at the orifice: 1.25 m/s ± 10 per cent;
   (b) Air flow rate: at least 1 l/min.;
   (c) Sampling head characteristics: a closed face sampling head should be used, to avoid filter contamination;
   (d) Intake orifice diameter: at least 4 mm diameter in order to avoid wall effects;
   (e) Filter or intake orifice position: as far as possible kept parallel to the face of the worker during the whole sampling period;
   (f) Filter efficiency: a minimum of 95 per cent efficiency for all particles sampled down to an aerodynamic diameter of 0.3 µm;
   (g) Filter homogeneity; maximum homogeneity of the lead content in the filter to allow for comparison between two halves of the same filter.

2. The lead-in-air sample collected in accordance with the procedures in point 1 is to be analyzed by atomic absorption spectroscopy or any other method which gives equivalent results.

ANNEX III

Methods of measuring biological indicators referred to in Article 4(2)

PbB: Atomic absorption spectroscopy;
ALAU: Davis[1] or equivalent method;
ZPP: Haematofluorimetry[2] or equivalent method;
ALAD: European standardized method[3] or equivalent method.

Appropriate quality control programmes will be established by the Commission.

1. Davis J. R., and Andelman S. L. 'Urinary delta-aminolevulinic acid levels in lead poisoning. A modified method for the rapid determination of urinary delta-aminolevulinic acid using disposable ion-exchange chromatographic columns'. Arch. Environ. Health 15, 53–9 (1967).
2. Blumberg W. E., Eisinger J., Lamola A. A., and Zuckerman D. M. 'Zinc protoporphyrin level in blood determination by a portable haematofluometer. A screening device for lead poisoning'. J. Lab. Clin. Med. 89, 712–723 (1977).
3. (a) Council Directive 77/312/EEC of 29 March 1977 on biological screening of the population for lead. OJ No L 105, 28.4.1977, p. 10 (Annex III).
   (b) A. Berlin and K. H. Schaller 'European standardized method for the determination of delta-aminolevulinic acid dehydratase activity in blood'. 3. Klin. Chem. Klin. Biochem. 12, 389–390 (1974).

ANNEX IV

Practical recommendations for the clinical assessment of workers referred to in Article 4(5)

1. Current knowledge indicates that large-scale absorption may produce adverse effects in the following systems:
   - hematopoietic;
   - gastro-intestinal;
   - central and peripheral nervous;
   - renal.

2. The dotor in charge of the medical surveillance of the worker exposed to lead should be familiar with the exposure conditions or circumstances of each worker.

3. Clinical assessment of the workers should be carried out in accordance with sound practice; it should include the following measures:
   - records of the worker's medical and occupational history;
   - physical examination and a personal interview with special attention to the associated symptoms of early lead poisoning;
   - evaluation of the pulonary status (for possible use of respiratory protective equipment).
   Blood analyses (and, in particular, establishment of the hematocrit level) and urine analysis should be carried out during the first medical examination and then regularly according to the doctor's judgement.

4. In addition to the decisions based on the results of biological monitoring, the examining doctor will establish the cases where exposure or continued exposure to lead is contra-indicated. The most important of these contra-indications are:

481

(i) congenital abnormalities:
 – thalassemia;
 – G – 6 – PD deficiency.
(ii) acquired conditions:
 – anaemia;
 – renal deficiencies;
 – hepatic deficiencies.

5. Use of chelating agents:
 The prohphylactic use of chelating agents, sometimes called 'preventive therapy' is medically and ethically unacceptable. Many chelating agents may be considered nephrotoxic when administered for long periods.

6. Intoxication therapy:
 To be carried out by specialists.

Council Directive

of 19 September 1983

on the protection of workers from the risks related to exposure to asbestos at work (second individual Directive within the meaning of Article 8 of Directive (80/1107/EEC) (83/477/EEC)

THE COUNCIL OF THE EUROPEAN COMMUNITIES,

Having regard to the Treaty establishing the European Economic Community, and in particular Article 100 thereof,
Having regard to the proposal from the Commission,[1]
Having regard to the opinion of the European Parliament,[2]
Having regard to the opinion of the Economic and Social Committee:[3]
 Whereas the Council resolution of 29 June 1978 on an action programme of the European Communities on safety and health at work[4] provides for the establishment of specific harmonized procedures regarding the protection of workers with respect to asbestos;
 Whereas Council Directive 80/1107/EEC of 27 November 1980 on the protection of workers from the risks related to exposure to chemical, physical and biological agents at work[5] laid down certain provisions which have to be taken into account for this protection; whereas that Directive provides for the laying down in individual Directives of limit values and specific requirements for those agents listed in Annex I, which include asbestos;
 Whereas asbestos is a harmful agent found in a large number of circumstances at work; whereas many workers are therefore exposed to a potential health risk; whereas crocidolite is considered to be a particularly dangerous type of asbestos;

Whereas, although current scientific knowledge is not such that a level can be established below which risks to health cease to exist, a reduction in exposure to asbestos will nonetheless reduce the risk of developing asbestos-related disease; whereas this Directive includes minimum requirements which will be reviewed on the basis of experience acquired and of developments in technology in this area;

Whereas optical microscopy, although it does not allow a counting of the smallest fibres detrimental to health, is the most currently used method for the regular measuring of asbestos;

Whereas, therefore, preventive measures for the protection of the health of workers exposed to asbestos and the commitment envisaged for Member States with regard to the surveillance of their health are important,

HAS ADOPTED THIS DIRECTIVE:

Article 1
1. This Directive, which is the second individual Directive within the meaning of Article 8 of Directive 80/1107/EEC, has as its aim the protection of workers against risks to their health, including the prevention of such risks, arising or likely to arise from exposure to asbestos at work. It lays down limit values and other specific requirements.

2. This Decision shall not apply to:
   - sea transport;
   - air transport.

3. This Directive shall not prejudice the right of Member States to apply or introduce laws, regulations or administrative provisions ensuring greater protection for workers, in particular as regards the replacement of asbestos by less-dangerous substitutes.

Article 2
For the purposes of this Directive, 'asbestos' means the following fibrous silicates:
- Actinolite, CAS No. 77536–66–4(*);[6]
- Asbestos grünerite (amosite) CAS No. 12171–73–5(*);[6]
- Anthophyllite, CAS No. 77536–67–5(*);[6]
- Chrysotile, CAS No. 12001–29–5;[6]
- Crocidolite, CAS No. 12001–28–4;[6]
- Tremolite, CAS No. 77536–68–6(*).[6]

Article 3
1. This Directive shall apply to activities in which workers are or may be exposed in the course of their work to dust arising from asbestos or materials containing asbestos.

2. In the case of any activity likely to involve a risk of exposure to dust arising

from asbestos or materials containing asbestos, this risk must be assessed in such a way as to determine the nature and degree of the workers' exposure to dust arising from asbestos or materials containing asbestos.

3. If the assessment referred to in paragraph 2 shows that the concentration of asbestos fibres in the air at the place of work in the absence of any individual protective equipment is, at the option of the Member States, at a level as measured or calculated in relation to an eight-hour reference period,
   – lower than 0.25 fibre per cm^3 and/or
   – lower than a cumulative dose of 15,00 fibre-days per cm^3 over three months,
   Articles 4, 7, 13, 14(2), 15 and 16 shall not apply.

4. The assessment provided for in paragraph 2 shall be the subject of consultation with the workers and/or their representatives within the undertaking or establishment and shall be revised where there is reason to believe that it is incorrect or there is a material change in the work.

Article 4
Subject to Article 3(3), the following measures shall be taken:

1. The activities referred to in Article 3(1) must be covered by a notification system administered by the responsible authority of the Member State.

2. The notification must be submitted by the employer to the responsible authority of the Member State, in accordance with national laws, regulations and administrative provisions. This notification must include at least a brief description of:
   – the types and quantities of asbestos used;
   – the activities and processes involved;
   – the products manufactured.

3. Workers and/or their representatives in undertakings or establishments shall have access to the documents which are the subject of notification concerning their own undertaking or establishment in accordance with national laws.

4. Each time an important change occurs in the use of asbestos or of materials containing asbestos, a new notification must be submitted.

Article 5
The application of asbestos by means of the spraying process must be prohibited.

Article 6
For all activities referred to in Article 3(1), the exposure of workers to dust

arising from asbestos or materials containing asbestos at the place of work must be reduced to as low a level as is reasonably practicable and in any case below the limit values laid down in Article 8, in particular through the following measures if appropriate:

1. The quantity of asbestos used in each case must be limited to the minimum quantity which is reasonably practicable.

2. The number of workers exposed or likely to be exposed to dust arising from asbestos or materials containing asbestos must be limited to the lowest possible figure.

3. Work processes must, in principle, be so designed as to avoid the release of asbestos dust into the air.
   If this is not reasonably practicable, the dust should be eliminated as near as possible to the point where it is released.

4. All buildings and/or plant and equipment involved in the processing or treatment of asbestos must be capable of being regularly and effectively cleaned and maintained.

5. Asbestos as a raw material must be stored and transported in suitable sealed packing.

6. Waste must be collected and removed from the place of work as soon as possible in suitable sealed packing with labels indicating that it contains asbestos. This measure shall not apply to mining activities.
   The waste referred to in the preceding paragraph shall then be dealt with in accordance with Council Directive 78/319/EEC of 20 March 1978 on toxic and dangerous waste.[7]

Article 7
Subject to Article 3(3), the following measures shall be taken:

1. In order to ensure compliance with the limit values laid down in Article 8, the measurement of asbestos in the air at the place of work shall be carried out in accordance with the reference method described in Annex I or any other method giving equivalent results. Such measurement must be planned and carried out regularly, with sampling being representative of the personal exposure of the worker to dust arising from asbestos or materials containing asbestos.
   For the purposes of measuring asbestos in the air, as referred to in the preceding paragraph, only fibres with a length of more than five micrometres and a length/breadth ratio greater than 3:1 shall be taken into consideration.
   The Council, acting on a proposal from the Commission, and taking account in particular of progress made in scientific knowledge and tech-

nology and of experience gained in the application of this Directive, shall re-examine the provisions of the first sentence of paragraph 1 within five years following the adoption of this Directive, with a view to establishing a single method for measurement of asbestos-in-air concentrations at Community level.

2. Sampling shall be carried out after consulting the workers and/or their representatives in undertakings or establishments.

3. Sampling shall be carried out by suitably qualified personnel. The samples taken shall be subsequently analyzed in laboratories equipped to analyze them and qualified to apply the necessary identification techniques.

4. The amount of asbestos in the air shall be measured as a general rule at least every three months and, in any case, whenever a technical change is introduced. The frequency of measurements may, however, be reduced in the circumstances specified in paragraph 5.

5. The frequency of measurements may be reduced to once a year where:
   – there is no substantial change in conditions at the place of work; and
   – the results of the two preceding measurements have not exceeded half the limit values fixed in Article 8.
   Where groups of workers are performing identical or similar tasks at the same place and are thus being exposed to the same health risk, sampling may be carried out on a group basis.

6. The duration of sampling must be such that representative exposure can be established for an eight-hour reference period (one shift) by means of measurements or time-weighted calculations. The duration of the various sampling processes shall be determined also on the basis of point 6 of Annex I.

Article 8
The following limit values shall be applied:
(a) concentration of asbestos fibres other than crocidolite in the air at the place of work:
   1,00 fibres per cm^3 measured or calculated in relation to an eight-hour reference period;
(b) concentration of crocidolite fibres in the air at the place of work:
   0,50 fibres per cm^3 measured or calculated in relation to an eight-hour reference period;
(c) concentration of asbestos fibres in the air at the place of work in the case of mixtures of crocidolite and other asbestos fibres:
   the limit value is at a level calculated on the basis of the limit values laid down in (a) and (b), taking into account the proportions of crocidolite and other asbestos types in the mixture.

Article 9

The Council, acting on a proposal from the Commission, shall, taking into account, in particular, progress made in scientific knowledge and technology and in the light of experience gained in applying this Directive, review the provisions laid down in Article 3(3) and in Article 8 before 1 January 1990.

Article 10

1. Where the limit values laid down in Article 8 are exceeded, the reasons for the limits being exceeded must be identified and appropriate measures to remedy the situation must be taken as soon as possible.

   Work may not be continued in the affected area until adequate measures have been taken for the protection of the workers concerned.

2. In order to check the effectiveness of the measures mentioned in the first subparagraph of paragraph 1, a further determination of the asbestos-in-air concentrations shall be carried out immediately.

3. Where exposure cannot reasonably be reduced by other means and where the wearing of individual respiratory protective equipment proves necessary, this may not be permanent and shall be kept to the strict minimum necessary for each worker.

Article 11

1. In the case of certain activities in respect of which it is foreseeable that the limit values laid down in Article 8 will be exceeded and in respect of which technical preventive measures for limiting asbestos-in-air concentrations are not reasonably practicable, the employer shall determine the measures intended to ensure protection of the workers while they are engaged in such activities, in particular the following:
   (a) workers shall be issued with suitable respiratory equipment and other personal protective equipment, which must be worn; and
   (b) warning signs shall be put up indicating that it is foreseeable that the limit values laid down in Article 8 will be exceeded.

2. The workers and/or their representatives in the undertaking or establishment shall be consulted on these measures before the activities concerned are carried out.

Article 12

1. A plan of work shall be drawn up before demolition work or work on removing asbestos and/or asbestos-containing products from buildings, structures, plant or installations or from ships is started.

2. The plan referred to in paragraph 1 must prescribe the measures necessary to ensure the safety and health of workers at the place of work.

   The plan must in particular specify that:

487

— as far as is reasonably practicable, asbestos and/or asbestos-containing products are removed before demolition techniques are applied;
— the personal protective equipment referred to in Article 11(1)(a) is provided, where necessary.

Article 13

1. In the case of all activities referred to in Article 3(1), and subject to Article 3(3), appropriate measures shall be taken to ensure that:
   (a) the places in which the above activities take place shall:
       (i) be clearly demarcated and indicated by warning signs;
       (ii) not be accessible to workers other than those who by reason of their work or duties are required to enter them;
       (iii) constitute areas where there should be no smoking.
   (b) areas are set aside where workers can eat and drink without risking contamination by asbestos dust;
   (c) (i) workers are provided with appropriate working or protective clothing;
       (ii) this working or protective clothing remains within the under-taking. It may, however, be laundered in establishments outside the undertaking which are equipped for this sort of work if the undertaking does not carry out the cleaning itself; in that event the clothing shall be transported in closed containers;
       (iii) separate storage places are provided for working or protective clothing and for street clothes;
       (iv) workers are provided with appropriate and adequate washing and toilet facilities, including showers in the case of dusty operations;
       (v) protective equipment shall be placed in a well-defined place and shall be checked and cleaned after each use; appropriate measures shall be taken to repair or replace defective equipment before further use.

2. Workers may not be charged with the cost of measures taken pursuant to paragraph 1.

Article 14

1. In the case of all activities referred to in Article 3 (1), appropriate measures shall be taken to ensure that workers and their representatives in the undertaking of establishment receive adequate information concerning:
   — the potential risks to health from exposure to dust arising from asbestos or materials containing asbestos;
   — the existence of statutory limit values and the need for the atmosphere to be monitored;
   — hygiene requirements, including the need to refrain from smoking;
   — the precautions to be taken as regards the wearing and use of protective equipment and clothing;
   — special precautions designed to minimize exposure to asbestos.

2. In addition to the measures referred to in paragraph 1, and subject to Article 3(3), appropriate measures shall be taken to ensure that:
   (a) workers and/or their representatives in the undertaking or establishment have access to the results of asbestos-in-air concentration measurements and can be given explanations of the significance of those results;
   (b) if the results exceed the limit values laid down in Article 8 the workers concerned and their representatives in the undertaking or establishment are informed as quickly as possible of the fact and the reason for it and the workers and/or their representatives in the undertaking or establishment are consulted on the measures to be taken or, in an emergency, are informed of the measures which have been taken.

Article 15

Subject to Article 3(3) the following measures shall be taken:
1. An assessment of each worker's state of health must be available prior to the beginning of exposure to dust arising from asbestos or materials containing asbestos at the place of work.

   This assessment must include a specific examination of the chest. Annex II gives practical recommendations to which the Member States may refer for the clinical surveillance of workers; these recommendations shall be adapted to technical progress in accordance with the procedure set out in Article 10 of Directive 80/1107/EEC.

   A new assessment must be available at least once every three years for as long as exposure continues.

   An individual health record shall be established in accordance with national laws and practices for each worker referred to in the first subparagraph.

2. Following the clinical surveillance referred to in point 1, the doctor or authority responsible for the medical surveillance of the workers should, in accordance with national laws, advise on or determine any individual protective or preventive measures to be taken; these may include, where approprite, the withdrawal of the worker concerned from all exposure to asbestos.

3. Information and advice must be given to workers regarding any assessment of their health which they may undergo following the end of exposure.

4. The worker concerned or the employer may request a review of the assessments referred to in point 2, in accordance with national laws.

Article 16

Subject to Article 3(3) the following measures shall be taken:
1. The employer must enter the workers responsible for carrying out the activities referred to in Article 3(1) in a register, indicating the nature and duration of the activity and the exposure to which they have been

subjected. The doctor and/or the authority responsible for medical surveillance shall have access to this register. Each worker shall have access to the results in the register which relate to him personally. The workers and/or their representatives shall have access to anonymous, collective information in the register.

2. The register referred to in point 1 and the medical records referred to in point 1 of Article 15 shall be kept for at least 30 years following the end of exposure, in accordance with national laws.

Article 17
Member States shall keep a register of recognized cases of asbestosis and mesothelioma.

Article 18
1. Member States shall adopt the laws, regulations and administrative provisions necessary to comply with this Directive before 1 January 1987. They shall forthwith inform the Commission thereof. The date 1 January 1987 is, however, postponed until 1 January 1990 in the case of asbestos-mining activities.

2. Member States shall communicate to the Commission the provisions of national law which they adopt in the field covered by this Directive.

Article 19
This Directive is addressed to the Member States.

Done at Brussels, 19 September 1983.

For the Council
The President
G. Varfis

---

1. OJ No. C 262, 9.10.1980, p. 7 and OJ No. C 301, 18.11.1982, p. 6.
2. OJ No. C 310, 30.11.1981, p. 43.
3. OJ No. C 125, 17.5.1982, p. 155.
4. OJ No. C 165, 11.7.1978, p. 1.
5. OJ No. L 327, 3.12.1980, p. 8.
6. Number in the register of the Chemical Abstract Service (CAS).
7. OJ No. L 84, 31.3.1978, p. 43.

ANNEX I

Reference method referred to in Article 7(1) for the measurement of asbestos in air at the place of work

1. Samples shall be taken within the individual worker's breathing zone: i.e. within a hemisphere of 300 mm radius extending in front of the face and measured from the mid-point of a line joining the ears.

2. Membrane filters (mixed esters of cellulose or cellulose nitrate) of pore size 0,8 to 1,2 micrometres with printed squares and a diameter of 25 mm shall be used.

3. An open-faced filter holder fitted with a cylindrical cowl extending between 33 and 44 mm in front of the filter exposing a circular area of at least 20 mm in diameter shall be used. In use, the cowl shall point downwards.

4. A portable battery-operated pump carried on the worker's belt or in a pocket shall be used. The flow shall be smooth and the rate initially set at 1,0 litres per minute ± 5 per cent. The flow rate shall be maintained within ± 10 per cent of the initial rate during the sampling period.

5. The sampling time shall be measured to within a tolerance of 2 per cent.

6. The optimal fibre-loading on filters shall be within the range 100 to 400 fibres/mm^2.

7. In order of preference, the whole filter, or a section of the filter, shall be placed on a microscope slide, made transparent using the acetone-triacetin method, and covered with a glass coverslip.

8. A binocular microscope shall be used for counting and shall have the following features:
   - Koehler illumination;
   - its substage assembly shall incorporate an Abbe or achromatic phase-contrast condenser in a centring focusing mount. The phase-contrast centring adjustment shall be independent of the condenser centring mechanism;
   - a 40 times bar-focal positive phase-contrast achromatic objective with a numerical aperture of 0,65 to 0,70 and phase ring absorption within the range 65 to 85 per cent;
   - 12,5 times compensating eyepieces; at least one eyepiece must permit the insertion of a graticule and be of the focusing type;
   - a Walton-Beckett circular eyepiece graticule with an apparent diameter in the object plane of 100 micrometres ± 2 micrometres, when

491

using the specified objective and eyepiece, checked against a stage micrometer.

9. The microscope shall be set up according to the manufacturer's instructions, and the detection limit checked using a 'phase-contrast test slide'. Up to code 5 on the AIA test slides or up to block 5 on the HSE/NPL mark 2 test slide must be visible when used in the way specified by the manufacturer. This procedure shall be carried out at the beginning of the day of use.

10. Samples shall be counted in accordance with the following rules:
    - a countable fibre is any fibre referred to in the second subparagraph of point 1 of Article 7 which does not touch a particle with a maximum diameter greater than three micrometers;
    - any countable fibre with both ends within the graticule area shall be counted as one fibre; any fibre with only one end within the area shall count as half;
    - graticule areas for counting shall be chosen at random within the exposed area of the filter;
    - an agglomerate of fibres which at one or more points on its length appears solid and undivided but at other points is divided into separate strands (a split fibre) is counted as a single fibre if it conforms with the description in the second subparagraph of point 1 of Article 7 and indent 1 of this paragraph, the diameter measured being that of the undivided part, not that of the split part;
    - in any other agglomerate of fibres in which individual fibres touch or cross each other (a bundle), the fibres shall be counted individually if they can be distinguished sufficiently to determine that they conform with the description in the second subparagraph of point 1 of Article 7 and indent 1 of this paragraph. If no individual fibres meeting the definition can be distinguished, the bundle is considered to be a countable fibre if, taken as a whole, it conforms with the description in the second subparagraph of point 1 of Article 7 indent 1 of this paragraph,
    - if more than one-eighth of a graticule area is covered by an agglomerate of fibres and/or particles, the graticule area must be rejected and another counted,
    - 100 fibres shall be counted, which will enable a minimum of 20 graticule areas to be examined, or 100 graticule areas shall be examined.

11. The mean number of fibres per graticule is calculated by dividing the number of fibres counted by the number of graticule areas examined. The effect on the count of marks on the filter and contamination shall be kept below three fibres/100 graticule areas and shall be assessed using blank filters.

    Concentration in air = (number per graticule area × exposed area of filter) / (graticule area × volume of air collected).

ANNEX II

Practical recommendations for the clinical assessment of workers, as referred to in Article 15(1)

1. Current knowledge indicates that exposure to free asbestos fibres can give rise to the following diseases:
   - asbestosis;
   - mesothelioma;
   - bronchial carcinoma;
   - gastro-intestinal carcinoma.

2. The doctor and/or authority responsible for the medical surveillance of workers exposed to asbestos must be familiar with the exposure conditions or circumstances of each worker.

3. Clinical surveillance of workers should be carried out in accordance with the principles and practices of occupational medicine; it should include at least the following measures:
   - keeping records of a worker's medical and occupational history,
   - a personal interview;
   - a clinical examination of the chest;
   - a respiratory function examination.

   Further examinations, including a standard format radiograph of the chest and laboratory tests such as a sputum cytology test, are desirable. These examinations should be decided upon for each worker when he is the subject of medical surveillance, in the light of the most recent knowledge available to occupational medicine.

Council Directive

12 May 1986

on the protection of workers from the risks related to exposure to noise at work
(86/188/EEC)

THE COUNCIL OF THE EUROPEAN COMMUNITIES,

Having regard to the Treaty establishing the European Economic Community, and in particular Article 100 thereof,
Having regard to the proposal from the Commission, drawn up after consulting the Advisory Committee on Safety, Hygiene and Health Protection at Work,[1]
Having regard to the opinion of the European Parliament,[2]
Having regard to the opinion of the Economic and Social Committee:[3]

Whereas the Council resolutions of 29 June 1978 and 27 February 1984 on action programmes of the European Communities on safety and health at work[4] provide for the implementation of specific harmonized procedures for the protection of workers exposed to noise; whereas the measures adopted in this field vary from State to State and it is recognized that they urgently need to be approximated and improved;

Whereas exposure to high noise levels is encountered in a large number of situations and therefore many workers are exposed to a potential safety and health hazard;

Whereas a reduction of exposure to noise reduces the risk of hearing impairment caused by noise;

Whereas, where the noise level at the workplace involves a risk for the health and safety of workers, limiting exposure to noise reduces that risk without prejudice to the applicable provisions on the limitation of noise emission;

Whereas the most effective way of reducing noise levels at work is to incorporate noise prevention measures into the design of installations and to choose materials, procedures and working methods which produce less noise; whereas the priority aim must be to achieve the said reduction at source;

Whereas the provision and use of personal ear protectors is a necessary complementary measure to the reduction of noise at source, where exposure cannot reasonably be avoided by other means;

Whereas noise is an agent to which Council Directive 80/1107/EEC of 27 November 1980 on the protection of workers from the risks related to exposure to chemical, physical and biological agents at work[5] applies; whereas Articles 3 and 4 of the said Directive provide for the possibility of laying down limit values and other special measures in respect of the agents being considered;

Whereas certain technical aspects must be defined and may be reviewed in the light of experience and progress made in the technical and scientific field;

Whereas the current situation in the Member States does not make it possible to fix a noise-exposure value below which there is no longer any risk to workers' hearing;

Whereas current scientific knowledge about the effects that exposure to noise may have on health, other than on hearing, does not enable precise safety levels to be set; whereas, however, reduction of noise will lower the risk of illnesses unrelated to auditory complaints; whereas this Directive contains provisions which will be reviewed in the light of experience and developments in scientific and technical knowledge in this field,

HAS ADOPTED THIS DIRECTIVE:

Article 1
1. This Directive, which is the third individual Directive within the meaning of Directive 80/1107/EEC, has as its aim the protection of workers against risks to their hearing and, in so far as this Directive expressly so provides,

to their health and safety, including the prevention of such risks arising or likely to arise from exposure to noise at work.

2. This Directive shall apply to all workers, including those exposed to radiation covered by the scope of the EAEC Treaty, with the exception of workers engaged in sea transport and in air transport.

For the purpose of this Directive, the expression 'workers engaged in sea transport and in air transport' shall refer to personnel on board.

On a proposal from the Commission the Council shall examine, before 1 January 1990, the possibility of applying this Directive to workers engaged in sea transport and in air transport.

3. This Directive shall not prejudice the right of Member States to apply or introduce, subject to compliance with the Treaty, laws, regulations or administrative provisions ensuring, where possible, greater protection for workers and/or intended to reduce the level of noise experienced at work by taking action at source, particularly in order to achieve exposure values which prevent unnecessary nuisance.

Article 2

For the purposes of this Directive, the following terms shall have the meaning hereby assigned to them:

1. *Daily personal noise exposure of a worker* $L_{\mathrm{EP},d}$

The daily personal noise exposure of a worker is expressed in dB (A) using the formula:

$$L_{\mathrm{EP},d} = L_{\mathrm{Aeq},Te} + 10 \log_{10} \frac{T_e}{T_o}$$

where:

$$L_{\mathrm{Aeq},Te} = 10 \log_{10} \left\{ \frac{1}{T_e} \int_o^{T_e} \left[\frac{p_A(t)}{p_o} \right]^2 \mathrm{d}t \right\}$$

T_e = daily duration of a worker's personal exposure to noise,

T_o = 8 h = 28 800 s,

P_o = 20 μPa,

P_A = 'A'-weighted instantaneous sound pressure in pascals to which is exposed, in air at atmospheric pressure, a person who might or might not move from one place to another while at work; it is determined from measurements made at the position occupied by the person's ears during work, preferably in the person's absence, using a technique which minimizes the effect on the sound field.

If the microphone has to be located very close to the person's body, appropriate adjustments should be made to determine an equivalent undisturbed field pressure.

The daily personal noise exposure does not take account of the effect of any personal ear protector used.

2. *Weekly average of the daily values $L_{EP,w}$*

The weekly average of the daily values is found using the following formula:

$$L_{EP,w} = 10 \log_{10} \left[\frac{1}{5} \sum_{k=1}^{m} 10^{0,1} (L_{EP,d})_k \right]$$

where $(L_{EP,d})_k$ are the values of $L_{EP,d}$ for each of the m working days in the week being considered.

Article 3

1. Noise experienced at work shall be assessed and, when necessary, measured in order to identify the workers and workplaces referred to in this Directive and to determine the conditions under which the specific provisions of this Directive shall apply.

2. The assessment and measurement mentioned in paragraph 1 shall be competently planned and carried out at suitable intervals under the responsibility of the employers.

Any sampling must be representative of the daily personal exposure of a worker to noise.

The methods and apparatus used must be adapted to the prevailing conditions in the light, particularly, of the characteristics of the noise to be measured, the length of exposure, ambient factors and the characteristics of the measuring apparatus.

These methods and this apparatus shall make it possible to determine the parameters defined in Article 2 and to decide whether, in a given case, the values fixed in this Directive have been exceeded.

3. Member States may lay down that personal exposure to noise shall be replaced by noise recorded at the workplace. In that event the criterion of personal exposure to noise shall be replaced, for the purposes of Articles 4 to 10, by that of noise exposure during the daily work period, such period being at least eight hours, at the places where the workers are situated.

Member States may also lay down that, when the noise is measured, special consideration shall be given to impulse noise.

496

4. The workers and/or their representatives in the undertaking or establishment shall be associated, according to national law and practice, with the assessment and measurement provided for in paragraph 1. These shall be revised where there is reason to believe that they are incorrect or that a material change has taken place in the work.

5. The recording and preservation of the data obtained pursuant to this Article shall be carried out in a suitable form, in accordance with national law and practice.

The doctor and/or the authority responsible and the workers and/or their representatives in the undertaking shall have access to these data, in accordance with national law and practice.

Article 4
1. Where the daily personal exposure of a worker to noise is likely to exceed 85 dB (A) or the maximum value of the unweighted instantaneous sound pressure is likely to be greater than 200 Pa,[6] appropriate measures shall be taken to ensure that:
   (a) workers and/or their representatives in the undertaking or establishment receive adequate information and, when relevant, training concerning:
   – potential risks to their hearing arising from noise exposure;
   – the measures taken in pursuance of this Directive;
   – the obligation to comply with protective and preventive measures, in accordance with national legislation;
   – the wearing of personal ear protectors and the role of checks on hearing in accordance with Article 7.
   (b) workers and/or their representatives in the undertaking or establishment have access to the results of noise assessments and measurements made pursuant to Article 3 and can be given explanations of the significance of those results.

2. At workplaces where the daily personal noise exposure of a worker is likely to exceed 85 dB (A), appropriate information must be provided to workers as to where and when Article 6 applies.

At workplaces where the daily personal noise exposure of a worker is likely to exceed 90 dB (A) or where the maximum value of the unweighted instantaneous sound pressure is likely to exceed 200 Pa, the information provided for in the first subparagraph must, where reasonably practicable, take the form of appropriate signs. The areas in question must also be delimited and access to them must be restricted, where the risk of exposure so justifies and where these measures are reasonably practicable.

Article 5
1. The risks resulting from exposure to noise must be reduced to the lowest level reasonably practicable, taking account of technical progress and the availability of measures to control the noise, in particular at source.

2. Where the daily personal noise exposure of a worker exceeds 90 dB (A), or the maximum value of the unweighted instantaneous sound pressure is greater than 200 Pa:
   (a) the reasons for the excess level shall be identified and the employer shall draw up and apply a programme of measures of a technical nature and/or of organization of work with a view to reducing as far as reasonably practicable the exposure of workers to noise;
   (b) workers and their representatives in the undertaking or establishment shall receive adequate information on the excess level and on the measures taken pursuant to subparagraph (a).

Article 6

1. Without prejudice to Article 5, where the daily personal noise exposure of a worker exceeds 90 dB (A) or the maximum value of the unweighted instantaneous sound pressure is greater than 200 Pa, personal ear protectors must be used.

2. Where the exposure referred to in paragraph 1 is likely to exceed 85 dB (A), personal ear protectors must be made available to workers.

3. Personal ear protectors must be supplied in sufficient numbers by the employer, the models being chosen in association, according to national law and practice, with the workers concerned.
   The ear protectors must be adapted to the individual worker and to his working conditions, taking account of his safety and health. They are deemed, for the purposes of this Directive, suitable and adequate if, when properly worn, the risk to hearing can reasonably be expected to be kept below the risk arising from the exposure referred to in paragraph 1.

4. Where application of this Article involves a risk of accident, such risk must be reduced as far as is reasonably practicable by means of appropriate measures.

Article 7

1. Where it is not reasonably practicable to reduce the daily personal noise exposure of a worker to below 85 dB (A), the worker exposed shall be able to have his hearing checked by a doctor or on the responsibility of the doctor and, if judged necessary by the doctor, by a specialist.
   The in which this check is carried out shall be established by the Member States in accordance with national law and practice.

2. The purpose of the check shall be the diagnosis of any hearing impairment by noise and the preservation of hearing.

3. The results of checks on workers' hearing shall be kept in accordance with national law and practice.

Workers shall have access to the results which apply to them in so far as national law and practice allow.

4. Member States shall take the necessary measures with a view to the doctor and/or the authority responsible giving, as part of the check, appropriate indications on any individual protective or preventive measures to be taken.

Article 8

1. Member States shall take appropriate measures to ensure that:
   (a) the design, building and/or construction of new plant (new factories, plant or machinery, substantial extensions or modifications to existing factories or plant and replacement of plant or machinery) comply with Article 5(1);
   (b) where a new article (tool, machine, apparatus, etc.) which is intended for use at work is likely to cause, for a worker who uses it properly for a conventional eight-hour period, a daily noise exposure equal to or greater than 85 dB (A) or an unweighted instantaneous sound pressure the maximum value of which is equal to or greater than 200 Pa, adequate information is made available about the noise produced in conditions of use to be specified.

2. The Council shall establish, on a proposal from the Commission, requirements according to which, so far as is reasonably practicable, the articles referred to in paragraph 1(b), when properly used, do not produce noise likely to constitute a risk to hearing.

Article 9

1. In the case of workplaces where the noise exposure of a worker varies markedly from one working day to the next, Member States may, for workers performing special operations, exceptionally grant derogations from Article 5(2), Article 6(1) and Article 7(1), but only on condition that the average weekly noise exposure of a worker, as shown by adequate monitoring, complies with the value laid down in these provisions.

2. (a) In exceptional situations where it is not reasonably practicable, by technical measures or organization of work, to reduce daily personal noise exposure to below 90 dB (A) or to ensure that the personal ear protectors provided for in Article 6 of this Directive are suitable and adequate within the meaning of the second subparagraph of Article 6(3), the Member States may grant derogations from this provision for limited periods, such derogations being renewable.

   In such a case, however, personal ear protectors affording the highest degree of protection which is reasonably practicable must be used.
   (b) In addition, for workers performing special operations, Member States may exceptionally grant derogations from Article 6(1) if its

499

application involves an increase in the overall risk to the health and/or safety of the workers concerned and if it is not reasonably practicable to reduce this risk by any other means.

(c) The derogations referred to in (a) and (b) shall be subject to conditions which, in view of the individual circumstances, ensure that the risks resulting from such derogations are reduced to a minimum. The derogations shall be reviewed periodically and be revoked as soon as is reasonably practicable.

(d) Member States shall forward to the Commission every two years an adequate overall account of the derogations referred to in (a) and (b). The Commission shall inform the Member States thereof in an appropriate manner.

Article 10

The Council, acting on a proposal from the Commission, shall re-examine this Directive before 1 January 1994, taking into account in particular progress made in scientific knowledge and technology as well as experience gained in the application of this Directive, with a view to reducing the risks arising from exposure to noise.

In the context of this re-examination, the Council, acting on a proposal from the Commission, shall endeavour to lay down indications for measuring noise which are more precise than those given in Annex I.

Article 11

Member States shall see to it that workers' and employers' organizations are consulted before the provisions for the implementation of the measures referred to in this Directive are adopted, and that where workers' representatives exist in the undertaking or establishments they can check that such provisions are applied or can be involved in their application.

Article 12

1. For the measurement of noise and checking workers' hearing, any methods may be used which at least satisfy the provisions contained in Articles 3 and 7.

2. Indications for measuring noise and for checking workers' hearing are given in Annexes I and II.

   Annexes I and II shall be adapted to technical progress in accordance with Directive 80/1107/EEC and under the procedure set out in Article 10 thereof.

Article 13

1. Member States shall bring into force the laws, regulations and administrative provisions necessary to comply with this Directive by 1 January 1990. They shall forthwith inform the Commission thereof.

   However, in the case of the Hellenic Republic and the Portuguese Republic the relevant date shall be 1 January 1991.

2. Member States shall communicate to the Commission the provisions of national law which they adopt in the field covered by this Directive. The Commission shall inform the other Member States thereof.

Article 14
This Directive is addressed to the Member States.

Done at Brussels, 12 May 1986.

For the Council
The President
W. F. van Eekelen

---

1. OJ No. C 289, 5.11.1982, p. 1; OJ No. C 214, 14.8.1984, p. 11.
2. OJ No. C 46, 20.2.1984, p. 130; OJ No. C 117, 30.4.1984, p. 5.
3. OJ No. C 23, 30.1.1984, p. 36.
4. OJ No. C 165, 11.7.1978, p. 1; OJ No. C 67, 8.3.1984, p. 2.
5. OJ No. L 327, 3.12.1980, p. 8.
6. 140 dB in relation to 20 μPa. If the maximum value of the 'A'-weighted sound pressure level, measured with a sound-level meter using the time characteristic I (according to IEC 651) does not exceed 130 dB (AI), the maximum value of the unweighted instantaneous sound pressure can be assumed not to exceed 200 Pa.

ANNEX 1

Indications for measuring noise

A. 1. GENERAL

The quantities defined in Article 2 can be either:
 (i) measured directly by integrating sonometers, or
 (ii) calculated from measurements of sound pressure and exposure duration.
Measurements may be made at the work place(s) occupied by workers or by using instruments attached to the person.
    The location and duration of the measurements must be sufficient to ensure that exposure to noise during the working day can be recorded.

2. INSTRUMENTATION

2.1 If integrating averaging sonometers are used, they shall comply with IEC standard 804.
    If sonometers are used, they shall comply with IEC standard 651.
    Instruments incorporating an overload indication are preferred.
    If data are stored on tape as an intermediate step of the measurement procedure, potential errors caused by the process of

sorting and replay shall be taken into account when analyzing the data.

2.2 An instrument used to measure directly the maximum (peak) value of the unweighted instantaneous sound pressure shall have an onset time constant not exceeding 100 µs.

2.3 All equipment shall be calibrated in a laboratory at suitable intervals.

3. MEASUREMENT

3.1 An on-site check shall be made at the beginning and end of each day of measurement.

3.2 Measurement of workplace sound pressure should preferably be made in the undisturbed sound field in the workplace (i.e. with the person concerned being absent) and with the microphone located at the position (s) normally occupied by the ear exposed to the highest value of exposure.

If it is necessary for the person to be present, either:

(i) the microphone should be located at a distance from the person's head which will reduce, as far as possible, the effects of diffraction and distance on the measured value (a suitable distance is 0,10 m), or

(ii) if the microphone must be located very close to the person's body, appropriate adjustments should be made to determine an equivalent undisturbed pressure field.

3.3 Generally, time weightings 'S' and 'F' are valid as long as the measurement time interval is long compared with the time constant of the weighting chosen, but they are not suitable for determining L_{Aeq, T_e} when the noise level fluctuates very rapidly.

3.4 Indirect measurement of exposure

The result of the direct measurement of L_{Aeq, T_e} can be approximated with a knowledge of the exposure time and the measurement of clearly distinguishable sound-pressure-level ranges; a sampling method and a statistical distribution may be useful.

4. ACCURACY OF MEASURING NOISE AND DETERMINING THE EXPOSURE

The type of the instrument and the standard deviation of the results influence the accuracy of measurement. For comparison with a noise limit, the measuring accuracy determines the range of readings where no decision can be made as to whether the value is exceeded; if no decision can be taken, the measurement must be repeated with a higher accuracy.

Measurements of the highest accuracy enable a decision to be taken in all cases.

B. Short-term measurements with ordinary sonometers are quite satisfactory for workers performing, at a fixed location, repetitive activities which generate roughly the same levels of broad-band noise throughout the day. But when the sound pressure to which a worker is exposed shows fluctuations spread over a wide range of levels and/or of irregular time characteristics, determining the daily personal noise exposure of a worker becomes increasingly complex; the most accurate method of measurement is therefore to monitor exposure throughout the entire shift, using an integrating averaging sonometer.

When an integrating averaging sonometer conforming to IEC standard 804 (which is well suited for measurement of the equivalent continuous sound pressure level of impulse noise) complies at least with the specifications of type 1 and has recently been fully calibrated in a laboratory, and the microphone is properly located (see 3.2 above), the results make it possible, with certain exceptions to determine whether a given exposure has been exceeded (see 4) even in complex situations; that method is thus generally applicable, and is well suited for reference purposes.

ANNEX II

Indications for checking workers' hearing

In the framework of checking workers' hearing the following points are taken into consideration:

1. The check should be carried out in accordance with occupational medical practice and should comprise:
    -   where appropriate, an initial examination, to be carried out before or at the beginning of exposure to noise;
    -   regular examinations at intervals which are commensurate with the seriousness of the risk and are determined by the doctor.

2. Each examination should consist of at least an otoscopy combined with an audiometric test including pure-tone airconduction threshold audiometry in accordance with 6 below.

3. The initial examination should include a medical history; the initial otoscopy and the audiometric test should be repeated within a period of 12 months.

4. The regular examination should be carried out at least every five years where the worker's daily personal noise exposure remains less than 90 dB (A).

5. The examinations should be carried out by suitably qualified persons in accordance with national law and practice and may be organized in successive stages (screening, specialist examination).

6. The audiometric test should comply with the specifications of ISO standard 6189-1983, supplemented as follows:

503

Audiometry also covers the frequency of 8 000 Hz; the ambient sound level enables a hearing-threshold level equal to O dB in relation to ISO standard 389-1975 to be measured.

However, other methods may be used if they give comparable results.

Council Directive

9 June 1988

on the protection of workers by the banning of certain specified agents and/or certain work activities (Fourth individual Directive within the meaning of Article 8 of Directive 80/1107/EEC)
(88/364/EEC)

THE COUNCIL OF THE EUROPEAN COMMUNITIES,

Having regard to the Treaty establishing the European Economic Community, and in particular Article 118 A thereof,
Having regard to the proposal from the Commission,[1]
In cooperation with the European Parliament,[2]
Having regard to the opinion of the Economic and social Committee:[3]
Whereas the Council adopts, by means of Directives, minimum progressively applicable provisions, with a view towards promoting the improvement, in particular, of the working environment, so as to protect the safety and health of workers;
Whereas the Council resolution of 27 February 1984 on a second programme of action of the European Communities on safety and health at work[4] provides for the development of protective measures for substances recognized as being carcinogenic and other dangerous substances and processes which may have serious harmful effects on health;
Whereas certain differences are revealed by an examination of the measures taken by Member States to protect workers against the risks related to exposure to specified work agents and work activities;
Whereas, therefore, in the interest of balanced development, these measures should be harmonized and improved as progress is made; whereas this harmonization and improvement should be based on common principles;
Whereas, to this end, Council Directive 80/1107/EEC of 27 November 1980 on the protection of workers from the risks related to exposure to chemical, physical and biological agents at work[5] contains such principles;
Whereas, under the terms of the said Directive, such protection must as far as possible be ensured by measures to prevent exposure or to keep it at as low a level as is reasonably practicable; whereas, also under these terms, for the provision of adequate protection of workers it is necessary to ban in the workplace certain specified agents and/or work activities which can give rise to serious effects on health in cases where use of other means does not make it possible to ensure adequate protection;

Whereas provision should be made in these circumstances to ban certain specified agents and/or certain work activities in the workplace, subject to certain exceptions and derogations;

Whereas representatives of employers and workers have a role to play in the protection of workers;

Whereas these principles need to be applied uniformly and speedily to encourage wherever possible the early development of alternative non-dangerous agents and/or work activities,

HAS ADOPTED THIS DIRECTIVE:

Article 1

1. The purpose of this Directive is to protect workers against risks to their health by means of a ban on certain specific agents and or certain work activities.

    The ban which is the subject of this Directive including the Annex is based on the following factors:
    - there are serious health and safety risks for workers;
    - precautions are not sufficient to ensure a satisfactory level of health and safety protection for workers;
    - the ban does not lead to the use of substitute products which may involve equal or greater health and safety risks for workers.

2. This Directive shall not apply to:
    - sea transport;
    - air transport.

3. This Directive shall not prejudice the right of Member States to apply or introduce, subject to compliance with the Treaty, laws, regulations or administrative provisions ensuring greater protection for workers.

Article 2

For the purposes of this Directive:
(a) 'substances' means chemical elements and their compounds as they occur in the natural state or as produced by industry, including any additives required for the purpose of placing them on the market;
(b) 'agents' means any chemical, physical or biological agents present at work and likely to be harmful to health;
(c) 'preparations' means mixtures or solutions composed of two or more substances;
(d) 'impurities' means substances which are a priori present in insignificant amounts in other substances;
(e) 'intermediates' means substances which are formed during a chemical reaction, are converted and therefore disappear by the end of the reaction or process;
(f) 'by-products' means substances which are formed during a chemical reaction and which remain at the end of the reaction of process;

505

(g) 'waste products' means the remains of a chemical reaction which need to be disposed of at the end of the reaction or process.

Article 3

1. To prevent the exposure of workers to health risks from certain specific agents and/or certain work activities in the cases referred to in Article 1, Member States shall impose a ban in accordance with the procedures laid down in the Annex.

2. The Council, acting by a qualified majority on a proposal from the Commission, in cooperation with the European Parliament and after consulting the Economic and Social Committee, may amend the Annex, in particular to include further agents or activities.

Article 4

In the case of the derogations provided for in the Annex, the Member States shall be obliged to ensure that employers comply with the following procedures and measures:

(a) an employer must take adequate precautions to protect the health and safety of the workers concerned; and

(b) an employer must submit at least the following information to the competent authority:
   - the quantities used annually,
   - the activities and/or reactions or processes involved;
   - the number of workers exposed;
   - the technical and organizational measures taken to prevent the exposure of workers.

In addition, the Member States may provide for systems of individual authorizations.

Article 5

1. Workers and/or their representatives in undertakings or establishments shall have access, in accordance with national law, to the documents submitted pursuant to Article 4 in regard to their undertaking or establishment.

2. The documents referred to in paragraph 1 shall contain the information necessary to ensure that workers and/or their representatives in undertakings or establishments are made fully aware of the health and safety risks connected with the agent or work activity to which they are or are likely to be exposed, together with the measures to be taken against such risks.

Article 6

1. Before 1 January 1995 the Commission shall submit to the European Parliament, the Council and the Economic and Social Committee a report concerning in particular experience gained in the application of this Directive and progress in scientific knowledge and technology.

506

2. The Council shall re-examine this Directive before 1 January 1996 on the basis of the report referred to in paragraph 1.

Article 7

1. Member States shall adopt the laws, regulations and administrative provisions necessary to comply with this Directive by 1 January 1990 at the latest. They shall forthwith inform the Commission thereof.

2. Member States shall communicate to the Commission the provisions of national law which they adopt in the field governed by this Directive.

Article 8

This Directive is addressed to the Member States.

Done at Luxembourg, 9 June 1988.

For the Council
The President
N. Blüm

---

1. OJ No. C 270, 10.10.1984, p. 3.
2. OJ No. C 72, 18.3.1985, p. 131.
3. OJ No. C 104, 25.4.1985, p. 6.
4. OJ No. C 67, 5.3.1984, p. 2.
5. OJ No. L 327, 3.12.1980, p. 8.

ANNEX

1. Subject to the conditions listed below, the following may not be produced or used:
   – 2-naphtylamine and its salts   (CAS No. 91-59-8);
   – 4-aminobiphenyl and its salts   (CAS No. 92-67-1);
   – benzidine and its salts   (CAS No. 92-87-5);
   – 4-nitrodiphenyl   (CAS No. 92-93-3).

2. This ban does not apply if the agents are present in a substance or a preparation in the form of impurities or by-products, or as a constituent of waste products, provided that their individual concentration therein is less than 0,1 per cent w/w.

3. Derogations from point 1 laid down by the Member States shall only be permitted:
   – for the sole purpose of scientific research and testing, including analysis;
   – for work activities intended to eliminate the agents that are present in the form of by-products or waste products;
   – for the production of the substances referred to in paragraph 1 for use as intermediates, and for such use.

4. The exposure of workers to the substances referred to in paragraph 1 must be prevented, in particular by providing that the production and earliest possible use of these substances as intermediates must take place in a single closed system, from which the aforesaid substances may be removed only to the extend necessary to monitor the process or service the system.

Council Directive

24 June 1982

on the major accident hazards of certain industrial activities
(82/501/EEC)

THE COUNCIL OF THE EUROPEAN COMMUNITIES,

Having regard to the Treaty establishing the European Economic Community, and in particular Articles 100 and 235 thereof;
Having regard to the proposal from the Commission,[1]
Having regard to the opinion of the European Parliament,[2]
Having regard to the opinion of the Economic and Social Committee:[3]
Whereas the objectives and principles of the Community environment policy were fixed by the action programmes of the European Communities on the environment of 22 November 1973[4] and 17 May 1977,[5] and having regard in particular to the principle that the best policy consists in preventing the creation of pollution or nuisances at source; whereas to this end technical progress should be conceived and directed so as to meet the concern for the protection of the environment;
Whereas the objectives of the Community policy of health and safety at work were fixed by the Council resolution of 29 june 1978 on an action programme of the European Communities on safety and health at work,[6] and having regard in particular to the principle that the best policy consists in obviating possible accidents at source by the integration of safety at the various stages of design, construction and operation;
Whereas the Advisory Committee on Safety, Hygiene and Health Protection at Work, set up by Decision 74/325/EEC,[7] has been consulted;
Whereas the protection of the public and the environment and safety and health protection at work call for particular attention to be given to certain industrial activities capable of causing major accidents; whereas such accidents have already occurred in the Community and have had serious consequences for workers and, more generally, for the public and the environment;
Whereas, for every industrial activity which involves, or may involve, dangerous substances and which, in the event of a major accident, may have serious consequences for man and the environment, the manufacturer must take all necessary measures to prevent such accident and to limit the consequences thereof;
Whereas the training and information of persons working on an industrial

site can play a particularly important part in preventing major accidents and bringing the situation under control in the event of such accident;

Whereas, in the case of industrial activities which involve or may involve substances that are particularly dangerous in certain quantities, it is necessary for the manufacturer to provide the competent authorities with information including details of the substances in question and high-risk installations and situations, with a view to reducing the hazards of major accidents and enabling the necessary steps to be taken to reduce their consequences;

Whereas it is necessary to lay down that any person outside the establishment liable to be affected by a major accident should be appropriately informed of the safety measures to be taken and of the correct behaviour to be adopted in the event of an accident;

Whereas, if a major accident occurs, the manufacturer must immediately inform the competent authorities and communicate the information necessary for assessing the impact of that accident;

Whereas Member States should forward information to the Commission regarding major accidents occurring on their territory, so that the Commission can analyze the hazards from major accidents;

Whereas this Directive does not preclude the conclusion by a Member State of agreements with third countries concerning the exchange of information to which it is privy at internal level other than that obtained through the Community arrangements for the exchange of information set up by this Directive;

Whereas disparity between provisions already applicable or being prepared in the various Member States on measures to prevent major accidents and limit their consequences for man and the environment may create unequal conditions of competition and hence directly affect the functioning of the common market; whereas the approximation of laws provided for in Article 100 of the Treaty should therefore be carried out in this field;

Whereas it seems necessary to combine this approximation of laws with action by the Community aimed at attaining one of the Community objectives in the field of environmental protection and health and safety at work; whereas, in pursuance of this aim, certain specific provision should therefore be laid down: whereas, since the necessary powers have not been provided by the Treaty, Article 235 of the Treaty should be invoked.

HAS ADOPTED THIS DIRECTIVE:

Article 1
1. This Directive is concerned with the prevention of major accidents which might result from certain industrial activities and with the limitation of their consequences for man and the environment. It is directed in particular towards the approximation of the measures taken by Member States in this field.
2. For the purposes of this Directive:
   (a) Industrial activity means:
       – any operation carried out in an industrial installation referred to in

Annex I involving, or possibly involving, one or more dangerous substances and capable of presenting major-accident hazards, and also transport carried out within the establishment for internal reasons and the storage associated with this operation within the establishment;
- any other storage in accordance with the conditions specified in Annex II.

(b) Manufacturer means:
- any person in charge of an industrial activity.

(c) Major accident means:
- an occurrence such as a major emission, fire or explosion resulting from uncontrolled developments in the course of an industrial activity, leading to a serious danger to man, immediate or delayed, inside or outside the establishment, and/or to the environment, and involving one or more dangerous substances.

(d) Dangerous substances means:
- for the purposes of Articles 3 and 4, substances generally considered to fulfil the criteria laid down in Annex IV;
- for the purposes of Article 5, substances in the lists in Annex III and Annex II in the quantities referred to in the second column.

Article 2

This Directive does not apply to the following:

1. nuclear installations and plant for the processing of radioactive substances and material;

2. military installations;

3. the manufacture and separate storage of explosives, gunpowder and munitions;

4. extraction and other mining operations;

5. installations for the disposal of toxic and dangerous waste which are covered by Community Acts in so far as the purpose of those Arts is the prevention of major accidents.

Article 3

Member States shall adopt the provisions necessary to ensure that, in the case of any of the industrial activities specified in Article 1, the manufacturer is obliged to take all the measures necessary to prevent major accidents and to limit their consequences for man and the environment.

Article 4

Member States shall take the measures necessary to ensure that all manufacturers are required to prove to the competent authority at any time, for the purposes of the controls referred to in Article 7(2), that they have

510

identified existing major-accident hazards, adopted the appropriate safety measures, and provided the persons working on the site with information, training and equipment in order to ensure their safety.

Article 5

1. Without prejudice to Article 4, Member States shall introduce the necessary measures to require the manufacturer to notify the competent authorities specified in Article 7:
   - if, in an industrial activity as defined in Article 1(2)(a), first indent, one or more of the dangerous substances listed in Annex III are involved, or it is recognized that they may be involved, in the quantities laid down in the said Annex, such as:
   - substances stored or used in connection with the industrial activity concerned,
   - products of manufacture.
   - by-products, or
   - residues,
   - or if, in an industrial activity as defined in Article 1(2)(a), second indent, one or more of the dangerous substances, listed in Annex II are stored in the quantities laid down in the second column of the same Annex.

The notification shall contain the following:
(a) information relating to substances listed, respectively, in Annex II and Annex III, that is to say:
   - the data and information listed in Annex V;
   - the stage of the activity in which the substances are involved or may be involved:
   - the quantity (order of magnitude);
   - the chemical and/or physical behaviour under normal conditions of use during the process;
   - the forms in which the substances may occur or into which they may be transformed in the case of abnormal conditions which can be foreseen;
   - if necessary, other dangerous substances whose presence could have an effect on the potential hazard presented by the relevant industrial activity.
(b) information relating to the installations, that is to say:
   - the geographical location of the installations and predominant meteorological conditions and sources of danger arising from the location of the site;
   - the maximum number of persons working on the site of the establishment and particularly of those persons exposed to the hazard;
   - a general description of the technological processes;
   - a description of the sections of the establishmer which are important from the safety point of view, the sources of hazard and the conditions under which a major accident could occur, together with a description of the preventive measures planned;
   - the arrangements made to ensure that the technical means necessary

511

for the safe operation of plant and to deal with any malfunctions that arise are available at all times.
(c) information relating to possible major-accident situations, that is to say:
   – emergency plans, including safety equipment, alarm systems and resources available for use inside the establishments in dealing with a major accident;
   – any information necessary to the competent authorities to enable them to prepare emergency plans for use outside the establishment in accordance with Article 7(1);
   – the names of the person and his deputies or the qualified body responsible for safety and authorized to set the emergency plans in motion and to alert the competent authorities specified in Article 7.

2. In the case of new installations, the notification referred to in paragraph 1 must reach the competent authorities a reasonable length of time before the industrial activity commences.

3. The notification specified in paragraph 1 shall be updated periodically to take account of new technical knowledge relative to safety and of developments in knowledge concerning the assessment of hazards.

4. In the case of industrial activities for which the quantities, by substance, laid down in Annex II or III, as appropriate, are exceeded in a group of installations belonging to the same manufacturer which are less than 500 metres apart, the Member States shall take the necessary steps to ensure that the manufacturer supplies the amount of information required for the notification referred to in paragraph 1, without prejudice to Article 7, having regard to the fact that the installations are a short distance apart and that any major accident hazards may therefore be aggravated.

Article 6
In the event of modification of an industrial activity which could have significant consequences as regards major-accident hazards, the Member States shall take appropriate measures to ensure that the manufacturer:
– revises the measures specified in Articles 3 and 4;
– informs the competent authorities referred to in Article 7 in advance, if necessary, of such modification in so far as it affects the information contained in the notification specified in Article 5.

Article 7
1. The Member States shall set up or appoint the competent authority or authorities who, account being taken of the responsibility of the manufacturer, are responsible for:
   – receiving the notification referred to in Article 5 and the information referred to in the second indent of Article 6,
   – examining the information provided,
   – ensuring that an emergency plan is drawn up for action outside the

establishment in respect of whose industrial activity notification has been given,

and, if necessary,

- requesting supplementary information,
- ascertaining that the manufacturer takes the most appropriate measures, in connection with the various operations involved in the industrial activity for which notification has been given, to prevent major accidents and to provide the means for limiting the consequences thereof.

2. The competent authorities shall organize inspections or other measures of control proper to the type of activity concerned, in accordance with national regulations.

Article 8
1. Member States shall ensure that persons liable to be affected by a major accident originating in a notified industrial activity within the meaning of Article 5 are informed in an appropriate manner of the safety measures and of the correct behaviour to adopt in the event of an accident.
2. The Member States concerned shall at the same time make available to the other Member States concerned, as a basis for all necessary consultation within the framework of their bilateral relations, the same information as that which is disseminated to their own nationals.

Article 9
1. This Directive shall apply to both new and existing industrial activities.

2. 'New industrial activity' shall also include any modification to an existing industrial activity likely to have important implications for major-accident hazards.

3. In the case of existing industrial activities, this Directive shall apply at the latest on 8 January 1985.

   However, as regards the application of Article 5 to an existing industrial activity, the Member States shall ensure that the manufacturer shall submit to the competent authority, at the latest on 8 January 1985, a declaration comprising:
   - name or trade name and complete address;
   - registered place of business of the establishment and complete address;
   - name of the director in charge;
   - type of activity;
   - type of production or storage;
   - an indication of the substances or category of substances involved, as listed in Annexes II or III.

4. Moreover, Member States shall ensure that the manufacturer shall, at the latest on 8 July 1989, supplement the declaration provided for in paragraph 3, second subparagraph, with the data and information specified

513

in Article 5. Manufacturers shall normally be obliged to forward such supplementary declaration to the competent authority; however, Member States may waive the obligation on manufacturers to submit: the supplementary declaration; in that event such declaration shall be submitted to the competent authority at the explicit request of the latter.

Article 10
1. Member States shall take the necessary measures to ensure that, as soon as a major accident occurs, the manufacturer shall be required:
   (a) to inform the competent authorities specified in Article 7 immediately;
   (b) to provide them with the following information as soon as it becomes available:
      – the circumstances of the accident;
      – the dangerous substances involved within the meaning of Article 1 (2) (d);
      – the data available for assessing the effects of the accident on man and the environment;
      – the emergency measures taken.
   (c) to inform them of the steps envisaged:
      – to alleviate the medium and long-term effects of the accident;
      – to prevent any recurrence of such an accident.

2. The Member States shall require the competent authorities:
   (a) to ensure that any emergency and medium and long-term measures which may prove necessary are taken;
   (b) to collect, where possible, the information necessary for a full analysis of the major accident and possibly to make recommendations.

Article 11
1. Member States shall inform the Commission as soon as possible of major accidents which have occurred within their territory and shall provide it with the information specified in Annex VI as soon as it becomes available.

2. Member States shall inform the Commission of the name of the organization which might have relevant information on major accidents and which is able to advise the competent authorities of the other Member States which have to intervene in the event of such an accident.

3. Member States may notify the Commission of any substance which in their view should be added to Annexes II and III and of any measures they may have taken concerning such substances. The Commission shall forward this information to the other Member States.

Article 12
The Commission shall set up and keep at the disposal of the Member States a register containing a summary of the major accidents which have occurred

within the territory of the Member States, including an analysis of the causes of such accidents, experience gained and measures taken, to enable the Member States to use this information for prevention purposes.

Article 13
1. Information obtained by the competent authorities in pursuance of Articles 5, 6, 7, 9, 10 and 12 and by the Commission in pursuance of Article 11 may not be used for any purpose other than that for which it was requested.

2. However this Directive shall not preclude the conclusion by a Member State of agreements with third countries concerning the exchange of information to which it is privy at internal level other than that obtained through the Community machinery for the exchange of information set up by the Directive.

3. The Commission and its officials and employees shall not divulge the information obtained in pursuance of this Directive. The same requirement shall apply to officials and employees of the competent authorities of the Member States as regards any information they obtain from the Commission.
   Nevertheless, such information may be supplied:
   – in the case of Artices 12 and 18.
   – when a Member State carries out or authorizes the publication of information concerning that Member State itself.

4. Paragraphs 1, 2 and 3 shall not preclude the publication by the Commission of general statistical data or information on matters of safety containing no specific details regarding particular undertakings or groups of undertakings and not jeopardizing industrial secrecy.

Article 14
The amendments necessary for adapting Annex V to technical progress shall be adopted in accordance with the procedure specified in Article 16.

Article 15
1. For the purposes of applying Article 14, a Committee responsible for adapting this Directive to technical progress (hereinafter referred to as 'the Committee') is hereby set up. It shall consist of representatives of the Member States and be chaired by a representative of the Commission.

2. The Committee shall draw up its own rules of procedure.

Article 16
1. Where the procedure laid down in this Article is to be followed, matters shall be referred to the Committee by the chairman, either on his own initiative or at the request of the representative of a Member State.

2. The representative of the Commission shall submit to the Committee a draft of the measures to be adopted. The Committee shall deliver its opinion on the draft within a time limit which may be determined by the chairman according to the urgency of the matter. It shall decide by a majority of 45 votes, the votes of the Member States being weighted as provided for in Article 148(2) of the Treaty. The chairman shall not vote.

3. (a) The Commission shall adopt the measures envisaged where these are in accordance with the opinion of the Committee.
   (b) Where the measures envisaged are not in accordance with the opinion of the Committee, or in the absence of an opinion, the Commission shall forthwith submit a proposal to the Council on the measures to be adopted. The Council shall act by a qualified majority.
   (c) If the Council does not act within three months of the proposal being submitted to it, the measures proposed shall be adopted by the Commission.

Article 17
This Directive shall not restrict the right of the Member States to apply or to adopt administrative or legislative measures ensuring greater protection of man and the environment than that which derives from the provisions of this Directive.

Article 18
Member States and the Commission shall exchange information on the experience acquired with regard to the prevention of major accidents and the limitation of their consequences; this information shall concern, in particular, the functioning of the measures provided for in this Directive. Five years after notification of this Directive, the Commission shall forward to the Council and the European Parliament a report on its application which it shall draw up on the basis of this exchange of information.

Article 19
At the latest on 8 January 1986 the Council shall, on a proposal from the Commission, review Annexes I, II and III.

Article 20
1. Member States shall take the measures necessary to comply with this Directive at the latest on 8 January 1984. They shall forthwith inform the Commission thereof.

2. Member States shall communicate to the Commission the provisions of national law which they adopt in the field covered by this Directive.

Article 21
This Directive is addressed to the Member States.

Done at Luxembourg, 24 June 1982.

For the Council
The President
F. Aerts

---

1. OJ No. C 212, 24.8.1979, p. 4.
2. OJ No. C 175, 14.7.1980, p. 48.
3. OJ No. C 182, 21.7.1980, p. 25.
4. OJ No. C 112, 20.12.1973, p. 1.
5. OJ No. C 139, 13.6.1977, p. 1.
6. OJ No. C 165, 11.7.1978, p. 1.
7. OJ No. L 185, 9.7.1974, p. 15.

ANNEX I

Industrial installations within the meaning of article 1

1. – Installations for the production or processing of organic or inorganic chemicals using for this purpose, in particular:
   – alkylation
   – amination by ammonolysis
   – carbonylation
   – condensation
   – dehydrogenation
   – esterification
   – halogenation and manufacture of halogens
   – hydrogenation
   – hydrolysis
   – oxidation
   – polymerization
   – sulphonation
   – desulphurization, manufacture and transformation of sulphur-containing compounds
   – nitration and manufacture of nitrogen-containing compounds
   – manufacture of phosphorus-containing compounds
   – formulation of pesticides and of pharmaceutical products.
   – Installations for the processing of organic and inorganic chemical substances, using for this purpose, in particular.
   – distillation
   – extraction
   – solvation
   – mixing.

2. Installations for distillation, refining or other processing of petroleum or petroleum products.

517

3. Installations for the total or partial disposal of solid or liquid substances by incineration or chemical decomposition.

4. Installations for the production or processing of energy gases, for example, LPG, LNG, SNG.

5. Installations for the dry distillation of coal or lignite.

6. Installations for the production of metals or non-metals by the wet process or by means of electrical energy.

ANNEX II

Storage at installations other than those covered by annex 1 ('isolated storage')

The quantities set out below relate to each installation or group of installations belonging to the same manufacturer where the distance between the installations is not sufficient to avoid, in foreseeable circumstances, any aggravation of major-accident hazards. These quantities apply in any case to each group of installations belonging to the same manufacturer where the distance between the installations is less than approximately 500 m.

Substances or groups of substances	Quantities (tonnes) ≥	
	For application of Articles 3 and 4	For application of Article 5
1. Flammable gases as defined in Annex IV (c) (i)	50	300[1]
2. Highly flammable liquids as defined in Annex IV (c) (ii)	10 000	100 000
3. Acrylonitrile	350	5 000
4. Ammonia	60	600
5. Chlorine	10	200
6. Sulphur dioxide	20	500
7. Ammonium nitrate	500 [2]	5 000[2]
8. Sodium chlorate	25	250[2]
9. Liquid oxygen	200	2 000[2]

1. Member States may provisionally apply Article 5 to quantities of at least 500 tonnes until the revision of Annex II mentioned in Article 19.
2. Where this substance is in a state which gives it properties capable of creating a major-accident hazard.

ANNEX III

List of substances for the application of article 5

The quantities set out below relate to each installation or group of installations belonging to the same manufacturer where the distance between the installations is not sufficient to avoid, in foreseeable circumstances, any aggravation of major-accident hazards. These quantities apply in any case to each group of installations belonging to the same manufacturer where the distance between the installations is less than approximately 500 m.

Name	Quantity ($\geq$)	CAS No.	EEC No.
1. 4-Aminodiphenyl	1 kg	92-67-1	
2. Benzidine	1 kg	92-87-5	612-042-00-2
3. Benzidine salts	1 kg		
4. Dimethylnitrosamine	1 kg	62-75-9	
5. 2-Naphthylamine	1 kg	91-59-8	612-022-00-3
6. Beryllium (powders, compounds)	10 kg		
7. Bis(chloromethyl)ether	1 kg	542-88-1	603-046-00-5
8. 1,3-Propanesultone	1 kg	1120-71-4	
9. 2,3,7,8-Tetrachlorodibenzo-p-dioxin (TCDD)	1 kg	1746-01-6	
10. Arsenic pentoxide, Arsenic (V) acid and salts	500 kg		
11. Arsenic trioxide, Arsenious (III) acid and salts	100 kg		
12. Arsenic hydride (Arsine)	10 kg	7784-42-1	
13. Dimethylcarbamoyl chloride	1 kg	79-44-7	
14. 4-(Chloroformyl) morpholine	1 kg	15159-40-7	
15. Carbonyl chloride (Phosgene)	20 t	75-44-5	006-002-00-8
16. Chlorine	50 t	7782-50-5	017-001-00-7
17. Hydrogen sulphide	50 t	7783-06-04	016-001-00-4
18. Acrylonitrile	200 t	107-13-1	608-003-00-4
19. Hydrogen cyanide	20 t	74-90-8	006-006-00-X
20. Carbon disulphide	200 t	75-15-0	006-003-00-3
21. Bromine	500 t	7726-95-6	035-001-00-5
22. Ammonia	500 t	7664-41-7	007-001-00-5
23. Acetylene (Ethyne)	50 t	74-86-2	601-015-00-0
24. Hydrogen	50 t	1333-74-0	001-001-00-9
25. Ethylene oxide	50 t	75-21-8	603-023-00-X
26. Propylene oxide	50 t	75-56-9	603-055-00-4
27. 2-Cyanopropan-2-ol (Acetone cyanohydrin)	200 t	75-86-5	608-004-00-X

Name	Quantity ($\geq$)	CAS No.	EEC No.
28. 2-Propenal (Acrolein)	200 t	107-02-8	605-008-00-3
29. 2-Propen-l-ol (Allyl alcohol)	200 t	107-18-6	603-015-00-6
30. Allylamine	200 t	107-11-9	612-046-00-4
31. Antimony hydride (Stibine)	100 kg	7803-52-3	
32. Ethyleneimine	50 t	151-56-4	613-001-00-1
33. Formaldehyde (concentration $\geq$ 90 per cent)	50 t	50-00-0	605-001-01-2
34. Hydrogen phosphide (Phosphine)	100 kg	7803-51-2	
35. Bromomethane (Methyl bromide)	200 t	74-83-9	602-002-00-3
36. Methyl isocyanate	1 t	624-83-9	605-001-00-7
37. Nitrogen oxides	50 t	11104-93-1	
38. Sodium selenite	100 kg	10102-18-8	
39. Bis(2-chroloethyl) sulphide	1 kg	505-60-2	
40. Phosacetim	100 kg	4104-14-7	015-092-00-8
41. Tetraethyl lead	50 t	78-00-2	
42. Tetramethyl lead	50 t	75-74-1	
43. Promurit (1-(3,4-Dichloro-phenyl)-3-triazenethio-carboxamide)	100 kg	5836-73-7	
44. Chlorfenvinphos	100 kg	470-90-6	015-071-00-3
45. Crimidine	100 kg	535-89-7	613-004-00-8
46. Chloromethyl methyl ether	1 kg	107-30-2	
47. Dimethyl phosphoramidocyanidic acid	1 t	63917-41-9	
48. Carbophenothion	100 kg	786-19-6	015-044-00-6
49. Dialifos	100 kg	10311-84-9	015-088-00-6
50. Cyanthoate	100 kg	3734-95-0	015-070-00-8
51. Amiton	1 kg	78-53-5	
52. Oxydisulfoton	100 kg	2497-07-6	015-096-00-X
53. 00-Diethyl S-ethylsulphinylmethyl phosphorothioate	100 kg	2588-05-8	
54. 00-Diethyl S-ethylsulphonylmethyl phosphorothioate	100 kg	2588-06-9	
55. Disulfoton	100 kg	298-04-4	015-060-00-3
56. Demeton	100 kg	8065-48-3	
57. Phorate	100 kg	298-02-2	015-033-00-6
58. 00-Diethyl S-ethylthiomethyl phosophorothioate	100 kg	2600-69-3	
59. 00-Diethyl S-isopropylthiomethyl phosphorodithioate	100 kg	78-52-4	

Name	Quantity (≥)	CAS No.	EEC No.
60. Pyrazoxon	100 kg	108-34-9	015-023-00-1
61. Pensulfothion	100 kg	115-90-2	015-090-00-7
62. Paraoxon (Diethyl 4-nitrophenyl phosphate)	100 kg	311-45-5	
63. Parathion	100 kg	56-38-2	015-034-00-1
64. Azinphos-ethyl	100 kg	2642-71-9	015-056-00-1
65. 00-Diethyl S-propylthiomethyl phosphorodithioate	100 kg	3309-68-0	
66. Thionazin	100 kg	297-97-2	
67. Carbofuran	100 kg	1563-66-2	006-026-00-9
68. Phosphamidon	100 kg	13171-21-6	015-022-00-6
69. Tirpate (2,4-Dimethyl-1,3-dithiolane-2-carboxaldehyde O-methylcarbamoyloxime)	100 kg	26419-73-8	
70. Mevinphos	100 kg	7786-34-7	015-020-00-5
71. Parathion-methyl	100 kg	298-00-0	015-035-00-7
72. Azinphos-methyl	100 kg	86-50-0	015-039-00-9
73. Cycloheximide	100 kg	66-81-9	
74. Diphacinone	100 kg	82-66-6	
75. Tetram ethylenedisulphotetramine	1 kg	80-12-6	
76. EPN	100 kg	2104-64-5	015-036-00-2
77. 4-Fluorobutyric acid	1 kg	462-23-7	
78. 4-Fluorobutyric acid, salts	1 kg		
79. 4-Fluorobutyric acid, esters	1 kg		
80. 4-Fluorobutyric acid, amides	1 kg		
81. 4-Fluorocrotonic acid	1 kg	37759-72-1	
82. 4-Fluorocrotonic acid, salts	1 kg		
83. 4-Fluorocrotonic acid, esters	1 kg		
84. 4-Fluorocrotonic acid, amides	1 kg		
85. Fluoroacetic acid	1 kg	144-49-0	607-081-00-7
86. Fluoroacetic acid, salts	1 kg		
87. Fluoroacetic acid, esters	1 kg		
88. Fluoroacetic acid, amides	1 kg		
89. Fluenetil	100 kg	4301-50-2	607-078-00-0
90. 4-Fluoro-2-hydroxybutyric acid	1 kg		
91. 4-Fluoro-2-hydroxybutyric acid, salts	1 kg		
92. 4-Fluoro-2-hydroxybutyric acid, esters	1 kg		
93. 4-Fluoro-2-hydroxybutyric acid, amides	1 kg		
94. Hydrogen fluoride	50 t	7664-39-3	009-002-00-6
95. Hydroxyacetonitrile (Glycolonitrile)	100 kg	107-16-4	

521

Name	Quantity (≥)	CAS No.	EEC No.
96. 1,2,3,7,8,9,- Hexachlorodibenzo -p-dioxin	100 kg	19408-74-3	
97. Isodrin	100 kg	465-73-6	602-050-00-4
98. Hexamethylphosphoramide	1 kg	680-31-9	
99. Juglone (5-Hydroxynaph- thalene-1,4-dione)	100 kg	481-39-0	
100. Warfarin	100 kg	81-81-2	607-056-00-0
101. 4,4-Methylenebis (2-chloroaniline)	10 kg	101-14-4	015-047-00-2
102. Ethion	100 kg	563-12-2	006-017-00-X
103. Aldicarb	100 kg	116-08-3	028-001-00-1
104. Nickel tetracarbonyl	10 kg	13463-39-3	602-053-00-0
105. Isobenzan	100 kg	297-78-9	
106. Pentaborane	100 kg	19624-22-7	
107. 1-Propen-2-chloro-1,3-diol- diacetate	10 kg	10118-72-6	
108. Propyleneimine	50 t	75-55-8	
109. Oxygen difluoride	10 kg	7783-41-7	016-013-00-X
110. Sulphur dichloride	1 t	10545-99-0	
111. Selenium hexafluoride	10 kg	7783-79-1	
112. Hydropen selenide	10 kg	7783-07-5	015-025-00-2
113. TEPP	100 kg	107-49-3	015-027-00-3
114. Sulfotep	100 kg	3689-24-5	015-061-00-9
115. Dimefox	100 kg	115-26-4	
116. 1-Tri(cyclohexyl) stannyl- 1H-1,2,4-triazole	100 kg	41083-11-8	
117. Triethylenemelamine	10 kg	51-18-3	
118. Cobalt (powders, compounds)	100 kg		
119. Nickel (powders, compounds)	100 kg		
120. Anabasine	100 kg	494-52-0	
121. Tellurium hexafluoride	100 kg	7783-80-4	
122. Trichloromethanesulphenyl chloride	100 kg	594-42-3	
123. 1,2-Dibromoethane (Ethylene dibromide)	50 t	106-93-4	602-010-00-6
124. Flammable substances as defined in Annex IV(c)(i)	200 t		
125. Flammable substances as defined in Annex IV(c)(ii)	50 000 t		
126. Diazodinitrophenol	10 t	7008-81-3	
127. Diethylene glycol dinitrate	10 t	693-21-0	603-033-00-4
128. Dinitrophenol, salts	50 t		609-017-00-3
129. 1-Guanyl-4-nitrosaminoguanyl- 1-tetrazene	10 t	109-27-3	

Name	Quantity (≥)	CAS No.	EEC No.
130. Bis (2,4,6-trinitrophenyl)amine	50 t	131-73-7	612-018-00-1
131. Hydrazine nitrate	50 t	13464-97-6	
132. Nitroglycerine	10 t	55-63-0	603-034-00-X
133. Pentaerythritol tetranitrate	50 t	78-11-5	603-035-00-5
134. Cyclotrimethylene trinitramine	50 t	121-82-4	
135. Trinitroaniline	50 t	26952-42-1	
136. 2,4,6-Trinitroanisole	50 t	606-35-9	609-011-00-0
137. Trinitrobenzene	50 t	25377-32-6	609-005-00-8
138. Trinitrobenzoic acid	50 t	35860-50-5 129-66-8	
139. Chlorotrinitrobenzene	50 t	28260-61-9	610-504-00-X
140. N-Methyl-N,2,4,6-N-tetranitroandene	50 t	479-45-8	612-017-00-6
141. 2,4,6-Trinitrophenol (Picric acid)	50 t	88-89-1	609-009-00-X
142. Trinitrocrescol	50 t	28905-71-7	609-012-00-6
143. 2,4,6-Trinitrophenetole	50 t	4732-14-3	
144. 2,4,6-Trinitroresorcinol (Styphnic acid)	50 t	82-71-3	609-018-00-9
145. 2,4,6-Trinitrotoluene	50 t	118-96-7	609-008-00-4
146. Ammonium nitrate[1]	5 000 t	6484-52-2	
147. Cellulose nitrate (containing > 12.6% nitrogen)	100 t	9004-70-0	603-037-00-6
148. Sulphur dioxide	1 000 t	7446-09-05	016-011-00-9
149. Hydrogen chloride (liquefied gas)	250 t	7647-01-0	017-002-00-2
150. Flammable substances as defined in Annex IV (c)(iii)	200 t		
151. Sodium chlorate[1]	250 t	7775-09-9	017-005-00-9
152. tert-Butyl peroxyacetate (concentration ≥ 70 per cent)	50 t 50 t	107-71-1	
153. tert-Butyl peroxyisobutyrate (concentration ≥ 80%)	50 t	109-13-7	
154. tert-Butyl peroxymaleate (concentration ≥ 80%)	50 t	1931-62-0	
155. tert-Butyl peroxy isopropyl carbonate (concentration ≥ 80 per cent)	50 t	2372-21-6	
156. Dibenzyl peroxydicarbonate (concentration ≥ 90 per cent)	50 t	2144-45-8	
157. 2,2-Bis (tert-butylperoxy) butane (concentration ≥ 70 per cent)	50 t	2167-23-9	
158. 1,1-Bis (tert-butylperoxy) cyclohexane (concentration ≥ 80 per cent	50 t	3006-86-8	

523

Name	Quantity (≥)	CAS No.	EEC No.
159. Di-sec-butyl peroxydicarbonate (concentration ≥ 80 per cent)	50 t	19910-65-7	
160. 2,2-Dihydroperoxypropane (concentration ≥ 30 per cent)	50 t	2614-76-8	
161. Di-n-propyl peroxydicarbonate concentration ≥ 80 per cent)	50 t	16066-38-9	
162. 3,3,6,6,9,9-Hexamethyl-1,2,4,5-tetroxacyclononane (concentration ≥ 75 per cent)	50 t	22397-33-7	
163. Methyl ethyl ketone peroxide (concentration ≥ 60 per cent)	50 t	1338-23-4	
164. Methyl isobutyl ketone peroxide (concentration ≥ 60 per cent)	50 t	37206-20-5	
165. Peracetic acid (concentration ≥ 60 per cent)	50 t	79-21-0	607-094-00-8
166. Lead azide	50 t	13424-46-9	082-003-00-7
167. Lead 2,4,6 trinitroresorcinoxide (Lead styphnate)	50 t	15245-44-0	609-019-00-4
168. Mercury fulminate	10 t	20820-45-5 628-86-4	080-005-00-2
169. Cyclotetramethylenete-tranitramine	50 t	2691-41-0	
170. 2,2′,4.4′,6.6′-Hexanitrostilbene	50 t	20062-22-0	
171. 1,3,5-Triamino-2,4,6-trinitrobenzene	50 t	3058-38-6	
172. Ethyiene glycol dinitrate	10 t	628-96-6	603-032-00-9
173. Ethyl nitrate	50 t	625-58-1	007-007-00-8
174. Sodium picramate	50 t	831-52-7	
175. Barium azide	50 t	18810-58-7	
176. Di-isobutyryl peroxide (concentration ≥ 50 per cent)	50 t	3437-84-1	
177. Diethyl peroxydicarbonate (concentration ≥ 30 per cent)	50 t	14666-78-5	
178. tert-Butyl peroxypivalate (concentration ≥ 77%)	50 t	927-07-1	

1.   Where this substance is in a state which gives it properties capable of creating a major-accident hazard.

NB: The EEC numbers correspond to those in Directive 67/548 EEC and its amendments.

524

ANNEX IV

Indicative criteria

(a) Very toxic substances

– substances which correspond to the first line of the table below.
– substances which correspond to the second line of the table below and which, owing to their physical and chemical properties, are capable of entailing major-accident hazards similar to those caused by the substance mentioned in the first line:

	LD 50 (oral)[1] mg/kg body weight	LD 50 (cutaneous)[2] mg/kg body weight	LC 50[3] mg/I (inhalation)
1	LD 50 ≤ 5	LD 50 ≤ 10	LC 50 ≤ 0.1
2	5 < LD 50 ≤ 25	10 < LD 50 ≤ 50	0.1 < LC 50 ≤ 0.5

1. LD 50 oral in rats.
2. LD 50 cutaneous in rats or rabbits.
3. LC 50 by inhalation (four hours) in rats.

(b) Other toxic substances

The substances showing the following values of acute toxicity and having physical and chemical properties capable of entailing major-accident hazards:

	LD 50 (oral)[1] mg/kg body weight	LD 50 (cutaneous)[2] mg/kg body weight	LC 50[3] mg/I (inhalation)

1. LD 50 oral in rats.
2. LD 50 cutaneous in rats or rabbits.
3. LC 50 by inhalation (four hours) in rats.

(c) Flammable substances

(i) flammable gases:
substances which in the gaseous state at normal pressure and mixed with air become flammable and the boiling point of which at normal pressure is 20°C or below;
(ii) highly flammable liquids:
substances which have a flash point lower than 21°C and the boiling point of which at normal pressure is above 20°C;
(iii) flammable liquids:
substances which have a flash point lower than 55°C and which re-

525

main liquid under pressure, where particular processing conditions, such as high pressure and high temperature, may create major-accident hazards.

(d) Explosive substances

Substances which may explode under the effect of flame or which are more sensitive to shocks or friction than dinitrobenzene.

ANNEX V

Data and information to be supplied in connection with the notification provided for in Article 5

If it is not possible or if it seems unnecessary to provide the following information, reasons must be given.

1. IDENTITY OF THE SUBSTANCE

Chemical name
CAS number
Name according to the IUFAC nomenclature
Other names
Empirical formula
Composition of the substance
Degree of purity
Main impurities and relative percentages
Detection and determination methods available to the installation
Description of the methods used or references to scientific literature
Methods and precautions laid down by the manufacturer in connection with handling, storage and fire
Emergency measures laid down by the manufacturer in the event of accidental dispersion
Methods available to the manufacturer for rendering the substance harmless

2. BRIEF INDICATION OF HAZARDS

– For man: – immediate ....
                          – delayed ....
– For the environment: – immediate ....
                          – delayed ....

526

ANNEX VI

Information to be supplied to the commission by the Member States pursuant to Article 11

REPORT OF MAJOR ACCIDENT

Member State:
Authority responsible for report:
Address:

1. General data
   Data and time of the major accident:
   Country, administrative region, etc.:
   Address:
   Type of industrial activity:

2. Type of major accident
   Explosion ☐   Fire ☐   Emission of dangerous substances ☐
   Substance(s) emitted:

3. Description of the circumstances of the major accident

4. Emergency measures taken

5. Cause(s) of major accident
   Known:
   (to be specified)
   Not known:
   Information will be supplied as soon as possible

6. Nature and extent of damage
   (a) Within the establishment
       – casualties   . . . . . killed
                                                            . . . . . injured
                                                            . . . . . poisoned

       – persons exposed to the major accident   . . . . .
       – material damage
       – the danger is still present
       – the danger no longer exists
   (b) Outside the establishment
       – casualties   . . . . . killed
                                                            . . . . . injured
                                                            . . . . . poisoned

       – persons exposed to the major accident   . . . . .
       – material damage
       – damage to the environment
       – the danger is still present
       – the danger no longer exists

7. Medium and long-term measures, particularly those aimed at preventing the recurrence of similar major accidents (to be submitted as the information becomes available).

ANNEX VII

Statement re Article 8

The Member States shall consult one another in the framework of their bilateral relations on the measures required to avert major accidents originating in a notified industrial activity within the meaning of Article 5 and to limit the consequences for man and the environment. In the case of new installations, this consultation shall take place within the time limits laid down in Article 5(2).

Council Directive

19 March 1987

amending Directive 82/501/EEC on the major-accident hazards of certain industrial activies
(87/216/EEC)

THE COUNCIL OF THE EUROPEAN COMMUNITIES,

Having regard to the Treaty establishing the European Economic Community, and in particular Articles 100 and 235 thereof,
Having regard to the proposal from the Commission,[1]
Having regard to the opinion of the European Parliament,[2]
Having regard to the opinion of the Economic and Social Committee:[3]
    Whereas Article 19 of Council Directive 82/501/EEC[4] requires the Council to review, on a proposal from the Commission, Annexes I, II and III thereof;
    Whereas the protection of man and the environment and safety and health protection at work call for the provisions of Directive 82/501/EEC to be strengthened with regard to some industrial activities which involve, or may involve, particularly dangerous substances;
    Whereas for some particularly toxic substances it is necessary to lower the threshold quantities set out in Annexes II and III in order that all industrial activities which involve, or may involve, these substances in quantities equal to or above the given threshold levels are covered by Article 5 of Directive 82/501/EEC, with a view to reducing the hazards of major accidents and enabling the necessary steps to be taken to reduce their consequences;
    Whereas it is necessary to cover the industrial activities which involve, or may involve, sulphur trioxide and liquid oxygen and the isolated storage of sulphur trioxide, as they may have serious consequences for man and the environment in the event of a major accident;

Whereas the industrial activities involving sulphur dioxide can pose a great hazard than the isolated storage of sulphur dioxide;

Whereas it is necessary to define more closely some substances or groups of substances and to amend the corresponding threshold quantities in order to reflect the different range of hazards posed by the different forms and types of these substances or groups of substances;

Whereas it is appropriate that the industrial activities involving ammonium nitrate, sodium chlorate and liquid oxygen and the storage of these substances fall within the scope of Annexes II and III to Directive 82/501/EEC, whenever the respective threshold quantities set out in these Annexes are exceeded;

Whereas it is appropriate that certain amendments should be made to Annex I to Directive 82/501/EEC;

Whereas it is necessary to make it clear that the list of processes set out in Annex I(1) to Directive 82/501/EEC is not exhaustive, but merely gives examples of some important operations, and that all other operations which could be used for the production, processing or treatment of organic or inorganic chemicals are also covered by his Annex;

Whereas the Advisory Committee on Safety, Hygiene and Health Protection at work, set up by Council Decision 74/325/EEC,[5] has been consulted,

HAS ADOPTED THIS DIRECTIVE:

Article 1
Annexes I, II and III to Directive 82/501/EEC shall be amended in accordance with the Annex hereto.

Article 2
1. In the case of existing industrial activities which will be subject to the provisions of Directive 82/501/EEC for the first time following adoption of this amendment, the declaration provided for in Article 9(3) of the said Directive shall be submitted to the competent authority within 24 months of notification of this Directive.

2. In these cases also, the supplementary declaration provided for in Article 9(4) of Directive 82/501/EEC shall be submitted to the competent authority within five years of notification of this Directive.

Article 3
1. Member States shall take the measures necessary to comply with this Directive not later than 18 months after notification of the Directive. They shall forthwith inform the Commission thereof.

2. Member States shall communicate to the Commission the provision of national law which they adopt in the field covered by this Directive.

Article 4
This Directive is addressed to the Member States.

Done at Brussels, 19 March 1987.

For the Council
The President
M. Smet

---

1. OJ No. C 305, 26.11.1985, p. 9.
2. OJ No. C 76, 23.31.1987.
3. OJ No. C 101, 28.4.1986, p. 10.
4. OJ No. L 230, 5.8.1982, p. 1.
5. OJ No. L 185, 9.7.1974, p. 15.

ANNEX

1. ANNEX I

Industrial installations within the meaning of Article 1

(a) In point 1, first indent, 'Installations for the production or processing of organic or inorganic chemicals using for this purpose, in particular:' is replaced by the following:
'Installations for the production, processing or treatment of organic or inorganic chemicals using for this purpose, amongst others:';

(b) In point 1, second indent, 'Installations for the processing of organic and inorganic chemical substances, using for this purpose, in particular:' is deleted, and the rest of this indent becomes part of the first indent.

(c) Point 4, 'Installations for the production or processing of energy gases, for example, LPG, LNG, SNG' is replaced by the following:
'Installations for the production, processing or treatment of energy gases, for example, LPG, LNG, SNG'.

2. ANNEX II

Storage at installations other than those covered by Annex I ('isolated storage')

(a) Footnotes 1 and 2 are deleted, together with the references to them in the text itself.

(b) The quantities of the substance chlorine are replaced by the following:

Quantities (tonnes) $\geq$	
For application of Articles 3 and 4	For application of Article 5
10	75

(c) The designation and the quantities of the substance ammonium nitrate are replaced by the following:

	Quantities (tonnes) $\geq$	
	For application of Articles 3 and 4	For application of Article 5
7. (a) Ammonium nitrate[1]	350	2 500
7. (b) Ammonium nitrate in the form of fertilizers[2]	1 250	10 000

1. This applies to ammonium nitrate and mixtures of ammonium nitrate where the nitrogen content derived from the ammonium nitrate is > 28 per cent by weight and to aqueous solutions of ammonium nitrate where the concentration of ammonium nitrate is >90 per cent by weight.
2. This applies to straight ammonium nitrate fertilizers which comply with Directive 80/876/EEC and to compound fertilizers where the nitrogen content derived from the ammonium nitrate is >28 per cent by weight (a compound fertilizer contains ammonium nitrate together with phosphate and/or potash).

(d) The following substance is added:

	Quantities (tonnes) $\geq$	
	For application of Articles 3 and 4	For application of Article 5
10. Sulphur trioxide	15	100

3. ANNEX III

List of substances for the application of Article 5

(a) Footnote 1 is deleted.
(b) The quantity of substance No 15 'Carbonyl chloride (Phosgene)' is replaced by the following quantity: 750 kilograms
(c) The quantity of substance No 16 'Clorine' is replaced by the following quantity: 25 tonnes
(d) The quantity of substance No 36 'Methyl isocyanate' is replaced by the following quantity: 150 kilograms
(e) The designation and quantity of substance No 118 'Cobalt (powders and compounds)' are replaced by the following:

Name	Quantity ($\geq$)
118. Cobalt metal, oxides, carbonates, sulphides, as powders	1 tonne

(f) The designation and quantity of substance No 119 'Nickel (powders and compounds)' are replaced by the following:

Name	Quantity ($\geq$)
119. Nickel metal, oxides, carbonates, sulphides, as powders	1 tonne

(g) The designation and quantity of substance No 146 'Ammonium nitrate' are replaced by the following:

Name	Quantity ($\geq$)
146. (a) Ammonium nitrate[1]	2 500 tonnes
146. (b) Ammonium nitrate in the form of fertilizers[2]	5 000 tonnes

1. This applies to ammonium nitrate and mixtures of ammonium nitrate where the nitrogen content derived from the ammonium nitrate is >28 per cent by weight and aqueous solutions of ammonium nitrate where the concentration of ammonium nitrate is >90 per cent by weight.
2. This applies to straight ammonium nitrate fertilizers which comply with Directive 80/876/EEC and to compound fertilizers where the nitrogen content derived from the ammonium nitrate is >28 per cent by weight (a compound fertilizer contains ammonium nitrate together with phoshate and/or potash).

(h) The quantity of substance No 148 'Sulphur dioxide' is replaced by the following quantity: 250 tonnes
(i) The following substance is added:

Name	Quantities ($\geq$)	CAS No	EEC No
179. Liquid oxygen	2 000 tonnes	7 782-44-7	008-001-00-8

(j) The following substance is added:

Name	Quantities ($\geq$)	CAS No	EEC No
180. Sulphur trioxide	75 tonnes	7 446-11-9	

Subject Index